The End of the Russian I
1905-193(

DOROTHY ATKINSON

The End of the Russian Land Commune 1905-1930

Stanford University Press, Stanford, California 1983

Stanford University Press
Stanford, California
© 1983 by the Board of Trustees of the
Leland Stanford Junior University
Printed in the United States of America
ISBN 0-8047-1148-8
LC 81-84457

Contents

List of Tables

Preface

The abrupt transition of a society from a long-established form of social organization raises a number of questions for the historian. When the institution abandoned is the commune, and the change is made by the first successful modern political party to call itself "communist," those questions hold special interest. The end of the Russian land commune is a topic that evokes grand themes of change and continuity, a topic that invites analysis of the relationship of society, economy, and polity.

Yet half a century after the sudden death of the commune—an institution rooted, according to some historians, in the primeval Slavic past—there is still a surprising lack of historical literature devoted to its demise. The time-clouded origin of the commune, in contrast, has been the object of extensive scholarly investigation and debate. The vast body of literature on this topic makes all the more remarkable the near absence of works on the final phase of the commune's history, since the imbalance in the investigation of its germinal and terminal stages by no means reflects the relative importance of the commune at the time of its extinction.

The historiographical neglect of the postrevolutionary commune seemingly results from a variety of factors. Under conditions of social upheaval and dislocation during successive wars, revolutions, and famines, the current of rural life flowed in shifting channels that often washed away their own traces. The systematic collection of local statistical material was disrupted, making the flow of events more difficult to follow. Part of the explanation, however, lies in the inevitable upstaging of institutional history by the more dramatic events of political history in a period of violent change. The urban-centered political history of the revolutions of 1917 and their aftermath has until recently all but monopolized the attention of historians, so that rural developments and the institutional structure of Russia's rural society and economy in this pivotal period have elicited comparatively little inquiry from either Soviet or non-Soviet scholars.

Those who have turned back of late to the study of the countryside in the 1920's have sometimes been surprised to find that the commune was not, after all, swept away either before or by the apocalypse. Not long ago a Soviet specialist was obliged to report, "The opinion has prevailed among our scholars right up to the present that the commune had already 'perished' before the October Revolution."[1] The recently published *Soviet Historical Encyclopedia* still advises readers that the commune was "decisively undermined by the Stolypin agrarian reform at the beginning of the twentieth century."[2] Yet, as this study will attempt to demonstrate, the commune was an enduring presence in the village on the eve of the Russian revolution and vigorously reasserted itself in the course of that event. Moreover, throughout the 1920's the commune was to play a major role in the life of the countryside, a role with political implications that contributed to the drastic restructuring of rural society at the end of the decade.

This study began as an investigation of the impact of the revolutions of 1917 on the communal organization of the peasantry. It soon became apparent that developments in 1917 could be properly understood only by extending the frame of reference back to the revolution of 1905–7 and ahead to the collectivization of agriculture launched at the end of the 1920's. The dozen years that followed the October Revolution, and the dozen that preceded it, are more than mere epilogue and prologue; they form integral parts of the final chapter in the history of the commune. The situation in 1905 was itself the product of an evolution that calls for discussion. Part I, therefore, gives a brief description of the historical development of the modern land commune and of conditions created by the emancipation of the peasantry in 1861.

The revolution of 1905–7 introduced the first major reversal in several centuries of a historical trend toward communal land tenure. The Stolypin agrarian reforms were designed to weaken and eventually to eliminate the commune in favor of individual landholding. A description of these reforms and a reappraisal of their effect on the commune in the decade before 1917 are offered in Part II of this work. The third part concerns the events of 1917: official policies and political programs bearing on the commune, peasant activities and organizations, and the massive redistribution of land that began in 1917 and continued in the following years. The study then turns to developments under War Communism in the period 1918–21, when a vigorous revival of the commune paralleled the appearance of new institutions in the countryside that would ultimately supplant it. Finally, Part V deals with the rural situation in the 1920's, pointing to the interplay of social, economic, and political factors related to the commune that contributed to the decision to collectivize agriculture.

The sources consulted for this study include legislative and statistical materials, publications of official agricultural and land agencies, administrative reports, monographs, political literature, memoirs, and the periodical press. Although a limited amount of material from the central archives in Moscow (TsGAOR) and in Leningrad (TsGIA) was available for the prerevolutionary years, access to archival materials for 1917 and beyond was denied by the Main Archival Administration. For the Stolypin era the existence of published documentary sources, along with well-documented accounts drawn from archival sources or from personal participation in agricultural administration, simplified the task of collecting data.[3] Yet inconsistencies in both the literature and the statistics suggested the need for a fresh look at departures from the commune before the revolution.

For the postrevolutionary period we have only scattered data on the commune, a fact long since lamented by a major historian of the institution.[4] There is, of course, a substantial body of literature on the history of Russian and early Soviet agriculture, including, in the West, the works of Vladimir Timoshenko, Naum Jasny, and Lazar Volin.[5] More recently, Western writers have begun to illuminate critical links between agricultural and political development. The work of Moshe Lewin has been particularly valuable, and E. H. Carr, R. W. Davies, and others have made important contributions.[6] Although the commune receives relatively little notice from these specialists, several later sections of this study draw on their findings on rural developments to help explain the history of the commune.

In recent years the Russian land commune in the twentieth century has emerged as a topic of interest among an international community of scholars, most notably those associated with the Centre for Russian and East European Studies at the University of Birmingham. A brief account of the village assembly in the mid-1920's by the political scientist Yuzuru Taniuchi was the first modern work to focus on political aspects of the communal organization of the peasantry.[7] His investigation was broadened and extended to the period of collectivization by Donald Male, another political scientist;[8] from a sociological perspective, Teodor Shanin has dealt more analytically with the commune in the twentieth century.[9] Welcome as these studies are, however, none claims to provide a history of the institution.

Soviet literature on the postrevolutionary commune falls into two categories: the work of the 1920's, and a small but growing body of recent scholarship. After collectivization the commune fell into relative obscurity, and only with the post-Stalin revival of interest in the agrarian history of the 1920's has the institution gradually come to claim increasing attention. Much of the early material is fragmentary and polemical, but the periodical press provided wide general coverage of the rural scene. Among the more valuable contemporary sources are the journals of the land organization agencies and the Agrarian Section (later Agrarian Institute) of the Communist Academy. As for recent material, the earliest serious investigator of the postrevolutionary commune is Viktor Petrovich Danilov; yet Danilov's interest in the commune has been secondary to a broader interest in postrevolutionary rural history in general.[10] His recent two-volume history of the Soviet countryside before collectivization devotes a comparatively minor section to the commune and to communal land tenure. Other Soviet scholars have given attention to the commune in more general works, have published articles on the subject, or have delivered reports on it at symposia on agrarian history. However, the only Soviet study devoted specifically to the postrevolutionary commune is a recent monograph by V. Ia. Osokina, which describes the institution in Siberia from 1920 to 1933.[11]

The present study makes no claim to cover all aspects of the commune or to detail its local peculiarities. What it does offer is a general historical description and analysis of a complex of institutional, social, and economic developments unfolding in an extensive and varied territory over the course of an eventful quarter-century. The focus is on European Russia, but other regions are occasionally discussed.

The history of the commune has an additional dimension, encompassing critical questions about collectivism and individualism in social development. What accounts for the relative strengths of each in different societies? And, a related problem, what is the relationship between collective property and the form of the state (whether "patrimonial," socialist, or other)? The commune is the locus classicus for the pursuit of such cosmic questions, but before discussion can proceed on that level, the place of the commune itself must be established.

Scholarship, like the commune, is a collective enterprise carried on by separate individuals. This study has drawn on the work of many researchers and is indebted to them all. A number of colleagues have also contributed in other ways to its progress over the past decade, and it is a pleasure to acknowledge their help. To Terence Emmons, Alexander Dallin, Wayne Vucinich, and Viktor Petrovich Danilov, who have generously shared their knowledge and perspectives on various topics covered here, a special note of thanks is due. Needless to say, all responsibility for the shortcomings of the work rests solely with the author.

D.A.

PART I

The Historical Evolution of the Modern Commune

The history of Russia, like the history of most of the world, has been until recent times a story of peasant society. In all peasant societies, human relations are profoundly influenced by relationships to the land, but in Russia a unique constellation of environmental and political forces gave these relationships exceptional significance. Throughout most of Russian history the most important institution governing land use was the commune. The use of the commune by the state and landowners to secure tax revenues and a labor force, and the practice of periodic land redistribution, which adjusted the supply of land and labor, gave a distinctive shape to Russia's rural society and economy by the beginning of the twentieth century.

1

Introduction

The Land Commune at the Beginning of the Twentieth Century

Until only a few decades ago most Russians lived close to the soil. At the beginning of this century, despite a recent surge of industrialization, Russia was a predominantly agricultural country, and even of the 13 percent of the population listed in the census as urban residents, many still spent part of each year in the countryside or were closely involved in other ways with rural life. Almost all Russians at the time belonged to communes of one sort or another. In addition to land communes there were urban communes, artisan communes, hunting communes, fishing communes, communes of salt miners, and many others. These differed greatly from one another, but all derived their legal identity as communes from the collective ownership and use of property.[1] Since the most important property in agrarian Russia was land, the most important commune by far was the land commune: in common parlance "the commune" (*obshchina*) meant "the land commune" (*pozemel'naia obshchina*). At the beginning of the century four out of every five peasant households in European Russia were among its members.

The commune united the peasants of a locality in a corporation that controlled the land they owned collectively. It elected its own officials and enjoyed some autonomy in matters of local administration and justice. Until 1903 members were mutually responsible for certain fiscal obligations. Under communal tenure a peasant's dwelling and garden plot were considered permanent, hereditary household property; arable fields, however, belonged to the commune and were redistributed from time to time among the member households. So that each family would get an equitable share of lands of varying quality, fields were divided into sections and subdivided into strips, then one or more strips in each section were allotted to every household, usually in proportion to the family's size or labor force. The plowland of each household con-

TABLE 1

Regional Distribution of Communal Tenure, 1905
(50 provinces of European Russia)

Region	Percent of house-holds under communal tenure[a]	Percent of all allot-ment land in communal tenure
1 Mid-Volga	100%	100%
2 Lake	100	100
3 Trans-Volga	99	99
4 Volga-Don	98	100[b]
5 Southern Steppe	98	94
6 Northern	97	99
7 Central	97	97
8 Dnepr-Don	68	72
9 Northwestern	28	21
10 Trans-Dnepr	23	29
11 Baltic	—	—
50 provinces	77%	83%

SOURCE: TsSK, *Statistika zemlevladeniia 1905*, pp. 174–75.

NOTE: The provinces in each region are shown in the Appendix, pp. 383–84. Regions are numbered as in the official data.

[a]The difference between figures in this column and 100 percent is the percentage of hereditary household tenure.

[b]The figures have been rounded to the nearest whole number. In the Volga-Don region the 2.1 percent of households that did not hold land in communal tenure held only 0.3 percent of all allotment land.

sisted of an assortment of these strips scattered among the commune's fields. Each family worked its own land separately, but the intermingling of strips and the prevailing system of agriculture made it necessary to coordinate field activities. The custom of grazing livestock on fallow and cropped fields, for example, required a common crop and a common system of crop rotation. The commune, acting through its general assembly or its officials, set the dates for planting and harvesting and generally synchronized the major agricultural operations of the community. It also regulated the use of certain lands that were considered "indivisible" and were used jointly by all members; depending on local conditions, such lands might include pastures, meadows, woods, and waters.

The "noncommunal" peasant minority held land in what was known as household tenure, a form of hereditary tenure that gave peasants permanent possession of their arable lands as well as their dwelling plots. Although cropland was not redistributed under this system, land divisions due to inheritance had led to the same pattern of small intermixed strips that was found on communal lands, and to the same sort of community regulation of agriculture. Here too there were indivisible lands used in common by all members. Technically, therefore, hereditary tenure communities constituted communes, also, although of a more limited sort.[2] Communes of this type, existing earlier not only in Russia but in many other parts of the globe, are still found today in parts of Africa, Asia, and South America. Yet the commune most important in modern Russian history, "the most peculiar of Russian institutions,"[3] was the redistributional commune.

In the central Great Russian core of the empire (in the north, the east, and much of the south of European Russia), the redistributional commune was virtually universal at the beginning of the twentieth century. Hereditary tenure was found primarily in the west. Land tenure statistics for 1905 (see Table 1) show little communal tenure west of the 30th meridian, and limited hereditary tenure east of that line. A short time after these figures were recorded tenure patterns began to change, and within a decade official data indicated a sharp shift away from communal tenure. But just as a streak on a seismograph can be evaluated only with the help of a previous record, so the commune's erratic course after 1905 is best tracked in the light of its previous history.

Terminology

Russians appear to have lived in communes since the beginning of recorded history. In different times and places these communes have been known by different names,[4] but historians have generally employed the term used by educated society for the modern redistributional commune, *obshchina*, to refer to communes at any point in the past. The use of a single blanket label for all variants of an institution reaching from pre-Kievan to modern times is problematic in that it emphasizes continuity at the expense of change, but it does make clear that throughout Russian history some aspects of the economic life of the masses have traditionally been encompassed in collective units: *obshchina* derives from the same root as *obshchestvo* ("society") and *obshchii* ("common").

The peasants, in contrast, used a more familiar and older term, *mir*, to refer to a rural community sharing the use of some land.[5] In the peasants' construction *mir* could be applied to communities observing either communal or hereditary tenure, since the community was understood primarily as a collectivity reified in the assembly of household heads. Educated society used the term in this sense also. Any community, then, could be called a *mir*, and a nonredistributional commune might occasionally be referred to as an *obshchina* to convey the notion of a group of joint landholders.[6] Perhaps because the concept of an immaterial landholding corporation was more abstract than that of an assembled community, *obshchina* was used more commonly in its attributive form—for example, in *obshchinnoe vladenie* ("communal tenure")—whereas *mir* appeared most often as a substantive.

The word *mir* has a wealth of meanings: in addition to "community" and "assembly," it also means "world" and "peace."[7] That these seemingly diverse meanings had a common historical origin is suggested by descriptions of the early Slavic assembly known as the *veche*, which the pioneering Russian sociologist Maksim Kovalevskii compared to the meetings of the most ancient Russian communes.[8] In these democratic gatherings of the populace, decisions were adopted by the unanimous agreement of the assembled community. When discussion failed to produce the obligatory unanimity, the recalcitrants settled issues by force: in the famous Novgorod veche, for example, opposing mobs battled on the bridge over the Volkhov, attempting to topple each other into the river. The same notion of forced unanimity as a guarantor of ultimate peace prevailed in the small world of the modern commune, where decisions reached by the collective were not only demonstrably enforceable, but morally binding on the individual. As the proverb put it, "What the commune orders, God ordains."[9]

Historical Development

Modern investigators of the redistributional commune believe that its development can be traced from the late fifteenth or the sixteenth century.[10] Peasant households in fifteenth-century Muscovy ordinarily held their fields in hereditary tenure, cultivated them independently, and had the right to buy, sell, or dispose of them freely. Neighboring households and settlements were linked in self-governing non-redistributional communes known as *volosts*, which served as territorial units for administrative and fiscal purposes.[11] Peasants within a volost commune were taxed collectively and shared the right to use certain local lands.

Among the peasantry land rights in general derived by custom from labor on the land, and tradition recognized a peasant's right to claim fields over which his "axe, scythe, and plow had passed."[12] In the peasants' view, it has been said, cultivated land belonged to those whose energy had created it from wilderness just as a child belonged to the parents who brought it into being.[13] As a matter of practical necessity, however, and perhaps as a result of kinship ties among the original settlers of villages, it was customary to reserve for common use certain lands and resources that were in limited supply but were essential to all households.

In the course of time communes assumed the right to distribute vacant and escheated land, and they began to play a stronger role in the land affairs of the peasantry. This development paralleled the government's gradual assertion of a proprietary sovereignty over all land,[14] for the property rights of individual households were subsumed under those of the commune just as the rights of more powerful landholders were superseded by those of the state.[15] In the middle of the sixteenth century, administrative reforms enacted by Ivan IV offered communes broad powers of self-rule under the *zemstvo* system, an optional arrangement giving peasants the right to elect local officials, who were then responsible to the state for maintaining public order and collecting taxes. The responsibilities were to prove more durable than the rights.

As the Muscovite state had grown, it had provided for its expanding force of military servitors by means of provisional land grants (*pomest'ia*), or service estates. Much of the land thus awarded was already occupied by peasants, and they usually remained on it, paying rent and performing services for their new landlords. Lands that were unpopulated were made attractive to peasant settlers by offers of loans and temporary tax advantages. Since without some form of rental income from the peasants land was of limited value to the holders of service estates or, for that matter, to the owners of hereditary estates (*votchiny*), landlords tried to bind peasants to their properties by debt contracts. Many peasants lost their freedom in this fashion. In the troubled later years of the sixteenth century, many peasants fled the harsh conditions of life in the central regions to try their luck on the open steppes and on the frontiers. Desertion of the land threatened not only the class available for state service, but the state itself. In order to secure a stable work force and to assure tax revenues, the state began to introduce regulations that deprived peasants of geographical mobility by requiring them to maintain permanent residence on the estate or property where the cadastral registers had recorded their names. By the middle of the seventeenth century enserfment was fully established.

The failure of the tentative mid-sixteenth-century attempt to create a stronger popular base under the autocracy through administrative reform meant the loss of peasant freedoms but did not lead to the disappearance of the commune. Peasants living on lands under the direct control of the state (the "black lands," often located in northern and outlying regions where there were few estates) were bound to the land along with the proprietary serfs, but retained their communes and generally enjoyed considerable autonomy in managing their own community affairs. By the end of the seventeenth century, however, there were almost four times as many serfs as state peasants.[16] Where peasants had been enserfed and the land put under the control of estate or monastic proprietors, volost communes were often broken up. In some cases a commune simply ceased to exist, but often the disintegration of the old multi-settlement volost was followed by the establishment of new communes within the boundaries of estates.[17] The elected elder (*starosta*) of the commune thus was called at times the "elder of the estate."[18]

Communes proved useful to landlords—and to the state—in a number of ways. In particular, it was convenient to tax a community of serfs or state peasants as a whole, and to make the commune collectively responsible for paying the total amount due. Taxes and feudal obligations were based primarily on land, and the commune—either independently or in consultation with the estate owner or state official—apportioned the total tax burden among its member households according to the amount of land held by each.[19] Households were assessed a certain number of *tiaglo* (or "load") units under a system in which the tiaglo represented a sum of tax money and also a corresponding amount of land. It was the legal responsibility of the estate holder to be sure that all of his landholding serfs carried a share of the state tax burden.

As the state expanded, a gap opened between mounting financial needs and an income limited by natural constraints on agricultural productivity as well as by a low level of economic development. In an attempt to make ends meet, the tax base was shifted in 1679 from land to households, since the household was a simpler unit of account, and one whose existence was more difficult to conceal from the tax collector than the extent of landholdings. Taxes increased precipitously. The peasants, already burdened with rising feudal obligations, reacted by consolidating households. It was in the landlord's interests to encourage this, since higher exactions by the state limited what they could hope to receive from their serfs.[20] The size of peasant households increased, therefore, although their number declined. The state failed to gain the full potential return from the reform, and its income remained insufficient to meet expenditures, which began to race upward in connection with the military and domestic projects of Peter the Great. In a new attack on the budgetary problem, in 1722 Peter introduced a direct tax on individual "souls"—nonnoble, tax-paying males.

Egalitarian Land Redistribution

The changes in the tax structure had an important effect on the commune. Before the late seventeenth century there appears to have been little communal land redistribution among households, even in the northern regions where communes remained strongest.[21] The earliest recorded instances of land equalization usually involved adjustments between neighboring villages—often in connection with the dissolution of volost communes.[22] Once the tax was fixed and equal for all individual households, however, the commune could no longer adjust the tax load in proportion to landholdings, but had to adjust landholdings in proportion to the tax. Instead of being considered simply a basis for assessment, land began to be considered a means enabling peasants to pay taxes, just as it was a means enabling estate holders to provide the military or administrative service they were obliged to render in place of taxes. By the beginning of the eighteenth century, the distinction between the provisional service estate and the permanent hereditary estate had all but disappeared, the property rights of all estate owners having been submerged in the preeminent domain of the state and its autocratic sovereign.

As previously, the commune was collectively responsible for the taxes of all its members, but it now began to try to find additional land for those whose inability to pay stemmed from a shortage of land relative to their supply of labor. The change was gradual, for many communes continued to observe earlier practices, treating the sum of the individual-soul taxes due from the entire commune as a burden to be apportioned among households according to their property status.[23] Alongside the old system of balancing taxes and land, however, there developed a system of balancing land and labor. Communes had routinely distributed newly acquired and vacant lands, but with increasing frequency they now also redistributed members' lands to adjust the size of holdings to the size of households.[24] At the same time, estate owners began to base their demands for labor and dues on the size of the work force in a serf household.[25] As a result, in the eighteenth century the tiaglo was gradually transformed into a unit of labor entitled to (or obliged to accept) a given amount of land and accountable for specific obligations. Under these circumstances, as one student has noted, "equal holdings were gradually instituted, not as a manifestation of a so-called egalitarian spirit of the peasantry, but simply as a consequence of the fact that in the majority of cases each peasant was capable of cultivating with his own means roughly equal quantities of land."[26]

Although some forms of land redistribution were carried out on a limited scale in the sixteenth and seventeenth centuries, the practice became widespread only in the late seventeenth century. It developed rapidly, however, and by the middle of the eighteenth century was dominant in central Russia.[27] Although the redistribution of land was often initiated by the state or by estate owners, the commune itself insisted on it in many cases. Recent investigations of early communal land redistribution suggest that when peasants were relatively well-off the initiative was apt to come from the landlord as part of a move to increase feudal dues, but that when general hardship prevailed, the peasants themselves asked for redistribution, hoping either to reduce their tiaglo obligations or to gain additional lands.[28] To the extent that redistribution improved the ability of the poorer households to meet their obligations, it heightened the utility of the commune to all landlords. The commune proved invaluable in 1731, for example, when landed proprietors were made formally responsible for the state tax obligations of their serfs. Many house serfs, for whom taxes now had to be paid, were converted to field workers, and the problem of providing them with land so that they could pay their own way was simply turned over to the communes.

Following the Pugachev rebellion, a major peasant uprising in the last quarter of the eighteenth century, administrative officials under Catherine II introduced land redistribution in communes in the north, hoping both to increase tax receipts and to promote rural tranquillity.[29] In the first half of the nineteenth century the practice was extended to other state peasants and to the appanage peasants living on lands belonging to members of the Imperial family.[30] Equalization of landholdings was often demanded by the peasants themselves, as occurred among the *odnodvortsy*, a group of state peasants originally awarded homesteads on the frontier in exchange for defending the border,[31] and among the Cossack rank and file, who insisted on redistribution within their own communities, where great inequalities in landholding had developed.[32] Poorer peasants typically called for redistribution and supported government efforts to introduce it, but peasants with relatively large holdings tried to block it.[33] The rule of mutual responsibility in all communes made land redistribution more palatable even to the relatively well-off, however, since the return from labor expended on extra land was subject to the claims of the commune if a tax deficit resulted from the inability of other members to meet their obligations.

Although there were differences in the size of holdings within the commune, land redistribution sharply limited the range of social differentiation among the peasants by repeatedly improving the position of the bottom stratum at the expense of the top. Therefore, even though it did not arise from an "egalitarian spirit," over the course of time the practice fostered the development of a social concept of egalitarianism. Evolving as a method of ensuring the fullest use of the labor supply on the land, redistribution was intended to provide each peasant household with at least the minimum amount of land necessary to meet its obligations to the state and the landlord. Yet the establishment of a uniform fiscal-labor unit (the tiaglo) as a basis for land distribution heightened social recognition of the "roughly equal" labor capacity of most individuals; since labor traditionally conferred the right to land, an equal capacity for labor implied an equal right to land.

Systems of Redistribution

As the practice of redistribution expanded, each commune adopted its own method of land allotment. Two basic schemes predominated: land was allotted to households either in proportion to the number of "souls" in them or in proportion to their total labor force. In the first case, the commune might distribute land to its "revision souls," that is, males listed in the last official census, or revision. If much time had elapsed since the census, the basis of allotment might be shifted to "present souls"—males actually living in the commune at the time of the redistribution. Under the other, more commonly used, system the entire labor supply of a household was taken into account. The basic unit of assessment, the tiaglo, was fixed by the estate owner, sometimes in consultation with the commune. It usually consisted of a man and his wife. Individuals, youths, and older peasants capable of work were rated as fractions of a unit. Land and obligations were assigned to a household in proportion to the number of its tiaglo units. Although more complicated than allotment by souls, this system was popular where land was scarce, and predominated first in the fertile black soil region, where peasant holdings were smallest. State peasants used the revision soul method, and serfs in the non–black soil region also tended to favor the simpler soul method of redistribution. By the latter part of the nineteenth century, however, it had become common practice in the non–black soil region to distribute land to households in proportion to the number of males of working age only. During this period many communes also began to count only the number of mouths to be fed in a household, reckoning the size of allotments "by eaters" rather than "by workers." Other systems of redistribution considered such factors as the amount of livestock and equipment available to work the land, and the outside employment of family members. Whatever the system adopted, however, the household receiving a share of communal land received with it a corresponding share in the commune's total tax bill, and members remained collectively responsible for the payment of the total sum due.

General redistributions of communal land took place irregularly, as the need arose, although some communes held them periodically.[34]

Where allotments were based on revision souls, general redivisions were usually scheduled at the time of a census, that is, about every twenty years. Shorter or longer intervals were not uncommon, but the requirements of the three-field system discouraged any general redistribution that did not coincide with the triennial cycle. Between general redivisions, which involved the holdings of all members, more frequent partial redistributions took place among a limited number of households; in some communes these limited transfers of land occurred annually. Voluntary adjustments between individual households could often be arranged without specific authorization from the commune, but communes could interfere in family affairs and at times brought about involuntary divisions of households and their lands.[35]

Regional Variations

The history of the redistributional commune varied in different parts of the country. Communal tenure developed vigorously in central European Russia. In the western region, where Russian territory had fallen under Lithuanian and Polish domination after the Mongol conquest, the ascendancy of a powerful nobility encouraged stronger traditions of private property. Although the western peasants became enserfed at about the same time as their brethren to the east, communal tenure failed to take root in the west, even after that region was reunited with the other Russian lands. The same was true of the Baltic provinces, which, before they were won by Peter, had long been under the influence of the Germanic Knights in Livonia. Communal tenure, therefore, was either absent or very weak in the west—in the Baltic region, White Russia, and the right-bank Ukraine.

The example of their west-Russian neighbors apparently affected landholders across the river in the upper left-bank Ukraine. A form of tenure similar to that in some northern provinces had developed in this region. As the families of the original settlers of a village grew and broke up into separate households, each descendant was recognized as having a fixed share of the village lands, except those in common use. A share represented the right to a fixed proportion of the land rather than to a specific piece of land, and the commune could redistribute parcels of land as required by changes in shareholding. In time, shares came to vary widely in size as they were subdivided among heirs, bought, and sold. In contrast to the northern regions, where communes proceeded to redistribute and equalize lands, many peasant holdings in this area of the Ukraine remained unequal and in the course of the eighteenth century came to be recognized as hereditary.[36] Farther south, however, in the territory known as New Russia, settlers from the central regions retained their earlier redistributional practices. By the end of the nineteenth century the southern border provinces and the rapidly growing southeast were solidly communal.

The redistributional commune was not limited to European Russia. As a part of the institutional baggage of Russian colonists, communes flourished beyond the Urals as well. In Siberia most colonization was a late historical development, and settlements were unevenly distributed. In remote regions where land was plentiful, such as Enisei province, households took over as much land as they could work and proprietorship was irrelevant. Siberian natives replied with perplexity to a nineteenth-century investigator: "Our boundaries, you ask? But who knows them! We think like this: our land is where our people live."[37] Where the population was denser, the commune had the right to recall unworked land held by a household and to reassign it, and in the heavily populated districts of western Siberia flanking European Russia, periodic adjustments in landholdings were effected by the commune. This system was similar to that of the traditional Great Russian redistributional commune, but holdings were larger and less fragmented, redistributions were less frequent, and households retained plots in the same location whenever possible.[38]

Correlates of Communal Development
Demography

The simultaneous existence of many different forms of communal tenure in late-nineteenth-century Siberia struck their leading investigator, Aleksandr Kaufman, as a tableau of various stages of communal evolution. Kaufman, like Kovalevskii, argued that evidence of the past was to be found in the "living history" of the present. Siberia, he concluded, showed that the transition from communal land use to communal land ownership was a function of population density.[39] Another student of the commune, K. R. Kachorovskii, reached similar conclusions. The "rights of work," in his view, had been gradually transformed under the pressure of population growth into the "right to work."[40] In agrarian Russia this still meant the right to land, but through the commune that right had been extended to all who were able and willing to work the land.

A number of scholars have postulated a direct link between the successive stages of communal landholding and rising population-to-land ratios;[41] yet it seems unlikely that population growth alone was responsible for the development of redistributional practices. Jerome Blum has pointed out that in the mid-nineteenth century the provinces of Poltava and Chernigov, with limited communal tenure, were far more densely populated than neighboring provinces that were solidly communal.[42] Even Kachorovskii, in his later work, came to question the validity of a correlation. The west Russian provinces, he noted belatedly, were heavily populated yet decidedly noncommunal.[43]

The evidence seems to suggest that population growth was a necessary but insufficient cause of the development of communal redistributional practices. A number of other processes accompanying that development may have contributed to it, the most important being the enserfment of the peasantry and changes in agrotechnology.

Serfdom and Agrotechnology

The relationship between the commune and serfdom naturally invites attention. The appearance of the modern commune paralleled or closely followed that of serfdom, and both institutions were concentrated in central European Russia. Communes served both the serf holder and the serf, and to varying degrees accommodated their mutual economic interests. These extended into the technical realm of agriculture.

Landed estates in Russia were not neatly divided into two separate sections of demesne and peasant land. They were a patchwork of lands belonging to the lord and his serfs. In fact, the estate itself could be in scattered parcels of land interspersed with those of other local proprietors or even state peasants; to complicate matters further, the boundaries of estates did not always coincide with those of communes. As a result, the cultivation of the demesne necessarily involved a landlord with operations on the land cultivated by his serfs on their own behalf.

The motley configuration of fields, originally a product of inheritance customs, was also due to developments in agrarian technology—in particular, to the three-field system, which made a gradual appearance beginning in the sixteenth century and was dominant in the central regions of European Russia by the mid-eighteenth century. Michael Confino has stressed the interrelatedness of that system with serfdom, labor dues, and the commune.* According to his analysis, the commune was tied to the three-field system because the trisection of already fragmented unenclosed land necessitated close synchronization of field operations. The new system—a distinct advance over pre-

---

*Following a path blazed by Marc Bloch, Confino argues that the technological mode adopted in agriculture determines or strongly influences the rural social structure. The integral fusion of the three-field system with social institutions blocked later agrotechnical progress, contends Confino, because any modification of the rural system was perceived as a threat to the entire social order. His argument provides a more concrete explanation of Russian agrarian backwardness than do conventional formulas on rural inertia. (Confino, *Systèmes agraires et progrès agricole*.) Complete citations for works referred to in the notes can be found in Works Cited, pp. 431–47; abbreviations are defined at the beginning of the Notes, pp. 385–430.

vious land-extensive, long-fallow practices—called for the division of arable land into three fields that passed in rotation through cycles of winter crop, spring crop, and fallow. To gain the benefits of the improved routine, all who had land rights in a given field had to coordinate their agricultural practices. The three-field system therefore enhanced the value of communal organization for the peasants, who were, in Confino's view, all the readier to accept communes because of their preconditioned "collective mentality." It also made the commune more useful to serf owners confronted with increasingly reticulated fields and more complex problems of agricultural management. At the same time, systemic requirements for order, and for a force capable of securing it, facilitated a far-ranging extension of the patrimonial authority of the estate owner. Where peasants worked directly on the demesne land for the benefit of their landlord, greater control of agricultural operations was possible. Thus the commune, serfdom, and labor dues developed along with the three-field system.

Although Confino's argument is persuasive, these institutions did not always appear together. As he himself notes, the absence of communes in the west proved no barrier to the establishment of the three-field system there. And although it is true that both serfdom and the commune were concentrated in central European Russia, the institutions were not coextensive. Communal tenure was more widespread than serfdom. There was relatively little serfdom in the far north or in other regions where communes eventually encompassed almost all peasant land; moreover, serfdom was strong in the western provinces, where there were virtually no communes. In fact, a close look at the geographic distribution of each institution in the mid-nineteenth century shows that the provinces with the lowest rates of communal tenure generally had higher-than-average percentages of serfs among their populations, while those with the lowest percentages of serfs were among the most strongly communal.[44]

A connection between the commune and the practice of demanding serf dues in the form of labor is no easier to establish. Although the demand for labor dues grew between the eighteenth and nineteenth centuries, when communes were sprouting vigorously, an examination of the patterns of growth fails to reveal a correlation. Some of the provinces with the highest rates of labor dues in the mid-nineteenth century were completely communal, others had no communes at all, and the remainder ranged fairly evenly between the extremes. In the twenty central provinces for which comparable eighteenth-century data are available, the proportion of serfs required to perform labor had actually declined slightly by the mid-nineteenth century.[45] Labor dues were in greatest demand in the west, the south, and the Urals region.

In fact, an examination of the pattern of nonlabor dues reveals a closer fit with the geographical distribution of communes. All of the provinces that showed a high rate of nonlabor dues in the nineteenth century were among the most strongly communal.[46] The reason is clear. Labor dues may have been collected from some two-thirds of the serfs, but since the serfs accounted for only about half of the peasantry at the time, no more than a third of the peasants were saddled with them, and the majority paid their obligations in the form of money or natural products. By the mid-nineteenth century there were almost as many state peasants as there were landowners' serfs.* The state peasants paid nonlabor dues, and virtually all of them were in communes. The relationship between labor dues and serfdom varied, but was far closer than the relationship of either to the commune.

Owners of large estates tended to favor nonlabor dues, except in the profitable black soil region, where almost all proprietors demanded labor of their serfs. Because of the prevailing field patterns and agricultural techniques, large estates were complex enterprises entailing high management costs. Serfs who did not pay labor dues had greater autonomy in the conduct of their own affairs, and the self-management of communes could help lower those costs for owners.

Given Russian field topography, the adoption of the three-field system intensified the need for organization in agriculture. It proved possible to satisfy that need in different ways. Both communal organization and seignorial authority were capable of coordinating field operations, and both the commune and serfdom developed alongside the new system of agriculture.[47] Speaking of the commune on large estates, V. A. Aleksandrov aptly describes it as the "organizing principle of all rural life."[48] Yet it was not the only such principle, for, as Confino perceptively observes, under serfdom "the seignorial domain represented a rigid unit of organization far more than a territorial unit."[49]

The manor and the commune were complementary, but not interdependent. In the western part of the country, serf holders imposed their own schemes of organization on the land without reference to communes. In central European Russia the commune developed alongside serfdom, taking on a broader or more limited role according to the degree of immediate control exercised by the estate owner. In the north and the more recently settled southern and eastern regions, where

---

*One important reason for the large increase in the number of state peasants was the secularization of ecclesiastical lands in 1764 and the transfer of the two million peasants living on them to the control of the state.

serfdom was weaker, the commune played a major role in the collective management of peasants' land and fiscal responsibilities.

The Role of the Commune in Peasant Life

The functions of the commune, however, extended beyond the management of land and finances. Although its activities and autonomy varied widely in different localities and under different landlords, the commune occupied an important part in the life of the peasant. Not only was it responsible for the equitable redistribution of land, but it alone provided protection against the loss of land. Under the law all of the land in an estate was the property of its owner. He was entitled to reduce the amount of land at the disposal of his serfs, or to alter any of their communal arrangements. In practice, however, this rarely occurred. The force of custom preserved the commune in its traditional territory, and the peasant in his traditional land rights. Instances of peasants being totally deprived of land were reported most often in the provinces of the Ukraine and in the western regions, where there were no communes.[30] That peasants viewed their communes favorably is suggested by the history of a group of serfs freed in 1803. Although these peasants were allotted land in hereditary tenure at the time of their emancipation, most of them continued to redistribute their lands according to their old communal conventions.[31]

Communes not only distributed community lands, but at times bought additional lands collectively. (The title to land purchased by serfs was registered in the name of the owner of the estate on which the commune was located.) The commune organized field operations, setting the dates for sowing, harvesting, and letting cattle out to graze on the stubble. When new households arose through marriage or family division, it was the commune that found land for them. Communes also established the amount of taxes and obligations due from each household. These included not only state and landlord dues, but also obligations levied by the commune itself. The commune could tax its members to meet community needs, and it could impose monetary, natural, or labor dues. Such dues were often substantial, amounting at times to half or more of the state tax or the landlord's impost.[52]

One of the most important duties faced by communes was filling the local quota of recruits for the army.* Military service was the most bur-

---

*See Aleksandrov, chap. 5. Attempts to avoid military service increased land redistributions, since large households often broke up in the hope of evading recruitment of a member. In 1731 family divisions among court peasants were restricted specifically to block service evasions. (Semevskii, 1:321, 2:xiv.)

densome of the many obligations demanded of peasants, and it was politically expedient for the government and the serf owners to let the
commune choose recruits. The number that had to be sent to the army
was based (after 1724) on the number of revision souls. Soldiers originally served for life terms; after 1793, they served for 25 years. A departing recruit was mourned by his family as if he had died. Until the
reform of 1874 universalized military service and reduced the term of
service to six years, communes could meet their quotas by purchasing
recruits and levying a tax on their members to cover the cost.

The commune settled family disputes, maintained social order, and
administered justice in routine cases on the basis of customary law.
Public welfare also fell within its competence. Admirers of the institution have pointed out that it provided for orphans, the widowed, the
aged, the dependents of soldiers, victims of fire, and others in need. In
a spirit of *paysannerie oblige* another proverb advertised, "A thread
from the commune becomes a shirt for the naked." After examining
estate records, however, a modern skeptic concluded that most communal assistance was limited to needy children, where charity might
represent a hardheaded investment in future workers and taxpayers.[53]
Other unfortunates were generally left to the care of relatives or were
obliged to fend for themselves.

Although communes had limited resources, they often attempted to
lay in stores of grain as insurance against crop failure. Such a supply
might be obtained from a part of the commune's land set aside and
worked collectively to provide for social needs; any surplus could be
sold to cover tax shortages. Some communes owned their own mills;
others rented them. Common needs, such as salt, might be met by
joint purchases, and occasionally there were more ambitious enterprises. V. I. Semevskii mentions a serf with some experience in trade
who persuaded the members of his commune to pool their capital in
business ventures.[54] Decisions of the commune were made at the general meeting (where only household heads voted) and were adopted—
generally by a simple majority—after debate and discussion. The estate owner or state officials, however, could influence or interfere with
democratic procedures.

By the middle of the nineteenth century, the commune served as
the basic de facto administrative and fiscal unit of European Russia. It
provided the essentials of local government, was responsible for routine but fundamental decisions affecting the agrarian economy, and
was the unofficial guardian of peasant customary law and order. On the
eve of serf emancipation, however, it became the target of reformist
criticism. The commune, it was charged, was an economic liability. It

perpetuated the irrational fragmentation of peasant lands, impeded transition to more advanced crop rotation systems, and was part of the outmoded system of serfdom. The nobility had been emancipated from state service in 1762, a century earlier; it was time, urged reformers, to emancipate the peasantry from service to the nobility and from all aspects of serfdom. Russia's defeat in the Crimean War had strengthened the case for modernization. As emancipation of the peasantry approached, the issue evoked widespread debate: was the commune indispensable, or was it an anachronism that should be abolished along with serfdom?

The Commune in the Nineteenth Century

The Debate on the Commune

Anticipation of emancipation drew unprecedented attention to the commune and its role in the life of the peasantry. According to a recent tally, an unprepossessing total of five works on the Russian commune had been published by 1855, although as recently as the 1840's reforms introduced by the Minister of State Properties, P. D. Kiselev, had strengthened the commune among state peasants and more recently still Baron August Haxthausen's three-volume study of Russian life and rural institutions (1847–52) had aroused general interest.[1] Given the scarcity of sources and the ideological climate, a lively difference of opinion was inevitable. What resulted has been described as a "historiographical brouhaha" without peer in Russian history[2]—by the time of the emancipation in 1861, over one hundred titles on the commune were in circulation, and in the last quarter of the century alone some two thousand new books and articles sustained the bibliographic explosion.[3]

The debate was framed in terms of the contemporary controversy between the Slavophiles and the Westerners: Was there a uniquely Russian history, national character, and destiny, or did Russian history merely replicate a general European pattern? On the Western side, nineteenth-century historians of the "state school" (notably B. N. Chicherin, S. M. Solov'ev, and K. D. Kavelin) argued that the modern commune had been created by the state as a "fiscal-administrative device" by a series of measures traceable perhaps to the late fifteenth or the sixteenth century. The modern commune took definitive shape only in the eighteenth century, in their view, and had little relation to ancient Russian communes, in which the distinctive practice of land redistribution was unknown. The Slavophiles (for example, K. S. Aksakov, A. S. Khomiakov, and I. D. Beliaev), on the other hand, insisted that the contemporary commune was directly descended from ancient prototypes. In their view, communes had formed the basic units of Russian social organization "from time without end, time beyond memory." The old and the new had a similar structure, they argued, and embodied the same egalitarian spirit of collectivism. Arising spontaneously to accommodate social needs, communes served the vital interest of the people.[4]

Many of the leading figures in the debate were politically prominent and attracted a large audience at a critical period in the formulation of the reform legislation. They represented all political sectors. Kavelin, for instance, had been tutor to the heir to the throne; both he and Chicherin were academic activists who helped to articulate liberal aspirations and anticommunal sentiments. The conservative Slavophiles were guaranteed a sympathetic audience in most bureaucratic circles, and several "liberal Slavophiles" won seats on the important Editorial Commission, which drafted the emancipation legislation in 1859–60.[5] Iu. F. Samarin and A. I. Koshelev, influential members of the gentry, advanced the merits of the commune in the Slavophile *Russkaia beseda*.

At the same time, the proto-socialists Aleksandr Herzen and Nikolai Chernyshevsky were writing in praise of the commune. Herzen's articles, smuggled in from abroad, reached the topmost levels of the government.[6] Raising the spectre of a renewed *Pugachevshchina*, a vast peasant uprising, he effectively exploited upper-class fears that social unrest might follow the disappearance of the commune.[7] Chernyshevsky, the remarkable journalist who was soon to become the social conscience of radical youth, agreed on the desirability of retaining the commune. Formulating the problem in Hegelian terms, he suggested that under favorable conditions Russia might pass via the contemporary commune from lower forms of communal landholding to the highest socialist form, skipping the "negation" of private property.[8] Such arguments in support of the commune brought the nascent revolutionary underground into uneasy alignment with the tradition-oriented Slavophiles.

The clash of opinions created a demand for information about the contemporary commune. After intensive discussion of the topic, the prestigious Free Economic Society launched a massive investigation of the countryside, and in 1880 it published a collection of materials for the study of the commune. By this time the new organs of local self-government, the zemstvos (see pp. 25–26) had begun to collect data themselves. Before the end of the century over two hundred district zemstvo statistical reports, covering over half of all existing communes, were available.

Despite the accretion of data, however, most scholars continued to adopt one or another of the two basic attitudes underlying the initial debate. Liberal historian Paul Miliukov, for example, developed the views of the state school, as did the historian of law Vasilii Sergeevich, whereas populist historian Vasilii Semevskii stressed the utility of the commune to the peasants and their own requests that it be introduced. In the controversy between Populists and Marxists toward the end of the nineteenth century, the familiar dichotomy was maintained, although to some extent the Marxists accepted elements of both earlier schools of thought.

The debate on the commune set a precedent by involving historiographic questions in the determination of policy on social reform. Yet the ultimate determinants of emancipation policy on the commune were undoubtedly the practical implications of its abolition.

Emancipation

Policy

Long reliance on the commune in matters of local jurisdiction and tax collection left the state with inadequate administrative machinery to replace it. If seignorial authority and communal authority were the basic alternative (or complementary) forces organizing rural life, then the abolition of the former with emancipation would require retention of the latter in the interest of social stability. No other immediate provision for local government at the village level was at hand. At a time when the public debt was swollen by military expenditures, finances were strained, and the burden of taxation was borne largely by the peasantry, the government was about to launch an emancipation that not only liberated the peasants but freed landlords from responsibility for peasants' taxes.[9] Under such conditions the mutual tax responsibility of the communes seemed a fiscal advantage that could not be surrendered. In addition, rapid proletarianization of the peasantry was anticipated as a by-product of any attempt to abandon communal organization; the political potential of such a development weighed heavily against any benefits that might result from dispensing with the commune. If the prevailing mood of the times favored an institutional pattern of local self-government, as has been argued recently, the mood only reflected the logic of circumstances.[10]

Both conservatives and radicals supported the commune, and even most of its liberal opponents were in favor of retaining it temporarily.[11] Not surprisingly, then, the emancipation statute of February 19, 1861, preserved the commune, though with an ambivalence that reflected the range of contemporary opinion. Ambivalence was to characterize official policy on the commune for almost half a century. Actually, retention of the commune was never seriously in doubt. Although a small group of provincial committees urged private land tenure for peasants, the majority of the committees and most members of the Editorial Commission favored communal tenure.[12] The views of Ia. I. Rostovtsev, the first head of the commission, were typical: the people needed a "strong authority" to replace the lord of the manor; furthermore, without the commune neither the gentry nor the government would be able to collect dues from the peasants.[13]

Legislation

The emancipation legislation was extensive and complex, covering vast areas with varying economic and social conditions. To encompass this diversity with a minimum of violence to local peculiarities, the legislation took the form of a general statute that provided the framework of emancipation, and four local statutes that dealt with different regions.

Additional regulations covered special groups and areas, including the lands of the Don Cossacks and Siberia. The Statute of February 19, 1861, was concerned primarily with gentry-owned serfs. The remainder of the peasant population (the appanage and state peasantry) was dealt with in similar legislation in 1863 and 1866.

In this juridical massif were two points of outstanding importance for the future of the commune: (1) the law recognized communal tenure, and (2) the newly "unbound" peasant was in effect now bound to the commune. The Imperial manifesto accompanying the legislation maintained the legal fiction that the nobility retained its property right over all its lands but was allotting part of the land to the peasantry "in permanent usage" in return for payment as prescribed by law. This "allotment land" was turned over locally to the peasants' "rural society" (*sel'skoe obshchestvo*), and the government paid the landowner up to 80 percent of the amount due from the peasants on the conclusion of an agreement between the rural society and the landlord. The peasants were to "redeem" the land by repaying the government in installments spread over a term of 49 years. House and garden plots remained in the hereditary possession of resident peasant families but reverted to the rural society upon escheat. The amount of land turned over to the society was determined by a system of regional norms and by negotiation with the landlord; lands were allotted to peasants as communal or hereditary household property in accordance with the local form of tenure. Where repartitional communes existed, the prevailing basis of distribution (revision souls, tiaglo, mixed, or other) was maintained. The Editorial Commission declared the allotment of lands and of corresponding taxes to be the distinguishing feature of communal tenure.[14] Land redistribution was judged a secondary characteristic.

Communal tenure thus defined was recognized as a historical fact and accepted as the basic form of peasant landholding; but in deference to the economic opponents of the commune and to the march of time, the commission left the door open for an eventual transition to private property "should the path of history take that direction." Hereditary household tenure was legally recognized as an intermediary stage along such a path and could be adopted by a two-thirds vote of communes where it had not previously existed.

Despite their juridical reinforcement of the institution, the members of the Editorial Commission seem to have considered the commune doomed to gradual extinction. At any rate, the Statute of February 19, 1861, made no provision for the conversion of private property into communal property, only for the reverse.[15] Although the legislation did not disturb the predominant redistributional tenure, most members of the commission acknowledged the adverse consequences of communal land redistribution, noting that it led to excessive fragmentation of holdings and stifled incentive to make improvements on the land. The commission discussed the merits of prohibiting or restricting land redistribution, but finally agreed that the numerous exceptions required would clutter the legislation with excessive detail. Instead, it decided merely to discourage redistributions by requiring that each be approved by a large majority of the householders within a commune. A 90 percent majority was first proposed; later a three-fourths vote was accepted as sufficient; and the final legislation reduced the requirement to a two-thirds majority.[16]

The Rural Society and the Volost

In an attempt to remodel on the basis of the existing structure, the government decided that a group of peasants who had been living on the same estate would be recognized by law as a rural society. The "rural society" (the legislation itself put the unfamiliar term in quotation marks) was composed of at least twenty members; smaller groups amalgamated to reach this minimum, if possible. The new legal entity could consist of an entire village, part of a large village, several small villages, or separate neighboring peasant landholders using some land in common or having other economic relations.[17]

The responsibilities of the rural society were spelled out in the emancipation legislation, and the societies were given the right to tax their members to meet these obligations. Most of their functions were within the traditional competence of the commune. In addition to such responsibilities as apportioning state taxes and selecting military recruits, the societies were required to maintain roads and waterways passing through their territory, provide fire protection for the community and for local woods, take certain public health measures, and cope with floods and pests. They were instructed to maintain granaries and were officially charged with the care of orphans, the aged, and those in need of assistance who had no relatives. In addition to these obligatory duties, the society could undertake to build and support churches and schools and to provide for other community needs, but taxes levied for such non-obligatory concerns were subject to the approval of the peasant volost.

Volosts not only had survived into the nineteenth century among the state peasants but had been given an expanded role in an administrative reorganization not long before the emancipation. A new system of volosts was now established to reinforce the administrative network between the peasants and the central authorities. As defined by law, a volost was composed of one or more neighboring rural societies within an administrative district (*uezd*) and originally included from 300 to 2,000 revision souls.[18] The peasants in the volost's territory elected representatives to a volost assembly, which was also attended by all of the elders and tax collectors of the rural societies within the territory. Just as the rural society elected an elder, the starosta, to preside over its meetings and serve as its executive officer, so the volost elected its own counterpart, the *starshina*. The assembly elected a peasant court that administered justice "according to the peasant tradition," thereby taking over one of the earlier functions of the commune. Peasants were thus joined in their economic (primarily land and tax) relations by the rural society and organized administratively by the volost. It has been suggested that the establishment of volosts as administrative units distinct from communes was a compromise between tendencies toward local autonomy on the one hand and autocratic centralization on the other.[19]

In addition to the volost, another new unit of local government was introduced under a reassuringly old name: the zemstvo. Launched in 1864, zemstvos were established at district and provincial levels. Delegates were elected by local property holders, were empowered to act on local economic needs, and had the right to impose taxes for that purpose. Although the founding legislation secured the predominance

of the nobility, communal peasants had the right as collective proprietors to elect representatives to the new organs of self-government and
were given a quota of over a third of the seats under the zemstvo electoral system.

After all these innovations, however, the unit of local government
closest to the peasants was still the familiar commune, now known officially as the rural society. The new term applied to all peasant communities, and its introduction marked an attempt at administrative
standardization. The legislators usually assumed a general coincidence
of the new units with pre-existing communes, and in later official documents the term "commune" (*obshchina*) sometimes appeared in place
of "rural society." On occasion, however, a distinction was drawn between the rural society as a whole, with its non-landowning residents
(village teachers, stationmasters, and so on), and the group of peasants
in the society who had rights to community lands.[20] In practice as well
as in juridical language, the line between the rural society and the
commune was blurred, and the old communes were generally preserved even where they did not—for one reason or another—coincide
with the new rural society. Separate small communes that fell within a
rural society often continued to control their own territories independently, though these lands had been legally assigned to the society as a
whole.

Land and Liberty

Besides retaining the commune, the emancipation legislation stated
that the peasant—rather, the peasant household—was not merely
granted a share of communal lands but was obliged to accept them,
along with a corresponding tax burden and mutual responsibility for
the taxes of the entire commune. A peasant who wanted to leave, even
temporarily, for outside work was dependent on the commune for a
passport. On the other hand, a peasant in arrears in his payments could
be sent out to work by the commune. Despite emancipation, then,
there were still serious constraints on the geographical mobility of the
peasantry.

The commune was not permitted to alienate any of its lands for a
period of nine years (until 1870) and then only with the authorization
of provincial officials. In theory a householder could redeem his house
and garden plot alone and renounce an allotment before undertaking
its redemption, but in practice this was difficult to arrange. Once collective redemption was underway, the difficulties increased: in addition to renouncing all claims to the commune's allotment land, obtain-

ing the consent of the head of the household, and paying current taxes, the peasant was obliged to pay half of the redemption assessment on his allotment (which was considerably above its market value) and then surrender the allotment to the commune.[21] Even then the commune could block separation by refusing to accept the other half of the debt. Where land was infertile and the taxes on it in excess of the value of its productive capacity, such a refusal was not unlikely. Only if a house-holder paid off the *entire* assessment on his allotment could he claim his scattered strips of field as permanent hereditary property, or take his leave.[22] Peasants in hereditary tenure communities could leave at any time if they could find someone to assume the redemption payments on their allotment; however, since these payments generally exceeded land rental costs, this was no easy matter.

In the two decades following the emancipation, fewer than 50,000 peasants were able under these conditions to redeem their allotments. By 1892, over 125,000 had done so, but a new law at the end of the following year forbade any withdrawal from the commune, even when an allotment had been fully redeemed, unless authorized by two-thirds of the membership. Thereafter, withdrawals fell off sharply.[23]

The restrictions on peasant mobility were designed to block any mass exodus from the countryside that could result in the urbanization and proletarianization of the population, developments viewed as threats to the autocracy and the social structure. They were also intended to ensure the manorial economy a rural labor force. The rationale was not devoid of a certain logic; the results, however, belied the intentions of the policy-framers.

The sweeping expropriation of the nobles' lands, which had been first recognized by the state as inalienable less than a century earlier, shows how shallow were the roots of private property in Russia. The transfer of those lands to the collective control of communes meant that the commune replaced the landlord as the effective rural authority. Communes now had the right, formerly held by the masters of serfs, to impose sentences of banishment. More ominously, the loan obligation virtually forced upon a peasant by the terms of the emancipation tied him to the land—replicating a situation that had led to enserfment centuries earlier. In the dynamic atmosphere of "the Great Reforms," contemporaries—even those debating the historical role of the commune—looked to the future more than at the past. State and society had needs that could still be filled by the commune. Yet from the perspective of a later century, leading students of the emancipation concur that the retention of the commune had negative consequences and was one of the main reasons why "the Emancipation was largely responsible for the social and economic crisis that resulted in the Russian Revolution."[24]

The Agrarian Problem
Population Growth and Allotment Size

Restraints imposed on the rural population combined with the agricultural practices of the commune to exacerbate the mounting agrarian problem of Russia in the late nineteenth and early twentieth centuries. Population pressure on the land, low agricultural productivity, high labor costs, and perhaps a restricted supply of skilled industrial labor were all related to these factors.[25] The total amount of land turned over to the peasants at the time of emancipation was somewhat less than they had been using previously.[26] But the amount of land held by any group becomes significant only when the level of its productivity is related to the needs of the population subsisting on it.[27]

Communal tenure tied the Russian peasant to a common system of crop rotation, preventing diversification or innovation. In the sixteenth century the three-field system represented an advance; three centuries later, it had become a drawback. The multitude of scattered, far-flung strips that constituted a household's holdings were monuments to economic irrationality. Not only the peasants' time and labor but much of the land itself was wasted, for each fragment of the field mosaic required access lanes. As liberal economic critics of the commune had pointed out, individual initiative was stifled under the system of periodic redistribution because any improvement or investment might pass to another landholder.

It has been estimated that under existing output levels, minimum subsistence required five to six desiatins of black soil per (male) soul.[28] (A desiatin equals 2.7 acres.) Yet according to official data the average allotment to former serfs (about 40 percent of the peasantry at the time of emancipation) was 3.3 desiatins.[29] Former state peasants (most of the remainder) received an average of 5.6 desiatins, and the small balance of appanage peasants got 4.1 desiatins. These figures reveal only part of the problem, for the peasants were deprived of essential woodlands and received disproportionately small meadow and pasture lands. In 1887 only a third of the privately held land was arable, but over half of the peasant allotment land was arable.[30] Peasant lands were mainly field lands, and while the land supply was short in general, the shortage of other types of land needed for a balanced agricultural economy was even more acute.

Given the relatively inelastic supply of land and the restraints on peasant mobility, the rise in population between the emancipation and the end of the century was bound to create a severe problem. Whereas the revision of 1858 recorded a population of 74 million, the census of 1897 returned 129 million for an Empire whose territory was enlarged only slightly. As a result of the growing population pressure, the average peasant allotment fell to 2.8 desiatins per soul by the end of the nineteenth century.[31]

Although the government tried to slow the fragmentation of holdings by requiring (in a law of March 18, 1886) the consent of two-thirds of the commune for family divisions, in practice this ruling, like similar regulations in the emancipation legislation, was largely ignored.[32] Following the famine of the early 1890's, another attempt materialized in a law of June 8, 1893, which forbade further partial redistributions of land and limited general redistributions to a minimum interval of twelve years. All redistributions were to be supervised by the land captains, new appointive officials introduced in 1889 to strengthen central authority in the countryside. The commune's voice in local affairs was weakened by changes in the zemstvo electoral system in 1890. Not only was the ratio of peasant delegates reduced, but representation became indirect, with delegates appointed by higher authorities from lists of candidates selected by volost assemblies. All of these measures were designed to improve the government's control of the rural economy.

The peasants themselves were vitally concerned about the diminishing size of allotments but in attempting to cope with the growing land shortage turned all the more frequently to redistribution.[33] A survey of communal redistributions in Aleksandrov district, Ekaterinoslav province, showed that 140 cases of general redistribution occurred between 1864 and 1904 in the 157 communes in the district. Up to 1895 only 19 of these major reshufflings of land took place; between 1895 and 1900 there was an average of 8 each year; and from 1900 to 1903 the annual average rose to 20. However, in the final year covered by the survey, 1903, the number jumped to 40—almost a third of all general redistributions carried out since the emancipation.[34] Land pressure led to a modification of the system of redistribution in the non–black soil region,[35] where it became common practice to distribute land to households in proportion to the number of males of working age that each contained, rather than simply to the number of males. This brought the land supply and labor force into closer correlation; however, the use of allotment systems based on males alone, even working males, began to draw occasional criticism. The "woman question" stirring

among elements of educated society had its rural echo. Although some
communes resisted taking any notice of females in the allotment of
land on the grounds that women neither paid taxes nor served as soldiers, others conceded that fathers who had the misfortune of having
only daughters should be given extra land to provide for them.[36] A de-
ceased peasant's widow or daughter was sometimes permitted to retain
his allotment, but often only until she married or until the next redistribution. The laws of 1886 and 1893 made it easier for peasants who
were well off to block repartitions, but the collective tax responsibility
of the commune meant that these peasants remained saddled with the
tax burden of their insolvent neighbors, who were becoming more and
more numerous. Tax-collecting police were authorized to seize and sell
the movable property (including livestock) of wealthier peasants to
help cover the arrears of fellow members. Surveys indicated that the
main motive of peasants who bought their way out of the commune
was not so much a taste for individualized tenure as the desire to escape mutual tax responsibility.[37] Still, a peasant who managed to take
his land out of the commune did not face a reduction of his allotment at
the next redistribution.

The Commune and Demographic Tendencies

The shrinkage of allotments caused by population growth was exacerbated by the nature of communal tenure. Not only did communes
repartition the land, but the system itself tended to keep the population on the land. The household head had to give permission for a
member to obtain a passport, and because land was generally allotted
to households according to their size, families could be reluctant to release their members. Although it is clear that the communal system
helped to lock the growing population to the land, it is not so clear why
the commune has been held responsible for the population increase
itself. According to one authority, "the main count in the indictment
against the *mir*, or redistributionary rural commune, as such, was that
it contributed to the development of agrarian overpopulation by re-
lieving the individual peasant from the responsibility for the excessive
increase of his family. The task of finding room for any new member
devolved on the whole commune, which did it at the expense of the
whole village, at the cost of relatively small individual sacrifices."[38]
This quite plausible argument is consonant with general observations
linking modes of property tenure with birth-rate patterns,[39] and is said
to explain differences in family structure that distinguish Russia from
western Europe.[40] But the fact that high birth rates were common in
communal areas does not necessarily mean that the commune was re-

TABLE 2

Communal Tenure and Population Growth, 1863–1914

(50 provinces of European Russia)

Region	Percent of households under communal tenure, 1905	Percent increase in population, 1863–1914	
1 Mid-Volga	100%	65%	
2 Lake	100	115	
3 Trans-Volga	99	115	
4 Volga-Don	98	80	103%
5 Southern Steppe	98	241	
6 Northern	97	74	
7 Central	97	82	
8 Dnepr-Don	68	94	
9 Northwestern	28	142	
10 Trans-Dnepr	23	148	136%
11 Baltic	—	68	
50 provinces	77%	109%	

SOURCES: TsSK, *Statistika zemlevladeniia 1905*, pp. 174–75; regional population increases are calculated from data in Rashin, *Naselenie*, pp. 44–45.

sponsible for population growth. A glance at the demographic data, presented in Table 2, suggests that the case remains to be proved.

In the first seven regions listed, communal tenure was nearly universal. The total population increase in these regions between 1863 and 1914 was an impressive 103 percent. But in the last three regions, where a minority of households held land in communal tenure, the increase was even larger—a hefty 136 percent. The two regions that experienced the lowest rate of population growth were at opposite ends of the scale of communal tenure. The solidly communal mid-Volga region had only a 65 percent increase—the lowest of any region—and the noncommunal Baltic was close behind with an increase of 68 percent.[*] On the basis of these data, it would be difficult to argue that the commune was responsible for population growth. Yet a closer look at the demographic materials shows that the question is not so easily dismissed. Birth rates in the communal regions were indeed higher in general than those in the remaining regions. (See the Appendix.) The birth rate in the mid-Volga region, for example, was half again as high as that in the Baltic provinces. But despite higher birth rates, the level of natural increase was typically *lower* in communal provinces because of higher mortality rates.

The death rate in Russia in the nineteenth century was often higher

[*] For a more complete breakdown of the data by provinces, see the Appendix.

in the countryside than in urban areas. Russian mortality rates in general were exceptionally high (an average of 34 per 1,000 for the period 1861–1913) and dropped far more slowly than Western mortality rates. Infant mortality in Russia was among the highest in the world and hardly declined at all in this period, although it dropped dramatically elsewhere. In the second half of the nineteenth century, one out of every four children born in European Russia died before its first birthday, and in some districts children below the age of five accounted for two-thirds of all deaths.[11] Communal tenure was strongest where conditions of peasant life were most difficult; since among peasants large families were generally wealthy families,* a higher loss of children in communal regions may have been enough to evoke a compensatory higher rate of births. The three western regions at the bottom of the scale of communal tenure had the lowest death rates. However, these general observations suggest only that the relationship of the commune to demographic tendencies calls for closer examination.

The Peasant Economy

Whether or not the social responsibility of the commune to provide land encouraged personal irresponsibility about family size, population pressure increased land hunger and led to soaring land prices. From an average of 12.6 rubles per desiatin in the period just before the emancipation, land prices rose to an average of over 100 rubles in 1910.[12] By the 1890's market prices had overtaken the inflated evaluations fixed in the original redemption agreements, and this contributed to an upsurge in the number of allotments redeemed.

Paradoxically, rising land prices were accompanied by falling grain prices and therefore by a decrease in the income that a peasant could hope to derive from the land. As a result of the general collapse of the international grain market in the late 1870's, Russian grain export prices declined steadily; beginning in the 1880's domestic grain prices followed an even steeper downhill slope.[13] Peasants could see only one solution: more land. Since hard times had shaken much of the gentry loose from the largely unprofitable pursuit of agriculture, peasants' readiness to pay high prices for land led to increasing sales and rentals. By 1905 approximately 40 percent of the land held by the gentry at the time of the emancipation had passed into other hands—most of it to peasants through collective purchases. About 40 percent of all land still privately owned was rented by peasants.[14] The Peasant Land Bank,

---

*Beginning at least as early as the seventeenth century, the word *sem'ianistyi*, meaning "having a large family," was synonymous with "wealthy." (Gorskaia, p. 229; Aleksandrov, p. 211.)

opened by the government in 1883 to facilitate credit arrangements, became increasingly important as an agent of transfer of state and gentry lands. Most of its transactions were with communes and peasant associations; only 2 percent of the loans granted between 1883 and 1895 were to individuals.[45] Mortgages of peasant land and the sale of allotment lands to nonpeasants were prohibited by a decree of December 14, 1893, which, in a significant reversal of previous policy, also stipulated that the right to leave the commune (guaranteed by Article 165 of the Statute on Redemption to a peasant who had paid in full for his share of allotment land) be subject to the consent of the commune. Since individual separations lessened the commune's land fund, the necessary two-thirds approval was not likely to be easily obtained. In the year 1893 alone close to a million rubles had been paid to redeem allotments; in 1894, following the imposition of the new restrictions, the total fell to 44,000 rubles.[46]

Official paternalism, like the Russian Imperial eagle, looked two ways at once. While the peasantry was being secured in (and securely locked into) its collective and class land rights, it was being drained to finance the government's policy of industrialization in the late nineteenth century.[47] Peasants were confronted not only with a rise in state taxes (largely in indirect taxation), but also with soaring zemstvo taxes, which climbed particularly sharply after the 1890 "counterreform" curtailed peasant representation.[48] Although zemstvo tax increases were accompanied by an expansion of zemstvo services in the countryside, a wide array of village needs were still met by the commune, and the budgets of communes rose also. Escalating "mir taxes" (taxes levied by the rural society and the volost) joined a mounting burden of peasant obligations.

The deterioration of the peasants' economic position was reflected by growing redemption-payment and tax arrears. In 1881 the outstanding redemption debt was reduced somewhat, and a few years later the soul tax was abolished. Crop failures and famine in 1891–92 brought further distress, however, and despite extensions of the payment period, the accumulated arrears amounted by the end of the century to a sum larger than the total annual tax bill. In the central black soil region, arrears in 1880 amounted to 15 percent of the annual levy; by 1896 they reached 127 percent.[49] In the hard-pressed agricultural provinces of the mid-Volga and Lower Volga regions, they soared as high as 400 percent.[50] High monetary obligations compelled the peasants to market more grain, even though agricultural prices were falling. Grain exports were the mainstay of the favorable balance of payments that the government considered essential to encourage foreign investment and provide capital for industrialization. Financial policy implemented the somber program of Finance Minister I. A. Vyshnegradskii (1887–92), who insisted that grain be exported even at the cost of going hungry. It was, of course, the peasant producers of the exported grain who were obliged to pay that cost. Grain production had increased by 36 percent between 1861 and 1891, but because of population growth production per capita had dropped by 12 percent.[31] This, plus a worsening of the peasant economy in general, made it increasingly difficult to maintain grain reserves against crop failure; as a result the poor harvest of 1891 created a famine of exceptional severity.

Government Policy

At the time of the legislation of 1893, the State Council called for a review of all legislation on the peasantry. In response, the Ministry of Internal Affairs drew up a list of questions on peasant affairs and dispatched copies to special committees of officials in the provinces, who were to investigate local conditions and submit reports. The review was conducted secretly so as not to raise "groundless hopes among the peasants," and the work proceeded slowly.[32] Meanwhile, in 1898 the Council of Ministers endorsed a proposal for an investigation of the needs of agriculture. Although the Tsar initially declined to authorize the establishment of an investigatory commission, a succession of bad harvests that hit the countryside at the turn of the century forced the government to give greater attention to the rural situation. An economic crisis in the industrial sector at the same time helped to emphasize the country's dependence on the strained rural economy, as well as the limitations imposed on industrialization by the agrarian problem. Not only the peasantry but also the nobility, the traditional serving arm of the autocracy, was in a critical and deteriorating economic position. For a number of reasons, then, it appeared essential to improve the state of agriculture.

In 1901 a commission was appointed to study conditions in the central agricultural region. The following year a Special Conference on the Needs of Agriculture was finally set up under the presidency of Sergei Witte, the sparkplug of Russian industrialization and Vyshnegradskii's successor as Finance Minister. This agency set up 618 local committees, whose 12,000 members set to work collecting data and opinions on the rural economy. The relationship between land tenure and the state of agriculture was among the questions submitted to the committee and was widely discussed. The majority of the committees (only 2 percent of whose members were peasants) reportedly viewed the commune as an "insurmountable obstacle" to agricultural improvement, a technical barrier to multi-field cultivation. A dissenting minority, although "valuing it primarily as a guarantee against proletarianization," noted the economic advantages of the commune in minimizing individual expenses (for pasturage, water, roads, and so on) and observed that the commune could be useful in introducing technical advances just as it had helped to introduce the three-field system.[33]

Witte had endorsed the commune on such grounds in the 1890's, but he emerged now as its vigorous opponent. By no means did the commune save the peasant from proletarianization, he argued; there was evidence of pauperization and of social differentiation among the peasantry even within it. In this conclusion he was in unwitting agreement with the Marxists—particularly with Lenin, who, while in Siberian exile in the late 1890's, had produced his substantial study of the agrarian economy, *The Development of Capitalism in Russia*. Once again pillars of the autocracy and their polar adversaries were united in their views on the commune, but now they were united in opposition to it. Both the minister and the revolutionary saw the commune as blocking economic progress, though Witte also saw a "great external correspondence between the commune and . . . the theoretical constructs of socialism and communism."[54]

The government's political concerns were heightened by a wave of peasant uprisings that rolled across the south, engulfing the provinces of Kharkov and Poltava in the spring of 1902. The challenge to law and the rural order provoked a number of responses. On March 12, 1903, the mutual responsibility of commune members for state taxes was abandoned, since collective responsibility had not prevented the accumulation of huge tax arrears and was only alienating the more prosperous peasants from the regime. Yet this momentous step promised little relief to the peasant masses, and in fact merely heightened the regressiveness of peasant taxes.[55] Although the repeal was essentially a conciliatory gesture toward the better-off peasants, it was hoped (at least by some) that the measure would also strengthen the commune by eliminating a source of antagonism among its members. Despite criticism of the commune, its supporters still had a strong voice in rural policy.

Following the 1902 disturbances, the review of peasant legislation that had been dragging on since 1893 began to move more rapidly. In July 1902 an editorial commission was set up under A. S. Stishinskii, the head of the Land Department of the Ministry of Internal Affairs, to draw up a new statute on the basis of the materials that had been collected. By 1904 a draft project had been prepared, but it was sent back to the provincial committees for further work, which continued into

1905. The proposed law was based on three principles: maintaining the separate status of the peasantry as a social estate, supporting the inalienability of allotment land from the peasantry, and defending the existing forms of peasant land tenure against any forcible legal change. The editorial commission, however, proposed that "land societies" be recognized as separate organizations completely independent of rural societies, and that measures be taken to permit any peasant to separate from the commune, with the right to receive his share of communal land in one consolidated piece.[56] These suggestions were fully in line with policy already marked out by the Tsar. On February 26, 1903, on the eve of the abolition of collective tax responsibility, an imperial manifesto, like a ritual incantation invoking stability in the face of change, insistently proclaimed the "inviolability" of the commune, while conceding that measures would have to be taken to facilitate individual departures from it.

The draft of the editorial commission and the materials it used were available to the Special Conference on the Needs of Agriculture. Stishinskii was among its members, and in the discussions on the peasantry in late 1904 and early 1905 he was among the conservative minority in the conference. Some members, including V. I. Gurko, the acting head of the Land Department and Stishinskii's close collaborator in the editorial commission, urged active measures to eliminate the commune. According to Witte's memoirs, this led the conservatives to characterize the conference to the Tsar as a "revolutionary club." Differences of opinion made it impossible for the conference to reach agreement on the general line to be followed in agrarian policy, but resolutions were adopted recognizing the right of individual peasants to claim their allotment land as personal property. Before the conference had completed its deliberations, it was unexpectedly shut down by the Tsar on March 30, 1905. Simultaneously, the formation of a new agency was announced: the Special Conference on Measures for the Improvement of Peasant Landholding. Under the direction of the conservative I. L. Goremykin, this body was to propose means of strengthening peasant land tenure without violating the private property rights of other landholders.[57]

One of the members of the earlier conference, Senator Khvostov, had protested that no group of true Russians could ever agree to the abolition of the commune,[58] and in 1902 the Tsar himself had recorded that he would never do away with the commune by a stroke of the pen.[59] Yet the agrarian crisis made it clear that change was necessary in the countryside. The emancipation, critics charged, had not changed things very much: "Before 1861 the peasants were bound to the commune by the estate owners; after 1861 they were bound to it by the state."[60] By 1905 even "true Russians" were beginning to feel that the bonds needed loosening, but, as in 1861, the government still held fast to the commune. To most of official Russia the commune was a fail-safe device upholding the social order and rural political stability. As such, it was to be tested in the events of 1905.

PART II

The First Agrarian Revolution
1905-1916

If revolution is thought of as radical change catalyzed by violence, then the innovations in the rural order after 1905 amounted not just to a reform, but to a full-fledged revolution. In this light, the violent upheavals of 1905 and 1917 can be viewed as successive episodes in a single prolonged agrarian revolution. On the other hand, insofar as the changes introduced after 1905 were carried out by a regime that successfully rode the first wave of violence, they can be considered a reform. In the perspective of contemporaries there was room for both interpretations.

3

The Second Emancipation

Just as the shock of the Crimean War triggered the "Great Reform"—the emancipation from serfdom, so the revolution of 1905–7 was said to have set off the "second Great Reform"—the emancipation from the commune.[1] For over half a century the government had based its policy on the premise advanced by Haxthausen, that the commune was a bulwark against revolution; it took a revolution to discredit that proposition. Conventional wisdom has it that the people lost some illusions about a benevolent "Little Father" Tsar when an unarmed procession of petitioners was fired upon on Bloody Sunday, January 9, 1905; the government also traded in some illusions about the people in the period that followed.

When war broke out with Japan in 1904, the peasants, already overburdened by heavy taxation, were subjected en masse to the most onerous of all social burdens: military conscription. Far from producing the "short victorious war" that had been promised, the military adventure turned into a national embarrassment that robbed personal sacrifices of meaning or dignity. Severe naval defeat forced a Russian capitulation, and a treaty of peace was signed with Japan in August 1905.

Pacification on the home front proved more difficult to arrange. Political tensions continued to mount throughout the country, and in October revolution broke out in the cities. Rural disturbances escalated rapidly thereafter both in number and in intensity.

Productivity and Politics

Even before the autumn uprisings the government had recognized the necessity of a change in the rural order. Various committees and conferences had been established to review the situation and to propose solutions to the "agrarian problem." The repeal of collective responsibility in 1903 was followed a year later by the abolition of the corporal punishment of peasants by volost courts. In May 1905 the Ministry of Agriculture was reorganized and combined with the Department of Colonization. A Committee on Land Affairs was established.* Resettlement of a part of the surplus rural population was one approach to agrarian problems;[2] another was an attempt to raise productivity.

The average yield of the Russian grain crops that accounted for over 90 percent of all cultivated land in the first years of the twentieth century was far below that of every major European producer and amounted to only one-third of the average of the leading countries of Europe.[3] Part of the problem was related to environmental factors, for zones of poor soil and unfavorable patterns of precipitation limited the potential of Russian agriculture. Yet other factors helped to depress agricultural productivity below its natural potential.

Among those factors was the commune. As its critics pointed out, the communal system of stripholding squandered land by necessitating extra access lanes; it also consumed additional time and effort. The fact that allotments had to be returned eventually to the commune's redistributional pool removed incentives for any long-term investment of capital or labor in the land. Agronomists blamed the commune for difficulties they encountered in trying to extend the cultivation of grass crops, and communes were held responsible for the wastefulness of the three-field system.[4] Under the more advanced systems of crop rotation used in the West, the proportion of land lying fallow had been greatly reduced. Whereas a full third of the land was always out of production in the three-field system, the corresponding Western ratios were: one-seventh in France, one-sixteenth in Germany, and a mere forty-eighth in England.[5] By opening new opportunities to Russian agriculture, the recovery of the international grain market after the turn of the century added weight to charges that the commune blocked the rationalization of agriculture essential for successful competition in the world market.

Yet attacks on the commune elicited a vigorous defense of the institution. Valid criticisms of agricultural practices, it was argued, were being illogically extended to the commune. The custom of fragmenting land holdings in small strips was just as much a problem under hereditary tenure as in communes, and the problem was said to be more readily remediable through communal land redistribution than under hereditary possession.[6] The advantages of collective action were

*The name of the ministry was changed at this time to the "Main Administration of Land Organization and Agriculture," but it reverted to "Ministry of Agriculture" in 1915. I use the shorter name throughout this period.

equally touted as a way of improving crop rotations. Zemstvo agronomists claimed more success in promoting grass crops by converting entire communes than by winning over individual peasants.

Many of the arguments raised in support of the commune, however, touched on extra-economic issues. Conservatives who saw the commune as an agency for rural social control considered it politically indispensable and turned a deaf ear to all criticism. This stance encouraged critics to protest that the economic interests of the country were being sacrificed to a dubious political expediency and to discount all arguments in defense of the institution. Increasingly, the commune became a political touchstone, a safe target for expressions of disaffection and a reductionist explanation for all agrarian woes. Not all nobles, or even all of the landed nobility, had an interest in preserving the commune, but as part of the old, dissolving order of landed property relations that had supported centuries of aristocratic privilege, the institution had a claim on the sympathies of this class. Gentry supporters of the commune, charged Witte, viewed it as "some sort of herd"; though it was undoubtedly more convenient from an "administrative-political point of view" to manage herds rather than individuals, the commune was stifling the countryside.[8] What was bad for the sheep, he reminded his peers, was bad for the shepherds.

Peasants in Revolt

The revolution of 1905–7 was a rural stampede that shook official confidence in the manageability of human herds. The unsuccessful and costly war with Japan, coming on the heels of intensive industrialization efforts and mounting social pressures, brought widespread grievances to a head. A mounting wave of popular protest crested in a paralyzing general strike in the capital in October 1905. Nicholas II, deeply alarmed, hastened to announce monumental concessions, and in the Manifesto of October 17 promised an elected representative legislature and legal recognition of basic political rights. The lumbering hulk of Russian autocracy had been cracked by the stresses of modernization. Or so it seemed.

The promise of a semiconstitutional regime effectively weakened the alliance of urban workers and intelligentsia. The apparent achievement of a common goal diluted the motive force for unification, and in the capital the revolutionary tide began rapidly to ebb. In the sprawling countryside events took a different turn. Spontaneous peasant uprisings continued throughout the autumn, and after a winter slump

picked up again in mid-1906. Different sectors of the country were
caught up at different periods: just as disturbances in Moscow peaked
after those in St. Petersburg, so the right-bank Ukraine and Poland became active after the central black soil region.[9] The disjunctions both
between city and countryside and between different regions enabled
the government to deal with each threat in turn and helped it to reestablish equilibrium.

Although the October Manifesto calmed a sufficient number of urbanites to permit control to be restored in the cities, it had little effect
on the peasants, whose complaints were largely economic. In a number of cases the manifesto itself actually provoked rural violence: some
peasants interpreted it as an invitation to take over gentry and state
lands, while others moved to direct action when frustrated in their expectations of a land grant.[10] Almost half of all peasant disturbances in
1905 occurred in the last two months of the year,[11] that is, after the
October Manifesto and—more significantly—after a second manifesto
announcing important concessions to the peasantry. This document,
the peasant equivalent of the October Manifesto, was issued on November 3. Under its provisions and those of accompanying decrees
sent to the Senate, redemption payments on allotment land were reduced by one-half for the following year and canceled entirely beginning in 1907.[12] This politically expedient gesture cost the government
less than 6 percent of its income, only a quarter of the amount brought
in by the vodka monopoly. In view of the economic condition of the
peasantry, Witte had proposed canceling the payments well before the
1905 outbreaks, but in vain. The repeal of the mutual fiscal responsibilities of peasant communities in 1903 also provided a logical opportunity to abolish these highly visible and unpopular payments, but the
government rejected this course. It has been suggested that redemption payments were kept in force after 1903 primarily because their
cancellation would have dissolved the only legal tie holding the commune together.[13] If this was indeed the rationale, there was historical
irony in the situation: if the modern commune was originally brought
into being to guarantee taxes, taxes were ultimately kept in being to
guarantee the commune.

The November Manifesto deplored peasant assaults on private property "in some districts" and enjoined the rural population to respect
the law and the rights of others. At the same time, the funding of the
Peasant Bank was increased and its lending rules were modified to facilitate purchases of land by peasant smallholders. Up to 90 percent of
the value of a property could be advanced or, with special authoriza-

tion, even the fully appraised value. The obvious intent was to invest the peasant with a stake in propertied society.

Whether because official news traveled slowly,* or because local estates offered more immediate attractions than the promised lands of a promised branch of the Peasant's Bank, the incidence of arson, pillage, and property seizure remained high. Less than 100 peasant outbreaks were officially recorded in 1904, but the number jumped to above 3,000 in 1905. In 1906 it declined to 2,600, a drop of less than 20 percent, whereas workers' disturbances fell by over 60 percent in the same period.[14] The spring and summer of 1906 witnessed peasant uprisings in half of all the districts of European Russia.[15]

Natural catastrophe contributed to the social crisis. Crop failures at the time were more acute than at any point since the calamitous famine of 1891–92, and in their geographic extent were almost as great. Poor harvests were endemic in Russian agriculture, but their impact was generally local. In 1904, for example, only 9 percent of the agricultural population lived in districts where the net per capita production of grain and potatoes was down to the famine level of twelve puds or less. (A pud is 36 pounds.) In 1905, however, a third of the population was in the area of critical shortages, and by 1906 half of the entire agricultural population of European Russia was reduced to this level.

The harvest was especially poor in the central agricultural and Volga regions, where the incidence of rural violence was highest during the revolution. In 38 districts with a total population of some ten million people the grain output fell below three puds per person. Saratov province, among others, experienced crop failures even more acute than those of the 1890's; the average yield of a desiatin of wheat or rye in the province in 1906 was only about two-thirds that of 1891.[16] Hunger, economic pressures, bleak prospects for relief, and lack of alternative resources combined to catalyze longstanding rural frustrations. Peasants seized what they could, and found themselves revolutionaries.

Even without the spur of famine, there was no shortage of revolutionary potential in the countryside in these years. Representatives of various political factions helped to develop that potential, not only by heightening the political consciousness of the peasants but by promoting their political organization. Moscow liberals, for example, encouraged peasants to form their own associations as part of a broad program to unionize a public denied political parties. In 1905 nearly 500 branch

---

*Even after 1910, in response to a questionnaire sent out by the Free Economic Society peasants in Kiev province stated that they had never been officially informed of the cessation of redemption payments. (Chernyshev, *Obshchina*, p. 178.)

unions took shape, boasting a membership of some 200,000 peasants.[17] At the first (illegal) meeting of the All-Russian Peasant Union in late July 1905, delegates articulated their grievances quite bluntly. Gross bureaucratic incompetence was declared rife at every level of government. In the ominous assessment of the deputies, "The wretched condition of the peasants today, come about because of too little land, because of too many taxes and too much gouging by the government, and because the people can't read and have no rights, is not about to be fixed up by the bureaucratic government we have now."[18]

Despite the rhetoric of union activists, most delegates wanted reform rather than an armed confrontation with the authorities. And despite Bloody Sunday, many peasants clung to the traditional view of a patriarchal Tsar whose good intentions were thwarted by malevolent bureaucrats. They were encouraged to persist in this habit by the language of imperial manifestos, which deliberately projected an image of benevolent paternalism.* The peasants often responded in kind. In Saratov province, for example, where peasant violence accounted for almost a third of all property losses reported for 1905, they sent their complaints directly to their "Little Father" when police made arrests "in spite of the Manifesto of October 17."[19] Police archives reveal that when the local governor imposed harsh regulations on the province, peasants sought relief at the same patriarchal fount of justice.[20]

One can ask whether peasants genuinely subscribed to the "myth of the Tsar" or whether they too were fabricating and exploiting it for political purposes—in their case, to legitimate resistance to other authorities.[21] The events of 1905–7 suggest that both were true. When it is functional, any system of beliefs reinforces itself, and the sociopsychic utility of the patriarchal model was undoubtedly enhanced by its political utility. Exploitation of the myth was not incompatible with a "naive monarchism" but was in fact complementary to it, and this may be the key to some apparent contradictions in peasant behavior at the time.

Resolutions (*prigovory*) adopted by rural societies in this period reflect a welter of aspirations and values, which often seem to be at odds with one another. Widely recorded during the revolution, these documents were a popular nonviolent device for the articulation of peasant wishes. Although many resolutions appear to have been spontaneous, peasants were also encouraged to compose them (or had them composed) by outside agitators. In some ways the "*prigovor* movement"

---

*The care given to the phrasing of such documents was evident in early 1906 when the State Council advised against publishing a manifesto because it threatened the peasants rather than addressing them with the customary kindness. (Dubrovskii, *Stolypinskaia reforma*, p. 96.)

was a rural analogue of the earlier urban "banquet campaign," marking a stage in the development and expression of political consciousness. One typical resolution from the southern village of Akimovo (which had 431 members) illustrates the conflict of sentiments in the countryside at the time. Dated December 20, 1905, it refers with an impressive if pointed sense of history to France in 1791 and to the fate of Louis XVI, talks of a return to the *Pugachevshchina*, yet calls upon the "Little Father" to "save his children."[22]

After the severe outbreaks of late 1905, the countryside quieted down in the early months of 1906. Yet many correctly anticipated a recurrence and intensification of rural disturbances with the coming of spring. In Witte's opinion, only an immediate land reform could forestall a renewal of outbreaks, and his view was widely shared.[23] Gentry landowners, panicked by the fiery autumn "illumination of the countryside," deluged the government with proposals designed to placate the land-hungry peasants. Some even called for the partial confiscation of private estate lands in the hope that at least some portion could be salvaged by landowners.[24]

The administration was at work elaborating its own land reform projects. One of these was the handiwork of the head of the Ministry of Agriculture, N. N. Kutler, who drew it up with the assistance of agrarian expert A. A. Kaufman. This plan, calling for partial, compensated expropriation of large estates and unused or permanently rented land, was rejected by the Council of Ministers in late December. By this time Moscow had been brought under control, rural disturbances had subsided, and panic was abating. Kutler was forced to resign. Any alienation of private property—however limited—was declared to be unacceptable; it would undermine the principle of property rights in general and lead to the destruction of the economy. The only proper policy was to maintain the inviolability of private property rights and to extend them to the peasantry.

The government had set its course: the solution of the agrarian problem was not to be sought in the expropriation of private property, but by individual appropriation by peasants of their own communal land. The fate of the commune may have been decided before the revolution, but the revolution gave pause to the defenders of communal tenure and gave sufficient urgency to the agrarian situation to convert an anticommunal tendency into an explicit legislative program.

Land Reform Projects

Beginning in 1906 several administrative agencies simultaneously worked on legislative proposals dealing with the structure of land tenure. The Department of State Lands at the Ministry of Agriculture worked out the decree of March 4, 1906, establishing provincial and district land organization commissions under the direction of a new Committee on Land Organization Affairs. This agency replaced the Committee on Land Affairs set up the previous May, and, to the irritation of the zemstvos, the local land commissions rendered superfluous the zemstvo commissions that had just been formed in response to a request from the Ministry of Finance to provide assistance to the Peasant Land Bank. The new land commissions were to be responsible for helping the bank arrange sales to peasants of private and state lands. These commissions were also to work on the resettlement of peasants on state lands, to arrange the rental of state lands to peasants, to work with rural societies to improve the conditions of land tenure and land use, and to act as intermediaries between peasants and private landholders in unscrambling lands that were intermixed or held in common.[25]

While the Ministry of Agriculture worked on these matters, the Ministry of Internal Affairs returned to its earlier legislative projects. A Special Conference under Gurko, now head of the Land Department, was assigned the task of coordinating proposals connected with the November Manifesto "concerning the rights of peasants to allotment land." Strictly speaking, the cancellation of redemption payments did not establish the right of individual peasants to claim their allotment land. A peasant's previously recognized right to take redeemed land out of the commune without the consent of other members had been revoked in 1893. Were it not for that repeal of Article 165, the November Manifesto would have opened the door to free departures with land from the commune. Yet the government was now required to untie the legislative binding with additional legislation.

Work on a draft law proceeded rapidly. Gurko's Special Conference immediately took the position that every member of a commune should have the right to demand at any time the separation of his share of communal land as personal property. A legislative project was elaborated on this basis in February 1906, incorporating provisions of the draft legislation worked out earlier.[26] Anticipating that the government might hesitate to enact a measure of such scope on the eve of the opening of the new legislature, the Duma, the conference drafted a set of corresponding temporary regulations, which were proposed for immediate adoption. Land reform, it was urged, would get underway more quickly by adopting the regulations; the peasants would be pacified, and the Duma would be more likely to move along policy lines already established. A sharp debate took place in the Council of Ministers and in the State Council on the advisability of adopting these provisional rules. Some proponents of immediate action argued that the government should take full responsibility for enacting land reform, and that the Duma should not be allowed even to discuss the matter of land legislation. The majority, however, preferred to avoid taking steps that could be interpreted as politically provocative. The promulgation of any legislation without the approval of the Duma was contrary to the pledge of the October Manifesto, and some feared that even provisional rules on so important an issue might be interpreted as a violation of the manifesto. Moreover, it was considered advisable to let the peasants have their say on the vital issue of communal tenure. There would be an opportunity for this in the Duma, where they had been given substantial representation. Yet Goremykin sounded a warning note. Should the Duma prove recalcitrant on the land issue and raise the question of confiscation of private property, it should forthwith be dissolved.[27]

Witte was among the minority pressing for immediate provisional legislation on the commune; his defeat on this point presaged his departure as head of the Council of Ministers. He was replaced by Goremykin. In the accompanying bureaucratic shuffle the portfolio of Internal Affairs was assigned to the governor of turbulent Saratov province, Petr Arkadevich Stolypin, whose firm suppression of revolutionary disturbances had attracted the attention of the capital.

When the Duma met, its approach to the agrarian problem was quite different from the official policy. A succession of land expropriation proposals in the assembly led rapidly to open antagonism. On May 8, soon after the opening of the new legislature, the Constitutional Democrats (Kadets), who had won the largest political representation in the elections, introduced their own solution to the land problem. This "project of the 42" had been formulated largely by Kutler, who, like Kaufman, was a member of the party. It proposed confiscating land in all holdings larger than a norm to be established for each locality; fair compensation for the land was to be awarded on the basis of local market prices.

The peasants, who occupied 40 percent of all Duma seats, were most strongly attracted to the program of the Labor Group (*Trudoviki*), a faction including diverse elements united by a commitment to radical land reform. On May 23 they presented their "project of the 104" in the Duma, calling for the establishment of a national land fund that would include all state and Church lands, as well as land confiscated from estates whose size exceeded a basic working norm. The fund was to belong "to all the people," and all who were willing to work land with their own labor were to have an equal right to its use. Compensation, if any, was to be at state expense. These propositions were highly controversial but had a sufficient number of supporters to guarantee a serious hearing. The even more radical program of the Socialist Revolutionary (SR) Party found less support. The "project of the 33" introduced by the SRs on June 8 demanded the elimination of all private property and recognition of the rights of all citizens, male and female, to the use of land.[28]

Although the extremism of the Labor Group and the SRs appealed to many peasants, others greeted the prospect of land confiscation with reservations or outright opposition. The interests of different groups emerged in open conflict as talk of expropriation brought home the realization that the peasants' own lands might become subject to confiscation along with those of other proprietors. Peasants well endowed with land became anxious about this, and the anxiety could extend to entire communities since in some localities the per capita landholdings of neighboring communes were quite disproportionate.

Some peasants communicated their fears directly to the Duma. Members of one community, for example, wrote to point out that they had paid high redemption prices on their land for forty years, and were not prepared to have it taken away without compensation.[29] Another group passed a resolution approving seizure of large private properties but insisting that peasant land be exempt from confiscation. These peasants, evidently well off and unabashedly self-interested, argued further that no confiscated land should be distributed to agricultural laborers since this would deprive larger peasant holdings of essential hired hands.[30]

The government was quick to respond to these concerns. On May 13, even before the proposals of the Labor Group and the SRs had been brought before the Duma, Goremykin warned that the government could not recognize the land rights of some while depriving others of those rights. In an aside clearly intended for commercial and industrial proprietors, he added that it was equally unthinkable to discriminate against the owners of landed property. In the weeks that followed, gubernatorial proclamations issued in the provinces announced to the public that the interests of all classes were equally safeguarded by the state and stressed that the category of landed proprietors included many peasants.[31] Peasants, advised the official press, should appreciate the government's firm defense of private property rights, "for if the rights of landowners of other social estates are violated today, then the rights of the peasants too can be violated tomorrow."[32] Some peasants undoubtedly responded to such warnings, but for most the question of the security of their property rights tomorrow paled before any prospect of increasing their land holdings today. A growing tendency to peasant radicalism became apparent as the session went on.

The Duma and Peasant Radicalism

The establishment of the Duma and the opportunity to elect representatives had a pronounced effect on the narrowly circumscribed political culture of the peasantry. Close contacts between peasant deputies and their constituents promoted rapid politicization of the countryside, and whatever confidence the government had possessed in the essential conservatism of the peasantry was soon shaken. When delegates took off from Saratov for the opening of the Duma in April 1906, a crowd of ten thousand gathered at the train station to see them off with a rousing chorus of the Marseillaise.[33] Peasant gatherings throughout the country sent enthusiastic greetings to the Duma, expressing high hopes and a determination to realize them. From Mogilev province, for example, came warm words addressed to the "friends of the people," and from village after village, to Astrakhan and beyond, the message was echoed: "Deputies! Our hopes are in you." Along with such greetings some peasants sent pledges of support in the "present and future struggle with the government."[34]

The readiness of at least a part of the peasantry to persist in confrontations with the authorities became more evident as the spring wore on. By the beginning of July defiant villagers from Redkin volost in the province of St. Petersburg were boldly informing the Duma, "We can expect neither land nor liberty while power remains in the hands of the present government."[35] To the most radical elements among the peasantry, it seemed unlikely that much real good could be expected of the Duma either, given its political constituency, and in June 1906 some of the organizers of a Congress of the All-Russian Peasant Union even called for new Duma elections.[36]

Most peasants, however, looked to the Duma for land reform, and interaction with Duma deputies contributed to the escalating militancy of the countryside. In Kharkov province, for example, a peasant member of the Duma Labor Group returned home at the end of May to confer with his fellow peasants, inquiring whether they wanted to acquire land through collective purchase on their own, buy it through the Peasant Land Bank, or receive it gratis from a state land fund (as proposed by the Labor Group). Assured by the villagers that they wanted only the last, he urged them to draw up statements to that effect and send them in to the Duma.[37] Similar visitations took place all over the country, and the local police sent in streams of warnings that the Duma deputies were creating havoc in the countryside. Late in May agents alerted the authorities that in the Volga area, in Kursk, and in Kharkov the peasants had been so inflamed by local agitators, including Duma deputies, that the agitators themselves were now trying to hold them back from untimely acts of violence.[38]

It rapidly became apparent to both local and central authorities that the work of mass political agitation was made possible by the opportunity to address peasants as a group in their community meetings (*skhody*). Without such meetings it was difficult to reach or organize the rural population because peasants, unlike urban workers, could not be approached effectively at their workplace. As the government became aware of the situation developing, peasant delegates to the Duma who attempted to meet their constituents at the village assembly began to find obstacles thrown in their paths. The peasants' own elected officials proved instrumental to the government in this matter. Since the starosta and starshina had to be confirmed in office by the local land captain and were subject to his supervision and authority, they tended to be among the more conservative, or at least the more cautious, elements of a community.

When the elders saw that the visits of Duma members were creating local ferment, they sometimes tried to avoid trouble by refusing to call an assembly to meet with them. In one instance, a starosta in Nizhnii Novgorod arrested villagers who tried to hold such a meeting after he had declined to convene it.[39] In Samara a land captain provoked riots when he refused to permit volost or communal assemblies to meet to discuss peasant questions raised in a letter from the local Duma representative. The problem, according to a police report, was that the rustics simply failed to understand the nature of the Duma. The peasants, it was reported, conceived of the Duma as a large volost assembly "capable of resolving the complicated and difficult land question in just a day or so."[40] On June 11, just a few days after presenting the government's reform proposals to the Duma, the new Minister of Internal Affairs, Stolypin, notified provincial officials that members of the Duma had no legal right to convene assemblies. Instructions were to be circulated prohibiting the holding of "illegal" assemblies, or of any sort of "so-called meeting" in rural localities.[41]

By this time it had become all too clear that whatever the state of their affections for the Tsar, the peasant masses were no anchor of political stability. Traditionalism proved remarkably elastic, and peasants who marched out in processions led by the village priest to greet their Duma delegates with bread and salt were likely to settle down on the spot to talk of revolution. Meanwhile, the commune, whose economic drawbacks had previously been glossed over by some for the sake of its assumed political expediency, perversely turned out to be useful in organizing peasant political opposition. In fact, in many places the peasants moved to revolution in the name of the mir. Folk wisdom maintained that "the Tsar is far and high, but the mir remains close by," and what was closer offered a more practical cover for the peasant. Contemporaries were well aware that not the peasant but the mir confronted the estate owner. Land was seized "for the mir," and property was plundered "on orders of the mir." [42]

Disenchantment with the peasants was evident in the speeches of the representatives of the nobility who gathered in the capital at the end of May to discuss the agrarian question. Stishinskii, now head of the Ministry of Agriculture, provided meeting quarters, and both he and Gurko were among the guests invited to attend sessions with an advisory vote. Understandably enough, gentry landowners were greatly concerned about the land expropriation schemes being raised in the Duma. The new legislature, in fact, was described as a revolutionary machine equipped with "five hundred Pugachevs." If the peasants conceived of the Duma as an enlarged meeting of the commune, then the nobles seemed to be thinking of the commune as a miniature Duma. "In other countries," complained Prince A. P. Urusov, "there is incomparably less land per capita than in Russia, yet there is no talk about land shortage because the concept of property is clear in the minds of people. But we have the commune—which is to say that the principle of socialism has destroyed this concept. The result is that nowhere else do we see such unceremonious destruction of property as we see in Russia." [43]

A week later, on June 6, the government began to unveil its own reform projects. The first, prepared by the Ministry of Internal Affairs, was presented to the Duma by Stolypin. It provided that the peasants be given equal civil and political rights with other social estates. Allotment land was to retain its special character as land reserved for the peasantry, but all peasant holders of such land were to be able to claim it as their personal property and would be free to leave the commune at will. The official gloss on the proposed law argued the need for change on the grounds that "the absence of personal property in allotment lands is interfering with the development among the rural population of correct views on private property in general." [44] A second legislative proposal, from the Ministry of Agriculture, was placed before the Duma on June 10. Introduced by Stishinskii, it provided for the physical consolidation of lands converted from communal to hereditary tenure. [45]

Except for a minority that supported the government, the Duma showed little interest in the official proposals and continued to press for at least partial expropriation of private lands. Meanwhile, in the countryside the number of peasant outbreaks jumped from 160 in May to over 700 in June, coming close to the high point of rural violence reached the previous November.[46] On June 20 the government published a lengthy statement on its land policy in the official press. After disputing the proposition that land shortage alone was responsible for the peasants' problems and recapitulating the government's policy on land legislation, the communiqué presented summary statistics on the amount of agricultural land in the country. Even if all the nonpeasant land were distributed to the peasantry, it claimed, the per capita gain would be insignificant—less than one desiatin for each male peasant. Furthermore, land confiscation once begun could hardly be expected to stop at nonpeasant lands. Justice would demand a wholesale egalitarian redistribution, and the result would be peasant holdings of less than four desiatins.

This simple calculation might have given pause to peasants with larger holdings (the majority), and what followed had equally disturbing implications for peasant have-nots facing the critically poor harvest of 1906. Without any large properties left to offer employment opportunities, asserted the government, a peasant would be overtaken by disaster when crop failures left him with inadequate income from his own land. Not only would outside agricultural work be unavailable to help families through hard times, but the government would no longer be able to help out by purchasing grain for famine relief, since most grain sold on the market came from the private sector. As a result of these considerations, concluded the statement, and not from exclusive concern for estate owners, the government would not permit the expropriation of land. "It is not the landowners who would bear the brunt of compulsory expropriation of their land, but the peasantry itself."[47]

The Duma hotly rejected this official line of reasoning and took its own arguments directly to the people. Early in July police reports indicated that Duma representatives all over the country were continuing to hold meetings with the peasants, despite the regulations to the contrary. On the first of July a peasant deputy reporting in Tver province on Duma activities and proposals for land confiscation prompted the local assembly to compose declarations that were dispatched at once to peasant newspapers. A few days later, under the influence of the deputy's speech, the peasants seized woodlands belonging to a local proprietor. Similar gatherings, followed at times by similar consequences, were reported within the week from rural communities throughout the country: from Orel, Ekaterinoslav, Poltava, Kharkov, Volynia, St. Petersburg, Penza. July 5 brought reports of the meeting of a Duma representative in Vladimir province with a "mass" of local peasants singing revolutionary songs and waving red flags. [48]

The State Council had already decided, on June 8 when the government was in the very process of presenting its land reform proposals, that the Duma would have to be dissolved at the first opportune moment. [49] That moment arrived a month later, following the failure of negotiations between the government and the Duma opposition. On July 9, without prior warning, the First State Duma was closed down by the authorities. Stolypin had just been appointed head of the Council of Ministers, retaining his post as Minister of Internal Affairs. In the manifesto issued to explain the dissolution of the Duma, the Tsar once again called upon the populace "as a father to his children," promising that peasants who needed more land would be provided with an honorable, legal means of obtaining it without violating the property rights of others.

4

The Agrarian Reform

In the summer of 1906 the government took steps to regain control of the countryside. On the one hand, it vigorously suppressed rural disturbances, introducing (after an attempt on Stolypin's life in August) a system of field courts martial to mete out summary justice to offenders. At the same time a series of measures, the first coinciding with the assassination attempt on August 12, released certain Crown lands (*udel'nyi zemli*—lands belonging to the Imperial family) for sale to the peasantry through the Peasant Land Bank. On August 27 another decree authorized the Minister of Agriculture to arrange through the land organization commissions for the sale to peasants (upon expiration of existing rental agreements) of some state lands rented to peasants in European Russia. Parcels of state woodland were to be designated for sale to the peasantry also.

Legislation

With relative tranquillity restored to the countryside, on October 5 the government issued a major decree repealing "certain limitations in the rights of rural residents and others of former taxpaying status"— limitations that had helped to keep the peasantry in a separate and unequal civil status even after emancipation. This decree extended to all citizens rights with respect to state service held previously only by nobles. Peasants were no longer obliged to obtain the permission of their communes or higher authorities for family divisions or to enter educational institutions, civil service, or monasteries. The decree recognized the right of peasants to choose their own place of residence, subject only to the passport regulations applying to other classes, and as a corollary, the right to leave any rural society upon renouncing the right to use its communal land (*mirskaia zemlia*), or upon alienating their plots of such land. Existing provisions of the law hindering such depar-

tures were voided (Article 4). Peasants were now permitted to belong
to more than one rural society simultaneously or to none at all (provided they registered in some volost), and the much-resented authority of the land captains was restricted. The right held by peasants
before 1890 to elect their own representatives to the zemstvo was restored, along with the right of peasant proprietors who owned a
qualifying amount of private land to participate in zemstvo elections on
the same basis as other nonnoble owners of private landed property,
regardless of membership in rural societies.

All of these measures had been passed without the authorization of
the Duma, required by the new Fundamental Laws of the State. Article 87 of the laws stated that emergency legislation could be submitted
directly to the Tsar by the Council of Ministers when the Duma was
not in session but required that the measures thus adopted be brought
before the Duma within two months of its reconvention. The reopen-
ing of the Duma had been set for February 1907, and Stolypin made
full use of the interim opportunity to implement the government's program under Article 87 without the Duma's obstruction. The transfer of
state lands for sale to peasants and the extension of civil rights were
relatively noncontroversial, and general approval of these government
initiatives helped to establish a precedent for Stolypin's use of the
emergency legislative power. The earlier steps prepared the way for
publication of the important decree of November 9, 1906, which was to
be the cornerstone of the government's agrarian policy in its final decade of existence.

The Decree of November 9, 1906

The new agrarian reform measure and the subsequent laws that extended it and gave it the retroactive sanction of the Duma structured a
bold attempt to transform the social and economic order of rural Russia. From its identification with the most forceful political personality
of the period, the program has been labeled the Stolypin reform or,
pejoratively, the *Stolypinshchina*, although the Prime Minister's personal role has sometimes been discounted.[1] Stolypin certainly did not
initiate the agrarian program, was not actively engaged in its formulation, and was relieved by an assassin in 1911 from responsibility for its
further implementation. Yet he had long advocated its basic policies
and was to support them vigorously.[2]

The decree of November 9, 1906, was brought forth under a disarm-
ingly modest title: On the Supplementation of Certain Regulations in

the Present Law Relating to Peasant Land Tenure and Land Use.[3] It opened with a reference to the cancellation of redemption payments as of January 1, 1907. After that date, since the land would be free of obligations connected with those payments, all peasants were to have the right to depart freely from the commune. This open-door policy had already been announced in general terms in the "equal rights" provisions of October 5, but the new decree made departures feasible by guaranteeing that householders (that is, the heads of peasant households) could take their land with them, and by establishing procedures to accomplish this.

It now became possible to convert a household's share of communal land into the personal property of the household head. The appropriator could simply assume hereditary title to his scattered strips, or once he had secured personal title he could request the commune to exchange his strips for an equivalent amount of land in a consolidated plot. If a request for a holding in one place was presented by any householder who had appropriated his land (or declared his intention to do so) before a general redistribution was actually underway, the commune was obliged to grant it insofar as possible when redistribution took place. At other times, the commune had the option of meeting such a request by making the necessary exchange arrangements with other strip holders or, if that proved too difficult, of offering to purchase the land of the separator. If the commune and the householder could not agree on the cash value of the holding, the volost court was to render a judgment, and the commune was required to pay the figure it set. If the peasant considered the price too low, however, he could reject payment and retain his strip holdings as individual property until the next redistribution, at which time consolidation was mandatory for the commune.

Where a general redistribution had not been held for 24 years, the householder was entitled to appropriate all the land (other than rented land) in actual use by the household at the time of separation.* Where redistributions had been held within that period, peasants who held land in excess of the share that would normally be allotted to the household at the next repartition (due to changes in family size since the last distribution, or other such factors) were permitted to retain the extra land upon paying the commune a price based on the original

---

*A. V. Peshekhonov pointed out at the time that communes trying to block individual appropriations of land could do so simply by renting out all of their land to members. As long as the terms and availability were equal for all, there was no legal bar to this tactic. Yet the peasants were either unaware of this option or reluctant to use it, since there seem to be no reports of such practice. See S. Maslov, pp. 8–10.

average redemption price of the land. Since land prices had climbed steeply, this provision gave special encouragement to departures from the commune by adding bargain prices to the prospect of permanent retention of above-normal holdings. Those who converted to hereditary tenure retained their previous rights in the commune's indivisible lands and special land funds.

A request for an individual appropriation was presented through the commune's starosta and required the approval of only a simple majority of the commune. A decision was required within a month after the request for separation of tenure, and where the approval of the commune was not obtained within that period the applicant could appeal to the local land captain for assistance. By a two-thirds vote any rural community, whether under communal or hereditary tenure, could elect to abandon the strip system and convert as a whole to consolidated holdings. Individual consolidations were not permitted in communities under hereditary tenure because the inevitable infringement of the personal property rights of others was considered justifiable only with the general consent of the community.

All land held in hereditary tenure was transferred from the status of household property to that of the personal property of the individual heading the household. This included land already under household tenure, land converted from communal to hereditary tenure by individual or group appropriation, and all of the house and garden plots of the peasants in communes. Joint ownership of such property was permitted only when a household's members were not a vertically lineal family. Gurko's project had called for completely abandoning household rights to property in favor of individual rights; however, the proposal met with resistance in the Council of Ministers, and Stolypin did not insist upon it.[1]

The decree of November 9, 1906, served as the legal basis of official agrarian policy until June 14, 1910. By that time the relationship between the Duma and the government had been considerably altered. Following the opening of the second Duma on February 20, 1907, Stolypin observed the Fundamental Laws by submitting to it (on April 4, within the stipulated two-month period) the measures adopted by the government under Article 87 in the interval between Duma sessions. The agrarian commission of the Duma turned the government land project over to a subcommission, which began its meetings early in May. Only one member of the subcommission—interestingly enough, a peasant—recommended that the Duma endorse the decree of November 9.[5] But before the group was able to submit its report, the second Duma, more radically polarized and contentious than the first despite government pressure at the polls, went the way of its predecessor.

The dissolution of the Duma on the third of June 1907 was accompanied by the promulgation of a new electoral law that greatly reduced the representation of the peasantry. The number of electors in the peasant curia was reduced from two-fifths of the total Duma electorate to one-fifth; the proportion of private landowners was boosted from a bare third to a full half. Peasants who would have qualified for participation in the landowners' curia by owning nonallotment land were now excluded from that body if they were members of rural societies. As a result, the expansion of the landowners' curia was accompanied by a sharp drop in the number of peasants within it. In elections to the first Duma a quarter of the electors in the landowners' curia were peasants. These peasants constituted 8 percent of the entire Duma electorate; added to the peasant curia electors, they had given the peasantry fully half of the total electorate. In the elections for the third Duma, however, peasants numbered less than 2 percent of all the electors in the landowners' curia.[6] This loss heightened the effect of the drastic cutbacks in the peasant curia, leaving the peasantry with less than a quarter of the total Duma electorate. Restriction of the representation of peasant proprietors of private land became even more significant with the passage of time, for between 1905 and 1915 peasants showed the highest gains in land acquisition among all private landholders. (See Table 10, p. 84).

The virtual exclusion of prosperous peasants from the landowners' curia appears to have been simply part of the general antipeasant reaction evident in the new electoral law. Yet it is strikingly inconsistent with the government's policy of encouraging departures from the commune and the establishment of individual farmsteads. If the government had, in Stolypin's celebrated phrase, "placed its bet on the sturdy and the strong," denial of political representation to the economically strongest group of peasants was a curious development.

Peasant losses under the new electoral system became landowner gains, and the political complexion of the Duma shifted accordingly. Although the agrarian question continued to hold an important place in Duma discussions, objections to the decree of November 9 were now directed largely to Stolypin's administrative methods. After accepting several amendments suggested by its own land commission and others introduced by the government, the third Duma gave its legislative sanction to the decree, which finally emerged as the law of June 14, 1910.[7]

The Law of June 14, 1910

The most important change introduced by the new law was its initial provision (Article 1) that in all communes where land had been allotted prior to 1887 but where there had been no general redistribution since the time of the original allotment the peasants were recognized as having transferred to hereditary tenure.[5] Allotments in such cases were to be considered the personal property of the household head, and certificates of individual title were to be issued on request. In these communities communal tenure was thus automatically converted to hereditary tenure. Furthermore, wherever hereditary tenure existed, a simple majority vote of the community was declared sufficient to permit a reorganization of the lands of all members into consolidated holdings. In communities under communal tenure two-thirds of the membership still had to agree for wholesale conversion, but peasants who had already converted to personal tenure were permitted to vote on the issue.

As under the decree of November 9, the commune had the option of offering to buy out a separator who requested the consolidation of his holding at a time other than a general redistribution if the request created special problems. But the law of June 14, 1910, went further by obliging the commune (without a purchase option) to accommodate any householder requesting consolidation at any time when, in the judgment of the district land organization commission, this could be arranged without particular difficulty. The commune was also obliged to consolidate holdings turned over to separators requesting this, if the departing group amounted to 20 percent of the membership or 50 members in communes with over 250 households. To promote consolidation further, the commune was permitted to make it compulsory in certain cases for peasants who had already appropriated their land. The new law reaffirmed that appropriated land, house and garden plots in communes, and all allotment land held in hereditary tenure was the personal property of the household head. Article 48, however, virtually dismissed women as heads of households by stipulating that land held by a household consisting of a mother and her children (as well as that of households whose members were not related in a direct line of descent) was to be classified, not as the personal property of the woman, but as the common property of the household.

The resolutions of communes and decisions of land captains concerning personal appropriations of communal land were to be submitted to the district conference (*uezdnyi s"ezd*) for confirmation. Any complaints by an individual or a commune had to be registered within 30 days of the announcement of a decision by a commune or land captain, and all complaints—including those relating to his own acts—had to be submitted through the land captain. He was to pass them on, along with his own report, to the district conference.

The legislation left no doubt that the government, with the support of the refashioned Duma, was intent on establishing a new class of independent peasant proprietors. Yet it was concerned about keeping this new yeomanry a class of smallholding peasants. The objective was to transform communal peasants into progressive, more productive, individual farmers, but in the process the slower-moving peasants were not to be forced out of the village en masse as landless proletarians. To this end the amount of allotment land that could be held by any peasant within a single district was restricted to a multiple of the emancipation allotment norm for the region.[9] Yet the recognition in October 1906 of a peasant's right to belong to more than one rural society clearly weakened the force of this restriction.

The Land Organization Statute of May 29, 1911

The agrarian reform legislation received its final major articulation in the statute of May 29, 1911, On Land Organization.[10] The new law for the most part simply described and systematized procedures for improving the physical layout of agricultural land, the sort of work carried out by the land organization commissions since 1906. It offered assistance not only to peasants but to smallholders of all social estates. All land organization work, according to the law, was to be initiated at the request of the landholder, and peasants in communes were no longer obliged to appropriate their lands before requesting consolidation or other forms of land work. The principle of the separation of lands was extended beyond individual households to groups of landholders and even to entire societies, all of whom were encouraged to disentangle and consolidate their intermixed holdings.

The 1911 statute provided for eight forms of land organization work: (1) separation (*vydel*) of the lands of separate settlements in rural societies; (2) separation of lands of small villages and parts of settlements; (3) separation of consolidated plots for individual members of rural societies and settlements; (4) full conversion (*razverstanie*) of the lands of rural societies or of settlements with separate holdings into consolidated plots for all members; (5) elimination of the intermixing of the lands affected by the statute with the properties adjacent to them; (6) conversion into consolidated plots of lands of different owners included in one deposition; (7) division of agricultural lands used jointly by peasants and private landowners; and (8) delimitation of lands subject to land organization from adjacent holdings when a preliminary establishment of outer boundaries was necessary for other land-organizing activities.

To the extent that it promoted individualized holdings, land organization work eroded communal tenure. Under the 1911 statute even the "indivisible" lands of communes could be divided and subject to individual appropriation. But the law provided that a minority who preferred to retain communal practices as a separate group could do so even when the rest of their commune converted to individual consolidated plots. Also, a group might separate from a commune but choose to function as a new commune, in a smaller, better-integrated territory. This option was offered in the hope of encouraging more rational land use in areas where peasants were reluctant to abandon communal tenure.

The consolidation of peasant lands could result in holdings that combined allotment and nonallotment land. Such mixed properties were considered private property under the law but could be registered by the owner as allotment land if there were no outstanding debts on the nonallotment section other than to the Peasant Land Bank. This point had been the most heatedly debated in the new law because of the complexities involved in joining lands of different legal status. Although a decree of November 15, 1906, had made it possible once again to mortgage allotment land to the Peasant Land Bank (and only to this lender),[11] allotment land retained other special characteristics as land that could belong only to peasants, and only in limited amounts to individual peasants. The peasants' rights of "personal property" (*lichnaia sobstvennost'*) in the form of dwelling plots or allotment land in hereditary tenure were not equivalent to the unrestricted rights of private property (*chastnaia sobstvennost'*) under the law. In addition to the other limitations noted, peasants who obtained personal title to their allotment land could not participate on this basis as individuals in zemstvo elections because possession of private property was required to qualify as an individual landowner.[12]

A peasant who wanted to consolidate his holdings could choose between two forms of land organization. He could request consolidation of his field plots but retain his house and garden plot in the village; a holding organized on this plan was known as an *otrub*. The alternative was to transfer the homestead from the village to the consolidated field land; this produced a farm called a *khutor*. Although more difficult to set up, the time-saving, more efficient khutor was the preferred plan from the official point of view, and the Peasant Land Bank was instructed to encourage the formation of these self-contained farms.

To make land organization more attractive to the peasantry, the government assumed most of the administrative and technical expenses of the work. The costs of surveying, registering titles, adjudicating, and so on were borne by official agencies. The actual work of land organization was carried out by the expanding network of land commissions established in 1906; peasants were responsible for maintaining and locally transporting the crew that came out to do work for them, and for supplying any additional labor needed for the work.

The Land Organization Commissions

Land organization commissions were established at the district and provincial levels to assist the Peasant Land Bank in arranging sales of land to peasants, combat the physical fragmentation and intermixing of agricultural lands, and help peasants rent or resettle on state lands. The district land organization commissions were headed by the district leader of the nobility and included a permanent member designated by the Ministry of Agriculture, the chairman of the district zemstvo, a representative of the judiciary, a tax inspector, a land captain, three representatives elected from the district zemstvo assembly, and three representatives of the peasantry chosen by lot from candidates nominated by the volost assemblies of the district. The governor of the province presided over the provincial commission, which consisted of the provincial leader of the nobility, the head of the provincial zemstvo board, a permanent member appointed by the Ministry of Agriculture, the head of the provincial office of the Ministry of Finance, the directors of the local branches of the Peasant Land Bank and the Nobles' Bank, a representative of the judiciary, a member of the provincial bureau on peasant affairs, the head of the regional office of Crown lands, and six members elected from the provincial zemstvo assembly, including three peasants holding allotment land.

In the first year of their existence, 1906, 178 district commissions were set up; even before the scope of their activity was extended by the law of May 29, 1911, they had been established in over 400 districts.[13] In 1913, 463 district land organization commissions were at work in the 47 provinces (468 districts) covered by land organization operations.[14] This included all of European Russia except the Baltic provinces. By 1914 the land organization administration had some 1,600 agronomists in the field, along with 2,000 assistants and 800 land organization specialists. It had established numerous model farms in various agricultural specialties, and had organized a number of hydro-technological projects.[15]

The commissions, which dealt with landowners in all social categories and with lands in all legal categories, were responsible for a broad array of organizational and meliorative works. By the beginning of 1915 close to 6 million applications for land organization of one sort or another had been received, according to official data. A surprisingly large number of these, ultimately about 2 million, were withdrawn by the applicants, but approximately half of the remainder had been acted upon.[16] Land organization work by this time had involved almost 2 million households, or roughly 15 percent of all peasant households. The most important form of land organization activity, encompassing over a third of the households involved, was converting whole villages into consolidated individual holdings. The next largest category of work, almost equally important, was separating the intermixed lands of different villages. This was followed by the separating from communes of individual peasants or groups of peasants who consolidated their holdings. (For a summary of all land organization work, see Table 3.)

Land organization work was categorized as individual if it involved the holdings of separate households, whether the work was undertaken on behalf of a single peasant or for an entire community converting to separate consolidated holdings. Approximately half of all work accomplished between 1906 and 1916 was of this sort, while the other half concerned various kinds of group activity. The balance between the two types of work, however, shifted over the decade. Because the creation of separate holdings was the most urgent of the government's concerns at the beginning of the reform period, individual work originally claimed most of the attention of the land organization staff. In 1908, 70 percent of all households serviced were in this category. But a heavy demand for group work gradually shifted the balance. By 1914 work on individual holdings involved only 43 percent of the households serviced.

Even within the category of individual work (which was devoted almost entirely to the formation of otrubs and khutors), collective action was important. Two-thirds of all consolidations came about as the result of conversions by whole communities, only a third as the result of individual decisions. Most consolidations (80 percent) were formed on the lands of rural societies. The rest were organized mainly on lands sold through the Peasant Land Bank, although a small number arose on lands acquired by the peasantry from the state. (Of some 200,000 desiatins of state land sold to the peasants through the land commis-

TABLE 3

Land Organization Work Completed as of January 1, 1915

(*47 provinces of European Russia*)

	Households		Land	
Type of work	Number	Percent of total	Amount (desiatins)	Percent of total
Individual:				
Conversion of entire villages into consolidated holdings	677,070	34%	6,651,444	40%
Separation of consolidated plots for householders	307,657	16	3,208,793	19
Group:				
Separation of lands of different villages	604,197	31	5,073,333	30
Elimination of intermixing of lands of adjacent properties	143,210	7	284,307	2
Delimitation of lands in mixed ownership	138,700	7	751,494	4
Other	95,250	5	862,087	5
TOTAL	1,966,084	100%	16,831,458	100%

SOURCE: Dubrovskii, *Stolypinskaia reforma*, p. 245.

sions during this period, 90 percent was transferred in the form of consolidated plots.)

According to Article 18 of the law of May 29, 1911, the land organization institutions themselves were to settle all disputes about the proper share of land due to an individual, a section of a community, or an entire rural society when the land in question was undergoing reorganization. They were also authorized to render final judgment (not subject to judicial review) in cases of disagreement arising from the work itself, including disagreements about the boundaries of the land subject to the work. Under Article 20, decisions about land organization arrived at by landowning communities or associations had to be verified and confirmed by the land captain within two weeks. All complaints of irregularity concerning the decisions themselves or the failure of land captains to confirm them had to be submitted to the district land organization commission.

Since land work often involved expenses that were not covered by the government—for example, the transfer of a dwelling when a khutor was formed—the land commissions offered government loans and occasionally outright grants (where social interests were served) to help cover such costs. Between 1906 and 1916 over 600,000 householders requested loans and another 120,000 asked for financial assistance with land organization procedures. The land commissions managed to meet the requests of fully half of each group. Approximately 31 million rubles was provided to peasants in the form of loans; another 1.3 million rubles was awarded in nonrepayable allowances.[17] But fieldwork rather than financing constituted the main contribution of the land commissions to the reform program. The financial aspects of peasant landholding were more central to the concerns of the Peasant Land Bank.

The Peasant Land Bank

The bank was an important agent in implementing the agrarian reform. It arranged sales to peasants from its own land fund, provided loans for purchasing private lands, and granted mortgage loans on allotment land. Before its founding in 1882, lack of long-term credit had limited peasants' ability to acquire land. When it began operations in 1883, strictly as a lending agency, the peasants in European Russia owned 10.7 million desiatins of private property, including all private land that they held collectively.[18] Almost all of the bank's loans in its first decades were made to collective buyers—to communes and peasant associations. Loans to individuals were rare and restricted in size. Interest rates charged by the Peasant Land Bank (initially 7.5–8.5 percent) were higher than those at the Nobles' Bank, but in its early years the bank normally required only a 10 percent down payment on land purchases. When the deteriorating position of the peasantry led to higher rates of loan default, the bank began to demand a third of the selling price. Nonetheless, under the pressure of population growth and shrinking holdings of allotment land, bank sales of private land to peasants continued to climb.[19]

By 1895 peasants had gained an additional 2.4 million desiatins of private land with the help of the Peasant Land Bank. In that year the bank was given the right to buy private properties in its own right for resale or lease to peasants. Interest rates had been lowered in 1894, and now down payments were reduced. The bank had also been allocated a small share of the annual revenue from the peasants' redemption payments as working capital. Land sales accelerated, and by 1905 another 5.9 million desiatins of private land had been acquired by peasants through the bank,[20] making them owners of over 24 million desiatins of private land, or about one-fourth of all privately owned land in the country.[21] The Peasant Land Bank had been responsible for

over half of the private property gains made by the peasants in the preceding two decades. Over the course of the following decade, however,
the bank was to become even more closely involved in transfers of private land to the peasantry.

In the panic of the revolution of 1905–7, there was a rush to unload
gentry property on the Peasant Land Bank. In 1905 the bank had purchased only 56,000 desiatins of gentry land with its own capital. The
following year it absorbed 1.1 million desiatins, and in 1907 it bought
another 1.5 million desiatins.[22] But this was only a fraction of the land
that it had been asked to purchase. In 1906, after the unleashing of the
"Great Fear" the previous autumn, the bank had been offered 7.6 million desiatins of land, most of it belonging to the nobility.[23] After 1907,
even more noticeably after 1908, panic-induced sales declined, but the
bank continued to make purchases from the dwindling land supply of
the nobles. In the decade between 1905 and 1915 the gentry lost 20
percent of its remaining lands.[24] But the fast-fading cherry orchards of
the nobility were not the only source of bank lands in this period.
From 1907 to 1916 the bank acquired 1.2 million desiatins of Crown
lands for sale to peasants.[25]

Convinced of the urgency of the peasant demand for land, the government committed part of its own land resources to the attempt to
divert peasants from land seizure to land purchase—the "honorable"
means of satisfying their needs that had been promised when the
Duma was prorogued in July 1906. The bank was central to this attempt and largely responsible for its measure of success. In October
1906 the bank's interest rates were reduced by the Senate to 4.5 percent (for a 55-year term). Regulations established the following month
made it possible for rural societies, peasant associations, and peasants
who held land in personal tenure to sell or mortgage it to the bank
to finance purchases of other land or to make agricultural improvements.[26] After some initial hesitation, probably due to lingering hopes
of a grant of expropriated lands, the peasants responded to the improved terms of purchase. Over half of all land ever transferred to
peasants through the bank was acquired as a result of transactions concluded in its final decade. As indicated by Table 4, from 1907 through
1915 the bank helped peasants to acquire over 8 million desiatins of
land, an impressive amount in view of the fact that the total private
land gain by peasants during this period was 9.8 million desiatins.[27]

The new official policy of individualizing peasant landholdings was
reflected in the pattern of the bank's loans. From its opening through
1905, 98 percent of the land it sold had gone to collective buyers and
only 2 percent to individual peasants. In 1906 sales from the bank's

TABLE 4

Transactions of the Peasant Land Bank, 1907–15

(million desiatins)

	Type of land	
Type of purchaser	Bank land[a]	Privately owned land[b]
Individuals	2.9	.8
Associations	.4 ⎤	3.8
Communes	.2 ⎦	
TOTAL	3.7[c]	4.6

SOURCE: *ARS*, pp. 173–74, 178.

[a] Land bought by peasants from the bank's land fund.

[b] Privately owned land purchased by peasants with the aid of bank loans.

[c] The total includes sales of 200,000 desiatins of bank land for which financing was not required. No breakdown of the purchasers is provided for collective purchases of private land.

land fund to communes and associations still accounted for 96 percent of its transactions, and the following year they had dropped only slightly, to 92 percent. Over the next few years the figures were to change radically.[28] By 1913 sales to groups were down to 5 percent of the total, and in the early months of 1915 (before bank sales were suspended in March) the amount of bank land sold to groups fell below one percent. Sales to individuals not only claimed the lion's share of the bank's land, but were larger on a per capita basis also. The average amount of bank land sold to individual purchasers between 1906 and 1916 was 14.6 desiatins; however, sales to peasant associations averaged 5.8 desiatins per household, and those to rural societies averaged only 2 desiatins per household.[29]

In addition to giving individual customers preferential treatment, the bank promoted the government's new agrarian policy by encouraging the formation of consolidated holdings. The down payment needed to purchase an otrub was reduced to only 5 percent of the selling price, and for khutors the bank could loan the full price, although the average down payment demanded for other properties was 20 percent of the bank appraisal of the land's value. Between 1907 and 1916 some three million desiatins of land sold by or with the help of the bank were formed into consolidated holdings. Slightly over one-fourth of these consolidations took the form of khutors; the remainder were organized as otrubs.[30]

Under the decree of November 15, 1906, the bank could give mortgage loans on allotment land only when it was held as personal property and only when it had been consolidated. In order to qualify for a loan, therefore, peasants in communes had first to establish separate title to the land. This could be accomplished by individual separations from a commune or by wholesale conversion of a commune to separate holdings, followed by consolidation of the appropriated holdings. After the law of May 29, 1911, the procedure was simpler because appropriation was no longer a necessary precondition of consolidation. In communities under hereditary tenure, since consolidations could not be effected individually, a majority decision to convert to consolidated holdings was the only means of qualifying for a loan. The all-or-nothing provisions of the law regarding these communities help explain why so many of the consolidated holdings that were formed resulted from group conversions. Although initially it was necessary to consolidate holdings of allotment land to borrow against them, a ruling of July 5, 1912, made it possible to get a mortgage on such land in order to consolidate it.

In a variety of ways, then, the Peasant Land Bank made departures from the commune advantageous and gave important financial support to the establishment of the new rural class envisaged by the reformers. The bank itself was only one of a number of mechanisms employed by the government after 1905 to implement the new agrarian policy. By enacting legislation that encouraged separations from the commune, by providing administrative machinery and technical assistance to facilitate the formation of unitary landholdings, by underwriting many of the costs involved, and by making land and credit available to those who desired to exchange, extend, or improve their holdings, the government had made a concerted effort to induce peasants to abandon the commune. How, then, did the peasants respond?

5

Changes in Communal Landholding

Peasant Landholding, 1905

From the time of the emancipation of the peasantry until 1906 only 140,000 households left the commune. This figure includes all departures under Article 165 and those that took place after 1893. In 1905, in 50 provinces of European Russia over three-fourths of all peasant households and over four-fifths of all allotment land were in communes. In these provinces 12.3 million households held 139 million desiatins of land legally reserved for the use of peasants and Cossacks; they included 9.5 million households with 115 million desiatins in communes and 2.8 million households with 23 million desiatins in hereditary tenure.[1]

Holdings in Cossack lands under communal tenure were usually far larger than the typical peasant holding of allotment land. Even discounting the Cossacks, the average holding in communes was larger than that of peasants with land in hereditary tenure. (See Table 6.) Global averages, however, conceal some important local differences, since the size of communal holdings varied considerably from region to region. The average size of holdings of allotment land is listed by region in Table 5.[2]

Not only did the size of average holdings differ sharply from one region to another, there was a broad range in the size of holdings within regions. Although the overall average allotment holding in European Russia was about 10 desiatins, the average was not necessarily typical.[3] Almost 70 percent of all such holdings were smaller, and in the black soil region 30 percent contained less than 5 desiatins.[4]

As Table 5 reveals, the size of the average holding in a region did not correspond to the extent of communal tenure. Although allotments in communes were typically larger than those in hereditary tenure, the largest regional average was in the Baltic, where all allotment land was

TABLE 5

Allotment-Land Holdings by Region, 1905

(*50 provinces of European Russia*)

Region	Average holding (desiatins)	Households under communal tenure (percent)
1 Mid-Volga	7.8	100%
2 Lake	11.2	100
3 Trans-Volga	18.3	99
4 Volga-Don	8.0	98
5 Southern Steppe	11.6	98
6 Northern	22.4	97
7 Central	7.9	97
8 Dnepr-Don	7.0	68
9 Northwestern	11.3	28
10 Trans-Dnepr	6.0	23
11 Baltic	36.9	—
50 provinces	10.2	77%

SOURCE: TsSK, *Statistika zemlevladeniia 1905*, pp. 174–75. The data cover 12 million households. Cossack and Bashkir lands were not included.

in hereditary tenure. Conversely, in the solidly communal mid-Volga region the average was below that for European Russia as a whole.

In some regions larger holdings of allotment land were associated with higher rates of population growth (the Southern Steppe, Northwest, Trans-Volga, and Lake regions). Yet there was no consistent correlation between the size of allotments and population growth, and the region with the smallest allotments (the Trans-Dnepr) had a high rate of growth.

Although it is difficult to correlate the size of allotments with the extent of communal tenure or the growth of population, one factor, the social background of peasant households, is unmistakably related to allotment size. Upon emancipation state peasants, as we saw earlier, received larger allotments than those given to freed serfs. Four-fifths of all households stemming from former state peasants were in communes in 1905. They accounted for exactly half of all communal households, but held 65 percent of all communal allotment land. In 1905 the holdings of these peasants averaged 13.6 desiatins.

Communes consisting of households of former serfs were in quite different, and disadvantageous, circumstances. They contained almost half of all households in communes, but held only 30 percent of the allotment land in communes. The average holding was only 6.8 desiatins. Moreover, although some of the land of former state peasants was, by virtue of its location or quality, less valuable as agricultural

TABLE 6

Allotment-Land Holdings by Households, 1905

(*47 provinces of European Russia*)

	Former status of household			
Category	State peasant	Serf	Crown peasant	Total
Percent of households:				
As percent of total peasant				
households	46%	50%	4%	100%
In communes	50	45	5	100
Under hereditary tenure	34%	65%	1%	100%
Average holding (desiatins):				
Of all households	12.5	6.7	9.6	9.5
Of households in communes	13.6	6.8	9.6	10.2
Of households				
in hereditary tenure	8.8	6.4	5.4	7.3

SOURCE: Calculated from data in TsSK, *Statistika zemlevladeniia 1905*, pp. xxx, 174–75.

NOTE: The data cover 11.5 million peasant households with 109 million desiatins of allotment land; Baltic peasants, Cossacks, colonists, and several special groups are omitted.

land than that of former serfs, as at least partial compensation former state lands were less apt to suffer from a shortage of the special land funds (hay land, woodland, and so on) that were frequently cut off from peasants' lands by estate owners at the time of emancipation.

Among peasants holding their lands in hereditary tenure, as among peasants in communes, the allotment holdings of former state peasants were generally larger than those of former serfs. As Table 6 reveals, however, the difference between the two groups was less pronounced where allotments were hereditary. Any discussion of later social differentiation among the communal peasantry must take into account the considerable differences in the size of allotments that existed at the time of the emancipation and had not been eradicated by as late as 1905.

Some of the critics who blamed the commune for the small size of peasant holdings were apparently unaware that the allotments of peasants not under communal tenure were generally even smaller than those of peasants in communes. At any rate, there was relatively little discussion of the fact in contemporary literature, which routinely held the commune responsible for the fragmentation of peasant holdings. As the data in Table 5 make clear, allotments had shrunk to their smallest in the Trans-Dnepr region, which had a high rate of population growth but little communal tenure. By tying peasants to the land, communes undoubtedly exacerbated the problem in some areas, but the large number of passports issued annually to rural residents by the turn of the century indicates that communes were not unwilling to release members when there were opportunities for more profitable employment elsewhere. The earnings of such members could help households meet their fiscal responsibilities and benefit the entire community when the local supply of land offered inadequate employment for the available labor force. Yet as the number of households grew (and legislation failed to halt the process), each redistribution of communal lands meant smaller allotments.

The Vitality of Redistributional Practices

The extent to which communes were still redistributing land was a subject of some discussion in the early twentieth century. Kachorovskii's turn-of-the-century study of 35 provinces indicated that most were still redistributing their field lands. He pointed out, however, that repartitions became fairly common only from the 1880's. At the time of his study he believed that there was evidence of growing resistance to redivision of lands among former serf households because of the extremely small size of their holdings; later he changed his views when additional data showed active redistribution even in communes with minimal land.[5]

In connection with its work on agrarian legislation, the Ministry of Internal Affairs investigated the incidence of land redivision in 28 provinces with extensive communal tenure. According to its report, many communes had not redistributed their lands at all since the original allotment following emancipation. Of the 73,000 rural societies included in the data, 48 percent had never redivided their land. Three percent had undertaken no redistribution for over 40 years, 13 percent for over 15 to 25 years, and 15 percent for over 10 years.[6] The government stressed the high rate of inactivity to explain the legislative provisions converting communes automatically to hereditary tenure; this was only to accept de jure what the peasantry had already effected de facto. The statistics on redistribution were officially interpreted as evidence that the commune had lost its vitality. Although this may have been a reasonable conclusion, the figures were challenged; since there was no attempt to compare them with pre-emancipation rates of redistribution, any conclusions based on them were necessarily tentative. There had been no general redistribution of lands at the time of emancipation, and apparently there had been relatively little wholesale redistribution in the years immediately following. Yet the official statistics themselves revealed that the frequency of redistribution was climbing steadily. Repartitional activity had clearly increased, and 20 percent of all communes had redistributed their lands in the last decade covered by the survey. That there had not been many general redivisions of land in the early years after the original allotment is hardly surprising. Many communes had been accustomed to redistribute after each census, and no census was taken between 1858 and 1897.

Other studies confirmed the picture of few early redistributions, but a growing number later. The investigation of communal redistributions in Aleksandrov district, Ekaterinoslav province (p. 29 above), showed a steep increase in the number of redistributions after the turn of the century. Similarly, a questionnaire circulated by the Free Economic Society in ten central agricultural and mid-Volga provinces in 1910 and 1911 revealed that of some 400 communes for which data were reported less than 8 percent had not redistributed their land.[7] Most repartitions, however, were recent. Almost 60 percent of the communes had redivided their lands in the decade between 1895 and 1906 (that is, after the legal restriction of 1893), and another 21 percent had held redistributions in the brief interval between 1907 and 1910. Although in the area from which the sample was taken strong communal traditions appeared to be holding firm in the face of the reform program, 10 to 15 percent of all household heads had separated their lands from communes at the time of the survey.

Appropriation, Conversions, and Consolidations of Communal Land

By 1910 individual appropriations under the reform had already passed their peak. After the decree of November 9, 1906, a considerable number of peasants claimed personal title to their share of communal lands, and by the end of 1915 some two million appropriations had been effected. The yearly record in Table 7 shows, however, that there was no overwhelming surge of departures from the commune, and that the greatest number occurred early. After a rather slow start in 1907 as administrative machinery was established and peasants became acquainted with their new rights, the number of applications for individual title to communal lands rose impressively in 1908 and 1909, then declined rapidly thereafter.

The gap between the number of applications and the number of appropriations completed was due only in part to a lag in processing. Only one-fourth of the applicants were able to reach an agreement with the commune within the stipulated period; the remainder had to turn to the local authorities to compel the commune to accept separation. Close to 10 percent of all applications filed were subsequently

TABLE 7

Personal Appropriation of Communal Allotment Land, 1907–15

(*39 provinces of European Russia and Stavropol province*)

Year	Applications for appropriation (000)	Appropriations completed (000)	Land appropriated (000 desiatins)	Avg. amt. of land appropriated (desiatins)
1907	212	48	4,316	7.7
1908	840	508		
1909	650	579	4,115	7.1
1910	342	342	2,303	6.7
1911	242	145	996	6.8
1912	152	122	785	6.4
1913	160	134	747	5.5
1914	120	98	594	6.1
1915	37	30	267	9.0
TOTAL	2,755	2,008	14,123	7.0

SOURCES: Chernyshev, *Obshchina*, 1:xiii; data in ARS, p. 145, from *Izvestiia zemskogo otdela MVD*, 1915, no. 7, pp. 242–43, and 1916, no. 8, pp. 218–19.

withdrawn either because they had been pushed upon reluctant peasants by overly zealous officials or because of the opposition of other members of the applicant's commune.[8] Yet some households were carried into hereditary tenure against the will of their members under the provisions for group conversion by a two-thirds vote of a commune. The fact that applications for individualized tenure dropped off after the first few years indicates a release of the backlog of pressure from those who wanted to leave the commune (many of whom had already in fact departed) and those who found it profitable to appropriate their communal land.

To some extent, however, the decline in applications reflects the effect of the law of June 14, 1910. By recognizing as automatically transferred to hereditary tenure all communes that had not held a general redistribution since their original allotment of land, the law made it unnecessary for their members to apply for a formal separation of title. Yet for legal evidence of personal property rights essential for the sale of land, for individual land organization work (until 1911), or for control of their own agricultural operations independent of communal decisions, peasants in these communes had to apply for official certification of personal ownership. As a circular of the Ministry of Internal Affairs advised local officials on January 27, 1911, the 1910 law failed to define the means whereby communes that had not redistributed their lands could be identified and subjected to the laws governing communities under hereditary tenure. As a result, all such societies were placed in an "extremely indefinite juridical position which could lead to utter confusion in their land relations under the law."[9] The only way of clarifying their status, in the view of the ministry, was to issue documents of certification either to these communes or to individuals within them, since formal recognition of the hereditary rights of any member would establish the status of the entire community. Local authorities, especially the land captains, were therefore instructed to make discreet inquiries concerning redistributions and to tactfully encourage requests for certification where favorable results could be expected. Despite such encouragement, however, the number of requests remained limited. The government, in an estimate that critics challenged as inflated, had declared that 3.5 million households belonged to communes that had not held redistributions. Kachorovskii, among others, considered the official estimate highly exaggerated. According to his investigation, no more than 10 percent of all households under communal tenure at the beginning of the century, that is, less than a million households, had not redistributed their lands.[10] By 1916 about 0.6 million had applied, individually or collectively, for certificates of ownership, and close to 0.5 million had actually obtained them.[11]

The number of householders who gained individual proof of personal ownership (317,000) was twice as high as the number of those who obtained it as members of entire communes requesting certificates (153,000), and the separate individuals owned less land on the average than householders in communes certified as a whole. The typical holding in both groups was below the average for European Russia, and it declined in size after the first year. Only in 1915, during the war, did the average size of certified holdings rise, and then fairly abruptly. (See Table 8.)

Although the total number of householders actually covered by certificates of personal ownership was only 470,000, the 317,000 householders who had received certificates as individuals managed by their action to identify their communes as not having redistributed their allotment lands. These householders came from communes in which there were some 1.7 million households, and this far more sizable group could therefore technically be recognized as having automatically converted to hereditary tenure. But such bookkeeping transfers had little effect on the peasants' landholding practices. These communes continued to hold their land as before, and in some cases even redistributed it.[12] Local authorities often refused to register such redistributions formally, but the government recognized realities by including in the official statistics only those householders actually applying for certificates of personal ownership.

TABLE 8

Certifications of Personal Ownership of Communal Allotment Land, 1910–15

(39 provinces of European Russia and Stavropol province)

Year	Issued to communes				Issued to individual household heads		
	Number	House-holders included	Land (000 desiatins)	Avg. land cert. per household (desiatins)	Number	Land (000 desiatins)	Avg. land cert. per household (desiatins)
1910	69	1,429	12	8.5	6,787	45	6.6
1911	2,623	75,356	460	6.1	91,894	526	5.7
1912	1,626	36,756	248	6.7	71,920	424	5.9
1913	571	26,367	176	6.7	71,392	390	5.5
1914	432	10,368	65	6.3	54,915	287	5.2
1915	84	2,627	28	10.5	19,981	135	6.7
TOTAL	5,405	152,903	989	6.5	316,889	1,807	5.7

SOURCE: Data from *Izvestiia zemskogo otdela MVD*, 1915, no. 7, pp. 242–43; and 1916, no. 8, pp. 218–19; in *ARS*, p. 145.

In gauging the effect of the reform on the commune, only the groups and individuals actually certified can be considered to be genuine conversions. Adding the 470,000 conversions to the roughly 2 million cases of personal appropriation of communal land gives a total of some 2.5 million households moving out of communal tenure by 1916. To this group of separators it may be necessary to add some of those who consolidated their holdings of allotment land after 1911, when prior appropriation was no longer necessary.

From 1907 through 1916 approximately 1.3 million households formed consolidated holdings on 12.7 million desiatins of allotment land with the help of the land organization agencies.[13] It is impossible to establish precisely how many of those who consolidated their holdings by 1917 had moved out of the commune, since the consolidators included peasants holding land in hereditary tenure as well as peasants whose lands had been in communal tenure. Data available through 1911 indicate that peasants under both systems of tenure consolidated their holdings at about the same rate, so peasants from communes may have accounted for 0.6 million of the post-1911 consolidations.[14] However, some of the ex-communal consolidators had appropriated their lands earlier and are already included among the other separators from the commune; others may be included among the post-1911 appropriators. The groups of appropriators and those receiving certificates of personal ownership also overlapped. Some of the peasants included among the 153,000 householders covered in group certificates had already claimed title to their lands as individuals and are counted twice in the statistics on separations.[15] Because it is not possible to determine the degree to which the various circles of separators overlapped and on the assumption that at least some of the doublecountings and undercountings in the statistics cancel out, the figure of 2.5 million documented separations is widely used to assess the effect of the reform on the commune. Although far from exact, it provides at least a rough measure of changes in land tenure.

The Statistics on Separations from the Commune

On the basis of the available data many scholars, both Soviet and Western, have concluded that in its scant decade of operation the reform program had a devastating effect on the commune. Communes, which held three-quarters of the peasantry in 1905, have been described as holding as little as a third of all peasant households a decade later.[16] Such conclusions appear unwarranted.

One source of major distortion has been the readiness of some writers to accept at face value the "separation" of the 1.7 million households blanketed under the automatic conversion legislation of 1910.[17] Since these households continued to hold and use their land exactly as before, there is little reason to consider them among the separators; even the government, as we saw, failed to list them among the certified households. Most authors follow the more reasonable course and do not include noncertified households among the separators, yet even the more conservative figure of 2.5 million introduces certain problems.

Of the 50 provinces included in the 1905 land statistics, 9 in the west had little or no communal tenure. The statistics of the Ministry of Internal Affairs therefore covered only the remaining provinces, except the Don region (which had special Cossack land arrangements) and Arkhangel province. The 40 provinces covered included Stavropol, which had not been surveyed in 1905 and where the extent of communal tenure was unknown but substantial. Data for these provinces indicate that the total number of appropriations by May 1, 1915, was 22 percent of the original number of communal households recorded in 1905.[18] As a result, some writers have reported a departure rate of 22 percent, apparently unaware that the number of appropriations in 40 provinces by mid-1915 was being compared with the number of households in 39 provinces in 1905. Apart from the minor problem of comparing slightly different areas, the use of 1905 data exaggerates the exodus from the commune. Separations occurred over a period in which the population was growing rapidly, with an average annual increase of over 2 percent in some regions; and allowance must be made for the appearance of new households when calculating the scale of departures.[19]

Between 1906 and 1916 not only was there a substantial natural increase in the number of peasant households, but there were also an increasing number of family divisions prompted by separations from the commune and by consolidations. Under these circumstances a separation from a commune did not necessarily mean a reduction in the number of households remaining within it. Since family divisions were more apt to occur among households within communes,[20] the mechanical increase in the number of communal households offset the higher rate of natural increase of the noncommunal population. It would be a relatively simple matter to assess the effect of the reform on the commune in quantitative terms if landholding statistics comparable to those of 1905 had been collected a decade later. Unfortunately, there are no similar data on the number of households or the land in communes at the close of the period.

There are, however, statistics on the number of peasant households at the beginning of 1916. According to corrected figures of the agricultural census taken that year, there were over 15.3 million peasant households in European Russia at the time.[21] In 1915, then, it can be estimated that there were about 15 million. Assuming roughly even rates of increase in the number of households under both forms of tenure, there would have been 11.5 million households in 1915 deriving from the households in communes in 1905. If 2.5 million of these had separated from the commune, then 9 million would have remained. Although hardly precise, this conservative calculation indicates that the households still in communes amounted to 61 percent of all peasant households in European Russia at the time, a substantial reduction from the 77 percent of 1905 but still a decided majority.

Analysis of the movement of land out of communal tenure is simpler since the quantity of allotment land, unlike the number of households, was fairly constant. The land data support the conclusion that communes still had a strong grip on peasant land at the end of the reform decade. By 1916 over 16 million desiatins (about 14 percent of the 115.4 million desiatins of allotment land in communes in 1905) had been individualized through appropriations and certifications.[22] The remainder, approximately 99 million desiatins, amounted to over 70 percent of all allotment land held by the entire peasantry. Even after allowance for additional losses through consolidations of communal land, fully two-thirds of all allotment land held by the peasantry remained in communes at the end of the old regime.

With respect to private land the situation was particularly interesting. Between January 1, 1905, and January 1, 1915, the amount of private land owned by peasants climbed from 24.6 to 34.4 million desiatins, a gain of 40 percent. Peasants owned 35 percent of the total 97.7 million desiatins of privately owned land in 1915. Part of the peasants' private land was in holdings of more than 50 desiatins, and Soviet historian A. M. Anfimov has suggested that these should not be counted among peasant lands, since only smallholdings below this level can be properly considered to be peasant holdings. According to his calculations, peasant holdings of private land with less than 50 desiatins amounted to 15.6 million desiatins in 1905 and 24.8 million desiatins in 1915.[23] Anfimov concludes that the real peasants (those who were peasants by virtue of their economic rather than their legal status) held only 25 percent of all private land in 1915 and were therefore not increasing their private holdings as rapidly as seems indicated. However, his own figures (which include the private land owned by rural societies and peasant associations) show that the share of private land held by peasant smallholders was increasing more rapidly than the aggregate amount held by the peasantry as a whole. The private lands held by smallholder peasants individually or collectively grew by almost 60 percent from 1905 to 1915.

One striking aspect of peasant land gains in this period has drawn little attention. In 1905 slightly over half (54 percent) of the land held privately by peasants was held by individuals, but by 1915 the share held individually had dropped to 49 percent. In other words, during the period of intense government effort to individualize proprietorship, the proportion of private land owned collectively by the peasantry (by rural societies and peasant associations) actually rose. The shift is all the more remarkable because of the much-publicized individualization policy of the Peasant Land Bank. As has been noted, the bank transferred its sales from collective to individual customers after 1906, particularly after 1908. Sales to groups claimed a mere 20 percent of all bank land sold in the period from 1906 through 1915, and even this modest figure was due only to the heavy turnover in the first few years before the new policy took full effect.[24] This development was widely advertised in the contemporary literature. But in addition to selling its own lands, the bank played an important part in the transfer of privately owned lands by providing loans to peasants; and in transactions where the bank acted only as a lending agency, the ratio of individual and collective buyers was reversed. Only 17 percent of the nonbank land went to individual buyers, and 83 percent was purchased by peasants collectively.[25] Since considerably more land was bought by peasants with the help of bank loans than was bought directly from the bank, the total amount of land involved in all group purchases outstripped the sum gained in individual acquisitions by a ratio of 54 to 46. As a result, although the private landholdings of individual peasants did increase from 1906 to 1915, the collective ownership of private land increased even more.

Peasant Landholding, 1915

In 1905 peasants held in all some 163 million desiatins of land, of which 73 percent was held by communes. By 1916 peasants held a total of 173 million desiatins. Since at that time communes held 99 million desiatins of allotment land and 4.6 million desiatins of private land, they still controlled three-fifths of all peasant land. (See Table 9.)

In sum, then, although the reform reduced the extent of communal tenure, the commune was still very much a part of rural life on the eve of the 1917 revolution. The number of households in communes had dropped from 77 percent to about 60 percent, and the amount of allotment land held in communal tenure had decreased from 83 percent to

TABLE 9

Changes in Peasant Landholding, 1905–15

	All peasant land		Land held by communes	
Category and date	Amount (million desiatins)	Percent of total	Amount (million desiatins)	Percent of all peasant land
1905				
Allotment land	138.8	85%	115.4	83%
Private land, owned by:				
Communes	3.7	2	3.7	100
Associations	7.6	5	—	—
Individuals	13.2 (4.3)[a]	8	—	—
TOTAL	163.3	100%	119.1	73%
1915				
Allotment land	138.8	80%	99.0	71%
Private land, owned by:				
Communes	4.6	3	4.6	100
Associations	12.9	7	—	—
Individuals	16.8 (7.3)[a]	10	—	—
TOTAL	173.1	100%	103.6	60%

SOURCES: TsSK, *Statistika zemlevladeniia 1905*, pp. 174–75; Anfimov and Makarov, pp. 85, 88.
[a] Data in parentheses show the amount included that was in holdings of less than 50 desiatins. All collectively held land was assumed to be in such holdings.

approximately 71 percent. However, the withdrawal of allotment land from communal tenure was only part of the shifting picture. Not only the appropriation of communal land by individuals but also the growth in peasant ownership of private land accounted for the diminishing role of communal tenure. Privately owned land increased from 15 to 20 percent of all land held by members of the peasant estate between 1905 and 1915.

Two particularly interesting developments were involved in this trend. First, private land gains were made at much higher rates by peasant smallholders than by peasants with larger holdings. Of the 3.6 million desiatins acquired by individual peasants, 3.1 million were in holdings of less than 50 desiatins. In the course of the decade, whereas the amount of individually owned private land increased by 28 percent among all peasants, it increased by 71 percent among peasant smallholders. Private land in peasant holdings of more than 50 desiatins increased by only 7 percent.

The acquisitions of the peasant smallholders were made at the expense of other social estates—nobles, merchants, the clergy—and

TABLE 10

Private Landholding, 1905–15

(million desiatins)

Type of land	1905	1915
All privately owned land	97.9	97.7
Individually owned land	81.9	73.0
All individual holdings up to 50 desiatins	6.2	7.8
Private land held by peasants	24.6	34.4
Individually	13.2	16.8
Collectively	11.4	17.5

SOURCE: Anfimov and Makarov, pp. 84–88.

often at the expense of other smallholders. The total amount of land gained by all individual proprietors (peasant and nonpeasant) of private land in smallholdings was only 1.6 million desiatins (see Table 10). Nonpeasant smallholders, therefore, were rapidly losing their private land to the peasantry. In 1905 peasants owned 68 percent of all private land in individual holdings of less than 50 desiatins; in 1915 they owned 94 percent. The general picture, then, is one of increasing individual ownership of private land among peasants, but almost entirely in the form of smallholdings.

Second, of the total amount of private land to come into the possession of peasants in this period (9.8 million desiatins), only about a third was acquired by individuals. The remaining two-thirds was purchased and owned collectively. Thus, during these years, when the amount of all individually owned land dropped by 8.8 million desiatins, the amount of private land owned by the peasantry collectively through associations and communes increased by 6.2 million desiatins. Peasants held, either individually or collectively, including holdings of all sizes, one-fourth of all privately owned land in 1905, and a full third of all such land in 1915. Adding the private property owned by communes to the allotment land in communal tenure in 1915 makes it all the more evident that communal landholding still predominated among the peasants at the end of the reform decade. Despite the growth of private landholding, the practice of collective tenure remained strong. In 1915, 67 percent of all land (allotment and private) held by peasants was held collectively.

Factors Influencing Changes in Tenure

In addition to the reform legislation and the policy considerations that shaped it, a number of factors—microeconomic, geographic, sociopsychological, and political—affected the shift in land tenure. The striking differences in the regional rates of separation suggest a point of departure in the search for forces influencing movement out of the commune.

Many of the separations from the commune occurred in regions where communal tenure had been weak. This fact led P. N. Pershin, in an early investigation, to conclude that the legislation per se did not destroy the commune, but simply permitted individualized property to move into a vacuum created by the "natural evolutionary" decay of an outmoded form of tenure.[26] Yet, as his own work demonstrated, many consolidations occurred in solidly communal areas of the south and southeast. Clearly, something other than institutional obsolescence was at work.

Contemporary analysts noted positive correlations among rates of separation from the commune, the formation of consolidated holdings, and emigration to Siberia. All were more marked in the black soil region, where the coincident patterns of mobilization of people and property reflected an economic transformation then taking place. Urban growth was strengthening the domestic market for agriculture, and an improved foreign market was providing a further impetus to commercialize the grain-producing agriculture of the south.[27] Yet communal tenure was an impediment to peasant entrepreneurship and threatened to further decrease the size of allotment holdings; therefore, separations from the commune became commonplace.*

Comparison of the number of separations with the regional price of land reveals a direct and unbroken correlation between the two.[28] (See Table 11.) The highest land prices were linked to the highest levels of separation. On the other hand, a comparison of the size of holdings with the rate of separation shows a generally inverse correlation: where land was most plentiful, the fewest separations took place. Land shortage alone fails to explain high land prices or social mobility, for the region with the smallest holdings had neither the most expensive land nor the most departures from the commune. Land prices were an index of economic development in rural areas where expanding market opportunities created incentives to individualize holdings.

In Siberia, which did not come under the Stolypin legislation, there was at this time an apparently spontaneous movement among peasants to individualize and consolidate lands. By 1913, in old-settler commu-

---

*The peasants' awareness of and responsiveness to market conditions is evident in their replies to a questionnaire of the Free Economic Society in 1910–11. Peasants submitted proposals for government price supports, for control of distribution, and even for diplomatic support in the international market. See Chernyshev, *Obshchina*, pp. 57–59.

TABLE 11

Regional Land Prices and Appropriations
of Communal Land, 1906–14

Great Russian communal provinces	Size of avg. holding (desiatins)	Avg. price of land per desiatin in 1906–8 (rubles)	Percent of households appropriating by 1914
I. Southern Steppe	8.5	172	40%
II. Volga-Central Agricultural	7.7	122	22
III. Central Industrial and Northwest	9.4	76	17
IV. Border provinces	18.5	33	7

SOURCE: Mozzhukhin, *Zemleustroistvo*, p. 34.

NOTE: Group I consists of Ekaterinoslav, Taurida, Kharkov, Kherson; Group II of Saratov, Simbirsk, Kazan, Penza, Tambov, Vorenezh, Kursk, Riazan, Orlov, Tula; Group III of Nizhnii Novgorod, Vladimir, Iaroslavl, Moscow, Kaluga, Tver, Pskov, Petrograd; Group IV of Vologda, Olonets, Novgorod, Perm, Viatka, Ufa, Orenburg, Astrakhan.

nities land organization work had been done on 6 million desiatins out of a total of 33.5 million, largely at local initiative and expense. Some 80 percent of this land was consolidated as unitary farms, with the same ratio of khutors (25 percent) as in the consolidations in European Russia. Beginning in 1911 half of the new allotments given to migrants were in the form of consolidated farms.[29]

The relative vitality of the commune as a land-repartitioning agency thus appears to have been less critical in separations than were local economic conditions. Similarly, it appears to have been less important than local geographic conditions in determining the form taken by consolidations.

The geographic distribution of consolidated farms followed a pattern that corresponded roughly to the pattern of separations, with concentrations in the northwest, south, and southeast of European Russia. The method of forming consolidated holdings showed an interesting variation, however. Whereas conversions by whole villages predominated in the north, northwest, and southwest, individual separations were far more common in the south and southeast. Another marked regional variation was the distribution of the two forms of consolidation: the khutor and the otrub. Khutors were concentrated almost entirely in the northwest and west. By 1913, 40 percent of the holdings in the northwest that had been consolidated through land organization work were fully integrated unitary farms; but in the south and southeast, although a majority of the consolidated holdings had been organized into two parcels, only 3 percent had been reduced to just one piece of land.[30]

These differences resulted from regional topographic and hydrographic features. The broken and varied terrain of the north had led to such extreme fragmentation that the benefits of consolidation were self-evident; an abundance of groundwater made possible the consolidation of peasant lands into completely unified holdings. Less fragmentation had occurred in the plains of the south and southeast, but the economic motives that have been noted prompted consolidation. Scarcity of water in the region, however, often made it necessary to keep homesteads in the village, near the local water source. In these fertile regions the average allotment was small and the value of a dwelling plot relatively high. A correspondent of the Free Economic Society reported from Kiev province that because house and garden plots there were often worth at least twice as much as a household's plowland, no peasant would consider moving from his dwelling site in the village.[31]

Apart from economic and geographic problems, intangible elements of the peasant *mentalité* inhibited separations from the commune in general and the establishment of khutors in particular. The Free Economic Society's rural correspondents frequently mentioned peasant concern about the inconvenience of being separated from the village: "In the commune everything is close to the peasant." As a troubled Tambov peasant saw it, a muzhik off by himself "has no store, no place to buy something quickly. There is no church. There is nothing. And that is why it is bad."[32] Resistance to a break with the familiar and fear of unaccustomed isolation, whether they bespeak rural conservatism, culturally conditioned collectivism, or simply basic human traits, were among the forces affecting peasant behavior. To the degree that increased market activity promoted an extension of rural social horizons, the commercialization of agriculture encouraged mobility. Yet many rural communities regarded the prospect of change with acute anxiety. Peasants did not want to leave the commune, reported one correspondent, because they feared they might then lose all their land and no longer "have a place even for a cock to crow."[33]

A typical village confrontation with land commission officials promoting individualization was vividly described by an enthusiastic land agent. Peasant hostility, suspicion, and resentment—particularly of the "cook's children," * who had abandoned the land for factory em-

---

*The notorious phrase of former Minister of Education I. D. Delianov was applied pejoratively by villagers to members of the commune who had gone off to work in the towns yet still claimed a share of the land. The new legislation permitted these "cook's children" to appropriate their share if they had maintained their claim through use of the land in any way—including renting it out. Such appropriations, made primarily for purposes of sale, were bitterly opposed by the commune.

ployment—created a tense atmosphere. "In this cottage, packed full with peasants, the fate of each household was being decided. Every man sensed that he was on the verge of some sort of crisis in his life, and before the eyes of each father of a family was the haunting question: And what if you lose? What if you get your land cut down?"[34]

Not all of the peasants were unwilling to surrender the security of the commune, and those who resisted separation were sometimes subjected to political pressure. The extent and degree of such pressure have been hotly disputed by critics and apologists of the government's reform program. Besides the provisions of the agrarian legislation that clearly favored separators by permitting them to leave the commune with extra land at little or no cost, the technical and financial assistance offered to separators, and the support of the Peasant Land Bank, all of which might be viewed as more or less legitimate techniques of policy implementation, there appears to have been some direct coercion—particularly at the local level. The land official quoted above worked in the field during the reform period. In an account written later he insisted that peasants had not been forced to leave the commune: "We propagandized, using no sort of pressure whatsoever, if only for the simple reason that we had no means at hand for exerting pressure."[35] Although this may have been true in his area, in others at least some heavy-handedness seems adequately established.[36]

Peasant protests about administrative pressure appear in the materials of the Free Economic Society and are recorded in official correspondence. Yet despite the urging of the central authorities and the fact that the land captains had exceptional authority to promote departures and stifle complaints, the picture that emerges from the sources is not one of policy introduced at bayonet point. Most often force appears to have come into play in response to active resistance by communal peasants to the withdrawal of part of their lands by separating households. In many cases, these separations had been prompted by local bureaucrats and were being carried out with little attention to the rights or concerns of the remaining peasants. Government land agents were accused, for example, of forcing communes to give separators some of their most valuable lands in the hope of encouraging others to depart also. When communes opposed proposals for separation or conversion, officials often tried to negotiate. In such cases they were apt to advise peasants that resistance was futile since sooner or later all would become private proprietors. If their arguments proved unconvincing, the local authorities could call for armed reinforcements. In one instance, in Samara in 1911, a village confrontation ended with the police opening fire on a threatening crowd. Ten peasants were wounded, three died.[37] Incidents culminating in such overt violence or resulting in such tragic consequences do not appear to have been common, but they reflect and undoubtedly contributed to rural tension. A good deal of bitterness followed individuals who departed from communes, and the government was obliged to provide physical protection for some of them. Peasants who obstructed the work of the land agents or interfered with separators' use of their individualized lands were arrested and fined.[38] As a more passive form of resistance, peasants sometimes refused to elect representatives for the seats allotted them on the local land organization commissions.

The fact that more than a quarter of all applications for appropriation were never completed has been interpreted as evidence of peasant resistance to separations initiated by local officials. It could, however, indicate communal resistance to peasant-initiated separations. In any case, close to 10 percent of all applications were withdrawn within a month without the commune's having taken action on them. Only 27 percent met with the agreement of the commune; all the remainder had to be completed through the land captain.[39]

Although communes in the non–black soil region were twice as likely as those in the black soil region to approve individual separations, the black soil region witnessed the majority of such separations. Along with the geographic distribution of group conversions and individual separations, this indicates that the movement out of the commune was more spontaneous in the north and northwest and that there was probably more administrative coercion in the southeast and in parts of the central agricultural region.[40] The reason for this regional difference was, again, related to differences among local economies. Within the southern and central grain-producing regions the open conflict of diverse peasant interests was a sign of growing intraclass differentiation as the peasantry became increasingly involved in the market economy.[41]

The question of what groups left the commune and why is a challenging one. The evidence, unfortunately, is limited. I. V. Chernyshev's analysis of the replies of the Free Economic Society's 1910–11 questionnaire, covering some 400 communes from the central agricultural provinces, indicated that peasants with holdings and families of all sizes separated. But departures were said to occur primarily among small families (43 percent of the replies) rather than among large families (6 percent). However, many respondents indicated that those with below-average holdings felt insecure at the prospect of going it alone and were reluctant to give up the chance of increasing their holdings at a future repartition. Repeatedly it was stated that the poor peasant simply could not exist without the commune.[42] Yet by separating from the commune a poor peasant would be able to sell his inadequate allotment and obtain capital for a new enterprise or for emigration. A better-off peasant was generally conceded to have the best prospects for individualized holding, but the replies pointed out that it was often more profitable for him to remain in the commune, where he could continue to dominate the village and to pasture his above-average supply of livestock on community land. And the "mir eater," who might own the village store, hire village labor, or rent the lands of departed smallholders, was not always interested in separating.[43]

Separators were motivated by different considerations. Some anticipated a reduction of land in the next repartition because of a change in family size or other factors; others appropriated their land in order to be able to sell it; still others separated in order to improve their agricultural practices by independent operation. More often than not, the amount of land held by a family actually corresponded to the share to which it was entitled. In the sample in the Free Economic Society's survey, over 10 percent of all separators had abandoned farming before leaving the commune. About 20 percent of the separators sold their lands, and another 12 percent rented theirs out. Nearly a quarter of the separators had consolidated their lands.

Another study, also in the central agricultural region, provides additional insight into the motives for separation. Conducted by I. V. Mozzhukhin, this investigation was restricted to Bogoroditskii district in the province of Tula. Solidly communal in 1905, this district led the province in the number of separations from the commune after 1907. By 1914 individual holdings had been formed on allotment and bank lands for about one-fourth of all its peasant households.[44] Mozzhukhin's field inquiry revealed some noteworthy differences between the motives of individual separators and those of peasants in group conversions. Not surprisingly, over half of the individuals leaving the commune did so in order to retain the largest possible amount of land. Only 9 percent of those involved in group conversions were similarly motivated. It is surprising, however, to find that 40 percent of the peasants in the latter group separated from the commune against their will. Even more unexpected is the finding that 17 percent of the individual separators had been forced to leave by the decision of the commune. Despite the fond hopes of the reformers, only one-fourth of each group had been motivated to leave the commune by a desire to improve their land economically, primarily through consolidation.

In his later comprehensive study of the agrarian reform, S. M. Dubrovskii draws heavily on the work of Chernyshev and Mozzhukhin in analyzing the social position and motivation of those who left the commune. At times Dubrovskii stresses that the predominant role in separations was played by the well-off peasants. On the basis of Mozzhukhin's data on motivation, he states that "a good half" of all separators were "land-grabbers," and he uses Chernyshev's figures to show that well-off peasants appropriated larger than normal allotments.[45] The average peasant, according to Dubrovskii, reacted negatively to the reform, and it was primarily the upper strata of the peasantry who took advantage of the opportunity to leave the commune at the expense of their fellow villagers. The fact that the earliest separations were the largest is cited as evidence of the rapid departure of peasants with extra land.

Yet when attention turns to the sale of allotments, the picture changes. Dubrovskii's emphasis turns from the concentration of land capital to the proletarianization of the rural masses, and through the other end of the glass the social composition of separators seems to shift. Evidence that 53 percent of all appropriations were made for sale suggests a different interpretation than does the statement that "a good half" of all separations were by wealthy land-grabbers. It might be possible to reconcile both views by concluding that only the social extremes were active in separations, but Dubrovskii points out that many middle peasants, too, left the commune for fear of being impoverished by the departure of the wealthier peasants with the best lands.

Investigators have been able to support a variety of conclusions about the status of separators, and Dubrovskii is not alone in his shifts of emphasis. George Pavlovsky, for example, reports: "It would appear that the two extreme groups among the members of village communities, namely, those possessing most land, on the one hand, and those with least land, on the other, were most numerous among the peasants who secured title-deeds for their holdings, and that the peasant middle-class was relatively the least numerous." But speaking of "peasants with average sized holdings" a few pages later, he states, "it was this group of peasants which responded most readily to the new legislation."[46]

Departures from the commune do appear to have been effected primarily by the social extremes. So contemporaries observed,[47] and data on consolidations and sales of appropriated holdings, representing respectively the upper and lower ranks of the peasantry, bear them out. Before examining such holdings, the question of which group of separators predominated can easily be laid to rest. Since the number of households that departed from communes was relatively greater than the withdrawal of land from communes, the size of the average appropriated holding must have been below the average allotment holding in communes. Thus most separators were smallholders who left the commune primarily in order to sell their inadequate holdings. Some of these peasants had already abandoned agriculture and were renting out their land. Appropriation in such cases made possible the sale of the land and removed it from communal control, but did not necessarily affect agricultural practices.

Peasant "Pioneers"

Efforts to eliminate the commune were essentially a clearing operation; the success of the reform depended on successful reconstruction by the peasants. The architects of the new policy believed that the introduction of agronomic improvements, different crops, or more advanced systems of crop rotation was likely to take place only where a peasant's land was physically separated from that of others and more or less consolidated. Where the new proprietor left his land in a patchwork of strips intermingled with those of his neighbors under the old three-field system or where individual rights to meadows, pastures, and woodlands remained submerged in a communal pool, the chance of any fundamental transformation of agricultural technique or significant increase in productivity was slight.

Yet in many cases land that had been appropriated from communes remained in exactly the same condition as before. Lands transferred to individual title often continued to be held as strips scattered among a commune's three fields, and agricultural practices on these lands were unchanged. An investigation carried out by the Department of Agriculture from 1912 to 1914 among some 3,000 independent smallholders revealed that the three-field system was still being used by 78 percent of the group.[48] In the communes questioned by the Free Economic Society, three-fourths of those who had appropriated their land as personal property had left it in strips, and according to Dubrovskii 90 percent of all appropriators continued to hold their lands in the form of dispersed strips.[49] It is clear that formal changes of title by themselves had no necessary effect on agrotechnology. The prospects for improved performance were most promising among the separators who actually consolidated their holdings; understandably enough, much contemporary attention was directed to these peasants.

The total number of consolidated holdings formed on allotment land between 1907 and 1917 was 1.3 million; an additional 0.3 million were formed on lands of the Peasant Bank and the state. Together, these holdings accounted for about 10 percent of all peasant households by January 1, 1917.[30]

Two-thirds of the allotment-land consolidations were formed by the conversion of entire communities into physically integrated farms; consolidations by individuals separating from communes largely accounted for the rest. As mentioned earlier, wholesale conversion was the only method of consolidation available to peasants in hereditary tenure communities. The intention was clearly to protect the individual property rights of hereditary strip holders, since these proprietors would otherwise be obliged under land reorganization rules to trade their strips to permit consolidation for others. Yet the result was paradoxical: peasants holding their land in hereditary tenure had no right as individuals to consolidate their strips, although individual peasants in communes could do so independently. And individual hereditary rights to land actually received less protection than the land rights of individuals under communal tenure insofar as the consolidation of all holdings in a community under hereditary tenure could be effected by a simple majority vote, whereas in communes the same sort of conversion required a two-thirds vote.

Consolidations on allotment land were undertaken by communal and noncommunal peasants at about the same rate. By 1913 approximately 6 percent of each group had completed consolidations.[31] Group conversion, as noted, was more common in the non–black soil region. In this area it was responsible for three-fourths of all consolidations, whereas in the black soil region it accounted for only half.[32]

The dynamics of consolidation followed a somewhat different course from that of separations. The latter reached a high point in 1909 and fell off thereafter, but applications for consolidation followed a somewhat steadier upward curve until in 1914 the war interfered with rural land reorganization. By 1917, 12.7 million desiatins of allotment land had been consolidated. Consolidations on lands sold by the Peasant Bank and the state added another 3 million for a total of 15.7 million desiatins, or 9 percent of all land held by peasants at the time. The size of the average consolidated holding was 9.9 desiatins, but varied with the origin of the land. On allotment land the average was 9.7 desiatins; on land sold by the Peasant Bank it reached 10.8 desiatins; and on the small number of consolidations formed on land sold to peasants by the state it was 14.4 desiatins.[33] The overall average of 9.9 desiatins approximates the general average for all allotment holdings (9.5–10.3 desiatins; see Table 6, p. 72, and n. 3 above). This is noteworthy, since many writers have stressed the large size of consolidated holdings. The average consolidation was indeed significantly larger than the average holding appropriated from communes (7.0 desiatins) but fell slightly below the average allotment holding within communes (10.2 desiatins).

Although otrubs were often smaller than the typical peasant holding, khutors were apt to be larger than the norm, in part because they contained more purchased land.[54] A 1913 budget study of peasant households in Simbirsk province showed that over 80 percent of the khutor land had been purchased, primarily from the Peasant Land Bank.[55] Another investigation found high ratios of purchased land in khutors in six other provinces.[56] Khutors tended to be large in Tula and ten other provinces for which Mozzhukhin obtained comparative information; this held true in Simbirsk and in nine out of eleven provinces for which the government published data on consolidations. Yet since the khutor was typically a large-family holding, the area of land per worker, although greater than among communal peasants, was not as large as the land data alone might suggest.

In addition to their large size and large families (which, of course, were related under the communal system), khutors had a higher ratio of males per family (i.e., a superior agricultural work force), a higher literacy level among their members, and younger than average households. In addition, they were relatively well provided with agricultural tools and livestock, and their physical layout conferred the maximum benefit of land reorganization.[57] With all these advantages the khutor peasants were expected to lead the way to a transformation of agriculture and the national economy. The contemporary literature is full of references to them as "pioneers," and Pershin later referred to them as "the more progressive and stronger part of the population."[58]

Thanks to the efforts of the Peasant Land Bank, the number of khutors on lands it sold or financed rose steadily in comparison with the number of otrubs, and by 1915 half of all consolidations being formed on such lands were khutors. But consolidations on bank lands were only a minor part of the whole, and khutors accounted for less than a quarter of all consolidations formed on allotment land.[59] As a result, although 10 percent of all peasant households had formed more or less unified farms by 1917, only 2 or 3 percent of all peasant holdings had been organized as khutors. To a lesser degree, many of the advantages of the khutor were shared by the remaining 7 to 8 percent of the peasants who had consolidated their lands.

The immediate benefits of consolidation—an end to the wasteful fragmentation of land, reduced travel time, the opportunity for individual innovation, and the availability of farm improvement loans—led to encouraging performance records. Optimism ran high. A publication of the Ministry of Agriculture on the results of land reorganization in twelve districts reported enthusiastically that the agrarian avant-garde was prospering.[60] And a steady increase in the number of applications for consolidation suggested that the peasants were responding to the government's cue.

Crop data revealed that the yield of consolidated holdings was consistently higher than that of other peasant land under all kinds of crops. Statistics gathered by the Free Economic Society showed that although the technical level of agriculture remained extremely low, some increase in the use of machinery was taking place and there was a general improvement in yields throughout the agrarian sector. Within that sector, however, marked differences were apparent. The net increase in yield reported by communal peasants was 6 percent. Those who had separated from communes without consolidating their land showed a gain of 13 percent. But separators who had consolidated their holdings reported an impressive 42 percent increase in output per desiatin.[61] That improvement had been effected without any basic change apart from the physical consolidation of the land, since the use of machinery on consolidated land was only slightly higher than on other land. These early findings were confirmed by data from later investigations.[62] The survey undertaken by the Ministry of Agriculture indicated particularly high yields in the northwest, where, as we have seen, khutors predominated. Consolidated holdings were more intensively farmed, but the degree of intensification decreased from the northwest toward the southeast. Diversification, improved crop rotation, deeper plowing, and better timing of crop cycles were all noted in connection with consolidated holdings, particularly on the larger holdings.[63]

On the other hand, progress had its price. One of the main indices of agricultural prosperity was the number of livestock—the major fund of non-fixed rural capital. Under communal tenure animals had been pastured on the commons, but a shortage of adequate meadow and grassland had been growing more acute from the time of the emancipation. With the division of communal lands the shortage became critical for separators with livestock. As the more prosperous and influential members of the commune, they had previously been able to control the use of pasture, often delaying the spring planting to provide a longer access to fallow. The transition to individual holdings called for stall feeding, but the new consolidator often lacked the resources to produce or provide the required feed. In the northwest the presence of natural meadows and greater crop diversification—particularly the introduction of grasses—allowed livestock to survive under consolidation. Elsewhere, especially in the south and southeast, the number of livestock declined on consolidated farms. As the peasants reported, the khutor might be good for people, but the commune was better for animals.

Although the loss of livestock could be considered a temporary problem of initial adaptation to individualization, other indicators suggest more serious difficulties. One contemporary skeptic observed that in the success of their agricultural operations consolidators on small holdings were not particularly different from households in communes. Only in the large khutors was better performance perceptible.[64] Moreover, the Simbirsk budget study revealed that khutor peasants, even though more productive, received a smaller net income than did peasants in communes. Despite a lower gross income, peasants in communes had more rubles left, even after spending more for food, rent, building repairs, and hired help. A relatively higher rate of expenditure for basic necessities generally signals a lower standard of living, yet in this case not only the rate but the absolute expenditure of the communal peasant for food and necessities was slightly higher. Although this may reflect the khutor's superior ability to provide its own food supplies, in conjunction with other lower expenditures it hardly suggests a favorable economic position. The explanation appears to be the higher capital investment required to establish a khutor, especially the high payments made for purchased land. The average peasant in a commune paid out only 6 percent of his income for land purchases, whereas the non-communal peasant expended a full quarter of his income in this way.

The higher land payments of the khutor farmers were not due solely to the greater extent of their holdings, but also reflected the higher cost of consolidated land. The average price of khutor land in Tula, for example, was 239 rubles per desiatin, whereas otrub land sold for 225 rubles, and the price of unconsolidated land was 161 rubles.[65] Land prices, high to begin with, rose rapidly with increased sales during the reform period. The average price of land sold by the Peasant Land Bank was not only higher than the average price of allotment land in the decade following 1905, but until 1911 it was higher even than the price of land sold through the Nobles' Bank.[66] The poor harvest of 1911, combined with mounting land costs, contributed to a subsequent decline in bank sales and to an extension of the role of private banks in providing credit for land purchases.[67]

According to the "organization-production" school of agrarian economics, based on studies initiated during these years, because of the consumer nature of his household economy the independent peasant is led to the highest level of intensification and to the most productive exploitation of small holdings. But because the investment of labor yields a higher return on larger holdings, there is a natural tendency toward more extensive agriculture. The independent peasant, therefore, will inevitably try to obtain the maximum land area and to work it with a minimal expenditure of capital and labor.[68]

This had been true of the peasantry as a whole since the emancipation. Under the pressure of growing population and shrinking landholdings, peasants bid market prices up until the increase in the cost of land not only vastly outstripped the increase in its productivity (by eighteen times in N. P. Oganovskii's calculation)[69] but even, at times, to a level where the annual cost of the land exceeded its return. High land prices (in addition to high taxes) prevented accumulation of the capital needed to raise the technological level of agriculture. Since the agrarian pioneers purchased relatively more land, they were hardest hit by the price inflation. Many found it impossible to meet their payments and were forced to sell out, or to sell off part of their land. Smallholders with few resources were particularly vulnerable.[70] A modern study of land mobilization in Voronezh province showed that 30 percent of the sales of consolidated holdings of allotment land resulted from deteriorating economic position. Speaking of the country as a whole, the investigator concluded that the existing level of peasant agricultural technology doomed the small khutor to "inevitable ruin, which at times came about even more rapidly than in the commune."[71]

Evidence that the problem was widespread can be found in the records of the Peasant Land Bank. Excessive land payments led to mounting arrears, and arrears in turn increased the annual amount due.[72] In 1910 arrears to the bank amounted to 9 million rubles. Within three years the deficit had doubled, and arrears equaled half the entire sum due in annual payments; by 1915 the figure had reached 68 percent.[73] A considerable part of the enterprising peasantry was clearly under economic stress, for beginning in 1912 the majority of the defaulters were the pioneers, the peasants on consolidated holdings. If the increase in peasant mortgages was a sign of "democratization," as an optimistic chronicler of the period reported,[74] then the increase in mortgage arrears indicates that the second emancipation was no less costly than the first.

Along with the increase in arrears, the number of peasant properties auctioned off by the bank for default increased rapidly. Relatively few peasants actually lost their lands in this fashion; only about 3 percent of the lands the bank helped peasants to acquire between 1906 and 1916 was sold at the gavel. Yet although peasants who purchased land indi-

vidually constituted less than one-fourth of all purchasers, these peasants lost over three-fourths of the land forfeited at auction. In the reform
period's initial years, defaults by collective purchasers predominated;
but from 1911 on, the amount of land lost by individual purchasers
exceeded that lost by collectives, and it grew steadily. Whatever the
potential rewards, pioneering involved greater risk. But it was not only
forced sales that parted the peasant from his property. The reform period also witnessed a flood of voluntary sales of allotment land.

Land Mobilization

Land sales increased in European Russia after 1907. The increase in
the amount of land sold was relatively less than the increase in the
number of transactions, indicating the turnover of smaller properties.[75]
From 1908 to 1915, 4.1 million desiatins of allotment land were sold by
1.2 million householders. Most of this land and the great majority of
sellers (3.8 million desiatins and 1.1 million peasants) had been in communes.[76] Therefore, sales were made predominantly by smallholders
who had separated from the commune. The allotment land sold in this
period amounted to one-fourth of the area taken out of communes as
personal property under the reform legislation, and the sellers of this
land amounted to almost half of the number of households who left the
commune. Investigation of regional variations in the pattern of allotment-land sales and analysis of archival data for Voronezh province led
a modern Soviet researcher to conclude that the putative reform was
actually leading peasants to "pauperization and proletarianization."[77]

Records of the Land Department of the Ministry of the Interior reveal that in 1914 over 100,000 peasants in 45 provinces of European
Russia sold allotment land in strip holdings, and another 17,600 peasants sold consolidated allotment land.[78] About half of each group sold
all their land. Peasants with the smallest holdings (up to 5 desiatins)
constituted the bulk of all sellers—almost 80 percent of those who sold
land in stripholdings and over 60 percent of those who sold consolidated holdings. The heaviest sales took place in the central agricultural
region, the right-bank Ukraine, and the southeastern Volga and steppe
regions. As a result of all these transactions, it is claimed, up to two-
thirds of all sellers of allotment land had become or were becoming
landless proletarians.[79]

The opportunity to sell appropriated communal land did help to mobilize many marginal smallholders. Yet according to the records half of
the peasants who sold their entire allotments, that is, about a quarter
of all sellers, had already abandoned agriculture. Thus the reform cannot be held responsible for all of the retreat from the land. Moreover, a

sale—even the sale of an entire allotment—did not necessarily mean withdrawal from landholding. Analysis of the motivation for land sales showed that about one-third of the sellers sold in order to improve their agricultural enterprise, primarily by purchasing other land, and almost one-fifth were prompted by a desire to resettle in Siberia or in some other province. The rest sold land either because the labor supply in their families was inadequate to continue farming (20 percent of all sellers) or because their economic position had deteriorated (15 percent). Seven percent of all sales merely transferred land to other members of the family.[80]

Given the chronic complaints of agrarian overpopulation and land shortage, at first glance it appears unaccountable that so many families should have been short-handed. It has been suggested that members of these families had gone off to seek industrial work since the land was unable to support them (the pauperization syndrome). Other factors could also have come into play. The fact that only a small labor force was available to a family would in itself account for the small size of its holding under the communal redistributional system. Mozzhukhin's data indicate that the group with an inadequate labor supply included households with widows, peasants too old to continue farming, and those incapacitated by illness; such households, faced with the prospect of diminished holdings at the next repartition, were likely to appropriate their land in order to sell it.[81] Insofar as their ability to do so was secured by the reform legislation, their break with the land might be considered a "result" of the reform, but without the reform they would undoubtedly have come to essentially the same state, merely substituting long-term rentals (until the next redistribution) as a legal fiction for sale in accordance with prevailing custom or, as Gurko records, even arranging illegal sales.[82]

One corollary of the pauperization thesis is the assumption that the land lost by peasants was being concentrated in the hands of an emergent peasant bourgeoisie: "kulakization" is seen as the obverse of "proletarianization." The report on sales of allotment land in Voronezh province refers to a concentration of property in the hands of kulaks; yet the data reflect no such development, and the author of the study suggests that this "concentration" is "not clearly expressed" in the data because of the declining importance of allotment land in the economy of the wealthier peasantry.[83] Peasant holdings of nonallotment land certainly grew rapidly during the reform period, but this says little about the redistribution of allotment land. The sale of allotment land was still limited to peasants, and the question remains: given that poor peasants sold their land, what group (or groups) of peasants bought it?

The records of land mobilization confirm that smallholders were the main sellers and that transactions typically involved small parcels of land. The regional distribution of sales followed a familiar pattern: most sales occurred in regions where land was scarce, prices high, and emigration common. However, from 1908 to 1912 for every 100 sellers there was an average of 96 purchasers among the communal peasantry, and 99.9 purchasers among peasants holding land in hereditary tenure.[54] This hardly suggests a strong concentration of landholding. More than half of the land sold by peasant smallholders was purchased by other peasant smallholders, and twice as much went to the group of smallest landholders as to the next higher group.

Furthermore, over a third of all allotment land sold went to previously landless peasants. Those who subscribe to the proletarianization model argue that the landless group was not typical of the poor peasantry, but included shopkeepers, "mir eaters," rural administrators, and speculators. Dubrovskii, for example, points out that previously landless purchasers bought 18 percent of the land sold by the Peasant Bank, in parcels almost twice the size of the average for all purchasers.[85] The pattern of purchases from the bank tends to reinforce the claim that landless purchasers of allotment land were not necessarily poor peasants. By limiting the amount of allotment land that could be held by an individual peasant, the law of June 14, 1910, made it necessary to conceal large-scale acquisitions. This may explain a part of the sales made to others within the family. Some peasants undoubtedly managed to buy up substantial holdings as land was surrendered by others, but their number appears not to have been large; some peasant smallholders who had been in communes became landless, but again this development was by no means universal. The entire group of sellers of allotment land was less than one percent of all peasant households in each year, and sales fell off in the later years of the reform period.[86]

From 1905 to 1915 acquisition of private property appears to have been a more important channel of land redistribution. Almost 10 million desiatins of private land were gained by peasants in that period, compared with the 4 million desiatins of allotment land that changed hands from 1908 to 1915. As has been pointed out, the bulk of the private property gains were made collectively, and over 3 million of the 3.6 million desiatins acquired by individuals were held by peasants with less than 50 desiatins. The land mobilization data, therefore, do not seem to support claims that land was becoming concentrated, and Mozzhukhin appears to have been on firm ground when he observed that "any sort of conclusion about the victory of capitalist sectors over the peasant economy is still more than premature."[87]

6

The Rural Economy

One of the major issues in the contemporary historiography of pre-revolutionary Russia is the interpretation of the development of the agrarian sector of the economy in the early twentieth century. Many Western and émigré scholars have pointed to the positive tendencies that were moving peasant Russia toward an improved state of affairs, arguing that the course of events would have led to a solution of the agrarian problem had it not been interrupted and reversed by war and revolution. Soviet scholars generally agree that capitalism, in accordance with the scheme of social development suggested by Marx and affirmed for Russia by Lenin's turn-of-the-century research, was gathering strength in prewar Russian agriculture. But this development is by no means seen as wholly positive, and in fact is held to have exacerbated certain aspects of the agrarian problem. Within Soviet historiography, moreover, there has been lively debate over the degree and direction of capitalist development in Russian agriculture in this period.[1]

Problem or Progress

Even the most cursory survey of agriculture at the time reveals the contradictory evidence that has contributed to the conflict of interpretations. First of all, the agrarian sector was relatively much larger in Russia than in the major contemporary Western national economies. At the time of the 1897 census, 87 percent of the Russian population was classified as rural, 84 percent belonged to the peasant estate, and 75 percent was directly engaged in agriculture. In England (the extreme case) only one-fifth of the population was rural; in France and the United States, less than three-fifths was. By 1913, despite advances in industrialization and in urbanization, little change had occurred in Russia in this respect; 85 percent of the population was still listed as rural in contemporary statistical sources.[2]

At the beginning of the century agriculture provided 45 percent of Russia's national income; in 1913 it still accounted for 43 percent. The constant ruble value of national income rose in this period by 39 percent, and that of agricultural output went up 34 percent.[3] The chief booster in the agrarian economy was an impressive gain of 37 percent in the net harvest of all grains between 1900 and 1909–13.[4] Increases were due partly to an extension of the area under cultivation and partly to an improvement in crop yields. Other contributing factors included a greater use of fertilizer and the use of more agricultural machinery and equipment.[5] Both the domestic production and the importation of such machinery and equipment rose in the early years of the century.

During this period, as we have seen, peasants purchased a considerable amount of additional land. The most important crop on peasant land had long been rye; although this remained true throughout the prewar years, wheat made substantial gains. In 1900, 40 percent of all cultivated land was planted in rye and only 21 percent in wheat; by 1915 the ratio was 31 percent to 30 percent.[6] Wheat growing expanded most vigorously in the Southern Steppe region, Siberia, and the Northern Caucasus area; in the older agricultural regions of central European Russia there was relatively little change.[7] Although rye continued to hold an edge over wheat on most peasant lands, the cultivation of wheat predominated on privately owned land. Yields of all grains were typically higher on private land.

The amount of grain marketed rose substantially from 1900 to 1913, but the peasants, who produced the bulk of Russian grain, brought a much smaller proportion of their output to market than did the proprietors of private land. Rye, the cheaper grain and traditional peasant foodstuff, was consumed primarily by its producers and in local markets.[8] In the export market, however, wheat was the most important commodity, and the volume of exports rose with or slightly ahead of the increasing output of the prewar years. Between 1900 and 1913 Russian grain exports rose by 55 percent; European Russia was exporting about one-sixth of its gross harvest of grain.[9] Slightly over half (52 percent) of all grain that was commercially transported to market was sent abroad, mainly through southern ports; the rest went to domestic buyers, who were gradually absorbing a larger share of all such grain as urban centers and the nonagricultural sector expanded.[10]

Grain exports were the mainstay of Russia's favorable balance of payments. Encouraged and supported by government policies, particularly by tariff and freight rates, they provided the credit necessary to finance state sponsorship of industrialization. Thanks to state support and to the international market situation, foreign trade in grain proved profitable for Russian agricultural entrepreneurs in this period. Whereas the volume of grain exports increased by approximately one-half from 1900 through 1913, their value almost doubled in the same interval due to price increases.[11] According to one calculation, the capitalist "profit norm" in Russian agriculture in 1913 averaged 14.9 percent.[12]

In addition to the overall increase in agricultural production and marketing in the early twentieth century, there were encouraging signs of diversification, with industrial and fodder crops making a stronger contribution to total output. There was yet another promising development: an improvement in the number of livestock.[13] At the same time, the cooperative movement was growing prodigiously. By 1914 credit, consumer, and producer cooperatives numbered over ten million households among their members.[14] All of this adds up to an impressive roster of achievements.

But there is a debit side to the agricultural ledger. Despite the advances in the agrarian economy, national income in Russia remained extremely low because of the low level of agriculture. In France, for example, where almost 60 percent of the populace was still rural, national per capita income was about four times higher than in Russia at the beginning of the First World War.[15] Although the extension of cultivated land had helped to improve Russian agricultural output, that development had important limitations. Much of the new land was in outlying regions or in Siberia. In the central regions of European Russia where land hunger was greatest, the increase in cultivated land between 1901–5 and 1911–15 amounted to only 6 percent.[16] Most of the land under cultivation still followed the three-field system and was still fragmented in stripholdings. Grain yields improved early in the century and again in the years immediately before the war, but the yields of the major grain crops remained extremely low, well below those of other leading world producers. Yields recorded by the statistical department of the Ministry of Agriculture showed average annual gains for rye of less than one percent from 1901 to 1915.[17] Other grain crops, particularly wheat, fared somewhat better. But in the early stages of the reform, from 1906 through 1911 (when crop failures and famine struck again), yields of both rye and wheat declined in European Russia; in 1906–10 the average annual gross harvest of rye dropped 10 percent below that of 1901–5, and wheat output, although it rose rapidly in Siberia and the Northern Caucasus region, was barely maintained in European Russia at a steady level. Only beginning in 1912 were recovery and renewed progress evident in the European part of the empire.[18]

Meanwhile, the population of this area had continued to grow rapidly, outpacing the growth of productivity.[19] By 1914 the population of European Russia is estimated to have been 37 percent larger than in 1897.[20] Grain exports also were rising rapidly, and the net result was a per capita grain balance within Russia that was exceptionally low in comparison with that in other countries.[21] The typical peasant's food consumption was inferior to that of the average urban worker, who was himself far from well nourished. A 1911 diet study in Kostroma province, for example, showed that workers consumed more meat, fish, eggs, white bread, and even vegetables than did peasants. The peasants, however, ate twice as much black (rye) bread.[22] Given the low consumption norm, it is noteworthy that the supply of rye, the peasants' main food, decreased absolutely in 1906–10 and rose by only 7 percent between 1901–5 and 1911–15.

Before the turn of the century almost two-thirds of all peasant households in the black soil region and four-fifths of those in the non–black soil region had been unable to get enough grain from their allotments for their personal consumption needs, and rural purchases of grain were rising steadily.[23] The acquisition of additional nonallotment land helped to meet part of these growing needs, but many peasant households were obliged to enter the market as buyers. For these peasants the steep rise in the domestic price of rye was disadvantageous. It is true that more wheat was available, but wheat prices were even higher than those for rye. In 1910–14, when the average domestic price of rye was 78.9 kopecks per pud, wheat was selling for 109.3 kopecks per pud.[24] The prime beneficiaries of the rising grain prices were the market-oriented wheat growers of the south and southeast. After 1912, a year in which many breaks occur in agricultural economic curves, grain prices declined. Along with this movement, reflecting U.S. competition in the international grain market and a drop in international grain prices, the country's foreign trade balance began to decline. In the first four months of 1914, the balance became negative.[25]

Even the surplus-producing proprietors who found the market profitable were apt to have complaints because the spiraling cost of land was reducing the profitability of grain production.[26] The land gains made by peasants were not only vitiated by the increase in the population but were secured at a cost that could be unsupportable. The cost of renting land escalated also, even more steeply than the purchase price of land. From the turn of the century to 1914, land prices in European Russia rose by about 50 percent, but the cost of renting land rose by 70 percent.[27]

Other bright features of the agrarian scene also had their darker side. Although the absolute number of livestock increased slightly, the growth in the population and the extension of the land area under cultivation meant that the number of animals per capita and per desiatin had actually declined.[28] The application of fertilizer still lagged far behind the practice of agriculturally advanced countries.[29] The production and importation of agricultural equipment and machinery showed impressive rates of growth largely because the base points were so low to begin with; moreover, its use was concentrated in large-scale and commercialized sectors of agriculture. Even there it was not an unmixed blessing: the introduction of agricultural machinery in the south was blamed for a decline in wages in the area that provided the country's greatest labor market.[30]

The growth of the rural labor surplus (and the allied phenomenon of the proletarianization of the peasantry) presents another set of problems. According to an official investigatory commission at the turn of the century, there was a labor surplus of 23 million workers in the countryside in 1901. This amounted to over half of the rural adult labor force. By 1913, it has been estimated, this surplus had risen to 32 million, despite the additional land in cultivation, migration to urban areas, Siberian colonization, and increased rural industrial employment.[31] The agricultural proletariat, in the interval, is said to have risen from 3.5 million to 4 million workers. The overabundance of labor depressed rural wages, particularly in agriculture. Female workers in the agrarian sector were especially disadvantaged, receiving wages far below those earned by men.[32]

Thus the period from 1906 to 1911 was hardly one of straightforward advances on all fronts. The crop failure of 1906 affected half of the entire population of European Russia; that of 1911, although not so extensive, struck some important grain-producing areas. In provinces of the Volga and Ural regions that had produced an annual average of over 800 million puds of grain (one-fourth of the country's total output) in 1906–10, the 1911 harvest was below 50 percent of the average. Hard-hit provinces in Siberia and the steppes fared even worse, with harvests below 40 percent of the local average. For a large group of provinces (including the above) that normally produced over half of the country's grain, the data show a harvest deficit of almost 40 percent. Over 20 million peasants are reported to have suffered famine as a result of the 1911 crop failures.[33]

In view of this, it comes as a surprise that grain exports for the year were exceptionally high, greater by over one-third than exports for the years preceding and following.[34] The explanation, presumably, is that the export transactions were concluded before the harvest shortages became evident late in the year. The fact that higher prices obtained in the international trade encouraged exports, but as the crop failures were revealed, prices in the Volga, Ural, and Caucasus regions as well as those in western Siberia fluctuated sharply.

The impact of the developments in 1911 on the peasantry is evident, although, as with the 1906 famine, the political implications of the situation have drawn relatively little attention. It is generally recognized that there was a rising incidence of political unrest starting in about 1912 and dramatized that year by the violent tragedy on the Lena gold-fields in Siberia. Less well known perhaps is the fact that the dispirited settlers returning from Siberia at the time amounted to over half of the number setting out for the territory as colonists with official encouragement.[35] Other indications of economic stress were the steep increase beginning in 1911 in the number of foreclosures on loans issued by the Peasant Bank and a rapid drop in the number of peasants who received loans from the bank. The problem extended beyond peasant proprietors; in 1912 payments collected by the government on the outstanding arrears on the old redemption dues dropped to less than a third of the amount paid the previous year.[36]

Between 1907 and 1914 some 20,000 peasant disturbances directed against the gentry and the "rural bourgeoisie" were recorded. Seventeen thousand of these occurred from 1910 through 1914.[37] An analysis of over 1,500 cases included in a Soviet documentary series on peasant disturbances indicated that only one-tenth involved action directed against political authorities. Half of the disturbances recorded in the volume covering 1907–14 were aimed at landlords and, interestingly, about a third involved opposition to departures from the commune. There is no way of knowing how representative the published documents are, but this sample indicates that peasant resistance to separations from the commune, along with moves to take land from landlords, rose abruptly in 1912.[38] Given the size of the rural population, however, the number of peasants involved in protest movements does not appear large. It was in the cities, where population was more concentrated and political culture more highly developed, that popular unrest was most evident, and as a result the attention of most political historians has been focused until recently on the stresses produced by industrialization and urbanization.

It has been suggested that one of the reasons for mounting urban tension before the First World War was a sudden influx of rural proletarians created by the agrarian reform legislation.[39] The urban work force increased after 1906, particularly during the years of industrial revival from 1910 through 1913. Yet the extent to which the reform legislation can be held responsible for this development is far from clear. The urban growth rate had outpaced that of the general population over the previous decades and had been moving ahead at an accelerating rate before the reform. The four-year period of industrial revival witnessed an increase of close to half a million in the number of urban workers precisely when the bulk of the half million certifications of individual title to land were issued under the law of 1910. Yet by far the greater part of the 2 million appropriations had already been effected before the 1910 legislation was enacted, and no upsurge in the work force was apparent then. Land sales statistics may explain part of the flow of peasants into the cities, but in view of the fact that there were significant numbers of landless and poor peasants among the purchasers of allotment land, peasants who might have drifted to the cities but for the reform, the net impact of land mobilization on the urban work force is difficult to assess.

The reform may have contributed to the proletarianization of part of the peasantry and to the movement of peasants into the urban work force, but even without the legislation these probably would have occurred as part of the broader course of economic development. A number of independent factors were propelling peasants into towns after 1909: the increasing pressure of rural population against the land, lower agricultural wages, higher food costs, the high price of land, the poor harvest of 1911. No less important was the pull of new opportunities. The establishment of more and larger factories offering employment to greater numbers of workers was reason enough for more peasants to appear in the cities. Between 1906 and 1913 the number of industrial establishments in the country rose by 26 percent, and the number of enterprises employing over 1,000 workers increased by 39 percent.

The pre-1906 movement of peasants into the industrial labor force suggests that they would have found ways to respond to the opportunity for urban employment even without formal release from the commune. The fact that peasant women formed an increasing share of the cities' labor force supports the conclusion that the general economic situation rather than the Stolypin legislation accounts for the movement out of the countryside. From 1906 to 1913 the female labor force in factories in Moscow province rose by 29 percent, whereas the male labor force increased by 17 percent. In 1913 women supplied 40 percent of the factory labor force in the province.[40]

A recent study of peasant proletarianization by Robert Johnson, although it accepts the thesis that the newcomers had an effect on urban life, draws attention to the counterflow of influence. As Johnson demonstrates, peasants who went to work in the cities maintained close contact with their villages and introduced new forces into rural life. Some of the provinces with the highest rates of rural unrest in 1905–7 had begun to send large numbers of migrants to the factories only shortly before, and Johnson suggests that migration was a "two-way street" that may have contributed to the spread of revolutionary discontent in rural areas.[41]

In any case, growth in urban centers meant a stronger concentration of grievances and improved opportunities for communication and politicization. To the extent that the reform contributed to that development, it defeated its own political purposes.

The War

The condition of Russian peasants during the First World War has been subject to interpretations as contrary as those of peasants' status in the years before the war. The Soviet historian Anfimov, for example, marshals evidence to support the thesis that the additional stress of wartime conditions set the final stage for revolution, not only in the cities, where the addition of industrial workers and refugees aggravated urban problems, but also in the villages. Military mobilization and the forced requisition of livestock led to a reduction in rural work power and to a decline in the area under cultivation, which resulted in a decreased supply of food. Heavier taxation, the loss of outside income, and the rising cost of living all contributed to mounting rural distress.[42] This picture contrasts sharply that presented by the émigré A. N. Antsiferov, who holds that the peasants improved their position during the war because of high grain prices, dependency allotments, payments for requisitions, savings on vodka (outlawed for the duration of the war), and other benefits.[43]

Peasants' own evaluations of their economic position were mixed. Respondents to the Free Economic Society's questionnaire in 1910–11 stated that agriculture seemed to be improving, but that most of the improvement took place among the well-off peasants—including those who left the commune in order to secure an advantageous position or to improve their operations. Poorer peasants considered it inadvisable to leave the commune, although some of the worst off had appropriated their land in order to sell it. When in 1917 the peasants of Kharkov province were asked to indicate whether local conditions in agriculture were improving or deteriorating, the majority of the respondents indicated improvement but, again, not for all. "Better for otrubs, but worse for communes" was the typical reply.[44] Anfimov, who reports on this survey, contends that the improvement claimed was merely the result of wartime shortages that raised grain prices. It was not the result of the Stolypin reforms, and it brought profits only to wealthier peasants with a marketable surplus. As for the peasants in communes, their position is said to have deteriorated inevitably after the departure of members with disproportionately large holdings that included some of the communes' best land: "The result [of such departures] was shrinkage of land and a worsening of the conditions of land use among the peasant majority that had remained behind in the communes."[45]

This is the conventional Soviet view, and it has much to commend it. Yet one element in the situation of the communal peasantry deserves more consideration than it has received. The analysis of departures from the commune in Chapter 5 indicated that, although some peasants separated from the commune with extra land and some largeholders left, more peasants left in order to sell holdings that were small. The average separator withdrew an amount of land smaller than the average communal holding. The result of the movement out of the commune, then, was to increase the amount of land per capita within the commune above what it would otherwise have been. Because of the continuous growth of the population, however, this was not immediately apparent. It was hardly Stolypin's aim to strengthen the landholding position of the communal peasantry; yet the reform, paradoxically, led to that unintended consequence. Without the reform the pressure on land within the commune would have been relatively worse.

Understandably, peasants in communes could fail to appreciate this back-handed benefit. Resentment of those who had departed with extra land or especially valuable land was easily stirred, and when the more fortunate separators visibly prospered on their consolidated farms during the war, former communal associates saw their newly proclaimed property rights as property wrongs inflicted on the rest. Separations met with growing resistance from communal peasants.[46] Half of the able-bodied men of the villages had been mobilized, and their families insisted on awaiting their return and participation in any further changes in local land tenure. Mobilization had more serious consequences for communal peasants than for khutor households with their larger male labor force. In Riazan province, for example, 36 percent of the communal households, but only 24 percent of the khutors, were without an able-bodied man by 1917.[47] Cases of opposition to land organization work outnumbered any other category of peasant disturbance in 1915.[48] The number of requests filed for certification of separate title dropped that year below the number of certifications processed as the land organization offices caught up on the backlog. Outbreaks of peasant violence against separators and against local land organization work led the Ministry of Agriculture in the summer of 1915 to circulate an instruction that the work was not to be pushed in the face of peasant resistance. In February 1916 a directive went out that no new work was to be initiated; land organization was to be confined to cases in process. On November 29, 1916, another and more drastic order was issued: all land organization work was to be suspended.[49]

The reform legislation had opened channels for the removal of legal and institutional restraints on rural economic development. It had brought indubitable benefits to some sectors of the peasant population, but it had proved no panacea: the agrarian problem remained a problem. A large part of that problem was a persistent lack of capital resources for economic development. Effective technological exploitation of Russia's agricultural potential called for a level of investment beyond the resources of the peasantry or of the Peasant Land Bank. Half of all consolidators had asked for government financial aid; a quarter had received it, but in limited amounts. The state itself lacked the resources to match its aspirations and looked to the peasantry, faute de mieux, to provide the means for industrialization. Under the circumstances, the reform effort to promote individual initiative in agriculture was a rural counterpart to the "patterns of substitution" discovered by Alexander Gerschenkron in the industrial sector.[50] In the village variant of this strategy, the intensive labor of the enterprising peasant was to provide the substitute for capitalization. But the task of developing industry proved simpler than that of curing agriculture.

The reform did not solve the agrarian problem, but neither did it create that problem, as its critics sometimes seem to imply. Perhaps what it did create was a new force among the economically depressed and displaced peasantry, the politically sensitive force that has been labeled a "rising tide of expectations." From 1906 to 1911 the tide surged. In 1912 there was a perceptible ebb. Peasant reaction to the reform legislation shows that despite an often hostile reception, some departed readily from the commune with anticipations of a brighter future: the proletarianized peasant who left for (or remained in) the city pocketed the price of his allotment with an unwonted sense of prosperity; the colonist set out for new territory with high hopes; the consolidator saw himself—in the words of a peasant delegate to the Duma—as a "little gentryman"; and the independent peasant producer looked forward to a profitable market. Yet the cities soon absorbed the slim capital of the new proletarians and left them worse off than ever, deprived of the economic and psychological cushion of a rural retreat.[51] Siberia sent back countless peasants who, having left the commune, found in fact "no place for a cock to crow." The consolidator saw his gentry illusions converted to gentry realities as mortgage payments drained his income. And the grain producer saw prices fall off again after 1912.

All these groups with their various degrees of discontent and disillusionment were in the minority that left the commune. What about the majority that remained? What was the net effect of the reform legislation on them? Insofar as the land organization commissions were able to simplify and consolidate the tangled holdings of adjacent villages and proprietors, the reform undoubtedly contributed to the efficiency of all agriculture, including the communal sector. Stripholding, the three-field system, and various other technological impediments obviously required correction, and to the limited extent that land reorganization corrected them, the reform was clearly beneficial. In unlocking the rural labor supply it opened the way for more flexible coordination of the basic productive resources of the economy. The transition that was in process was far from cataclysmic, but it was incontrovertible.

Whether the reform offered a long-range solution to the agrarian problem is a question that could have been answered only in a broader frame of time. Its brief duration has made its impact difficult to assess. Agricultural statistics reveal that the yield and productivity of major grain crops declined in the first half of the reform decade, but improved in later years. It would be unreasonable to hold the reform responsible for the initial decline, since poor harvests due to natural conditions in 1906 and 1911 adversely affected the record. Yet it is equally problematic to credit the reform with the better agricultural performance of the later years in view of the fact that the improvement in yields occurred at about the same rate on the lands of private proprietors and on peasant allotment land.[52]

Opinions about the results and significance of the reform indicate that the historiography of the commune remains the touchstone it was over a century ago. Writers who share a sympathy for individualism and for economic systems based on individual enterprise have tended to see substantial and positive results issuing from the reform.[53] They speak enthusiastically of the rapid eradication of the commune, and present the reform as a genuine revolution accompanying and in large part responsible for major improvements in agriculture. On the other hand, those who more keenly appreciate the social merits of collectivism have (for a variety of reasons) viewed the reform and its effects

on the communal peasantry quite negatively. This disparate group includes earlier writers of the neo-Populist persuasion, along with Soviet
scholars who reflect Lenin's appraisal of the reform as a "Prussian" development promoting the concentration of landed property. Its negative outlook is shared by a diverse company of political critics of the old
regime who generally fault the government's procedures more than
they disagree with the reform objectives.[54]

Among the criticisms brought against the reform are the charges
that the law and local officials made departures from the commune advantageous to separators at the expense of the commune, that those
who held the largest and best lands were encouraged to leave, that
common lands were often reduced to impractical dimensions, and that
the ability of the commune to accommodate the land to the growing
population was hampered. The result of these developments, conclude
the critics, was a deterioration of the economic position of the communal peasantry. In fact, as we have seen, the departure of smallholders
from the commune improved the per capita land ratios in communes;
yet the charges amount to a serious indictment of tsarist agrarian policy—all the more serious since more peasants were in the commune at
the end of the reform period than even the critics have appreciated.
Curiously enough, because of the statistical problems discussed above
and perhaps also because of attitudes and expectations about the development of capitalism in Russia, both the supporters and the opponents of the reform have tended to accept a somewhat exaggerated estimate of the number of peasants who departed from the commune in
these years. A lack of the economic resources for investment essential
to successful individualization and an unwillingness to relinquish the
modicum of economic and social security provided by the communal
system kept most peasant households within the commune a decade
after the introduction of the "open door" policy.

Stolypin had declared that the successful establishment of the government's agrarian reform would require twenty years of peace. Before
even half of that time had elapsed, Russia was involved in the First
World War. In the course of the war not only did the reform measures
come to a close, but the government itself was brought to an end. Perhaps the best gauge of the success or failure of the reform is the fate of
its sponsors. The anticommunal policy of the government had both
economic and political goals. Although evaluation of its economic
achievement remains controversial, appraisal of its success in enrolling
political support for the autocracy has been rendered more simple by
history.

In the panic of 1905 the "lessons of history" were market wisdom.

References to the French Revolution and to 1848 were common, and the stabilizing role of *le petit propriétaire foncier* was an article of political faith. But a lesson closer at hand was overlooked. In the agrarian disturbances early in the century the greatest rural violence had erupted in the adjacent provinces of Poltava and Kharkov. Yet in their modes of land tenure the two were at opposite poles, with 18 percent and 93 percent of their respective households in communes. As 1917 was to show again, the political temper of rural Russia was not so much a result of the conditions under which men held land as of the conditions in which the land held men.

PART III

The Dialectic of Revolution
1917

The revolution that put an end to tsarism in February 1917 resulted from a conjunction of political circumstances, deteriorating economic conditions, social pressures, and a wide array of other historical ponderabilia. Even the weather may have contributed something to the balance that finally tipped for revolution—1917 inflicted an unusually cold February on the war-strained, hungry population of the capitals.[1] The exceptionally warm days of August 1914 that witnessed flower-strewn military parades trumpeting through the streets had long since cooled, and much with them.

7

Policies of the Provisional Government

The outbreak of revolution in February was a political expression of society's demand for a change in the state's order of priorities; the second phase, in October, followed as a result of the inability or unwillingness of the Provisional Government to minister to that demand. Popular demands were made clear in the trinity of revolutionary slogans: Peace, Bread, and Land. These simple watchwords stripped complex political issues to their barest essentials; they arose from the basic human struggle for life and for the means of sustaining it. The slogans alone fail to explain the course of developments, yet peace, bread, and land hold the key to why October followed February in the revolutionary calendar. The foreign policy of the Provisional Government—whatever its merits or logic—was hardly calculated to appeal to the pacifist inclinations of a war-weary people, and the military failure of the June offensive intensified popular discontent. As for bread, the efforts of the Provisional Government to secure a more adequate supply of foodstuffs for the army and the cities aroused rural hostility but failed to provide a solution to mounting supply problems. Ineffective response in both areas had major political consequences, but it was land that ultimately led to the most critical disaffection.

The failure of the first provisional government to satisfy the popular desire for peace led to its replacement in May by a coalition government. Failure to solve the problem of food supply under the ongoing stress of war contributed heavily to the political tensions that subsequently brought a succession of increasingly radical coalition governments to power. The second coalition was formed in July, the third and last in September. None of these governments, however, managed to address the perennial land problem in a manner that satisfied the peasantry. This failure opened the way for a new stage of revolution and a new form of government.

Food Supply

The war, as we have seen, disrupted Russian agriculture by wrenching away much of its manpower, livestock, and supplies. Yet some losses proved less damaging than they might have been under other conditions. The previous rural labor surplus cushioned the military drain of manpower, and prisoners of war were brought into the fields to help make up the deficit.[1] Much of the rest was supplied by rural women, who took over the work done earlier by men. By the end of the war three-quarters of the total rural work force was female. As a result of initially successful adaptation to changing circumstances and with the help of benign climatic conditions, the 1915 harvest exceeded the average for the previous five-year period in European Russia and the Northern Caucasus by over 10 percent. Yet under the stress of wartime conditions the area under cultivation steadily declined. By 1916 there was 11 percent less land under crops in these regions than in 1914, and grain output had dropped correspondingly.[2] Since exports had been halted, the drop was not necessarily serious in itself. But the extra demands of the army and of a shifting population, combined with the mounting problem of food transport, led to local shortages that increased in number and severity.

In the autumn of 1915 the Ministry of Agriculture, seeking to discourage speculation in grain and to assure the flow of military supplies, introduced a policy of fixed prices for grain purchased by official procurement agencies.* Producers who refused to sell voluntarily could be obliged to surrender their grain and in such cases were subject to a 15 percent reduction in payment. Since the 1915 harvest was ample and the official prices were set at the level of market prices, there were initially no problems. But the system of dual prices (fixed for government purchases, free on the private market) soon ran into difficulties as inflationary pressures overtook the economy. Market prices escalated rapidly, and price differentials encouraged speculative trafficking in grain. Official agencies were flooded with consumer complaints protesting the high prices of grain. As a result, on September 9, 1916, after lengthy review and considerable debate in government circles, a uniform system of fixed prices (adjusted to local conditions) was adopted for all trade in grain.[3]

---

* Fixed prices were first introduced by a regulation of October 5, 1915, to provide for needs of the army and of certain workers in defense industries. Initially established for oats, they were soon extended to rye, wheat, flour, and barley. (*EPR*, p. 166, p. 471, n. 76, 1.)

Because the fixed prices were by now considerably below market potential, because the 1916 harvest was smaller, and because transportation problems were worsening, the state procurement organs faced increasing difficulties in meeting military and urban needs. Before the end of the year the Ministry of Agriculture had elaborated a detailed program for compulsory deliveries of grain from all regions of the country. Quotas were established for each province and broken down within provinces for their constituent territorial-administrative units. The scheme was a model of planned efficiency; the reaction to it, however, was strongly negative. Protests and petitions flooded into the ministry, insisting that the quotas were impossibly high. Some local officials requested a lowering of the amount demanded of them; others reported that the peasants, claiming local shortages, refused outright to make any deliveries. At the same time a steady barrage of complaints was directed at the prices fixed for grain. Peasants accused estate owners of trading illicitly at higher prices and avoiding official transactions, whereas the more vulnerable muzhiks were forced by the government to accept artificially low prices. Prices on essential but increasingly scarce consumer items had not been fixed, and the terms of trade were highly disadvantageous to agriculturalists. Rural discontent ran high in the winter of 1916–17, and intense dissatisfaction with the government's policies was widespread in the final months of the old regime.[4] Yet it was the failure of those policies to provide adequately for the hungry cities that proved fatal. The growing bread lines grew by the end of February into ranks of revolutionaries.

The critical problem of food supply was taken up immediately by the Provisional Government, established at the beginning of March. In an emotional appeal to the rural citizenry, the Duma called on those who had grain to save the motherland, to save their sons and brothers in the army, by bringing their grain at once to railway stations and storage depots.[5] A number of food supply commissions and committees were established in rapid succession. The new government turned first to the provincial zemstvos, instructing them to organize provincial and lower-level food supply committees and to requisition grain from large landholders and trading organizations.[6] Before these orders could be carried out, a new line had been taken. On March 9 a State Food Supply Committee was formed under the Ministry of Agriculture to handle all matters relating to food. A few weeks later, on March 25, a law simultaneously placed all grain supplies under state regulation and established a network of provincial, district, municipal, and volost food supply committees. Trade in grain became a state monopoly, and local food committees were ordered to requisition all surplus grain supplies above consumption and seed needs as established by the provincial committee. Owners were to be reimbursed at the official fixed rates, which were now raised by about 60 percent.[7]

When the law of March 25 was published, the Provisional Government took formal note of its responsibility to improve the supply of such basic consumer goods as iron, textiles, and kerosene and to establish fixed prices for them. The promise was repeated periodically in the months that followed, but little was ever accomplished.[8] Peasants had scant incentive to surrender their grain for depreciated currency with which almost nothing could be bought. Under the circumstances it made more sense to those with a surplus to consume more grain at home, either personally or as fodder for livestock, or to convert it (illegally) into moonshine. Yet relatively few peasants were fortunate enough to be faced with such options. Those who were forced into the market as buyers shared the central authorities' concern with shortages and distribution problems.

By the end of April the government had turned to rationing in an attempt to improve the distribution of grain supplies; two months later it was necessary to lower the per capita norms that had been established. The rationing system set a maximum amount that could be purchased by individuals, but provided no assurance that the stipulated quantity would be available. Early in May a new ministry was created to deal exclusively with matters of food supply. Effective July 1, it soon acquired a broad array of functions and responsibilities that ranged from extending the area under cultivation to distributing basic consumer goods. The Minister of Food Supply became chairman of the State Committee on Food Supply, and the network of food supply committees became subsidiary agencies of the new ministry.[9] The committees were authorized to take undelivered grain by force and pay only half of the fixed price when the surplus crop was not brought in voluntarily. Efforts were made to draw cooperatives, along with commercial enterprises, public organizations, and private individuals, into the difficult task of procuring grain. New ranks of officials, provincial and district commissars, were drawn from zemstvo executive boards and given broad powers to facilitate the implementation of grain policy.[10]

Despite this multi-pronged attack on the supply problem, the official procurement targets were not met. Committees, commissars, and collectors representing various agencies and groups jostled one another in the countryside, competing for grain and contributing to the mounting confusion. Data from the Ministry of Food Supply, although incomplete, indicate that for the agricultural year 1916–17 procure-

ments amounted to only two-thirds of the quotas set in November
1916. From February through October they reached barely one-half of
the targeted goals.[11] The agricultural situation continued to deterio-
rate. The harvest figure for the entire country in 1917, although below
the average for 1909–13, showed some improvement over 1916. But in
European Russia, where the bulk of the population was located, and in
the Northern Caucasus area, the harvest was almost 20 percent below
that of 1916.[12] Data compiled by the Ministry of Food Supply on the
amount of surplus or shortage in each province showed a net surplus of
grain in the country, but most of the surplus was located in southern
areas occupied by the enemy and later lost under the terms of the
Treaty of Brest-Litovsk. Without this territory the balance was negative, with a deficit of some 150 million puds.[13] The greatest shortages
were in fodder grains, but this had a direct impact on food supplies
since instead of slaughtering livestock agriculturalists were likely,
where possible, to divert food grains to maintain their animals.

As a result, deliveries to the military and to the cities fell off during
the summer of 1917. The low point came in August, when less than 20
percent of the state purchase quota was met. Bread rations for residents of Moscow were cut once again and fell to about 200 grams a day.
In some cities the ration dropped to 100 grams.* Attempts to exert
more pressure on the peasants only evoked greater hostility. Concerned that the peasants might be withholding grain in the hope of
later price increases, the central authorities issued a notice early in August stating flatly that there would be no such increases. Within a few
weeks, however, the situation had become so critical that a major price
hike was announced in the desperate hope of luring grain out of the
countryside. On August 27 grain prices were abruptly raised to double
the levels established on March 25. The move, as indignant provincials
warned, was hardly calculated to inspire confidence in the declarations
of the government, but it appears to have somewhat improved deliveries.[14] Its effect is difficult to assess, however, since the arrival of the
harvest season in itself would undoubtedly have improved the flow of
grain. The higher prices, of course, represented an additional burden
on peasant purchasers of grain, and critics of the increase (including
peasants and numerous local officials) warned central authorities that it
would only exacerbate an already inflationary situation.[15]

---

*Keep, p. 178. The likelihood that urban shortages were not due solely to a lack of
supplies is suggested by a letter from peasants in Tver province who advised officials in
April that there was enough grain in the province to feed the capital for five months but
no one was coming to buy it. The claim may have been exaggerated, but peasants without reserves would hardly have invited purchasers. See Gaponenko, *Revoliutsionnoe
dvizhenie v aprele*, p. 581.

During the late summer and the fall, reports indicated that the peasants were acutely unhappy about the unavailability and high prices of articles of prime necessity. Demands that fixed prices be established for such items alternated with or accompanied demands that the grain monopoly be abolished and complaints about grain prices. But the most strident demand of the peasants was the call for land, and it was increasingly articulated in actions as well as in slogans.

Land Policy

Despite the large part that land questions played in the economic and social life of the preceding decade, the land question as such was relatively quiescent in the period immediately before the February Revolution. Once it became evident that the structure of the state itself could be changed, however, the possibility of changing the structure of land relations appeared more feasible.

In its first pronouncements on the major tasks ahead, the new government had little to say about the land question. In mid-March all appanage property was declared to be state property, and by the end of the month the lands that had been owned personally by the former Tsar were similarly nationalized. State lands were to continue in agricultural use under existing rules, although sales of such land were now suspended and rental leases were limited to a year.[16] There was no general statement on the land question until March 19, when an official announcement asserted, a bit belatedly, that solving the land problem was "the most serious socioeconomic task of the present historical moment."[17] According to this declaration, which was to become the cornerstone of the land policy of the Provisional Government, a solution was to be sought not by violence and land seizure but by legislation adopted by representatives of the people. The formulation of the necessary laws would require study of the quantity, distribution, and mode of tenure of all land in the country. The Minister of Agriculture was instructed, therefore, to establish a committee to collect and prepare materials for this purpose as expeditiously as possible.

Despite the importance of the work to be done and incoming reports of rural unrest, which made that work more urgent, it took a month to set up the committee. On April 21, in the midst of antiwar demonstrations brought on by the foreign policy of Kadet minister P. N. Miliukov, the Provisional Government issued a statement on the formation of land committees.[18] A main committee was created, and a triple-tiered pyramid of local land committees was established below it. Land committees were to be formed everywhere at the provincial and district levels. Volost land committees were optional and could be set up at the initiative of district land committees or of the local populace. The primary task of the committees was to prepare for land reform and to devise interim solutions to urgent land problems pending the convening of a Constituent Assembly.

The Main Land Committee was responsible for elaborating a draft law on land reform on the basis of data it collected and materials presented to it by the lower-level land committees. It was to submit its reports and proposals to the Provisional Government through the Minister of Agriculture, who was among its members. The committee could propose the suspension of previous legislation that might impede orderly resolution of the land question by the Constituent Assembly, or that was creating "misunderstanding" among the populace because of its incompatibility with the new state order. It could also recommend the abolition of positions and institutions dealing with land affairs if their functions were considered superfluous under the new conditions, and it could advise the government on the reassignment of their property and technical personnel to other agencies. In general, the main committee was to coordinate the government's activities and organs concerned with land relations.

Given the complexity and gravity of its assignments, it is perhaps not surprising that the main committee turned out to be quite large. Along with the Minister of Agriculture and his assistant, it included over 25 appointed members, plus representatives of provincial land committees, peasant organizations, political parties, public agencies, and scholarly economic societies. In addition, representatives of government offices and invited experts could participate with an advisory vote. In all, over 200 persons with diverse and often strongly conflicting views were present at its meetings. Under the circumstances it was difficult to function effectively, and the full committee met for only three sessions (May 19–20, July 1–6, and August 25–29). The basic work of the Main Land Committee had to be carried out by its executive council; even within this smaller group there was a tendency to bureaucratic aggrandizement. The council established at the first general session had 22 members; at the second session it was expanded to 34, and membership rose subsequently to 50.[19]

The provincial and district land committees, in addition to collecting materials and implementing the land regulations of the central authorities, were to coordinate with local government in managing local state properties, settle local land disputes in accordance with existing legislation and the rulings of the Provisional Government, prevent actions leading to the depreciation of land and agricultural properties (unless such acts were in social or state interests), bring before the main committee cases where such property was taken from private persons, and consult with local food committees and other state agencies on the most appropriate use of these properties in the light of government rulings. Members of the provincial land committee were drawn from the provincial zemstvo, the city council of the provincial capital, the district land committees, and the local judiciary. The Ministry of Agriculture appointed a representative, and, as in the Main Land Committee, invited experts were allowed an advisory vote. The district land committees were similarly composed but also included several technical specialists (zemstvo agronomists and statisticians) among their members.

Where volost land committees were established, they were to consist of five members and three alternates. According to the April directive, representatives were to be elected by the volost zemstvo or, pending the establishment of volost zemstvos, elections were to be regulated by the district land committees. In practice, however, representatives were generally elected by the volost assembly.[20] The functions of the volost committees were not defined in the April resolution; this opened the way for independent action by these groups and made it difficult for the higher-level land committees to control their activities. Yet the conflicts that developed between committees at different levels would probably have arisen in any case because of their differing constituencies and objectives. The immediate practical concerns of the peasants were not necessarily the most pressing concerns of officials, who, however well informed and well intentioned, were at a greater distance from the village and brought different perspectives to the question of land relations. The proportion of peasants in the land committees increased sharply in the lower levels, and the volost committees were composed almost entirely of peasants. Initially some of the peasant representatives on these committees were drawn from the more conservative elements in the community, elements traditionally more acceptable to the authorities, but such representatives tended to be replaced in time by more radical village spokesmen.[21]

The local committees got off to a rather slow start. Their number and time of establishment were not always recorded with the central authorities, but the papers of the Main Land Committee indicate that by mid-June, almost two months after the decision to establish them, only 30 percent of all provinces and 18 percent of all districts had land committees. Most provincial and district committees were established in late June and July. By September there were 46 provincial committees and 425 district committees (representing 92 percent of all districts) in operation in European Russia. The establishment of the "voluntary" volost committees was inadequately registered, but appears to have been far more widespread than the government anticipated. Financial support had been allocated for land committees in only 20 percent of all volosts, but data for 54 provinces show that by September volost land committees had been formed in 11,680 volosts (80 percent of the total in these provinces).[22] The peasants were clearly willing and eager to take a direct role in handling local land relations, and in some places land committees sprang up spontaneously before the official call for them.

The land committees at all levels faced formidable difficulties. As a research and planning organ, the main committee was dealing with a dynamic land situation that refused to lend itself to systematic analysis; as agencies engaged in practical matters of land regulation, dealing daily with problems of property seizure, rent relations, and land use, the local committees lacked sufficient authority or the means to enforce unpopular policies. Unable to pursue any measure that might limit the freedom of action of the Constituent Assembly, the land committees were also constrained by the competing jurisdictions of other agencies with equally broadly defined responsibilities. The food committees, for example, were frequently involved in land questions when matters of crop production arose, and despite government efforts to delineate separate areas of responsibility for the parallel sets of committees, ambiguity and conflict persisted.

In addition to the lack of inter-agency coordination, there were problems with the coordination of different levels within the same agency. These were a by-product of the administrative disintegration of the countryside and antedated the committee system, but the committees failed to provide an alternative form of administrative coherence. Harassed land owners in Saratov complained to the central authorities that the newly formed administrative organs in the province had absolutely no contact with one another and carried on their affairs independently: "The village committees take no account of the volost committees, the volost authorities take no account of the district, and so forth."[23]

Although the Main Land Committee was criticized as an "organ with an inadequately defined function,"[24] the essential problem appears to have been its inability to take effective action. The role intended for the land committees was outlined clearly enough from the start. Their establishment signaled the fact that the new regime could not rely on the administrative machinery of the old. Yet because the Provisional Government was reluctant to establish a firm new order without the sanction of a representative national assembly, the land committees fell into an administrative breach. The second session of the Main Land Committee, meeting early in July, requested that the land committees be given complete interim regulatory control over agricultural lands. Similar requests were persistently repeated by local committees and by peasant organizations, which argued that such a move was in the interests of the entire economy.[25] Yet the government hesitated.

Part of the problem stemmed from the fact that in order to delegate authority a government must first possess it. The Provisional Government was never secure enough to risk the diffusion of central authority. Then, too, the country did not have *a* Provisional Government, but a succession of provisional governments—which tended to be more provisional than governing. The Kadet Minister of Agriculture, A. I. Shingarev, was followed by the SRs V. M. Chernov and S. L. Maslov. None ever had a free hand.

Even during the critical July Days, when popular demonstrations filled the streets, Chernov, speaking of a future transfer of land to those who worked it—his party's policy and strong point—was careful to stipulate that this *ought* to be the basis of land reform. All he could offer, however, was a promise that the government would propose it to the Constituent Assembly for consideration.[26] In June it was announced that elections would be held in September and that the assembly would convene by the end of that month. However, in August the elections were postponed to November 12 and the meeting of the assembly to November 28.

One reason for the delay was a growing conviction among leaders that more time was needed to prepare reform projects, particularly projects for land reform. As the Main Land Committee struggled with its herculean task under the presidency of Professor A. S. Posnikov, the agrarian specialist, it found widespread support in public circles. Private organizations, in fact, had taken the lead in the work on land reform.* The League of Agrarian Reform, arising from the influential Moscow Society of Agriculture, dedicated itself to preparing materials for land reform legislation at its first congress on April 16–17. Branches of the league sprang up throughout the country as other eminent societies and specialists responded to the opportunity to help reshape land relations. In Petrograd the venerable Free Economic So-

---

* However, in 1916, when the Economic Council of the Union of Towns proposed a meeting of leading economic specialists and scholars throughout the country to formulate a program on major questions of economic policy, the agrarian question was at the very bottom of the lists of topics the council and the Free Economic Society suggested for discussion. (TsGIA, *f.* 91, *op.* 2, *d.* 446.)

ciety, which had long been at odds with the old regime over its land policies, decided after some hesitation to sponsor a local division. Led by the renowned academic economist M. I. Tugan-Baranovskii, this branch became the theoretical center for agrarian legislative projects.[27] The league hoped to clarify agrarian issues and to prepare for land reform by informed discussion and the dissemination of popular and scientific literature. Meanwhile, the economic section of the All-Russian Zemstvo Union was energetically at work, gathering materials to contribute to the reform enterprise.[28]

None of these groups was identified with any one political party, and none had an organizational program for land reform. For one optimist in the Free Economic Society, the diverse political sympathies of members posed no obstacle to their uniting in a general program of agrarian reform since, in his view, no single party had yet worked out such a program.[29] Whatever the merit of the observation, reports of league congresses show a wide range of opinions on the direction the reform should take.[30] Pamphlets were rushed to press as different groups hastened to present their analyses. Proposals that had been raised in 1905–7 were resurrected and reexamined. A 1906 brochure on "Confiscation or Compensation" was reissued with a blurb proclaiming that it was "never more contemporary."[31]

While the fine points of the debate on land reform were being spun out in the conference halls of Petrograd and Moscow and in the occasional sessions of the Main Land Committee, the peasants in the countryside were often deciding land controversies at the point of a pitchfork. The renewed eruption of rural violence and the revival of the possibility of land expropriation led once again, as in 1905–7, to a flurry of land sales and speculative transactions. Some of the sales were fictitious: estates and large properties were divided into small parcels that were "sold" to individual family members in an attempt to reduce the size of holdings to anticipated norms of inalienability. In other cases land was sold to foreign interests or was mortgaged. The peasants saw such moves as attempts to keep them from getting control of land to which they were entitled, and sent numerous requests to the Provisional Government to block these maneuvers.[32]

In April, Chernov proposed a law to halt land transactions. Opposition spearheaded by the Kadets prevented its passage; however, a draft of the proposed law served as the basis of a circular telegram sent out to notaries by Minister of Justice P. N. Pereverzev on May 17 announcing the temporary cessation of all transactions in land.[33] The gentry strongly protested this measure, complaining that its impact on landowners, banks (as mortgage holders), and the economy in general would be disastrous. As a result, the instruction was rescinded in June. By then Chernov had become Minister of Agriculture, and he again tried to freeze the land situation. Only after his hand was strengthened by the call of the All-Russian Congress of Peasant Deputies for prohibition of land transfers, by evidence of popular unrest in the July Days, and, most importantly, by the resignation of the Kadet ministers and of Prime Minister G. E. Lvov in early July, was he successful. Total prohibition of transactions had drawn sufficient resistance to force some compromise. The decree published on July 12 allowed land transfers in individual instances that met with the approval of the provincial land committee and were confirmed by the Minister of Agriculture.[34] Without this special approval, no land transaction concluded after February was to be recognized as valid. Property that was marked for public auction was to be placed under the interim economic management of the Peasant Land Bank, the Nobles' Land Bank, or the Department of State Properties.

Land sales were not the only moves to concern peasants in 1917. Changes introduced or threatened by land organization work continued to be a source of discontent throughout the first half of the year. Although the tsarist government had responded to the growing dissatisfaction of the peasants by ordering a suspension of land organization work at the end of November 1916, the organizational structure remained in place, and some work in the countryside apparently continued under the heading of unfinished business. When revolution broke out two months later, the new Minister of Agriculture, the Kadet A. I. Shingarev, promptly issued instructions that land organization activity was to continue.[35] By this time, however, peasant opposition to the work was even more widespread, and a flood of petitions to halt work underway or to undo completed arrangements revealed the seriousness of the problem.

From the point of view of the peasant majority, still in communes, there were two problems with the land organization program. The first was the preferential treatment of separators in the division of lands arranged by agents of the land organization commissions. Not only did peasants often feel that they had been unjustly deprived of their best land or of an unreasonable amount of land, but the reorganization of fields required to permit withdrawal of consolidated plots was said in some cases to create special hardships for the agricultural operations of the commune. In the years before the war, peasants in communes had turned repeatedly to the Tsar with petitions to save them from the ruinous effects of land organization.[36] Now they turned to the Provisional Government with similar requests, but with additional complaints because of the second problem they confronted, which resulted from the war. Peasant women wrote (or found literate villagers to write for them) to protest land organization work that was being carried out against their wishes in the absence of their husbands and sons.[37] Peasants withdrawing their land from communes were said to be taking advantage of those who were away at the front defending the land with their lives. One large commune in Voronezh province petitioned in early April to forestall imminent land organization work demanded by a group of its members who had decided to separate with consolidated holdings. Since the group amounted to one-fifth of the total membership, the commune was obliged under the law to conduct a general redistribution of its lands. But one-third of the household heads were away at war, and the remaining members of the commune felt it would be impossible to defend their interests adequately. The would-be separators were said to be interested primarily in selling their land, and the petitioners warned that redistribution would wreak havoc with the spring planting.[38]

Other peasants who were unhappy about land organization decided to take matters into their own hands. The residents of six rural communities in Perm province held a general assembly at the office of the volost administration late in April and decided to get rid of all individual boundary markers, reestablish kitchen gardens in their previous location, and "destroy everything done by the land organization commissions and confirmed by law." Two "orators" who were rash enough to point out that this ran counter to the provincial commissar's instruction to await the Constituent Assembly were placed under arrest and dispatched to the district commissar as counterrevolutionaries.[39]

In the face of growing conflict between separators and peasants in communes, the Provisional Government decided to put an end to separations and to the work of the land organization commissions. On June 28 a resolution was adopted terminating the issuing of certificates of personal ownership under all previous laws (including Article 65 of the Emancipation Redemption Statute and the law of June 14, 1910) and ending appropriation of communal allotment land and land organization work provided for by the law of May 29, 1911, or other legislation. Under certain conditions a limited amount of work already in process could be completed upon the recommendation of the provincial land commission and with the permission of the Main Land Committee. The provincial and district land organization commissions were to be disbanded, their staff members and directors dismissed or transferred to other agencies. The papers and property of these commissions were to be turned over to the new provincial and district land committees, and their technical personnel (land surveyors) were placed under the Main Land Committee for service with the new committees.[40] Despite its formal adoption by the Provisional Government at the end of June and reports of confusion arising from the simultaneous existence of the old land organization commissions and the new land committees, the resolution was not published for a full month.[41] This poorly publicized and little-noticed enactment finally brought an official end to Stolypin's ambitious program of land reform. That program had been roundly attacked before the revolution for one reason or another by every political party now influential in the government (only the Octobrists and the Nationalists had supported it), but it had taken five months to eliminate it formally.

By the end of the summer, with costly and unsuccessful war still draining the country, the cities still hungry, and the aroused peasants turning increasingly to their own direct approaches to land reform, the Provisional Government had little grounds for complacency. Beginning in the latter part of September, reports from the provinces, from the Main Land Committee, and from the ministries repeatedly stressed the urgency of enacting interim agrarian legislation to regulate land rent and other issues causing rural discord. Prime Minister A. F. Kerensky called on the local land committees to bring order into land relations and to see that agricultural lands were fully utilized "to save the national economy from final ruin."[42] To make this possible, it was again suggested that all agricultural land be placed under the control of the committees. With this end in mind, several official agencies drafted legislative proposals that were submitted to the Provisional Government by mid-October.[43]

The belated attempt to increase the authority of the local land committees is understandable in light of the disintegration of central authority and the rising violence in the countryside. Yet it can be seen as an abandonment of policy. As the government was well aware, the lower-level land committees, especially the volost land committees, were by this time far more concerned with local peasant interests than with government policy and more responsive to their local communities than to their bureaucratic superiors.[44] Even this attempt proved abortive. The Third Coalition Government decided to defer action on the draft laws on the grounds that they should be discussed first in the new Council of the Republic (formed in September after the country was proclaimed a republic) and in the future Constituent Assembly.[45]

8

Agrarian Programs of the Political Parties

The land policy of the Provisional Government, which appears in retrospect indecisive and temporizing, was, at least in part, the product of a divergence of views on basic political goals. This divergence defined the limits of the politically possible, for until October no single group could gain enough support to realize its program. To a large extent the agrarian programs and policies of the major political parties in 1917 determined the course of Russian history, and they form an essential part of the history of the commune. Those parties, reading from February to October, were the Kadets, the Mensheviks, the SRs, and the Bolsheviks. Despite interparty disagreements, intraparty differences, and a great deal of fractionalization on agrarian issues, there were features common to the programs of all; thus what proved most important was not what they represented in general but where they stood on particular issues.

The Kadets

When the February Revolution eclipsed the parties of the right, the Kadet Party (also known as the Party of People's Freedom) lost its central position in the political spectrum. The old center became the new right, and the Kadets found themselves the prime target of the ascendant left. Though they had found support among the liberal landed gentry, the rural intelligentsia, and some Cossacks, the Kadets never attracted a strong following among the peasants. Despite vigorous efforts to win rural backing, they had only 4 percent of the representatives in the peasant electoral assemblies for the first Duma in 1906.[1]

In 1917 the Kadet agrarian program remained essentially unchanged from what it had been in 1905–7: expropriation of estates above a labor norm (that is, above a unit based on the average amount of land needed for subsistence farming; its size might vary regionally according to local conditions), with the land to be transferred to the peasants and with compensation to be paid to the former owners. As a typical liberal party in the Western political tradition, the Kadet Party upheld principles of private property, the rule of law, and parliamentary procedure. However, as a party of Russian liberals, responding to a unique configuration of domestic political, economic, and social conditions, it was prepared to modify the existing system of private property, using legal and parliamentary means.

At its seventh congress in March 1917, the party decided that resolution of the agrarian question would have to await the end of the war. Any earlier attempt to restructure land relations would threaten to reduce agricultural productivity and interfere with the war effort, to which the Kadets were committed. Some delegates, although accepting this decision, urged adopting an agrarian program with a broader appeal to the peasantry. Immediate radicalization of the Kadet position on at least some agrarian issues was not only essential, in their view, but should have top priority among the party's concerns. Since the central committee had been unable to draft proposals during the congress, a special commission was elected to work out a draft of a new agrarian program, and another congress was scheduled for fuller discussion.

Debate on the agrarian question at the eighth congress in May revealed deep differences among the delegates. Some called for the free and unencumbered transfer of land to the peasants; others argued that the breakup of large estates and the transfer of land to poor peasants would cause a disastrous drop in field production. Some minor points were carried by the more radical delegates, but the conservatives held the day.[2]

The program that was adopted (or reconfirmed) along with a supplementary statement entitled Principles of Land Reform declared that all agricultural land should pass into the hands of those who worked it. The Kadets supported compulsory expropriation of all privately owned land above a definite labor norm, but certain categories of land (expanded at the eighth Kadet congress) were excepted from confiscation: home garden plots, orchards, vineyards, and other intensively cultivated lands whose output might suffer from their division. A proprietor cultivating his land with his own agricultural equipment and draft animals might retain land up to a higher norm if there were no local land shortage. On the decision of the responsible institution that the maintenance of a large estate was in the interests of the economy, its proprietor could retain it intact regardless of its size. To avoid disrupting agricultural production, many Kadets had insisted on preserving large, technologically advanced agricultural enterprises, which were to be left temporarily in the hands of their owners.[3]

Different viewpoints were voiced about property rights to the alienated lands that were to be transferred to the peasants. Some Kadets wanted the land given out as private property. F. I. Rodichev, for example, claimed that the Stolypin reforms had created a sense of property that had to be reckoned with: "All of the Russian people want land as private property."[4] V. A. Kosinskii argued similarly that private property was psychologically essential to ensure the most intense cultivation of land. Their critics, however, objected that such views opposed "Kadetism to socialism, individualism to collectivism," and urged the party to adopt a middle ground. The suggestion might have seemed misplaced to Western liberals but was in line with the majority view, and the party called for a degree of nationalization rather than the extension of private ownership. The land expropriated from largeholders was to be placed in a state land fund and distributed to landless and smallholder peasants for use for an unlimited period.

Compensation for the expropriated land was considered a moral and practical obligation. Since other types of property (industry, capital, small landholdings) were not to be expropriated, compensation would be the only way of avoiding discrimination and injustice. The party newspaper, *Rech'*, cited Marx in justifying compensation as the cheapest way of throwing off landlordism.[5] Compensation was to be "at fair valuation" but on a sliding scale, with largeholders receiving less per unit of land than smaller proprietors. Part of the cost of compensation (about 6 percent) was to be paid by the recipient of the land; the rest was to be provided by the state. Thus the direct burden on the peasant who received the land would not be heavy, but the peasantry as a whole could anticipate taxation to cover the state's expenses.

Peasants, of course, had no more interest in compensating the gentry for the land in 1917 than in 1905 or, for that matter, in 1861. A peasant representative from Saratov had delivered that message loud and clear in the Duma: "God created man and put the land in his hands, yet we do not have it. Why? I will tell you straight out: You have stolen it from us. But we, gentlemen, have come to take it. The land is ours. We have come not to buy, but to take."[6]

As defenders of the right to buy—and sell—land, the Kadets also found themselves at cross-purposes with the peasants on the issue of prohibiting commercial transactions in land. They opposed the policy adopted by the Provisional Government after their departure because they considered it an infringement of economic freedom and because they anticipated an adverse impact on the shaky economy.

Although the Kadet Party recognized the economic drawbacks of the commune, it had consistently opposed the Stolypin program on the grounds that it was harmfully accelerating a development that should have been left to its own inevitable evolutionary course. The Kadet program, therefore, called for an end to the forcible destruction of the commune and demanded that departures from it be regulated in the interests of those who remained behind as well as those who left. The Kadets supported strongly the abrogation of the Stolypin land legislation and the closure of the land organization commissions, and they welcomed the April statute on the new land committees with equal enthusiasm. *Rech'* even compared it with the rescript of November 20, 1857, which prepared the way for the emancipation, and expressed the hope that the land committees' preparation for reform would facilitate the peasants' peaceful and patient wait for the Constituent Assembly.[7]

"Patience" soon became the official watchword of the parties brought to power by a people grown impatient. The Kadet Minister of Agriculture, Shingarev, a former zemstvo doctor and the author of *The Dying Village*, a sympathetic study of rural poverty at the turn of the century, was now writing circulars warning the villagers sternly that "willful seizure of the lands and property of others" would be "punished to the full extent of the law."[*] The Kadets became identified in the popular mind as the party of law and order—the old order. Within a short time they fell from a position of political predominance to that of frustrated bystanders, excluded entirely by the end of the summer from the last provisional government. The unpopularity of their agrarian program was not the only cause of their political defeat, but it was a sufficient one.

As William Rosenberg's insightful analysis of the party has shown, the Kadets, for all their intellectual commitment to liberalism, shared the Russian intelligentsia's traditional fear of the "uncultured masses," the "dark people," and assumed a paternalistic posture. They justified their reluctance to support unreservedly the "class interests" of the peasantry by claiming to remain above all class interests. This served as a convenient screen for their own narrow electoral base, for "as national nonpartisan liberals rather than defenders of sectarian interests, party leaders could argue they 'deserved' power even if they lacked

---

[*] *EPR*, p. 221. Shingarev was Minister of Agriculture in the original Provisional Government and Minister of Finance in the first coalition government. After the October Revolution he was arrested as a member of the Central Committee of the Kadet Party, and in January 1918 he was murdered in a prison hospital. The second edition of his study (1907) was republished in 1937 as an appendix to a later investigation of the same villages that was designed to show the improvements introduced under the Soviet government. See Shuvaev, *Staraia i novaia derevnia*.

massive popular support."⁸ Without that support, however, it proved impossible to retain power in revolutionary Russia.

The Mensheviks

The agrarian program of the Mensheviks was designed to fit their theoretical conception of the course of Russian history. Anticipating an interlude of capitalist development after the bourgeois revolution, they accepted the necessity of political cooperation with the more democratic elements of society while conditions ripened for a transition to socialism. As a result, their agrarian program shared certain characteristics with that of the Kadets. It, too, called for expropriation of private holdings above a certain norm and for the transfer of this land, along with that of churches, monasteries, and the Imperial family, to public ownership.

Both the Mensheviks and the Bolsheviks, as factions of the Marxist Social Democratic Party, expected the next revolution to be made by the proletariat and were therefore interested primarily in that social sector rather than in the peasantry. Initially both factions had subscribed, at least in theory, to the same agrarian program. Yet their members had differed on agrarian issues even before the great schism at the party congress in 1903, and were far from agreement on the reworked party program of 1906.

The most distinctive feature of the Menshevik agrarian program was "municipalization," that is, the transfer of large parcels of land to autonomous local agencies for distribution among peasants or for use in the public interest, as locally determined.⁹ Regional authorities were to establish in accordance with local conditions the norms above which land would be appropriated. All communal land and individual peasant holdings below the local norms were to be inalienable. The Mensheviks feared that an attempt to nationalize all land would propel the peasants into the ranks of the counterrevolution. To prevent the accumulation or reconstitution of large holdings, they proposed in 1917 that the purchase of peasant lands be restricted to public agencies.¹⁰

Another point in the Menshevik program stipulated that rent for the use of confiscated land was to be paid to the state at locally established rates and that the zemstvos were to provide for social needs such as education and medical care.¹¹ On the other hand, the state was to assume outstanding obligations on the expropriated lands, with the cost to be met by a progressive income tax. P. P. Maslov, the principal architect of the Menshevik program, was in favor of partial compensation for the alienated land, but the party rejected the proposal and refused to agree to any compensation. It also rejected proposals for the compulsory preservation of large, highly cultivated estates, leaving discretion in such cases, again, to the local authorities.

On the question of halting land sales and mortgages on land, the Mensheviks opposed the Kadets and joined their socialist colleagues. The All-Russian Conference of Mensheviks in May 1917 called for an immediate government decree prohibiting all private transactions in land, except those specifically authorized by the land committees. The Mensheviks wanted the committees to be given full responsibility for regulating gentry-peasant relations, normalizing rents and wages, establishing conciliation chambers to resolve land disputes, and arranging the rental and cultivation of unworked gentry lands.[12]

The Mensheviks' position on the commune, like that of most other parties, was somewhat contradictory. Recognizing the drawbacks of the system of communal tenure, they condemned it as an economic anachronism and as a class restraint on the control of landed property.[13] G. V. Plekhanov, the eminent Menshevik leader and theorist, was convinced by his study of the institution that its demise was inevitable;[14] yet in the years after 1905 the party had criticized the Stolypin agrarian program on the familiar grounds that it was artificially forcing that demise. On the other hand, to the extent that the agrarian reform accelerated the development of capitalism in the countryside it could be viewed as progressive (*per aspera ad astra*). The Mensheviks' proposal to declare communal land inalienable and purchasable only by public agencies seemed unlikely to spur any such development, but they believed that capitalism was developing within the commune and would continue under its own historical momentum to bring about the dissolution of the institution. The retention of local control over land after a successful bourgeois revolution was preferable to full nationalization of land, they argued, because local control would best safeguard the peasants' land interests if a political restoration or reaction were to occur.

The Socialist Revolutionaries

Unlike the Kadets and Mensheviks, who found little support among the peasants, the SRs were a peasant party with a strong political base in the countryside. They had more followers among the peasants than did any other party. Initially the only SR in the Provisional Government was the maverick Kerensky, who accepted the post of Minister of Justice without the authorization of his party. The SRs, however, dominated the Petrograd Soviet, with which the government was obliged to share its authority in the *dvoevlastie* ("dual power") interval between February and October. At the All-Russian Congress of Soviets (June 3–24), SRs were the largest group present, with 285 representatives among the 1,090 delegates participating. There were 248 Menshevik delegates and 105 Bolsheviks.[15] When the soviet approved the participation of the socialist parties in the government, the SR leader Chernov succeeded Shingarev as Minister of Agriculture in May. Since the SRs retained the post through later shifts in coalition, they would appear to have been in a favorable position to promote the agrarian policies that were the mainstay of their program.

In contrast to the Social Democrats (SDs), who held that society was divided into classes by the different relationships of groups of individuals to the means of production, the SRs recognized only two basic social groups: the exploiters and the exploited. The central problem in social relationships, according to SR theorists, was the problem of distribution, and it was this that gave importance to control of the means of production. Gross inequities in the existing system of distribution amounted to social exploitation, and the exploited included both workers and peasants. Because peasants constituted the bulk of the population, they were necessarily the primary target of socialist concern. Peasants were exploited by means of private property in land, which prevented a just distribution of the products of labor applied to land. The SR solution, proposed in essence by the Trudovik delegates in the first and second Dumas (the "Project of the 104" and its successors), was the "socialization" of land. The term "socialization," which came into use in 1902, initially signified simply the nationalization of land with land use available on equal terms to all members of the working agricultural population. It soon came to mean also that the right to distribute lands was not to belong to the state but to communes and their territorial unions.[16] Land was to be redistributed to those who worked it, on egalitarian principles and on the basis of consumption norms (i.e., in amounts adequate to provide for basic necessities). Land currently held in excess of that norm was to be taken from its owners without compensation and redistributed by communes.[17]

To the SRs, the commune was a gangway leading from contemporary bourgeois society to the future socialist society. Although peasants in communes worked their land individually, they held it collectively, and under the influence of the egalitarian distribution of all land they would become psychologically conditioned for collective labor. In an interesting elaboration of this point, one SR theorist noted that in the field of industry the socialist organization of production had to proceed from collective labor to collective ownership of the means of production. In Russian agriculture, in contrast, it would have to proceed from collective ownership of the means of production to collective labor. Capitalism had created collective labor in industry, and it was necessary only to introduce social control over the means of production to achieve socialization there. History had created social control over the agricultural means of production in the form of the commune, and it was necessary only to introduce the collectivization of labor to bring about the socialization of agriculture.[18] Historical development had thus shaped an essential difference in the economic positions of the proletariat and the peasantry: whereas the proletariat could grow and gain through the development of capitalism, the peasantry would benefit only from the socialization of land—which was contrary to the development of capitalism. It followed, then, that the interests of the two exploited groups were not identical, and that the program of the peasant-minded SRs would necessarily differ from that of the proletarian-oriented SDs.

When private property was eliminated and every peasant had equal use of the land, the question of individual versus collective cultivation would become a simple matter of technical and economic advantage rather than an issue of principle. The commune would completely destroy the petty bourgeois peasant tendency to "property fanaticism." The SRs insisted that their modern conception of the commune was far more realistic than the naive idealization of their Populist predecessors.[19] Like their contemporary political opponents, they saw negative features in the commune, but more than any other political party they were confident that these were mutable and were greatly outweighed by the positive features of the institution. In contrast to other socialists, who wanted land transferred to "municipalities" or the state, the SRs—and here perhaps they revealed the anarchist strain in their background—wanted to eliminate not only private property in land, but the very notion of owning land. "We will not make land the property of the commune," said Chernov, "or the property of the region. We will not even transfer it simply to the ranks of contemporary 'state property.' We will make it nobody's. And precisely as nobody's, it will become everybody's—people's property."[20]

In 1905 the SRs had called for the seizure of lands by the peasants, but after the February Revolution party leaders opposed such action. Both Chernov and Semen Maslov, who succeeded him as Minister of Agriculture in September, warned that disorganized land snatching could result in an extremely unequal distribution of land that might benefit wealthier peasants alone. Rumors of land seizure were inducing desertions from the front by peasant soldiers afraid of being bypassed, and actual seizures were aggravating the nation's economic problems by causing a further decline in the area under cultivation. Therefore the SRs, like the Kadets and Mensheviks, urged the peasants to wait for the Constituent Assembly. Direct peasant action could be justified in 1905, they announced, since then nothing could be expected from the Duma. Now, however, there was every reason to await the Constituent Assembly.

Although the SRs joined the chorus counseling the peasants to be patient, they were more ready to take interim measures on agrarian issues than were most of their political associates. As noted above, they secured the prohibition of commercial transactions in land after a struggle of several months. They were strongly opposed to the Stolypin reform legislation and were instrumental in its elimination. The SRs urged their colleagues in the Provisional Government to transfer control of local land affairs and agrarian problems to the land committees. This was only to be expected, since the SRs were the political party most strongly represented within the land committee structure and grew stronger there as the months went by. At the first meeting of the Council of the Main Land Committee in May, the SRs held a third of the seats. By August not only had the council expanded considerably, but the SRs had increased their representation to 60 percent of its membership, and another 18 percent was politically allied with them.[21] In the local land committees, SR representation was high from the start and remained so throughout the life of the committees. Yet the attempts of the SRs to transfer power legally to the committees were repeatedly blocked.[22]

At least part of the reason for the SR's failure to realize their agrarian program more fully was their lack of a concrete plan of action. Discussion of the program at the third party congress in May 1917 was largely limited to a reaffirmation of its socialization plank, and promises to review the entire agrarian program were subsequently put aside. "It is a remarkable circumstance," noted one investigator, "that the land problem in conjunction with which this party had grown up and waxed strong, should have suffered from inattention."[23] In fact, the SR leadership appears at times to have been living in a different world from that of the peasants for whom the party claimed to speak. Though the SR literature of 1917 is full of admonitions to the restless peasants and demands for law and order, the party leader was later to complain of peasant conservatism: "If [the peasants] have revolutionary significance, it is only insofar as they . . . abandon their point of view for that of the proletariat."[24]

One of the party's agrarian experts, elected in May to its central committee (devoid of peasant representatives), confessed that the thought of socialization "causes a good deal of alarm when you begin to think of proceeding to its practical realization."[25] Uneasy leaders do not inspire confidence, and the confidence in SR leadership shown earlier at the polls began to melt. In the September elections to the Moscow City Council the SRs won only 14 percent of the vote, as compared with 58 percent in June.[26] In the countryside no such fall-off was evident, but a shift to the Left SRs took place as differences within the party became more pronounced.

The Left SRs had become more active after the February Revolution; by May they had constituted themselves as a distinct faction within the party and had their own newspaper. Differences between them and their fellow party members sharpened during the summer. By fall the Left SRs were ready to break off relations with the non-socialist parties in the coalition government. They had little sympathy for the Democratic Conference or for the Council of the Republic. In agrarian matters, they had been the first to call for the transfer of full interim power over land matters to the land committees; the rest of the party had come over to that position more gradually. The Left SRs urged that the committees be given complete control of all agricultural land, including gentry lands, but they were prepared to leave nominal ownership of the land unchanged until the meeting of the Constituent Assembly.[27]

Intraparty differences were plastered over to preserve some semblance of unity among SRs, but the plastering itself may have been responsible for the party's ineffectiveness since it limited freedom of action.[28] By September a group of old SRs was complaining that it was no longer possible to speak of the party's position on any given point: there were at least several positions on every issue.[29] As summer gave way to autumn, the protracted wrangles over the proposed law on the land committees seemed to confirm the contention of the Left SRs that nothing good could come of cooperation with the "bourgeois" parties. On October 24 the draft legislation was once again discussed by the Provisional Government in an evening session in the malachite drawing room of the Winter Palace, but the matter remained unresolved.[30] On the following evening the heirs of February were escorted out of that elegant hall under arms, and within 24 hours the history of Russian land relations and of the commune had turned another page.

The Bolsheviks

Eight months had passed and the parties in power had done little to resolve the land problem despite the many important points on which their programs agreed. All accepted the necessity of basic land reform. All were prepared to alienate or confiscate lands above a set norm and turn them over to the peasants along with state, Imperial family, and Church lands. All opposed peasant seizure of lands as inefficient, unjust (to different groups, for different reasons), and harmful to the economy. And whether they waited for "expropriation with compensation," "municipalization," or "socialization," all were prepared to wait, and all told the peasants to wait, for a Constituent Assembly that kept receding in time.

It was not the idea of land reform, or even the nature of the reform, that prevented effective political cooperation and action, but hesitation before its implications. Land reform was the key to social transformation: a means that would inevitably shape the end. Since the ends in view differed radically, cooperation on the means proved impossible. When the Provisional Government and its coalitions proved unable to satisfy their needs, the peasants looked for more effective agents. In the increasingly popular slogan "All Power to the Soviets," the critical words were the first two. "All Power" promised positive action in place of negotiation and denial. The tradition of autocracy made absolute power comprehensible; the frustrations of the interval since February made it acceptable. "Soviets" did not necessarily mean Bolsheviks. In fact, the slogan was abandoned by the Bolsheviks after the July Days, when the possibility of their winning control of the soviets looked dim. Only in September, when they had taken a leading role in the Petrograd and Moscow Soviets of Workers' and Soldiers' Deputies, was it revived, and it was then that Lenin decided the Bolsheviks should attempt to take power. Despite the fact that the party was still weak in the peasant soviets, Lenin confidently asserted, "Only a Bolshevik government will satisfy the peasantry." The apparent paradox of the party of the proletariat coming to power in a peasant country disappears when one looks at the Bolshevik's agrarian program in 1917.

Before the 1905 revolution the Bolshevik wing of the SDs had given scant attention to the elaboration of an agrarian program. Although Lenin had studied Russian rural problems, the conclusions presented in his numerous publications had not been followed up in political programming. In illustrating how capitalism had crept into the countryside, Lenin provided considerable evidence of agricultural backwardness and pointed to economic and institutional restraints on further development. He viewed such features as *otrabotka* (the renting of land for payment in labor) and the system of communal land tenure as post-emancipation survivals of a feudal, serf-holding economy. The contradiction between the impulse toward capitalist development and the drag of feudal elements in agriculture would contribute to the bourgeois revolution; but since the revolution would be made by the most politically conscious and active sector of society—the industrial proletariat—the Bolsheviks, along with the Mensheviks, directed their program to urban workers.

Yet as early as 1902 Lenin had written that the Russian SDs would try to utilize the experience of the West by making earlier and more urgent efforts to attract village forces to the SD movement. Much could be taken from abroad, he wrote, "but in the agrarian field perhaps we shall work out something new."[31] The Party, he urged, should come out for the small peasant, involve itself in "alien" (nonproletarian) questions, and persuade all the working and exploited masses to look to it as their leader and representative.[32]

At the time of the uprisings of 1905, the official SD agrarian program was the modest and unimaginative platform adopted by the second party congress in 1903. Its main point was support of the peasants' old demand for the return of the *otrezki*—the pieces of land cut off from peasants' holdings and retained by the gentry at the time of the emancipation.[33] In the course of the intervening half century, many of these had reverted through purchase to the peasantry and boundaries had become blurred, so the demand was more symbolic than substantive. The scope and strength of the peasant uprisings in 1905 indicated that a reappraisal of the rural situation and its revolutionary potential was in order, and a new agrarian program was called for at the Tammerfors Conference in December 1905.

Though he had previously endorsed nationalization of land in principle, Lenin had opposed as premature a proposal to include partial nationalization in the 1903 program.[34] However, the events of 1905 (including the demand of the Peasant Congress for nationalization) changed his position. "There cannot be the slightest doubt," he wrote early in 1906, "that the idea of national property in land is now extraordinarily widespread among the peasantry [and] . . . bears a revolutionary-democratic character."[35] In answer to criticism that the peasants were leading their leaders, he replied pragmatically that the SD agrarian program could not have been more concrete before a mass peasant movement since the effect of capitalism on the peasants, their readiness for revolution, was "too difficult or impossible to decide on the basis of theoretical considerations alone."[36]

The agrarian program he proposed as a member of the Agrarian Commission of the fourth congress of the SDs in February 1906 called for confiscation of all gentry, Imperial family, Church, and state land. Peasant committees were to arrange for the immediate distribution of the land and, if the revolution was successful in establishing a republic and a democratic state structure, "then the party will seek the repeal of private property in land and the transfer of all lands into the common property of all the people."[37] Without the establishment of a democratic state, nationalization was not desirable since it could be used as an instrument of exploitation by the dominant classes. The peasants were to be warned that mere seizure of land was not enough: the revolution had to be carried out to the end and its political objectives realized or their victory would be insecure. The Bolshevik "Divisionists" (including Stalin), who wanted gentry lands divided among the peasants as private property, opposed nationalization. They insisted that the peasants were interested only in their own property and had but a hazy notion of nationalization, which they were using as an ideological cloak for their desire to take gentry land. Lenin agreed, but accused the Divisionists of the error that Marx had detected in the early materialists: they knew how to explain the world, but the point was to change it. The peasant idea of transfer to the state of land that was "God's," "the state's," or "nobody's" was a lever that could be used to develop their political consciousness. Peasants could be brought to understand that if land were controlled by the state, then the state would have to be democratized to protect their interests.[38]

The agrarian resolution finally adopted by the fourth ("united") congress of the SDs in 1906 represented a compromise of various viewpoints. It included "municipalization" of confiscated lands, "nationalization" of a land fund for colonization and of forests and waters of statewide importance, and the "division among the peasants of former gentry lands that had not been cultivated as large units."[39]

Although Lenin objected to the "municipalization" (or, as he termed it, the "provincialization") of the Menshevik program, he felt that as a practical matter the distribution of lands would inevitably fall to local authorities. But he assailed Menshevik "agrarian bimetallism": the attempt to fuse a new system with the old by nationalizing only part of the land and exempting allotment land.[40] He criticized the SRs, on the other hand, for thinking it feasible to both end trading in land and preserve an open-market economy. In his view, they were mistaken in assuming that socialization and egalitarianism would lead to socialism because they were oblivious to the class struggle among the petty peasantry. Yet Lenin was keenly interested in the socialization projects of the peasant delegates to the Duma and personally verified the signatures on the "project of the 104" to ascertain their peasant origin. Peasant discontent was a revolutionary wellspring, and socialization (or nationalization) was politically expedient. However, the SRs, in relying on the commune, were running against the tide of time, unaware that the commune had outlived itself and was "condemned to collapse by the whole course of historical development."[41]

The Stolypin anticommunal program put the Bolsheviks, like the Mensheviks, in an awkward theoretical position. Although they condemned the reform and denied that it improved the condition of the peasantry as a whole, they considered it historically progressive because it had quickened the pace of capitalist development by concentrating the means of production (agricultural land and inventory) and encouraging social differentiation and rural proletarianization. Lenin considered communal organization superior to individualism insofar as the commune organized the production of at least its own members ("if it did even that"), whereas individualism destroyed social ties. Yet he conceded that capitalism too gave a social character to production and bonded "masses of individuals."[42]

The commune created a number of problems for Party theorists. The first concrete point in the history of the Russian Marxists' agrarian program had been a demand, directed against the Populists in 1888, for peasants' right to leave the commune.[43] But the institution always had its attractions. Despite the fact that the contemporary commune was primarily a "fiscal-serf burden" on the peasantry, observed Lenin in 1902, it was also a "democratic organ of local government" and "a fraternal or neighborly association"; the Party, he vowed, would never help anyone to destroy it.[44] The worst features of the commune in his view were mutual tax responsibility and members' inability freely to sell or renounce allotments. The first drawback had been eliminated in 1903, and Stolypin had largely removed the other. But his methods were branded as an invitation to the "plunder of the commune by the kulaks." To the historically minded Bolsheviks, the Stolypin program was "agrarian Bonapartism" and Stolypin himself was a latter-day Guizot, wooing the peasants to the tune of "Enrichissez-vous!" These sentiments by no means prevented Lenin from dismissing liberal critics of the reform out of hand. When liberals complained of bureaucratic interference in the lives of the peasants and lamented the use of force, he wrote, they became "reactionary whiners," for without force, without a revolutionary break, there could be no breakthrough, no rural progress.[45]

The Bolsheviks therefore could condemn the reform without actively opposing it, but they were left without a full-fledged agrarian program of their own. Their main concern was with the political implications of the peasants' path to progress. Was agrarian development likely to proceed in Russia along the reformist "Prussian" path leading to the formation of large landed estates or the revolutionary-democratic "American" path leading to independent small farmsteads? Stolypin, as we saw, had declared that successful implementation of his reform would require twenty years of peace; the Bolsheviks, uneasy spectators of the "inevitable" unfolding of capitalism, conceded that under certain conditions and given enough time the government might in fact be able to control the path of agricultural development. This, warned Lenin, would force the Party to renounce any agrarian program in a bourgeois society.

Time and events decreed otherwise. By 1917 war had brought the government's land program to a formal halt and had improved the prospects for nationalization. War, wrote Lenin, accelerates the development of state economic control under capitalism and facilitates the transition to socialism.[46] This made it possible in his view to push on immediately after the February bourgeois-democratic revolution toward the proletarian revolution and socialist objectives. In the famous "April theses" in which he advanced this position (to the consternation of many of his colleagues), Lenin vehemently opposed continuation of the war and any cooperation with the Provisional Government. His agrarian proposals were summarized in just one thesis—the sixth of ten. In it he called for the creation of a soviet of *batraks* (agricultural proletarians) to assume responsibility for an agrarian program, the confiscation of all gentry lands, and the nationalization of *all* (his emphasis) land, with model farms to be created at public expense on large estates and placed under the control of the batraks.[47]

Although Lenin's April proposals struck some Bolsheviks as precipitous, ready theoretical and political arguments were at hand to support a land nationalization policy and peasant seizure of land. As he had pointed out earlier, the Russian bourgeoisie was not yet "territorialized" in the sense Marx had in mind when describing countries with advanced capitalist agriculture. In a prolonged democratic interval, a system of individual land ownership would undoubtedly appear in Russia, and once it did, the transition to socialism would become more difficult than it would be if land could be nationalized at once with the support of "the radical bourgeoisie—the peasantry."

In addition to accepting full nationalization of all land, the Seventh Conference of Bolsheviks (April 24–29), in adopting the Party's first new agrarian program since 1906, called for the confiscation by peasants of all lands of the gentry, Church, Imperial family, "etc." All land was to be turned over to peasant soviets or to other "democratically elected autonomous local organs independent of the gentry and the bureaucrats." The conference proposed the formation of large model farms on gentry estates. The Party was to strengthen the alliance between the proletariat and the poor peasants and to organize the agricultural proletariat.[48]

Lenin shared Stolypin's view of the peasants as essentially passive proprietors temporarily radicalized by extreme economic pressure. "Millions of people won't go to revolution on order, on the advice of the Party, just because the Party tells them to, but only when driven to it by impossible living conditions."[49] While enlisting the support of the petty bourgeois peasants, the Party, he warned, should not forget their class sympathies with the bourgeoisie. The proper tactic was to try to split the poorer, more radical peasants—the batraks and semi-proletarians—from the rest. Separate organizations and soviets were to be organized for these groups. The April program predicted, accurately enough, that the movement of the poor peasants would "determine the fate and the outcome of the Russian revolution."[50]

The key to the success of that movement, according to the Bolsheviks, was organization. Point 5 of the program read: "The Party advises the peasants to take the land in an organized way." Peasants were told to organize their own revolutionary committees and assume power. Local units were to elect district and regional committees. Alongside or within these general peasant committees or soviets the Party was to form special units of agricultural laborers and poor peasants. At the same time, the peasants were encouraged to seize the land— immediately, without compensation to former owners and without waiting for the Constituent Assembly. "Take the land, take it at once," urged Pravda, "but take it in an organized way, without anarchy— under the control of the peasant soviets."[51]

Chernov criticized the notion of "organized seizure" as an illogical compound of two mutually contradictory concepts—despite his own 1905 enthusiasm for the same compound.[52] But far more than the logic of terminology was involved in the angry political attacks provoked by the Bolsheviks' policy on land seizure. The Bolsheviks, it was charged, were threatening to undo the achievements of the revolution, preventing the reestablishment of domestic tranquillity, and inviting anarchy—if not counterrevolution—all from purely partisan political motives.

Lenin replied in detail to criticisms of his faction's land policy.[53] To the charge that the confiscated land was not equitably distributed, he replied that the land was being held only temporarily, not as the property of those who seized it. It might be distributed unevenly among the peasants for the time being, but that was preferable to its far more inequitable retention by the gentry. Wealthier peasants were said to be claiming disproportionate shares of the newly acquired land because they possessed the inventory needed to work it, but the poor peasants would be even worse off if land relations were to be left to the "voluntary agreements" with landlords endorsed by the other political parties. Only the well-off peasants could afford the rents that such agreements inevitably entailed. A later redistribution of land would be arranged by the central authorities: either by the Constituent Assembly or by an All-Russian Soviet of Soviets if such an authority was created by the peasant-worker masses.

The complaint that news of land seizures was luring soldiers from the front was handled gingerly. Indifference could have fed rumors of Bolshevik treason circulating since the return of Lenin and some of his colleagues through Germany after the February Revolution. The government, in fact, was able to exploit public uneasiness about the possibility of Bolshevik collaboration with the Germans to drive Lenin into hiding and to place some of his co-workers in jail after the July Days. On this sensitive point, therefore, Lenin confined himself to observing that desertions from the military were motivated only by a fear that land was being distributed as private property; since that was not Bolshevik policy, criticism on this score was misdirected. Finally, the charge that land seizures were leading to a decline in cultivation and productivity was dismissed as totally unreasonable. Why would the peasants work less land, or work the land less well, when it was free than when they had to pay rent for it? If productivity had declined because of the breakup of large estates or because of a lack of peasant inventory, then it would be advisable to organize the collective cultivation of former estates with gentry inventory, a proposal included in the Bolshevik agrarian program.

In an enthusiastically received address to the All-Russian Congress of Peasant Deputies in May, Lenin drew a sharp distinction between the land policy of the Bolsheviks and that of the Mensheviks and SRs. It was clear to all these parties, he stated, that land should belong to the people, and that all gentry land should be given to the peasants without compensation. But only the Bolsheviks proposed that the peasants "should take all the land at once, without waiting for the Constituent Assembly, and without paying any kind of rent to the gentry."[54]

The appeal of the Bolshevik position on these points became increasingly evident. When 242 peasant instructions to delegates of the May Peasant Congress were compiled by SR editors in August to produce a Model Instruction, the peasant demands it embodied came closest to the SR program insofar as it called for a transfer of land to the state or the commune, and for an egalitarian distribution of the land with periodic redistributions. But as autumn approached and the harvests came in, the peasants became increasingly restless. The SRs were accused of playing a waiting game for political advantage, and Stalin labeled them "headless philosophers" who had betrayed the peasants.[55] The Bolsheviks by then were in an excellent position to capitalize on the peasants' dissatisfaction with the Provisional Government, since they had dissociated themselves from it and criticized it from the beginning. More and more peasants were finding it difficult to refuse the Bolshevik invitation to help themselves to the land, and although the Bolsheviks did not particularly endorse the peasants' desire to redistribute the land and equalize holdings, they did not object to it, either. "Let them do so," advised Lenin. "The important thing is the transfer of political power to the proletariat." Party agitators, now being sent in rising numbers to the countryside for political work, were told to pay close attention to the Model Instruction because it embodied what the peasants really wanted. The message they were to carry to the peasants was simple: only the revolutionary proletariat, led by the Bolshevik party, could make their wishes come true.[56]

By the end of September, Lenin was describing the situation within the country as one of "imminent crisis" and as "the greatest turning point in Russian history." "In a peasant country, under a revolutionary republican government which has the support of SR and Menshevik parties . . . , a peasant uprising is mounting. It is improbable, but it is a fact."[57] To many still-hesitant Bolsheviks, it seemed equally improbable that their "proletarian" party would be able to ride a peasant revolution to power. Yet, thanks largely to the Bolshevik agrarian program, that improbability too became fact.

9

The Peasantry in 1917

In 1917 as in 1905, revolution brought an unexpected opportunity for land-hungry villagers to take a direct part in reordering local land relations. The prospects for success in any such endeavor hinged on the degree of organization they could muster and on the amount of revolutionary pressure they could sustain on the crumbling but still resistant structure of land relations in the countryside. This the peasantry had learned from 1905, so the lessons of the Bolsheviks served as reminders more than as instructions.

Peasant Organizations

One of the most remarkable phenomena of rural life in 1917 was the appearance and proliferation of new peasant organizations. Unfortunately, this development has been little studied because the sources are poor and scattered; however, recent work has begun to shed light on the complex dynamics of rural organizations at the time.[1] Some of the new "committees" that sprang up in 1917 (the committee was the predominant form of organization) arose spontaneously in the villages. They appeared immediately after the February Revolution in some localities, and soon scarcely a hamlet was without a burgeoning crop of committees. Local groups often sent delegates to district congresses of peasants, which in turn dispatched others to provincial congresses. Many committees were formed as a result of specific government directives; others arose under the influence of unofficial outside forces. Some of the new organizations were short-lived apparitions, "one-day wonders" as they were caustically dubbed.[2] Others were subsumed by or transformed into different committees. A considerable number, such as the food committees and the land committees, formed part of a multilevel organization that covered the entire country. But incorporation of local units into a system of this sort did not, as we have seen, guarantee coordination between higher and lower levels or control of the lower by the higher. In short, the organizational situation defies orderly schematization; nonetheless, the general nature of developments is clear.

In early March self-generated peasant committees began to take shape in scattered villages in a number of regions, and within a few weeks the first provincial congresses of peasants were taking place.[3] The lower-level committees appear to have been created most often by the decision of the village or volost assembly; although their functions and authority were apt to be vaguely defined, their general mandate was to replace the local administrative infrastructure of the old regime. At times the committees grew quite large, and in such cases an executive committee might be elected to conduct affairs. The composition of the committees, the manner of their election, and their titles varied greatly from one rural locale to another. There were "committees of people's power," "committees of social security," "revolutionary committees," and "committees of mutual aid," to name just a few. On March 19 the formation of peasant committees was given a vigorous boost when the Provisional Government instructed its district commissars to create volost committees to carry out local administrative functions until volost zemstvos could be established. These provisional volost committees were to draw on other local bodies already in existence (food committees, cooperatives, and volost committees that had already been elected) and were to include local landowners and the rural intelligentsia.[4]

The law establishing the volost zemstvo, long awaited by Russian liberals, was confirmed on May 21. The peasants showed less enthusiasm for the new institutions than the government had anticipated. Delegates to the first All-Russian Congress of Peasants clearly expected the volost zemstvo to become part of the local administrative scene,[5] but when elections were held in the late summer the institution's reception in the countryside was cool. The long-standing peasant mistrust of the old zemstvo institutions was combined with a growing disenchantment with the Provisional Government and a change in the political temper of the villages. The new all-class volost zemstvos were to take over functions that the peasant volost committees had become accustomed to handle. The volost committees were predominantly peasant in social composition, especially after the first few months.[6] The peasants had little interest in sharing their new-found authority in local affairs with other social elements that had traditionally dominated zemstvo activity. As a result, when elections were held in late August and early September the voting turnout was very light, often insufficient to elect delegates. Cases of violence were reported in connection with the elections in a number of localities: electoral lists were destroyed, polling places and voting equipment were wrecked, and officials were beaten and arrested.[7] In some areas, however, hard-fought electoral campaigns were conducted by political organizations competing to get their candidates into the zemstvos.[8] The volost zemstvos were never firmly established and proved to be a short-lived innovation, yet they added temporarily to the growing list of rural organizations.

Some of the new organizations in the countryside were created by or in response to outside forces not directly connected with the government. A multitude of urban-based associations such as trade unions, factory committees, and especially political parties sent emissaries out to rural areas to promote their several causes and to organize support groups.[9] Among the more effective emissaries were members of the zemliachestvos, associations of workers who had come from the same region and banded together in the cities for mutual aid. Although the workers' groups had been established earlier and remained the most common, by 1917 soldiers and sailors also had formed zemliachestvos. More politicized and better informed than their village kinsmen, with whom they were in close contact, the members of these organizations were important links between town and country and influential forces in shaping rural opinion. The zemliachestvos often sent their own delegates to district and provincial peasant soviets and peasant congresses. Although they were nonparty organizations, they rapidly became arenas of political struggle in 1917. In Petrograd, where the zemliachestvos were strongest, a central bureau was formed in September under Bolshevik leadership. The charter of the united zemliachestvos published on October 22 declared that the "most immediate objective of the zemliachestvo organizations is the unification of the proletarian and semi-proletarian peasant masses for a common stand for their political rights, and to satisfy the economic and educational needs of the countryside." The program adopted by the united soviet called for the immediate confiscation of all land and its transfer to the people without compensation; the document ended with a flourish that nicely illustrates the Bolshevik adaptation of international Marxism to Russian conditions: "Proletarians of the world, unite. Long live Land and Liberty." By this time the united zemliachestvos of Petrograd and Kronstadt alone were linked with over twenty different provinces and had a membership of some forty to fifty thousand workers, soldiers, and sailors. In early autumn their activities intensified: they collected funds, distributed literature, and organized special courses for emissaries to be sent out to the villages. Before the October Revolution these orga-nizations had sent out thousands of political propagandists and agita-tors to rural areas in diverse parts of the country.[10]

One of the more striking forms of peasant organization to result from the urban-rural exchange was the rural Red Guard. Well aware of En-gels's conclusion that the Paris Commune of 1871 failed because it lacked sufficient popular armed force, after the February Revolution Lenin immediately urged that armed detachments of workers and poor peasants be formed. The first Red Guard units were formed in March and April, primarily from urban workers in the Party. Soon afterward, or in some cases alongside, rural units came into being. From April through October a total of 148 Red Guard units were formed in the central industrial region—75 of them rural, 73 urban. Over two-thirds of these units were created in September and October.[11] The rural units consisted primarily of workers from factories located in the coun-tryside, but by autumn the Military Organization of the Bolshevik Central Committee was calling for a "Peasant Red Guard." On October 12 the first number of the organization's new newspaper, *Derevenskaia bednota* (*The Village Poor*), called upon the peasants to take over gen-try lands with the help of the Red Guard. Two weeks later, on the eve of revolution, the paper apparently attempted to legitimate these revo-lutionary instruments in terms calculated to appeal to the petty bour-geois mentality. In addition to urging the peasants to take the land at once, the paper advised them to create a Peasant Red Guard "for the protection of the property and security of all citizens." The land was to be distributed by a soviet of peasant deputies or by a peasant revolu-tionary committee elected by the entire peasant community ("mir").[12]

The idea of peasant soviets was advanced in 1917 by different groups for different reasons. Bolsheviks, SRs, the Peasant Union, and the cooperatives were among their sponsors. The Petrograd Soviet had arisen spontaneously at the time of the February Revolution, reviving the revolutionary tradition of 1905, and numerous soviets of workers and soldier deputies sprang up to form a political base for that powerful organization. Soviets of peasant deputies were slower to develop and more loosely structured. Those that appeared early in the countryside were quite diverse in size, social composition, and purpose, and were not easy to distinguish from the many other peasant committees of the period. However, as the movement to organize soviets among the peasants spread, they assumed a definite political aspect and were in-corporated into the nationwide system of soviets as it took shape. Their backers were on the radical side of the political spectrum and viewed them as a form of popular check on the Provisional Government.

The first All-Russian Congress of Peasant Deputies in May adopted a resolution calling for the creation of soviets of peasant deputies all over the country.[13] These soviets, "organs of the peasantry on guard for the new order and for political-revolutionary work," were to unite the peasantry from top to bottom, descending from the All-Russian Soviet of Peasant Deputies through provincial, district, volost, and village soviets of peasant deputies (with a number of intervening categories to encompass all the territorial-administrative subdivisions of the country). Their tasks were: (1) to clarify the land question and to introduce such measures as possible while awaiting the Constituent Assembly; (2) to prepare the peasants for the assembly; (3) to supervise and control official agencies to assure adherence to democratic principles; and (4) to represent the peasants in all governmental and social organizations.

The congress itself had been organized with the help of the resurrected All-Russian Peasant Union, which had been quiescent since 1906. The Peasant Union, along with the cooperatives, had provided funds for the congress and hoped to provide leadership for the peasant soviets. By the end of the summer, however, that hope had been defeated, and the union slid back once more into obscurity. It was the SRs, also active in organizing the Peasant Congress, who captured the leading role at the congress and in the peasant soviets.[14]

The first Congress of Peasant Deputies was attended by well over a thousand delegates.[15] It elected an executive committee of 250 members and a presidium of 30. In the latter, most influential group there were 25 SRs but no Bolsheviks. Despite the strong impression created by Lenin's address to the delegates, the assembly followed the SR program in voting to leave final resolution of the land question to the Constituent Assembly. But the congress, which had as many soldiers as peasants among its delegates, also voted to continue the war "to a victorious conclusion."[16] This, of course, was in May, before the costly and unsuccessful June offensive and before the further deterioration of conditions in the countryside.

Although the congress and its officials promoted the organization of peasant soviets, it did not enjoy the same authority over the lower peasant soviets as did the Petrograd Soviet over the lower workers' and soldiers' soviets. As a perceptive investigator noted, "there was no peasant equivalent to the Petrograd Soviet,"[17] and the observation points to a significant difference in the status of the peasant institutions.

The SRs supported peasant soviets as ideal agencies of local self-rule and popular control pending the establishment of permanent arrangements by the Constituent Assembly. They took an active part in creat-

ing the peasant soviets and managed to retain their predominant position within them (and within most peasant organizations) up to and
even beyond the October Revolution. The Bolsheviks, who also promoted the formation of peasant soviets, viewed them rather differently, as revolutionary organs capable of challenging and ultimately replacing the Provisional Government. The Bolsheviks were initially less
successful in securing representation within the peasant soviets (both
the SRs and the Mensheviks won greater support), but they gained
ground in the fall and benefited from gains made then by the Left SRs.
Despite Lenin's call for the formation of separate soviets for agricultural laborers and poor peasants, few of these came into being.[18]

In addition to the direct organizational work sponsored by the Party,
Bolsheviks in the zemliachestvos took active part in the creation of
peasant soviets, as did the Party's rural Red Guard. Some peasant soviets were formed by converting peasant committees into soviets. Land
committees, for example, were sometimes simply absorbed and transformed into the land departments of peasant soviets. Zemstvos too
might be converted into peasant soviets after October. The desire to
free the soviets from financial dependence on the zemstvos was often a
factor in such cases, since the early provincial and district soviets of
peasant deputies were supported by contributions from zemstvos and
cooperatives.[19] Yet according to a recent Soviet study, "the peasants by
no means always understood the difference between the liquidated and
the newly formed organs of power. The class and party composition of
the first volost soviets were not sharply distinguished from the composition of the zemstvos."[20]

Before the October Revolution peasant soviets were far more firmly
established at the higher territorial-administrative levels than at the
lower. By October provincial soviets of peasant deputies existed in 67
out of 82 provinces in the country, and district soviets of this type had
been created in two-thirds of the districts of European and Asiatic Russia. At the volost level or below, however, peasant soviets were rare. In
29 provinces of European Russia (provinces where higher-level soviets
were most common) no more than 11 percent of all volosts had peasant
soviets. The figure for the country as a whole was undoubtedly well
below this, and soviets at the village level were virtually unknown.[21]

A frequently encountered explanation for the low number of volost
soviets before October is that the many other peasant committees
made them unnecessary.[22] On the other hand, it has also been suggested that the peasants' traditional village and volost community
meetings made it possible to conduct local affairs without peasant soviets.[23] The land committees were clearly present in force at the lowest

levels of rural administration, where peasant soviets were a rarity before October. Yet the long-established practice of dealing with land questions through meetings of the commune not only persisted, but was strengthened in 1917. Of the many organizational forms joining the peasants in the pursuit of their common interests after February, the commune remained the most vital, the most widespread, and the most cohesive at the immediate local level.

The "Peasant Movement"

The thrust of all peasant activities directed against the established order is described in the literature of the time and in modern Soviet texts as the "peasant movement." The movement is seen as directed toward revolution, and its strength is measured both quantitatively (the number of incidents occurring, the number of peasants involved) and qualitatively (the type of activity, the degree of political consciousness). In 1917 it was in evidence immediately after the February Revolution, and it developed markedly in the months that followed.

March brought reports of local peasant uprisings and violations of property law in many provinces. Throughout the country estates were looted and burned, rental agreements were repudiated, timber was felled illegally, and landowners and their agents were arrested. Prisoners of war were removed bodily from estates and forbidden to work for the estate owners, and agricultural laborers unilaterally established new wage rates.[24] The Provisional Government, from the initial Kadet-dominated phase to the final all-socialist stage, reacted to news of the rural disturbances with acute uneasiness. Once the decision was taken to defer settling the land question until the meeting of the Constituent Assembly, all extralegal ("revolutionary") action taken by the peasants with respect to land relations was viewed as a threat to the revolution. Circulars sent out by the central authorities to the countryside alternated (or sometimes combined) entreaties with threats.

Beginning with its first statement on the land issue on March 19, the Provisional Government inveighed against land seizure as theft by violence, "the most foolish and most dangerous means in the area of economic relations."[25] Yet in some cases peasants took possession of unused land and began to cultivate it; given the critical food situation this was clearly in the national interest. Reasoning or rationalizing along these lines, in late March a provincial congress of peasant deputies in Samara passed a set of temporary rules concerning land use. Intended to govern land relations in the province until the meeting of the Constituent Assembly, these regulations gave broad authority to volost "committees of people's power." The committees were empowered to redistribute among those willing to work them all lands and inventory not currently in use. The rental price of such land was fixed at only one-fourth of the prewar level because of the "huge risk" faced by the sower, the lack of "work hands" in peasant households, and the disproportionate prices of manufactured goods and grain. The committees were authorized to renegotiate all long-term rental contracts concluded earlier with any landowner—private, public, commercial, or communal. All commercial transactions in land were prohibited.[26] These rules were accepted by the Samara provincial Soviet of Peasant Deputies and the provincial executive committee.

Two weeks later, on April 11, the Provisional Government sent out a directive that provided for the transfer of unsown land to local food committees, which could rent it out to peasants. But this announcement, aimed at securing and improving the flow of food supplies and sent out under the signatures of Prime Minister Lvov and Minister of Agriculture Shingarev, showed far greater concern than had the Samara peasants for the property rights of landowners. Not only were they to be compensated at a "fair price" for any land taken over by the committees, but all landowners were promised compensation for any financial loss suffered as a result of crop damage on their land due to acts of violence.[27] The regulations adopted in Samara were declared illegal, and the Ministry of the Interior instructed the provincial commissar to block their implementation. When the Samara provincial Soviet of Peasant Deputies turned to the executive committee of the All-Russian Soviet of Peasant Deputies in June for support against the government in this matter, pointing out that the Samara land regulations were in accord with the resolution of the first All-Russian Congress of Peasant Deputies that had called for control of land affairs by local land committees, the executive committee declined to interfere. Moreover, after denying that the resolutions passed by the two bodies were alike, it reminded the Samara Soviet that the resolution of the All-Russian Soviet could not, in any case, be considered a "law subject to immediate enactment."[28] This is a good example of what the inferior status of the All-Russian Soviet of Peasant Deputies meant at the local level. The "dual power" shared by the Petrograd Soviet and the Provisional Government was a real political force, however murky its content and ill-defined its limits. Yet the most eminent leaders of the peasantry, urbanites and members of the intelligentsia, not only failed to share in the central power but seemed readier than their rural followers to accept that state of affairs.

As reports of rural violence kept flooding in to the government, orders were sent out to all provincial commissars to take measures to defend property. In language reminiscent of the tsarist admonitions of 1905, the government protested rural lawlessness, and once again a war-weakened militia was sent to restore order in the countryside.[29] Predicting that matters would worsen, Shingarev urged privately at the end of April that measures be passed to satisfy the land needs of the peasant population as soon as possible, without waiting for the Constituent Assembly. Yet publicly he called only for a cessation of disturbances, warning the volost land committees that property seizures would be punished and invoking moral sanctions against those who would "irresponsibly take advantage of the present difficult circumstances to satisfy their personal interests."[30] When moral exhortation proved ineffective and disorders continued to mount, the government relied increasingly on military force. Early in July the commander on the southwestern front, General L. G. Kornilov, demanded that all agrarian disorders within the territory under his jurisdiction be brought to a halt. Legal prosecution of all violators was ordered, with fines or prison terms to be imposed on the guilty. When Kornilov became Supreme Commander of the army at the end of the month, his order was extended throughout the country, and all district and provincial commissars were made responsible for its observance.[31] But the government received little assistance in this respect from the land committees it had established to deal with the prime cause of rural unrest. The committees at the lower levels all too often simply acted as the peasants' agents in bringing about the changes they demanded. In July and August alone nearly 2,000 members of land committees were arrested and jailed.[32]

On September 8, with Kornilov himself imprisoned by the panicked government on charges of counterrevolution, his order was reissued almost word for word by the new Supreme Commander, Prime Minister Kerensky.[33] Yet the steady deterioration of conditions in the weeks that followed obliged the government, at a meeting held on September 28, to consider additional measures "to combat the growing anarchy in the country, and particularly agrarian disorders." A decision was taken at this point to set up special committees to combat peasant disturbances in certain provinces. With the help of these committees the provincial commissars (or the military authorities in war zones) were to use "every means at their disposal" to suppress agrarian disorders.*

---

* *Krasnyi arkhiv*, 1936, no. 78, pp. 96–97; *EPR*, pp. 259–60. The committees were to include local representatives of the central administration and judiciary as well as representatives of local government (e.g., heads of zemstvo boards and of food committees) and of local social organizations dealing with land questions.

Most investigators who have studied peasant disturbances between February and late October have pointed to changes in the type of incident that predominated at different times. Typologies have been variously constructed, but it is generally agreed that the earlier incidents of peasant activism involved milder and more limited forms of attack on the existing order. Typically these involved partial seizures of private fields and meadowlands, compulsory renegotiation of wages and rental contracts, and arrests and expulsions of estate owners and administrators. Later activities tended to be more far-reaching, involving greater destruction and more frequent seizure of entire properties, even though the overall number of land seizures declined in the fall. Disputes over land rental figured less prominently in the later rural disturbances, but acts of violence and clashes over the use of woodlands became more common. The most intense violence took place in the central agricultural region, the Volga region, and the right-bank Ukraine. In September, 105 gentry estates in Tambov province alone were raided; in October, 106 manor houses were razed in just four districts of Tula, and 98 estates in Orel were liquidated. In these two months 164 landed properties in Penza were attacked, and acts of pillage, arson, land seizure, and arrests comprised over three-quarters of all peasant "incidents" in the province of Voronezh.[34] Yet events in these provinces were not typical of the whole country or the entire period: acts of destruction amounted to a minor (though highly important) part of the peasant movement; perhaps a fifth of the total number of incidents that took place during the peak autumn months fell into this category.[35]

The regional differences that became evident and the changes that occurred resulted from specific local and temporal factors. Land was most frequently seized in areas of acute land shortage, particularly where peasant land shortages existed alongside relatively large private holdings. In the central agricultural region, the region of greatest disturbance, the average peasant holding was 4.6 desiatins, and the average nonpeasant holding of private property was 219 desiatins.[36] In the food-producing regions it was the supply policies of the Provisional Government that evoked waves of protest during the summer. The government's grain monopoly was the target of disturbances in a quarter of all the volosts in Kazan, and in some districts such protests predominated over all other types of unrest. In September, a widespread demonstration in the province involved over 5,000 participants and lasted two and a half weeks.[37]

Seasonal variations in the agricultural cycle were clearly related to some aspects of the pattern of peasant activities: conflicts over meadowlands erupted at haymaking time; seizure of field crops occurred when the crops were ready to harvest; illegal chopping of trees and seizure of woodlands increased as autumn drew on and the need for firewood became more pressing. In the same fashion, the seizure of arable land declined somewhat once the growing season was past, but as the intensity of agricultural labor slackened the total number of incidents in the peasant movement rose.

One aspect of the movement was the phenomenon described in Soviet historiography as the "second social war," that is, the struggle within the peasantry fanned by hostility toward wealthier peasants, particularly those who had separated from the commune. Attacks against these peasants began in the first days after the February Revolution. Within a few months reports had come in from Penza, Voronezh, Orel, Viatka, Novgorod, Kazan, Simbirsk, Saratov, and other provinces describing clashes between the communal peasants and local peasants on khutors and otrubs. Even where the property of the gentry remained initially untouched, in some cases lands were forcibly taken from peasant households that had separated and consolidated their holdings.[38] Not only was the "extra" land of such households reclaimed, but the entire holding, including purchased land, might be taken over for redistribution, with the former holders obliged to reenter the commune. In some cases the communal peasants requested the permission of the central authorities to return the land to communal tenure, but more often they simply took matters into their own hands. Complaints from the dispossessed consolidators prompted the Ministry of Agriculture to telegraph local land committees that land use was to continue on its previous bases and that the compulsory elimination of consolidated holdings was "impermissible."[39] The call of the first All-Russian Congress of Peasant Deputies for an equal distribution of land among those who worked it gave impetus to the peasant movement and to attacks against individualized peasant properties, especially larger holdings. Moves against otrubs increased in a number of provinces, including Kazan, where zemstvo provincial records show that expropriations of the property of wealthy peasants occurred in over one hundred volosts.[40]

The highest rate of incidents of this sort occurred in the Volga region. This area had witnessed the greatest number of individual separations from the commune, and the communal peasants there had resisted them most strongly. The resulting atmosphere of hostility provided the background for a particularly virulent outburst of social antagonism. From March through June over one-third of all peasant incidents in the lower Volga region involved the complete liquidation of khutors and otrubs, and the rate of such incidents continued to grow. From March through October, they constituted 44 percent of the total for this region, and similar figures are reported for parts of the Ukraine.[41]

It is difficult to arrive at an estimate of the relative strength of the attack on individualized peasant property, first because the data on incidents involving property rights are far from complete, and second because actions directed against peasant property were far less likely to appear in the official records of the period than were those directed against gentry estates. The high rates of destructive activity found in the central agricultural region were not typical of the peasant movement as a whole, nor was the intensity of the "second social war" in the Volga region and the Ukraine. Acts of destruction constituted a minor part of the entire peasant movement, and the seizure of peasants' lands amounted to a minor share of all incidents of land seizure. The prime target of the peasants was the private property of the gentry, and the "first social war," encompassing the peasants' assault on that property, overshadowed the second.

Nonetheless, several Soviet investigators have attempted to calculate the relative weight of the "second social war" in the peasant movement, with results that give increasing importance to this phenomenon as more data are brought to light (or more zeal is invested in proving intraclass differentiation and conflict). According to materials of the Main Land Committee, reported to the executive committee of the All-Russian Soviet of Peasant Deputies in August by the SR N. Ia. Bykhovskii, during the months of June and July a total of 1,318 gentry properties, but only 72 khutors and otrubs, were attacked by peasants. A recent Soviet investigator has objected to Bykhovskii's report as tendentious and incomplete; since the SRs were inclined to minimize elements of social conflict within the peasantry, his comments may be valid.[42] Yet the calculation made by Bolshevik scholar Dubrovskii in 1927 shows only 6 percent of all peasant moves directed against the property of khutors and otrubs.[43] Dubrovskii's data too have been faulted by modern Soviet investigators. Attacks against consolidated peasant properties often involved "tens and even hundreds" of individual households, they report, yet were recorded as a single episode, whereas assaults on gentry property were recorded individually. As an example, the data of the Main Land Committee show only 15 cases involving khutors and otrubs in Viatka province for the eight-month period from March through October; yet investigation of a volost where one incident was reported revealed that 282 consolidated holdings were liquidated after a bitter struggle and their 2,000 desiatins of land returned to the commune.[44] One study based on a larger number of cases (line c in Table 12) stated that 11 percent of all incidents were directed against the "rural bourgeoisie."[45] This figure was raised again in short order by a subsequent study that unearthed an even greater number of incidents and attributed 20 percent of the entire peasant movement to actions taken against kulaks and peasants on khutors and otrubs. According to this tally (described by its author as still incomplete), from April through August there were over 1,880 incidents of this sort. In some areas (Penza, Saratov, Kazan, Simbirsk, and elsewhere) they amounted to well over the indicated 20 percent.[46] An increasingly higher percentage of incidents involving khutor and otrub property might be anticipated as more cases are uncovered by the detailed study of local sources that has been undertaken only lately.

Not surprisingly, the assault on peasant holdings drove some peasant proprietors to ally with the landowning gentry. By the fall the new All-Russian Union of Landowners had established 337 local branches. Samara alone had 4,000 members. In Penza the great majority of members of the ten district branches of the union consisted of peasants who held khutors and otrubs. This was also true in Orel, where more otrubs had been formed on purchased land than in any other province.[47] Peasant proprietors everywhere formed a substantial part of the membership of this and most similar organizations that sprang up in 1917 in a futile attempt to hold on to private property being washed away in the rising tide of revolution.

The first congress of the All-Russian Union of Landowners, which opened on June 1 (well attended by peasants), strikingly illustrates the dilemma of the helpless landowners. As the president's opening remarks reminded his audience, "landowners and agriculturalists [had] been the support of the state throughout the entire existence of Russia."[48] Yet the state had also been the support of the landowners. Given the symbiotic relationship between them, the destruction of one left the other vulnerable. Reports from the countryside in 1917 spoke of a widespread negative attitude toward private property among peasants, and there was now no effective state protection of the existing property order, no defense against the demands of a peasantry long accustomed to viewing private property in land as a means of exploitation. That view, moreover, had only been reinforced for most peasants by the anticommunal reform of the previous decade.

At a time when some of the highest Provisional Government officials were anxiously (if only privately) talking of the need to enact immediate land measures to pacify the peasants, Gurko was urging the Union of Landowners to demand that no law be passed on the land question before the convening of the Constituent Assembly.[49] No law was passed, but neither was there any security for rural landed proprietors. As the summer drew to a close the countryside dissolved into chaotic violence. Over three-quarters of all districts in the country were caught up in the peasant movement, and in the more populous central regions hardly a one remained unscathed.[50] With rural conditions approaching anarchy, the government appeared to be in the grip of political paralysis. In mid-October an order went out to all commissars from the Minister of Internal Affairs: they were not to interfere in land matters within the competency of the land or food committees or even to take part in their decisions. Further, as representatives of the Provisional Government they were not to subscribe to any statements concerning how the Constituent Assembly should resolve the land question.[51] When the government met on October 24 to discuss the draft laws on the regulation of land relations and on the land committees, it decided—as noted above—to defer action for further discussion. Among the reasons offered for that decision was the opinion, advanced with the obstinate confidence of the proverbial ostrich with its head in the sand, that "with winter approaching, the crisis of land relations is significantly abating."[52]

Although such contemporary perceptions of the peasant movement appear faulty in hindsight, that hindsight itself has been progressively transformed. The overall dimensions of the peasant movement in historiography have an elasticity rivaling that of the "second social war," since later investigations have progressively expanded the count of the early statistical reports on peasant activism in 1917. (See Table 12.) The contemporary statistics of the militia, for example, did not include the numerous incidents in which the police were not involved, and even the most recent data do not always indicate the number of households affected. Not only are the aggregated incidents of unequal weight, but successive investigations yield an ever-growing mountain of incidents whose appearance raises questions about the whole body of quantitative data: since more complete data are available for some localities than for others and since there are distinct regional differences in the behavior of peasants, the additional data could be skewing the global picture. The absolute figures thus clearly have their limitations. Nonetheless, most accounts show a similar dynamic for the peasant movement and therefore tend to reinforce the same general picture of its development, even when they differ on the number of incidents involved.

Whatever the numbers involved, the sources agree on a steady in-

TABLE 12

The Peasant Movement, March–October 1917

(number of incidents)

Period	Date of source				Actions of peasant committees[a] affecting land relations (e)
	1917(a)	1971(b)	1975(c)	1977(d)	
March	16	183	190	257	4
April	193	445	508	879	63
May	253	580	682	1,232	101
June	562	836	1,036	1,809	247
July	1,100	900	1,358	1,860	282
August	665	569	856	1,461	171
September	599	693	1,033	1,690	131
October	729	1,210	1,635	2,176	220
TOTAL	4,117	5,416	7,298	11,364	1,088

SOURCES: (a) Data of the Police Administration, Ministry of the Interior of the Provisional Government, Kostrikin, "Krest'ianskoe dvizhenie," p. 41; (b) Kravchuk, pp. 88, 107, 178, 203; (c) Kostrikin, *Zemel'nye komitety*, pp. 224, 269; (d) Kostrikin, "Krest'ianskoe dvizhenie," pp. 39–41; (e) Kostrikin, *Zemel'nye komitety*, pp. 217–18, 268, 307.

[a] Including land committees.

crease in peasant activity into July, a slackening in August, and a sharp climb to new heights in October. This pattern has been variously explained, but two questions related to it are still being debated. The first is: why was there a slump in midsummer? Western scholars point to the demands of the agricultural cycle as a good part of the reason why peasants were unable to become involved at that time.[53] Soviet scholars, however, have stressed political factors and explain the lull as a result of government armed repression in the countryside or growing conservatism among the land committees (see line e, Table 12). The second question has to do with the nature of the intensified peasant movement in the autumn: was it an "organized" movement or an elemental eruption of revolutionary forces? The debate revives shades of the old Bolshevik ideological controversy on spontaneity versus will. On the one hand, the peasants are said to have been reacting with violence to accumulated frustrations with the policies of the Provisional Government, reacting in opposition to zemstvo conservatism and in response to official repression. On the other, it is argued that the mounting activity and increasing violence manifested with the approach of autumn were due to the deliberate decision of the peasants (with or without the organizational assistance of the land committee and other local bodies) to put an end to the old order of land relations.[54]

This was what the Bolsheviks had been urging all along, and despite the strong hold that the SRs still retained on the peasants the Bolsheviks had been gaining ground among them.

In April Lenin had stated the case with typical political pragmatism: "Peasants, soldiers, and workers are a huge majority in the state. This majority wants all land transferred immediately into the hands of soviets of peasant deputies. No one can block a majority *if* it is well organized . . . aware [and] . . . armed."[55] With the approach of October, calling on his colleagues to take over the government, he argued forcefully that the Bolsheviks and the Left SRs constituted a majority "in the soviets, and in the army, and *in the country*" (Lenin's emphasis). There was no reason to wait longer, he insisted. The Provisional Government had no support; even the SRs referred to "Kerensky and Co." as "Stolypinites." No one would defend such a government, nor would anyone want to fight against a new government that offered peace, and land to the peasants.[56]

10

The Redistribution of Land

The Bolsheviks took power in Russia on October 25, 1917. On the evening of October 26, at the meeting of the second All-Russian Congress of Soviets of Workers' and Soldiers' Deputies, the first major item of business was ratifying a declaration read by Lenin that the new government would begin immediate negotiations for peace. Next came a decree on land.

The Decree on Land

According to accounts left by V. P. Miliutin, first Commissar of Agriculture in the Soviet government, the first draft of the decree was drawn up by himself and Iu. Larin on the evening of October 24.* Thus at the very time when the Provisional Government was deciding to defer action on a land law, its opponents were taking decisive action on that critical matter. The final version of the decree was written by Lenin and presented to the congress after approval by the Bolshevik faction.

Unlike the first Congress of Workers' and Soldiers' Soviets, the second congress was strongly Bolshevik. Various accounts place the number of their deputies at close to half or even well over half of all delegates present.[1] Peasants, on the other hand, were harder to find at the congress: only 19 of the 402 soviets represented were peasant soviets—a fact that undoubtedly contributed to the Bolsheviks' strong showing.[2] But the peasants had every reason on this occasion to throw their sup-

---

* Lutskii, "Leninskii dekret," pp. 16–17. Lutskii minimizes the contribution of the first draft, suggesting that it was rejected by Lenin since no copy is extant. Yet Miliutin, while acknowledging Lenin's decisive role in the formulation of the final document, apparently felt some pride of authorship since he wrote about the draft while Lenin was still alive and could have refuted him. Most accounts make no mention of the draft and indicate that Lenin composed the decree on the evening of the 25th and on the 26th. See, for example, the collectively authored publication of the Institute of State and Law of the Academy of Sciences, *Leninskii dekret "O zemle" i sovremennost'*, p. 31.

port behind the party. Not only were the Bolsheviks proposing immediate action on the land question, but they were offering exactly what
the peasants themselves had demanded—the second section of the decree was, word for word, Part II of the Model Instruction compiled
from the 242 peasant instructions.

The strange scene of the party of the proletariat advancing the peasant program was rendered even more incongruous by an episode that
interrupted the congress proceedings. No sooner had Lenin finished
reading the Decree on Land than the platform was invaded by an angry member of the executive committee of the peasant soviets. Two
SRs who had been ministers in the Provisional Government had been
imprisoned (along with others) in the revolutionary takeover, and the
immediate release of these "chosen representatives of the peasants"
was hotly demanded. Calm was restored when Trotsky announced that
the Military Revolutionary Committee had already decided "on principle" to release the men. Attention returned eventually to the land
decree, and it was passed with only one dissenting vote at 2:00 A.M.
The peasant delegates "were wild with joy," according to an observer.
And the Bolsheviks had reason to congratulate themselves on having
proved that they were "the only people in Russia who had a definite
program of action while the others talked for eight long months."[3]

More important, they had given the peasants just what the peasants
wanted, but with the warning that these gains could be secured only
by securing the revolution. Nationalization of land was to help the
peasants understand and accept the nationalization of banks and heavy
industry. If the economic significance of these matters escaped the
peasants, the political significance was clear: it was the Bolsheviks who
had delivered the promised land.

The Decree on Land was a brief document.[4] The first section declared that: (1) gentry property in land was abolished at once without
compensation; (2) gentry, Imperial family, monastery, and Church
lands, with all inventory, structures, and appurtenances, were placed
at the disposition of volost land committees and district peasant soviets
until the time of the Constituent Assembly; (3) destruction of confiscated property would be punished by revolutionary courts (district soviets were to keep order in, and keep account of, confiscated property);
(4) changes made on large properties before their final disposition by
the Constituent Assembly were to be based on the Model Instruction; (5) the lands of ordinary peasants and Cossacks were not to be
confiscated.

The remainder of the decree consisted of the Model Instruction.

Under its provisions private property in land was abolished forever. Land could not be bought, sold, mortgaged or rented, "or alienated by any other means." All land (the ten types enumerated included "state," "public," and "peasant"—with "etc." added for good measure) was alienated without compensation, was converted into "people's property," and passed into the use-tenure of those who worked it. The right to public support was to be available to those who suffered from the property revolution, but only for as long as was necessary for them to adapt to the new conditions.

All mineral rights and water and forest resources that were of nationwide importance were turned over to the state. Local waterways and woods were transferred to the use of communes under the regulation of autonomous local agencies. Highly developed lands such as orchards, nurseries, and animal-breeding farms were not to be divided but were transferred to the state or to communes according to their size and importance. The inventory on all confiscated land was to be turned over to the state or to communes, but no inventory was to be confiscated from smallholders.

All citizens of the Russian state, without distinction of sex, had a right to the use of land as long as they were capable of working it with their own or their family's labor. Hiring labor, however, was forbidden. If members of a land society became unable to work their land, the society was to cultivate it for them until their recovery or for up to two years. An individual who permanently lost the ability to work land because of age or illness lost the right to land but was to receive a pension from the state.

Land use was to be egalitarian: the land was to be divided among the peasants according to labor or consumer norms depending on local conditions and at local option. The forms of use-tenure were to be "completely free." Peasants could choose to hold land in hereditary or communal tenure, to hold it in *artels* (collective farms; see Chapter 12) or as khutors. Confiscated land was to go into a public land fund to be divided among those willing and able to work it. The land was to be periodically redistributed depending on population growth and agricultural productivity, but peasants were to be reimbursed for the cost of any improvements when their land was returned to the common pool.

A final paragraph added by Lenin described the decree as an expression of the will of the "huge majority of conscious peasants of all Russia" and declared it to be a provisional law that was to be put into effect as soon as possible—specifically, before the Constituent Assembly.

This remarkable document—as unique in its popular origin as in its revolutionary promulgation—is undoubtedly an authentic reflection of peasant attitudes toward the land. Lenin accepted it as such and therefore chose it as the first piece of Soviet agrarian legislation despite the fact that some of its features contradicted the Bolshevik program. A Soviet scholar's comparison of the Model Instruction with some of the local peasant instructions on which it was based has revealed that the Model, published in the peasant soviet newspaper, was an accurate summary of the individual instructions.[5] It would appear, however, that the SR editors who compiled and printed it may have been inclined to select SR terminology. For example, the phrase *sobstvennost' gosudarstva* ("property of the state") in the original instructions became the familiar SR *vsenarodnoe dostoianie* ("people's property") in the Model.[6] The Model speaks of "confiscation," but none of the instructions investigated used precisely that word, though the same intent was clear.

The correspondence of the Model with the SR program went beyond phraseology. Although Lenin accused the SRs of deceiving the peasants with false promises—a refrain that has persisted ever since in Soviet scholarship[7]—he made no attempt to deny the SR influence evident in the peasant instructions and in the Bolshevik land decree. While reading the decree to the congress he was interrupted with shouts proclaiming it an SR document. Acknowledging the fact, he dismissed it as irrelevant. The important thing was not the origin of the decree but its enactment. "As a democratic government we cannot ignore the call of the lower ranks of the people even though we may not agree with them."[8] Later, when taunted that the Bolsheviks were a fine party if they had to steal the SR program, he retorted that on the contrary, the SRs were a fine party if they had to be defeated and driven out of office for the worthwhile parts of their program to be realized.[9]

Yet the Bolsheviks were not comfortable with all they had promulgated in the Decree on Land. Although much of its content was prefigured in the agrarian resolution adopted at the Seventh Party Conference in April, the provisions of the decree for egalitarian land use and land redistribution were decidedly unpopular with Bolsheviks. Describing them as "utopian illusions" of the peasants, fostered by the SRs, Lenin nonetheless reluctantly decided to accept them as a political necessity. According to a recent study, Lenin may not have arrived at that decision until the very eve of the revolution. Until the appearance of the Model Instruction in August, he spoke out frequently against egalitarian land use. Having studied the Model intently, however, he indicated in late August that the Bolsheviks should make no move to block the peasants from the redistribution they so obviously sought. But this was not to say that the Party should sponsor such wrongheaded notions. For the next two months Lenin made no further remarks on the subject, even when speaking in detail about the peasant instructions or about land policy. His decision to compromise on this point may have been influenced by the nature of the peasant movement in the autumn or may have been a concession demanded by the Left SRs as the price of political alliance.[10] In any case, he confidently expected that the peasants would soon discover egalitarianism to be a mirage, vanishing with free access. The decree on land was intended, then, not just as a law, but also as an exercise in developing political consciousness (in addition, of course, to the immediate goal of winning peasant support). "In the fire of life," predicted Lenin, "applying [the decree] in practice, introducing it locally, the peasants themselves will find out where the truth lies. . . . Life is the best teacher, and it will show who is right."[11]

The Decree on Land was deliberately written in the most general terms in order to permit its accommodation to varying local conditions. Every attempt was made to put the new law into effect with the greatest dispatch. The villages were to be informed at once of what had been done, and by whom. "Millions of copies" of the Decree on Land were distributed in short order by "thousands of party emissaries" to the far corners of the country. Special agitprop (agitational-propaganda) workers were sent into rural areas to discuss the new government's agrarian policies and to answer peasant questions. Lenin, who had urged a decade earlier that the peasants' hazy notion of a transfer of land "to the people" should be exploited for political propaganda, took a lively personal interest in the details of the publicization of the decree.[12]

In its wholesale abolition of property in land and its overturning of the old system of land relations, the Decree on Land was a revolutionary measure. Even today, it is considered "the broadest, most radical, and most revolutionary transformation of a land system ever known to humanity," a relevant model for the juridical transformation of the agrarian structure of socialist countries.[13] From one viewpoint it signaled "the first step" in a new stage of development by transferring control over the basic means of production into the hands of the state. Yet from the peasants' point of view it meant primarily the old, familiar redivision of lands—augmented with gentry fields. In the long perspective of Russian land relations, also, there was something familiar about it, for the new stage recalled an earlier, less abrupt but no less significant development: the de-territorialization of the old boyar "nobility" by the medieval Russian autocratic state.

Chernyi Peredel: The "Black Redistribution"

If Lenin was prepared to have the peasants test their illusions in "the fire of life," the peasants for their part were quite ready to light the torch. The desire for a universal and fundamental reallotment of all the land—the age-old dream of a *chernyi peredel* or "black redistribution"—resurged in 1917 on an unprecedented scale. The term derived from the distant past when the tax-bearing peasants (the "black people") lived on unassigned state lands (the "black lands") directly administered by agents of the prince.[14] A general redistribution of all the land among the peasants had long been a popular ideal, and in the late nineteenth century it became a Populist goal. After the split of the Land and Liberty group in 1879, the antiterrorist populists took the name *Chernyi peredel* for their organization and for its short-lived newspaper. In the initial issue of the paper, editor Plekhanov, explaining the choice of title, wrote, "These two words hold the solution to the peasant problem on which all the rest depend in turn."[15]

An element in the notion of an equal share of life-supporting land for each individual went beyond purely economic considerations. In a society where the masses had long been deprived of political voice and social status, where land traditionally meant power and prestige, the desire for a *chernyi peredel* represented a broad range of unarticulated aspirations for political and social as well as economic rights. In 1917, a "semimystical" paroxysm of egalitarianism is said to have swept the countryside under the banner of this slogan, catching up even with some private landowners, who voluntarily renounced part of their land rights.[16] Yet it would hardly be realistic to attribute the widespread redistribution of land that occurred to an outburst of revolutionary fraternalism.

The mechanics of redistribution were only vaguely, and somewhat inconsistently, defined in the Decree on Land. Article 2 of the first part of the decree declared that the distribution of expropriated lands would fall to the volost land committees and district Soviets of Peasant Deputies, yet Article 8 of the second part (the Model Instruction) stated that the land would be distributed by local and central agencies ranging from communes to regional institutions. Although the soviets were the preferred agents, few peasant soviets, as we have seen, had been organized by October. Soviets of Workers and Soldiers had no land departments as a rule and in organization were not directly connected with the countryside.[17] As a result, the volost land committees established by the Provisional Government and dominated by the SRs became the official apparatus of confiscation and redistribution.

The Decree on Land provided that the land fund be subject to periodic redistribution to meet population growth and to improve agricultural productivity. However, there was no indication of how, or according to what rules, this redistribution was to take place. On November 5 in a Reply to Peasant Questions Lenin indicated that the volost land committees were to take all gentry land immediately into their custody and assume responsibility for it as people's property.[18] But detailed instructions were not sent out to the committees for another month. In the interim the Left SRs broke with the SRs to form an independent party and entered the Bolshevik government. The Left SR A. L. Kolegaev was given the post of People's Commissar of Agriculture.

In December the Soviet of People's Commissars (Sovnarkom) adopted a new statute on the land committees that called for reelection of the local committees and the inclusion within them of representatives from the soviets. The Main Land Committee was dissolved. At the same time an Instruction on the Regulation of Land and Agricultural Relations by the Land Committees was approved and published.[19]

This document provided more specific directives for the takeover of gentry property and, to a lesser extent, for its protection and disposition. The volost land committees were to elect land commissars or special "distributional soviets." These commissars, with the assistance of the land committees, the peasant soviet, the volost zemstvo, and witnesses from the community, were to compile a detailed inventory and appraisal of each confiscated property. Not only the land but also the agricultural inventory on it, including live inventory, structures, stocks of agricultural products, and supplies, was to be taken. The inventory lists were to record the quantity and quality of each item. After these registers were compiled, land commissars were to remain on the confiscated properties to guard them against looting, attempts to transfer any of the property, or other forms of loss. The committees were instructed to distribute the land equally to all who were prepared to work it with their own labor. Inventory was to be distributed to the needy. Highly developed properties were not to be broken up but were to be run by the committees themselves, and the inventory necessary for their cultivation was to remain on them.

Behind the reelection of the land committees was the hope of reducing SR influence within them and of securing firmer control of the rural situation through them. However, the new committees turned out to be far from satisfactory to the government. The problem, as described by one Soviet scholar, was that "the volost land committees forming the basis of the entire system of land committees were elected by the entire population by a universal, direct, equal, and secret vote, that is, in practice they often included even kulak elements."[20] After the dispersal of the equally unsatisfactory Constituent Assembly, which met finally and briefly in January but was closed down by the government before there was any possibility of action on the land question, the need for the land committees was reconsidered. On January 13, 1918, the third All-Russian Congress of Soviets of Peasant Deputies was formally united with the third Congress of Soviets of Workers' and Soldiers' Deputies. From this point on there was to be a single system of Soviets of Workers', Soldiers', and Peasants' Deputies. The united congress then approved a Basic Law on the Socialization of Land, a product of the Left SR agricultural administration that had been accepted by the Bolsheviks as part of the political alliance of the two parties.* The new law was shorn of all reference to the land committees and placed the distribution of land completely in the hands of the land departments of soviets. The land committees were subsequently either gradually eliminated or transformed into the land departments of the soviets.[21]

The Law on Socialization was confirmed by the All-Russian Central Executive Committee (VTsIK) on January 27, but its publication was deferred to coincide with the anniversary of the emancipation on February 19.† It embodied familiar principles of socialization advanced in the earlier SR program. All private property in land, subsoil, waters, forests, and natural resources was permanently abolished. Land was to be turned over for the equal use of all who worked it personally, and it could not be sold, bequeathed, or privately transferred. Unlike the SR program and the earlier Decree on Land, the new law made no mention of communes in connection with the redistribution of land. Along with the volost land committees, they simply disappeared from the legislation. Specifying the norms, methods, and priorities of land distribution, the law spoke only of the land departments of the soviets when it came to the actual implementation of land distribution.[22]

Yet just as in the Decree on Land the talk of using peasant soviets

---

*V. V. Kabanov, "Razrabotka osnovnogo zakona o sotsializatsii zemli," in Volkhov, p. 83. The congress actually approved only the first ("basic") part of Kolegaev's draft and authorized the government to confirm later sections to be worked out by a special commission.

† February 6, old style. The calendar was changed on February 1, which then became February 14, new style. Subsequent dates in the text are given according to the new calendar.

TABLE 13

Land Acquisitions by Peasants and the Formation of Soviets in Volosts, by Month, 1917–18

(*percent of documented cases*)

Period	Land acquisitions	Formation of soviets
Through October 1917	15%	2%
November	11	1
December	19	7
January 1918	15	39
February	8	34
March	8	13
April	8	3
May	1	1
Sometime in spring 1918	9	—
At other times	6	—
TOTAL	100%	100%

SOURCE: Makarova, p. 116. Data on the formation of soviets covers 1,357 volosts in sixteen provinces; that on the land acquisitions covers 533 volosts in six of these provinces.

had run ahead of the existence of such soviets, so the Law on Socialization somewhat anticipated developments. Questionnaires sent out by the Ministry of Agriculture and by the Moscow Oblast Executive Committee (summarized in Table 13) show that land confiscation tended to precede the formation of soviets in volosts.

In most cases, land was taken over initially by the land committees, and it was often already redistributed before the appearance of a volost soviet. The rapid disappearance of gentry property was due in part to a continuation of the autumn flare of rural violence, fanned by the heady news of the Decree on Land. Few individual proprietors, gentry or peasant, were persuaded without the use or threat of force to surrender their lands and possessions. The new revolutionary government tried, as had the old, to control the violence, but unlike the Provisional Government it encouraged and assisted the transfer of property to the peasants. One of the effective instruments employed in that process was the Red Guard. From November 1917 through June 1918 an additional 413 Red Guard detachments were formed in the fourteen central provinces. About two-thirds of these (268) were composed of peasants, and 27 more were rural detachments of workers.[23] Demobilized soldiers played an important part in the formation of the later units.

The physical dispossession of former gentry landowners was only the first step in the process of redistribution. Although the allotment of specific lands to individual households inevitably took place at the local

level, redistribution might involve higher agencies at some stage. Because the confiscated lands themselves were not evenly distributed,
there was some attempt by district and higher authorities to balance
household holdings among volosts. Transfers of land were sometimes
arranged to improve the relative position of the volosts with the least
land. For example, volosts with small holdings were occasionally given
rights to use confiscated lands located in other volosts, and neighboring volosts were obliged to transfer or exchange some of their lands in
the interests of all the villages involved. Most intercommunity redistribution of land took place within volosts or among volosts within a
district, and land transfers that extended beyond district boundaries
were rare.[24]

In most land transfers among communities and in almost all those within
villages, the familiar mechanisms of redistribution were brought into play.
The peasants knew one way to distribute the land: the commune. In
the course of the *chernyi peredel* that swept the countryside in 1917
and 1918, the commune was revived and extended beyond any of its
previous historical frontiers. Never before had so much land been under the immediate control of the peasantry. Never before had it been
so clear that the commune, whatever its origins and drawbacks, served
the peasants as well as the state. The old, traditional village organization proved to be the indispensable executor of the peasants' revolutionary testament. This was doubtless due in part to the absence of
other competent and acceptable agencies in the countryside. The People's Commissariat of Agriculture (Narkomzem) sent out a force of land
surveyors in the spring of 1918, but the amount of assistance available
from agricultural specialists was limited.[25] The commune was not only
already on the spot and best informed about local conditions, but it
filled a wider variety of peasant needs related to land redistribution.
Villages with a claim to a neighboring estate, to nearby ecclesiastical or
state lands, or to the fields of local consolidators had to find a way to
distribute them with some pretension to the equity in whose name
their confiscation was justified—and without which continued violence was inevitable. Not only did the commune have established techniques for measuring, dividing, and distributing the land, but the collective will that it was said to represent provided moral justification for
dispossessing individuals. In order to emphasize this principle (as well,
no doubt, as to ensure community solidarity through mutual com-
plicity) reluctant fellow villagers were sometimes forced by the commune to accept shares of confiscated property.[26]

The right to confiscate homes and personal property along with land
and agricultural inventory was not clearly established at first. On No-

vember 21 the Commissariat of Agriculture instructed a volost land committee that only the latter were subject to alienation under the Decree on Land, and that residences and their furnishings should be left at the disposal of their owners. Yet only a few days later the same agency informed all provincial and district land committees that estate houses were to be put to community service as schools, hospitals, shelters, or theaters. Although the instructions issued to land committees in December failed to clarify the situation, directives sent out in April 1918 in connection with the Law on Socialization called for the land departments of soviets to expel former estate owners from their erstwhile properties.*

Gentry landowners were the primary, but not the only, target of confiscations. Church and monastery lands as a rule were transferred entirely to the local land fund and redistributed. Clerics and monks who were willing to work the land could apply for an allotment on the same basis as others. At the time of the October Revolution, there were 1,061 Orthodox monasteries in Russia and about one hundred more belonging to different churches. They had a membership of 92,000 (21,000 men and 71,000 women) and owned over a million desiatins of land of various types. Although some of the monastery land was confiscated at once, the peasants were reluctant to turn out nuns. However, in 1919 and 1920, under pressure from local authorities, many of the remaining establishments were converted into agricultural collectives. By 1922 almost three-quarters of the Orthodox monasteries and most of their land had been secularized; the rest were located in territory separated at the time from the Soviet state.[27]

A questionnaire sent out by the Central Statistical Administration (TsSU) in the summer of 1922 elicited information on land redistribution from 228 districts (1,133 settlements) in twenty-nine provinces. In about half of the 1,067 settlements responding on this point there had been no change in the amount of allotment land; 66 percent had held redistributions. Those that had gained land had an average addition of 314 desiatins per settlement. Respondents to a question on the origin of the additional land (464 replies) indicated that most of it (61 percent) came from gentry property, 10 percent derived from Church and monastery land, and 19 percent was from the land of peasants. Much of the peasant land that was taken over had been in consolidated holdings and much was purchased land. In some areas up to four-fifths of the

---

*Selunskaia, *Izmeneniia*, 1917–1920, pp. 199–201. Gentry whose lands were confiscated and who had no other source of income were entitled, if they were unable to work, to receive a monthly minimum subsistence stipend at the discretion of the provincial land committee. The Law on Socialization gave them the right to receive a pension equivalent to that given at the time to soldiers.

property purchased by peasants had been alienated and redistributed, and less than half of the khutors and otrubs on allotment land had survived.[28]

In some localities the long-smoldering resentment toward consolidators was vented in clearly punitive actions. In Vladimir province, for example, all land in khutors and otrubs was ordered transferred to communes; buildings on the land had to be removed at the owner's expense, and the former proprietors were required to move.[29] In 60 settlements in one district of the province, all consolidators were deprived of land allotments.[30] The liquidation of consolidated farms was especially evident in the communal strongholds of the central agricultural and Volga regions, where hostility against separators had been a conspicuous element of the peasant movement before October.[31] However, there were substantial local and regional differences in the treatment of khutor and otrub peasants. In some cases only purchased land was requisitioned; in others allotment land too was subject to alienation. In the central agricultural region, for example, allotment land was included in redistributions in Tambov, Riazan, and Orel, but not in Tula.[32] Of 24 provincial decrees analyzed by one investigator, 15 stipulated that all land be subject to redistribution regardless of prior ownership; regulations adopted at the district level typically specified limits for holdings of enumerated categories of land. Peasants in some localities were allowed to retain their consolidated holdings but had them cut back to the local norm. In some places, consolidators were treated sympathetically and allowed to keep one and a half times or even twice the norm (on the grounds that they were technically advanced agricultural units); in others they were forced to surrender all of their land to the commune, accept a normal allotment, and return to the old strip system of communal agriculture.[33]

Though some peasants were forced back into the commune during the *chernyi peredel*, others apparently returned voluntarily. Where redistribution was conducted by the commune, only its members had a voice in the process. A land official working in the countryside at the time recorded the inquiry of one calculating peasant about whether he could rejoin the commune in order to receive an allotment of gentry land and then separate from it again.[34] Presumably this was not an isolated case, and similar motives may have prompted others to take their chances once more with the commune.

The redistribution of land was a major and widespread phenomenon after October, but it did not occur everywhere, nor did it necessarily encompass all the land where it did take place. Materials collected by the Commissariat of Agriculture show that general redistributions involving all the land and all the peasants of a commune took place less frequently than did partial readjustments.[35] Sometimes only the newly acquired lands were parceled out, and only among the landless or poorest peasants, although at least some of the old lands of the commune were often involved as well. Allotment holdings were frequently untouched except for "surplus" land, or where there was little agricultural land available for confiscation. In Vologda province, for example, all of the land was redistributed in 36 volosts, partial redistributions took place in 79, and none occurred in 34.[36]

The original Decree on Land called simply for egalitarian use of the land based on local labor or consumer norms. Subsequently the Law on Socialization specified "consumer-labor" norms as standards to be established on the basis of a nationwide census of the existing land and population. Independent norms were to be set up for different zones based on the type of field cultivation practiced in the area. The amount of land to which a household was entitled was to be calculated from the zone norm applied to the amount of labor power and the number of mouths to be fed in the household. Children below the age of twelve were considered incapable of field work and did not qualify for allotments as labor units but were reckoned as consumer units. Because the projected census could not be carried out in time to provide immediate guidelines (zone norms never were worked out) the norms actually used were fixed by local authorities or, more realistically, the commune simply divided the available land among those whom it accepted as having a legitimate claim.[37]

The most common basis of distribution in local practice was the consumer norm—the number of eaters in a household. In mid-1918 some 600 volost soviets in eighteen provinces of central European Russia indicated in response to an official questionnaire that about 70 percent of their redistributions had been conducted on this basis. In the TsSU sample taken in 1922 this was the criterion used in 88 percent of the villages investigated.[38] Nine percent had allotted land on the basis of the number of males in households, 2 percent considered the total work force in the household, and 1 percent held on to the old "revision soul" as the basis for redistribution. The consumer norm was the most radically egalitarian approach to redistribution, but not always the most practical one. In households where the number of mouths considerably outran the number of work hands it could lead to an allotment that was too large to cultivate without the use of hired help, a practice now forbidden. To avoid this problem there was often some attempt to take the household's labor force into account, even when its consumption needs were given priority.[39]

The norms themselves varied considerably from one locality to another. District norms in Riazan province were from 0.9 desiatins to 1.8 desiatins per person; in Samara they extended all the way from 1 to 8.5 desiatins.[40] The spread within districts sometimes reflected an attempt to deal with differences in land quality: higher norms could be set for land of inferior quality. The difficulty of weighing the qualitative as against the quantitative aspects of land for redistributional purposes was a constant problem. In order to speed up the distribution of land in time for spring planting, norms were most often established simply by dividing the total amount of available land by the number of people qualifying for it. The resulting "arithmetical norm" ignored the economic value of the land. Productivity was not taken into account, and households receiving equal amounts of land could find themselves the recipients of quite unequal values.

Yet determination of the value of newly acquired land could be cumbersome. In Tula province an effort to differentiate types of land economically led to the establishment of 46 categories.[41] Other local approaches, some fairly sophisticated, sought to establish norms properly weighting the quality, quantity, and income of the land, but in general a fine-honed balance proved immediately unattainable.[42]

The dynamics of redistribution, as of most other peasant activities, were influenced by the agricultural cycle. Fields allotted for spring crops were distributed in the early spring, meadowland and fallow were divided in the summer, winter cropland in the fall.[43] In the first flush of legal land seizures, fields that had been sown with a winter crop presented a special problem. Gentry lands were immediately confiscated, but in order to avoid crop losses fields were left intact for the growing season, and the local soviet (or land committee) was made responsible for harvesting them. This was arranged by hiring landless laborers or organizing artels. When the sown fields belonged to large-holder peasants who had themselves planted the crop, the land was often left with them until after harvest. If such land was confiscated payment might be made for the labor and seed invested in it.

By the spring of 1918 the bulk of the confiscations had been completed and most of the confiscated land intended for spring crops had been temporarily allotted.[44] The new land was generally redistributed on a temporary basis, often for only one crop season or for one year. At first this was to allow for the decisions of the Constituent Assembly. Later it was a convenient way of facilitating compromises and of providing for the return of soldiers and, increasingly, for the influx from the cities. The temporary nature of allotments of redistributed land was specified in the instructions accompanying the introduction of the Law on Socialization on April 11, 1918. As economic conditions in urban areas deteriorated with the intensification of the food shortage and the closure of factories, many of the "cook's children" returned to the countryside. An average of six families (40 individuals) reappeared in villages in the TsSU investigation, and in some regions the average was as high as nineteen families per village. In addition, new families who had never belonged to the village appeared and claimed the right to work the land under the new legislation. Almost all of the "returners" and nearly half of the newcomers were given allotments by the communes investigated. The rate of acceptance was highest in central Russian regions with a strong communal tradition.[45]

By the latter half of 1918 general redistributions involving allotment land as well as new lands were more widespread.[46] One reason for this was the collapse of resistance by the better-off peasants. In some areas they had put up a strong and temporarily successful opposition to redistribution, but by the fall they were obliged to succumb to the demands of the poorer peasants, who were now encouraged by officially backed committees of poor peasants. Meanwhile the organizational support of the wealthier peasants had been cut off: in July 1918 the Union of Landowners was closed down by the political police.[47]

In the years after 1918 the shake-up of the land tenure system continued, although on a diminishing scale. Some of the lands allotted temporarily in 1917 and 1918 were redistributed again in 1919 and in 1920 in accordance with a 1919 statute, Socialist Land Organization and Measures for the Transition to Socialist Agriculture. Lands that had been redistributed among villages and volosts on this basis were legally secured to them in 1922.[48] In areas affected by the war or by civil war, in remote regions, and where local conditions reinforced the resistance of former property owners, redistribution was delayed. But as the position of the new government stabilized and its authority was extended, the *chernyi peredel* was extended. In 1917–18 it primarily affected the central European provinces; following the civil war it spread over the rest of the country, and it continued on the peripheries throughout the 1920's.[49]

The amount of land acquired by the peasants as a result of the long-awaited *chernyi peredel* is a vexing question. Data of the Commissariat of Agriculture for 32 provinces show that of 24.2 million desiatins of agricultural lands formerly held by the gentry, the state, or the Church, 16.4 million had been transferred to the peasants by November 1918.[50] However, the data for that early period were incomplete, and the process of redistribution continued well beyond 1918. Another set of commissariat data on agricultural land turned over to the peasants in 28 provinces of central European Russia for late 1918 and early 1919 moved the figure up to 30 million desiatins; and it was estimated that another 8 to 10 million desiatins had been taken from largeholder peasants and redistributed.[51]

For many years, right up to the present, it has been routinely repeated in the literature that the peasants gained 150 million desiatins of land from the revolution.[52] Some years ago Soviet historian V. P. Danilov attempted to track down the derivation of this global figure, only to conclude that the available sources made it all but impossible to specify exactly how much land the peasants received after October; only after critical analysis of the existing sources and intensive nation-wide study of local materials would it be possible to arrive at a reasonably accurate answer. Returning recently to the challenge, Danilov reviewed a formidable mass of relevant land statistics from before and after the revolution.[53] His careful investigation has permitted some correction and refinement of the figures on land transfers, but reveals problems with the data that tend to confirm his earlier conclusion.[54] On the whole, it suggests that the established figure of 150 million desiatins in peasant land gains is considerably inflated.

In 1927 TsSU published aggregate data on landholding in the USSR and in the RSFSR (Russian Republic) for that year and for 1917. According to that material, during the decade peasant holdings of agricultural land had increased in the country as a whole by about 74 million hectares, rising from 240 to almost 315 million hectares. This included a gain of 48 million hectares within the RSFSR, where peasant holdings rose from 185 to 233 million hectares.[55] (See Table 14.)

Danilov states that the data on the RSFSR (compiled by the Commissariat of Agriculture), despite the absence of figures for the autonomous republics, provide the most accurate general information on land redistribution. The most important flaw in these statistical records, in his opinion, is a failure to include peasant acquisitions of woodlands after the Forest Code of 1923 authorized the transfer of extensive local wooded property to the peasants for agricultural use. Correcting for that omission, he concludes that peasants in the RSFSR had actually received an additional 10 to 12 million hectares by 1927, and several million more by the end of the decade.[56] This raised peasant land acquisitions to 61–62 million hectares. A methodical search of local source materials for the autonomous republics and regions enabled Danilov to establish gains in peasant landholding in these territories that raised the total peasant land acquisition for the RSFSR to 77 million hectares of land and woods for the twelve years following the revolution, an increase of 29 million hectares over the earlier figure.[57]

TABLE 14
Peasant Land Gains, 1917–29
(million hectares)

Area	1917	1927/29	Percent increase
USSR:			
Source (a)	240	315	31%
Source (b)	240	337	40
RSFSR:			
Source (a)	185	233	26
Source (b)	185	262	42

SOURCES: (a) TsSU, *Itogi, 1917–1927,* pp. 118–19. The RSFSR data are based on materials of the Commissariat of Agriculture, RSFSR, but do not include the autonomous republics or regions.

(b) Danilov, "Pereraspredelenie," pp. 261–310. RSFSR data include the autonomous republics and regions with the exception of Khiva, Bukhara, and Tadzhikistan.

Material on the other republics, with the partial exception of the Ukraine and Belorussia, is said to be less reliable than that for the RSFSR. A check of the data on peasant gains outside of the RSFSR indicated the need for a downward revision of figures by 6 million hectares. The bottom line of Danilov's complicated ledger, then, is a net increase of about 23 million hectares in peasant land throughout the country. Instead of the earlier global figure of 74 million hectares, we can now substitute 97 million hectares. But this amounts to only 89 million desiatins. Although Danilov points out that the data are still incomplete and that the "transfer of new lands to the peasants in the course of collectivization" must be taken into account, the peasants' revolutionary landfall falls far short of the legendary 150 million desiatins.

Moreover, the new figures, like the old, consider all land that was privately owned by individuals in 1917 as transferred to the peasants by 1927. Yet, as indicated in Table 10 (p. 84), in 1917 individual peasants in European Russia owned 16.8 million desiatins. If this amount is deducted from the 1927 total, the gain drops to about 72 million desiatins.[58] Although the changes in landholding after the revolution should by no means be minimized, in considering the amount of land turned over to peasants it must be also kept in mind that up to 20 million desiatins of nonallotment land had been rented by peasants in 1917 and were therefore already in their use.[59]

Regional and local studies show that the land acquired by the peasants as a result of the revolution was far from evenly spread throughout the country. Data for the central agricultural region for 1917–18 indicate a gain of 28 percent over the peasants' prerevolutionary allotment land.[60] In the Ukraine, in contrast, there was a gain of 61 percent between 1916 and 1923 in the amount of agricultural land (without woods) held by the peasants. With subsequent additions and the inclusion of woodlands the increase may have reached 76 percent.[61] On the local level the disparities could be more extreme, ranging from no gain at all (or even a loss for previously well-endowed communities) to acquisitions that doubled the prerevolutionary fund of peasant land.[62]

The average amount of land received by a peasant also varied considerably with the locality. Nowhere did it reach really large dimensions, and where land was scarcest the average per capita acquisition was quite small. In some provinces it came to less than a tenth of a desiatin; only in Astrakhan, Samara, and the Don region did it climb above a desiatin. In the provinces of central European Russia the increment averaged only between a quarter and a half of a desiatin per person; in five central agricultural provinces it averaged 1.5 desiatins per household, ranging from 1.2 desiatins (Kursk) to 2.2 desiatins (Tula).[63] Yet since the land gains were not distributed in equal parcels, the average may be misleading. Landless peasants and peasant smallholders profited most, and sometimes improved their relative positions dramatically.[64]

Increasing the holdings of the lowest strata of the peasantry, in part at the expense of the upper strata, led to a flattening of the social pyramid. The number of landless peasants dropped by 1919 to less than half of the figure for 1917, while the group at the other end of the scale, with holdings above 10 desiatins, was cut to a quarter of its former size (see Table 15). The state's "regathering of the lands" had resulted in a substantial leveling of rural society.

Among the factors contributing to the rise in the number of smallholdings was an increase in family divisions. These were motivated in part by a desire to keep family holdings below norms of confiscation and to maximize the number of claims for allotments. Attempts to qualify for larger holdings by adopting children are said to have been among the reasons the family law code of 1918 prohibited adoptions.[65] Family divisions, which affected less than two percent of all households per year in prerevolutionary times, are said to have taken place in a total of over ten percent from 1917 through 1920.[66] Although the tendency toward fragmentation of family units might be viewed as individualistic, it developed simultaneously with the collectivist tendency toward social reconsolidation in the rejuvenated commune.

The economic consequences of land redistribution rapidly became apparent. By 1919, 96.8 percent of all agricultural land was in the hands of peasant cultivators.[67] Over 3 million landless peasants had received allotments, and gentry property had been virtually eliminated. The peasants had been freed from land payments amounting annually

TABLE 15
Changes in Landholding, 1917–19
(percent of peasantry)

Amt. of cropland owned	1917	1919
None	11.5%	6.6%
1–4 desiatins	57.6	72.2
4–9 desiatins	25.8	19.7
Over 10 desiatins	5.1	1.5
TOTAL	100%	100%

SOURCE: TsSU, *Trudy*, 6:21.
  NOTE: The data cover 225 districts in 25 provinces.

to over 700 million gold rubles. An outstanding debt of 1.4 billion gold rubles owed to the Peasant Land Bank was canceled, and the actual savings gained by the peasants as a result has been calculated at 3.5 billion gold rubles when interest payments, penalties, and the cost of state subsidies to the bank are added to the debt principal.[68] The metamorphosis in the structure of land relations, however, was accompanied by a decline in the average size of land holdings and a loss of technical efficiency. Along with other factors, this contributed to a steady decline in agricultural productivity and in marketing. Part of the problem lay in the lack of inventory of the peasant smallholder, part in diseconomies of scale. The negative economic aspects of the redistribution of land were acknowledged at the time but were called inevitable. To justify the government's policies, sympathetic observers pointed to the example of Hungary, where the failure of a communist revolution in 1919 was attributed to the fact that the land was not turned over to the peasantry.[69] The economic cost of redistribution, therefore, was viewed as part of the price of successful revolution.

The political result of redistribution was twofold: the destruction of the economic base of the government's opposition and the creation of active support for the new regime among the peasants. Insofar as it deprived the gentry and Church of their property and seriously weakened the position of the better-off peasants, the *chernyi peredel* was politically opportune, whatever theoretical objections to it the Bolsheviks entertained. During the critical year following the revolution, it kept the peasants involved with local affairs and gave many, at least for the time being, a sense of forward motion, a sense that the potential for a better life was being realized.

But the "fire of life," as Lenin anticipated, left cold ashes in some quarters. Asked whether they were content with the existing division of land and with the communal system, slightly over half of the 1,023 settlements that replied to the 1922 TsSU questionnaire reported some dissatisfaction. Almost one-fourth of these villages (i.e., about an eighth of the respondents) stated that all peasant strata were unhappy with the prevailing land arrangements. Most of the remainder indicated that it was the poor and middle peasants who were dissatisfied; only one-sixth reported that the wealthier peasants were grumbling.[70]

On the basis of materials in central and provincial archives, Danilov concluded that the peasants had almost immediately lost faith in the *chernyi peredel*. "It cannot be said that in 1918–20 the peasantry fully rejected the principle, but the fact is that disenchantment with egalitarian land use was already beginning in 1918."[71] The highest rate of discontent shown in the TsSU sample was in the Volga (especially the Lower Volga) and central agricultural regions, precisely where the greatest amount of unrest had been in evidence before the revolution. Yet it is no easy matter to interpret the 1922 responses because the settlements reporting from the Lower Volga region had experienced one of the highest rates of land redistribution (52 percent), while those in the central agricultural region had the lowest (6 percent).

There was an obvious incongruence between the intended improvement of the peasants' situation through land redistribution and the actual deterioration of agricultural productivity. This was only one of a number of contradictions apparent in the course of revolutionary events. One of the most striking is the fact that the Bolsheviks, while maintaining an uncompromising position on the inevitability of class war within the peasantry, sponsored (however unenthusiastically) an egalitarian redistribution of land that assumed the existence of a unified community of interests, a notion totally antithetical to the concept of class struggle. In this the Bolsheviks, however logically inconsistent, were highly realistic. In contrast, it was quite unrealistic of the SRs to expect the wealthier peasants to surrender their advantageous position without a struggle.

Another contradiction was apparent in the conflicting impulses of the peasants. On one hand was the desire of each household for its own (larger) land holding, on the other a longstanding dislike of large private properties as a source of exploitation. Thus, the ambivalence of the Bolshevik stance in October was matched by the peasants' own perceptions of property. As much as anything else, it was this cognitive resonance that won the peasants over to support the Soviet government. As Lenin was to acknowledge in 1921: "We won out in Russia because we had on our side not only the indisputable majority of the working class . . . , but also because immediately after our seizure of power half of the army, and in the course of several weeks nine-tenths of the peasantry, came over to our side."[72]

The accord between the Bolsheviks and the peasants was tenuous to the extent that it rested on a temporary compromise on the part of the Party. The contradictions in the peasants' attitudes toward property were solidly reconciled within the commune, however, for there the desire for both a holding of one's own and protection against exploitative private control of the land were satisfied.

Within the limits of the supply of agricultural land, the *chernyi peredel* was unable to satisfy the exaggerated hopes of the peasants. Yet in the peasants' attempt to apply their own solution to the land problem the Russian land commune "reached the apogee of its power and of its development,"[73] in the judgment of a contemporary scholar who had studied the institution for decades—and had helped to establish the prerevolutionary opinion that the commune was an obsolescent institution. The whole trend of the anticommunal agrarian revolution of the previous decade was abruptly reversed by the 1917 revolutions. The commune that had been whittled back in the course of the preceding decade blossomed over virtually all of the agricultural land in the country. By 1920 the commune encompassed almost all rural households for which data is available.[74] The Stolypin negation of the commune after the revolution of 1905 had undergone in its turn the negation of the revolution of 1917, and the commune had entered a new historical phase.

PART IV

Communes under War Communism 1918-1921

In the spring of 1918 two developments combined to produce a critical challenge to the Soviet government. First, the costly Treaty of Brest-Litovsk brought respite from one war but released hostile military elements within the country to mount an internal offensive. Then, as civil war spread, the growing food crisis in the cities led the government to put pressure on the peasants, arousing a strong negative reaction and some active resistance.

Attempts to deal with the difficult rural situation, with food supply problems and their political implications, led the government to sponsor a number of institutional innovations and developments: the committees of poor peasants, the system of rural soviets, and new forms of collectivized agriculture. This was a period of rapidly changing conditions when policies were improvised, modified, and sometimes abandoned in a process of trial and error as the new regime struggled for survival. The new political bodies and forms of economic organization that appeared in the countryside during the years of War Communism posed a threat to the traditional hegemony of the commune in local economic and administrative affairs. Despite this threat and the disastrous effects on agriculture of war, revolution, and civil strife, the commune continued to provide the basic framework structuring the rural economy and to be a major element of social stability in the life of peasants.

11

Organizational Conflict in the Countryside

The period of War Communism, from the spring of 1918 to the spring of 1921, is simpler to define than the policy of War Communism. It has been suggested, in fact, that there was no such thing as a policy of War Communism, if policy is understood to involve a deliberate choice among perceived alternatives. The government's measures have been described instead as a series of specific military and "communist" reactions to a succession of critical problems.[1] The decision to react with military and communist measures may in itself have been a deliberate choice; sidestepping the philosophical problem of human options, it seems reasonable to assume that a government's actions reflect its policy. Although the Soviet government dealt with a wide range of concerns between 1918 and 1921, undoubtedly "food requisitioning was the basic part, the main element, in the policy of 'War Communism.'"[2]

Food supply problems led to the creation of the Committees of the Poor late in the spring of 1918. Well before the appearance of the committees, organized bands scouring the villages for caches of grain and food supplies had become a familar feature in the countryside. Such bands were sent out by factories and other organizations in the hungry cities to find food for their members; military units lacking provisions similarly sent out their own foraging detachments. But these piece-meal efforts had done little to alleviate the problem.

Immediately after the October Revolution the new government had confirmed the official grain monopoly, simultaneously promising to improve the flow of essential consumer goods from industry to the villages. However, the peasants, as before, proved reluctant to turn over their grain for low fixed prices paid in a depreciating currency in a market almost devoid of consumer goods. The situation failed to improve. In January 1918 only 7 percent of the grain supplies designated for Moscow and Petrograd were actually delivered. The following month the rate was pushed up to 16 percent, but by April it was down to 6 percent, and in May it sank even lower.[3] Not all of the problem could be attributed to the peasants' economic resistance or, as sometimes charged, to "kulak sabotage." The loss of important grain-producing areas during and after the war and the control of major agricultural areas by elements hostile to the government seriously curtailed the flow of grain to the urban centers. By the summer of 1918 most of the territory that had produced a marketed surplus in 1917 was in the hands of enemies of the regime or cut off from the center: the Ukraine, Siberia, the Don and Northern Caucasus region, and part of the Volga territory.[4] Within the area still under central control, agricultural productivity had been adversely affected by the *chernyi peredel*. Nonetheless, it does seem likely that some of those who had a surplus deliberately withheld grain. Since industrial commodities were not available, a peasant had little incentive to surrender his surplus; increased personal consumption or stockpiling in the hope of future price increases was still preferable.

At the end of March 1918, over one billion rubles was assigned to the Commissariat of Food Supply "for barter with the village."[5] Specific consumer goods were to be made available to the commissariat to exchange directly for the grain and other food products required to fill state quotas.[6] But there was little beyond paper with which to barter. As food shortages in the cities forced factories to close and workers to retreat to the villages, industrial goods grew scarcer. By April 1918 a third of the factories in Petrograd were shut down.[7] On November 25, 1917, the government had declared a state monopoly on the distribution of all agricultural equipment and machinery, both domestic and imported,[8] but it was unable to utilize market demand for such goods to obtain grain from the peasants since so little equipment was available. The production of agricultural machinery and implements in 1917 was only 15 percent of the prewar level, and imported agricultural machinery even in 1916 had amounted to less than one percent of that in 1913.[9]

The period in late spring and early summer when stores from the last harvest are depleted and the new planting is not yet productive is traditionally the lean season in rural Russia. During this period in 1918 there were many reports of starvation. Food supplies on the free market (meat, produce, whatever was available) were sold at exceptional prices, and a black market trade in grain flourished. The daily bread ration in Moscow and Petrograd dropped to 50 grams.[10]

Unable to draw essential food supplies out of the countryside, the government decided, in the interests of the urban population, the Red Army, and its own political survival, to force them out. An assault on the entire peasantry was considered unnecessary since it was assumed that the bulk of surplus grain was held by the wealthy peasants, the kulaks. Launching a campaign to improve the flow of foodstuffs, the government employed the tactic that the Party had urged all along in relations with the peasantry: the exploitation of class rivalries. Poor peasants were to be enlisted in the struggle against wealthier peasants.*

The Committees of the Poor

In May 1918 several important decrees were issued by the All-Russian Central Executive Committee and the Council of People's Commissars of the RSFSR reorganizing and giving exceptional authority to the Commissariat of Food Supply in the "struggle with the rural bourgeoisie concealing and speculating in grain."[11] A food supply dictatorship was established. All surplus grain was ordered turned over to the state at fixed prices, and anyone refusing to surrender grain above the amount needed for seed and household consumption was declared an enemy of the people, subject to at least ten years imprisonment and expulsion from the commune. In order to deal with such enemies and to confiscate their grain, the Commissariat of Food Supply was empowered to raise an armed force of workers and poor peasants, a "supply-requisition army." These decrees were soon followed by another on June 11, On the Organization of the Village Poor and the Means of Supplying It with Grain, Basic Commodities, and Agricultural Implements.[12]

Committees of the rural poor were to be organized in villages and volosts to assist local procurement agencies in taking grain surpluses "from kulaks and the wealthy." In return for their services they were to be given control of the local distribution of grain, basic necessities, and agricultural equipment, as well as the right to determine who was to receive them. To provide the peasants with incentives to collect grain rapidly, the government offered a bounty. All Committees of the Poor (*Kombedy*, as they soon became known) were to be rewarded by receiving free the grain to which members were entitled under local

---

*The moot question of whether the different strata within the peasantry actually constituted distinct classes evoked considerable and prolonged discussion among Marxist theorists, but there was no disputing the difference between the relationships of a landless, horseless *batrak* and a well-off kulak to the means of production. Marx, in different contexts, spoke of a peasant class and of peasant classes. See Lefebvre, pp. 120–21; Selunskaia, *Izmeneniia, 1917–1920*, pp. 222–25, reports that the data available do not make it possible to establish the number of poor peasants, but show that only 2 percent of the peasants at this time can be classified as "clearly kulaks."

norms, provided they completed by July 15 the requisition of all local grain designated as surplus by provincial and district authorities. Committees that completed collections by mid-August were to be supplied with grain at a 50 percent reduction in the government's fixed price, and those finished by the end of August were to receive a 20 percent cut. Similar though lesser bargains were offered in basic consumer goods and agricultural equipment.

Since the requisitions were supposed to be directed against the better-off peasants, these not only were ineligible for membership on the Committees of the Poor, but could not participate in elections for them. Yet newly arrived outsiders were eligible to vote and to be elected along with the local inhabitants. This provided a firm foothold for the contingents of urban workers who were arriving in the countryside in growing numbers as official detachments of the food supply army. Members of these armed units (*prodotriady*), determined to ferret out grain, unhampered by personal attachments, and unintimidated by local potentates, were ideal candidates—from the government's point of view—for the Committees of the Poor.

The first task stipulated for the supply detachments was to develop the poor peasants' political consciousness, to make them aware of their own interests. In the process the instructors were to get peasants to reveal hidden grain stores. In their zeal, or desperation, these paramilitary units often extended the definition of "surplus" to include grain required by peasants for their own subsistence; the label "kulak" was stretched to fit anyone who had or was suspected of having confiscable supplies. The other major task of the supply detachments was to organize the rural poor, and in this connection they played an important role in forming the committees.[13] During the period of War Communism, over 125,000 men were sent into the countryside in supply detachments. The figure includes 45,000 for the "army" of the Commissariat of Food Supply, 75,000 in military supply detachments for the regular army, and 5,000 workers enlisted for work in food supply organs.[14] Many of them were Communists (the new name was adopted in March 1918), and more were Party sympathizers. In the summer and fall of 1918 they served as the sparkplugs of the Committees of the Poor. They were joined by the workers who flowed back to the villages as factories closed and by the returning politicized soldiers.

Committees of the Poor sprang up most densely where industrial workers (and food shortages) were concentrated, but they appeared most rapidly in the central agricultural region, to which the great bulk of the food detachments were sent.[15] Over 80 percent of the committees were organized in September and October 1918, largely as a result of energetic measures taken to enlist workers and poor peasants to collect the harvest, measures that included dispatching special "harvest-requisitioning detachments" into the countryside. By December Committees of the Poor appear to have been established in a majority of the villages in the area under Soviet control; over 130,000 had been organized in 33 provinces of the RSFSR.[16] According to data for Tambov province, only a half to two-thirds of their members were local peasants. Workers from the cities comprised about one-fifth of the members of village committees, were presidents of a fourth of them, and held the post of treasurer (dealing with all requisitions) in two-thirds.[17]

Under the influence of the committees, the poorer peasants, with their newly enhanced "awareness," began to confiscate not only grain but land from the more prosperous peasants. During the period of committee work, peasant land figured more prominently in the *chernyi peredel*, and it was because of the work of the committees that most of the *general* redistributions of land occurred in the latter half of 1918. The alliance of poor peasants and proletarians during the civil war was based on an economic pact. As Lenin put it, "The peasant got all the land and was defended from the gentry and the kulaks by the workers' state; the workers got food from the peasantry on credit pending the revival of heavy industry."[18]

The tactic of divide and rule applied to the peasants was unacceptable to the Left SRs. In their view the government's policy should have aimed to integrate the peasantry on the basis of the equal right of all to land rather than to fragment it into hostile sectors. Already at odds with the Bolsheviks over the Brest treaty and unable to block the formation of the committees or the seizure of peasant lands, they came to a final parting of the ways with their former allies in July.[19]

Working in conjunction with the food detachments, the Committees of the Poor proved an effective agency of supply. The size of the new crop was reckoned in the fields before harvest to prevent concealment. Thanks to the efforts of the committees, the state procurement organs collected two and a half times as much grain in the second half of the year as they had in the first six months.[20] In addition to collecting grain, the committees were involved in a number of other activities. Some helped to set up agricultural stations that made equipment available to others, played a role in establishing early agricultural collectives, or opened rural schools. They also assisted with the distribution of government publications in the countryside. In the first year after the revolution, the newspaper *Bednota* (*The Poor*) had a circulation of 33 million, whereas *Pravda* was issued in 25 million copies.[21]

Yet, as the sorcerer's apprentice discovered, useful tools can get out of hand. The Committees ran into conflict with local soviets and began to challenge their authority. Although the committees had not been invested with political powers, they all too quickly absorbed the lessons of their Communist instructors and decided that while the poor were inheriting the earth they might just as well take over its governance. Conflicts were most frequent in the central black earth region, where the shortage of land intensified the hostility of the poor peasants not only to the gentry, but to the wealthier peasants. Some of the wealthier peasants who had status and influence within the villages were among the members of the early lower-level soviets; thus the free hand that was given to the committees often struck, directly or indirectly, at the local soviets. The two organizations competed for financial support. By the beginning of December 1918 the committees had received 8.5 million rubles from the Commissariat of Food Supply. This gave them an independent footing in the countryside, which was strengthened both financially and politically when they were authorized to levy fines for nonobservance of their regulations. In cases of conflict with local soviets, they were in a position to defy the soviets and even to move against their members.

At the end of October 1918 the government announced an extraordinary one-time revolutionary tax of 10 billion rubles to be collected from the urban and rural bourgeoisie. Of the billion to be collected in Moscow province, one-fifth was to come from the towns, four-fifths from the districts. In rural areas special commissions were to be set up, selected from members of the committees, to allocate the tax locally; the committees were to decide exactly who should be subjected to the tax in each locality and to give lists of those designated to the commissions. In parts of the Volga region where exactions were heavy (Samara and Saratov faced a tax bill of 400 million rubles each), some "kulak" households were completely liquidated.[22]

As the Committees of the Poor became more numerous and assumed a vigorous role as rural despoilers, incidents of unrest flared once again. The summer and fall of 1918 were marked by widespread disturbances that were officially described as counterrevolutionary acts of kulaks, fomented by disgruntled SRs. In response to this "counterrevolutionary" resistance by peasants, the Committees of the Poor increasingly took local matters into their own hands, dominating and at times even eliminating the weak local soviets.[23] The implications of the challenge to the entire soviet system were not lost upon the government, nor were the implications of rural discontent to be ignored at a time when the Czech uprising, mounting White resistance, and the greater likelihood of foreign intervention because of the end of the world war, made domestic unrest particularly dangerous.

Repeated explicit prohibitions of interference by the committees in affairs beyond their competency indicate the growing concern they evoked in official circles.[24] They were criticized openly, and certain mistakes were acknowledged. In particular, it was announced that the exclusion of the middle peasants from the ranks of the committees was a serious error. The committees were faulted for not having understood that the attack on the kulaks should not extend to the middle peasants, who were to be enlisted as allies.[25]

What had happened was clear. The government's "wager on the weak" had proved a dangerous tactic. Thanks to the *chernyi peredel*, many of the peasants had shifted from the poor to the middle group, and the Party was faced with a classic political "dilemma of progress." To the extent that it had been successful in reducing the category of poor peasants it had undermined part of its own political base. Having helped to transform the bulk of the poor peasants into middle peasants, the Party had to adjust its policies accordingly. Outright dissolution of the committees, which would doubtless have provoked considerable resistance, was avoided.[26] Instead, after the harvest was in it was announced that they had fulfilled their immediate function and were to be reorganized: they were to be fused with the local soviets through a process of reelections for the lower-level soviets at the end of the year and in early 1919. Within a short time the Committees of the Poor had disappeared, except within the Ukraine, where they survived for some time. "Kulaks" were excluded from participation in the elections and from the reconstituted soviets, but the party switched from its previous position of "neutrality" toward the middle peasants to a new "firm alliance" with them that was to continue as the official line for the next decade.[27]

The soviets had not been alone in facing the competition of the committees. During the revolution the commune had dealt for the first time with organized local groups that made and imposed decisions about the use and distribution of land. Yet the land committees had been formed of members of the commune and were generally established by the commune itself. On the whole they had worked with the commune, and those that survived as land departments of soviets had continued to do so. In some cases the Committees of the Poor also were elected by general assemblies of the commune,[28] and where this occurred it tempered relationships between them. The two often cooperated, and sweeping redistributions of peasant land called for by the committees were carried out by the communes. But outside influences played a greater role in the formation of the Committees of the Poor, and in areas such as the central agricultural region, where the commune was strongest and the land-poor peasants most radical, the potential for collision was great.

Given the gap between the theoretical egalitarianism of the commune and the actual (albeit limited) stratification within it, a challenge to communal authority might have been anticipated from the committees. Had they continued to exist and to arrogate local authority, they would have presented a threat to the traditional communal system of local self-government by the entire land-sharing community. That threat, like the Committees of the Poor and the land committees before them, was taken over by the rural soviets that emerged and took root in the years of War Communism.

The Formation of Rural Soviets

The lower-level soviets had a slow and unsteady start in the Russian countryside. Data on the earliest local soviets are fragmentary, but the available information indicates that volost soviets had been formed in less than 2 percent of all volosts in fourteen provinces of the central industrial region before October 1917.[29] Lower soviets were virtually unknown at the time. Following the October Revolution, the situation changed rapidly. Although there is some disagreement on the exact dynamics of the process, a considerable number of volost soviets were organized in the first few months of 1918.[30] By the end of March they existed in three-quarters of the volosts in 19 central provinces.[31] These early soviets, however, sprang up without a uniform system of internal organization and lacked hierarchical or horizontal linkages. Generally, the lowest level of soviet formed in the countryside was the rural soviet (the *sel'skii sovet*, or *sel'sovet*), but in some smaller localities a lower "village soviet" (*derevenskii sovet*) was established.[32]

With the promulgation of the first Soviet constitution in July 1918, the soviets were given a more systematic format. A uniform, multi-layered organization was outlined, based on the principles of "democratic centralism"—that is, elections to each level were to proceed from the bottom up, discussion of matters under consideration was to be held at all levels, but decisions adopted by superior levels were to be accepted without dispute by lower echelons. The system was consonant with the medieval universalism and unanimity of the mir, extended now from the political microcosm of the commune to the wider scale of the state.

Rural soviets were to be formed in all rural settlements, with one deputy for every 100 members of the population. They were to serve as the local units of state authority and were to meet at least twice a week. Their functions were rather loosely defined. They were to carry out the rulings of higher state organs, concern themselves with improving cultural and economic relations, resolve local problems, and coordinate all soviet activities within their areas. Each rural soviet was to have from 3 to 50 members, and soviets in settlements with over a thousand inhabitants were to elect an executive committee (*ispolkom*) of up to 5 members. All persons who had reached eighteen years of age and who were engaged in socially useful labor could participate in elections, but undesirable social elements (such as persons hiring labor for profit, those living on unearned income, traders and middlemen, clerics, former police, and members of the former ruling house) were disfranchised and debarred from office.

Above the rural soviet there was to be an ascending hierarchy of volost, district, provincial, and oblast congresses of soviets, each with its own executive committee to carry on work between sessions. The committees were authorized to set up departments to deal with their various concerns. Volost congresses of soviets were composed of representatives elected from the rural soviets (originally 1 for each 10 members, but starting in December 1919, 1 for each 100 local residents); district soviet congresses also were formed of delegates from the rural soviets (1 for every 1,000 residents). The provincial congresses drew their delegates from members of urban soviets as well as from volost congresses of soviets. But whereas each urban delegate represented 2,000 residents, each rural delegate represented 10,000 residents. The unequal representation was said to be justified by the higher organizational and cultural level of the workers, and was intended to secure a leading role for workers in the soviet system.[33]

The tidy organizational scheme outlined in the constitution suggested a complete administrative transformation of the countryside. But under the prevailing conditions it proved impossible to put the system into effect during the period of War Communism. A realistic appreciation of that possibility had led to a loophole provision that permitted the government to sidestep the issue of rural administrative control at a time when it had other and more urgent problems. According to a note under Article 57 of the constitution, the administration of local affairs was to continue where feasible under the immediate control of the general assembly of the local electorate, which was recognized as the highest authority within its own territory. After the difficulties created by the Committees of the Poor, the government was content for the time being to leave most local matters in the hands of the traditional assemblies. In practice this meant that the commune not only remained in place but retained its accustomed authority in the life of the village, although rural soviets (where they existed) were now to function alongside.

Under such circumstances the fledgling rural soviets had little chance of acting as strong agents of the central authorities. Rather than replacing the assembly by the rural soviet, the 1918 constitution, according to one view, opened the way for replacing the rural soviet by the assembly.[34] The hard-pressed government made no consistent attempt to introduce universal soviet administration at the village level in this period. Local affairs, more than ever before, became the domain of the commune. When M. I. Kalinin, a former peasant himself, was participating as head of the All-Russian Central Executive Committee in numerous "agitrain" propaganda excursions into the countryside, he constantly urged the peasants to solve their own land problems through the village assembly.[35]

Following the reelections in the winter of 1918–19—the first general elections held on the basis of the new constitution—rural soviets emerged in greater numbers and, thanks to the election of many activists who had served on the Committees of the Poor, somewhat more politicized. Half of the newly elected members of the rural soviets and an even larger proportion of their leaders had been committee workers.[36] But there were also numerous reports of illegal elections of kulaks and other "undesirables." The only election records of rural soviets in 1919 found in the central archives cover 321 volosts in fifteen provinces.[37] Slightly over a million electors were qualified to participate in the elections in this territory, and 41 percent actually did take part. The turnout was not particularly impressive, but was a considerable improvement over the 5 to 7 percent participation rate reported for volost zemstvo elections before the October Revolution.[38]

Eighty-one percent of the voters were men, 19 percent women. The voting pattern for rural women was complex. In general, the percentage of women among the electorate was higher where the turnout was higher, but neighboring communities could show sharp differences. In the rural-soviet election held in one village of Strelinskii volost (Kaluga province) all of the voters were men, but in the election in a neighboring village in the same volost the majority of the voters were women.[39] In Voronezh province less than one percent of those who took part in the elections were women, whereas in Kostroma women accounted for 41 percent of all voters. Of the 14,000 (approximately) delegates for whom information is available, only 0.2 percent were women.

The educational level of the delegates to rural soviets was not high. Only one percent had a mid-level education, two-thirds had a primary education, and a third had never been to school. More surprising, despite the incorporation of committee activists in the reelected soviets, less than 3 percent of the delegates were Communist Party members. The rate of Party membership was about the same for rural soviets in both agricultural and industrial provinces, and had actually dropped slightly from 1918 membership rates. The decline was attributed to the loss of politically active elements to the Red Army. An increase in the proportion of delegates reporting no party affiliation was clearly the result of official measures taken earlier to oust SRs and Mensheviks from the soviets on the grounds that they were supporting counter-revolution.[40] The limited information available on the social composition of rural soviets in 1919 suggests that the numbers of poor and middle peasants were about equal.[41]

By the end of 1919 rural soviets were more firmly established than in 1917, but the system of soviets still had serious shortcomings at the local level. In some localities there were no soviets, and in many more they existed only in name. Where they were functioning, because of their broad membership they often proved too cumbersome and inefficient for the exceptional requirements of War Communism. On the basis of the constitutional provision for 1 delegate per 100 inhabitants, about 10,000 delegates should have been elected in 1919 from the million qualified peasants covered in the archival data. Yet the data show that close to 30,000 delegates were actually elected, almost 3 for every 100 residents.[42] At times some of the smallest rural soviets (often five or six of them) joined forces to form an "area rural soviet" (*raionnyi sel'skii sovet*), which had not been envisaged in the general plan.[43]

The need to consolidate and streamline the sprawling networks of official agencies was felt more keenly at the center as time went on, and it extended beyond the rural soviets. Starting in early 1919 the food supply detachments had increased significantly in number. In an attempt to improve the coordination and effectiveness of the units, in August the entire Food Supply Army was separated from the Commissariat of Food Supply to become part of the country's internal defense forces. In territories close to war zones and behind the constantly shifting lines of combat, special revolutionary committees (*revkomy*) had sprung up in 1918. In 1919 they spread widely: provincial, district, volost, and rural revolutionary committees appeared in many regions and assumed complete authority. They often existed alongside local soviet executive committees and at times included their members, but under conditions of military control the soviets played a secondary role. At the beginning of January 1920, with much of the country freed from active hostilities, the revolutionary committees were largely eliminated by a decision of the central Defense Council.[44] As part of the same organizational thrust, a new decree was issued just six weeks later reshaping and redefining the functions and responsibilities of the rural soviets.

The Statute on Rural Soviets of February 15, 1920, bore, in the words of a contemporary, "the clear imprint of its epoch."[45] Given the nature of that turbulent epoch, it is not surprising that the new law— initiating what was to become a long-term if not necessarily irreversible process—strengthened the "centralist" principle at the expense of the "democratic."[46] The number of rural soviets was reduced, their authority was heightened, and the whole system was administratively tightened. Rural soviets were now proclaimed the highest organs of authority within the territory they served, and observance of all their rulings was declared mandatory for the entire population of that territory.

The formation of rural soviets was limited now to settlements with at least 300 residents. Smaller villages and separate households were given the option of joining with neighbors to reach the necessary minimum or of continuing to deal with local problems through the general assembly of electors. Villages that included more than one land commune were to form a single rural soviet elected by the entire population of the village. The soviet was still limited to 50 members. It was to elect a president but was no longer to have an executive committee unless the population it served exceeded 10,000. Where executive committees did exist, they were limited to 3 members. In settlements where a volost executive committee (*volispolkom*) was located, an executive committee of the local rural soviet was ruled unnecessary; the volost executive committee was to serve as the executive for the local rural soviet. However, the long tradition of communal home rule apparently caused this provision to be observed in the breach in rural soviets, although a comparable ruling for urban soviets was accepted without difficulty.[47] In line with the general curtailment of the number of rural soviets and their executive staff, the frequency of their meetings was to be reduced from the earlier two per week to only two a month.

The new legislation was clearly intended to cut back the unwieldy apparatus of rural soviets in the interest of greater efficiency. However, the functions listed in the second section of the decree were broader than before. In addition to carrying out the rulings of higher agencies, maintaining order, and raising the economic and cultural (the order was now reversed) level of the population within its territory, the rural soviet was now to draw the masses into "the building of a new life." In the course of this creative endeavor it was to assume no less than 53 different responsibilities in the fields of administration, agriculture, economics, food supply, labor obligations, military affairs, defense, public health, and social security. Members were warned (section 3) that if they did not fulfill their formidable duties, they would answer "to the full severity of revolutionary laws."

The contradiction between the organizational contraction and the functional expansion of the rural soviets suggests that the second section of the statute of February 15, 1920, should be taken as a statement of ultimate goals rather than of immediate intentions, a statement reflecting the heroic style of the day.[48] It is notable that a new statute on the higher-level volost executive committees issued just a month later specified less than a quarter as many functions.[49]

Following the introduction of the new law on rural soviets, each province was given a special instruction on reelection procedures that took local conditions into account and permitted modifications in the electoral norms in accordance with population density. The aim was to reduce the number of rural soviets where population distribution would otherwise have led to more than were considered administratively desirable. In Viatka province, for example, where the minimum norm of 300 inhabitants would have led to the formation of some 10,000 rural soviets, the norm was raised to 500, resulting in the establishment of approximately 3,000 rural soviets.[50]

As a result of the new legislation, in many areas the number of rural soviets dropped significantly, in some localities to half of the previous level or less. Records of the Commissariat of Internal Affairs covering 101 districts in 37 provinces, primarily in central Russia, show that there were approximately 25,000 rural soviets in this territory in the second half of the year. Most of the rural soviets (over 70 percent) served a single population center, but a fourth of them covered two to ten villages. Nearly a third of the soviets existed in villages with a population below the minimum specified by the law. Data on the participation of the peasantry in the elections for rural soviets in 1920 are even more fragmentary than those for 1919, but it appears that peasant voting levels remained static or declined.[51]

Rural soviets were almost entirely composed of peasants, although factory workers in the countryside were permitted to form their own rural soviets or to join neighboring ones. At higher levels in the soviet structure, the number of peasant deputies decreased. At volost congresses of soviets peasants made up 95 percent of all delegates; at district congresses they accounted for 65 percent; at provincial congresses—only 37 percent. On the executive committees of soviets they were less well represented, supplying only 20 percent of the members of district executive committees and a slim 8 percent of the provincial executive committees.[52]

The proportion of Communist Party members in the soviets increased at each level, whereas that of peasants declined. Party membership in the rural soviets remained at a low 3 to 4 percent, but rose at volost congresses to 9 percent, at district congresses to 43 percent, and at provincial congresses to 79 percent. Communists controlled an even larger share of the seats on the executive committees: 78 percent at the district level and 90 percent at the provincial.[53]

The participation of women in the soviet system remained extremely low, although it was significantly higher in some industrial areas where women were employed. Urban women were far more active politically than were peasant women. Whereas female participation in rural soviets was quite unusual, almost 10 percent of the delegates to the Moscow City Soviet and close to 20 percent of those in the Petrograd City Soviet were women. As a result of the urban/rural differential, the representation of women in the soviet system, slight as it was, tended to improve at the upper levels. At district congresses of soviets in 1920, 2.3 percent of the delegates and 1.6 percent of those elected to district executive committees were women; on the provincial executive committees, 2 percent of the members were women. Moscow province, a textile manufacturing center employing many women, led with four women on its provincial soviet.[54]

Between 1917 and 1919, increasingly frequent congress meetings and growing attendance at them attested to an overall strengthening of the soviet system. But in 1920, although the number of provincial congresses continued to increase slightly, the number of district congresses dropped sharply, reflecting organizational tightening and the concentration of authority at higher levels.[55]

Another reflection of these developments was the reorganization of the departments of the executive committees. A dozen different types of departments were now specified at the district level; three more were to be established by provincial executive committees. Departments were to be responsible to the immediate executive committee as well as to the corresponding department of the high committee and to the appropriate people's commissariat.[56] Following their reorganization in February 1920, the rural soviets were deprived of the right to form departments. It appears, however, that few had done so earlier.[57]

Appointments to volost land departments (consisting of a department head, an assistant, and a secretary) were subject to confirmation by the district land department. Although both the district and provincial land departments had subsections organized on the plan of those of the Commissariat of Agriculture, the volost land department had none.[38] According to one source, "quite often a land department was not even created, and the volost executive committee decided land matters on its own."[39] However, since there were some 8,400 volost land departments in 1919, it would appear that land departments did exist in most volosts.[60]

The functions of these units were formally more limited than those of the district and provincial land departments and consisted to a large degree in carrying out the instructions of the higher bodies.[61] The volost land departments, however, were charged with responsibility for seeing to it that land was used properly by the individuals and institutions to whom it was assigned. They were to consider and decide all petitions for redivisions of land, and along with the district land departments they were to control and direct the rural soviets in enacting land reform and organizing agriculture on socialist principles. Thus the practical fulfillment of the government's chief declared objectives for the agrarian economy was relegated to the lowest level of the soviet administrative hierarchy, whereas political authority and support for those objectives were concentrated at the top. All land departments were under the authority of the Commissariat of Agriculture, and provincial and district land departments received funds from it. Volost land departments, however, were subsidized by the Commissariat of Internal Affairs.[62]

The financing of the rural soviets was a makeshift affair. The entire soviet system depended to some extent on the collection of local taxes, but the higher levels were provided with the major part of their estimated requirements out of the general state budget, whereas the lower levels received little if any budget support. As early as November 19, 1917, the Council of People's Commissars ruled that local soviets were to support themselves by levying local taxes. Unless they had evidence of the inability of the local populace to provide for them, their requests for financial assistance from the central government were to be denied. The soviets were authorized to call on the Red Guard and the militia to collect taxes they imposed, and deliberate nonpayment of such taxes was punishable by up to five years imprisonment.[63]

The weakness of the local soviets and the tradition of communal authority led to the practice of discussing and voting in assemblies on the taxes the soviets proposed. When a tax was accepted by the community, it was generally levied on the entire population on a per capita or per desiatin basis. Sometimes, however, soviets passed special taxes on the wealthier peasants, either alone or along with rural industrialists and other nonpeasants. In some instances, phony soviets were created on paper as a means of obtaining funds from the central government.[64] Starting in 1919, volost executive committees that had previously been dependent on local funds were given some state support, but the rural soviets continued as a rule to depend on whatever, out of an official list of assessable taxes and fees, they could collect locally.[65] Where peasants were taxed by the rural soviet, the volost soviet, and the district soviet, there was often a strong negative reaction against the whole soviet system.[66]

At the close of the period of War Communism the rural soviet, despite its widespread establishment and the formidable description of its responsibilities and authority under the law, was far from being an effective agency of local government. The rural soviets in 1921 were still fewer than the Committees of the Poor had been at their peak. Whereas there had been over 130,000 committees in 33 provinces of the RSFSR in 1918, there may have been as few as 64,000 rural soviets in 53 provinces and regions of the RSFSR in 1921.[67] The average rural soviet had only four members, and throughout the period of War Communism most rural soviets met less frequently than was stipulated by the law. Volost congresses of soviets, originally scheduled to meet at least once a month, were officially cut back to meetings held at least every three months. Although these volost congresses were supposed to elect the delegates to the provincial soviets, such elections were actually held in only five provinces in 1920. In most cases, the district congress of soviets elected the provincial delegates. Elections for the rural soviets were held irregularly, and the turnout of the peasant electorate did not improve.[68]

Given the difficult conditions the new government faced throughout this period, there was probably little more that could have been done to strengthen the rural soviets. On the other hand, the central leadership may have considered it advisable to let things ride in the villages. Despite the responsibilities assigned to them in the field of political education and propaganda, the rural soviets showed surprisingly little political involvement, insofar as involvement can be measured by Party membership. Between 1918 and 1920 Communists actually dropped from 61 to 43 percent of the delegates at district congresses of soviets, and in 1921 less than a third of the members of the volost executive committees belonged to the Party. The fact that peasant participation in the upper-level soviets declined as Party membership increased did not speak well for the bond between the countryside and the political center, and the organizational retrenchment of February

1920 tended to weaken the ties between the soviet and the village. Staffed by few dedicated Communists, the rural soviets that emerged from the period of War Communism were feeble agents of the central government and played a limited role in local government.

The commune, on the other hand, came through the period of War Communism considerably strengthened as a result of the redistribution of land and decidedly democratized (at least on paper) thanks to land legislation and the constitutional extension of voting rights. A genuine economic democratization was evident in the changed social composition of the peasantry. Far from having been replaced by the new rural soviets, the commune, in accordance with long-standing tradition, continued to be utilized by the state as a basic administrative and fiscal unit in the countryside.

12

Forms of Land Tenure

The spirit of innovation and experimentation that characterized the period gave rise to new forms of landholding under War Communism. Russian Communists viewed communal tenure in Russia as an expression of bourgeois individualism in land relations, and sought new forms of collective tenure for a new socialist economy after the revolution. A genuinely classless society, they held, called for collective labor on the land and collective use of all productive resources. Yet while novel modes of collective landholding were being enthusiastically introduced, communal tenure flourished, and in some areas a taste for fully individualized tenure was manifest.

Communal Landholding

The position of the commune outlined in the Decree on Land was altered in some respects by legislation issued under War Communism. The decree had delineated a major role for communes, placing various types of property (specific lands, woods, waters, confiscated inventory, and so forth) under their direct control and providing for them to distribute confiscated land and to redistribute peasant land periodically. Yet the Law on Socialization transferred many functions previously assigned to communes to the land departments of soviets. The right of communes to use land for agriculture was reaffirmed, but preference in the allotment of land by land departments was to be given to collectives.* As a corporate personality, the commune was officially considered more a person than a corporation. The statute of February 1919 on socialist land organization placed it, as we have seen, among the "individual" holders of land.

Under War Communism change vied with continuity in the commune. The membership of the commune was broadened by the inclu-

*In allotments to colonists the priorities were reversed.

sion of formerly separate peasant households and urban residents returning to the countryside, and it was altered socially by the admission of many landless peasants. With the drop in the proportion of wealthy peasants, the enlarged membership was in a better position to prevent the "mir eaters" from dominating the commune, and the old patriarchal order was undermined by the new legal right of all members eighteen and over to participate in the communal assembly and, most importantly, to separate from their households with a share of land.

Although these developments undoubtedly affected social and personal relationships, the general pattern of life within the commune remained much the same. For the most part only household heads made decisions in the communal assembly; women still took little part in its deliberations. The economically stronger peasants often continued to exercise more authority in the commune than did their neighbors. Political democratization did not necessarily work against rich peasants. Since wealthier households were generally larger than the average, a vote for all adults in the commune (where this practice was observed) could mean relatively more votes for the prosperous.

Allocation and redistribution of land by the commune continued much as before, but now extended over the newly acquired land, including the land in khutors and otrubs that were reabsorbed by communes after the revolution.[1] One reason for the heightened activity in this area was the heavy demand for land by new arrivals from the cities. Ex-urbanites scrambled for every scrap of land as the only means of obtaining food, and they turned to communes for help. Although the food problem contributed to the revival of land redistribution in communes, especially in the consuming industrial regions and near urban centers, it was only one of many factors involved. General land hunger, the need for some acceptable mode of distributing the confiscated lands, a decade of accumulated resentment against those who had separated from the commune, the legal obligation to provide for newcomers, and doubtless also an element of egalitarian utopianism all contributed to the unprecedented scale of communal land redistribution witnessed in the *chernyi peredel*.

The constant turnover of land and the uncertainties attendant on a succession of temporary short-term allotments had a negative effect on agricultural production that soon led the government to curtail, and in some cases to prohibit, land redistributions. As early as the Law on Socialization of February 1918, instructions were issued that all allotments assigned by land departments were to be in the form of single parcels of land wherever possible in order to avoid the detrimental effects of stripholding. Instructions to this effect were repeated in con-

nection with the land organization statute the following year. Shortly
thereafter, in March 1919, the Commissariat of Agriculture sent a circular to the land departments of the executive committees of soviets
prohibiting redistributions of temporary allotments until they could be
accompanied by land organization procedures outlined in the statute.
Exceptions could be made only with the approval of district land departments, confirmed by provincial land departments, and were limited to partial redistributions.[2]

The Commissariat of Agriculture published general regulations governing land redistribution on July 1, 1919.[3] Though these stated that
all redistributions unaccompanied by land organization work were undesirable in principle, particularly where a redivision had occurred
within the past year in connection with the acquisition of new lands,
they permitted partial redistributions that had the sanction of the local
land department. Volost land departments were allowed to permit redistributions that involved technical improvements, were required by
the transfer of part of a commune to collective tenure, or were necessary to eliminate flagrant injustice or economic drawbacks. A request
for authorization of a partial redivision had to be supported by a majority of the members with full electoral rights in a commune. To receive
official consideration, general redistributions had to be requested by
two-thirds of such members.

Because widespread land redistribution continued, particularly
where it had been delayed by civil war, on April 30, 1920, the Council
of People's Commissars issued a decree restating the provisions of the
earlier regulations in more forceful language.[4] Redistributions uncon-
nected with land organization work were prohibited, and exceptions
were to be made only to permit economic improvements and conversion to collective forms of tenure (rectification of injustice was abandoned). Requests for general redistribution were to be considered by
district land departments, but only when presented by two-thirds of
the commune members with electoral rights; requests for partial redistributions were to be addressed directly to volost land departments
by the parties concerned. General redistributions were to be conducted at intervals no shorter than three full cycles of whatever crop
rotation was used by the commune—in a typical three-field rotation,
for example, a period of nine years. The decree warned that all redistributions not conforming to its provisions would be considered void
and the persons and institutions involved would be held responsible
before the law.

Yet these rulings appear to have had little effect on the actual procedures involved in redistribution or on the commune's autonomy in

managing its internal land affairs. If enforced, they would have limited the commune's authority to determine the frequency of redistributions (although less rigidly than the prerevolutionary twelve-year restriction). The peasants themselves wanted to end the turnover of land and welcomed land organization work as a solution to the problems of scattered and far-flung strip holdings. But the work progressed slowly, dissatisfaction with existing land arrangements was high, and additional lands continued for some time to become available. As a result, redistributions continued throughout the period of War Communism.[5]

Just as the emergence of the modern Russian land commune was linked historically with periodic land redistribution, so the wave of postrevolutionary land distribution was closely bound up with the resurgence of the commune. The extent of that resurgence is evident in the statistics collected by the TsSU in the agricultural census of 1920. Data on the total number of rural households in each of 47 provinces or administrative territories are available, as well as the number of households in communes for all but 8 of these. In the 39 provinces or areas for which both sets of figures are available, 96 percent of all rural families were in communes in 1920. This high figure reflects the absence of data for the Baltic provinces and for some other northwestern and Ukrainian provinces, but indicates what had taken place in the old communal areas. Since the census category of "all rural families" included rural residents who were outside of communes and not directly involved in agriculture (millers, train and post station attendants, etc.), the figure indicates that almost every household working on the land had been drawn into the commune. By 1922 the number of consolidated farms in Stavropol province had fallen from 25 percent of the prerevolutionary total to less than one percent; in Samara it fell from 19 percent to one-tenth of one percent; in Saratov from 16 percent to hundredths of a percent. In Moscow province khutors and otrubs dropped from 9 to 3 percent, and in the province of Petrograd from 29 to 23 percent.[6]

The causes of the reinvigoration of the commune were diverse. In addition to its utility as a mechanism for distributing newly acquired lands, the commune was a means of recovering lands claimed previously by separators. Individual peasant largeholdings (and sometimes smallholdings) were often (re)incorporated into the communal land fund. The commune was also the logical agency to distribute and regulate the use of expropriated agricultural inventory after the revolution. Over and beyond such mechanical functions, however, the commune, from the early days of the revolution, gave organizational coherence to the village. In the face of a collapse of other agencies of local government, the commune attended to a wide array of peasant needs, kept rural life running in familiar patterns and served as a stabilizing force in the countryside.

In the postrevolutionary extension of the commune, the technical drawbacks of communal land organization were also extended. The disadvantages of stripholding and distant plowland remained acute. Plans were developed for a comprehensive land organization program to continue the work carried on by the tsarist regime after the revolution of 1905, and in April 1919, a central land agency (Tsentrozem) was established under the Commissariat of Agriculture to direct all land organization work. The new organization, operating with a staff of fewer than 2,000 land organizers in its first year, was directing some 3,500 to 4,000 workers by the end of 1920.[7]

The basic task preoccupying this agency from 1919 to 1921 was the allotment of land to volosts and communes. Although work on the elimination of narrow strips and distant landholdings was a relatively minor part of its early efforts, this grew to be the most important land-organizing activity (in terms of area involved) in 1921. The allotment of land to state farms and collective farms was a minor function, and land organization work directed to the establishment of individual farms (khutors and otrubs) was so insignificant in these early years as to be commonly unlisted in general tabulations. It amounted to only a small fraction of one percent of the total work accomplished.[8]

Agrarian Individualism

The minuscule amount of land reported organized as separate farms would appear to reflect a general reaction against individual holdings. Provincial land department records show only rare requests for the organization of individual farms—or, as one report put it, for "transfer to the old Stolypin form of land use."[9] As one contemporary pointed out, surveying costs on individual farms were three to four times higher per land unit than similar work done on communal land. "Agrarian individualism," it was observed, "is aristocratic and expensive."[10] Others revived the argument that the existence of the commune would facilitate the introduction of agronomic improvements, difficult or impossible to effect under individual tenure.[11]

Given the evidence of extensively revived communal landholding after the revolution, it would not be unreasonable to conclude that the agrarian individualism so solicitously nurtured in the preceding decade had been completely uprooted by the revolution. Individual landholding may have been "too expensive" in a variety of ways; the official statistics on the organization of individual farms in the postrevolutionary years suggest that peasants were unwilling to pay the social cost and sought security, perhaps even survival, in the commune.

Yet there is also evidence of a different sort. Investigation of the records of applications for the establishment of separate farmsteads has revealed that they were not only rare, but were ignored by land officials. The amount of land organization effected in this area, therefore, is not necessarily an accurate gauge of the strength of peasant separatism. The advocate who pointed to the advantages of communal tenure in the introduction of agricultural improvements warned at the same time (in 1921) that it was impossible to ignore "the growth of *individualistic tendencies* among the peasantry."[12] Other agrarian experts, well acquainted with the contemporary situation, spoke of "the extreme individualistic bent of the population" during this period and referred to the massive spontaneous growth of "an individualistic land tendency."[13]

Such statements are difficult to reconcile with the data showing the strong predominance of communal tenure. There seem to be two reasons the statistics on tenure fail to show a postrevolutionary current of agrarian individualism: (1) the movement was geographically restricted and (2) it was at least partially concealed in official records. In the days following the revolution when individual homesteaders (or their lands) were being driven back into communes, the greatest number of independent farmers survived in the northwest, where they had been most vigorously established and where they had most often come into existence by the decision of an entire commune to convert to separate consolidated holdings. Sympathetic land officials in the area helped khutors resist returning to the commune by pointing to clauses in the new land legislation that stressed the desirability of consolidated landholding.[14] Not only did the peasants there mount fewer attacks on separated farms, but on occasion they used the opportunity of a general redistribution to convert to consolidated field allotments for each household. The resulting arrangement was equivalent in effect to full conversion to otrubs, although the commune's indivisible lands were still used jointly and the arable land was still subject to redistribution.

In some areas, particularly in Smolensk province, a new form of semiindividualized tenure became popular. Small clusters of households (frequently a group of five, hence the name *piatidvorki*) would join forces to form a mini-commune with many of the characteristics of an otrub.[15] There were also many outright transfers to khutors and otrubs "both with the sanction of the local land organs as well as—and in general—without it."[16]

A trend toward consolidated and individual landholding is said to have been perceptible in 20 provinces,[17] but it appears to have reached significant dimensions only in Vitebsk (where Latvian influence was strong), in Smolensk, and to a somewhat lesser degree in the surrounding territory of Novgorod, Petrograd, Pskov, and Gomel. Reports from land departments in these areas repeatedly stressed that the local population was demanding, and forming, separate farms and separate small settlements.[18] By 1920 the movement was gathering momentum and is even said to have assumed "an elemental character." This was precisely when the campaign for the "socialization" of agriculture was at its peak. Local land officials were caught between pressure from above to implement a collectivist policy and pressure from below to reorganize agriculture on diametrically opposed individualistic lines.

Under such conditions it was not surprising that applications for individual farms would be ignored and that such farms would fail to be recorded when they were formed. As a Smolensk land department complained, it was impossible for local land officials to stop the "willful" conversion of land to khutors while the officials were dependent on the local population.[19] Lands that were no longer in communal tenure or that were in a substantially modified form of communal tenure might nevertheless continue to be listed as communal. And the figures for communal tenure were not the only ones concealing the existence of individually held land. As the policy of socialization turned the khutor into forbidden fruit, peasants who wanted to form independent farms banded together to create "fictitious artels," which they organized to suit their purposes and cloak their separate holdings. Local officials who knew what was going on nevertheless sanctioned the formation of such artels in the hope that collective cultivation would eventually appear in them, and perhaps in the hope, too, of presenting a more acceptable land account for official audit.[20]

It is obviously not possible to quantify the strength of this regionalized agrarian individualism. Some idea of its scope may be deduced from the statistics for land held as khutors and otrubs in these provinces in 1922, when land policies had relaxed somewhat. In Vitebsk 33 percent of all agricultural land was held individually, in Smolensk 28 percent, in Petrograd 23 percent, in Novgorod 22 percent, in Pskov 15 percent, and in Gomel 13 percent. These figures can be compared with an average of 1.6 percent for the other 42 provinces and territories listed by the TsSU. There was a marked regional concentration of agrarian individualism in the west. The 1922 data (resulting from spot studies covering no more than 10 percent of the territory) showed communal tenure to be virtually universal in the major agricultural regions of the country, but somewhat less predominant in the industrial provinces and covering only 65 to 70 percent of the peasants' land in White Russia and the northwest.[21]

The strength of individual tenure in the western provinces stemmed from a number of regional peculiarities. The nature of the broken terrain, the proximity of Western models, and the example of relatively prosperous noncommunal neighbors influenced the peasants there. In addition, the area had been characterized before the revolution by intensive agriculture, industrial and urban development, and the growth of commerce, all of which presented new opportunities but called for more flexibility than the existing communal system afforded. This combination of circumstances had led to the creation of the many individual farms. The average khutor, as we have seen, was more productive than the average communal holding, and once the revolution had freed the land of mortgage payments, greater productivity promised greater prosperity. Moved by such considerations, some peasants took advantage of the opportunity to establish individual farms or small settlements.[22]

In the remainder of European Russia communal tenure was unchallenged. The dual nature of the commune, with its elements of collectivism and individualism, had found a parallel in the government's policies. Whereas the Stolypin program had fostered individualism through establishing separate farms, assigning individual property rights to heads of households, and supporting personal independence from the family and the commune, the Soviet extension of electoral and property rights to all (politically acceptable) persons over eighteen could be said to have advanced the same principle of individualism. Simultaneously, however, the Soviet government was promoting collectivization and the subordination of the economic interests of individuals to the economic interests of society.

The Social Control of Land

The Party conference of April 1917, following Lenin's proposal, had called for social control of large-scale gentry agricultural enterprises. This meant placing such units under public or social agencies. The Decree on Land provided for this by stipulating that enterprises of this sort were to be run by the state or by the local commune. Instructions issued to the land committees in December 1917 required that certain types of agricultural lands were to be preserved intact and not distributed among the peasants. These lands included orchards and nurseries, seed farms, stock-breeding farms, plantations raising sugar beets, tobacco, or hops, model farms and experimental stations, and fields belonging to agricultural or other schools. All such enterprises, soon to become known as state farms (*sovkhozy*), were placed under the control of the land committees pending reorganization "on new bases." The land socialization measures in the spring of 1918 provided for the formation of state farms on the confiscated lands of large proprietors, enlarged the fund of non-redistributable land, and transferred the control of such land to the local soviets.[23]

At the same time as the state farms were taking shape under official sponsorship, different forms of agricultural collectives appeared in the countryside, more or less spontaneously but with the active encouragement and support of the authorities. These collective farms (*kolkhozy*) took several forms: the *kommuna*, a new form of radically egalitarian commune; the *TOZ* (*tovarishchestvo po obshchestvennoi obrabotke zemli*), an association for the common cultivation of land; and the more familiar artel. Throughout the first year after the revolution there was considerable debate on just where the government should throw the weight of its limited resources. Some favored all-out backing of the *kommuny*, but others, finding these new collectives reminiscent of the ill-fated communes of Robert Owen and "utopian socialism," called for the organization and management of agricultural enterprises directly by the state as more consistent with the theoretical postulates of Marxian "scientific socialism."

A decision was not taken until late in 1918, when it was resolved to pursue all forms simultaneously. On November 2, 1918, the Council of People's Commissars created a special fund of one billion rubles for loans and assistance to collectives and to communes transferring to collective cultivation of their land.[24] The development of socialism in agriculture, however, was to be encouraged rather than forced, and frequently repeated policy directives placed beyond question the official intention to proceed without compulsion. Lenin warned that too rapid a development could be harmful, even ruinous in view of the inadequate material base for a socialist transformation of agriculture.[25] Struggling with civil war and facing resistance provoked by requisitioning, the government had no desire to risk another confrontation with the peasants simply to accelerate a movement it considered inevitable.

That it was intended to be inevitable was manifest from the start. By prescribing the development of collective enterprises in agriculture as one of the functions of the land departments, the Law on Socialization of February 19, 1918, made clear that an ultimate transformation of the land structure was projected. Collectives were to be formed "at the expense of individual enterprises, in the interests of a transition to a socialist economy."[26] The law stipulated that in the distribution of land preference was to be given to collectives and to settlers forming collectives, and that collectives were to be given preferential "cultural and material assistance" to promote "the most rapid achievement of socialism." Socialization, then, was more than simple nationalization or state ownership. Increasingly, it came to mean social control of land through direct state management or through agricultural collectives.[27]

The shift to "vertical centralism" under War Communism left no doubt who controlled the land. According to the statute of February 14, 1919, Socialist Land Organization, all land was declared part of a single state fund under the immediate direction of state authorities.[28] For the first time the policy of collectivization of agriculture "for the final elimination of every sort of exploitation of man by man" was fully elaborated in a major legislative enactment, and all forms of individual land use were declared obsolescent. Agricultural land was to be distributed first to state enterprises, then to various forms of collectives, and finally to "individual" land users (communes, separate families, and single persons). Certain categories of land were to be denied to "individuals."

Considerable attention was devoted to the organization of state farms. The declared purpose of these farms was to (1) raise agricultural productivity and extend the crop area, (2) create the conditions for a full transfer to communist agriculture, and (3) establish advanced agronomic centers. All highly developed agricultural lands, such as orchards, vineyards, and sugar beet and cotton plantations, were to be turned over to the state farms. (The sugar beet industry and all livestock-breeding establishments other than those of working peasant households had already been nationalized in 1918.)[29] The statute of February 14, 1919, placed all highly developed agricultural enterprises of nationwide importance under the direct control of the Commissariat of Agriculture; those of lesser significance were assigned to the various levels of local administration and fell under the jurisdiction of their land departments.

Next to the state farms in line of priority, the decree provided for the establishment of agricultural *kommuny*. These were to be formed as voluntary associations to pursue agriculture on communist principles of production and distribution. District land departments were to allot land from the local fund to those who wanted to form a *kommuna* or, if the group was adequately supplied with land already, to assist it in exchanging its scattered holdings for a consolidated tract. Inventory was to be provided from the confiscated stock of private and Church properties.

In return for state support, the *kommuny* were to turn over all their surplus production above the norms established for consumption. They were placed under the control of the Commissariat of Agriculture and were under the financial supervision of the local land department. Their agricultural operations were to conform to the regional plan established by the commissariat or the provincial land department. Each *kommuna* was to elect a soviet of three to five persons, and its president was to serve as economic manager after confirmation by the district land department.

The statute also provided for other and looser forms of collectivism. Members of traditional communes were encouraged to pool their labor for specific crop operations and to share equipment. One article (96) went further in facilitating the transfer from individual to collective land use than had any single provision of the Stolypin legislation in encouraging the opposite trend. It declared that the decision of a simple majority of the members *present* at an assembly sufficed to establish common cultivation of all the land in a commune. Should a group of members who wanted to work their lands in common be unable to secure a majority, the commune was required to allot them a unified piece of land in proportion to their aggregate shares at any time they so demanded. The land thus set apart for joint labor could be organized as an artel or as a *TOZ*, neither of which was subject to the land redivisions of the commune. Members of these collectives, however, retained the right to participate in the commune's decisions on land matters.

The switch to more active promotion of collectivization early in 1919 initiated a phase in official land policy that was to persist throughout the remainder of the period of War Communism. Coming at a time when the Committees of the Poor were being abandoned and the government was coming to terms with the changed social structure of the countryside through its "alliance" with the middle peasants, this new emphasis appears at variance with other aspects of contemporary rural policy. Yet it falls into the general pattern already observed in connection with the committees and the rural soviets: the government consistently pressed for the socialization and centralization of the countryside, but accepted the limits of the possible as defined by peasant resistance.

Along with other considerations moving the government toward stronger support of collectivization was an ideological compulsion to translate socialist theory into practice. It was one thing to exploit the peasants' proprietary instincts to shape an agrarian program that led to political power, but not to direct that power to the realization of social-

TABLE 16

Progress of Socialization in Agriculture, RSFSR, 1918–21

Year	State farms	Collective farms			Total
		Kommuny	Artels	TOZy	
1918	3,101	975	604	—	4,680
1919	4,063 (516)	1,961	3,605	622	10,251
1920	5,928 (1,636)	1,892	7,722	886	16,428
1921	6,527 (2,136)	3,313	10,185	2,514	22,539

SOURCE: Snegirev, "Zemleustroistvo," p. 30.
NOTE: Figures in parentheses indicate the number of "ascribed" state farms included.

ist goals was to undercut the legitimacy of the revolution. Given the frustrations and anxieties of the period after October, the difficulties of partial nationalization in industry, and the melting away of the urban proletariat, the government was bound to want some demonstrable measure of socialist achievement in the countryside.

Theoretical considerations only sharpened the compelling material and technical arguments favoring collectivization and state control of agriculture. Foremost among such arguments was the critical need to raise agricultural productivity and to relieve the country's food shortage. In 1919 large areas were in enemy hands. Spring sowing in the agriculturally important Volga region was disrupted by the advance of General A. V. Kolchak's anti-Bolshevik forces; General A. I. Denikin's army occupied large areas of the south; and hostile Cossacks controlled much of the Don region. During the harvest season fighting swept over the central agricultural provinces, reaching almost as far as Tula. Within the area nominally under Soviet control, there was widespread peasant resistance to forced requisitions and deliberate cutbacks in the area cultivated. Under such conditions the advantages of government control of field production through state-managed farms were obvious; the formation of *kommuny* whose surplus production was automatically assigned to the state fund was almost equally to be encouraged.

The economic logic of pooling agricultural machinery and equipment, which were in extremely short supply, also made collectivization desirable. Shortages were aggravated by the uneven distribution of inventory; many of the poor peasants who had received land in the *chernyi peredel* lacked the tools and animal power necessary to work it. These factors, coupled with official encouragement of collective landholding, led to the growth of socialized forms of agriculture during this period, as indicated in Table 16. Different sources vary in absolute numbers, but generally agree on the overall pattern of development.[30]

In the first year after the revolution government policy combined with the *chernyi peredel* to make the state farms the most common form of socialized agriculture. After 1920 the creation of state farms tapered off, mainly because fewer larger properties remained available for such development as time went by. (Ninety-eight percent of the land in the state farms had been privately owned.)[31] The state farm was a relatively large unit, averaging 530 desiatins in 1920.[32] However, the average varied greatly from one region to another, ranging from 160 desiatins in the central industrial region to 2,612 desiatins in the Lower Volga area.[33] In this period state farms typically employed from 20 to 24 workers, but each worker generally provided for about two "eaters" (sometimes more) who subsisted on the farm. The average number of eaters per state farm was somewhat larger (74 individuals) than the average for collective farms (about 63).[34]

Some of the early state farms were assigned directly to institutions or enterprises in much the same manner as land and serfs had been "ascribed" to state-supported industries in an earlier epoch. The ascribed farms were organized like the other state farms, but their labor force was frequently supplemented with industrial workers sent out to man the plows and to organize a return flow of provisions and/or raw materials for the factory.

State farms, unlike collective farms, separated labor on the land not only from land ownership but from all control over the land. State farm employees were entitled to a share of the product of their labor, but that labor gave them no more right to the land itself than factory workers had to the industrial machinery they used. Although the party of the proletariat waxed enthusiastic over the potential of the new "grain factories" in the fields,[35] the peasants, long conditioned to the proposition that "the land is ours," were sometimes less excited. On occasion, efforts to form state farms on local estates were resisted by the peasants as depriving them of the fruits of the revolution. In the mid-1920's the creation of state farms was said to have been a "great political mistake," particularly in the outlying Soviet republics.[36]

The Early Collectives

All of the major forms of collective farm—the *kommuna*, the artel, and the *TOZ*—were organized on principles of common cultivation. Members shared collective rights over their land and managed it collectively. Yet there were great differences among the types of collectives.

Kommuny

Initially the most popular, and in many ways the most interesting, of the early collectives was the *kommuna*. The first *kommuny* sprang up spontaneously. Official support was quick to follow, however, and was so pronounced that one scholar has charged that analysis of the Commissariat of Agriculture's activity "could lead to the impression that *kommuny* were the only form of collective agriculture in 1918."[37] The government's policy has been defended, on the other hand, as a response to the peasants' own expression of interest in *kommuny*, an interest especially evident among the poor peasants. The very name of the new collectives, "resonant with the ultimate goal of the Bolshevik Party—the building of communism," was said to attract sympathy to them.[38]

A few *kommuny* appeared in late 1917, and by mid-1918 over 500 were reported to be in existence. Most of the first collectives for which data are available were formed on peasant allotment land, but it soon became more typical for them to arise on confiscated gentry land. By the end of 1918 they were popping up like mushrooms after a spring rain, and the Commissariat of Agriculture was inundated with their requests for financial assistance. Many of the early *kommuny* were formed of family members and groups of relatives. Their members were generally young (under 40), and had a high proportion of dependents (mostly young children) to workers.[39]

Peasants in the *kommuny* were more restricted in their land rights than were members of other collectives. According to the first model charter for *kommuny*, approved by the Commissariat of Agriculture on July 21, 1918, peasants forming or entering a *kommuna* surrendered all of their property except personal possessions. If members decided to leave, the *kommuna* was not obliged to return any of their contributions. A subsequent version of the charter permitted departing members to retain household effects but, like the earlier one, left it to the general assembly of the *kommuna* to determine whether anything more could be withdrawn.[40] Such provisions had little appeal to relatively well-off peasants but offered no drawback to those who had little or nothing to contribute. Not surprisingly, most members of *kommuny* were poor peasants or rural proletarians.[41] Data for 520 *kommuny* in 1918 and 1919 show that only slightly over half of their members were peasant agriculturalists; most of the remainder were craftsmen and workers.[42]

Members of *kommuny* lived, ate, and worked together, shared virtually all their belongings, and divided the product of their labor equally. Life, according to the model statute, was to be based on communist principles: "Everything belongs to everyone and no one in the *kommuna* may call anything his own except for personal objects. Everyone in the *kommuna* works according to his ability and receives according to his needs, depending on the economic condition of the *kommuna*." This early blueprint for a communist utopia was modified somewhat in later specifications, as it was modified by the social realities of life where *kommuny* were established.[43] For many peasants the communist ideal was deeply unsettling. In the reelections for soviets in late 1918 and early 1919, alarming rumors circulated that all peasants were going to be forced into *kommuny*.[44] Along the same lines, it was reported in the nonofficial press in 1918 that the Bolsheviks were about to nationalize women.* Both central and local authorities worked vigorously to prevent such misunderstandings and to allay peasant fears, but the *kommuny* were clearly based on social principles that threatened some traditional rural values.

Many *kommuny* were formed by immigrant groups, some of which arrived well provided with agricultural machinery and equipment. After the revolution almost half a million people in 83 different groups, as well as several thousand separate individuals, are said to have requested permission to come or return to Russia for agricultural work. The groups forming agricultural collectives showed a strong preference for *kommuny*. Collectives of this type were formed by Finnish, Dutch, Czech, German, Austrian, Swiss, Canadian, and American groups. Immigrants from the United States (workers and returning Russian peasants) soon predominated. By 1925, 70 percent of the members of immigrant *kommuny* were from the American continent, and only 30 percent were from Europe.† Some of the immigrant *kommuny* were highly successful and became model farms; others, however, were less fortunate and like most other *kommuny* encountered serious difficulties.

Thanks to government support, the *kommuny* tended to be better endowed than other collectives in amount of land (2.2 desiatins) and

---

*Sobolev, p. 207. The newspaper in which the report appeared, *Vechernaia zhizn'*, May 3, 1918, was promptly shut down.

†Grishaev, *Kommuny*, p. 152. See the glowing report in *Pravda*, May 1, 1929, on the *kommuna* "The Sower," located in the Northern Caucasus. Originally founded by American immigrants, it came to include ten different national groups and was renowned for its high productivity. Another success story mentioned by *Pravda* was the American *kommuna* "Lenin" (March 27, 1928). Yet another immigrant *kommuna* was the "California," formed in 1922 by 153 settlers from America and allotted a tract of 2,008 desiatins, also in the Northern Caucasus (Rybinskii, p. 74).

inventory per capita, but many were very small agricultural units without adequate means of supporting their members. There were about 40 individuals in the average *kommuna*. In the larger, better-provided establishments, however, the complexities of management were often beyond the abilities of their inexperienced members.[45] Such problems contributed to the decline of the *kommuny* during the years of War Communism, although whether that decline was absolute or only relative to the growth of other forms of collective agriculture remains unclear.[46] According to some sources, including Table 16, p. 217, there was an increase in the number of *kommuny* throughout the period except for a slight drop in 1920;[47] other sources show a peak in 1919 and a steady decline thereafter. Recent data show 1,340 *kommuny* in 1918; 1,993 in 1919; and 1,494 in 1920. The role of the *kommuny* in the economy, as well as their impact on peasant life in general, was obviously limited, but they were a unique experiment before which, in Kalinin's view, "all the previous experiments of Owen appear microscopic."[48]

Artels

By 1919 the number of *kommuny* had already been overtaken by the number of artels, and artels were to remain the predominant form of agricultural collective throughout the period of War Communism. The artels were invested with less lofty social goals than the *kommuny*, and they focused on narrower economic objectives. They recognized to a greater extent the individual material interests of their members, and according to one contemporary, they provided the "intermediate form" the peasants were seeking "between the khutor and the *kommuna*."[49] Artels appealed to a somewhat more prosperous group of peasants and required an entrance fee in money and/or property.

The first model charter for artels, adopted on May 19, 1919, permitted members to retain all of their land and property above the level of the entrance requirement.[50] If members departed, their money was to be returned, and other property might be returned at the discretion of the artel. Upon the approval of the local land department, departing members who had contributed land were to be allotted a piece of the artel's land corresponding to the regional norm.

The amount of labor each member had to contribute to the collective effort was prescribed by the general assembly of the artel; once this requirement was met, members could spend the rest of their time working for themselves. Members' livestock and equipment (beyond the required contributions) were to be made available for common use when needed by the artel, but were recognized as individual property.

An attempt was made to establish a cost accounting system by assigning a value to the artel's products distributed among members and balancing this against the work time recorded for each member. However, the system was complicated by an instruction that products were also to be distributed according to need. The need to provision privately owned livestock was to be taken into account by the artel in distributing its products, but the income from the private sector of a household's economy was to be considered also.

Although the artel was run by an assembly of all its members, it elected an executive soviet headed by a president—"the artel starosta," as the model statute dubbed him, borrowing the title of the elected head of the commune. The average artel in 1920 had less agricultural land (1.7 desiatins) per person than the average *kommuna*, but had a greater labor force, with an average of close to 60 individuals.[51] Almost a third of the land in artels was former allotment land.[52] Despite the fact that artels received less official support and less material assistance from the government, by the end of the period of War Communism they outnumbered *kommuny* by at least three to one.

TOZy

The simplest and most loosely structured of the collectives was the *TOZ*, or association for the common cultivation of land. As its name indicates, it was a group whose members tilled their fields jointly. Members retained their own inventory and received a share of the total output in proportion to their share of the land that was cultivated in common. The system eliminated some of the disadvantages of stripholding since boundary lines could be ignored, and the efficiency of field operations was increased by better utilization of the available pool of labor and inventory.

Small communes occasionally converted to this form of collective work, and in some cases members of a commune established a *TOZ* for joint labor on undivided communal lands or on empty land, while retaining their separate lands in the commune and working them independently. The *TOZy* were the slowest form of agricultural collective to develop after the revolution, but by 1921 they accounted for about one-sixth of all collectives, gaining at the expense of both *kommuny* and artels.

Dynamics

The relative importance of the different types of collective farms shifted considerably during the period of War Communism, as is evident in Table 16 (p. 217). Although all forms of collectives increased in number over the period, the proportion of *kommuny* dropped sharply, whereas artels gained rapidly. The reasons for the shifts are evident. The declining role of the *kommuny* was linked with both the ebbing of the early tide of egalitarianism and the diminishing availability of land grants once the confiscated lands had been redistributed. Moreover, the presence of many nonpeasants and poor peasants in the *kommuny* shows that this new form of collective was most attractive to the economically least secure. Artels and *TOZy*, on the other hand, appealed to peasants who were somewhat better off. During this period, the general redistribution of land promoted many peasants from the category of landless or poor to the loftier social status of middle peasant. (In prerevolutionary Russia 65 percent of all peasants were categorized as poor peasants; after the revolution up to 65 percent were middle peasants.)[53] As the socioeconomic position of the peasants changed, their interest in collectives shifted accordingly.

Despite generous grants of land and money, loans, priority allocation of equipment, and tax benefits, the collectivized sector of the rural economy enveloped less than one percent of the population by the end of War Communism.[54] In the central regions of the country, where the agricultural collectives were concentrated,[55] the commune—a form of agricultural collective precisely "between the khutor and the *kommuna*"—provided an adequate measure of collectivism for most peasants.

13

The Limits of Economic Elasticity

Economic strains imposed by war and resulting food shortages, the conditions that contributed to the downfall of both the tsarist regime and the heirs of February, improved but little after the October Revolution. The rise of political opposition in the civil war period actually helped the government to secure its hold on power by focusing attention on political issues and creating a scapegoat for economic difficulties. The polarization of forces during the era of War Communism drew many more firmly behind the government, if only because the opposition lacked greater appeal and the middle of a battlefield is notoriously inhospitable. At the same time, the summary justice of martial law was an effective aid in wiping political scoreboards clean. Whatever benefits the new regime may have derived from it in political consolidation and stabilization, however, the period of War Communism was economically disastrous. After the fighting had died down, the economic troubles remained—and loomed larger than ever before.

Land Cultivation and Productivity

In a country whose population is overwhelmingly peasant and whose income is derived mainly from agriculture, the state of the national economy hinges on the state of the agrarian economy. The basic resource of any agrarian economy is land, and the amount of land under cultivation (at a given level of technology and with an adequate labor force) largely determines output. Thus the amount of land under cultivation during the years of War Communism is a rough indicator of the state of the economy, and the steady decline in crop area signals unremitting intensification of economic difficulties.

According to data published by the TsSU in 1924 (see Table 17), the area planted in grain averaged 90 million hectares from 1909 through 1913, but dropped to 63 million hectares in 1921. The average prewar

TABLE 17

Area under Grain and Grain Production, 1909–21

Year	Area sown in grain (million hectares)		Gross grain production (million tons)	
	Source (a)	Source (b)	Sources (a) and (b)	Source (c)
Avg. 1909–13	90	—	62	65
1913	—	94	—	—
1917	87	—	54	55
1920	69	87	34	45
1921	63	80	28	36

SOURCES: (a) TsSU, *Trudy*, 18: 122–23, 131. Data (converted here into hectares and tons) do not cover the Far East, Turkestan, or the trans-Caucasus.

(b) Poliakov, p. 58 and 64. Data on sown area taken from TsUNKhU, *Sotsialisticheskoe stroitel'stvo*, p. 176.

(c) *SDD*, 1:284. Data converted to tons.

output of this territory was 62 million tons, but by 1921 was only 28 million tons. These statistics were territorially incomplete and were criticized on other counts as well. The data of the old Central Statistical Committee (TsSK) used by the TsSU for prewar figures were said to be too low and were revised upward in the 1920's. However, the new figures calculated by the TsSU differed from those adopted by the State Planning Commission (Gosplan), and the data were subsequently revised further.[1] The various data sets confronting the researcher differ not only in the adjustments made, but also in the areas and number of grains covered. In 1934, TsSU revised downward the data on prewar sown area and harvests, and as late as 1960 yet another downward revision of the harvest figures was introduced. The last change was officially attributed to the reclassification as peasant land of lands rented by peasants from gentry landowners (previously recorded as gentry land); since peasant land was less productive, the figure for overall output was correspondingly lowered.[2] This explanation of the adjustment has been questioned,* but whatever the reason behind the revision, its effect was to reduce the prewar production figures *below* the original TsSK figures, which were universally acknowledged in the 1920's to be too low.

Any assessment of the postrevolutionary agrarian economic situation must take note of the problem with prerevolutionary data. Movement can be measured only from a fixed point, and the prewar point of de-

* Wheatcroft maintains ("Reliability," p. 171) that even if *all* landowners' land were transferred to the peasant category, the resultant output figure would remain above that recently adopted by the TsSU. The new figures appear in TsSU, *Sel'skoe khoziaistvo SSSR: statisticheskii sbornik* (1960), p. 196.

parture is not easily established. The range of figures for the 1913 harvest, for example, extends from 76 million to 110 million tons.[3] The
choice of data strongly influences (or is influenced by) interpretations
of postrevolutionary conditions. Soviet historian Iu. A. Poliakov, for
one, objects to the continued use of the early TsSU data on the amount
of sown land and uses instead the later figures, which show a much
smaller decline: 16 percent rather than 31 percent.[4] Yet statistics from
the early 1920's indicate that in European Russia the drop amounted to
about 40 percent of the prewar grain area and was even worse than the
summary TsSU data suggest.[5] On the other hand, the figures may have
been distorted by the understatement of peasants seeking to minimize
their grain-requisition quotas. Poliakov's quandary illustrates the problems created by the statistical hodgepodge: having rejected the 1924
TsSU data on sown area as too low, he was obliged for want of a better
source to utilize the accompanying data on grain production.[6] However, combining the two sets of figures that he accepts (a process he
avoids) would suggest an even more drastic drop in the productivity of
the land than emerges from the TsSU data alone.

The statistical dissonance in the field is less important than the general agreement about the existence (if not the extent) of a major economic setback in the years following the revolution. There is also broad
agreement that the drop in productivity was more severe than the decline in the area under cultivation. Recently published TsSU data show
a drop of 45 percent in gross agricultural production (including field
crops) in comparison with 1913, and Naum Jasny speaks of an overall
decline of almost 50 percent by 1921/22.[7]

The reduction in the amount of land cultivated is especially striking
in view of the land acquisitions by peasants in this period. In addition
to the relative gains made by the peasants in the *chernyi peredel*,
there was simply more land available per person because of the substantial decline in the population resulting from wars, revolutions, and
related phenomena. The amount of agricultural land per capita increased between 1917 and 1922 in most regions of the country.[8] The
census taken on August 28, 1920, indicated an overall population decline of about 12 percent, with higher rates of loss for European Russia.[9] Additional casualties occurred during the remainder of the year
and throughout 1921 because of some continuing fighting and because
of famine. Total losses since 1914 were said to exceed 20 million, and
were especially heavy among males of working age.[10]

How much the decline in the rural labor force affected cultivation is
difficult to assess. Previous agrarian overpopulation and the influx of
city dwellers cushioned its effects; despite continuing internal strife,

the return of soldiers after the war relieved manpower shortages. The partial census returns for 1917 show one male in four missing from rural areas, but by 1919 this figure had been halved.[11] It appears unlikely, therefore, that the cutback in cultivation and the more drastic fall in productivity were caused by a lack of labor.

Different approaches have been taken to explain the shrinkage of both area and yield. Soviet historians stress the unfavorable conditions of the civil war, when fighting interfered with agriculture and often made it impossible. They have pointed, too, to the disruption inherent in the redistribution of land, inefficiencies resulting from the breakup of larger economic units, the dispersal of inventory, and devastating periods of drought.

Problems connected with the redistribution of land undoubtedly took their toll, and the statistical sources confirm the inadequacy of agricultural inventory throughout the period. A quarter of all draft animals were lost between 1916 and 1921; by 1920 over 27 percent of all peasant households in the RSFSR were completely without draft power.[12] The overall amount of agricultural machinery and equipment in the country in 1920 was approximately the same as in 1910; but some items were in critically short supply, and all of the inventory was older and distributed over a larger number of households.[13] Importing of agricultural equipment, which had virtually stopped after the outbreak of the First World War, resumed for a brief interval in 1917 but contributed almost nothing more to inventory for the rest of the period of War Communism.[14] Records of official distribution of the inadequate domestic production of agricultural equipment show some improvement of output in 1919 over 1918 levels, but a decline in 1920.[15] Efforts to promote efficient utilization of the available supply by establishing central rental and repair stations could not remedy basic deficiencies.

The damage that can be attributed to the civil war is difficult to evaluate. On the basis of regional crop-production statistics, the agricultural economist V. P. Timoshenko noted that "the regions most affected by the civil war show smaller declines than regions in which the civil war terminated early and which were under the complete control of the Soviet government for a longer period."[16] Although the Soviet statistical sources cited above do not agree with Timoshenko's figures, they confirm his contention that the Ukraine and Siberia, both the scene of active civil warfare, witnessed a below-average decline in crop area between 1916 and 1921.[17]

The essential cause of the decline in agriculture, according to Timoshenko and some other non-Soviet writers, was the food-procurement policy pursued by the government under War Communism.[18] Increasingly draconian supply measures culminated in the decree of January 11, 1919, which introduced the full requisitioning of all grain above a consumption norm and declared trading in the requisitioned products to be a state crime.[19] Many peasants reacted by curtailing production to personal subsistence levels.

Food-Intake Patterns

Although the relative weight of the various factors involved in the decline of output is open to debate, there is little disagreement about their cumulative effect. The statistics on crop area and output tell an unadorned story of hungry people. As Marx was hardly the first to observe, "people must be in a position to live in order to 'make history.' But life involves, before everything else, eating."[20] Few needed to be persuaded of that fact in revolutionary Russia. The makers of history were incessantly concerned with the problem of food shortages during the years of War Communism.

There were significant differences between rural and urban consumption of food during the period, and between intake in the food-producing and the food-consuming regions. The partial agricultural census of 1919 (covering 34 provinces) and the census of 1920 showed, as might have been anticipated, that urban proletarians were consistently getting less to eat than peasants, and that the producing provinces were better fed than the consuming provinces. Town dwellers were getting about a third less food (measured by the daily caloric intake of an adult) than rural residents, although inhabitants of the two capital cities were faring somewhat better than those of other towns.[21] The diet of both rural and urban populations consisted primarily of bread and potatoes.[22] The potato crop had fallen below the prewar level, but by only about 15 percent, and it had become a more important part of the general food supply than previously.

According to summary data published later, in the agricultural year 1919/20 the intake by weight of grain per capita was only three-fourths of the prerevolutionary level in the consuming provinces but was almost normal in the producing provinces.[23] However, grain provided an increased share of the diet since the sources of meat and dairy products were shrinking. (Livestock had declined by a third between 1916 and 1920.)[24] Even where grain consumption was maintained at previous levels, therefore, the total food intake was reduced and deteriorated in quality.

The low point in food consumption for workers in the cities came in 1918,[25] just before the government embarked on its requisitioning policy and began to promote socialization in agriculture. The situation in the countryside was rather different. In rural areas the low point in consumption was not reached until the winter of 1920–21.[26] By then an extraordinary situation had come into being: the food-intake level of the producing zone had fallen relatively lower than that of the consuming zone. The normally higher per capita consumption of the producing region was down to 67 percent of the prewar level, whereas in the consuming zone intake was still at 81 percent of the prewar level.[27]

This unusual circumstance resulted from poor harvests and crop failures caused by adverse climatic conditions. The drought responsible for much of the damage was not severe, but it affected regions bereft of reserves of food or seed grain. In the hard-hit Volga region, famine began to claim a heavy toll, and a "hunger migration" sent large numbers wandering through the countryside in search of food. By February 1921 the grain-producing area that normally yielded a surplus to fill deficits elsewhere in the country was itself reduced to only two-thirds of the local per capita consumption norm. Everywhere peasants were getting less food than before. As Lenin was to acknowledge, "the crop failure of 1920 worsened the position of the peasants beyond belief."[28]

And it was among the peasants that support for the government was weakest. As hunger spread, disaffection began to stir openly in the countryside. Communist Party members and their families became the targets of growing rural hostility in the winter of 1920–21. In Tambov province an antigovernment army of peasants organized with the help of local SRs took control of a sizable area, seizing rail lines and disrupting the meager flow of food supplies.[29] Similar uprisings broke out in western Siberia; although the insurgency there was less organized, it swept over a larger area. Heavy fighting in February placed important grain-carrying railroads in the hands of the rebels.[30] This was the state of affairs confronting the government when in late February and early March the troops and sailors stationed at the Kronstadt fortress outside Petrograd (many of them newly arrived from the countryside) rose in revolt with a demand for "soviets without Communists."

The ominous political situation was a direct outgrowth of the steadily deteriorating economic situation. When conditions continued to worsen after the guns had become silent, the government was forced to come to terms with the peasants' growing resistance to its policy of requisition. Efforts to promote the socialization of agriculture had met with a limited response. It was evident that the government was pulling in one direction, the peasantry in another. By the spring of 1921 the limit had been reached. Lenin, openly admitting peasant opposition, announced a need to reappraise policy: "If any Communist imagined that the economic base—the economic roots of small-scale agriculture—could be transformed in three years, then he of course was a dreamer. And there is no hiding it, quite a few such dreamers were in our midst."[31]

Long before, the historian Paul Miliukov had pointed out that major reform periods throughout Russian history had been regularly prompted by economic needs and connected with military endeavors.[32] The developments of War Communism, essentially the struggle of a new regime to feed a nation and an army while facing serious challenges to its own survival, offer another illustration of the conjunction. The many institutional innovations of the period were attempts to develop new mechanisms of administrative control; socialization of agriculture was intended, like nationalization of "the commanding heights" in industry, to increase the state's control of basic economic resources.

Noting similarities between administrative changes after 1917 and Peter the Great's reform of 1719, a contemporary of the modern reforms predicted that the new would prove as short-lived as the old.[33] Although many innovations of the period had disappeared or faded by the end of War Communism, some of those that remained were to become permanent, major features in the organization of Russian social and economic life.

The inauspicious early soviets and the agricultural collectives gave no indication at the time of the role they would ultimately play in the countryside. The system of communal land tenure seemed firmly entrenched. There were a number of reasons—long- and short-range benefits, social attitudes, and a lack of viable alternatives—to explain why the peasants had flocked to communes after the revolution. Why they stayed in them emerges more clearly from a reconsideration of the record of the previous decade.

Who left the commune when the door was finally blown open by the revolution of 1905? The poorest peasants and the wealthiest peasants. In the great leveling of the *chernyi peredel* these groups, if they did not disappear, were substantially reduced.

Who stayed in the commune after 1906? The economically insecure, the smaller families, those with little inventory, little opportunity for market enterprise, or little chance of outside employment. Under the conditions prevailing during War Communism, virtually the entire rural population fell into these categories.

The monarchy, the Church, and even the family had to greater or lesser degrees been institutional casualties of the revolution. Only the commune survived intact.

PART V

Old Economic Policy and New Social Policy 1921-1929

Rural developments between 1921 and 1929, a relatively placid interval between the turbulence of War Communism and the high drama of collectivization, have until recently received comparatively little attention in historical literature. Only in the last few decades (that is, since Stalin's death) have Soviet historians begun serious scholarly investigation of the countryside in the 1920's, and major Western scholarship in the field has followed a similar pattern. Yet it has become increasingly apparent that rural developments not only influenced, but were in large measure responsible for, many of the more highly publicized political conflicts and policy decisions during this critical, pivotal decade in the reshaping of Russian society.

Official policy moved through distinct stages in the 1920's. Analysis of agrarian policy has led some investigators to speak of three successive phases: the early years from 1921 to late 1924, characterized by a cautious, hands-off approach and a retreat from the harsh tactics of War Communism; the middle years from 1925 through 1927, bringing more active support for (as well as more vociferous opposition to) the rural status quo under the slogan "Face to the countryside"; and the final, turbulent years from the end of 1927, when the Party "set a course for collectivization," until late 1929 and the whirlwind drive that radically and permanently changed the structure of rural society.

This is a useful scheme, but developments in different areas of interest did not always proceed at the same rate. In the history of the commune the first two periods are essentially one: the period of coexistence. Events in 1928 and 1929 followed a different course, yet in many ways represent the culmination of tendencies that can be traced in the earlier period. Throughout every stage of development, however defined, the commune remained the most important administrative institution dealing with the immediate concerns of peasants; its predominance in the countryside was to prove a significant factor in the social, political, and economic evolution of the country as a whole.

14

Communes under NEP

The political crisis of 1905 had persuaded the Imperial government to sign a death warrant for the commune; the economic crisis of War Communism prompted the Soviet government to renew its lease on life. Although on both occasions economic and political problems were closely intertwined, in 1921 as in 1905 the government basically responded to the political situation. Addressing a group of officials on March 15, 1921, Lenin announced, "The question of the replacement of requisitions by a tax is primarily and essentially a political question." In a country composed largely of small agricultural producers, transitional measures would be necessary in the passage to socialism. "We must not try to hide anything, but must say candidly that the peasants are dissatisfied. . . . We must reckon with this . . . and reexamine our policy."[1]

According to the Party's most eminent historian at the time, M. N. Pokrovskii, the danger of counterrevolution did not stem from the upper bourgeoisie or from the gentry landowners. The power of those groups, though formidable, was based on material possessions, and these could be taken away. The petty-bourgeois peasants, on the other hand, were aflame with revolutionary enthusiasm ignited in their bourgeois revolution, and this was the real danger confronting the Soviet regime.[2]

The historian's assessment was confirmed in the field. The military commander M. N. Tukhachevskii, dispatched to Tambov after regaining control of Kronstadt for the government, observed that the peasants referred to the local insurrection as "their revolution"; in his view, the situation had to be dealt with as a war and not just as rural disturbances.[3]

On March 21, 1921, following several weeks of discussion and publication of the measure within the Party and in the press, the government issued a decree that ended requisitioning and substituted a fixed tax in kind.[4] The level of taxation was reduced, and peasants who had paid their taxes were free now to dispose of the rest of their crops as they chose. Trade was legalized, and barter was encouraged.[5] The "New Economic Policy" (NEP) thus introduced marked a reversal of the socialization trend of the later War Communism period. It was, in fact, a reversion to—or more accurately, toward—old economic policy.

Two days later a directive issued to all land departments prohibited the compulsory allocation of land for state or collective farms and limited the land that could be placed in new collectives to the amount previously held by members.[6] A general relaxation of land policies accompanied an official return to the original neutrality toward forms of tenure that had been proclaimed in the first days of the new regime. As a Soviet scholar has noted, the land legislation of 1921–22 had something in common with that of 1917–18. Both provided a juridical framework for a "long siege" that was interrupted by the "blitz attack on capitalism" of War Communism.[7]

Juridical Status

The question of land tenure and the need to clarify existing land laws in view of the changes in economic policy came up for immediate discussion in 1921. By May 1922 a Basic Law on Land Use had been elaborated and adopted; its provisions were refined and confirmed in the Land Code that became effective in the RSFSR on December 1. The new code, variants of which were subsequently adopted in the other republics, superseded previous land legislation.[8]

If there remained any lingering doubt that land had been nationalized, the new legislation dispelled it. The opening lines of the 1922 code of the RSFSR declared the right of private ownership of land, subsoil, waters, and forests "forever abolished." All land was explicitly proclaimed the property (*sobstvennost'*) of the state, and all agricultural land was placed under the control of the Commissariat of Agriculture. At the same time the prohibition of commercial transfer of land use rights was reaffirmed. Any proprietorial or entrepreneurial instincts the peasant may have had, whether "petty" or more presumptuous, were thus firmly checked. Most Russian peasants had been unable at the beginning of the century to buy or sell the land they worked because it was the property of the commune; in the Soviet period they remained unable to do so because all land had become the property of the state.

The form of tenure in which households or groups utilized this state property remained an open option under the code. Households could hold land in consolidated holdings (khutors and otrubs), in communes, or in collectives. Any landholding community could retain its existing form of tenure or could transfer to another form upon the decision of the members. Households wishing to separate from communes could do so at any time with the consent of the commune, or even without the commune's consent at the time of a general redistribution. Separations without consent could be effected at other times only if the group of separating households numbered one-fifth of the membership, or 50 households in communes with 250 or more households. These last provisions, which will be recognized as directly out of the Stolypin legislation, were prompted by the same considerations as had inspired their adoption earlier: the separation of individual households, or of only a few households, was apt to seriously disrupt the agricultural operations of the community because of the complex layout of peasants' intermixed stripholdings.

There was another parallel between the 1922 Land Code and an earlier law. Just as the emancipation legislation had introduced a note of confusion by using the unfamiliar and undefined term "rural society," so the Land Code raised questions with the equally vague new name "land society" (*zemel'noe obshchestvo*).[9] One contemporary analyst suggested that the term was deliberately left undefined to allow for the anticipated development of a new type of land commune.[10] Another, ignoring the Stolypin legislation, offered the explanation that a new name was required to distinguish the old "compulsory" commune ("rural society") from the new voluntary organization.[11] The principle of voluntary membership in the land society had, in fact, drawn serious opposition while the legislation was being formulated, but was finally approved on the recommendation of a special commission appointed to study the question.[12]

"Land society" legally designated any group who jointly used some or all of their land and settled questions related to land use in group assemblies.[13] The term therefore covered some collectives and groups of independent households sharing the use of any land; however, general references to the "land society" in the 1920's were understood to mean the commune. Official documents of the period used the terms "commune," "land society," and "rural society" interchangeably. The Georgian land code, for example, had no section dealing with the "land society" as such but spoke specifically of communal tenure.[14] As for the peasants, they continued to refer, as previously, to "the commune" and "the society" without distinction.[15]

Under the new legislation the authority of the land society was expressed in its general assembly. The assembly was to be guided by the

Land Code and by local customs insofar as they did not contravene the law. According to Article 51 of the code, the assembly was to decide all matters affecting the land society as a whole: the mode of tenure, land supply, land organization work, separations from the society with land, the redistribution of land, agricultural questions (crop rotation, pasturing, and so forth), arrangements for use of the common land,* the disposition of vacant land, and similar matters of general concern. All land users of either sex eighteen years of age or older (and in special cases even younger individuals conducting independent land operations) could participate and vote in the assembly. For most routine affairs a majority of member households constituted a legal quorum whose decisions were binding on all members. To resolve more fundamental questions, such as a change in the tenure system, a vote of representatives of two-thirds of all member households and at least half of all members with full voting rights in the society was required. The difficulty of achieving a quorum in large communes led to a law of 1926 permitting the formation of "secondary assemblies" composed of delegates elected by subgroups of households (1 for each 10 households in communes with 250–500 households, and 1 for each 20 in communes with over 500 households).[16]

Meetings of the assembly were open to the public and could be attended by any local resident or interested visitor. All who were present could take part in its discussion and debates, but only the members of the commune, those who were recognized as having a right to use its land, were allowed to vote.[17] This followed longstanding practice, for traditionally nonlandholding members of the community could take part in the assembly and have a voice in the resolution of local questions not related to landholding.[18] The statute of March 14, 1927, however, distinguished between assemblies of the land commune (*zemel'nye skhody*) and general village assemblies (*sel'skie skhody*).[19] From this point on, the former were supposed to be restricted to land users and confined to land questions, while the latter were to be open to all local residents with full constitutional rights and could discuss all *but* land questions.

The 1922 Land Code (Article 9) guaranteed the right of any individual to use land for agriculture with his or her own labor. But the provisions of the code repeatedly referred to the household rather than the individual. Jurists debated which of the two was the "subject of the law," and the prevailing opinion was that households constituted

---

*The type of land included in this category varied in the different republics. In the Azerbaidzhan code, for example, all ponds, wells, and reservoirs were under the direct control of the land society. (Novitskii, "Zemel'noe obshchestvo," p. 92, n. 1.)

the legal users of land.[20] Technically, a household could consist of a single person without a family, but the requirements of agriculture were such that few peasant households were so constituted.[21] The land allotted to a household was assigned to its use without a specific time limit, but in communes all land except houses and garden plots was subject to redistribution. A household could be deprived of its allotment only if it had abandoned the land for six years, if it had forfeited the land as a judicial penalty, or if the land were required for state or social needs, such as ways of communication or mineral exploitation (Article 186). On the other hand, the household could renounce its land at any time. Upon renunciation, as upon abandonment or escheat, the land reverted to the communal fund.

Since the household was the basic organizational unit in agricultural production, there were practical reasons for considering it the landholder under the law. The return to the principle of household, as opposed to individual, tenure was a reversion to pre-Stolypin practice. Although the code left more discretionary control of the land in the hands of users than had previous Soviet legislation, it restricted the use rights of both the household and the commune in certain respects. For example, the commune was responsible for land redistribution but was not at liberty to schedule it at will. General redistributions were limited to a period of no less than three full crop rotations (or, according to a provision added in 1923, no less than nine years where no regular rotation system was in effect); partial reassignment of lands could be made only with the consent of all parties involved, and not more than once per rotation period. The intent of such regulations was to prevent excessive fragmentation of landholdings by limiting the frequency of redistribution. Yet redistribution could be brought about against the wishes of a majority. In the Ukraine, where membership in a land society was obligatory for all peasant landholders, redistribution undertaken to improve the system of land use could be compulsory even in societies composed entirely of khutors and otrubs. And a 1926 amendment to the RSFSR code provided that a minority of any size could bring about a redistribution of lands where none had taken place since November 1917 and significant inequalities in holdings existed.[22] In White Russia there was no periodic redistribution of the land, but household holdings could be readjusted on an individual basis if they failed to conform to the local norm.[23]

One of the important concessions made to the peasants in the 1922 code was the authorization to lease land under special and temporary circumstances. Land could be leased only where hardship or lack of inventory made it impossible for its holders to cultivate it themselves, and then for only one crop rotation period, or three years. This limited dispensation, prompted by evasions of the former prohibition and by recognition of the likelihood of their increase under NEP, was broadened by a VTsIK circular of October 24, 1923, and subsequent legislation in 1925 ending the disfranchisement of agriculturalists who used hired labor.[24] Since communes were engaged in both leasing land (as lessors and as lessees) and hiring workers, these modifications of the earlier regulations were significant for them. However, communes' renting out of part of their land was sharply criticized in some circles as an egregious contravention of the principle that only those who worked the land themselves had a right to it. As a result, in mid-1924 the Council of Commissars of the RSFSR adopted a ruling that restricted to individuals the right to lease out land and permitted communes to rent land only from the state land fund.[25] For a number of reasons this policy proved impractical and unenforceable, and it was abandoned the following year in connection with a shift to a more conciliatory line. An amendment to the Land Code in 1925 recognized the right of land societies to lease out their lands either to individuals or to groups; in 1926 the term of leasing was extended to two rotations or up to twelve years, and hiring of labor was liberalized.[26]

The right of the commune to engage in practices permitted to individuals followed logically from the code's recognition of the land society as a juridical person. According to Article 64 the society as such had the right to "acquire property, conclude contracts, bring claims and answer charges in court, and bring matters before other institutions."[27] Precisely because the commune was recognized as a juridical person, individual members could not refuse to accept responsibility for its contractual obligations. A member might legally protest, for example, the specific share of a debt contracted by the commune that had been assigned to his household, but he could not repudiate responsibility for some part of the debt, even if he had voted against contracting it. Thus, in the words of a legislative analyst of the period, the legal status of the commune made it possible "to strengthen the social responsibility of members of the society with respect to social obligations, and to establish the firm responsibility of each for all."[28] Here then was another example of continuity through change: a reaffirmation of the principle of mutual responsibility that strikingly illustrates the traditional component inherent in the new socialist ideology.

Because of considerable differences in the size, constituency, and local problems of different land societies, it was not possible to prescribe uniform detailed regulations governing their use of land and other functions. The Land Code (Article 48) indicated that rules for land use and for other land-related economic affairs were to be defined by the society itself in a charter or in a corresponding resolution adopted by the membership. Many communes, however, appear to have operated simply on the basis of established local tradition without ever drawing up any formal document. In an attempt to strengthen the rule of written law in rural land relations, on January 5, 1926, the Commissariat of Agriculture issued a regulation requiring every land society to adopt a charter and published a model charter to assist them in doing so.[29]

The 1922 legislation, which defined land relationships for the next half-dozen years (and in some respects continued to do so formally for decades), was said at the time to embody the principle of "juridical neutrality" for all forms of land tenure. But as observers remarked, although the law permitted a choice of tenure, it by no means followed that the state had to "remain passive with respect to realities."[30] It was possible to transfer to any form of tenure, but the provisions of the law made it easiest to transfer to collective landholding, particularly to forms encompassing collective cultivation. There was much to be said for the observation that "in place of 'juridical neutrality' it would be more correct, closer to the letter, the sense, and the intent of the law, to speak of the 'juridical priority' of collective forms of land use."[31] Yet it is also true that until 1928 official priorities did not intrude in NEP legislation to the point of seriously constraining the commune in the exercise of its traditional and expanded functions.

Practices and Problems

What the law decreed was not necessarily what the peasants practiced. Village life encompassed a range of activities and relationships that had long been regulated by custom rather than formal law, and custom proved tenacious. Moreover, the laws themselves—articulating the norms of a new order while attempting to compromise (for a time) with parts of the old—were constantly being reshaped in response to changing conditions.

One anomaly of the legal situation was the fact that participation in the general meeting of the community remained open to all of its members, including those who had been deprived (for social or political reasons) of the right to vote for members of soviets. The rationale for this was the fact that only the soviet was formally considered a part of the administrative system, and the soviet did not necessarily coincide territorially with the land society.[32] Yet refusal to recognize the commune as part of the system was inconsistent with provisions of the law making the society responsible for the administration of local affairs. In any case, disfranchised members of the community could continue as (or become) members of the commune.

The membership might also include individual local households (khutors and otrubs) that shared the use of some land with other members of the commune. Where such households were sufficiently concentrated, they could form their own land society. Membership in a land society was not obligatory in the RSFSR, but in some cases scattered consolidators chose to join the local commune as a special category of members whose lands were not subject to redistribution. Similarly, small collectives formed on lands that had belonged to communes frequently remained component units within the original commune rather than establishing a new land society. Of a group of 25 collective farms covered in one investigation, 20 belonged to larger land societies.[33]

The communal assembly continued to concern itself with all aspects of village life, partly through force of tradition and partly because of the absence of other local agencies competent to resolve village problems. The elimination of the zemstvo system of local self-government gave it new room to exercise its powers. Over the course of the half century between the emancipation and the October Revolution, which ended its existence, the zemstvo had come to play a large role in rural society, providing a wide array of educational, medical, agronomic, and other services. New Soviet agencies assumed some of the functions that had been carried out previously by the zemstvos, but in some areas the commune stepped into the breach.

The primary function of the commune remained regulating land use and land relations within its territory. It was responsible for distributing land among its members and established the rules of land use. The assembly now elected a "plenipotentiary" (still referred to popularly as the starosta) who was authorized to handle routine land matters for the commune and represented it before official agencies and in court. Where the territory of the commune and the rural soviet coincided, the soviet served as executive for the commune, and a plenipotentiary was not elected. In any case, basic questions were resolved by the general assembly. As noted, the commune could rent out its land or rent additional land for its members to use. It hired herdsmen and watchmen for the community as a whole and could conclude contracts and agreements with state and cooperative agencies, contract debts with credit institutions, and issue loans. The commune had its own budget and sources of income (primarily from self-taxation) to cover expenditures authorized by its membership. It decided collectively on accepting new members, and assumed responsibility for certain social obligations. The law did not circumscribe the scope of its functions, and in practice it defined them itself. Generally poor communications with the center tended to reinforce its local autonomy. Official rulings and legislative revisions often remained unknown in rural areas long after they had been adopted; once received in the localities, they were apt to be applied according to the temper of the community.

Attendance at the village assemblies was often low. Estimates range from 10 to 15 percent of the membership up to a rare 40 to 50 percent.[34] However, meetings were convened fairly frequently, depending on local custom and the problems requiring discussion. They were generally not scheduled regularly. Voting was usually reserved for household heads; since few households were headed by women, few women were among those who made decisions at the assembly despite the equal rights guaranteed by the constitution. Women, in fact, were said rarely to be present at the meetings. A typical 1925 newspaper article on "Women in the Village" reported that women attending assemblies were treated with derision and were not permitted to speak.[35]

Nonetheless, voting records for elections to soviets show that the political participation of rural women in this arena rose substantially in the course of the decade. In 1922 women constituted over one percent of the deputies to rural soviets in only 4 out of 46 provinces and administrative territories. The highest rate of female participation was in Tsaritsyn, where 2.8 percent of the delegates were women. In the elections of 1924/25, however, women won 9 percent of the seats in rural soviets in the RSFSR. By 1927 women accounted for 12 percent of all representatives elected to rural soviets in the RSFSR, and almost one-third of all qualified women were voting in elections for soviets.[36] Although comparable data are not available for participation in the communal assemblies, the social change reflected in the electoral patterns for soviets undoubtedly had some effect there. In urban areas female political participation was higher than in the countryside. In 1927, 19 percent of the delegates to local soviets in the towns were women. The participation of urban women in the labor market affected their political participation rates, and the same factor may have helped to politicize rural women. According to some studies, as much as 40 percent of the hired agricultural labor force was female in the mid-1920's.[37] However, agricultural employment provided less opportunity for association and political development, and a strong residue of patriarchal tradition kept women less active in rural public life.

The same set of traditional attitudes limited the role of younger members of households in the village assemblies. In time, this gave rise to a charged situation because of demographic developments: the loss of population during the years of war, revolution, and civil strife had shifted the age profile, and the average age of the populace had dropped. Starting in the latter half of 1922, birth rates rose rapidly, reducing the average still further.[38] By the time of the 1926 census, over half of the rural population was under twenty years of age. The total population by this time had regained the prewar level and numbered 147 million. Almost 121 million (82 percent) lived in rural areas, and 115 million (112 million of the rural population plus 3 million living in urban localities, or 78 percent of the total population) were supported basically by agriculture. The peasant practice of putting children into the labor force at an early age meant that less than 12 percent of the entire rural population in the country ten years of age and over was not self-supporting.

Self-support did not necessarily mean economic self-sufficiency, since most individuals (particularly self-supporting women) worked within the interdependent family economy under the authority of the household head.[39] That authority tended to be maintained within and by the commune, even over adult males, although they were more likely than women or youths to have a voice in the deliberations of the commune.

In the course of the decade the number of households increased more rapidly than the total population. Family divisions, which had markedly accelerated from 1917 to 1920, dropped between 1920 and 1922 because of economic conditions. Starting in late 1922, however, they rose once again, and the rate of divisions remained high throughout the decade.[40] The division of a household and its property could be effected by any member who had full civil rights and was eighteen years old; any newly formed household could demand additional land from the commune if its share of the divided land fell below the commune's distributional norm.[41] In large part as the result of such divisions, the number of households throughout the country rose from 21 million in 1916 to 25 million by 1927.[42] Some of the increase, of course, was from natural growth, and the total would have been even higher had unions of families and liquidations of households not cancelled out some of the divisions. From 1920 through 1925 over a quarter of all households in the consuming region and over a third of those in the producing region underwent one or more basic structural changes.[43] By the middle of the decade a substantial number of households were newly formed social units.

The motives for household divisions varied. One Soviet investigator has suggested that there were two distinct groups of reasons for the breakup of familes during the NEP period.[44] The first set reflected a certain social ferment, and its agents of change included progressive agricultural innovators, partisans of collectivism and cooperativism, proponents of women's liberation, and opponents of the "old, often semipatriarchal order." The second group of factors was largely economic and was said to be related to "capitalist tendencies" in the countryside. This included the desire for economic independence ("petty proprietary inclinations") and attempts to escape taxation through purely formal or fictitious divisions.

Whatever the reasons, the net result was a drop in the size of the average family between 1916 and 1927 from 5.7 members to 5.1. This had social and economic implications that contemporaries were quick to elaborate. As noted earlier, larger peasant families had always been stronger and more prosperous. Household divisions, by reducing the size of the production unit, typically reduced its resources and weakened its productive capacity. According to the theories of Chaianov and the organization-production school, family divisions were a normal part of the cycle of "demographic differentiation" characteristic of the peasant economy.[45] Young families were normally smaller and poorer than the average because of the high ratio of dependent young children to the number of workers. In time, they grew into larger units with a more favorable ratio, growing more prosperous in the process. Finally, large, well-off families split up as grown children broke away to establish their own households, and the new, younger households began to reenact the basic pattern. To members of the school, the developments of the 1920's seemed to confirm their theory. Thanks to the gains of the revolution, the position of the peasantry as a whole had been improved, and it was primarily the larger and more prosperous households that were breaking up. This development was not without its benefits, since per capita productivity increased where there was a higher ratio of dependents to workers in the peasant household.

The notion of demographic differentiation met with little sympathy among the rising new schools of Marxist agrarian theoreticians. Emphasis on the cyclical mobility of the family, they protested, only obscured the more critical processes of social differentiation taking place in the countryside and overlooked elements of social antagonism within the household. What was actually unfolding in households, in the opinion of writers such as L. N. Kritsman and M. I. Kubanin, was an economic struggle among members of the family, a struggle intensified by the development of a market economy. The entrepreneurial head of the household was exploiting other members of the family, who were in the position of mere laborers. Despite the juridical equality that had been established by the revolution, there was a growing economic inequality resulting from the control of family income by the household head.[46] Whether or not this was a new phenomenon, the 1926 census provided evidence that young workers in agriculture were a particularly dependent category. Almost half of the agricultural labor force, it was revealed, worked in the capacity of "helpers of the head of the household," and two-thirds of this group (or one-third of the entire agricultural labor force) was below twenty years of age.[47] Not all Marxists agreed, however, on the significance of generational conflict, and some found the emphasis of their colleagues on this issue excessive. Dubrovskii, for example, scathingly proposed a new slogan to them: "Proletarian and kulak sons, unite!"[48]

Intrafamilial conflicts did play some role in the breakup of households. According to *Komsomol'skaia pravda*, 30 to 40 percent of all family divisions were due to the contemporary generation gap. But more than a twentieth-century chapter of *Fathers and Sons* was unfolding—the new official social climate reaching into the village, especially the new legislation, was making it possible to modify the traditional family structure.

One example of this was the new protection given to women's property rights in divorce. Divorce itself was a new phenomenon and remained a rarity in the countryside, yet its impact on more urbanized areas had repercussions there. In the country as a whole, the divorce rate had been statistically insignificant, and summary prerevolutionary demographic data often did not even list it. By 1927, however, 3.1 divorces were recorded for every thousand people in the European part of the RSFSR.[49] (The marriage rate at the time was 10.2 per thousand.) The statutory right of women to leave the household and the right to claim a share of its property (confirmed in the 1927 Marriage and Family Code), although limited in their immediate application in rural areas, undoubtedly had some effect on peasant attitudes. The potential for mobility had changed considerably since the days of tsarist Russia, when the law required a married woman to reside with her husband and divorce was unknown in the village.

The changes that were taking place within the family and the household merely strengthened the role of the commune in the life of peasants. The increased number of households created new demands for land redistribution. Communes had no control over the rights of households to subdivide their land when families divided, but the Soviet government was no less concerned than its predecessor about the economic consequences of such division. Land officials were instructed to prevent excessive fragmentation of holdings, and provincial executive committees were authorized to establish regional norms below which land could not be divided. Several statewide legislative projects were formulated with a view to controlling the minimum size of holdings, but like similar tsarist projects they were never enacted.[50]

Despite the many official attempts to limit the practice and despite the restrictions in the Land Code, the redistribution of communal land continued. As Marx had observed almost a century earlier, speaking of Western Europe, peasants resisted any attempt to limit their right to divide the land. All such efforts violated deep-rooted peasant notions of justice founded on principles of egalitarianism. In the mid-1920's agencies of the Commissariat of Agriculture and the Workers' and Peasants' Inspectorate reported that widespread redistributions were taking place annually in many central agricultural provinces, in the Ural region, and in the Northern Caucasus. A check of some 500 communes in Voronezh showed that almost 80 percent had conducted redistributions before the end of the legally stipulated nine-year term, and almost half of them had done so within a three-year period. In 1923 and 1924 redistributions were registered for almost 30 percent of the RSFSR, and the Workers' and Peasants' Inspectorate noted that many others were not registered.[51] Considering the extensive scale on which redistribution appears to have been carried out at the time, it may be a sign of the commune's success in this area that only 2 percent of the disputes brought before the land commissions in the mid-1920's had to do with the redistribution of land.[52]

An attempt by the Land Code to introduce the establishment of a uniform unit of distribution (e.g., "eater" or "worker") within localities appears to have met with little response among the peasants. The law advised that communes using a different unit from that announced by local authorities were not obliged to undertake a premature redistribution merely to conform to the new standard, but this solicitude seems to have been unnecessary. Most communes simply continued to employ their accustomed units of redistribution. In this minor matter as in more important questions, the government, having indicated its own preferences, was prepared to accommodate those of the peasants. In the latter part of the decade, there was a policy shift in favor of redistributions where they could be used to undermine the wealthier peasants or to promote collectivized forms of agriculture. This shift was already evident in the 1926 amendment to the code that permitted a minority to bring about redistributions in certain cases. In 1928 a Union law authorized two new exceptions to the minimum period between redistributions: cases of transfer to an "improved form of economy" and cases involving the "necessity of a struggle with kulaks." In general, however, the government discouraged redistributions, and it was a sign of the peasants' persistence rather than of official approval that they continued on such a scale throughout the period.

Land Organization Work

A more pronounced ambivalence emerged in policy on land organization work. The government supported such work for technical reasons, but there was considerable concern about the social implications of some forms of land organization. This concern, coupled with the competition of other demands on the budget, kept land organization activity at a fairly low level throughout most of the decade. In the later years the nature of the work was modified, and efforts were made to strengthen the program.

In the 1920's all of the agricultural land in the country was divided into land organization sectors, each with its own staff. In 1925 there were over 500 such sectors in the RSFSR, with approximately 7,000 employees.[33] By 1927 the number of sectors had risen to about 850, but staffing remained a problem. The number of land surveyors and land organizers working in the entire country at the end of that year was only 11,500; and a complaint was raised at the Fifteenth Party Congress in December that such a limited staff was far from adequate for the tasks confronting the agrarian economy.[34]

In the initial years after the revolution, almost all land organization activity had come under the category of "inter-village" land work and was directed to distributing and equalizing land among communes. The Land Code of 1922 called for more work to improve crop rotation practices and to eliminate or reduce both the intermixing of strips of land and the often inordinate distance separating lands from their peasant cultivators.

The need for such work was evident; prerevolutionary land organization efforts had only begun to address these problems, and some of the progress made had been undone by subsequent developments. If the communal organization of the peasantry remained essentially unchanged, so did the problems of land organization within communes. The drawbacks of stripholding continued to afflict the central, western, and northern regions of the country. In the province of Vologda, for example, almost every peasant household held over 75 pieces of land; in Pskov 12 percent had their arable land dispersed in over 100 strips.[35] The disadvantages of plots that were too far away particularly plagued peasants in the large communes of the southeast. A third of the households in Samara held field lands located more than ten kilometers away from the village, and over two-thirds of the peasants in Orenburg were in the same situation.[56]

When a plot of land was too small or too far away, a peasant often made no attempt to cultivate it. In land-scarce areas where holdings were smallest the size of the commune itself could influence land utilization, and in large communes the distance to the fields could be so great that cultivation was uneconomical. A study of Voronezh province showed that in communes with up to 50 households only 6 percent of the peasants with the smallest holdings (up to 6 desiatins) failed to cultivate them, yet in communes with over 1,000 households, almost 60 percent of those with holdings of the same size were not cultivating their land.[57] Thus utility was a function of size and location, not a matter of size alone.

Between 1922 and 1927 some 98 million hectares of land were affected by land organization work in the RSFSR. The bulk of the work was still on inter-village land organization, but this now included a broader range of activities, including work on separating the intermixed lands of neighboring communes. Although the law of May 22, 1922, had declared a freeze on landholding by recognizing the claim of all "volosts, villages, and other agricultural units" to the land in their possession at the time and by prohibiting further equalizations of land between them, the land organs were authorized to proceed with the separation of significantly scrambled lands. In fact, such work was one of the forms of land organization that could be made compulsory.[58] Although inter-community work predominated, organizational work on land within communities grew increasingly important. Of the 98 million hectares organized in the RSFSR during this period, over 42 million were in the "intravillage" or "internal" category. This amounted to roughly one-sixth of all peasant land.

Work on the broadening and consolidation ("comassation") of strips formed an insignificant part of land organization activity in the early 1920's but increased steadily thereafter and amounted to 39 percent of all internal land organization effected in 1927.[59] The beneficial effects of such work are suggested by studies showing that just doubling the size of strips could save up to 40 percent of the animal time and one-fourth of the man-hours invested in their cultivation.[60] Fewer strips in a holding not only lowered the cost of production, but raised the level of output.[61] Yet these benefits were limited to relatively few peasants. Broadening and consolidating had been carried out on only 7 percent of all peasant land in the country by 1928. Moreover, this sort of work was often connected with the introduction of multi-field systems of rotation, and because of the greater number of fields the net result at times was an increase of, rather than a reduction in, the total number of strips within the commune.[62] In 1927 the old three-field system was still employed on the vast majority of peasant holdings, and multi-field rotations were in use on only about one-sixth of the sown land in the RSFSR. Yet the introduction of advanced rotation systems may have been helping to bring more land into use. The average peasant household at this time held 6 hectares of arable land, but was actively cultivating 4.7 hectares (including its own and rented land).[63] A high proportion of rented land could be expected to be under cultivation, but even allowing for this the ratio is an improvement over the two to three that would result from the three-field system alone.

One of the most important forms of land organization work in the 1920's was the breakup of large communes into smaller land units, either as distinct subsections or as independent new settlements (*poselki* and *vyselki*). By 1928 about a third of all current work was in this category, and almost a tenth of all peasant land in the country had been involved in it.[64] This sort of activity was especially important in the southeastern steppe, where the absence of natural barriers had led to the formation of huge communes with extensive landholdings. More than half of all settlements in this area contained over 300 households, so that many peasants found themselves the nominal users of land too far away to be economically exploited. A similar situation prevailed in the central black soil region, where over 40 percent of the population lived in communities with over 200 households.[65]

Being organized in large land units had negative consequences in a number of other areas. Evidence suggests that as communes grew larger, the percentage of poor peasants rose and the percentage of well-off peasants declined. The larger the commune, the larger the peasant holding had to be for worthwhile cultivation, since land was likely to be located farther away from the village. Smallholders in small communes were better supplied with livestock than were peasants with holdings of the same size in large communes, and the proportion of peasants without horses rose with the size of the commune.[66] There was good reason, therefore, to try to break up the large communes.

Between 1922 and 1927 about one-sixth of the agricultural land in the black soil region was separated from larger land units by means of land organization. Typically the new *poselki* or *vyselki* contained about 25 households, and detachment usually improved agricultural performance.[67] In Samara, where exceptionally large communes had been recorded in 1922, a quarter of all peasant households were brought into this form of land organization, and the new communes averaged less than half the size of the old. A 1925 investigation of 136 of the new units found that crop yield was 30 percent higher than on neighboring "unorganized" land, and gross income was 33 percent higher.[68] Similar results were obtained from the subdivision of large communes in the Northern Caucasus region.[69]

Other aspects of land organization were less satisfactory from the government's standpoint. After the heady period of land socialization from 1919 to 1921, when most intravillage land work was devoted to the formation of collectives, land organization for this purpose dropped precipitously. By 1922 it was down to three percent of all land organization work; in 1925, it fell to a low of one percent; and in 1927 it still accounted for only two percent of the total.[70] By the end of that year two-thirds of all state farms in the RSFSR were still awaiting the benefits of land organization.[71] Two-thirds of the collective farms had been organized "externally" (i.e., their lands had been separated and delimited), but about 90 percent of all collectives lacked internal land organization.[72]

Mounting criticism of this state of affairs was accompanied by growing criticism of land work devoted to the formation of individual consolidated farms. There had been a steady refrain of such complaints, but in the earlier stages of NEP it had been muffled. The superior performance of many of the consolidated holdings, their more advanced forms of rotation and higher crop yields, had won this form of tenure the support of many agrarian experts. In 1926 a report presented at a conference of land agency officials argued for strict observance of the provisions of the Land Code respecting the peasants' freedom of choice with reference to land tenure. Officials were urged not to place "administrative obstacles before the populace in the selection of any particular form (communal, khutor, otrub, and so forth)."[73]

Under NEP the individualistic tendencies evident earlier in the western and northwestern regions received fuller expression. As we have seen, the formation of individual holdings was a limited phenomenon even in these regions, and was almost unknown elsewhere in the years of War Communism. Relaxation of official attitudes toward the peasantry after 1921 led to a stronger, or at any rate more open, movement toward separate consolidated farms, especially in the areas where they had previously been most popular. By 1923 the establishment of khutors and otrubs accounted for over 10 percent of all land undergoing organization procedures, for a whopping 38 percent of all such land in the western provinces, and for 23 percent in the northwest.[74]

In Smolensk, the extreme case, a third of all peasant land was in khutors and otrubs by 1925, and a projected local plan of land organization called for 70 percent of the land to be in this form at the end of a decade. Contemporary journals spoke of "khutormania" in Belorussia, and enthusiastic land officials in Nizhnii Novgorod sought the stamp of higher approval by advertising the creation of "Red khutors" as progressive models of the new socialist economy.[75] In the western region, from 1922 to 1927 the area in khutors and otrubs grew by over a million hectares to include 16 percent of all agricultural land. In the northwest it increased to 11 percent of the agricultural land. Elsewhere, however, it remained generally insignificant, with the possible exception of the central industrial region, where it reached almost 5 percent.[76]

The revival of individual landholding under NEP, limited as it was, did not take place without "administrative obstacles." As early as 1923 steps were taken to discourage the move to consolidated holdings by establishing a differentiated scale of payments for land organization work. Fees for a transfer to individual landholding were considerably higher than those for a move to collectivized tenure. Credit was made available for land organization in September 1924, but those who wanted to form khutors or otrubs got lowest priority in the granting of loans.[77] In October the Commissariat of Agriculture sent a circular to its land offices informing them that official policy opposed the formation of individual farms. Local agencies were to accept no more applications for the conversions of entire villages to khutors.

By early 1928 the Third Provincial Congress of Soviets, meeting in Moscow, was roundly condemning the individualistic "zemstvo approach" of the personnel of land organization agencies.[78] By then the proponents of collectivism were in a stronger position; however, they had never abandoned the field. The October 1924 circular of the Commissariat of Agriculture had instructed land officials to draw the population "to other forms of tenure from which the transfer to collectives would be less difficult." The formation of small settlements was to be encouraged, and land officials were actively to promote collective land tenure "beginning with the simplest types of collectivization of labor on the land." Khutors were to be granted only such land as was unsuitable for the use of small group settlements.[79]

In September 1926 the Central Executive Committee and the Council of People's Commissars adopted a resolution assuming the expense of land organization work for the "poorest part of the peasantry," leaving it up to the separate republics to define that social sector within their own boundaries.[80] The Fourth Congress of Soviets of the USSR, meeting the following April, called on the state to assume a greater share of the expense of land organization and pointed to the lack of such work as a basic obstacle to the improvement of agriculture.[81] On the eve of the tenth anniversary of the October Revolution in the fall of 1927, the government responded by announcing that all land organization work for the poorer middle peasants as well as the poor peasants would be at state expense. Meanwhile, a sharper class line had been taken on credit policy, and loans for land improvement were limited to poor and middle peasants.[82]

The cumulative effect of these measures and of the hardening official policy against individual consolidations was a sharp decline of activity in the formation of khutors and otrubs. By 1928 it had fallen to less than one percent of all land work.[83] Despite official discouragement, consolidated farms continued to develop in some parts of the west. In Vologda okrug, for example, their number increased between 1926 and 1928.[84] The same was true in Pskov okrug, where they covered 44 percent of the land in 1929; in Smolensk 60 percent of all peasant households were said to be in khutors in 1929.[85]

That few poor peasants left the commune for the khutor was not necessarily a matter of preference. The establishment of an independent farm, as in the Stolypin era, required an investment beyond the resources of the poor. In words that echoed the replies sent in to the Free Economic Society in 1910–11, peasants told officials of the Workers' and Peasants' Inspectorate that "everyone" wanted to separate from the commune, but means were lacking.[86] A peasant in search of means could no longer sell or mortgage his land legally. Yet it seems that a way was sometimes found around the law, just as it had been before 1905, when the law prevented the sale of communal property. Privately arranged transfers of shares from departing members to replacements were recognized by communes in the 1920's and duly recorded.[87]

Although individual separators tended to be relatively well off, life on a khutor may have been no less a struggle than previously, despite the consistently higher performance of consolidated farms. Land costs were no longer a direct factor, but the need for and scarcity of capital remained a problem. As the decade wore on, taxes became a special burden. A detailed socioeconomic study of land use in Voronezh province in 1926 concluded that it was more difficult for poor peasants to maintain themselves on khutors than in communes, and reports of individual farmers returning to communal tenure began to be heard in increasing numbers beginning in the middle of the decade.[88] Such reversions (occurring most often among otrubs) do not appear to have been a widespread phenomenon, but they were sufficiently common to command attention in a set of regulations issued by the Commissariat of Agriculture in September 1927.[89] In Leningrad province communal

tenure grew at the expense of individual tenure by almost 5 percent
from 1925 to 1928, and even in Smolensk a number of khutor villages
reconstituted themselves as small *poselki*.[90]

The land organization work accomplished in these years helped to
improve the physical layout of part of the country's agricultural lands.
Yet the work was limited in extent and was hampered by the conflict of
different viewpoints on its social and political objectives, conflict both
within the agencies responsible for land affairs and between those
agencies and their critics. One of the first steps of an efficient land program would have been to register all landholdings as required by the
Land Code. However, lack of funds, lack of an adequate organization,
and lack of rural cooperation prevented the fulfillment of the plan. The
project had called for only half of the land to be registered by 1928, but
performance was considerably behind schedule, and land organization
workers throughout the period complained of slow progress.[91]

Except for helping to establish individual tenure within specific,
limited areas that had previously shown strong tendencies in that direction, land organization had little effect on the predominance of communal tenure in the 1920's. Within the commune, land organization
helped mitigate some of the negative features of traditional land arrangements, and the improvements that were introduced led some enthusiasts of the period (and after) to speak of the emergence of a "new
type" of commune, pointing particularly to the smaller, physically reorganized communes of the latter part of the decade.[92] Contemporaries
who attributed new features and potentialities to the commune in the
1920's stressed the advantages of the new land arrangements, and such
"revolutionary" innovations as the end of mutual responsibility and the
"new" freedom to leave the commune at will. The progress cited was
real enough, but the roots of the revolution extended farther back than
1917.

The "new, improved" commune of the times was seen by some as
the logical stepping-stone to the communist future of the countryside.
Others argued that the demands of socialist agriculture were incompatible with the system of communal tenure. On the eve of collectivization, the technical improvements that had been introduced through
land organization, though beneficial and promising, had affected only a
minor (though not an insignificant) part of peasant landholdings. From
1917 to 1928, about a third of all peasant land underwent some form of
inter-community reorganization, but less than a fifth was reorganized
within communities, and on less than a tenth was there any advance
against the still predominant three-field system.[93] Land work, along
with the tempo of collectivization, was accelerated in 1928, but com-

plaints about the slowness and inadequacy of the work continued through the end of the decade.[94]

Elements of change were evident in the countryside and the commune in the 1920's, but they unfolded against, and sometimes obscured, strong underlying elements of continuity. The commune (or some communes) may have been improved, but in many ways it remained the old commune. The law of March 14, 1927, that attempted to separate assemblies of the commune from general assemblies of the community was generally ignored in the villages. The old communal assembly carried on much as it always had, and on the whole the peasants appeared content that this should be so.[95] Just as the New Economic Policy recalled the old, the "new commune" was a classic example of "plus ça change. . . ."

The Number and Size of Communes

Although there are differences of opinion on the attributes of the commune in the 1920's, there is little question that the communal form of land tenure was then far more extensive than before the revolution. The TsSU data on landholding at the beginning of the decade, mentioned above, showed that communal tenure had become predominant nearly everywhere by 1922 and was almost the only form of tenure adopted by the peasants in most of the country. The widespread movement back to the commune after 1917 was a sharp reversal of the officially encouraged prerevolutionary trend, and the extended hold of the commune on peasant land remained firm throughout the NEP interlude. The amount and proportion of peasant land in different forms of tenure in 1927 are summarized in Table 18.

As might have been expected, the number of communes increased after the revolution with the upsurge in communal landholding. Unfortunately, since the commune was not considered part of the official soviet administrative system no official account was kept of their changing number.[96] And not only did the number change, but that change had important implications for organizational management of the rural economy and society.

In 1917 there were 110,000 rural societies in the RSFSR. When the first rural soviets were formed, there was a fair coincidence of the two institutions. The number of these soviets in the RSFSR in 1921 may have been as high as 100,000.[97] There was therefore at least a rough correspondence for a time between the commune and the rural soviet, and ample opportunity for their interaction at the lowest level of rural administration. The number of communes was growing, but the num-

TABLE 18
Peasant Land Tenure in the RSFSR, 1927
(million hectares)

Region	Communal		Individual — Khutors		Individual — Otrubs		Collective		Total[a]	
	Area	Percent	Area	Percent	Area	Percent	Area	Percent	Area	Percent
Northeast	6.9	97%	.04	—	.13	2%	.02	—	7.1	100%
Northwest	9.3	89	.39	4%	.76	7	.03	—	10.5	100
West	5.3	81	.97	15	.29	4	.03	—	6.6	100
Central Industrial	22.8	95	.24	1	.97	4	.07	—	24.1	100
Central Agricultural	16.2	99	.05	—	.03	—	.13	1%	16.4	100
Viatka-Vetluga	8.0	100	.01	—	—	—	.02	—	8.0	100
Mid-Volga	17.9	96	.01	—	.02	—	.83	4	18.7	100
Lower-Volga	23.3	98	—	—	.30	1	.41	2	23.7	100
Ural	22.3	98	—	—	.75	3	.13	—	22.7	100
Northern Caucasus	22.0	95	.04	—	—	—	.48	2	23.3	100
Siberia	52.6	94	.28	—	2.9	5	.22	—	56.0	100
Far East	15.7	100	—	—	—	—	—	—	15.7	100
TOTAL[a]	222.4	95%	2.1	1%	6.1	3%	2.4	1%	232.9	100%

SOURCE: TsSU, *Itogi, 1917–1927*, pp. 120–21.
[a] Rounding of the figures has introduced minor discrepancies in the totals.

ber of soviets was increasing also. At the same time, there was a general proliferation of other administrative-territorial units in response to changing conditions after the revolution. The number of volosts, for example, had increased by 1921 to over 4,400 more than before the revolution.[98]

As early as February 1920 a special commission was established by the VTsIK presidium to redesign the existing administrative structure in the interests of greater efficiency and "to meet the specific needs of a socialist state." Local commissions (provincial and district) were created to assist in the work, and the entire project was soon taken over by the new State Planning Commission. Starting in 1923 a new system of territorial divisions based on economic regions was gradually introduced. The old system of provinces, districts, and volosts was replaced or supplemented by a new apparatus of *oblasts* (or *krais*), *okrugs*, and *raions*—all of which were larger units than those they succeeded. Whereas there had been 15,000 volosts in the country in 1922 before the introduction of the reform, there were fewer than 5,000 remaining by 1925.[99]

The process of "regionalization," as the reform was called, included enlarging the local soviets and reducing their number.[100] As a result, the expanded territory of the soviet was now likely to encompass a number of communes. By 1928 there were fewer than 56,000 rural soviets in the RSFSR, and only 73,000 in the entire country. The average rural soviet covered almost 8 settlements; some extended over far more.[101] In Pskov province, for example, 80 settlements were included within the boundaries of a single rural soviet.[102] The number of settlements was not necessarily identical with the number of communes, since several small settlements could be joined in one commune and large settlements might include more than one commune. However, the coincidence of commune and settlement was high and grew closer over time. In general, there were more settlements than communes, but the instructions issued on January 5, 1926, indicated that a membership of only three households was sufficient for registering a land society.

The administrative reorganization, therefore, by reducing the number of rural administrative organs created a greater distance between the village communes and the formal order of government. The problem was compounded by the continued growth in the number of communes throughout the 1920's. Initially, the number had increased primarily as the result of the postrevolutionary redistribution of land and the accompanying extension of communal tenure. Later, new communes were created when large communes were broken up. In the

Don okrug of the Northern Caucasus region, for example, 13 old communes that were reorganized between 1923 and 1926 gave rise to 369 new land units.[103] By 1928 the number of communes in the RSFSR was reported to be approximately 319,000, and over 400,000 were said to exist in the country as a whole.[104] At this time there were about 425,000 settlements in the RSFSR and about 550,000 in the entire country, so the correspondence of commune and settlement was fairly high.[105]

Since 222 million hectares of land were in communal tenure in the RSFSR in 1927, the average commune there had about 700 hectares in its use. There were then about 17 million peasant households in the RSFSR.[106] If 95 percent of these were in communes, the average commune had about 50 member households and included about 260 individuals. Although these average figures can serve as a rough yardstick, they may also, as is so often the case, tend to obscure rural realities. The size of communes varied considerably from one area to another. Data covering almost 17,000 communes in 30 provinces of the RSFSR in 1922 show them ranging in size from an average of 105 hectares in Ivanovo-Voznesensk province to an average of 3,511 hectares in Samara province.[107] The smallest communes were located primarily in the northwest and in the central industrial region; the largest were in the southeast and (to a lesser degree) in the central agricultural zone. Communes in Belorussia were small, but in the Ukraine the average holding was over a thousand hectares. Whatever their size locally, communes were to be found nearly everywhere, and in increasing numbers, throughout the 1920's.

15

Agrarian Dynamics

Two questions face students of Russian rural economy in the 1920's: What happened in agriculture? and What did contemporaries (in particular, the political leadership) think was happening? The first question leads to agrarian history; the second, to political history. But both lines of inquiry are intertwined in the history of the commune in this period. Political perceptions that were influenced by agrarian developments in turn had a major effect on later events.

The Recovery of Agriculture

The general pattern of agricultural development under NEP is reasonably clear. The rural economy entered NEP seriously disrupted by cumulative postrevolutionary stresses capped by drought and famine in 1920 and 1921. Although the effects of that disruption were still evident in 1922, there were also signs of recovery. Peasants greeted the end of requisitioning by returning to the fields with greater enthusiasm, and more settled conditions in the countryside contributed to an economic revival. Although there was a lag before the area under cultivation was expanded, favorable climatic conditions led to a bumper harvest in 1922, and the peasants' new freedom to sell their surplus in the marketplace provided an incentive to increase production. Before the end of the year Lenin was reporting that peasant opposition to the regime had come to an end. "The peasants are satisfied with their present situation. . . . We consider this more important than any sort of statistical evidence. No one can doubt that the peasantry is the decisive factor with us."[1] The critical corner had been turned.

The best single indicator of the state of Soviet agriculture in the 1920's is the production of grain. The rural economy was essentially a grain economy, with 85 percent of all cultivated land under grain. An increase in output in 1922 was followed by further improvement the next year—the sown area was extended, and crop output increased. In 1924 the area under grain continued to grow, although the harvest was slightly smaller because of climatic conditions. The next two years, however, proved to be the agricultural high point of the decade. Crop area continued to expand, yields reached a peak, and harvests were excellent. By 1925 the total area under all crops had regained the pre-war level, and in 1926 grain plantings (which had lagged slightly behind the general advance) were also back to prewar figures. During the last three years of the decade, the agricultural situation appeared to have stabilized. Grain production fell slightly in 1927 but remained well above the level of all but the last two peak years. In 1928 the area under grain declined somewhat as the cultivation of technical crops such as sugar beets and flax was extended, yet high grain yields kept the grain harvest at a steady level. In 1929, in contrast, the grain area was expanded to an all-time high, but a severe winter in 1928–29 killed part of the winter crop, contributing to a mild falloff in the harvest.

The difficulty of establishing the level of prewar agricultural production creates problems for measuring accurately the performance of the Soviet rural economy under NEP against the standard of prewar performance. The current Soviet data on NEP and prewar production are summarized in Table 19; the effect of the 1960 TsSU revision of prewar data (see p. 225) is to improve the relative performance of Soviet agriculture in the 1920's.[2] According to the figures previously used, grain production never returned to the high level of 1913 before collectivization. The year 1913 was an exceptional one, and production was above the average for the period; however, according to the recently revised data, Soviet output in the mid-1920's not only reached, but exceeded that prerevolutionary pinnacle.

Yet agricultural performance, however measured, lagged behind the recovery of the economy as a whole. Between 1925/26 and 1928/29, when the Soviet national output increased in ruble value by 27 percent, income from agriculture rose by only about 9 percent.[3]

As has been noted, one of the factors accounting for fluctuations in the harvest was the weather. The effects of climate on agricultural production in the 1920's were evident, and the question of crop output was urgent enough to promote serious study of agro-meteorology in the Soviet Union at this time.[4] Another basic reason for the slower progress of agriculture within the economy was the inadequate supply of machinery and equipment. Between 1922 and 1929 the state in-

TABLE 19
Grain Production under NEP, 1922–29
(territory of USSR as of September 1939)

Year	Area sown in grain (million hectares)	Yield (tons per hectare)	Harvest (million tons)
1909–13, avg.	—	.69 (.74)	65.2 (67.6)
1913	94.4	.81 (.85)	76.5 (80.1)
1922	66.2	.76	50.3
1923	78.6	.72	56.6
1924	82.9	.62	51.4
1925	87.3	.83	72.5
1926	93.7	.82	76.8
1927	94.7	.76	72.3
1928	92.2	.79	73.3
1929	96.0	.75	71.7

SOURCES: TsSU, *Sel'skoe khoziaistvo SSSR, statisticheskii sbornik* (1960), p. 196; TsUNKhU, *Sotsialisticheskoe stroitel'stvo*, pp. 176–77, 203; figures in parentheses are from *SDD*, 1: 283. The two sets of figures for 1909–13 are clearly not based on the same sown area. On the successive revisions of the data, see Wheatcroft, "Reliability."

vested only 85 million rubles (at 1926/27 prices) in the production of agricultural machinery, and most of this went to repair or rebuild existing facilities. Not until 1926 did domestic production of agricultural machinery regain prewar levels, and no new construction for this purpose was undertaken before 1928.[5] Imports of agricultural machinery rose erratically under NEP, but remained well below prewar levels.[6] The supply of agricultural tools and equipment improved somewhat over the course of the decade, but as late as 1928 three-quarters of the spring sowing was still being done by hand, and almost half of the entire grain harvest was gathered by hand. Only one percent of the spring plowing was accomplished by tractors that year, and the number of horses had not quite regained the 1916 level at that time.[7] Since the number of households in the countryside had substantially increased, there was a much lower ratio of horsepower to households than before.

Even when agricultural inventory was available, high costs often made it inaccessible to peasants. In an attempt to broaden utilization of the available supply, a network of credit associations was developed in the late 1920's. By 1929 almost 22,000 credit unions had been organized for the purchase of agricultural machinery, and these associations claimed a membership of over 400,000.[8] Tractors were in especially short supply and high demand. Initially, they were sold to anyone who could afford to purchase them, but complaints about the advantages thus derived by wealthier peasants, coupled with glowing reports about the effectiveness of the collective use of tractors, led to restrictions on sales to individuals by the end of the decade.

Tractor "columns" (later known as "stations") were established in 1927 and were soon servicing entire agricultural communities, as well as state and collective farms. In mid-1929 the Grain Center (Khlebotsentr), which united grain cooperatives, had 45 columns with a total of about 1,200 tractors under its control. These columns serviced 17,000 households in 226 communes and 208 collectives.[9] At this time there were approximately 35,000 tractors in the country, the great majority in cooperative use.[10]

The cooperative was the most rapidly growing form of rural association in the 1920's. Since the launching of NEP, Lenin had written of the advantage of cooperatives as bridges to socialism in the countryside.[11] The impressive prewar growth of cooperatives had been interrupted by the turn of events, and agricultural cooperatives in particular had experienced a sharp decline in the period of War Communism. In 1914 there had been 24,000 cooperatives of this sort, but by 1921 the number was down to 6,000. Under NEP the movement revived and flourished. In 1927 there were 136,000 cooperatives of all kinds in the country, including 70,000 agricultural cooperatives with 10 million members. By 1929 over a third of all households belonged to some form of cooperative.[12]

Meteorological, mechanical, financial, and organizational factors all played a part in determining agricultural output under NEP. Yet the level of output, and even the relative levels of prewar and Soviet output, derive their importance primarily from their effect on the population, an effect most immediately evident in food consumption.

Food Consumption

Declining levels of food consumption had been a source and sign of the deepening crisis of War Communism. Under NEP the situation improved markedly, but not until more than a year after the introduction of the new policies was there a return to higher levels of food intake. The early months of 1922, in fact, were the hungriest season in postrevolutionary Russia. Two years of drought and a severely reduced area of cultivation brought food supplies to their lowest point, and even the substantial supplies provided by the American Relief Administration under Herbert Hoover could do no more than partially mitigate the suffering of millions. At the beginning of 1922 the average individual in the producing region was eating less than half as much grain as before the war, and in the consuming zone intake was only three-quarters of the earlier level.[13] It was the good harvest of 1922 that finally turned the situation around.

By the fall of 1922 grain consumption had rebounded everywhere almost to prewar levels, and the next two years brought a full restoration of the earlier rates of grain intake per capita. In late 1924 and early 1925 grain consumption fell off somewhat, but it soon recovered, and intake remained at (or close to) the prewar level during the next two years. The autumn of 1927 saw another drop, and rural grain consumption dipped to the lowest level since 1922. As in the prewar period, per capita grain consumption was generally higher in the producing region, although the consumption differential was slightly less than before.

Yet grain was not the only item consumed, and a drop in the proportion of grain in a diet can indicate qualitative improvement. Consumption data do show a growing supply of other foodstuffs in the 1920's. Between 1922 and 1927 rural consumption of meat, eggs, milk, and dairy products increased. There was also more sugar on the table. The consumption of potatoes declined, however, and the intake of fruits and vegetables dropped substantially.[14]

In terms of the total caloric intake per capita of the adult rural population, the data show improvement after the low point in early 1922 to a high in the fall of 1924. After this peak, consumption fell slightly. Interestingly enough, despite the heavier consumption of grain, the per capita caloric intake (as well as the intake of food by weight) was consistently less in the producing region than in the consuming region.[15] Those who produced the most food were actually eating less, and eating a more restricted diet, than the rural population in the consuming regions. Urban consumption, however, was the lowest of all. (See Table 20.)

How did conditions under NEP compare with the prewar situation? According to one set of figures, the per capita consumption of food (by weight) of the rural population from 1896 to 1915 was higher than that of 1927/28 in grain, fruits, vegetables, fish, and salt.[16] In the later period consumption of meat and potatoes was about the same as in the earlier, or slightly higher. Some improvement over prewar consumption levels was evident in milk and dairy products, eggs, and sugar. The data do not suggest any dramatic advance over prewar consumption levels that were far from ideal, and qualitative upgrading of some aspects of the diet appears to have been offset by deterioration of others. The general situation is summarized in Table 21.

Although the limits of improvement in general were set by the over-

TABLE 20
Average Daily Food Consumption under NEP, 1922–28
(data for October, in grams)

| | Rural population | | Urban population | |
Year	Consuming region	Producing region	Workers	Employees
1922	2,168	1,771	1,476	1,436
1924	2,173	1,877	1,555	1,535
1925	2,029	1,791	1,434	1,422
1926	2,023	1,858	1,458	1,469
1927	2,016	1,725	1,427	1,363
1928	1,986	1,844	1,440	1,425

SOURCES: TsSU, *Itogi, 1917–1927*, pp. 355–56, 361–62; TsSU, *Sel'skoe khoziaistvo, 1925–1928*, pp. 402–5, 408–11.
NOTE: The October figures are typically 10 to 15 percent higher than those for February.

TABLE 21
*Average Annual Per Capita Food Consumption
of the Rural Population, 1896–1928*
(kilograms)

Period	Consumption
1896–1915	670.6[a]
1923/24	685.9
1927/28	649.1[b]

SOURCES: Kerblay, p. 894; TsSU, *Statisticheskii spravochnik za 1928*, pp. 850–51.
[a]This is the average of the range of different sources cited by Kerblay. The lower end of the range for the entire period, 1896–1915, is 658.7, the upper end 682.5.
[b]Kerblay's data do not include figures for fish or sugar consumption for 1927/28. These have been estimated at 7.6 kilograms and 7.2 kilograms respectively on the basis of the TsSU data for 1928 and have been added to the consumption total of 634.3 kilograms derived from Kerblay's data for 1927/28.

all performance of agriculture, the changes in consumption patterns were clearly related to sectoral shifts within agriculture. From 1925/26 to 1928/29 animal husbandry increased the value of its output by 15 percent, technical crops (including sugar beets) by 11 percent, but grain by less than 3 percent.[17]

Harvest and Marketplace

The Soviet government, like the tsarist government it replaced, looked to the peasants to supply the nation with food and with the capital necessary for industrial development. Once the policy of food requisitioning ended, the agriculturalists had not only to produce food but to market it if these objectives were to be met. Without an adequate quantity of foodstuffs in the marketplace, the requirements of the urban populace, the military, and the consuming region could not be satisfied. Even within the producing region local marketing was important for the balanced distribution of food supplies.

Given the rapid recovery of Soviet agriculture under NEP, grain marketings might also have been expected to rebound. Yet marketing was a problem almost from the start, as emerged acutely in the "scissors crisis" of 1923. In that year grain output exceeded the previous good harvest by 12 percent thanks to the extension of land under cultivation. With the adoption of NEP, the government had increased the production of consumer goods to encourage exchange. Prices of agricultural products had gone up, and the terms of trade had improved for the peasants. The alliance of peasant and proletarian was to demonstrate its mutual benefits in the marketplace. What confronted the peasants there in 1923, however, was hardly reassuring. Since the fall of 1922, when agricultural and industrial prices were in the same relationship to one another as before the war, agricultural prices had dropped steadily, and prices of manufactured commodities had skyrocketed. The rapidly widening angle between the two intersecting price levels on a graph led Trotsky to speak of a "scissors," and the name became a label for the problem.[18] The nature of the scissors was easily demonstrated, but responsibility for it was not so easily assigned.

It was said that peasants were deliberately withholding grain from the market in a speculative calculation that grain prices would rise. Before the revolution the peasants, particularly the poor peasants, had been forced by their heavy fiscal obligations to sell their crops immediately upon harvest even though prices were lowest then. Now there were fewer poor peasants, and the monetary obligations of the peasants had been lightened. To some worried observers it appeared that the peasants were exercising their new options and holding grain back in anticipation of a spring price rise. The crisis, therefore, could be blamed on the profit-seeking tendencies of a peasantry that was "holding up the towns to ransom."[19]

Yet there was another side to the story. The managers of the state industrial trusts had fixed the high prices on consumer goods. The problem in 1923, unlike that earlier, was not a lack of such goods; on the contrary, expensive consumer goods piled up in storehouses for lack of buyers while prices were adamantly maintained by profit-seeking managers hoping to sell high once the peasants had sold off the harvest. Such were the early fruits of state capitalism under NEP.

Viewed from this perspective, the peasants were more victims than villains.

One of the first results of the crisis was the decision taken by the Twelfth Party Congress in the spring of 1923 to promote the export of grain.[20] This would have the effect of raising grain prices, it was held, and would stimulate the revival of agriculture. At the same time (although this point figured less prominently in the discussion), the resumption of exports promised a source of capital for the development of heavy industry. There was growing concern in the Party that such development, essential to the future of the country, was being slighted under NEP, whereas light industry was receiving preferential treatment. But only in the fall, when the scissors crisis peaked, did the government became sufficiently alarmed to take action. By October 1923 the industrial price index (based on prewar prices) was over three times higher than the agricultural index.[21] To say, as E. H. Carr does, that the "free interplay" of NEP market forces had broken down may be to overstate the case for market freedom, given the fixed prices on consumer goods. In any event it was state action that brought about an easing of the crisis at the end of the year.[22] The industrial trusts were forced, by government restriction of their credit and the imposition of direct price controls, to lower their prices. The crisis ebbed.

The situation that developed in 1923 crystallized a number of concerns and issues that were to persist throughout the remainder of the decade. To the consternation of some observers, the "battle of the scissors" indicated that the vaunted alliance of peasant and proletarian in the new society was anything but stable because of the antagonism of their interests in the old marketplace. Moreover, the clash of those interests seemed to threaten the entire new order.

Analysis of the market behavior of the peasants has recently led students of the period back to the work of the organization-production school and its eminent spokesman, A. V. Chaianov. According to Chaianov and his colleagues, peasant households have peculiarities that cause them to operate differently from capitalist enterprises. James Millar has recently suggested that, although Chaianov failed to recognize the fact, the prime distinguishing feature of the peasant household is that the family labor force generally represents a fixed (overhead) cost, which does not vary with changes in the output of the household.[23] Because of this, a deterioration in the general terms of trade is likely to lead to an intensification of the family's efforts rather than to a withdrawal from the marketplace, especially if there is a generally accepted notion of a minimum standard of living, "or if the previous level of living exerted any continuing influence."[24] Since there are some goods and services that the peasant household cannot do without (or chooses not to) and cannot produce for itself, even the least monetized "subsistence" household will make every effort to remain in the market, often shifting in the process to the production of more valuable, but more labor-intensive, products. According to this theory, the unfavorable turn in the terms of trade in 1923 should have led to an intensification of peasant labor in an attempt to produce more units for sale to compensate for the lower prices. Instead, the peasants are said to have withdrawn from the market for classically capitalistic considerations of price and profit. There is some question, however, about whether a withdrawal occurred at all.[25]

In 1923, once attention was drawn to the growing gap between agricultural and industrial prices, political leaders became anxious about the anticipated behavior of the peasants in the market. Anxiety led to a sense of vulnerability. Yet in the spring, when the crisis was first defined, there was apparently no great shortage in the domestic market, or the decision to export grain would hardly have been adopted. Consumption data show an increase in food intake in early 1923 over the fall of 1922.[26] Less grain than authorities hoped for appeared on the market later in the year, but a number of factors could help to account for this. The harvest was still well below the prewar level (by 15 to 40 percent, depending on the figures used). Lower output was offset to some extent by the lower level of exports, but prewar consumption levels had not yet been fully recovered at the beginning of 1923. In addition, apart from immediate physical needs, the famine may have generated psychological drives for heightened consumption and for the stockpiling of depleted grain reserves. In this sense, the "previous level of living" undoubtedly did influence decisions about marketing.

The peasants, therefore, had ample reason to retain a larger part of their output even without reference to market prices. Given those prices, they could easily have elected, in effect, to "purchase" more of their own grain. The fact that prices on agricultural goods remained relatively low indicates that no great shortages developed. The only "ransom" in evidence was in the high prices of manufactured consumer goods, and the crisis abated when those prices were brought down.

The most important point, however, is that leaders saw the peasants as deliberately hoarding grain as a pressure tactic against the government, and for some that perception reinforced a preconception of the peasant as an antagonist. The thesis that deteriorating terms of trade promote intensification of the efforts of peasant households might be supported by the continued increase in the sown area. Yet the experi-

ence of War Communism suggests an important corollary: intensification of efforts (beyond the point of subsistence) is likely to occur only
when the household has control over the output of its labor.

By the spring of 1924 the prices of agricultural and industrial products had moved closer to their prewar relationship, and grain consumption was back to prewar levels. But autumn brought new problems. The harvest was down somewhat due to a drought in the Volga
and southeastern grain regions, and a number of coincident political disturbances—attacks on rural press correspondents, rumors of
counterrevolution, and an uprising in Georgia—revived apprehen-
sions not only about the reliability of the food supply, but about the
peasantry as well. As the reduced size of the harvest became evident in
the summer of 1924, grain prices streaked upward. By August 1924
they were twice as high as the previous August. The Commissariat of
Domestic Trade set maximum prices for state purchases, and all exports of grain were halted. But private traders were able to bid for the
peasants' grain at higher prices, and the peasants showed little interest
in selling to government procurement agencies at the lower official
prices. By the end of the year the state had been able to acquire less
than a third of the intended purchases, and grain imports had to be
authorized. The official price maxima were first raised, then abandoned.[27]

According to the political groups that earlier had been most worried
about the scissors, and those who later shared somewhat the same perspective, "the cities were once more being held to ransom."[28] Yet was
this the case? The grain harvest of 1924 was 10 percent below that of
1923, and the population was slightly larger. The recurrence of
drought had unquestionably stirred memories of the recent famine.
There is no doubt that the peasants preferred to eat or stockpile what
grain they had rather than to sell it at low prices; whether their marketing decisions were intended as entrepreneurial blackmail is less
clear.

To some political leaders, the majority at this time, the self-interest
of the peasants appeared unfortunate, but not basically hostile. It was a
fact of life that could be turned to the general advantage. Just as the
Party had won the political struggle in 1917 by responding to peasant
interests, so it could win the economic struggle by convincing the
peasants that their interests were still being advanced. As conditions
improved it would be possible, gradually, to inculcate a broader view of
self-interest, a view in which the goals of the individual and of society
as a whole could be seen to coincide under socialism. In the summer of
1924, as the harvest problem emerged, a slogan was launched: "Face to

the countryside!"[29] Repeated on all sides, this was soon to become the keynote of the heyday of NEP. Political unrest was evident in the countryside, and there was no desire to fan it with unpopular policies.

When it became clear that the peasants would not accept the low state prices for their grain, the official reaction was a retreat. Since 1917 all Party congresses had been convened in the spring. By now the importance of the harvest for policy decisions had become so obvious that the annual Party congress for 1925 was deferred to the fall, when the size of the harvest would be known. Meanwhile, the face turned to the countryside was a most benign countenance. In an attempt to encourage agricultural enterprise and improve output, taxes were reduced, restrictions on leasing and hiring were loosened, and prices were left open to market influences. N. I. Bukharin went so far as to address the peasants using the very term with which Lenin had mocked the Stolypin "agrarian Bonapartists": "Enrich yourselves!" Although the slogan was disavowed within the Party, it remained publically unchallenged, and despite an explicit disclaimer by Bukharin, it seemed to announce a new "wager on the strong."[30]

A decision to lower taxes was taken in the spring of 1925. By summer it was evident that the harvest was going to be an exceptionally good one. Expectations of large government procurements ran high, and an ambitious program of expanded exports was projected. These best-laid hopes, however, went astray when the crops came to market. The amount of grain offered for sale was far below anticipation, and prices, after a brief dip early in the fall, climbed steadily. The government had abandoned price ceilings, but had set price guidelines for official purchasing agencies in the expectation that the large harvest would cause prices to fall. So likely did this seem, in fact, that the state was prepared to support minimum prices for grain to avoid a repetition of the scissors problem.[31] Instead of a flood of grain on the market and a price drop, however, there was a limited supply and a rise in prices. An important factor contributing to the last was the competition of different government agencies, which in effect bid against one another in an attempt to make early purchases. The situation was eventually brought under control, but the immediate effect was to raise prices beyond a point at which state agencies could acquire grain. The private market took over, and as a result little grain was obtained by the official organs. Although prices paid by the state were later raised, they continued to lag behind open-market prices. At the end of the year the government was offering only two-thirds of the price available in the private market for rye, and its price for wheat was relatively almost as low.[32] Once again, it became necessary to suspend all exports.[33]

This unexpected setback in the presence of the most bountiful harvest since the revolution was a rude jolt that set into motion some fundamental reappraisals of the situation. State planning appeared to be at the mercy of peasant preferences, whether the government employed the stick of War Communism or the carrot of NEP. Increasing concern about the class nature and orientation of the peasantry began to appear in political circles.

Yet political considerations were peripheral to the peasants' immediate concerns. True, the harvest was a generous one, but there was a shortage of consumer goods at the time. To prevent a repetition of the scissors, the prices on industrial goods had been held down; and as grain prices rose in 1925, the agricultural price index actually rose briefly above the index for industrial prices, in a development that was exceptional for the decade.[34] Peasant purchasing power quickly drained the available stock of consumer goods from store shelves. With little to buy and lower taxes to pay, the peasants had scant incentive to surrender their grain for low state prices. It had once been possible for Imperial ministers to decree "We may go hungry, but we will export"; now it was possible for the peasants to decide "We will eat." And eat they did. The consumption statistics reveal that whereas grain intake dropped slightly in the fall of 1925 in the consuming region, it rose in the poorer-fed producing region.[35] Moreover, the government's disappointment in its grain procurements did not mean that the cities were deprived of food; low procurements meant only that food was more expensive. The caloric consumption of the urban population was higher in the fall of 1925 than it had been at any previous point since the revolution.[36]

Nonetheless, the procurement problem, arising after a good harvest and following a number of concessions to the peasants, created misgivings. The loss of exports left the government facing a substantial negative trade balance.[37] Criticism of official rural policy was more openly voiced, and toward the end of the fall Bukharin felt obliged to retract his "incorrect" phraseology.[38] The following spring a decision was taken to raise agricultural taxes and to redistribute them so that the wealthier peasants, assumed to be hoarding grain, would be forced to bring more of it to market.

For the time being, little more was done about the situation. Bukharin continued to defend the gradualist policy of bringing the peasants around to socialism through the marketplace, and, along with like-minded colleagues, he remained in control. Critics of conciliatory policies toward the peasants had been undermined in political struggles at the Fourteenth Party Congress late in 1925, and the alliance of peasant and proletarian had been reaffirmed. Despite the concern over exports, the recovery of agriculture almost to prewar levels induced a degree of complacency. The population was being fed, and further advances could be anticipated. Attention now turned increasingly to the challenge of industrialization.

Developments in 1926 only confirmed the general feeling that the agrarian economy could be left to its own devices, however imperfect, for the time being. The area under grain finally returned to its prewar extent, the harvest hit a new high (close to the exceptional output of 1913), and procurements proved no problem. Supplies of industrial goods were adequate, and food supplies were available at a lower cost. Stocks of grain held by government agencies almost doubled between October 1926 and January 1927.[39] Grain exports climbed, and the foreign trade balance became positive again.[40]

The satisfactory state of agricultural affairs in 1926 appeared to vindicate the defenders of NEP. Had it continued, the later history of the decade might have been quite different. But in 1927 some old problems reappeared. The harvest was down from the 1926 peak, yet it came in at the respectable level of the previous year. The difficulty arose, once again, from price ratios. Because agricultural prices had dropped in 1926, retail prices on industrial goods were officially lowered early in 1927. The price reduction stimulated sales and led to another "goods famine," with the by-now-predictable result that the peasants marketed less grain. Yet, as in the earlier episodes of low marketing, other factors were involved. For one thing, rural needs were steadily increasing with the growth of the population. Although the area sown in grain had returned to the prewar level, the growth in the population meant that there was only 88 percent as much sown land per capita.[41] Increased taxation had helped to bring more food to market, but as exports were boosted to the high point of the decade in 1927, the food intake of the entire population fell to the lowest level since the introduction of NEP. Under the circumstances, it is hardly surprising that the peasant producers of grain were little inclined to take their output to market. Grain procurements dropped once more, exports were curtailed, and government stocks dwindled. The grain stores held by state agencies shrank by almost a third in the last quarter of the year.[42]

Despite its recovery to prewar levels by 1926, Russian agriculture failed to advance significantly after the middle years of the decade. Given the limited investment in the agrarian sector of the economy, its performance was perhaps creditable enough. Land organization work undoubtedly contributed to improvement, and peasant responsiveness to opportunity was demonstrated by the shift to more profitable technical crops, livestock, and dairying. Yet Russian crop yields remained extremely low in comparison with those of other European countries, and agricultural "backwardness" appeared an ever more serious constraint on economic development as ambitious plans for industrialization moved forward in the later years of the decade.[13]

The recurrent problem of government grain procurements brought together and heightened two concerns of the central authorities. The first had to do with the level of agricultural productivity; the second, with control of output. The data indicate that output in the 1920's was generally adequate to feed the population (at or near the low prewar level), but too close to basic consumption needs to assure an exportable surplus as long as the peasants retained some voice in the matter. As for domestic supply, the problem was essentially the hybrid nature of market mechanisms. There was a fundamental inconsistency in the NEP acceptance of a free market for agricultural products alongside price guidelines for state purchasing agents and fixed prices on industrial consumer goods. Under this eclectic scheme there was no chance for the "invisible hand" of market forces to adjust supply and demand, and little opportunity to achieve equilibrium in market relations through economic planning.

Once the productive level of prewar agriculture had been regained, the need to raise that level and to resolve the problem of distribution still confronted the government. The leaders generally agreed on the importance of both objectives, but the question of how to achieve them raised a storm of debate.

16

The Great Debates of the 1920's

The critical situation confronting Soviet leaders at the end of the period of War Communism had made it necessary to set aside broader systemic and theoretical questions while energies were directed to more immediate problems of survival. In the struggle to meet those challenges, the new regime had been forced to relegate other concerns to the background. At the beginning of NEP the questions of how to fashion a socialist society out of the recalcitrant stuff of petty-bourgeois peasants and how to refashion the economy into a fully socialist system were less urgent than placating the peasantry and feeding the populace. But once the economy showed signs of revival and the regime grew more secure, discussion of the paths to socialist development was reopened.

On the ultimate goal of establishing a purely socialist economy there was little disagreement. Such an economy would in itself secure the socialist nature of society. Yet when it came to the problem of how to approach that goal, there were different viewpoints. Collisions of economic opinions gave rise to political antagonisms, but political factionalism also influenced the nature of economic opinions. A major debate centered on the question of how to industrialize and on the relationship of industry to agriculture. Discussion of these issues cut across and intensified a parallel debate concerning rural social developments. This in turn drew attention to the institutional structure in the countryside, and led to the debate closest to our immediate concerns—the debate on the commune. The controversy on the commune involved less prominent contenders and received less notice in the literature, yet the questions of social organization and economic management that it concerned were no less fundamental to Soviet society. Because it was so closely connected with the other debates of the period, a review of those heated discussions will help to establish the context in which it took form.

Development Strategies

Of the many socioeconomic controversies that punctuated the NEP period, the industrialization debate has probably received the most attention. Leading political personalities figured most conspicuously in this contest, and in it the issues were set out most explicitly. The entire debate was colored by the Marxian view of industrialization as a necessary condition of any modern state. Whether the establishment of a socialist state as such required industrialization was a question that elicited little if any discussion. It was irrelevant for a number of reasons.

For one thing, in Marxian historical perspective the industrialized nations were at the head of the march of time. To be highly industrialized meant to be modern, to be progressive, to be riding the crest of the wave of social development. There was also a general assumption (derived from Marx's view of the inevitability of struggle between successive socioeconomic formations) that the surrounding capitalist world would be hostile, and that the survival of socialism consequently depended on the strength of the state—including its military-industrial strength. This outlook was reinforced by international developments in the 1920's, especially by the failure of socialist attempts to gain political control elsewhere. Finally, there was the undeniable fact that industrialization, as the progenitor of the proletariat, served the sociopolitical interests of the "party of the proletariat."

Industrialization, therefore, had a strong appeal and the idea of remaining a predominantly agrarian economy met with little sympathy. The literature of the 1920's, reviewing Marx's concept of an international division of labor with world industrial and agricultural sectors, left no question about the place intended for the Soviet Union in any such division. Miliutin, who held a number of responsible posts in agricultural administration and state planning throughout the decade, referred in the agrarian journal of the Communist Academy to longstanding fears—going back to the revolutionary Decembrists of the early nineteenth century and even beyond—about the danger of Russia's becoming a mere agrarian appendage to capitalist countries.[1] Although all the leaders accepted the desirability of a high level of industrialization, however, they differed not only about how to proceed toward that end, but also at what pace.

Industry had suffered an acute setback during the period of War Communism, with overall production falling even more severely than in agriculture. At the low point in 1921 production of basic industrial commodities was down to a minor fraction of the prewar output. Production of pigiron had dropped to less than 3 percent of the 1913 level;

less than a third as much coal was being produced, and less than half as much crude oil.[2] By 1926/27 prewar output figures had been regained (except for iron), and growth continued in the later years of the decade. The rate of growth, however, had slackened, and there was concern about a "declining curve."[3] The conviction that industrial development was not proceeding rapidly enough was reinforced by the recurrent "goods famines" that marked the decade.

A diagnosis of the problem and a prescription for a radical cure were advanced by a group of economists and political leaders who, to varying degrees, shared Trotsky's outlook. The economic case for this group, which came to be known as the "Left Opposition," was drawn up by Bolshevik economist Evgenii Preobrazhenskii.[4] According to his analysis, industrial capital had been seriously depleted during the disturbances of War Communism, when much industry was shut down and abandoned. As recovery proceeded and preexisting plants returned to operation, rapid advances toward prewar levels occurred; but as the limits of plant capacity were approached, growth was bound to taper off. At the same time, however, effective consumer demand was mounting above the prerevolutionary level because of the greater numbers and greater disposable income of the peasants. The situation called for substantial increases in capital outlay to be concentrated primarily in "the production of means of production," that is, in heavy industry. Because of the long interruption in capital replacement, large injections of capital were required in short order. Current production, already inadequate, would begin to decline as obsolescent plants wore out.[5]

But how was this large amount of capital to be obtained? The old regime had exported agricultural products to finance industrialization, and had encouraged foreign investment. Political circumstances limited the possibilities of the latter, and the peasants' new freedom to dispose of their crops made exports uncertain. The solution, said Preobrazhenskii, was to force savings via price policy. Marx had described a "primitive capitalist accumulation," achieved by means of land enclosure and the expropriation of the peasantry. What was called for in the Soviet situation, declared Preobrazhenskii, was an analogous "primitive socialist accumulation."[6] The labor value represented in agricultural products had to be exchanged for a smaller investment of industrial labor. The difference between what the peasants produced and what they received in return could be accumulated by the state as socialist capital.

The key to successful socialist accumulation was maintaining a barrier between the domestic and the foreign market. Foreign goods

could be bought on the average at half the cost of the same goods produced within the country, Preobrazhenskii acknowledged. Yet imports
had to be restricted. Accumulation could take place only "by forcibly
tying our internal market to our technically backward industry while
selling the exported products of the peasant economy at the prices prevailing on the world market, and by subordinating our import program
to the task of accumulating basic capital and replenishing stocks of circulating capital."[7]

Naturally, the peasants could be expected to protest the lack of a fair
return for their labor, but the appropriation of their surplus through
the proposed mechanism was less likely to evoke resistance than would
direct taxation. There was a risk that the substantial delay involved until an increased supply of consumer goods became available might
cause the peasants to hold back their own production. However, the
enforced drop in consumption rates that had taken place during the
years of war and revolution had accustomed the population to doing
without goods, and this would make it easier to keep those rates low.
In time, a gradual increase of real income would accompany industrialization, and this would help to keep matters under control. In the interim, the state would have to use force where necessary to implement
the proposed policy. Here again, Marx was quoted to lend authority to
the prescription. The methods of primitive accumulation, he had written, "depend in part on brute force. . . . They all employ the power of
the state. . . . Force is the midwife of every old society pregnant with a
new one. It is itself an economic power."[8]

Preobrazhenskii's approach to the problem of Soviet industrialization was first elaborated in articles that appeared in 1924 in the wake of
the scissors crisis. It was published in fuller form two years later in a
widely read work entitled *Novaia ekonomika* (*The New Economics*).
The title was apt. A New Economic Policy implied the existence of a
New Economics, and the work seemed to promise a new theoretical
guide to the resolution of practical problems faced by the first socialist
state in history, a bridge between the conceptual framework of Marxism and the concrete problems faced by Soviet Marxists. The need for
such a bridge was evident. At the beginning of NEP Preobrazhenskii
had pointed to the problem: although Marx had said that any indus-
trially developed country could serve any less advanced country as a
picture of its future, not one of the more highly industrialized states of
Europe or America could serve as a model for backward Russia. An
unexpected "zigzag of history" had established the dictatorship of the
proletariat in a less developed country, and Russia would have to find
her own way to industrialized socialism.[9]

Yet just as the New Economic Policy turned out to be in large part a return to older economic policies, the core of the New Economics espoused by the Left Opposition was a return to the old tsarist policy of capitalizing industry by enforced agricultural exports. The progress achieved by moving from capitalist accumulation to socialist accumulation could be measured by the uncertain distance between capitalist exploitation and socialist exploitation. What was new, perhaps, was the perception of conflicting interests, struggle, and inevitable antagonism in the economic world both within and without the country. "Behind our miserable domestic-commodity exchange," wrote Preobrazhenskii, looms the "huge and threatening shadow of the world market." Moreover, "even our collaboration with the poor and middle peasant is only a special form of struggle for the collectivization of agriculture." Cooperation with the private sector of the economy under NEP was a "forced cooperation," a prison in which "we are simultaneously the jailors and the jailed."[10]

To those who refused to accept this outlook and rejected the program of the Left Opposition, its proposals seemed to call for a return to War Communism and to invite a repetition of its consequences. In the mid-1920's Bukharin and A. I. Rykov (later labeled as the leaders of a "Right Opposition") had greater authority in questions of economic policy. Although they and like-minded analysts did not challenge the Left's general assessment of the problems facing the economy and agreed on the need for industrialization, they objected strongly to the tactics suggested. Given the experience of War Communism and the lesson of the scissors crisis, it would be folly, they contended, to try to extract the peasants' surplus through pricing mechanisms. This would lead only to reduced demand and would limit industrial growth.[11] Direct taxation could be used to finance a selective program of capital investment. Balance should be maintained in the development of agriculture and industry, and commodity production should parallel growth in heavy industry. Support should be given to labor-intensive industries in order to utilize the available labor supply, but monopolistic control and state regulation were apt to be less effective in maximizing exploitation of resources than were individual incentive and initiative.[12]

It was in line with the last point that Bukharin, the leading Bolshevik theoretician and the most eminent spokesman of his group, had advanced his notorious slogan "Enrich yourselves!" The assumption was that what was good for the peasants was ultimately good for the proletarians, good for the economy, and good for the Party. The classic Marxist element of class and systemic antagonism was fully accepted by the Right, but the desirability of tempering and circumventing conflict where possible was also accepted. The differences between Left and Right involved substantive issues, but were to some degree a matter of temperament and world view: in the one case, a perception of the possibility of "spheres in harmony," in the other a Hobbesian vision of "worlds in collision." Bukharin, significantly, was one of the first economists to stress the new concept of dynamic equilibrium in the development of socioeconomic systems.[13]

The substantive differences between the two sides in the industrialization controversy extended beyond methodology. The extent and rate of industrialization commanded a great deal of attention, and discussion of them was closely bound up with the question of agricultural policy. Whatever the method of extraction, the agricultural sector was going to have to provide the surplus for investment, the labor force for industry, and (ultimately) the market for industrial products. Yet agriculture itself was in sore need of capital investment, and there was much debate on the relative share of total capital expenditure that should be allotted to it. Rates of return from the agricultural and industrial sectors were compared and disputed, and the subject of investment priorities was heatedly debated.[14]

Some, such as Lev Shanin of the Commissariat of Finance (Narkomfin), held that the bulk of investment should be made in agriculture because relatively small amounts of capital, strategically placed there, would yield the greatest economic return. Since only a limited supply of goods could be offered to the peasants initially in the process of capital extraction, the level of investment would necessarily be low at first. But as agriculture progressed and exports rose, the rising level of peasant demand and of capital accumulation would permit industrial expansion. The current economic disequilibrium was due, not to the inadequate development of industry, but rather to the excessive weight of heavy industry in comparison with light industry. Except for essential investment in transportation, therefore, the available supply of capital should be directed mainly to agriculture, and policy should be aimed at exporting agricultural products.[15]

The proposal received scant consideration. Despite the contention that it would actually lead to the most rapid development of industry, such a pattern of investment suggested the preservation of a primarily agrarian structure, with all the connotations that had for contemporaries reared on Marxian economics. So distasteful was the prospect that S. Strumilin, an economist in the State Planning Commission, had even argued against resuming grain exports in 1923 on the grounds that this would return the country to the role of an "agricultural colony

of the bourgeois West," with negative consequences for the development of Soviet industry.[16] As the drive for intensive industrialization
picked up steam, the agrarian journal of the Communist Academy
published a pertinent article by economist Evgenii Varga (erstwhile
Minister of Finance in the abortive Hungarian socialist republic) reviewing the Marxian concept of an international division of labor and of
world industrial and agricultural sectors.[17] The fact that Russian agriculture was considered particularly backward made industrialization
seem all the more progressive, and even those who urged large invest-
ments in agriculture in the 1920's did so in the name of the "industrialization of agriculture." Lenin had used the term earlier to refer to the
development of the industrial processing of agricultural products, but
at this time it picked up a variety of meanings, ranging from the simple
introduction of machinery to that plus a basic reconstruction of agricultural productive processes and relationships.[18]

Varga pointed out that machinery was the basic indicator of industrialization; to the agricultural industrializers, machinery was the
prime need of the agrarian economy. Many enthusiasts of economic
development at the time believed with Lenin that electrification was
the keystone of industrial development, and in the 1920's mechanization was to agriculture what electrification was to industry. The tractor
became a symbol of modernity and progress. But tractors, like other
agricultural machinery, were in short supply. Foreign tractors were imported under duties that were used to subsidize domestic production.
However, domestic output was inadequate (as well as qualitatively inferior), and sharply dwindling imports were limited by trade balances.
Between 1925 and 1929 the annual domestic production of tractors
rose from about 700 to 2,800, but imports fell from over 12,000 in
1925/26 to a low of 2,400 in 1927/28 and were back to only 6,600 in
1928/29.[19] The problem of agricultural mechanization thus swung back
to the general problem of industrialization. Almost every technical improvement that was called for in agriculture—machinery, chemicals,
electricity, processing—depended on the development of industry.

Yet that development was dependent on capital that had to be obtained somehow from agriculture. Even the "superindustrialists" on
the Left were prepared to see a limited share of capital resources invested in the mechanization of agriculture. Preobrazhenskii's view of
the general requirements of the economic situation was radically different from that of Shanin, but just as Shanin accepted the need for
some nonagricultural investment, so Preobrazhenskii called for a massive supply of tractors.[20] The call for tractors, however, and for mechanization in general was predicated on the assumption that agriculture

would be organized in large-scale units and that machinery would be used collectively. Lenin had stated that if 100,000 tractors could be provided to collectives, the peasants would flock to join them. By the end of the decade, as we have seen, most tractors were assigned to collectives, cooperatives, and the machine-tractor stations. But on the eve of collectivization the total number in the country was still less than half of what Lenin had called for, and he had specified "first-class tractors . . . with gas and mechanics." [21]

Nonetheless, the reported successes of the collective use of tractors encouraged further investment in agricultural machinery, and brought both sides in the industrialization debate into agreement in principle. Yet the mechanization of agriculture had social implications, and on these the Left and Right were most strikingly at odds. While Bukharin was encouraging the rustic enterpriser to get rich (for the good of the cause), Preobrazhenskii was demanding tractors specifically and exclusively for poor peasants. [22] The socialization of agriculture was the ultimate aim of both factions, but the Left was far more concerned about, and preoccupied with, the rural class struggle. That issue, in fact, became a distinct topic of debate as discussion of contemporary rural social development broadened into a major controversy in its own right.

Social Differentiation

The social composition of the peasantry and the impact of NEP on social stratification were topics of intense concern to the political leaders of the 1920's. Along with the return to capitalist practices, it was assumed, there was bound to be an increase in social differentiation, a polarization resulting from growth of the social extremes at the expense of the center. Part of the peasantry could be expected to decline to proletarian status; part would develop into prosperous petty bourgeois kulaks, whose interests and political outlook would be opposed not only to those of their less fortunate fellow peasants, but to those of the Party as well.

As early as 1921 Preobrazhenskii predicted that the growth of kulaks would lead to an inevitable clash between the socialist government and the peasants. [23] And Lenin was hardly reassuring when he raised the question "Can capitalism return in Russia?" The spirit of the flea market persisted, he warned his audience, "in the spirit and in the actions of every petty proprietor [khoziain]. This . . . is the basis of capitalism. While it exists, capitalists in Russia can return and can become stronger than we. . . . As long as we live in a country of petty peasants, capitalism will have a stronger economic base in Russia than communism."[24] In 1923 the young Dubrovskii was already writing of the "re-cidivism" of capitalism under NEP, and cautioning that this should not give rise to panic.[25]

Throughout the NEP period the problem of social differentiation drew a great deal of attention. An index of agrarian literature covering 1922 to 1926 included approximately 500 titles on this subject alone.[26] Starting in the mid-1920's, interest became preoccupation, and some of the leading agrarian journals were given over to the discussion. By 1927 it involved practically every prominent economist in the country.[27] One of the most important arenas of debate was the Communist Academy. Its Agrarian Section, established in 1925, was renamed the Agrarian Institute in 1928. Many of the younger Marxist scholars working in the independent, prestigious Scientific Research Institute of Agricultural Economics found this new branch of the Communist Academy a congenial environment for pursuing their own research interests and developing new approaches to rural studies.[28] The Scientific Research Institute, headed by Chaianov, housed an eminent group of established scholars whose orientation became increasingly unacceptable to their rising Marxist colleagues.

Most of the senior researchers associated with the institute were members of, or sympathetic to, the organization-production school. Before the revolution these economists had been on the cutting edge of research on the peasantry, and in the 1920's they continued to make important theoretical advances. The center of their studies was, and remained, the peasant household. In their view, the peculiarities and production elasticities of peasant households defied standard modes of economic analysis (including Marxism). There was no explicit rejection of Marxism, however; in fact, they insisted that their findings were in no way incompatible with the general theory. Their own investigations led them to conclude that intensive small-scale peasant production, the peasant family farm, could maximize agricultural productivity under certain conditions, and the question of the optimal size of farms was high on their list of research priorities.[29]

For the younger group of "agrarian Marxists" other problems took precedence: rural social structure; class, intraclass, and even intrafamilial conflict; the distribution of the means of production; and the use of hired labor.* Their investigations yielded a widening stream of alarming evidence of social differentiation in the countryside. Because of the political implications of these findings, some of the senior "es-

---

*The agrarian Marxists included L. N. Kritsman, A. Gaister, I. Vermenichev, and M. I. Kubanin. They published numerous articles on these topics in the journal of the Agrarian Section of the Communist Academy, *Na agrarnom fronte.*

tablishment" scholars turned to the problem in their own research. Signs of differentiation among the peasants were acknowledged, but there was said to be little reason for concern, since the appearance of some prosperity among the peasantry was a healthy sign of rural economic progress.[30]

By the mid-1920's the Marxists were moving away, both institutionally and in their research orientation, from their non-Marxist tutors. Within a short time the question of social differentiation among the peasants had become a political touchstone. By the end of the decade rural studies had become ensnared in factional struggles, and scholars found themselves locked into hostile camps. But it was not only the rural specialists in the academic community who became entangled in disputes. Many prerevolutionary agrarian experts in government service, such as N. D. Kondrat'ev at the Conjuncture Institute of the Commissariat of Finance and N. P. Oganovskii of the Commissariat of Agriculture, became targets of criticism.

The growth of concern about the kulaks stemmed from a number of mutually reinforcing factors: economic, ideological, and political. Every time a procurement problem arose in the marketplace, alarms were raised that a hostile peasant force lay in wait in the countryside, ready to starve out the new regime at the first opportunity. The ideology of class struggle sustained and promoted this outlook. But the official policy was one of alliance with the peasants, and since the wealthiest peasants held, or were believed to hold, most of the agricultural surplus, they alone, labeled with the old pejorative tag "kulak," were identified as the rural enemy. It was not the peasants who were "holding the towns to ransom," it was the kulaks.[31] And the clenched fist of the kulak was seen behind every untoward political incident or development in the countryside.

When the scissors crisis was followed in 1924 by signs of rural unrest and by almost equally disturbing signs of peasant indifference to the elections for rural soviets, concern about the political reliability of the peasants was activated. Political workers were dispatched to the countryside to enlist more active peasant support, and measures were taken to ferret out possible pockets of resistance. In March 1925 former members of the gentry who had been permitted to remain on a portion of the land they had once owned (scaled down to the local peasant norm) were deprived of the right to reside on such land and were ordered expelled from the locality. The announced reason for this harsh measure was that a "significant part" of the group had been involved in counterrevolutionary activities or had been exploiting the peasants through their influence on the commune, the hiring of labor, or other suspect practices.[32] Behind the move was the fear, openly expressed by Molotov in a 1926 report, that the revival of capitalism under NEP would encourage the remnants of the old "petty bourgeois political parties" (Mensheviks and SRs) to make new attempts to revive their organizations and influence.[33] Any such attempts seemed most likely to be spearheaded by the dispossessed gentry and supported by the kulaks. Together, these groups might pose a serious challenge to the regime.

Although there was general apprehension about the menace of a countryside that was alien to most political leaders—the majority of whom, like Marx, were "city boys"—there was little agreement on the extent of the danger, and less on how to deal with it. Here debate unfolded. For despite the firm conviction that the kulak existed (*cogito ergo est*), the general agreement that his tribe would increase under NEP, and the pervasive concern about the implications of this for the Soviet regime, there was no clear understanding of how to define a kulak and no certain knowledge about just how many there were. In fact, the very term "kulak" was so ambiguous that in 1925 an article in *Bol'shevik* proposed abandoning it entirely.[34] That very ambiguity may have made the label so useful; in any case, the suggestion fell on deaf ears, and the opprobrious title remained a vital part of the sociopolitical lexicon of the times.

Who was the Soviet kulak?[35] Interest in the question spread beyond political and scholarly circles. As early as 1924 the publication of a collection of letters sent to *Bednota* revealed widespread concern with identifying this bogeyman. Many peasant correspondents protested that any success achieved by a hard-working peasant was enough to brand him a kulak,[36] and Stalin, in a folksy conversation with peasant correspondents, agreed that "if a peasant puts on a new roof, they call him a kulak."[37] That criterion was hardly satisfactory, but what was a proper test?

Beginning in 1925 with a survey conducted by the TsSU, a variety of statistical and analytical studies dealing with the evidence on social stratification were produced. The first TsSU efforts were much criticized by the agrarian Marxists and were subsequently revised. A. I. Kriashcheva, responsible for much of the work, was said to be tainted with Populist ideology, and as a result, it was charged, the earlier categories of investigation had failed to record what were now seen as the "most important qualitative shifts," the class differentiation of the village.[38] Starting at the end of 1926 the collection of census data was reorganized in order to permit fuller analysis of socioeconomic processes in the countryside.

An increasing number of reports on differentiation were issued by the agrarian Marxists in the Communist Academy; studies of social stratification were conducted in the Scientific Research Institute of Agricultural Economics; and data bearing on the subject were collected by the Commissariats of Agriculture and Finance, the State Planning Commission, and other official agencies.[39] Although all this data was widely quoted, there was no agreement on just what it proved. The evidence used by some to raise the alarm was cited by others to assuage concern. Because there were no generally acceptable criteria to determine a peasant's social status, researchers based their work on whatever factors they considered most significant, or whatever data were available. As a result, some studies classified peasants by the amount of crop land held, others by possession of livestock or by ownership of the means of production in general. Of particular importance to the Marxists were the amount and kind of labor hired by a household, the land rented, the inventory rented out, and the money loaned. Any of these factors, or any combination of them, might be taken into account in various schemes of social classification.

Not only were the criteria for classification diverse, the categories marked out in different studies varied also. Some referred simply to "poor peasants," whereas others distinguished the agricultural laborer (*batrak*) from the poor peasant (*bedniak*). Middle peasants could be "weak" or "strong." But the wealthier peasants presented the greatest difficulty. Most frequently they were simply called "kulaks," but sometimes studies referred to a broader category of the "well-off" (*zazhitochnye*), which might include "upper middle" peasants, and there was talk, too, of a narrower, more elite "upper crust" (*verkhushka*).

Under the circumstances, it was no easy matter to delineate the kulak. Molotov admitted as much at the Fifteenth Party Congress in December 1927. Despite an abundance of data, he confessed, it was an "almost impossible task to calculate any sort of general percentage of agricultural bourgeoisie [kulaks] for the entire USSR."[40] Undaunted, however, he attempted just such a calculation. Selecting as the most appropriate criteria the hiring of labor and the renting of land, he concluded that households that could properly be considered kulak (i.e., those involved in both hiring and renting) amounted to 3.7 percent of all peasant households in the country. The growth of capitalist elements was therefore still of "quite insignificant magnitude." Yet, citing the investigations of several of the agrarian Marxists, he cautioned that in some areas a more rapid differentiation appeared to be taking place. Other estimates nudged the figure up or down somewhat, but most fell fairly close to this appraisal, assigning between 2 percent and 5 percent of all peasants to the kulak category.[41] To some the figures were proof of galloping kulakization; others found them reassuring.

Comparison of TsSU data for 1920 and 1925 indicated that the leveling process begun after the revolution continued throughout the first half of the 1920's. Within this period there was a further decline in the number of peasants without land.[42] Moreover, data from the Workers' and Peasants' Inspectorate comparing the same areas in 1910 and 1926 showed that the number of large landholders (those with anywhere from over six desiatins to over sixteen desiatins, according to regional norms) was consistently smaller in the later period. Comparison of the number of households with more than one horse led to the same conclusion: "The role of the upper strata is negligible now in comparison with prerevolutionary times."[43] The "kulak" group, amounting by general agreement to no more than 5 percent of the peasant population in 1928/29, had included 15 percent of all peasants before the revolution.

Classification of a sample of the peasantry by income in the mid-1920's showed that the top group received an average of only 50 to 60 percent more income per capita than the lowest group.[44] The per capita averages are particularly important because differences in household size could create an erroneous appearance of social differentiation. Families labeled as kulaks were typically much larger than the average peasant family. In 1926, when the average peasant household had five members, the average "kulak" household numbered eleven.[45] The old rule still held true: a large peasant family was apt to be a more prosperous family, in all likelihood, for some of the same reasons as in the seventeenth century. At any rate, it would be difficult to prove that the coincidence of size and status was the result of capitalist differentiation. Under the communal system of land redistribution, a larger family still received more land. The larger landholding of the household was not in itself evidence of greater per capita wealth, and household data in general may be misleading for this reason. In 1927 kulak households had only about 20 percent more arable allotment land and hayfields per capita than the average for all peasant households in the country.[46] However, larger households stood to benefit more from their holdings even without extra land. Their larger allotments permitted efficiencies in land utilization that could contribute to greater prosperity. Similarly, the general underemployment of the rural labor force meant that larger families could introduce a more cost-effective division of labor within the household.* Surplus labor could more easily be

---

*This was limited to some extent, however, by the fact that large kulak families generally had a higher ratio of dependents to workers than other peasant families. See *SDD*, 1: 224–27.

released for outside employment that increased household income, and large families received greater benefits from pooling the surplus production (or earnings) of their members, since more substantial resources became available as a result.

Whatever the basis of social classification, most investigations placed the great bulk of the peasants in the middle group. About two-thirds of all peasants fell into this category after the *chernyi peredel*, whereas the poor peasants were generally said to comprise a quarter to a third of the total.[47] Just as large family size could be enough to place a household in the kulak category, so a small peasant family could find itself labeled "poor" because of its lesser holdings. For this reason family divisions played a role in the process of social differentiation. But the nature of that role was complex: some researchers indicated that household divisions contributed to the growth of poor households; others found that they swelled the numbers of middle households.[48]

In any case, the middle peasant was clearly the predominant figure in the countryside, and remained so throughout the 1920's. Rather than witnessing the growth of the social extremes at the expense of the center, the last years of the decade saw the poor peasantry declining somewhat, the middle peasantry waxing, and the ambiguously defined kulaks increasing only very slowly.[49] As for the use of rentals as a criterion of intraclass stratification, data of the Workers' and Peasants' Inspectorate reveal that two-thirds of all renting (in terms both of the number of households and the amount of land involved) was done by middle peasants.[50] Less than 7 percent of all sown land was rented in 1927, according to Molotov's report at the Fifteenth Party Congress, and kulaks took only a minor share of this.[51] Census data for 1927 show that the average kulak household rented about two and a half times as much arable land as the national average for all peasants; but given the larger size of these households, the difference per capita was not so great. Moreover, kulaks rented out land also, and just as much per household, on the average, as the average amount rented out by the peasantry as a whole.[52] All of this hardly suggests acute differentiation; nonetheless, mounting concern about capitalism creeping into the countryside led to a tightening of legislative controls on land renting once again in 1928.[53]

Not only were the middle peasants responsible for most land rental, but they were responsible also for most of the hiring of labor. About half of all kulak households hired labor, but they accounted for only 8 percent of all households employing hired help.[54] About a quarter of all middle peasants hired agricultural workers. These households, however, made greater use of day laborers, whereas kulaks were more likely to hire term labor (for a month, a season, or a year). The employment of labor does not appear to have been particularly profitable for kulaks. Budget studies indicated that labor costs were as high or higher in these households as in those that did not employ outside labor, with the result that kulak enterprise was relatively profitable only by comparison with that of the lower-middle peasants.[55]

After the relaxation of restrictions against hiring in 1925, the number of peasants who hired out as agricultural laborers rose. Between 1926 and 1927 the number of term workers in nonsocialized agriculture went up from 2.3 million to 2.4 million. Yet the number employed by individual households actually declined slightly in this year. All of the increase (and then some) was due to increased hiring by communes. The same pattern was repeated the following year: the number of term workers employed by individual households dropped (now more substantially), but the number hired by communes increased.[56] Communes hired agricultural laborers primarily as herdsmen for members' livestock, but they also employed workers to take care of community needs and to ease seasonal needs for labor.

If it was difficult to build a solid case against the kulaks on the grounds of concentration of landholdings or exploitation of labor (both of which were undoubtedly present in some cases), it was somewhat easier to do so on the charge of control of the means of production. Here again, however, the data are subject to different interpretations. The census of 1927 showed 71 percent of the peasantry in the "middle" category, and this group held 79 percent of all agricultural equipment and means of production.[57] When classified socially by ownership of the means of production, only 3.2 percent of the peasantry fell into the kulak group (owning assets amounting to over 1,600 rubles). Yet this small group held 16 percent of all the means of production and 31 percent of all agricultural machinery. Moreover, the "well-off" category of kulaks and upper-middle peasants, amounting together to one-sixth of the entire peasantry, owned almost three-quarters of the small stock of complex agricultural machinery.[58] Thus there was some basis for concern on the part of those who were predisposed to "view with alarm" whatever was going on in the villages.

Behind the alarm, of course, was a fear that the village might be able to dictate its own terms in disposing of agricultural output. Kulaks, like prerevolutionary estate owners, were apt to have a larger marketable surplus than other producers, and were therefore apt to have more influence than other peasants on the level of government procurements.

Starting in 1925, when procurements became a major problem, it was widely assumed that shortages were due to the hoarding of grain

TABLE 22

Grain Marketing by Sector, 1913 and 1926/27

(percent)

Date and sector	Gross output as percent of total	Percent of output marketed	Percent of total marketing
1913			
Kulaks	38%	34%	50%
Middle and poor peasants	50	15	28
Landowners	12	47	22
TOTAL	100%	—	100%
1926/27			
Kulaks	13%	20%	20%
Middle and poor peasants	85	11	74
State and collective farms	2	47	6
TOTAL	100%	—	100%

SOURCE: Nemchinov, p. 58.

by kulaks for speculation or worse. L. B. Kamenev at that time presented the Central Committee with TsSU statistics indicating that the top 3.5 percent of the peasants held 30 percent of the surplus (marketable) grain, and suggested that "political methodology" called for examination of the situation.[59]

Although the data were subjected to criticism, Kamenev took the floor at the Fourteenth Party Congress at the end of the year to insist that the criticism did not alter the basic issue: "We can debate how strong the kulak is . . . such a percent or such a percent," but the kulak remained to be reckoned with.[60]

According to controversial data supplied to Stalin by the statistician V. S. Nemchinov (Table 22), the gross output of grain in 1926/27 was only slightly below the high level attained in 1913—78 million tons as compared with 82 million in the earlier year.[61] Marketing, however, had dropped drastically. From 21 million tons in 1913, it had plummeted to 10 million in 1926/27. The poor and middle peasants, who had previously contributed only about a quarter of all marketings, were now accounting for three-quarters of the total, but the share contributed by kulaks had shrunk greatly. In 1913 kulaks had marketed almost 11 million tons of grain; in 1926/27 they brought only 2 million tons to market. The conclusion drawn from these figures was that the kulaks were responsible for the decline in marketing and for the state's procurement difficulties. The sketchy data were widely publicized in the late 1920's and were enlisted in the mounting attack on the kulak.[62]

The data on marketing, as well as those on grain output, have been the subject of considerable controversy.[63] Yet apart from problems concerning the accuracy of the data or the manner of obtaining them, problems that have received some attention in the literature, several interesting points seem to have drawn little notice. Before the war the kulaks had marketed 34 percent of their output, and they were faulted in the late 1920's for marketing only 20 percent. The marketing of poor and middle peasants had dropped also as a share of their total output, but only from 15 to 11 percent. That decline was less dramatic and drew less comment, but its effects were far more pronounced, since this group was producing the bulk of all grain in 1926/27. If the kulaks had continued to market at their prewar level, they would have added only 3 million tons to total marketing in 1926/27, according to the data. Yet if the marketing of the rest of the peasants had remained at the previous level, it would have added almost 10 million tons to the market supply of grain, and by itself would have maintained the earlier balance.

The problem, therefore, was related to the reduced marketing of all peasants. The data show that kulaks actually provided a larger share of all marketings in 1926/27 relative to their share of the total output. Before the war kulaks supplied half of the grain on the market and produced 38 percent of all grain. In 1926/27 they accounted for 20 percent of all grain placed on the market, but were producing only 13 percent of the total output. Moreover, if kulaks accounted for 15 percent of the peasants before the war and provided 50 percent of marketed grain, then the 2 to 5 percent of peasant households supplying 20 percent of all marketed grain in 1926/27 were providing a larger share of all marketings relative to the size of the group. Rather than proving that they were responsible for the state's procurement difficulties, the data showed that not only were the kulaks marketing relatively more than other peasants, but (in view of their reduced numbers) they were actually providing a relatively larger share of the market supply than before the war.

Given the government's economic needs and objectives, kulak interest in the market might have been turned to the state's advantage through such policies as were advocated by Bukharin. Yet data demonstrating the existence of that interest were interpreted as evidence of a kulak withdrawal from the market. Economic logic was restructured in the light of partisan politics. The problem of the kulak, of the peasants in general, of agriculture, and of industrialization became involved in the intensifying factional struggles of the period. At mid-decade the "opposition" consisted of the Trotsky-Preobrazhenskii bloc, whose views on a number of points differed from those of the predominant "propeasant" group led by Bukharin. The program of the opposition was defeated at the Fourteenth Party Congress at the end of 1925, but the bloc was joined in 1926 by Kamenev and G. E. Zinov'ev. The faction soon lost out, however, in the political infighting that followed. Increasingly, talk was heard about the existence of *two* "deviations"—one on the Right as well as that on the Left. The "black panic before the muzhik" attributed to the Left was said to be paralleled by an equally erroneous Right tendency to underestimate the kulak danger.[64]

Paradoxically, only after the "antipeasant" Left was defeated did the campaign against the kulak begin to emerge in full strength. The situation recalls another famous schism in the history of the country: the attack on Patriarch Nikon's Old Believer opponents that gathered force after his downfall in the seventeenth century. In both cases, ideology and politics were inextricably intermeshed. With due qualification, the same might be said of the last of the great debates of the 1920's—the controversy about the commune. Closely linked with the other major disputes of the decade, it was inevitably influenced by the direction they took.

The Controversy over the Commune

In the early years of civil war and War Communism, Bukharin and Preobrazhenskii had collaborated to produce a popular primer on communism.[65] In it they agreed that the future belonged to large-scale socialist agriculture. They agreed, too, that communal landholding had no place in that future. A decade later they were still agreed on the basic premise, but disputed the point at which yesterday's future becomes the present. The place of the commune in the Soviet countryside and in the transition to socialism had become one of the major issues in the round of contemporary debates.

The controversy over the commune fused the debate on developmental strategy with that on social stratification. Like those issues, it began to emerge only in the middle of the decade. Debate on the role of agriculture in the economy led to debate on the role of the commune in agriculture; debate on the social differentiation of the peasantry led to debate on the role of the kulak and the poor peasant within the commune.

The point of departure was public discussion of draft legislation designed to clarify basic principles of land tenure.[66] Publication of the proposed statute in the summer of 1926 brought the commune to the center of attention, and the ensuing discussion revealed major differences of opinion about the institution. The ambivalence that had characterized attitudes toward the commune for the better part of a century was still clearly in evidence. On one hand the commune was seen as an archaic survival of a backward past, on the other, as an ideal passageway leading to socialized agriculture.

The arguments were summarized in an exchange that took place later in the year in the Agrarian Section of the Communist Academy between the former Menshevik N. Sukhanov and the young agrarian Marxist M. Kubanin. Sukhanov began by stating that the whole question of land tenure hinged on the problem of the commune, but that the commune was a problem only because of the rigid outlook of the "communophobes." Retaining the old liberal ("Stolypin-bourgeois") view of the commune and focusing on its serf origins, mutual responsibility, and compulsory rotation, opponents of the institution were oblivious to recent changes. The revolution, after all, had effected a reversal of values. Thus a free press was a good thing while the proletariat was struggling for power, but became a negative feature in a period of attempted bourgeois counterrevolution; a standing army had been an evil in the hands of imperialists, but became a positive institution as a defender of the proletarian state. In a similar turnabout the revolution had transformed the commune from an obstacle to economic development into an instrument that could facilitate advancement.

After reviewing the legal status and economic functions of the commune, Sukhanov addressed the charge that communal tenure inhibited progress by discouraging individual initiative. This he dismissed as an argument of bourgeois liberals. According to them, "the independent bourgeois enterprise, large or small, must have full freedom for its development. Society, in the form of the state, must help it (give subsidies, suppress foreign competition, etc.), but it must not by any means bind or restrain it. The independent proprietor, large or small, must interfere in the affairs of the state (bourgeois democracy), but society must not interfere in his affairs (the principle of freedom)." In contrast to such views Sukhanov described the proper outlook of a socialist: "The progress of the individual is nothing to us; the progress of the masses—everything." If the commune interfered with individual economic rights, so did the state. Traits that were looked on negatively, the commune's "restraint, interference, regulation, and dictatorial rights," should be viewed positively as assets in the state's march toward socialism. It was precisely through these traits that the economic dictatorship of the rural soviet was secured wherever the commune and the soviet were juridically joined.[67]

If the commune could impose backward practices on its members, it could also impose progressive practices, argued Sukhanov. Charges that it was responsible for fragmented holdings were untrue: in the noncommunal western regions, landholding was even more splintered. Though progressive elements tended to leave the commune (for individual tenure), it did not follow that the weaker groups left behind were less capable of improvement. Such a notion, he insisted, was counter to Soviet ideology. The commune was an instrument of progress and socialism. The "established theory" of the evolution of the rural economy was based on the expectation that individual households would be gradually joined in production units through the growth of cooperativism. Communal organization facilitated this development by creating ties among groups of land users and accustoming them to common land use and collective action.[68]

The point most likely to sway his audience Sukhanov saved for last: "As a dyed-in-the-wool believer [*ortodoks*], I must, in conclusion, make reference to Marx."[69] The reference was to a draft in the recently discovered 1881 correspondence with Russian revolutionaries on the topic of the commune.[70] Referring to the innate dualism of the commune, with its blend of social ownership and individual use, Marx had written that there were two alternative possibilities in communal development, with either the collective or the individual principle inevitably coming to predominate. The outcome would depend on historical circumstances.

The Russian commune, said Marx, was without historical precedent: "Common property in land gives it a natural base for collective adaptation, and its historical means of capitalist production provide ready material conditions for cooperative enterprise organized on a broad scale. It can, as a result, make use of all the positive devices produced by the capitalist system. . . . With the help of machinery . . . it can gradually replace a fragmented economy with a complex economy . . . it can become the immediate point of departure for the economic system toward which contemporary society is striving, and give rise to a new life without prior resort to suicide."[71]

Marx has given us his teaching, concluded Sukhanov, and it remains for us to make use of it. Reminding his audience that the rural soviet was already legally responsible for implementing the decisions of the commune where the two coincided territorially, he suggested that they be joined everywhere. The commune was already largely a public-law institution. In order to make it entirely so, it would be necessary only to deprive members of the right to separate from it with land and to give all residents of its territory a voice in the communal assembly.

If a case could be made for the commune in the Soviet system,

Sukhanov had made it. His argument denied the social objection to the commune, termed economic objections political distortions, transformed drawbacks into organizational virtues, and even produced evidence that Marx considered mechanization feasible within the communal system. If his presentation had been allowed to stand, defense of the commune would have been incumbent on all the orthodox. But a rebuttal was published simultaneously.

Opening his attack with a quotation from Lenin about self-styled Marxists who lacked an elementary comprehension of revolutionary dialectic, Kubanin proceeded to a methodical excoriation of his opponent. The "original" dialectic of this "communophile," he charged, represented the latest Neo-Populist defense of the commune in defiance of the logic of facts. If it were to be taken seriously and implemented in Soviet rural policy, it could cause great harm.[72]

Sukhanov had stated that "the land society" was the official title of the commune in Soviet legislation, thereby showing, said Kubanin, that he did not understand the difference between the two. (This shot missed its mark, as readers were quick to point out. The two terms were not strictly interchangeable, but all communes were land societies under the law.)[73] More important, Sukhanov failed to understand the nature of the class struggle in the countryside and within the commune. The notion of "progressive" kulaks leaving the commune was not based on facts, claimed Kubanin. Actually, kulaks stayed in the commune in order to exploit the village, whereas the poor left the commune when possible.[74]

Kubanin then offered his own description of the commune, with evidence from contemporary newspapers of kulak malfeasance within it: opposition to land organization, manipulation of the commune (and of the rural soviet), control of redistribution, and so forth. According to the reports of rural correspondents, those leaving the commune included all groups but kulaks. (The revelation that many of the rural correspondents themselves had left the commune raises the question of whether they were likely to label separators as kulaks, but that point was not discussed.)

Kubanin dismissed as utopian the contention that the commune provided an indispensable mechanism for regulating agriculture. The "true believer" had overlooked class analysis: regulation of whom by whom? (*kto kogo?*). Here again Kubanin showed himself a scholar of the new breed: social differentiation and the conflict of class interests were central to his approach. Sukhanov had acknowledged the problem of the kulaks, but proposed to limit it by forbidding further withdrawals of land from the commune. To Kubanin, such a move would only improve the position of the kulak within the commune, and was sure to be interpreted by the peasants in this light. By calling for a compulsory commune and by describing the Soviet Land Code as similar to Stolypin legislation (in permitting departures with land) Sukhanov, he charged, showed a complete lack of understanding of Soviet policy. Lenin had emphasized that the use of force against the peasants was inadmissible. They could not be compelled to stay in the commune, nor would they be forced out of it.

As for the use of pronouncements from Marx, Kubanin noted that similar tactics had been employed in recent émigré literature. In fact, several points raised by Sukhanov had been discussed there by SR writers, and Kubanin suggested that the "coincidence" was revealing.[75] Like the émigré analysts, Sukhanov completely misinterpreted Marx. Though Marx had said that the commune could be saved as a socialist base by revolution, he had in mind a revolution at the time he was writing, that is, before the development of capitalism in the 1880's and 1890's and before capitalism had infiltrated the commune.

The comments to which Kubanin referred had been made by Marx and Engels in the preface to the Russian edition of the *Communist Manifesto* in 1882.[76] They had not actually been among the remarks cited by Sukhanov, but had been circulated by others at the time in defense of the commune.[77] What Sukhanov had quoted was part of a draft letter written by Marx in 1881 in response to a request from the Populist Vera Zasulich for a statement of his views on the Russian commune. The reply to Zasulich did not speak of the need for revolution. Marx obviously had difficulty formulating his conclusions on the commune, and had composed four drafts of the letter.[78] The epistle that was finally dispatched, like the earlier drafts, reflected a guarded optimism about the role of the commune in Russia's future. It was carefully hedged, however, with cautions about the necessity of favorable circumstances.

The author of *Capital* was then near the end of his life. He was well aware of the weight his word carried (Zasulich had approached him as one would the Delphic oracle, declaring that an answer was "a matter of life and death, especially for our socialist party"), and of the fact that his pronouncements would affect the historical assessment of their author. His struggle with successive, circumspect drafts is evidence of the quandary in which he was placed by a request for a statement that could be published in Russia. The brief reply that was finally dispatched contained an apology that a piece suitable for publication could not be sent (which may explain why the letter itself was not published at the time). Its hopeful but cautious conclusion that the commune could provide "a base for the social rebirth of Russia" was a model of Delphic augury.[79] "It would be necessary first," Marx added, "to eliminate the pernicious influences to which it is subject on all sides, and then to secure normal conditions of free development for it."

These rather vague and tentative formulations lent themselves to quite different interpretations and became a standard part of the ammunition exchanged in debates on the commune in the 1920's. Kubanin's attack on the institution was actually a weak piece (rhetoric discounted) that extrapolated broad conclusions from very limited data. Yet it helped to remove the aura of Marx's authority from upholders of the commune and effectively smeared them with the brush of Neo-Populism.

Marx was not the only socialist authority whose writings on the commune were subjected to exegesis in the course of the controversy. Chernyshevsky too was reexamined in the light of the contemporary situation. In 1928, the centennial of Chernyshevsky's birth, *Pravda* quoted Lenin to the effect that this revolutionary hero was a "socialist-utopian" who had dreamed of a transition to socialism through the old semi-serf commune, unable to foresee in the 1860's that only the development of capitalism and the creation of a proletariat could bring about the conditions for a transition to socialism.[80]

The many supporters of the commune were not easily discouraged, however. Other participants in the discussion within the Communist Academy stressed the value of the commune as an economic unit that permitted the government to deal with the peasants in organized communities rather than as separate households.[81] Without the commune, they contended, land relations, and relations with the peasantry in general, would be chaotic. The same points were repeated somewhat later in the Party journal, *Bol'shevik*.[82] There the author directly challenged Kubanin's claim that the kulak always dominated the commune. He readily conceded that kulaks controlled some communes, but said that there were many examples of poor and middle peasants using the commune to harness the kulak. Moreover, communal tenure was presented as the form that best promoted a transition to socialized agriculture, particularly where the communes' lands had been reorganized and broken up into the more efficient *poselki* and *vyselki*.

The author of the *Bol'shevik* article not only denied Kubanin's criticisms of the commune, but also rejected Sukhanov's proposal to convert the commune into a public-law institution, contending that the fusion of commune and rural soviet Sukhanov had suggested was impractical. The commune had its role to play; the soviet, another. Those who felt that the soviet could simply assume the functions of the commune were forgetting that it was "impossible to regulate the economic relations of small-scale peasant production by bare administrative measures. It is not to be imagined that the rural soviet could immediately direct the production of all this scattered mass of peasant households. That is utopia."[83]

The debate on the role of the commune in the transition to socialism thus led to a consideration of the relationship of the commune to the rural soviet. That relationship, a subject of relatively little concern in the earlier years of NEP, was to become an increasingly important issue in the later years of the decade. All of the debates of the period involved disputes about the correct answers to critical economic and social questions of the day. Yet the choice of questions was itself a major part of the debates. When the agrarian Marxists put forward the question *kto kogo?* they were changing the framework of the long-standing debate on the uses of the commune. In the context of the relationship between the commune and the soviet, the question being raised was: Which institution was going to control which?

17

Dual Power in the Countryside

The rural soviets had a checkered history in the early years of Soviet power. Springing up after the October Revolution—in part spontaneously, in part as the creation of the central government—they were assigned an ambitious role in the countryside, but were left pretty much to their own devices to fill it. As we have seen, after a confused initial period of conflict with other agencies harboring pretensions to local authority (notably, the Committees of the Poor), the rural soviets were reorganized in 1920, and their formal responsibilities under the law were expanded.

One of the basic problems faced by these new institutions was the fact that they had no ready-made slot to occupy. Most other newly created organizations in some way replaced earlier institutions that had been abolished, but there had been no administrative agency comparable to the rural soviets before the revolution. The volost zemstvos were the closest counterpart, but these had barely appeared on the scene when they were abandoned in 1917. It was one thing for the law to ascribe an impressive range of functions to the rural soviet, another to translate the legislative model into an operating organ of rural administration. The difficulty was compounded by the existence of an institution outside of the formal administrative structure, the commune, which had been, and continued to be, responsible for many of the functions assigned to the rural soviet.

Commune and Rural Soviet

With the introduction of NEP a number of changes occurred in the lower rural soviets. In 1921–22 the volost land departments were eliminated, and local land affairs were left under the supervision of the volost executive committee.[1] Both the rural soviet and the volost executive committee were modified by new legislation adopted in January

1922.[2] In connection with the general overhaul of the administrative system and the reduction in the number of administrative units, the number of rural soviets was sharply cut back. They could be formed now only in villages with at least 400 inhabitants. A delegate was to be elected for every 200 residents, and the size of the rural soviet was limited to 25 members. (The previous corresponding figures were 300, 100, and 50.) As before, the soviet could have an executive committee only where it represented over 10,000 rural inhabitants, but this committee was now to consist of two members rather than three. An attempt was made to stabilize the soviets and to stop the constant turnover of personnel by depriving rural soviet members of the right to leave office before the end of their terms without the consent of the volost executive committee. Members of that agency, in turn, could not abandon their posts without permission from district authorities.

The 1922 legislation described the functions of the rural soviets in fairly brief and general terms, much as did that of 1918. They were to carry out the instructions of the higher organs of government, to raise the economic and cultural level of the rural population, and to promote public participation in the latter endeavor. The "building of a new life" and much else in the ambitious program of 1920 was quietly put aside. The volost executive committee was declared responsible for the observance of all laws (including regulations on agriculture and land use) by the population within its territory. Disputes between individuals over land were transferred in the RSFSR from the various agencies previously responsible for their adjudication to a new system of land commissions that was established in May 1922. The commissions served at various administrative levels as the basic land courts of the country throughout the period of NEP.[3]

It was not long before the next important set of changes was introduced. The combination of the scissors crisis in 1923 and the political disturbances in the countryside in 1924 focused attention on the rural arm of government once more, and led to the adoption of a new Statute on Rural Soviets on October 16, 1924.[4] The new law was more detailed than its predecessor and to some degree extended both the functions and the authority of the lower soviets. The supervisory role of the volost executive committee was made more specific in matters of land organization, in land rentals, and in the execution of decisions of the land commissions.[5] The number of rural soviets was further reduced, but the limits on size and membership were relaxed. Once again, one delegate was to be elected for every 100 rural residents (rather than every 200), and the soviet could now have up to 100 delegates (rather than 25).

The sphere of competence of the rural soviet was extended over a broader range of activities. Certain functions previously assigned to the volost committees were now turned over to the soviets, and they were authorized to initiate agricultural improvements, help in the formation of collectives, participate in certain land disputes, register rental contracts, and develop school systems, libraries, and health facilities.

The legislation defined somewhat vaguely the relations between the rural soviet and the commune. The soviet was to convene the communal assembly, but was instructed to carry out all of its legal resolutions. It was to represent the commune before higher agencies and to transmit its petitions to them. In these matters the soviet served as the agent of the commune. However, the commune was subject to all legal rulings of the soviet within the territory under the soviet's jurisdiction. This rather ambiguous state of affairs was the subject of considerable discussion over the next several years. There appeared to be two authorities directing the countryside, and references began to be heard to a rural "dual-power" system, recalling the interlude in 1917 when the Provisional Government ruled side by side with the Petrograd Soviet.

Starting about the middle of the decade, proposals to clarify the relationship between the commune and the rural soviet were broadly publicized and debated—from the sessions of the Communist Academy to the pages of the peasant press. One result was the adoption on March 14, 1927, of a new law in the RSFSR, the Statute on General Assemblies (*skhody*) of Citizens in Rural Settlements.[6] In a dramatic break with longstanding tradition, this legislation provided for the establishment of a new type of village meeting. From now on there were to be two kinds of assembly in the countryside: general assemblies of the local populace as well as the traditional assemblies of the commune. The general assembly was to be open to all citizens of the community with full voting rights, including landless residents (agricultural proletarians, herdsmen, teachers, blacksmiths, etc.) who were not members of the commune. It was to meet under the supervisory authority of the rural soviet, and its decisions were subject to confirmation by that body. The communal assembly was to be closed to all who were not members of the commune, and was to restrict itself to discussing local land affairs.

The provisions of the law of March 14, 1927, would have brought about a major change in the nature of the customary communal assembly, had they been accepted. But contemporary accounts agree that the law was almost universally ignored.[7] The peasants saw nothing to be gained in substituting two time-consuming meetings to dispose of matters that had always been taken care of in one. They continued, therefore, to conduct community affairs as before, and left it to the authorities to worry about whether a meeting was a general or a communal assembly.

The peasants' indifference in this matter was paralleled by their general indifference to the rural soviet. Low levels of participation in the elections to the soviets were typical, but when the participation rate of qualified voters in elections to rural soviets fell from 37 percent in 1923 to 29 percent in 1924, the central authorities became alarmed. Apathy on the one hand and violence on the other (the attacks on rural news correspondents and the Georgian unrest) moved the government to action. Complaints were heard that the practices of local bureaucrats during elections had discouraged peasant participation. Rural elections were typically held by voice vote, and according to one contemporary account, "deputies for soviets and for executive committees were nominated (or, more accurately, as obligatory recommendations, were appointed) as previously from above, or by the local party organization."[8] Reviewing the situation, a Conference on Socialist Construction convened by the Presidium of the Central Executive Committee decided to invalidate all elections in which fewer than 35 percent of the qualified voters had participated. Detailed new instructions were issued, a vigorous campaign was waged to get out the vote, and new elections took place.* The outcome was a rise in the electoral participation rate to about 40 percent.[9]

One of the reasons for the decline of interest in the elections for rural soviets in 1924 was the disappearance of many soviets as a result of the new statute introduced that year. The number of rural soviets in the RSFSR dropped from 80,000 in 1923 to 50,000 in 1924. This placed a greater distance between the village and the soviet, and weakened interest in the elections. Electoral data showed that the level of participation moved inversely to the number of villages included within the rural soviet.[10] Recognition of the problem led to some increase in the number of rural soviets over the next few years, but the growth in the number of delegates far outpaced it, with the result that the soviets, in line with the general policy of enlarging administrative units, grew to be larger organizations over the second half of the decade. In 1924/25 the average rural soviet had fewer than 14 members; by 1928/29 it counted more than 32. (See Table 23.)

---

*Where 35 percent of the electorate had participated, the earlier results were retained. In areas where elections had not yet been held, they were to take place under new electoral regulations.

Meanwhile, intensive efforts were maintained to involve the peasants more actively in elections and to improve the Party's links with the countryside. Party cells were few and far between in rural areas (only one for every 25 to 30 settlements at mid-decade), and the role of the Party in the rural soviets was much weaker than in lower urban soviets. Beginning with the electoral campaign of 1924, a number of drives were undertaken to "revitalize" the soviets in the countryside. Thanks to these efforts, electoral participation rates showed steady improvement. By mid-decade about two-thirds of the adult rural population of the RSFSR was voting in elections for soviets. Comparison of participation rates for 1930/31 and those for 1924/25 reveals an additional 28 percent of the rural population taking part in the elections.

Most of the gain (about 75 percent of the total increase) was achieved by drawing women into the electoral process. (See Table 23.) In the earlier year fewer than one rural woman in five were voting; in 1930/31 more than three in five were doing so. Since the number of women exceeded the number of men in the rural population (by about 8 percent), the relative weight of women in the electorate was even higher than their participation rate might suggest.* In 1927 women accounted for 12 percent of all delegates elected to rural soviets; in 1929, for 19 percent. An even more striking change was the appearance of women as presidents of rural soviets. In 1927 only one percent of all the presidents of rural soviets were women, but by 1929 women held 7 percent of these posts.[11]

Although efforts to increase the number of Party members in rural soviets met with some success, at the end of the decade fewer than one-sixth of all delegates to rural soviets were Communists. (See Table 23.) With the addition of Communist Youth (Komsomol) members, the number rose to almost a fifth of the membership. Party members controlled the leadership of rural soviets to a somewhat greater extent, but even there the party was not dominant. Before the "revitalization" campaign of 1927, Party members served as presidents of only about one-sixth of the rural soviets; by 1928/29 they accounted for almost a third.[12] In the volost committees Party members were more numerous, but the distance between the volost and the village was greater. The average rural soviet in 1928 covered six to eight settlements, with 300 to 400 households and 1,500 to 2,000 residents: on the average, there were fourteen rural soviets on a volost in the European RSFSR, and twenty per volost in the country as a whole.[13]

There were far fewer rural soviets than communes. As indicated

---

* According to the December 1926 census, the number of females in the rural population was 62.6 million; the number of males was 58.1 million. (*SDD*, 1: 24.)

TABLE 23

Rural Soviets in the RSFSR, 1922–31

Category	1922	1923	1924/25	1925/26	1927	1928/29	1930/31
No. of rural soviets (000)	120.0	80.0	50.7	51.6	54.8	55.3	52.1
No. of delegates (000)	500	500	700	857	955	1,800	930
Avg. no. of delegates per rural soviet	4.2	6.3	13.8	16.6	17.5	32.5	17.8
Percent of electorate voting	22	37	41	48	48	61	69
Percent of female electorate voting	—	—	20	28	30	47	62
Percent of party members in rural soviets	—	—	6	6	8	9	14
Percent of Party and Komsomol members in rural soviets	6	8	9	10	13	15	20
Percent of Party members among presidents of rural soviets	—	—	16	14	19	31	57

SOURCES: Kukushkin, p. 290. The data on the number of rural soviets are from NKVD, *Administrativno-territorial'noe delenie Soiuza SSSR*, p. xxv, except for 1922 and 1923, which come from Kukushkin, pp. 57, 75, and are approximate.

NOTE: Where two years are indicated, the figures are for January 1 of the later year.

above, there were approximately 319,000 communes in the RSFSR in 1928, with the average commune including only about 50 households and 260 individuals. The commune was clearly much closer than the rural soviet to the peasants. Although the soviet had been authorized to convene the communal assembly, it did so ordinarily only where the two units coincided territorially and the soviet was serving as the executive of the commune. Rarely did the soviet take a directing role or even exert significant influence over the commune. That hardy institution appeared to be carrying on much as before, impervious to outside influences. According to an irate observer reporting to *Bednota* in 1925, the new land society was nothing more than the "old prerevolutionary commune, living by the old tradition of the mir, with a common class 'consensus,' with 'democracy,' . . . with all the antisoviet aspects of its way of life."[14] As for its relations with the rural soviet, a contemporary report on one volost describes a situation that appears to have been fairly typical. The soviet there was said to exist in name only, and the commune concerned itself exclusively with local affairs. Yet any official proposition formally placed before it the commune duly approved for the record and solemnly resolved "to fulfill by 100 percent."[15]

In 1926, when the debate on the commune broke out in full force, the journal of the Commissariat of Internal Affairs insisted that the question of the authority of the rural soviet over the commune was not a proper matter for debate. There could be no question about the predominance of the soviet. The rural soviet was an organ of government; the commune had no official status in the administrative system.[16] Yet there was clearly a difference of opinion on the issue within official circles since at the same time the Commissariat of Agriculture was advising its agents that under the provisions of the Land Code the rural soviet had no authority over the land society.[17]

At the end of 1926 the Workers' and Peasants' Inspectorate began an investigation of the functioning of the lower soviets. To the consternation of higher authorities, the rural soviets were found to be playing a quite minor role in the countryside. Not the soviets, but the communes were dealing with the major economic and cultural needs of the village. At times the commune even elected the president of the rural soviet, and some communes reportedly discussed and approved the work plan of the soviet.[18]

As increasing attention was turned to the problem of rural administration, it became apparent that neither the rural soviet nor the volost committee had effective control over the commune. Numerous reports, official and unofficial, emphasized the fact. The decisions taken by communal assemblies were supposed to be filed with and reviewed by the volost committee. Yet, as an investigation in Tambov province revealed, most decisions reported (and "far from all" were reported) were simply recorded without comment at the volost office.[19] In Saratov province the situation was apparently much the same. Here there were at least 100 communes in each of the large volosts, and every commune met several times a month. To keep a close watch over their manifold activities was beyond the physical capabilities of the ill-staffed, overworked volost committee.[20]

The commune's activities extended to almost all aspects of community life. The agenda of an assembly might include such matters as local roads, insurance, bridge repair, aid to fire victims, and landmarks, as well as designating guardians for orphans and renting out the village bull. According to the tally of the Workers' and Peasants' Inspectorate, the largest category of questions (39 percent of the total) discussed at assemblies had to do with land. Next came financial and tax matters (16 percent), administrative questions (15 percent), cultural life (9 percent), public welfare (8 percent), and miscellaneous concerns.[21] Although some of the questions dealt with by the commune were taken up in the rural soviet, the commune was usually in a better position to resolve local problems.

Since the rural soviet generally covered a number of settlements, delegates were likely to come from different localities and might have to travel some distance. Often the president and the secretary alone handled the business of the rural soviet. Meetings could be difficult to arrange and in many soviets were held infrequently. One local study revealed that although the commune met at least once a week and at times even daily, the rural soviet had convened only five to eight times in the course of the year. This commune was said to decide "absolutely all questions, so that there was nothing left for the rural soviet to do." [22] Another local investigation showed that many assemblies of the commune took place during an interval when not a single meeting of the soviet was held. [23] This was not unusual in some localities; in others the rural soviet met fairly often. It seems to have been a general rule, however, that whatever the number of soviet meetings, the commune met more frequently. [24]

Attendance was another matter. According to the Land Code, representatives of half of all member households had to be present for a legal quorum of the assembly; in order to change the form of land tenure, half of all eligible voters, including representatives of two-thirds of all households of the land society, were required to be present. The 1927 statute on general assemblies called for the presence of only 25 percent of all persons with voting rights living within the area, yet even this more moderate level of attendance proved difficult to achieve. Inability to gather a quorum was a general problem. In 1927, an investigation by the Workers' and Peasants' Inspectorate of assemblies in 25 settlements in different regions found attendance below 20 percent in almost half, and below 30 percent in most of the remainder. Reports from a number of other localities indicated that attendance of 10 to 15 percent was fairly typical. [25]

They suggested too that one reason for the low attendance was the persistence of traditional attitudes. In many localities the household head was considered the only proper representative at the meeting, and others were not expected to appear. This was particularly true of women. [26] Although their participation in soviet elections and in the soviets themselves was increasing, peasant women were not welcome at the assembly. There were many reasons why women did not attend assemblies, reported rural correspondents. Some claimed the cursing that went on when debate became heated and the heavy tobacco smoking drove women from the meetings. [27] (The relative purity of air and language at the soviet was apparently not recorded.)

A more general deterrent to peasant attendance at assemblies was the time-consuming nature of the meetings. They could drag on for days, and sometimes more than one meeting was called in a single day.

Any time that there was a matter of general interest to discuss, a meeting could be called, and there appeared to be no end to the matters with which the commune concerned itself.

To contemporaries, the commune, "by occupying itself with almost all questions of rural life," was approximating the old commune, which "apparently had passed unscathed through the whole epoch of revolution."[28] Reports circulated of communes contributing to the support of the Church or being involved in other untoward behavior, and warnings were heard that the lack of proper socialist control over their activities left them open to kulak influence.[29] With concern mounting about differentiation in the countryside, it took little to convince urban leaders that the new capitalist kulak was none other than the old "mir eater," still dictating to the old commune.

The question of social influences was extended to the rural soviet. The central authorities had two concerns: on the one hand, the relationship of the rural soviet to the commune; on the other, the soviet's relationship to the regime, its commitment to the goals of the state that it represented. One of the main objectives of the revitalization campaigns was to improve the social as well as the political composition of the soviets. Along with a desire to strengthen Party representation among the delegates, there was a determination to build a broader base of non-Party support among the peasants.

According to data available at the time, the percentage of rural-soviet delegates without horses was below that of horseless peasants in general, and the number of delegates exempted from taxation because of poverty was also lower than the overall rate.[30] These findings were disturbing, since they suggested that the poorer peasants, on whom the Party felt it could most rely, were inadequately represented in the lowest echelons of rural administration. The scanty evidence at hand indicated that the middle peasants predominated in rural soviets. The percentage of poor and wealthy peasants was variously estimated and appears to have shifted with the size of the soviet and the number of settlements it contained. One investigation found middle peasants dominant in 80 percent of the rural soviets analyzed; poor peasants took the leading role in 12 percent, kulaks in 8 percent. Another showed a higher representation of poor peasants, rising in some areas to over 50 percent of the membership of rural soviets, and revealed no more than 8 to 10 percent kulaks.[31] Although the preponderance of middle peasants was no great cause for alarm, it did not give much ground for confidence that the rural soviet had a social bias that would automatically align it with the central government in any collision with the commune.

When grain-supply problems reappeared late in 1927, the question of rural control gained greater urgency. In the 1920's the commune had first become a subject of open debate after the procurement difficulties of 1925; it was to become a more open target of criticism with the recurrence of those problems starting in 1927. The law of March 14, 1927, on rural assemblies was passed in an attempt to strengthen the role and authority of the rural soviet in public life. Yet, as we have observed, that legislation had little effect. Later in the year it was followed by several other moves designed to improve the position of the rural soviet with respect to the commune. A decree adopted in the Ukraine on October 12, 1927, authorized rural soviets to supervise the activity of all land societies within their territory and to review and register all their decisions. When the soviet considered a decision illegal, it was empowered to prevent its enactment.[32]

During the same month instructions were issued in connection with new Union legislation on land use. One of the objectives of the new law, it was stated, would be to secure a "directing role" for the rural soviet in its relations with the commune. The new law would exclude those who had been deprived of the right to vote in elections for the rural soviet from voting in assemblies of land societies. At the time, about three percent of the population was disfranchised, including family dependents of the disfranchised, who were also deprived of electoral rights. These households paid a special tax to the rural soviet in lieu of liability for service on it—a unique form of taxation, not only without representation,[33] but specifically for nonrepresentation.

At the end of the year the Fifteenth Party Congress emphasized the need for additional measures to strengthen the rural soviet in its dealings with the commune. The congress provided a sympathetic forum for renewed charges that an ominous dual power prevailed in the countryside. In his report on social statistics provided by the Council of People's Commissars, Molotov stressed the importance of more vigorous rural soviets to combat the growth of kulak influence in the countryside. "Up to now, when we have vitalized the soviets the kulaks have often turned to the land societies and have tried to entrench themselves there. [Kaganovich: "Right!"] Now we will finally beat them out of even these last trenches."[34]

After the congress the refrain "dual power" was heard on all sides. Commenting on the congress's directives, *Pravda* complained early in 1928 that the rural soviets so far had had "almost nothing to do with the socioeconomic problems of the village."[35] *Bednota* chimed in, observing that the commune was still "master of its own affairs," while the rural soviet merely looked on.[36] In the spring a report of the Workers' and Peasants' Inspectorate to the Council of People's Commissars, RSFSR, again reiterated the dangers of the dual power of commune and soviet.[37] Meanwhile, the Ukrainian law of October 12, 1927, was given wide and laudatory publicity.

The Ukrainian initiative demonstrated that it was easier to strengthen the rural soviet where traditions of communal self-rule were weaker. This was evident in other regions, where soviets played a more vigorous role in local life. Of the Azerbaidzhan Republic, for example, it was reported that "in the majority of Turkish villages all work is concentrated in the soviets and nothing is left for the assembly"; yet in other villages "the soviet is often no more than the executive organ of the assembly."[38] Since all of these villages were under the same general set of laws, it was obviously not law that determined the relative status of commune and soviet. The general disregard of the statute of March 14 showed the limits of legislating change; there was little correspondence between the role cut out for the rural soviet by law and the role that it actually played in rural life. As one legal analyst noted, the commune had a "greater weight than followed directly from the law."[39] Part of that weight was simply a residual of communal traditions, but part was due to the inadequacy of the soviet as a financial counterweight to the commune.

Financing Rural Administration

The weak financial position of the local soviets was a persistent problem for the government, but it was hardly a new problem. In Russian administrative history, financing local government had long been troublesome. The traditional solution to the problem had involved a certain accommodation of state to society. Since the administrative reforms of Ivan the Terrible in the middle of the sixteenth century, local populations (or their ruling elites) had periodically been offered a degree of autonomy in running local affairs in exchange for their financial contributions to the centralized administration. This arrangement had two direct consequences: (1) the burden of meeting rural needs fell directly on the local populace and remained largely outside of the state budget; and (2) the rural administrative structure remained poorly articulated, comparatively underdeveloped. As discussed earlier, this situation had contributed to the decision to retain the commune at the time of the emancipation of the serfs in the nineteenth century. However, whereas the commune had been retained in the 1860's because no adequate administrative substitute was at hand, in the 1920's its very existence appeared to be blocking the establishment of other, preferable administrative institutions. At the same time, because the commune was still providing for essential local needs, it was not lightly to be cast aside.

After the emancipation the tsarist government had sponsored the development of the zemstvo system, an alternative system of rural self-governance designed to address local needs.[40] However, the zemstvo uneasily straddled the breach between the central administration and the countryside, and was never fully accepted by either. As far as the peasants were concerned, the zemstvo had represented first and foremost an additional tax bill. Although some peasants supported the institution, the predominant reaction to its elimination after the October Revolution was relief. Under the circumstances, the government was hesitant to impose local taxes to support the rural soviet. The result, however, was to leave that agency virtually without resources, since it was inadequately provided for in the state budget.

In the late 1920's all observers generally agreed that the main reason for the existence of dual power in the village was the absence or inadequacy of the rural-soviet budgets. Early postrevolutionary legislation had attempted, unsuccessfully, to centralize all budget administration; abandoning that course in 1921, the government had made no immediate provision for lower local budgets. Not until 1923 were arrangements made for regular volost budgets, and even these were not widely established before 1925. The volost was given control of state enterprises within its territory from which some income could be derived. It received part of the single agricultural tax and could collect certain stipulated taxes (on transportation, transient trade, licenses, fees, fines, etc.). But out of its income it was obliged to maintain the state farms, provide or rent buildings for public agencies and institutions, establish social services, build roads, and meet other responsibilities—including supporting the volost executive committee and aiding the rural soviet within its territory.[41]

Yet the problems of the volost were as nothing compared with the plight of the rural soviet. The lowest organ of the soviet administrative system had almost no resources to draw upon. Rural-soviet budgets were a rarity. The Volga German Autonomous Republic had provided for them in 1924, transferring sources of land income to the soviets, but this was exceptional.[42] Independent budgets for rural soviets were given guarded approval starting in late 1926, but only for large settlements with strong local economic resources.[43] Not until the issue of dual power surfaced did the financial status of the rural soviets come in for serious attention. At the Fifteenth Party Congress the financial situation of the rural soviets was described as deplorable and in need of immediate improvement. Their total income was placed at 16 million rubles, whereas "land societies and other peasant associations" were said to have an income amounting (according to various sources) to 70, 80, or 100 million rubles.[44] Materials of the Commissariat of Finance covering 29,000 rural soviets in the RSFSR showed that only 3.2 percent had independent budgets in 1926/27.[45]

Although the soviet was authorized to issue mandatory regulations concerning certain public services (communications, sanitation, fire protection, etc.), it could not, under a 1925 ruling, levy a local tax to provide such services without the consent of the assembly.[46] Financial aid furnished by the volost executive committee was limited (when available at all) to small sums assigned for specific purposes. Moreover, the pay of the presidents and secretaries of rural soviets was notoriously low, although their jobs could be highly demanding. Some officials received no payment at all for a substantial outlay of time and effort—a factor that eliminated many poorer peasants from the positions. The average monthly pay for a president or secretary of a rural soviet was about 20 rubles, at a time when the plenipotentiary of a land society was receiving 35 to 40 rubles, a state farm worker was paid 40 rubles, and the average monthly wage of a worker in Moscow was 75 rubles.[47] As a result, few highly qualified peasants were interested in holding these positions. Within a six-month period, out of a group of 807 presidents of rural soviets, 123 had quit and 58 had been dismissed.[48] The record of the secretaries of rural soviets was comparable.

The officials of the rural soviet were expected to familiarize themselves with all of the laws, instructions, and circulars sent out by higher authorities and to translate these into local practice. According to the report of VTsIK secretary A. S. Kiselev to the All-Russian Congress of Soviets in June 1929, over 6,500 pieces of literature had been sent out to each rural soviet in the previous six months alone.[49] The reception of such literature can be gauged from a contemporary description of the workings of one soviet. "In conformity with good Russian tradition, all papers received . . . are filed by the secretary with the notation 'for information' or 'for guidance.' Into cartons 'for information' and 'for guidance' fall all papers not dealing with taxes, including many of the brilliant productions of circular literature from district, provincial, and central authorities who are troubling themselves over the rural soviets."[50]

It was no accident that papers dealing with taxes received special handling. Both the volost committee and the rural soviet were burdened with tax work. The rural soviet, or its president, was described in the same account as a "mere tax agent, harassed and under threat of administrative and judicial punishment."[51] From the peasants' point of view, reported another source, the soviet appeared "not as the director of the economic life of the village, but in the role of a tax collector."[52] According to *Pravda*, the rural soviets were concerned mainly with exerting administrative control over the population: they collected the agricultural tax, carried out the instructions of higher agencies—in short, "busied themselves with everything connected in the popular mind with the notion of *pressure*, rather than help."[53]

The chief sources of regular income for the rural soviet were a share of the agricultural tax and any income from land or buildings that might be assigned to it.[54] But these sources proved too limited to permit the rural soviet to carry out its assigned role. Under the circumstances, it was hardly surprising that soviets frequently turned to communes for financial aid. A delegate at a congress of soviets in Saratov voiced a widespread complaint: "On every question—on the repair of schools, on the hiring of a watchman, and so forth—every day it is necessary to talk with the general assembly, every day it is necessary to beg for money."[55] From Kursk the president of a rural soviet wrote to *Bednota* describing his woes. Advised by the volost committee that he would have to find means to cover the soviet's clerical expenses, he had appealed to the commune—but in vain. The peasants had dismissed him with the comment that they had no need of such services. To add insult to injury, they suggested that he had entered the soviet only to avoid hard work. Such a view, commented the writer, was held only by the "sick" or the "unconscious," but the rest of the peasants had refused to support the soviet on the grounds that they were already paying enough in taxes.[56]

Other communes proved more cooperative. In 1927 many were providing regularly in their own budgets for the soviets, and more were providing irregularly. The main sources of the commune's income were land rentals and self-taxation; additional income was derived from various fees or charges that depended on local conditions (the use of the commune's mill, the services of the community bull, etc.). Land rentals and self-taxation were the major sources of income and apparently were of about equal importance.[57] There was no official accounting of the budgets of land societies, but self-taxation was clearly the most elastic source of income and one that was available to all communes. It had traditionally been the village's way of providing for its needs and was based on the familiar principle of mutual responsibility. If the assembly decided on a measure that involved an expenditure, the cost was divided among the households in the community and collected by the commune's officials. In some cases (e.g., the construction or maintenance of roads or other public facilities) the required contribution might take the form of labor rather than money.

Because the peasants themselves determined the need for the outlay and because of the deep-rooted convention that decisions of the community were binding on all, the system of self-taxation was universally accepted by the peasants. It appeared to provide a reasonably satisfactory means of meeting many of the needs of the village. However, the egalitarian aspect of the system drew fire from the authorities, and with good cause. In line with the commune's general principle of equal shares for all members, a tax was generally distributed as a uniform amount to be collected from each household or "per eater." Since the income of households and individuals was not uniform, the tax was actually regressive and fell more heavily on the poorer peasants. Comparison of the part played by self-taxation in the total tax payments made by households showed that in different regions it took from 13 to 69 percent of the payments made by poor peasants, but only 4 to 52 percent of the total paid out by wealthy peasants.[38]

The government, therefore, tried to eliminate self-taxation or at least to restrict it to labor obligations. But there was a great deal of peasant resistance, and a compromise was offered. In 1924 it was ruled that taxes voted by the assembly could be collected only from those who had voted for them. This evoked wide protest. The peasants argued that if the assembly were unable to impose a tax on the entire community, antisocial elements would be able to avoid their fair share of public expenses. Those who were disfranchised, for example, could refuse to contribute to the soviet. In view of the peasant opposition and because there was no viable substitute at hand to provide for rural needs, the government backed down. On August 24, 1927, a statewide decree authorized self-taxation in money, natural products, or labor, by general assemblies or by "separate groups of citizens" for local cultural and economic purposes.[39] The ends to which self-taxation could be applied were to be defined by the separate republics to meet their particular requirements. A tax approved by a simple majority of a general assembly was binding on all members of the community, provided that a quorum of half of the electorate was present at the meeting. A resolution on self-taxation had to be submitted to the volost or raion executive committee; if that body presented no objection within two weeks, the resolution was to be carried out by the rural soviet. In making this concession to the peasants, the government called for a more progressive distribution of self-imposed taxes. From now on, the soviet would allocate shares of the self-tax burden among households in the community, taking into account their economic strength. Collecting the tax was also to be its responsibility.

Given the new role of the soviet, the fiscal and political potential of self-taxation led to a radical change in the government's approach. Within five months a new ruling lifted the requirement that half of the electorate be present at an assembly imposing self-taxation. Exceptions to a previously stipulated limit on self-taxation (a maximum of 35 percent of the agricultural tax) were now authorized upon the approval of higher local authorities.[60] Almost simultaneously the RSFSR published a decree listing an extensive range of rural needs that could be addressed by self-taxation, including educational, cultural, and public health institutions (schools, libraries, reading rooms, clubs, nurseries and nursing homes, hospitals, clinics, etc.) and a broad array of social and economic services (social security, fire protection, means of communication and transportation, grain reserves, veterinary and agronomic stations, etc.).[61] Self-taxation, in short, could be applied for just about any measure contributing (in the judgment of the local soviet authorities) to the improvement of the local economy or the welfare of the populace. Following adoption of a resolution on self-taxation, the rural soviet was to designate within three days the share due from each household in proportion to the sum of the (progressive) agricultural, industrial, and income taxes it paid. Poor peasants, and citizens in government service who were not conducting an economic enterprise of their own and did not stand to benefit from the objective of the tax, could be exempted from payment.

The expansion of the rural soviet's role in self-taxation was greeted by Party stalwarts as a step in the right direction. And there were other steps. In 1927 the RSFSR began moves to empower rural soviets to require labor service for certain public purposes from residents of their territory. In addition, rural soviets with independent budgets were given the rights of juridical persons, making it possible for them to conclude contracts and negotiate binding property agreements.[62] But there was a good deal of grumbling in Party circles in 1928 about the fact that the commune, on the whole, remained a far stronger institution economically. Communes were still able to initiate self-taxation, although poor peasants might now to some degree escape it. The financial situation of the soviet still left much to be desired. At the beginning of 1928 only 5 to 6 percent of all rural soviets had independent budgets; a year later the situation had improved, but 85 percent still lacked an independent budget.[63] Most still looked to the commune for assistance, and the result of this financial dependency was a loss of independence in policy. The soviets were supposed to be the spokesmen of the government in the countryside, but under the circumstances they were in no position to speak up in opposition to the commune. Local reports indicated that the soviets preferred to avoid conflict with the assembly, left responsibility for decisions in its hands, and remained "neutral."[64] The implications of the situation were not overlooked when the matter came up for discussion at the Fifteenth Party Congress, and dual power continued to occupy a prominent place in the press in the months that followed.

The Question of Dual Power

In the course of the exchanges at this time, the journal of the Communist Academy aired the argument that since all land belonged to the state, all income from land should go to state agencies and not to "private-economy" associations such as the commune.[65] All land held by communes that was not being worked directly by members should be transferred, it was urged, to the rural soviets. The proposal was endorsed by *Bol'shevik*, which carried it further by calling for the compulsory establishment of independent budgets for rural soviets.[66] The underlying considerations had little to do with the fiscal aspects of rural government: at their core was the issue of political control. Certain social elements had been disbarred from participation in the elections for soviets in order to prevent them from having any influence in government, yet these elements were permitted to take part and vote in communal assemblies. To the extent that the rural soviet was subject to the decisions of the commune in budget matters, a back door had been opened for a political role for the disfranchised.

The other disturbing aspect of the situation was the kulak. With the assumed growth of capitalist elements in the countryside, the resources of the wealthy peasants were expected to grow, and their influence within the commune was expected to increase. The domination of the commune by petty bourgeois elements was a serious enough problem, but the domination of the rural soviet by the commune was, in Kiselev's words, "absolutely intolerable." Political leaders therefore considered the relationship between the rural soviet, the commune, and the rural budget one of the "most vulnerable" parts of the soviet system.[67]

Although the debate on the role of the commune in the transition to socialism continued throughout 1928, there was little debate on the relationship between the commune and the soviet. It was generally agreed that there was much to be desired in that area. As the case was put at the Fifteenth Party Congress, until the commune was under the firm control of the rural soviet the revolutionary slogan "All power to the soviets" would remain unfulfilled, and "elements of dual power [would] be preserved in the countryside."[68]

Yet what sort of "dual power" actually existed? The label was something of a euphemism for the unpalatable situation revealed in contemporary reports. The commune emerges repeatedly in those accounts as the "master" of the countryside, a "state within a state," and "the center of village life," whereas the rural soviet "takes a back seat," is "passive," and is "weak."[69] If there was a contest, it was decidedly one-sided. The commune, for better or for worse, was a real force in the life of the peasants, whereas the soviet often had little more than title to a role. The country might be under the dictatorship of the proletariat, but the countryside was under the dictatorship of the commune. This had been true throughout the decade following the revolution. By the end of 1927, however, perceptions of the situation had begun to shift, and new developments began to change the situation itself.

The Grain Crisis and the Economic Plan

In the years immediately following the October Revolution, circumstances made it difficult for the new government to move as rapidly as desired toward a "socialist reconstruction" of society and the economy. Notable success was achieved in securing the "commanding heights" in industry, finance, and trade, but food supply problems prevented the extension of comparable control over the agricultural sector. The critical situation in 1920–21 forced a retreat from the compulsory policies of War Communism to the relative deregulation of NEP. The market was reopened to small-scale private trade, the peasants regained the right to dispose of their output as they chose, and the government fell back on a system of procurement agencies purchasing grain at fixed prices to meet the needs of the cities and the army.

There was no theoretical basis for NEP, no economic system underlying it. The policy amounted to a political compromise with the economy, a compromise that grudgingly tolerated elements of capitalism within the skeletal framework of a developing socialist economy. Throughout the decade there was constant tension between the antagonistic principles of state control required for socialist planning and the free interplay of economic forces essential for market equilibrium. Yet despite occasional malfunctioning (the scissors crisis and the 1925 procurement problem), the uneasy balance that was maintained between competing systemic demands permitted economic recovery in both industry and agriculture. With the economy essentially restored to prewar levels by 1926, the question of the direction and tempo of further development led to the great debates.

But while the battle of words was raging, its outcome was being shaped by the policies adopted and the actions taken by the major state economic and planning agencies. Starting in the middle of the decade both the Supreme Economic Council (Vesenkha) and the State Planning Commission moved toward greater and more centralized control of the economy. The growth of administrative regulation (e.g., price controls) was one sign of this gradual shift; another was the formulation of increasingly ambitious economic plans devoted to large-scale industrial development. Those who took more cautious approaches, including the staff of the Commissariat of Agriculture, found themselves increasingly closed out of the centralized planning process.[1] As it turned out, the very gains achieved by the compromise with capitalism undermined the position of the compromisers and strengthened that of the most ambitious planners for socialism.

Once the economy had substantially recovered, goals that had been set aside earlier were reconsidered. Yet advancing toward those goals meant abandoning the retreat that had permitted stabilization, and risked destabilization. Given the government's shaky hold on the countryside, this was a sobering prospect. The question of the dynamics of economic development was therefore all-important, and economic planners in the mid-1920's faced a challenge of extraordinary complexity as they attempted to delineate the limits of the possible. There was no yardstick in history by which to scale a proper rate of socialist transformation of the economy, but there was a good deal of enthusiasm for the project, and an upwelling of optimism fed by a prematurely suppressed current of revolutionary heroics.

Although annual "control figures" for the economy had been developed in the earlier years of the decade and various draft plans had been sketched out, the implementation of a concrete, long-term economic plan for the entire country was possible only after basic recovery. In mid-1927, as planning efforts intensified, the Council of People's Commissars called for the creation of a Union-wide plan to promote and coordinate the development of the different economic regions and to ensure "maximum utilization of their resources for the industrialization of the country."[2] The State Planning Commission, where partisans of ambitious planning targets had recently won out over more cautious rivals, was given sweeping authority over the planning agencies of the separate republics. Although the Five-Year Plan for economic development was not submitted for formal approval until the spring of 1929, it covered a period beginning with the economic year 1928/29 and was already being put into practice at the time it was officially endorsed by the Sixteenth Party Conference in April 1929.

From 1927 to the official adoption of the First Five-Year Plan in the spring of 1929, planning goals escalated remarkably. The State Planning Commission ultimately submitted two variants of the plan: a basic version (embodying fairly ambitious targets), and an extravagant best-case or optimal variant that was said to be feasible only if a number of uncontrollable variables (such as the weather) turned out favorably each year. Despite the odds, and over the strong objections of dissenting economists (some of whom had pressed earlier for high targets, but now drew back in dismay), enthusiasts who voiced confidence in the force of revolutionary will carried the day. Not only was the optimal plan adopted, but some targets were subsequently raised to even higher levels. The history of the First Five-Year Plan cannot be pursued here, but its development and the expectations that fed into and flowed out of it were critical to developments on the agrarian scene in these years. It was the government's commitment to launching the economic plan that converted a familiar problem, reappearing in late 1927, into a crisis that spelled the end of NEP—and an end to the commune.

The Development of the Crisis

The resolutions of the Fifteenth Party Congress in December 1927 embodied a set of directives on the Five-Year Plan. Immediate targets for agriculture were to include an increase in yield, expansion of the sown area, and balanced development of the different fields within the agrarian economy. There were said to be three ultimate objectives of agricultural development: (1) greater consumption, (2) the growth of exports (to provide for essential imports and for the accumulation of foreign currency reserves), and (3) the supply of raw materials for industry.[3]

Undoubtedly, it would have been a welcome turn of events if food consumption could have been raised while the other objectives of the plan were being attained, but this provision was probably a politic expression of hopes for the future rather than the priority item its listing suggested. Despite the failing fortunes of the Left, a decision had already been taken to pursue intensive industrial development. (In the plan approved by the Sixteenth Party Conference, investment in industry was to increase over the previous five-year level by close to 300 percent, whereas investment in agriculture was to grow by only about 60 percent.)[4] The contributions of agriculture to industrialization envisaged in the other two points in the congress directive, especially in the second, were therefore more urgent. Agricultural exports would help cover the cost of vital imports. A call for extremely high targets for agriculture (equivalent to those actually adopted in 1929) was already being voiced by Ia. A. Iakovlev, assistant commissar of the Workers' and Peasants' Inspectorate, at the 1927 congress.[5] Iakovlev, again, presented a decision of the Central Committee that was adopted among the resolutions of the congress. According to this statement, which echoed remarks in Stalin's address to the congress, the "*basic task*" of the Party in the countryside at the time was to unite small-scale individual peasant households and transform them into large-scale collectives.[6] Yet, like Stalin and others who spoke on this theme at the congress, Iakovlev emphasized that collectivization could proceed only with the consent of the peasants, and would take place gradually.

While the delegates were optimistically passing resolutions on various desiderata in agriculture, developments barely given notice at the congress were taking an unfavorable turn. In line with the steady pattern of NEP recovery, the area sown in grain in 1927 showed a slight increase over the previous year. However, less favorable climatic conditions led to lower yields, and the harvest fell below the bumper crop of 1926 by about 6 percent. (See Table 19, p. 259.) This alone was sufficient to create a predictable drop in the amount of grain available to official procurement agencies in the fall and winter of 1927–28, but the shortages that developed had not been anticipated. When reports of procurement difficulties began to come in during the autumn, they were initially discounted as having only local significance. There were some worried references to procurements at the Fifteenth Party Congress, but no real discussion of the problem. By the time the congress broke up in mid-December, however, the gravity of the situation was becoming apparent. Procurements were lagging well behind those of 1926, and they were particularly low in December. The 300 million puds of grain collected by the government in the last three months of 1927 amounted to only 70 percent of collections for the same quarter of the previous year. By the beginning of 1928 there was talk once more of a crisis.[7]

The reasons for the recurrence of supply problems were a topic of considerable discussion. Trade Commissar A. I. Mikoian, writing in *Pravda*, denied that crop yields were the real source of the problem, since the reduction in the level of marketing was greater than the decline in agricultural output.[8] The root of the trouble, he maintained, was the increased purchasing power of the peasants relative to the supply of consumer goods. Forty percent of all agricultural income was realized in the first quarter of the agricultural year (beginning in July), but only 25 percent of industrial output became available within that quarter. To add to the problem, light industrial output and textile production were behind schedule in the current year, and taxes were not collected on time. The peasants, therefore, had no incentive to part with their grain.

The contention that the goods shortage was responsible for the grain shortage was repeated frequently in the press at the beginning of the year. There were reports of efforts to send goods out to the country-side, even at the cost of stripping the cities to obtain them.[9] At the same time there was much talk of the need to raise taxes. It was at this point that self-taxation (now under the direction of the rural soviets) received a strong boost from the central authorities. The agricultural tax was substantially increased for the coming year, and the peasants were invited to participate in a government loan through a lottery opened in February.[10] Goods, taxes, and lottery alike were intended to siphon off the excess purchasing power of the peasants and to motivate them to sell grain.

The same objective might have been pursued through price manip-ulation, but this was a complicated matter. Retail prices on industrial goods had been reduced in 1927, but that move had contributed to the goods famine. Higher prices on the goods that were available would have taken up more of the peasants' income and would have been more in keeping with the NEP goal of market equilibrium, yet high prices on industrial goods had contributed to the development of the earlier scissors crisis and were currently unpopular with the leadership since they were associated with the policy of the discredited Left.

Another line of approach would have been to increase the official prices paid for grain. This would have increased peasant purchasing power, but a similar move in 1925 had been effective in getting the peasants to bring out their grain. Official procurement prices for grain in 1927/28 were only 15 percent above prices for 1913, whereas the general index for wholesale prices of agricultural products stood at 157 and that for industrial products at 188. Official grain prices were well below those on the private market. In 1925/26 the annual average price paid for all agricultural products in the socialized market was 92 percent of the average paid in the private market. In 1926/27 it fell to 85 percent, and in 1927/28 it dropped to 64 percent.[11] Although low prices were a major factor in the peasants' reluctance to sell to procure-ment agencies, the government resisted attempts to raise them.[12] In line with plans for industrialization, it was determined to keep food costs as low as possible. Moreover, an increase in grain prices had led earlier to a decline in industrial crops; an increase now might produce the same unwanted consequences. There was also a political aspect to the question: accepting higher grain prices might have seemed an endorsement of the Right position on the peasants and might have strengthened that faction.

One of the factors accounting for the falloff in procurements in 1927 was population growth. According to data submitted by Rykov to the

Fifth Union Congress of Soviets, the per capita production of grain in 1913 had been 584 kilograms, but in 1927/28 it was down to 490 kilograms.[13] Thus the margin between the consumption needs of the producers and the volume of their output was narrower. Population growth was compounded by economic growth and by the industrial mobilization of the labor force out of the countryside into the cities. From 1926 through 1928 the number of workers and government employees rose by 3 million.[14] A substantial increase in industrial investment and in construction took place in 1926/27. This meant more jobs in urban areas and accelerated the movement into the towns; it also meant that former producers of agricultural goods were joining the ranks of consumers, so that urban needs were rising not only in absolute terms but relatively as well.

There were therefore a number of explanations for the grain crisis, and a number of palliatives addressed to solving it. But no trickle of goods to the villages, no threatened tax, no lottery lure was likely to bring in adequate food supplies promptly enough to meet immediate needs. There was an army to be fed and cities to supply, cities that had approached a revolution through bread lines not so long ago. Official stores of grain were shrinking rapidly, the prospect of exports was fading fast, and the dream of building "socialism in one country" was threatened with a rude awakening.[15]

The solution that recommended itself to Stalin and his clique was direct requisitioning. This amounted to a return to War Communism and was strongly opposed by the "pro-peasant" faction as abandoning NEP and the alliance with the peasantry on which it was founded. Objections were overruled. The situation was said to be exceptional. Under War Communism requisitions had been the ordinary method of grain collection, but now requisitioning was an extraordinary measure, to be employed only temporarily. As for the alliance, it remained firm. It was not the peasantry as a whole that was "hoarding" grain. It was the kulak.

War Communism Revisited: The Crisis and the Commune

January 1928 saw the reintroduction of "exceptional" measures that distinctly recalled the procedures of War Communism, despite the disclaimers of the authorities responsible. Military terminology came back into daily use as the countryside was swept by a new "grain campaign." Once again, Party cadres were mobilized and sent out to give battle on the "grain front." One of the most effective weapons employed in the attack on the peasantry was Article 107 of the criminal code of the RSFSR (Article 127 of the Ukrainian code). Introduced in 1926 as a means of controlling speculation, it provided penalties of up to five years' imprisonment and confiscation of property for those who deliberately caused a price rise by speculative practices. These included "failure to offer . . . goods for sale on the market."[16] Although not originally intended for this purpose, if interpreted literally the provison could be used to take action against a peasant simply for possessing a store of grain.

Rural soviets were put to work collecting data on local grain holders, and local officials were pressured to increase government procurements. A group of high officials (close colleagues of Stalin) went out to lead the campaign personally in critical grain-producing areas.[17] Stalin himself took the offensive in Siberia, accusing local bureaucrats who showed reluctance to use Article 107 of collusion with kulaks and threatening to purge legislators who hesitated to apply it.[18] To avoid the appearance of an all-out war against the peasantry (and perhaps because by this time there was a conviction in some quarters that the true malefactors in the countryside were wealthy hoarders) the campaign was waged as an attack on the kulaks.

It was reasonable enough to assume that wealthier peasants would have a higher share of surplus grain relative to their output. But since the wealthy were in a small minority, there was no reason to think that they controlled the bulk of grain held by peasants. If the wealthier peasants were inclined to hold on to grain in the hopes of a price rise, other peasants with grain to spare were apt to share the same outlook. Stalin, for one, was well aware that the middle peasants possessed most of the grain, and he acknowledged as much.[19] Although repeated complaints were heard about grain being taken from middle and even poor peasants, the fiction was maintained that "surpluses" were to be collected only from the kulaks. Local authorities naive enough to take this at face value found it impossible to produce sufficient grain to satisfy procurement demands. But undoubtedly most got the point of the *Pravda* article on "natural selection" (February 9, 1928), which stated flatly that the current campaigns would show which rural officials were unfit to serve the Soviet state and which should survive.

The heightened attack on the kulak, already anticipated in the slogans of the Fifteenth Party Congress, created some concern among the peasants as a whole. A press report on the plight of one "advanced" villager is illustrative. Although this former Red Army man had always considered himself a poor peasant, he had been doing somewhat better of late and now feared that he would be listed as a well-off peasant.

Since prospering peasants were "talked about like strangers," he had decided it was preferable to return to poverty.[20]

With the help of the extraordinary measures, such a move was easily arranged for any peasant who happened to have some grain set aside. But what was most extraordinary about the measures employed in the villages at this time was the development of a new technique for extracting grain from the peasants—the so-called "Ural-Siberian method" or the "method of social pressure."[21] This amounted to a Soviet retooling of the venerable practice of "divide and rule," aimed at harnessing the authority of the commune in the service of the state. The method emerged initially as the unplanned byproduct of a conjunction of circumstances, but once its utility was recognized, it was developed by the authorities into an effective instrument in the procurement campaign. Ultimately, it was to play an important role in collectivization.

The use of social pressure was closely connected with the practice of self-taxation. When the campaign for grain procurements was organized at the beginning of 1928, control figures were sent out from higher authorities to volost and raion executive committees. The committees in turn drew up grain targets for each village, assigning responsibility for collecting these "fixed quotas" (tverdye zadaniia) to the rural soviets. The soviets were assisted by special emissaries dispatched to the countryside especially for this purpose and armed with broad authority to take whatever measures were required to ensure the delivery of the grain demanded. The amount due was treated as a tax on the community, and at this point the recent legislative changes in administering self-taxation gained new significance. On the one hand, they provided a legal basis for the role of the local soviets in the grain collection process. Although the rural soviets themselves played a limited part in the campaign, the outside agents and agricultural plenipotentiaries who spearheaded the procurement drive legitimated their operations under the umbrella of the authority of the rural soviet. On the other, the law made it possible to transfer responsibility for individual levies to the assembly. The confrontations bound to result from requisitioning, therefore, would take place among the peasants themselves rather than between peasants and the state; at the same time, the principle of submission to the decisions of the commune would facilitate acceptance of the requisitions. In short, the method, in a dialectical tour de force, joined the tradition of collective responsibility with the ideology of class struggle.

This use of self-taxation was a logical if unintended consequence of the newly established role of the rural soviet and an acknowledgment that the peasants themselves were in the best position to know who actually had grain. In Siberia and the Urals territory, where there was a more pronounced degree of social differentiation than that typical of the country as a whole, local officials were quick to make use of "social influences" in the procurement campaign and to recommend the tactic to the central authorities—hence the name "Ural-Siberian method." The application of social pressure followed the adoption of a decision by the assembly, and the government made it simpler for a minority of poor peasants to secure the adoption of a measure. The law of January 10, 1928, recognized an attendance of only one-third of the eligible voters as a legal quorum for purposes of self-taxation if an earlier meeting for the purpose had failed to produce a quorum of one-half.[22] Since a simple majority of those present sufficed to give binding force to a resolution on self-taxation, a group amounting to only about one-sixth of the enfranchised citizenry could legally impose a tax on the entire community. This greatly simplified the process of requisitioning, which, as might have been expected, ran into strong resistance from the peasants.

Attempts to mobilize poor peasants appear initially to have met with limited success, but gained ground starting in mid-February with the arrival of urban activists in the countryside.[23] The typical procedure was for local officials, reinforced by a plenipotentiary, to convene a meeting of the village assembly. The problem would be explained, and the quota for the village would be announced. The assembly was then required to vote formal acceptance of the quota and to allocate it among the individual households with the help of the rural soviet. The difficult part, from the point of view of those responsible for collections, was obtaining approval of the quota. Meetings were often protracted until a compliant quorum was found, and sometimes went on far into the night. At times, the quorum was simply disregarded. Those who refused to vote for the quotas were intimidated by having their names taken down, and opposition to self-taxation was often taken as prima facie evidence of a peasant's kulak status. Once the quota was accepted by the assembly, any refusal to deliver the grain demanded was punishable under the law. Among the measures taken to compel acceptance were arrests, searches, confiscations, roadblocks to intercept shipments of grain, arson, and shootings.[24] In the milder forms of pressure, those who failed to surrender the amount demanded (an amount not necessarily based on any evidence of actual holdings) were fined, had their names published, were excluded from the village cooperative, or were not allowed to purchase even essential goods from the cooperative store.[25]

The April 1928 plenum of the Central Committee and Central Control Commission acknowledged that grain had been seized outside of the judicial procedures required under Article 107, that private trade in grain had been illegally prohibited, and that various other "excesses" had been perpetrated. It was admitted too that "administrative pressure" had been exerted on the middle peasants. All of this, however, was said to have resulted from incorrect interpretation of the Party's policy by local officials. NEP was solemnly reaffirmed as the proper and only possible route to a socialist transformation of the economy.[26] This seeming retreat from the more militant phase of the campaign was a concession both to critics on the Right and to the fact that the assault on the peasantry had achieved some immediate successes. But the plenum decision to award poor peasants 25 percent of all grain taken henceforth from kulaks was a clear sign that the attack had not been called off. Insisting that the Party held firmly to the Leninist policy of alliance with the peasantry, Stalin derided "those comrades" who believed that the alliance covered the entire peasantry, including the kulaks. Anyone who thought so, he warned, had "nothing in common with Leninism" and was "not a Marxist, but a fool."[27]

In an interesting digression, Stalin went on to compare the grain shortage in 1928 and the move against the kulak to the famine of 1921 and the government's move against the Church at that time. The earlier crisis had permitted Lenin to confiscate Church valuables in the name of aid to the starving masses, winning popular support for a measure that would otherwise have been difficult to carry through. The same kind of opportunity had arisen, in Stalin's analysis, in the later situation. The crisis (which he now declared "liquidated") had permitted the government to carry out a campaign against the kulak, a campaign that was recognized by the masses as in their interests and was therefore supported by them.

In order to reach such conclusions it was necessary to overlook the considerable evidence of peasant resistance to the procurement campaign, but this Stalin was able to do without undue difficulty, having apparently—and conveniently—convinced himself and others that use of the Ural-Siberian method meant popular backing for the government's policy. The only evidence that carried real weight was the mounting stock of grain that had been accumulating since January in state warehouses. In the last three months of 1927 procurements had been down by 128 million puds compared with the previous year's collections; in the first three months of 1928 they were 110 million puds *above* those of the previous year. *Pravda* had reported exultantly (no doubt by way of encouragement) at the beginning of the campaign that use of Article 107 was proving marvelously effective; applied to grain hoarders it worked "like icy water splashed on the head, bringing them around quickly." Wherever pressure had been applied, it was said, procurements had improved.[28] The extraordinary measures thus appeared to have been extraordinarily successful, at least in the short run, and Stalin saw no point in abandoning them.

Previously, Stalin had avoided the strong antikulak stance of the Left. Now, with the Left defeated, he inveighed increasingly against the kulak as the main economic power and problem in the countryside. Strong measures were called for, although it was necessary—for political reasons—not to alienate the middle peasants. That would threaten the worker-peasant alliance. Yet in his view that critical bond, even when construed as excluding the kulak, was not to be thought of as a "moral alliance." "The union of the working class and the peasantry is a marriage of convenience [*po rashchetu*], a union of the interests of two classes . . . with their mutual profit in view."[29]

The campaign was not called off, therefore, but after March there was some letup in the application of extraordinary measures. Now, however, there was a drop in procurements, and collections for the quarter from April through June fell below those for the same period in 1927. The falloff may have meant only that peasant stocks were down to a point where there was little more to be had, especially since poor weather had destroyed part of the winter crop in the Ukraine and Northern Caucasus. But partisans of pressure tactics were inclined to other interpretations, and in the July plenum of the Central Committee sounded the crisis alarm once again. For the time being, however, their adversaries held the day. Reporting on the plenum, Rykov announced the immediate repeal of the extraordinary measures. Not only had they been ineffective, he charged, but by hurting the poor and middle peasants they had caused a deterioration in the regime's relations with the countryside. A review by the supreme court of the RSFSR of applications of Article 107 in Tiumen okrug, Siberia, had revealed that poor peasants were involved in 25 percent of all cases, middle peasants in 64 percent, and kulaks in only 7 percent. This was not just a matter of statistics, warned Rykov, but of "political resonance in the countryside." Each such case started waves of concern among the peasants, who had not forgotten War Communism.[30]

Despite the introduction of a moderate increase in official grain prices, procurements continued low throughout the summer. Climatic conditions were blamed, but a good harvest was anticipated for the fall. As autumn approached procurements showed signs of improving, but there were complaints that local authorities had returned to using extraordinary measures.[31] There was no end to the pressure on the peasants because there was no end to the government's need for grain. The Five-Year Plan was scheduled to begin in the fall. Revolutionary ideals, economic goals, and political ambitions were flowing together, propelling targets ever higher, pressing for new triumphs.

At the end of May a lead article in *Pravda* stressed that exports (and the imports that depended on them) were the key to solving many economic problems.[32] Yet the government found it impossible to increase its grain exports. On the contrary, it became necessary in 1928 to cut them back sharply, and even to import some grain. In 1928 as in the period of War Communism, grain requisitioning led to a reduction in the sown area. The total harvest was slightly above that of the previous year but below expectations, especially in the principal food crops— rye and wheat.[33] At the close of the year the atmosphere was still one of crisis. Procurements had slumped again in the fall, and although the drop was not as serious as in 1927, the November plenum of the Central Committee was obviously whistling in the dark when it stated that the situation was under control.[34] In December bread lines were reported in Moscow. Exports had trickled to a halt.[35]

A comparison of the data on grain procurements and exports for the decade yields some surprises. (See Table 24.) Despite the government's strong interest in increasing its sales of grain abroad, exports did not keep pace with the growth of procurements. Stalin had drawn attention to the fact in June, and at this point he introduced V. S. Nemchinov's data on grain marketings into the discussion on procurements.[36] (See Table 22, p. 286.) By claiming that the low level of marketing (particularly by kulaks) was responsible for the country's economic difficulties, Stalin set the stage for the policies that were to follow. Yet the procurement and export data suggest (and he himself had acknowledged) that the problem of shortages was caused essentially by the state's rising demand for grain for internal use. In 1926/27 the amount of grain consumed in urban areas was already 27 percent greater than in 1913, and between 1926/27 and 1929/30 government allocations of grain to the cities and the army rose by 50 percent.[37] During the summer of 1928, in the face of continuing procurement difficulties, the Council of People's Commissars announced a cutback in the number of grain consumers to be supplied directly by the state.[38] But the requirements of the Five-Year Plan led to a substantial upward revision of procurement quotas for the following year in spite of the smaller harvest of food grains.

From 1928 on, it was constantly repeated that the country's economic difficulties stemmed from a contradiction between the large-scale socialized (i.e., progressive) industrial sector and the small-scale

TABLE 24

Grain Procurements and Exports, USSR, 1913 and 1920–30

(thousand tons)

Year	Procurements		Exports
	Source (a)	Source (b)	Source (c)
1913	—		9,587
1919/20	3,480		—
1920	—		4
1920/21	6,012		—
1921/22	3,814		—
1922/23	5,916		748
1923/24	6,842		2,661
1924/25	5,248		599
1925/26	8,935	8,415	2,069
1926/27	11,319	10,590	2,178
1927/28	—	10,382	344
1928/29	—	8,302	99
1930	—		4,846

SOURCES: (a) TsSU, *Itogi, 1917–1927,* p. 379; (b) Carr, *Foundations,* 1: 2: 943; (c) TsUNKhU, *Sotsialisticheskoe stroitel'stvo,* pp. 382–83. See also Davies, *Socialist Offensive,* pp. 432–33.

individual (i.e., backward) agricultural sector. There was an element of truth in this, a contradiction indeed. But it extended beyond questions of scale or occupational sector. The fundamental contradiction lay in the irreconcilability of total planning with a free market.

The grain crisis made this painfully apparent. When the government scooped up the available consumer goods in the cities and sent them to the countryside, hoping to induce peasants to sell grain, private traders rushed out to buy up the merchandise and take it back to town for profitable resale. When agricultural products were sold by state and cooperative stores at low official prices, private traders bought them for resale at higher prices in other areas or (in large cities) even within the same city.[39] The development of industry *as planned* made control of agricultural resources mandatory. To secure an adequate supply of grain at a price the government was prepared to pay would clearly require in the long run something more than exceptional measures. The market could have provided for the needs of industry and of the industrial labor force only at a cost that the planners were unwilling to pay. A higher return to the peasants would have meant, at least initially, a slower rate of industrial growth. Given this situation, changes in the organization of the agrarian economy were indicated.* The role of private trade in the market had been declining steadily since 1925/26,

---

*Otherwise, as Moshkov acknowledges, p. 65, planned deliveries of grain to the government at unprofitable prices would have led, as earlier, to a reduction of the sown area to the subsistence minimum.

when it accounted for over a quarter of the total, but the greatest drop—from 17 down to 9 percent—came with the introduction of the plan in 1928/29.[40]

Early in 1928 Stalin began to argue, with increasing conviction, that the only long-range solution to the grain problem was conversion to collectivized agriculture. The process would necessarily be gradual, but it was essential to keep moving in that direction. Meanwhile, it was critical to block the development of capitalist tendencies, since the growth of rural capitalism would hinder the transition to socialism. By every means possible the kulaks had to be restrained, debilitated. This line of reasoning appeared as self-evident to Stalin and his supporters as it appeared suicidal to Bukharin and the Right. But by the end of 1928 the Right was in a shaky position; within a year it had been decisively defeated.[41]

Stalin had spoken of the influence of the kulak on the rest of the peasantry, and the literature of the period is full of references to the dominance of the "mir eater." Undoubtedly, the better-off peasants, who were able to make loans to needy neighbors, to rent out equipment, or to provide employment for idle hands, were apt to command a special position in the village. Undoubtedly, some who enjoyed such positions exploited them, and their fellow villagers into the bargain. Yet, as Pokrovskii had observed, power that is based on material things can be destroyed by simply taking those things away. When the Fifteenth Party Congress decided to "advance the attack on the kulak," this tactic was brought into play. Grain confiscations were the most direct form of taking, but there were other ways. Taxation, too, rapidly became confiscatory.

Fiscal Policy

NEP began and ended with policy shifts that found their clearest expression in the notations of the fisc, and the records of state and local taxation neatly trace the jagged lines of official policy toward the peasants. It opened in March 1921 with the abandonment of requisitioning as a form of taxation. At that time fixed taxes in kind had been levied on the peasants, and output above the level of taxation could be disposed of freely by sales to government agencies or through private trade. In March 1922 the "single natural tax" was introduced, unifying previously separate natural taxes and establishing units of equivalency for different agricultural products in terms of a pud of rye or wheat. The amount of tax due was based on the amount of arable land held. Various other taxes were collected from the rural population in addition to the natural tax. In 1923 all of these were consolidated in the "single agricultural tax." The total tax was lowered from 380 million rubles (value) in 1921/22 to 340 million in 1922/23, and the poorest households (primarily those without livestock—about 20 percent of the total) were exempted. The agricultural tax brought in about 14 percent of the state budget in 1923/24, when agriculture accounted for 60 percent of the national income. Starting in 1924, following reform and the stabilization of the currency, the tax became payable in money rather than produce.[42]

In the early years of NEP, then, the general policy of "retreat and regroup" was mirrored in the steps taken to lighten and regularize taxation. At mid-decade the line of "face to the countryside" was even more strikingly reflected in the tax structure. The single agricultural tax was considerably lowered, dropping in 1925/26 to 250 million rubles.[43] Changes introduced in the bases of assessment in 1924/25 benefited both the poorer and the wealthier (livestock-owning) peasants. The procurement problem of 1925, however, drew attention to the "surplus" purchasing power of the peasants, and as a result the agricultural tax was extended in 1926 to cover additional sources of agricultural (and some nonagricultural) income. The tax was also made somewhat more progressive. The number of poor peasants granted exemption increased to 28 percent, and the share of the total tax paid by "kulaks" rose to 21 percent.[44]

The state consistently made use of the tax system to promote developments in agriculture that it favored. After the middle of the decade, for example, substantial tax benefits were provided to encourage livestock farming and the extension of technical crops. This proved effective as far as immediate goals were concerned, but had the unfortunate side effect of contributing to the 1928 decline of the area sown in grain. In another direction, reductions from the regular tax norms were allowed for collective farms and cooperatives. (This particular form of incentive was to become an important tool of policy implementation in the final years of the decade, and will be pursued later in connection with collectivization.) Starting in 1927, important changes took place in two other aspects of rural taxation: the fiscal treatment of the kulak and the state's use of self-taxation.

The tenth anniversary of the October Revolution was an important milestone in the history of the Soviet Union. The time span itself conferred a reassuring legitimacy on the young state. Publicity given to the achievements of the decade, emphasis on the growth of industry, and claims about the recovery of agriculture all created a sense that a stable base had been secured from which it was possible, and imperative, to move forward. The anniversary marked and stimulated a change in psychological climate, a shift to the climate of confidence (at times, of overconfidence) that was responsible for the runaway targets of the Five-Year Plan. At the same time, awareness of its own audacity in the planning enterprise, and of the risks involved in charting a new economic course, heightened the government's anxiety about both domestic and international concerns. Bourgeois or foreign saboteurs were soon found lurking in every administrative and factory woodpile, leading to a series of famous trials of these would-be "wreckers" of a brave new world. In the countryside, it was the kulak who gave a face to all of the rural forces, real or imaginary, active or passive, that might resist the forward movement that now seemed possible.

The atmosphere at the Fifteenth Party Congress at the end of 1927 reflected the changing mood. There was evidence of a desire to move on somehow to bigger and better things—industrialization and collectivization—although the precise goals to be set and the specific means of attaining them were not defined. In talk of financing desirable projects, it was enough to suggest that the peasant's "little kopeck" might answer the need.[45] But the government's tax designs on the peasants had already been spelled out in October. A manifesto issued in honor of the anniversary freed 35 percent of the peasants from the agricultural tax.[46] Since this exceeded the number of poor peasants by most reckonings, the tax-exempt included the poorer part of the middle peasants as well. In addition, tax arrears were canceled for poor peasants and reduced for peasants in the middle ranks, so that the number actually exempted in 1927/28 came to 38 percent.[47] The agricultural tax brought in 320 million rubles in 1927/28, only 3 percent less than in the previous year. That meant that a smaller group of peasants was carrying just about the same total tax burden; in 1927/28, the poorest 33 percent of the taxpayers contributed 6 percent of the tax, and the wealthiest 6 percent paid 33 percent.[48]

After the grain crisis broke out in 1928, the agricultural tax was raised sharply. In 1928/29 it was budgeted at 400 million rubles. The basis of collection was shifted in 1928 to household income, and the taxable income from a peasant's agricultural land was calculated by multiplying a regional income norm per land unit by the number of units held by a household. Local authorities could decide whether to use arable land or sown area as the basis of assessment. In either case, this method of assessment worked to the disadvantage of large families. Holdings of equal size were taxed alike without allowing for the number of individuals sharing the (presumedly equal) income from each unit of land. Since larger families tended to be wealthier families, there was some justification for this; however, large families of poor and middle peasants were penalized. Not only land income was subject to the single agricultural tax. All income was to be counted now for tax purposes, including that from nonagricultural sources and from non-labor sources such as renting agricultural machinery (this provision was clearly aimed at the kulaks).[49]

The antikulak provisions of the tax regulations could be viewed simply as a follow-up of the general directive of the Fifteenth Party Congress that called for the "most progressive system of income taxation" aimed at the "growing income of the wealthiest strata of the village."[50] Yet the abruptness and severity of the measures adopted appear to be due not so much to the congress as to the grain crisis that developed right after it. Within a few months after the crisis broke the Central Committee and the Council of People's Commissars introduced, on April 21, 1928, an important innovation in rural taxation: the "individual tax."[51] All households with a high level of income not derived from labor were to have their incomes assessed on an individual basis rather than by the "normative method" used for others. For these households the maximal tax rate was raised to 30 percent as compared with a "normal" maximum of 25 percent. Not more than 2 to 3 percent of all households were to be subject to the individual tax according to the law. In fact, however, the tax was applied far more broadly.

Many wealthier households whose income derived solely from their own labor were individually assessed, and many middle-peasant families were also subjected to the individual tax. According to Stalin, up to 12 percent of all peasant households were affected, in some localities even more.[52] A review of individual tax assessments ordered by the Central Committee of the Party after numerous complaints found that almost half of the households so assessed were those of middle peasants. These were released from the individual tax; the remainder—less than one percent of all households in 1928–29—paid out 23 percent of their income on the average, contributing 14 percent of the total agricultural tax collected for the year. It is especially noteworthy that, despite all the rhetoric about the alliance with the middle peasantry, the better-off elements among that group were also subjected to special tax pressure in 1928–29. A "correction" in the normative method of assessment provided for a surtax of 5 to 25 percent on households whose aggregate income *from all sources* reached a stipulated figure: 400 rubles in the RSFSR and the Ukrainian Republic, 350 or 300 rubles elsewhere. In 1928/29, 16 percent of all households in the RSFSR were calculated by the normative method to have a total income of 400 rubles or more. Republican and regional officials were given discretionary authority to take family size into account, and to exempt from the surtax households whose per capita income did not exceed 50 rubles.[33] The shift to taxation on the basis of household income evoked wide protest and led to a sharp jump in the number of household divisions, particularly among the more prosperous households.[34] This tendency was reinforced by an instruction issued to local authorities early in 1928 directing that "surplus" lands were to be taken from kulaks and handed over to poor peasants.[35]

Whatever their social or political repercussions, the new tax policies brought unexpected fiscal rewards in 1928/29. Although the agricultural tax had been calculated to bring in 400 million rubles in that year, the amount actually collected—thanks largely to overenthusiastic application of the individual tax—was at least 10 percent higher; between 1925/26 and 1928/29 the agricultural tax had grown by about 80 percent, whereas the peasants' income may have increased by 13 percent.[36] By 1929 a far larger tax bill was being paid by a smaller share of the peasantry, and it was being levied far more progressively. Under the law the top 4 to 5 percent of all peasant households were to pay 30 to 45 percent of the agricultural tax, but in practice many middle-peasant households were being subjected to heavy tax pressures. In the face of intense and vociferous opposition, the Sixteenth Party Conference in April took note of the need to lighten the tax burden on the middle peasants. According to a resolution it adopted, greater care was to be taken to avoid improper imposition of the individual tax, and the agricultural tax was to be lowered by at least 50 million rubles.[37]

The decline in sown area led to an array of new tax concessions: land that was newly brought into cultivation was to be tax exempt for two years (but not for kulaks); a 10 percent reduction was offered to land societies adopting improved agricultural procedures (5 percent for individual households where the society as a whole would not adopt improvements); and a 15 percent reduction was offered for conversion to a multi-field system of crop rotation. Some allowance was granted to large families, household income below 500 rubles was now exempted from the surtax, and the surtax was reduced to 5 to 10 percent in place of the previous 5 to 25 percent. At the same time, it was made clear that the tax pressure on the "most wealthy kulak households (no more than 3 percent of the general number of peasant households in the USSR)" was to be firmly maintained. Party and government agents were warned officially that deterioration of a taxpayer's position was no excuse for reluctance to enforce tax policies.[38]

The changes in the tax structure over the last half of the decade clearly signal the shift in policy toward the peasants. At the beginning of the period the Left was calling for "socialist accumulation" by control of the market and pricing policy, and the Right was insisting that taxation was a preferable means of economic regulation. By the end of 1929 both Left and Right had been defeated politically, but policies that had been advocated by each were being implemented. The private market had been practically eliminated; low fixed prices were being maintained on the chief products of agriculture; and taxation was being transformed, in Bukharin's impassioned words, into "tribute" exacted by "military-feudal exploitation of the peasantry."[59] Both approaches to state control of the peasants were being pursued simultaneously, with a rigor unanticipated by their original proponents.

From a purely fiscal point of view, the effect of the agricultural tax may have been far greater on peasant households than on the state budget. The budget was growing rapidly (it doubled between 1925/26 and 1928/29), and the tax contributed only a minor and shrinking share. Two-thirds of the agricultural tax remained in the hands of local organs of government, and the major source of state revenues was indirect taxation.[60] By official account, in 1927/28 the agricultural tax provided only 5 percent of total budget revenues—about the same share as was contributed by the old redemption payments in 1905. Like that burdensome levy, it had a political significance that may have outweighed its economic import.[61] As Kalinin frankly admitted in the fall of 1928, the changes introduced in connection with the tax that year amounted to an "archpolitical campaign," and *Pravda* announced with equal candor early in 1929 that the agricultural tax would henceforth be used "in greater measure than previously as a lever on peasant households to achieve the economic and political tasks that the Party has set itself."[62]

Even more important in its political implications, however, was the government's shift with respect to self-taxation. This conversion, described above, was at the heart of the social pressure method of dealing with the peasants. In effect, the government used this line of approach to tie itself (via the rural soviet) in with the traditional communal system of peasant self-government and to manipulate that system in the interests of state policy. The development has only recently drawn some attention in historical literature, and there has been a tendency to treat the Ural-Siberian method simply as part of the general turn to measures of compulsion taken in 1928. Although it is true that administrative influence, pressure, and outright coercion reinforced the tactic of social pressure, the method was distinct from the measures, and in the long run may have been more important. Violence often drove the peasants together, but the newfound method, exploiting the principle of communal self-rule, succeeded in driving them apart. It refined the use of taxation as an instrument of class policy, and with its help self-taxation was developed into an instrument of intraclass warfare.

Once a part of the peasant community had been persuaded (or intimidated) at an assembly to accept a grain quota or other obligation, the rural soviet could use administrative measures to compel all members of the community to meet its levies, all in the name of peasant democracy and under the banner of "revolutionary legality." Pointing out the benefits of self-taxation in 1928, Kalinin acknowledged that unwarranted pressure had been applied in introducing its new form. Pressure was necessary, he argued, but it should be social pressure (with official encouragement and support), not administrative pressure. Care should be taken that a majority actually did vote for a tax; then this majority should make sure that the minority conformed to its decision.[63] A similar note was sounded later in the year, when self-taxation was lauded as a means of meeting local needs while the state was carrying the burden of industrialization. On this occasion, however, local Party and soviet officials were explicitly instructed to enlighten the poor and middle peasants about the benefits of self-taxation so that the kulaks, who paid for most of it, would be unable to block it at assemblies.[64]

Self-taxation had been limited in 1927/28 to a maximum of 35 percent of the agricultural tax; the 115 million rubles reported in self-taxation for that year amounted to 36 percent of the agricultural tax.[65] In 1928/29, when the agricultural tax was substantially raised, self-taxation was set at a maximum of 25 percent of that tax, but some regions were allowed to go as high as 50 percent. Although the government encouraged self-taxation, it wanted the peasants to be able to pay the agricultural tax. By this time, however, the peasants were confronted not only with the higher agricultural tax, but also with indiscriminate application of the individual tax, the surtax, and other new financial demands. The result was that, although agricultural-tax receipts were higher than anticipated, self-taxation dropped to 97 million rubles, of which only 75 million was actually collected.[66] The rate of effective self-taxation therefore was only 17 percent of the agricultural tax. The sum of the agricultural tax and self-taxation collected during the year (440 million rubles + 75 million) was almost 20 percent higher than in 1927/28 (320 million rubles + 115 million). The government's response was to raise the general maximum for self-taxation to 50 percent of the agricultural tax and to authorize the rural soviets to impose steep fines on peasants who failed to meet their obligations (up to five times the amount originally due).

Direct taxation was not the only kind of financial pressure applied to kulaks in the last years of the decade. In addition to the increase in taxation, there were increasing restrictions on credit and on the acquisition of agricultural machinery by individuals. The new policies in these areas flowed from the directives of the Fifteenth Party Congress, but, like taxation, their development was accelerated by the grain crisis. The limitation of credit to kulaks paralleled an attempt to make more credit available to poor and middle peasants. However, since peasants in these groups were greater credit risks, it became more costly to provide credit to individuals, and this reinforced a growing tendency to shift credit resources to collectives.

The total amount of credit available for agricultural production increased from 55 million rubles in 1923/24 to 908 million in 1929/30. However, the amount available to individual households, 32 million at the beginning of the period, rose to a peak of 255 million in 1927/28, then fell to 49 million in 1929/30. In relative terms, it went from 58 percent to 45 percent to 0.5 percent of the total.[67] In 1927 the terms of credit were improved for collectives of poor peasants, and local authorities in the RSFSR were authorized to prohibit sales of tractors to individuals.[68] Class restrictions on credit and preferential treatment for poor and middle peasants were introduced in the RSFSR in 1928, with the result that kulaks obtained less than one percent of all credit in the republic for the year.[69] In 1929 all credit was denied to kulaks; the access of upper peasant strata to agricultural machinery was limited in the RSFSR to a maximum of ten percent of planned output.[70] Peasants were classified for these purposes on the basis of their income as established in the revised tax rolls.[71] Grain-procurement difficulties early in 1929 led the Council of People's Commissars to authorize an increase in the sale of machinery to kulaks (up to 20 percent of the total) in certain grain-producing areas as an inducement to release more grain; however, this decision was promptly overruled by the Central Committee of the Party.[72] As a result of the new policy, the proportion of all tractors in the hands of individual peasants declined from over 10 percent in 1926 to less than one percent by October 1929.[73]

Credit for other purposes was similarly withdrawn from the kulaks. The amount of credit available to purchase draft animals, for example, reached a maximum of 100 million rubles in 1927/28. The following year it was cut drastically. In the RSFSR only 36 million rubles was available in credit in 1928/29 for such purchases, and under the accumulating burden of financial stresses the better-off peasants began surrendering their livestock to the poorer peasants. The number of households without draft animals declined in many regions between 1927 and 1929, and the livestock holdings of kulaks also declined, furthering the growth of the middle peasants at the expense of both social extremes.[74] Within this period kulaks lost 30 to 40 percent of all their means of production.[75]

Yet the deteriorating position of the kulaks had no effect on state policy. Little matter that taxes had been raised, credit cut off, machinery and draft animals lost, and grain confiscated; little matter that sales of grain were unprofitable at official prices, and that there were no industrial goods to buy: a peasant who reduced the area of cropland under cultivation was accused of conducting a "grain strike" against the government, was declared a kulak under the law, and could lose his land. From 1927 through 1929 the area sown in grain by kulaks dropped from 8.2 million to 4.7 million hectares (from 13 to 7 percent of the total area under grain).[76] The battle on the grain front called for an enemy, and the kulak had become a sort of psychic lightning rod, drawing attention from the fact that the entire peasantry was under attack. Concern about the kulak was no doubt genuine, but the grain crisis provided an opportunity to forge the myth of a "kulak menace" into a serviceable instrument of broader policy.

The peasants were not always easily persuaded of the myth. Communes were given primary responsibility for withdrawing lands from "vile people who have cut back their sown area"; rural soviets and higher local officials were authorized to take action when communes were insufficiently aggressive in the matter. In practice, communes did prove reluctant to initiate the necessary juridical procedures, and most instances of deprivation of land were initiated by the authorities.[77] The method of social pressure thus had its limits, but it was an invaluable tool for legitimizing unpopular policies in the countryside and for deflecting some of the hostility they aroused. Viewed politically, the kulak served (and in a sense was created to fill) the role once occupied by the local tsarist *chinovnik*, the bureaucrat responsible for all ills and for frustrating the designs of the benevolent higher power. There was ample evidence in the late 1920's of the reemergence of that Manichaean strain in the political culture—a strain that was to find full expression later in the Stalinist "cult of personality." But there was also something new and different in the political ambience of the countryside. God was no longer "high above," and the Tsar himself was leading the attack on the surrogate chinovnik.

It would have been strange indeed if the multi-pronged assault on the economically stronger sector of the peasantry had not met with some active resistance. According to press reports of the period, kulaks not only resisted but mounted a major counteroffensive, and tales of kulak violence in the countryside were given wide currency in the last two years of the decade. At the beginning of the procurement campaign in 1928, there were frequent reports of kulak opposition to self-taxation, but for the most part the initial resistance appears to have been passive or obstructionist. Yet as the heavy-handed tactics of the grain-collecting authorities continued, instances of rural violence multiplied. The July plenum in 1928 announced that the "revolutionary measures" adopted in connection with the grain campaign had provided an opening for kulak agitation against soviet power.[78] The number of rural correspondents of newspapers had grown by this time to over half a million, and these individuals, accessible and vulnerable, sometimes fell victim to rural hostility against the regime. In 1927, 13 correspondents were murdered; in 1928 (after they had been instructed to see to it that "not one kulak" won election to the rural soviets), 32 were slain in the first eight months of the year alone.[79]

Toward the end of the year a full-scale return to administrative methods of grain collection led to a rising incidence of what the press began to call "kulak terrorism." Cases that could be expected to fan antikulak sentiment were nationally publicized. Prominent press coverage was given to an attack on a woman correspondent that led to the death of her daughter, and to the murder of a local Party member who had called for the removal of kulaks from the assembly (500 local factory workers were said to have applied for Party membership after his funeral).[80]

The case that received the widest press coverage at the time, however, was the notorious Ludorvaiskii affair. The incident was brought to light through a winter trial at which the members of the commune and the rural soviet of the village of Ludorvaiskii were held to account for the public flogging of some poor peasants. The victims had been accused of letting their cattle wander into the fields of others, but according to the prosecutor the real reason for the brutal treatment was their attempt to bring about a redistribution of land that was opposed by the kulaks. The trial presented a grim picture of both kulak and commune. In Ludorvaiskii there had been no redistribution of land for 50 years. When the commune's starosta (who was one of the accused and also a member of the rural soviet) tried to excuse his actions by stating that he had merely carried out the orders of the commune, the prosecutor showed little sympathy. "And if they told you to kill a person would you do it?" The starosta: "I would kill." By the time the trial had run its course, the evils of kulak control of communes had been thoroughly demonstrated to the Soviet public.[81]

The coincidence of soviet elections and the revival of a strong procurement campaign in the winter of 1928–29 led to the intensification of violence in the countryside. From December 1928 to February 1929, 101 cases of terrorism (murder, assault, and arson) were recorded for the Moscow juridical region, as compared with 13 for the previous year.[82] A rash of articles at the time linked the kulak, "kulak intrigue," and "kulak sabotage" with the Church. Yet in the midst of the ongoing smear campaign Kalinin (hailed as the "all-Union starosta" on the occasion of his tenth anniversary as president of the Central Executive Committee) admitted publicly that the kulaks commanded influence in the village because they did in fact help their fellow peasants out "and not just before elections." However, the kulaks' good deeds were inspired by self-interest, and therefore the government would have to replace them locally with cooperatives and other such bodies. The class struggle in the countryside, he warned, would have to be fought with determination and for a long time, since "the resistance in the village initially will be enormous."[83]

Throughout the months that followed evidence of resistance mounted, but the fragmentary data do not suggest any massive counterattack on the regime. In 1928, 700 cases of terrorist activity were reported in the RSFSR, and the first nine months of 1929 witnessed 1,000 such cases. From 1927 to 1929, 300 procurement agents were said to have been killed.[84] For the most part, however, the peasants appear to have reacted to official pressure by reducing the extent of cultivation, breaking up large households, and getting rid of the inventory that marked a muzhik as a "kulak."

The Basic Principles of Land Use

Official policies clearly affected agricultural performance, although it is difficult to separate the effects of policy from those of other factors, such as the adverse climatic conditions in some areas at this time. A report presented at the Sixteenth Party Conference in April 1929 indicated a further decline per capita in the area sown in grain. Again, the major food crops were most affected. The area under rye had declined by 8 percent in comparison with 1927/28, the area under wheat by 11 percent.[85] Part of the earlier decline in sowings could be attributed to the peasants' shift to industrial crops and other forms of agriculture that had become more profitable as a result of the government's agricultural policies. Livestock and dairy farming, as noted above, had benefited from those policies. Yet animal husbandry showed signs of trouble after 1928. The number of animals had reached a peak in that year and generally stood above the levels of 1916. (Horses were an important exception—still about 6 percent below the 1916 figure in 1928.) But the fund of livestock in the country fell markedly in 1929. By 1930 the number of large-horned cattle had dropped by 16 percent and was below the 1916 figure, and the number of other animals (including horses) had declined similarly.[86]

Talk about deteriorating agricultural performance was anathema to expansionist-minded circles pushing for high targets in the winter of 1928–29, and those who were rash enough to point to the evidence were soon politically overwhelmed.[87] Yet concern about the state of agriculture was apparent in a December statement of the Central Executive Committee, "Measures to Raise Yield."[88] It was now declared an objective of the Five-Year Plan to increase yield by 30 to 35 percent. In order to accomplish this, the agricultural sections of rural soviets were to be revitalized and strengthened, and they were to be responsible for introducing simple measures to improve output in the agrarian economy. The announcement ended with observations on the complexity of the tasks facing land organs and on the shortcomings of Union-level direction of land affairs.

Turning directly to the latter problem at the same session on December 15, 1928, the Central Executive Committee approved a major piece of land legislation that had been under discussion for some time, the Basic Principles of Land Use and Land Organization.[89] This Union law, which was to serve as the fundamental land law of the country for decades, supplemented but did not replace the RSFSR Land Code of 1922. However, the Basic Principles introduced some important changes in the land order. According to the new law agricultural collectives, along with poor and middle peasants, were to have preferential rights to the use of land. Moreover, those rights extended qualitatively to the best and the most conveniently located land.

Land societies and their members were assured of the use of their lands without time limit. As before, the land could be lost if it was renounced by all members, if it was not used or was used illegally (by sale, mortgage, bequest, or unauthorized rental), if a household had no heirs, or if it was needed for state or social purposes. The Union republics could stipulate additional causes for land loss, and could pass legislation regulating redistributions of land.

Voluntary "cooperativization" of the peasantry was declared the basic means of the socialist transformation of agriculture, and a number of tax and credit benefits were established for collectives. Other provisions of the Basic Principles restricted the rental of land to hardship cases and limited it to a maximum of six years (three on the decision of local officials); land rented out by kulaks was to be taken away from them. Peasant households were permitted to hire help only if the able members of the household themselves worked alongside and the hired labor was strictly auxiliary. It was the responsibility of the rural soviet to supervise households for conformity to these regulations, and to register all land rental contracts.

The chapter of the law dealing with the land society and the rural soviet grew out of the debates raging over the previous two years on the relationship between the two. Not surprisingly, the issue was settled in favor of the soviet. First of all, the new legislation redefined the membership of the land society. From now on it was to include not only members of households that belonged to the society, but also all those who participated in its agricultural work or in that of member households—all hired hands, herdsmen, blacksmiths, and so forth. Minors maintaining an independent household were recognized as members with full rights, provided they were not kulaks. The right to vote in the assembly and the right to be elected as an official of the society were limited now to those who had the right to vote for soviets. Having failed in its 1927 attempt to establish separate assemblies of enfranchised citizens under the control of the rural soviets, the government at this point simply converted the land societies into bodies of similar constituency.

More important, the land society was subordinated to the rural soviet. Where the territory of the two organizations coincided the soviet was to conduct the business of the land society; elsewhere, the land society could elect this as an option or could elect a special plenipotentiary or board to run its affairs. In matters of land use and land organization the rural soviet was to direct the work of land societies, to confirm decisions regarding the form of land use and the plan of land organization, and to determine who was eligible for preferential treatment or exemption from paying for land organization work. If the soviet considered a decision taken by a land society to be against the law, counter to the goal of "cooperativization," or against the interests of the poor, it could send back the decision for reconsideration. If a reconsidered decision did not meet with its approval, the soviet had the right to countermand it. The land society had two weeks to appeal such a ruling to the volost or raion executive committee.

One of the most critical provisions of the new land law was discreetly lodged in a brief article (Article 52) that left it to the Union republics to pass appropriate legislation defining the rights and obligations of the rural soviets with respect to lands, woods, and waters "subject to transfer to their immediate use." This was to serve as the basis for a gradual transfer to the rural soviets of the income from lands and various enterprises previously collected by communes, contributing to the growth of rural-soviet budgets.[90]

The commune was now formally subject to the rural soviet in certain important areas, but as the earlier law on village assemblies had proved, the peasants did not unduly trouble themselves about legal formalities. The fact that there were far more communes than rural soviets helped to strengthen the role of the commune in the countryside, and the number of soviets declined after 1928. Proposals to increase their number in order to bring them closer to the peasants were dismissed with the objection that only large units could command the authority and the economic resources appropriate to organs of the Soviet government.[91] One of the means by which the government sought to reinforce the rural soviets was increasing the representation of poor peasants within them. In the electoral campaign conducted just after the adoption of the Basic Principles, intense efforts were made once again to revitalize the soviets. A strongly worded official proclamation issued in January 1929 in connection with the elections warned of the dangers of imperialist aggression as growing economic depression engulfed the collapsing world of capitalism.[92] The international situation, it was argued, made industrialization urgent. But industrialization was being held back by the slow growth of agriculture, which limited exports. For these compelling reasons it was essential to eliminate all kulaks from rural soviets. Thanks to vigorous agitational work founded on such arguments, not only kulaks but a fair number of middle peasants were replaced by poor peasants in the elections.[93] The turnout of voters was higher than ever before, and peasant women in particular voted in unprecedented numbers. The representation of poor peasants and women in rural soviets was greatly strengthened.[94]

Despite these changes, the rural soviets remained unsatisfactory agencies of central authority. Charges of dual power continued to be heard, and although the financial status of the rural soviets was improving, the great majority were still without independent budgets at the end of the decade.[95] It proved impossible to transform the soviets overnight into fully effective instruments of rural policy, and when a task of immediate urgency arose—as in the mobilization of a spring sowing campaign in 1929—the government continued to dispatch party activists and urban workers to do the job. "The central economic organ in the village," acknowledged the Party newspaper at the time, "is often not the rural soviet, but the commune."[96]

All of the major political, economic, and legislative responses to the grain crisis discussed so far brought the government into more direct contact with the commune. This was equally true of other lines of approach to the perennial problem of procurement. All roads to the peasant, and to the peasant's agricultural output, appeared to lead through that "central economic organ."

Agricultural Contracting and Land Organization

The task of securing control of the agrarian economy was far too important an endeavor to leave solely to the rural soviets. While attempting to strengthen and work through those instruments, the government pursued a number of other policies. The most promising was the system of contracting.

Earlier in the decade, state enterprises had contracted in advance with peasant producers for their output. The first agricultural contracts had been limited largely to industrial raw materials; such crops as sugar beets, cotton, oil seeds, and tobacco were often purchased by industrial processors at fixed prices before they were harvested. Only after the procurement problem of 1927, however, was a concerted move begun to extend the contract system to grain purchases. At the Fourteenth Party Congress at the end of the year the advantages of the system were extolled, and contracting was described as a major step toward the socialization of agriculture.[97]

Contracts provided guaranteed deliveries to the state at fixed prices in return (initially) for monetary advances or credit. Peasants accepting a contract received (or obtained a preferential right to buy) agricultural machinery or tractors. In other cases, the right to call on the services of a local machine-tractor station was the attractive feature.

Contracting quickly demonstrated its virtues as a relatively painless means of obtaining grain from the peasants, and 1928 witnessed a rapid growth of the system.[98] Miliutin described it in July as an effective aid to procurement, but stated that it covered an inadequate area.[99] A drive was announced by the Council of People's Commissars to extend grain contracting during the autumn sowing campaign. Peasant producers were to be offered advances, seed was to be made available to those in areas where winter crops had failed, and bonuses were to be offered for early deliveries.

The 1928 contracting campaign failed at first to meet expectations. The campaign had started late and was overly optimistic in calling for all contracts to be concluded within a month. According to early reports the plan had not been fulfilled; peasants had not been supplied with seed.[100] But deteriorating procurements in the fall provided the impetus for a new and more extensive contracting campaign. Plans called for doubling the grain area under contract within a year. Before the year had passed, however, the target had been overtaken. The area contracted rose from 6 million hectares in 1927/28 to 19 million in 1928/29.[101] By April 1929, at the time of the Sixteenth Party Conference, contracting extended over 15 million hectares, and Kalinin's report envisaged further growth.[102] Before 1927/28 all agricultural land under contract amounted to only 2 percent of the cultivated land in the country. During that year it rose to 11 percent; by 1929 it had expanded to one-third of the entire cultivated area.[103]

Communes played an important part in the spread of agricultural contracts. Most of these "grain futures" were concluded with producers' groups; only about 10 percent of all contracts were signed with individual peasant households in 1928. At the outset the rapidly growing agricultural cooperatives dealing with the Grain Center were the primary grain contractors, but as other state agencies swung over to adopt the system an increasing number of communes became involved.

Just as the government was finding it possible to make use of communal self-taxation to secure needed grain supplies, so it turned to contracting with communes for the same end. According to official instructions, contracts were to be offered on a voluntary basis to "entire land societies, production units, and groups of cultivators."[104] About a quarter of all group contracts covering winter crops in 1928 were concluded by communes; however, the role of the communes was actually more significant than the figure suggests, since these included over 40 percent of all households under contract and 45 percent of the area covered. Communes received about half of the entire sum given out in contract advances during the year.[105]

The contract proved an effective means of getting the peasants to upgrade their agricultural practices. Contracts could stipulate the kind and quality of the seed to be used, require the application of manure to the fields, and specify the time of sowing. In 1929 a basic set of agricultural standards, the "agrominimum," was adopted for contracts. Rural soviets were instructed to secure the adoption of such norms by land societies. To facilitate this, a new group of officials was brought into being, the agroplenipotentiaries.

A circular letter sent out by VTsIK to rural soviets on April 10, 1929, provided for the establishment of the new office. Unlike the plenipotentiaries elected by the land societies to handle land affairs, the new officers were to be chosen by the rural soviet (either from its own members or from nonmembers) and were to serve as its representatives in the land society. There was to be one agroplenipotentiary for each land society or, in large societies, one for each 50 households. The new official was to work under the immediate instruction of the sectional agronomist and to report to him and to the rural soviet on the fulfillment or nonfulfillment of assigned "agrotasks." Those tasks included introducing measures to improve agriculture, assisting the peasants in meeting the norms of the agrominimum, and calling meetings of the land society to discuss measures undertaken in connection with agriculture. In 1929, 125,000 land societies adopted resolutions on the agrominimum, and over 220,000 agroplenipotentiaries were elected.[106]

The uses of the commune in upgrading agricultural practices were immediately evident. Dealing with the entire village as a single production unit was a great convenience. Not just the commune's organization of the peasants, but the whole web of communal traditions proved invaluable. Those traditions could be called upon to oblige all peasants in a community to observe a contract or a resolution on standards adopted by their commune. Official pronouncements stressed the importance of the "collective responsibility of all members of a production unit or a land society concluding a contract for the fulfillment of its terms."*

By the summer of 1929 the contract system, according to an ebullient Party announcement, was extending over "tens of millions of hectares" and leading "millions of peasant households" within the sphere of a unified plan, securing the peasants' marketable surplus for the state.[107] The contract system seemed to offer a solution to the grain-procurement problem acceptable to both the state and the peasantry. The state would be assured of grain delivery; the peasants would get advances, credit, machinery, fertilizer, and agronomic assistance. Moreover, the production standards stipulated in the contract would contribute to the general improvement of agriculture.

This promising picture was warped by changes that overtook the system. The cash advances provided earlier to contracting peasants began to disappear. The limited amount of money allocated for this purpose was made available only to poor peasants (i.e., those capable of delivering least grain in return) and was restricted largely to the collective purchase of means of production. Although little was to be heard now about immediate financial benefits, peasants were at least guaranteed that the prices they received for their grain would be higher than

*The wording was identical in the Party document and in the law.

official procurement prices at the time of delivery. In return, however, they were obliged to accept an extended list of responsibilities. Contracts could require peasants to join consumer and agricultural cooperatives, to contribute to collective purchases of agricultural equipment, and to make deliveries to the state on credit.[108]

Those under contract were legally bound to (1) raise agricultural products of stipulated quantity and quality as directed by the state, (2) deliver these products at the agreed time, and (3) adopt specified measures to raise the technical level of agriculture and the level of collectivization. The state for its part was obliged to (1) supply the peasants with means of production and "so far as possible, with consumer goods within the limits of the supply plans for the corresponding regions and villages," and (2) organize agrotechnical services and provide organizational cooperation in implementing the contract measures. Since nationalized land was the primary means of production provided by the state, the contract partners hardly gained equally from the arrangement. If a peasant failed to meet his obligations, the full weight of the state was available to reinforce the contract, yet there was no mechanism for protest or appeal if the state failed to meet contract terms.[109]

In addition to contracting, the government actively promoted land organization work in the final years of the decade. As discussed above, most of the earlier effort in this area had been concentrated on "external" work, that is, on separating the lands of different villages, but there was a shift later to more intensive forms of land organization within communes and other landholding entities. This trend was encouraged when the Basic Principles in 1928 called for more work on the problems of stripholding, distant holdings, and systems of crop rotation. But the most important development in land organization work toward the end of the decade was the growing attention devoted to land in collectives. According to an article in *Pravda* early in 1928, only 65 percent of all collectives had experienced the benefits of external land organization by that time; a mere 11 percent had been fortunate enough to have had their lands reorganized internally.[110] The state farms were even worse off; two-thirds of those in the RSFSR had had no land organization at all.[111] The new land law at the end of the year strengthened the position of collectives by giving them preference (along with poor and middle peasants with little or no land) in the allotment of land. All land organization work for these groups was to be at government expense.[112]

The law stipulated that land organization work was to be carried out in observance of the right to a free choice of the form of land use, but it also made clear that the work was to facilitate the collectivization of

agriculture. Requests for the formation of consolidated individual holdings were to have lowest priority and were to be denied if the creation
of such units would contribute to the growth or strengthening of
kulaks. Land organization could be initiated by the rural soviet or by
higher soviet authorities as well as by land users, and the Union republics were authorized to issue legislation providing for compulsory
labor service from the population where necessary.[113] At the beginning
of 1929 it was evident that much remained to be done. *Pravda* greeted
the new year with the mournful observation that in the twelfth year
after the revolution more than half of all agricultural land had not yet
been reorganized.[114] Work on the formation of khutors and otrubs had
ground to a halt. In Moscow province, for example, work on consolidations had fallen from 10 percent of all land organization activity in 1924
to less than one percent in 1928. But in that year the process of "liquidation" was begun; 2,600 khutors and otrubs—almost a tenth of the
total in the province—were eliminated.[115] Work involving the breakup
of large communes into *poselki* continued on the assumption that the
smaller units could be induced to convert to joint cultivation of the
land if provided with a tractor.[116] But the need for land organization in
collectives was considered most urgent; the failure of many collective
farms was attributed to the lack of such work.

Reviewing the unsatisfactory progress of land organization work, the
agrarian Marxists had no difficulty in finding an explanation for the prevailing sorry state of affairs. According to the indignant Kritsman,
there were simply too many survivals of prewar bourgeois attitudes in
land work, too much emphasis on individual work, and too little attention to the need for a "class approach."[117] His attack on the staff of land
organization agencies joined a general and mounting attack directed
against all of the "bourgeois" agricultural specialists.

The political developments of the period have been traced by others
and need not be pursued in detail here. Just when the Five-Year Plan
was being inaugurated, the grain crisis, sending a chill blast over the
exuberant hopes surrounding it, strengthened the fears about and mistrust of the peasantry that troubled much of the Soviet leadership. The
"propeasant" Right was undermined, opening the way to a resumption
of the requisition policies and strong-arm tactics of War Communism.
The successes of the grain campaign further discredited the Right and
reinforced the position of those who stood ready to take a hard line
against the troublesome peasants.

The caption of a lead article in *Pravda* in 1928 might have served as
the epitaph of the late 1920's: "Apply pressure on all levers." References to "levers" were common at the time. The notion that society

was manipulable, and that leaders were responsible for manipulating it correctly, was part of the revolutionary mentality. For Stalin it formed a greater part than for some others. His outlook permitted no tolerance of opposition, ambiguity, or contingency. The responsibility for manipulating levers correctly meant seeing to it that they did not fall into the hands, Left or Right, of those who held incorrect views. A petty bourgeois peasantry that threatened to interfere with the attainment of revolutionary goals had to be brought under control, levered by any means—including the commune. The lever that was to prove in the long run the most effective, spelling the end of the commune, was the collectivization of agriculture.

19

The Commune and Collectivization

The collectivization of agriculture had never ceased to be a goal of the Soviet regime under NEP. However, the view that collectivized agriculture had to be approached gradually through voluntary cooperativism, a view elaborated by Engels and endorsed by Lenin, became the official outlook in the 1920's. Only at the end of the decade did a different perspective emerge.

Socialized Agriculture in the 1920's

From the scanty evidence available, the history of collectives under NEP emerges as a chronicle of frustration and failure.[1] The condition of socialized agriculture in the 1920's gave little reason to expect that a socialist transformation of the countryside was imminent. Between 1921 and 1927 the number of collective farms in the country fell from 16,000 to 14,800, but the struggles of the collectives for survival were more intense than the moderate decline might suggest. Each year about a quarter of all collective farms failed and were liquidated; only by being replaced with new units did they endure as well as they did.[2]

Among the state farms, also, a steady attrition occurred. In 1922/23 there were 5,700 state farms in the RSFSR, but by 1925/26 only 3,300 remained. However, the total amount of land held by state farms remained almost constant, so that although the number of farms was shrinking, the size of the average unit was expanding.[3] In 1927 the state farms held one percent of the total area sown in grain and were contributing 1.6 percent of gross production; collective farms had slightly under one percent of the land under grain and less than one percent of all peasant households, and were producing one percent of the gross output.[4]

A change had taken place in the popularity of the different forms of collective. At the beginning of NEP artels predominated, and *kom-*

muny had a substantial numerical lead over *TOZy*. But by 1927 the artels and especially the *kommuny* (in which almost all property was held in common) had lost ground. The *TOZy*, the loosest form of collective, had gained. *Kommuny* now accounted for only about 10 percent of all collectives, artels for about half, and *TOZy* for slightly over 40 percent.[5]

The average collective farm in 1927 was an unprepossessing enterprise. It had only thirteen member households, 50 to 52 hectares of land under cultivation, three or four horses, and six or seven cows. The few *kommuny* were the largest collectives, with an average of over 100 hectares; artels averaged about 60 hectares, and *TOZy* about 50 hectares of socialized land. Households in artels and *TOZy* also held nonsocialized lands individually. These added up to an additional 26 hectares on the average in artels; in *TOZy* the aggregate nonsocialized holdings of member households amounted to 57 hectares—an area larger than the collectivized land.[6]

As a rule, a half to two-thirds of the members of collectives were poor peasants. The poorest gravitated toward the *kommuny*. With little or no property to contribute, these peasants were the most willing to accept a high degree of socialization. Peasants with more resources were attracted to the *TOZy*, especially to those formed specifically for the purchase and common use of heavy machinery.[7]

One consequence of the socioeconomic background of the members of collective farms was a lower ratio of draft animals in collectives than among the noncollectivized peasants. The collectives suffered too from a shortage of agronomic assistance and from inadequate land organization work. Attempts to equalize the amount of work demanded of members led to conflicts over accounting procedures and record keeping, and efforts to establish equal pay for workers had an adverse effect on the intensity of labor contributions and on peasant initiative. Such problems brought many collectives to ruin.[8]

On the other side of the ledger there were some bright spots. From the official point of view, the collective farmers were the socialist avantgarde among the peasants; as a result the collectives were relatively well endowed with land. Poor peasants who joined collectives were generally raised in the process to the status of middle peasants in per capita land supply. Thanks also to government support, peasants in collectives were better supplied with agricultural machinery and implements. In addition, collective farms more frequently practiced multicrop rotation. Due to these advantages, collectives often managed to obtain yields that were above the general peasant average.[9] This higher performance was advanced as reason enough to promote the development of collectivized agriculture when attention turned to economic planning in the later years of the decade.

The Fifteenth Party Congress, held at the end of 1927, became known as the "Collectivization Congress," since at this point the Party was said to have "set a course for collectivization." Yet the point appeared more significant in retrospect than at the time. The course marked out at the congress was not charted for a rough or particularly rapid passage. Congress directives still laid great stress on cooperativism, and a number of speakers, including Stalin, indicated that the transition from fragmented individual holdings to large-scale socialized agriculture would be a gradual process based on mechanization.[10]

The onset of the grain crisis in 1928, however, whetted official interest in collectives. As a result of the crisis, attention became focused on one characteristic of socialized agriculture that particularly commended itself to the government: the level of marketing. In 1927 the noncollectivized peasant producers of grain marketed 17 percent of their output; the collectives, however, placed 28 percent of the grain they produced on the market, and this went for the most part directly to government agencies.[11] The state farms marketed a higher percentage of their output than did the collectives: nationwide they turned 41 percent of their gross production over to the government in 1927, and those in trusts in the RSFSR surrendered an impressive 60 percent.[12] According to the Nemchinov data cited by Stalin in the spring of 1928, although the combined output of collective and state farms in 1926/27 was less than two percent of the total grain production, these farms supplied 6 percent of all marketed grain.[13] The share of collective and state farms in total production was still minute, but the marketing data made the prospect of growth in the socialized sector especially appealing in the light of grain-procurement problems.

The high productivity of the state farms and the more substantial share of their grain output turned over to the government made them particularly attractive to economic planners. Throughout 1928 there was strong emphasis on developing this sector of agriculture, and plans were announced for creating great "grain factories" covering up to 30,000 hectares.[14] During the summer and fall many new state farms sprang up. The scale of planned expansion demanded a higher level of investment and a change in investment allocations.[15] In 1927/28 the government spent 62 million rubles on collective farms and only 40 million on state farms; the control figures for 1928/29, however, were 75 and 105 million rubles respectively.[16]

Although the development of state farms was still high on the list of priorities in agriculture in early 1929, at the Sixteenth Party Conference in April attention was clearly shifting to the rapidly growing collective farms.[17] In 1927 the state farms marketed three times as much grain as the collective farms; in 1928 they marketed twice as much. In 1929, although the amount of grain marketed by state farms continued to rise steadily, the total came to only two-thirds of the amount marketed by collective farms.[18] By the end of the year the state farms had taken a back seat to the collectives, and at the November plenum they were described as agricultural enterprises of a future, more advanced type.[19]

The program of all-out collectivization was no chance by-product of agricultural policy, but the dynamics of the movement were clearly not the product of prior policy decisions. The directives of the Fifteenth Party Congress, as noted, did not call for a rapid transformation of agriculture, and throughout 1928 and early 1929 there were repeated official statements that it would take some time to reach collectivization. A Central Committee resolution of July 10, 1928, declared: "In order to resolve the grain problem, to eliminate the danger of a rupture between town and country, . . . we must . . . assist in raising the productivity of small and middle peasant households, *which will remain the basis of the grain economy in the country for a significant time yet*."[20] Later in the year, at the November plenum Bukharin proclaimed that the country still was and "would long be" a petty bourgeois land, in need of "levers other than repression" to overcome its economic problems.[21] Rykov too spoke of collectivization as a process that would go on for a long time.[22] Admittedly, these two were spokesmen for the Right, but similar views prevailed in all political camps. At the plenum Molotov had conceded that prevailing conditions were "completely inadequate for the rapid transfer of the basic mass of peasant households to a large-scale collective economy. The transformation of scattered peasant households into great collectives is a difficult task and a task for a long period."[23]

Not only was there general agreement that collectivization would require time, but it was still largely accepted in principle that the process would have to be effected through voluntary cooperativism. This was the position taken in the Basic Principles of Land Use at the end of 1928, and to underscore the point for those inclined to disregard it, Lenin's widow, Nadezhda Krupskaia, repeated his views on the subject in an article in *Pravda* on January 20, 1929. Coercion, she stressed, could play no part in the prolonged process of collectivization: "A revolution in agriculture *from above* is impossible" (emphasis in the original).

At the end of 1928 collectivization seemed unlikely to pose an immediate threat to the commune. Although collectives had doubled in number during the year, they claimed only 2 percent of all peasant households. Taking note of the recent gains, a writer in the journal of land organization urged that more attention be directed to the "new, improved" commune. If further collectivization efforts were to raise the number of collectivized households "even ten times," he pointed out, 80 percent of all peasant households, over 20 million individual households, would still remain outside the collectives.[24] Well into 1929 the commune still appeared very much alive and as well as it had ever been.

Not only did the commune seem to have a future, but the peasant household seemed likely to endure as an economic unit within it. The Sixteenth Party Conference in April 1929 went to some lengths in making this clear. Along with promoting large-scale socialized agriculture, the Party pledged continued cooperation with the nonsocialized poor and middle peasants. "Even with the maximal possible development of state and collective farms," it announced, "the basic growth of agricultural production in the years immediately ahead will fall on individual poor- and middle-peasant households; the petty economy has not and will not soon outgrow its [productive] possibilities."[25]

The climate of collectivization, however, had already begun to change. Recent gains in the movement were described at the conference as welling up *"from below"* (emphasis in the original), and outstripping the planned growth of a "technical base" for collectivized agriculture.[26] One of the major factors affecting the situation was the prolonged grain crisis. The harvest of 1928 was marginally larger than that of the previous year, but procurements were lower. In the critical food grains (rye and wheat) they were down by 20 percent.[27] Given the government's rising needs, the shortfall was a disturbing reminder of the vulnerability of the Five-Year Plan.

By the start of 1929 food shortages in the cities had become critical enough to require rationing. Beginning in February, ration books were distributed to workers in the major cities, permitting limited purchases of bread at controlled prices. Nonworkers were obliged to make out as best they could on the (rapidly vanishing) private market, where supplies were scarce and prices doubled. In summer, tea and sugar were rationed also; later in the year meat was added to the list. The ration books were used to establish norms for the distribution of other foods that were in short supply, though not officially rationed.[28]

The development of state farms promised the ideal long-range solution to the grain-supply problem, but short-range needs made it essential to get hold of peasant grain rapidly. The creation of state farms required land as well as other scarce resources, and few peasant land-holders were likely to surrender their land willingly to work as laborers on such farms. Yet a fair number of poorer peasants might be induced to join collectives, and the output of collective farms was accessible through the expanding contract system. The optimal variant of the Five-Year Plan adopted in the spring of 1929 called for a significant increase in the output and marketing of collectives. By the end of the plan in 1932/33 socialized agriculture was to provide 16 percent of all grain production but 43 percent of marketed grain, with 26 percent to come from collectives and 17 percent from state farms.[29]

One of the most direct forms of state support for collectives was granting special tax benefits. As early as 1926/27 members of the more socialized collectives were permitted a flat 25 percent deduction in the agricultural tax; members of *TOZy* received a deduction of 10 percent. In 1927/28 the tax advantages were increased. The tax assessment on a collectivized household was not to exceed the average for the non-collectivized peasants of the area. In the Ukraine and several other republics, the tax on households in collectives was established at the level of the local average minus 25 percent. In the RSFSR and elsewhere, if the per capita income of a collectivized household was above the local average, it was calculated as average, less 25 percent; if it was below the local average, it was reduced by 25 percent. (Members of the less fully collectivized *TOZy* still received a more modest 10 percent discount.) These reductions were an even greater benefit than might appear. According to the tax rolls for 1927/28 the collectivized peasants had an average per capita income of 57.5 rubles, whereas the average for noncollectivized peasants was 47 rubles. Thus, calculating the income of the collective household at the local average amounted in itself to a 22 percent reduction, and the total tax saving for collective farmers was close to 50 percent.[30]

The resolution of the Central Executive Committee and the Council of People's Commissars on the single agricultural tax in April 1928 brought further fiscal benefits to members of collectives. Member households of *kommuny* received a deduction of 60 percent if their per capita income was not above the local average, 30 percent when it was. Households in artels received a corresponding reduction of 40 or 25 percent. Members of collectives with a per capita income below 30 rubles were declared tax exempt. The general effect of the changes was to increase the advantages for the poorer peasants and to raise somewhat the taxes of the better-off members of collectives. Peasants in *TOZy* were granted a tax deduction of 20 percent.[31]

Tax benefits were not the only advantages enjoyed by collectives.

TABLE 25

Growth and Decline of Collective Farms, 1927–30

(percent of peasant households in collectives)

Month	Percent	Month	Percent
June 1927	0.8%	January 1930	18.1%
June 1928	1.7	March 1930	57.2
June 1929	3.9	April 1930	38.6
October 1929	7.5	June 1930	24.8

SOURCE: Davies, *Socialist Offensive*, pp. 442–43.

Additional incentives, as indicated above, were provided in the form of land grants, preferential treatment in land organization work, and priority allocation of land, agricultural machinery, and credit. In its instructions on the development of collectives, the April 1929 plenum stressed the need to improve the supply of complex agricultural machinery, especially tractors. Party workers and officials were urged to promote the transfer of entire villages to collective forms of labor and to use agricultural contracts and machine-tractor stations for this purpose. The formation of *TOZy*, the simplest form of collective, was to be encouraged, but these units were then to be developed into higher forms (artels and *kommuny*).

The success of the government's policies is evident from the growing number of collectives. (See Table 25.) The modest number of peasant households in collectives, which doubled from 1927 to 1928, doubled again in the following year. Starting in mid-1929 the rate of growth took off on an even more sharply accelerating curve. By the end of the year almost a fifth of all peasant households were in collectives, and a few months later over half of all households were collectivized.

On the anniversary of the revolution Stalin published an exultant article in *Pravda* (November 7, 1929), entitled "The Year of the Great Turning Point." The peasants, he announced, were joining forces in a massive, world-historical movement into collectives. The accuracy of the statement and the importance of the movement that was taking place are beyond question. Collectivization was indeed a historic turning point, and the great turn came in the summer of 1929. But what accounted for the stampede into collectives from that point on?

Commune and Kulak

Undoubtedly the most important element in any explanation of the peasants' entry into collectives is the mounting pressure that was brought to bear on them. This increasing force, nominally directed against the kulaks, was exerted in significant measure through the commune. The Ural-Siberian method, first applied successfully in 1928, was reinforced and extended in 1929.

At the time of the "Collectivization Congress" in 1927, Molotov had drawn a bold line linking the kulak and the commune. The enemy in the countryside, battening on capitalist exploitation, endangering the worker-peasant alliance and the Soviet state, was said to have taken refuge in the commune whenever he was under attack.[32] In theses prepared for the Central Committee and the Sixteenth Party Conference, Kalinin returned emphatically to the problem of the kulaks. The recovery of agriculture, he claimed, had gone as far as possible under the prevailing system. Further advance would depend on the old question: *kto kogo?* "Who will direct the development of the economy, the kulaks or the socialist state?"[33]

Stalin answered that question in no uncertain terms at the April plenum in 1929. The familiar argument that the kulaks were responsible for the grain problem was reiterated yet again. Kulak withholding of grain was just part of the resistance of capitalism to the inexorable advance of socialism, and "organized pressure" would be necessary to overcome this resistance. Poor and middle peasants would have to be mobilized against the kulak in the campaign to increase the collection of grain. This could be achieved using the commune:

"The significance of the Ural-Siberian method conducted on the principle of self-taxation is precisely that it makes it possible to mobilize the laboring stratum of the village against the kulak for the purpose of strengthening grain procurement. Experience has shown that this method gives us positive results . . . in two areas: first, we immobilize the strata of the village holding surplus grain, thereby facilitating supply of the country; second, we mobilize the poor and middle masses against the kulak, educating them politically and organizing them into a mighty, multi-millioned political army in the countryside. . . . The latter is one of the important results of the Ural-Siberian method of grain procurement, if not the most important. True, this method is sometimes joined with the application of extraordinary measures against the kulak, which evokes comical howls from comrades Bukharin and Rykov, but what is so bad about that?"[34]

A short time later the method was rendered even more effective by the adoption of new legislation. On June 28, 1929, a resolution of VTsIK and the Council of People's Commissars, RSFSR, gave legal force to the decisions of peasant general assemblies endorsing grain-collection levies and allocating quotas among households. An analogous decree was published in the Ukrainian Republic on July 3. If a household refused to comply with these decisions, the rural soviet could impose penalties ranging from the fivefold fine to confiscation of property. As Mikoian pointed out at the time, this legislation was of "enormous importance" in mobilizing the forces of "social influence" in the countryside. Anyone who opposed the decision of the commune was now subject to "economic, sociopolitical, and administrative measures."[35]

Any group of peasants that refused to cooperate in grain deliveries was now liable to prosecution under new provisions of the criminal code (Article 61) extending well beyond the still-operating Article 107. Penalties for collective resistance included fines, imprisonment (up to two years), forced labor, confiscation of property, and exile. Part of the fines collected was to be placed in a fund for collectivized poor peasants.[36] At the end of July, when the RSFSR decree was published, the Central Committee issued instructions that the grain quotas planned for each village were to be discussed by the general assembly of its citizens. Assemblies in the RSFSR were then instructed to elect delegates to special squads to be attached to rural soviets for the work of grain collection.[37]

During the summer, when all of these mechanisms were set in place to make use of the commune in the grain campaign, the coming harvest was expected to be bountiful. Whether optimistic predictions flowed from confidence or whether they were announced to create confidence is a moot point.[38] In any case, the expectations proved unfounded. The harvest of 1929 was slightly below that of 1928, and the production of food grains was 5 percent lower. Collection quotas, however, had been set in accordance with harvest predictions and were maintained at the higher levels. Moreover, the procurement campaign in the fall was pushed through at a far more rapid pace than previously. In 1928/29, 15 percent of the harvest had been collected in procurements in the course of the entire year; in 1929/30 22 percent of the total output was collected, almost entirely within the first six months of the agricultural year, that is, by the end of December 1929.[39]

Collections had been successively extended to include all grain "surpluses," not only those of the collectives and of peasants under contract, but wherever "extra" grain was to be found. In effect this marked the end of NEP, despite the fact that the private market had not been officially closed.* Under such circumstances there was a good deal of resistance, much coercion, and great tension in the countryside. It has

---

*According to Moshkov, pp. 63–65, the legislation of June 28 and July 3, 1929, signaled the end of NEP and provided the juridical basis for the subsequent moves against the kulaks.

been estimated that a quarter of a million peasant households were fined or taken to court in the course of the grain campaign.[40] Many kulaks (as earlier, this inevitably included middle and even poor peasants who were caught up in the drive) were deported or had their property confiscated. Often such actions resulted from decisions of the assembly, decisions prompted by local officials and especially by the new order of plenipotentiaries enlisted from Party activists and workers who were sent out to the countryside in droves at this time.[41] Resolutions of the peasant assemblies on grain deliveries were enforced by the local militia and the courts as authorized in the recent decrees.

It is no easy matter to determine the extent to which "antikulak" resolutions of the assemblies were the result of the "naked administrative pressure" so evident at the time. To what extent did they reflect real social antagonisms in the village, and to what degree did they simply express the instinct for self-preservation? Did the peasants on the whole respond opportunistically to the assault on their more prosperous neighbors, or did they resist in a demonstration of communal solidarity? The government's motives in the attack on the kulak are clear; the peasants' role is less obvious.

In some areas measures taken against kulaks had broad popular support. This was most apparent where social differentiation was strongest. In Siberia, for example, where almost all of the peasants were in communes, there was considerable antagonism between later settlers and the wealthier "old residents." The poorer peasants at times succeeded in taking advantage of their new preferential land rights (established under the Basic Principles of 1928) to force redistributions that gained them the best and closest lands, whereas kulaks received the worst and most distant holdings.[42] Meetings of poor peasants in the Volga and North Caucasus regions were said to have demanded prosecution of kulaks who resisted grain collections, and there were frequent press reports of massive support in the villages for the campaign against the kulak.[43]

The press, to be sure, was under official control, but it provides evidence that sometimes peasants presented a united front to resist the authorities. *Pravda*, for example, in an antireligious campaign unleashed a barrage against peasants who "sing the refrain, 'We are all God's children' and protest that there are no kulaks among them."[44] Other peasants were reported to be grumbling about the costs of industrialization policies, maintaining that the only real kulaks were the high-paid engineers in town.[45] Some communes insisted on assigning equal quotas to all members for grain deliveries rather than dividing the assigned village quota among the better-off households alone. By this time, after several years of antikulak measures, the number and economic strength of those who could be labeled kulaks had declined considerably, and in many villages there was little significant differentiation. But the authorities frowned on such egalitarian practices. Those who supported equal quotas were branded kulaks or kulak henchmen, regardless of their economic status. In some cases peasants refused to bid at auctions for the confiscated property of kulaks, or bought the property and returned it to its former owners.[46]

Peasant attitudes toward the kulak appear to have been an unstable compound of admiration, envy, sympathy, and resentment, in proportions that varied with local circumstances and could shift with changing conditions and degrees of pressure.[47] There were undoubtedly elements of intraclass antagonism within the commune that lent themselves to political exploitation, but the basic conflict within the institution was more complex. It involved a collision of values shared by all the peasants: the principles of collectivism and individualism, of mutual responsibility and self-interest, which had found mutual accommodation in the commune, were set against each other by government policies.

Opposition to collectivization by any peasant sufficed to identify him in the eyes of the authorities as a kulak, and simply not to enter a collective farm was to "stand aside from the fundamental class struggle with the kulak."[48] A description of the collectivization of one Siberian village illustrates the techniques that were utilized to promote the movement. Reluctant peasants there were presented with a proposal to join a collective farm. When it came time for a vote, those who were opposed were asked to speak out. Since none dared vote against the measure, it was declared adopted.[49] In another case, a commune in the Lower Volga region voted against joining a collective. The organizers of the meeting then rephrased the question, asking "Who is against Soviet power?" When there was no reply, it was recorded that the village had voted "unanimously" for collectivization.* In some instances the vote of a minority of households in the commune (usually a group of poor peasants organized for the purpose) was declared binding on the entire membership, nonjoiners were arrested or threatened with exile, or the peasants were simply told that collectivization was compulsory.[50]

If peasants or "kulaks" attempted to resist collectivization, their land might be confiscated and they themselves banished from the commu-

---

*Izvestiia, April 19, 1930. Kiselev's article in this issue details a number of similar cases. In one general assembly of peasants where only 50 peasants appeared (out of 407 households), 27 voted against collectivization, yet the minority vote was declared sufficient to collectivize all 407 households.

nity. The land and inventory taken from the dispossessed generally became part of the indivisible fund of the collective farms and confiscation thus became an important source of land for collectives. Iakovlev,
who became head of the newly established Union-wide Commissariat
of Agriculture at the end of 1929, reported at the Sixteenth Party Congress the following July that lands formerly held by kulaks made up 15
to 22 percent of the indivisible funds of all collectives in the country.[51]
The new commissar, a man to fit the moment in agriculture, had gone
on record in *Pravda* earlier with the complaint "We are often un-
believably cowardly in applying to the peasants the socially obligatory
actions that can give the quickest effect, but which one must know how
to organize, joining persuasion with compulsion."[52]

There was more evidence of compulsion than of persuasion in areas
where collectivizers encountered agricultural individualism. In Smolensk province, a leading khutor region since the Stolypin reform, the
conflict was especially bitter. Incidents of peasant resistance to collectivization in this area are well documented in the Smolensk archive
that became available to Western scholars after the Second World War.
Yet these materials must be used carefully since Smolensk, as we have
seen, was an extreme case.[53]

The harshness of the struggle for collectivization there was evident
even in contemporary press accounts. According to a report published
late in 1929, about 30 percent of the poor peasants in one locality were
led by special "agrobrigades" of workers and agrarian specialists to request land reorganization. Gradually, it was said, a majority of poor
and middle peasants were won over to their position. Seeing the writing on the wall, the kulaks proposed that small communes (*poselki*) be
formed. But when the majority decided to form a large collective instead, the kulaks capitulated and agreed to enter on equal terms with
the other peasants. The poor peasants, however, rejected this "maneu-
ver" and refused to let kulaks join the collective farm. A number of
kulaks were then evicted from the area, and the home of one was converted into the center of the new collective. The remaining pioneers of
agrarian individualism thus found themselves among the pioneers of
agrarian collectivism. The separate dwellings of these peasants were
removed from the fields by the collective labor of the group, and anyone who chose to leave the new collective, "Forward to Socialism," had
no right to claim the return of any land.[54]

These developments were repeated with local variations throughout
the country. In the summer and fall of 1929, as the collectivization
movement showed signs of accelerating, the question of admitting
kulaks came up for repeated discussion. With each successive advance,

official policy toward the kulak hardened. The old defenders of the
kulaks were forced into humiliating capitulation. At the November
plenum the leaders of the Right, Bukharin, Rykov, and M. P. Tomsky,
admitted the error of their former positions, denying that they had
ever objected to an antikulak offensive.[55] Shortly afterward, the agrarian economists A. V. Chaianov and N. P. Makarov of the organization-
production school followed suit, acknowledging their earlier mistakes
and announcing support for collectivization.[56] At a meeting of the
agrarian Marxists on December 27, Stalin described as ridiculous the
question "Can the kulak be let into the collective farm?" He insisted,
"Of course he cannot be allowed in the collective. This is impossible
because he is the sworn enemy of the collective farm movement."[57]
The real bombshell, however, was dropped in another of Stalin's statements at that meeting, an announcement that the Party had gone from
a policy of restraining the exploitative tendencies of the kulak to a policy of "liquidating the kulak as a class."

A resolution adopted on January 30, 1930, and instructions that followed on February 1 (both still unpublished) established three categories of kulak.[58] The first group (whose membership was to be defined
by the political police) included those who were considered actively
hostile to the Soviet regime. Their property was to be confiscated,
they were to be imprisoned or interned in labor camps, and their families were to be deported to distant regions. The second category contained kulaks guilty of oppressing other peasants or actively opposing
collectivization. After their property was confiscated, they were to be
deported, but they were allowed to retain a small amount of movable
property. The relatively inoffensive kulaks in the last group were to be
allotted small plots of land on the outskirts of the collective or in some
other locality within the region. The constituency of the second and
third categories was variously determined in different localities, with
rural soviets, poor peasants, meetings of the collective farm, and general assemblies of citizens playing greater or lesser parts in the process.
Tax lists provided some guidance in designating kulaks, but the criteria
of selection in general were arbitrary, leaving victims of personal attack
defenseless and without recourse. Like most other state operations
of the period, the move against the kulak had its Plan, its "control
numbers." Quotas were assigned to each region, divided up, and subdivided down to the level of the village.[59]

Countless peasants, not only the wealthiest, frantically divested
themselves of property and livestock in an attempt to avoid being classified as kulaks. The slaughter of livestock resulting from this "self-
dekulakization" and from the determination of resentful peasants not

to surrender their animals to the collectives into which they themselves were being herded brought about a severe decline in animal
stock that would not be overcome for years. Yet the cost in livestock
was little compared to the human cost of the campaign that "liquidated" the kulak "as a class" and as a symbol of the economic and political independence of the peasantry. Along with the kulak, the social
legitimacy of all agrarian individualism was liquidated—including that
of the commune.

Commune and Collective Farm

In giving legal force to the decisions of the commune on grain collection, the new regulations introduced in the summer of 1929 had drawn
the commune into the official administrative system, as had earlier decrees on peasant self-taxation. As a result of these measures the commune had been transformed into a "public-law institution," as its proponents had advocated in the debates of 1926–27. In the process,
however, it was made into an instrument of its own destruction. State
enforcement of communal authority came about because of the government's interest in the peasants' grain output and tax budget. Control of the countryside, of its economic life and political tendencies,
was to be secured by taking advantage of differences among the peasants and enlisting the support of the poor and middle majority (or, if
need be, minority) in the commune. But the adoption of this tactic in
dealing with the peasants had important unintended consequences.

It has been said of 1929 that "insofar as the concept of 'rural democracy' was concerned, the role of the village assemblies now counted for
very little."[60] Yet precisely the vitality of that concept (whatever its
limitations) and of the commune that embodied it gave the Ural-
Siberian method its efficacy. True, the assemblies were ineffective in
resisting or lowering the grain quotas assigned to them. Nonetheless,
their acceptance of the quotas, even when secured by intimidation, le-
gitimized the collection process and helped to avoid a more direct confrontation with the peasants. Even the use of outright compulsion,
thanks to tradition that may have predated the bridge on the Volkhov,
did not destroy the legitimacy of a decision taken by the commune.

But the grain-collection campaign did not turn out to be the most
important for the commune. It was absorbed by the collectivization
campaign, and successes achieved by the techniques and sanctions developed for the first campaign made possible the successes of the next.
A direct attack on the commune had never been seriously contem-
plated; legislative restrictions on the institution had failed to alter its

essential nature. Yet in the tumultuous course of the collectivization campaign the commune was to disappear, almost unnoticed.

That collectivization was an unplanned consequence of the grain crisis was openly acknowledged in the summer of 1929. If there had been no grain difficulties, admitted Mikoian, the government would not have created collective and state farms on such a scale at that time.[61] In connection with the grain campaign a whole network of agents had been sent out into the countryside. When collections were completed in record time, many of these activists were put to work in the service of collectivization. In November a plenum resolution called for dispatching to the countryside "no less than 25,000 workers with adequate organizational-political experience" to reinforce and direct a movement that was unaccountably running ahead of the most optimistic projections.[62] Under the approved optimal variant of the Five-Year Plan, less than 10 percent of all peasant households were to be in collectives by 1933, but by the end of 1929 almost 20 percent of the peasantry was already enlisted on the rolls of collective farms.

One of the immediate consequences of this rapid growth was a decline in the overall rates of mechanization and land organization in collectives. From mid-1928 to mid-1929 the number of tractors per unit of sown land in collectives dropped to below half the starting level, and the explosive growth of collectives beginning in mid-1929 meant a far more radical decline after that point.[63] Moreover, the lands of the new (and for that matter, of many old) collectives were often in disarray: separate land parcels acquired from kulaks (expropriated "surplus" lands and confiscated holdings) and land contributions of individual households who joined collectives were frequently interspersed among the holdings of noncollectivized peasants. This impeded joint cultivation and made it impossible to use the short supply of heavy agricultural machinery with maximum efficiency. On the other hand, the shrinking amount of land per capita in collectives meant that a higher ratio of labor was available to work it. This advantage could not offset the deterioration of other conditions, however, and the yields of collectives dropped by almost 10 percent between 1928 and 1929.[64]

Until about the middle of 1929 there had been universal agreement that the rate and scale of collectivization would be limited by the availability of machinery, that the number and size of collectives would gradually increase as the supply of tractors and heavy equipment increased. The "model collectives" that attracted peasants were always heavily equipped.* In discussions of land organization work in 1928

* One example was the Leningrad artel "Colossus II," which had 37 households, 2,000 hectares of common land, three tractors, two threshing machines, two binders, a number of seeders, and so forth. (Seleznev and Gumarov, p. 32.)

there was a general consensus that although the formation of some large collectives was desirable, the wholesale collectivization of large settlements was out of the question for the present because of the lack of tractors. Land organization policy was directed at breaking up large communes into smaller, more efficient settlements that could be persuaded to convert to collective cultivation as the services of more machine-tractor stations became available.[65]

Yet by the spring of 1929 the increase of collectives over the previous year combined with the grand promise of the Five-Year Plan to give rise to a more ambitious call for large-scale collectives. Land organs in the countryside were urged to assume new roles as "organizers of a great socialist agriculture and directors of an agricultural revolution in the rural economy."[66] Mass conversions of entire villages were to be encouraged, and supported with a greater supply of agricultural machinery. New tractor factories were to be built. To construct collectives on the basis of wooden ploughs, declared Rykov at the Fifth Union Congress of Soviets in May, would only discredit socialization.[67]

Starting in the spring of 1929 there was increasing talk of the collectivization of "whole villages," but less discussion of the need for a technical base for such a movement. The fact that mechanization was beyond immediate attainment was no longer to be permitted to stand in the way. Under the influence of galloping enthusiasm the creation of large-scale socialized agricultural enterprises became a goal in itself, apart from any economic calculation of optimal size or any reasonable expectation of economies of scale. As "gigantomania" gripped the collectivizers, extensive favorable publicity was given to "The Giant," the largest of the state farms, and to a mammoth collective farm of 135,000 hectares in the Urals that united 84 smaller collectives under the same name.[68] Every effort was made to mechanize such showpiece enterprises, and unions of small collective farms were encouraged even where agricultural machinery was not available.

To accommodate the situation a new theory was concocted, which Stalin elaborated to the agrarian Marxists at the end of the year: although the peasant nag and plough were not advanced means of production, the quantitative aggregation in a collective of even those means provided in itself an improved basis for production.[69] The notion that tractors were necessary for large-scale agriculture was publicly dismissed as "sheer stupidity."[70] What was essential was the consolidation of peasant households and their land into large collectives. The conversion of entire communities would make possible the "solid collectivization" of agriculture, with unbroken expanses of land that could be cultivated jointly, making the best use of the machinery available.

The movement to collectivize entire villages rather than separate households began to gain ground in the summer of 1929. The term "solid collectivization" (*sploshnaia kollektivizatsiia*) was heard on all sides later in the year. Employed loosely, it indicated simply a substantial degree of collectivization; in specific contexts it could designate a definite percentage of collectivization of households or land. At a conference of large collectives held in July 1929, it was given an operational definition: "solid collectivization" meant that collectives were "being organized in villages and included the majority of the population of the village."[71] Widespread transition to this form of collectivization followed the successful establishment of large mechanized collectives in certain regions (the Northern Caucasus, the Urals, and Siberia) where geographic conditions favored extensive cultivation and the availability of virgin land made experimentation possible. Most of the early collectives in the RSFSR had been formed in the north and northwest, where large landowner estates had been concentrated, but the greater part of those formed in 1928 were in the south and southeast.[72] The conditions that made large collectives successful were lacking in many regions, but in the growing enthusiasm for a heroic scale in all things, this consideration was of little moment.

The conversion of "whole villages" meant in most cases, of course, the conversion of whole communes. The techniques already developed for utilizing the authority of the commune for purposes of state policy had an enormous impact on the drive for collectivization. Only with the general transfer to the method of enlisting entire communes did the movement begin to accelerate steeply, and the process was greatly facilitated by the legislation adopted in the summer of 1929. The fact that most new collectives were initially just rebaptized communes is suggested by their size. At the end of 1929 the average collective included about 60 households, just about the same as the average commune.[73]

According to a regional Party secretary in the summer of 1929, it was possible to ensure the total collectivization of all peasants by replacing the recruitment of individual members "by a method forcing the opposing minority to join." The "minority," he added, "was not always a minority in fact."[74] The success of this tactic spelled the success of the snowballing collectivization movement in the winter of 1929–30. Yet success came faster than anticipated. Only after it became apparent that the move into collectives was overtaking all expectations, only after reports of "stormy" and "elemental" rates of collectivization began coming in late in 1929, did the leadership come out for full-scale and immediate collectivization.

"What is *new* in the present collective movement?" asked Stalin in his jubilant article on the "Great Turning Point" in November. His answer: the "new and decisive" element was that peasants were entering collectives not separately but by "whole villages" and even entire administrative districts.[75] The conclusion that he drew, widely echoed at the November plenum, was that the middle peasants had been seized by an enthusiasm for collectivization. At the plenum it was announced that the current "gigantic scale and unexpected rates of economic development" were proving that it was possible to catch up with and overtake the leading capitalist countries in "a historically minimal period." New methods had led to the collectivization of entire settlements; intermediate administrative territorial units were becoming solidly collectivized. The next task would be the solid collectivization of whole regions. All of the stops to collectivization were pulled. Planned-growth targets were thrown to the winds as the plenum warned against taking any "formal-bureaucratic approach" to collectivization in this "new historical stage in the socialist transformation of agriculture."[76] In the flush of rising confidence organizational efforts were redirected from the *TOZy* to the more fully socialized artels. Between June and October 1929 the relative proportion of *TOZy* among all collectives had grown from 60 to 68 percent, whereas artels had dropped from 29 to 23 percent. By mid-1930 the general proportions of the two forms of collective had been approximately reversed.[77]

On January 5, 1930, the Central Committee approved a resolution providing for the complete collectivization of the Volga and Northern Caucasus regions (where collectivization was farthest advanced) by the autumn, or no later than the spring of 1931. The other grain-producing areas were to be basically collectivized within the following year.* The collectivization movement that swept the countryside in late 1929 and early 1930 was an event of genuinely epic proportions, and was viewed as such at the time. Contemporary reports breathe a spirit of self-conscious heroics, a sense of being present at the Creation. The great transformation of the countryside that was taking place was said to be proof of the correctness of the Party line. But the official explanation of why the change became possible precisely at this time came down to the alleged change of attitude by the middle peasants, a change said to have been brought about by the Party's policies. No doubt there were some middle peasants, just as there were some poor peasants and even some better-off peasants, who were caught up in the vision of the new

---

* *Kollektivizatsiia*, pp. 258–59. The resolution stressed the "necessity of a firm struggle against all attempts to hold back the development of the collective movement due to lack of tractors and complex machinery."

and better life that was promised through collectivization. In one sense the socialization of land was the ultimate *chernyi peredel*, the highest realization of the egalitarian principle. If it had been impossible before to bring about a genuine equality through the redistribution of land, it would be possible now to guarantee a different form of equality by eliminating individual landholdings.

Although there were undoubtedly some enthusiasts of collectivization among the peasants (especially where tractors and agricultural machinery were to be had), there is little evidence that the majority were eager to exchange household holdings for collectivized fields. If the peasants did not welcome collectivization, how was it possible to bring about this massive transformation? The use of the organizational structure and traditional authority of the commune was clearly an important means of effecting the change, but why did the commune capitulate? Active resistance was often overcome by outright coercion, yet if the peasants had maintained a united opposition the government would hardly have pushed for immediate, all-out collectivization. It was not prepared to risk mass rural rebellion. The real push—the revision of planned targets, the dispatch of the "25,000-ers"—came only *after* evidence that communes were converting to collectives.

Numerous reports from the countryside speak of a voluntary movement toward collectivization. These might be discounted as politically inspired, yet accounts that refer openly and critically to coercive techniques being applied in the countryside also report that the peasants were moving into collectives of their own volition.[78]

The treatment of kulaks certainly played a role in the psychological collapse of peasant resistance to collectivization. They had served as a village model of the better life to which the less fortunate peasants aspired; when they were destroyed, the peasants' incentive for material self-improvement through individual effort was undermined. The policies of War Communism had been directed against the entire peasantry and had evoked active resistance. Those of the late 1920's, however, were nominally aimed at the kulaks alone and led to a more limited and passive resistance. The Ural-Siberian method amounted to turning the tables on the kulaks in the commune. If the commune had once been manipulated in the interests of the rich minority, it was now being manipulated in the interests of the poor minority. Yet that minority on its own could scarcely have manipulated the commune into accepting collectivization against the wishes of the majority, and not all poor peasants opted for collectivization, given a choice.

Poor peasants, however, were the most likely to be attracted to collectives, and the strong inducements that were offered for joining—

extra land, tax benefits, the availability of credit and agricultural machinery, and so forth—were designed to win them over. As all these advantages were heightened, as more land was taken from kulaks and given to collectives, and as recruitment efforts and pressure tactics were increased, the number of poor-peasant households that found it to their advantage to leave the commune began to mount. Departures of individual poor-peasant households from communes accounted for most of the growth of collectives from the Fifteenth Party Congress until mid-1929.[79] These departures from the commune led to impressive growth rates for the collectives, primarily because there were so few collectives to begin with. In comparison with the overall number of households remaining in communes in mid-1929, the collectives were still insignificant: less than four percent of all peasant households had been collectivized at that point.[80] However, the departure of those households from communes may help to explain the subsequent rapid acceleration of collectivization.

Peasant allotments in the commune were still predominantly in scattered and intermixed strips, so it was extremely difficult to make individual separations without affecting the entire commune. This was why the Stolypin legislation, although it strongly encouraged departures from the commune, had limited them to times of general redistribution or occasions when a significant number of households wanted to leave together. These provisions of the earlier legislation had been maintained by the Soviet government after the revolution— for the same good reasons. Those reasons were still valid at the end of the 1920's, and individual departures could wreak havoc with agricultural organization and production within the commune. Yet in the attempt to promote collectivization in early 1929, the government authorized unrestricted individual departures from the commune with land for those who decided to join collectives.[81]

The various incentives provided were strong enough to attract some peasants out of the commune, and the sudden and obligatory turnover of lands that this involved could severely disrupt the commune's agricultural operations, even when the number of households was relatively small. Under the circumstances, it could be easier for the commune to throw in the sponge and convert to a collective farm rather than struggle with the instability of its field organization.

Other considerations too promoted the wholesale conversion of communes into collectives. The law provided that if a majority decided to collectivize, dissenting households had the right to retain their lands separately. Yet the households most likely to resist collectivization were those with the largest and best holdings. Resistance to collectivization placed them in the same category as the deeply resented "separators" of the Stolypin era, and they were often denied the right to withdraw their lands. In many cases the only real options were to join the collective or to depart landless. The official antikulak policy coincided here with the interests of the bulk of the communal peasantry, and "social influence" undoubtedly reinforced and worked alongside administrative pressure in such cases. There is no question about the presence or the overriding importance of "administrative measures" in collectivization, but the element of voluntarism that is stressed in Soviet accounts may have had some limited basis in fact: the collective offered some peasants a chance to improve their relative status, and others an exit from a situation that had been made impossible.

When the great wave of transfers began to swell after the harvest in 1929, the government, taken by surprise, rode along euphorically with a call for solid collectivization. The Party workers and directives sent out at this point led to more intense pressure on the peasants, and the collectivization drive took off. At the end of the year a revision of the Land Code was passed in the RSFSR authorizing the transfer of "improperly used" land from the commune to the collective.[82] Only when it became clear in the spring of 1930 that chaotic conditions in the countryside threatened the spring planting was there a letup of the pressure on the peasants. Central authorities ordered a stop to coercive measures of collectivization. At the beginning of March Stalin published his famous article "Dizzy with Success," placing all of the blame for the "excesses" that had taken place on local officials.[83]

Just as in 1917 the withdrawal of an anticommune policy had led to a sweeping reentry of peasants into communes, the official retreat in the spring of 1930 resulted in a great flow of peasants back into the old institution.* (See Table 25, p. 353.) Given the option of life in the commune without administrative pressure, the peasants clearly preferred it. But the prospect glimpsed by the leadership in the heady winter of 1929–30 was not to be surrendered to peasant preferences. The drive was resumed the following fall, and within the "historically minimal period" of the next few years it succeeded in bringing virtually all peasants into collective farms, this time permanently.

The role played by peasant women in the process of collectivization has received little attention. Almost all accounts present a picture of

---

*In September, when the number of households in collective farms reached bottom and there was less coercion, the size of the average collective was again close to 60 households. The average had risen sharply during the winter frenzy of mass collectivization, when collectives had been joined to create large units—most of which existed only on paper and disappeared by the time of spring planting.

adamant opposition to collectivization by the female peasants, and in both contemporary and later sources this opposition is viewed as a manifestation of the unfortunate backwardness typical of rural society and of its female half in particular. The stereotype may have its basis in widespread female attitudes, but it ignores certain features of the social situation in the countryside and obscures some interesting developments.

Women had strongly resisted "communalization" of the household in the early postrevolutionary socialization movement, and this tendency reappeared as the move for collectivization got underway in the late 1920's. At the beginning of 1928 *Pravda* bemoaned the fact that individual landholding seemed necessary to satisfy the "individualistic female spirit."[84] Women were said to be especially susceptible to kulak agitation against collectives, and in a number of cases were reported, armed with sticks, pitchforks, and axes, to be leading attacks in the fields against members of collectives.[85] Workers, such as the "25,000-ers," sent out to the countryside to organize collectives complained that female audiences were hostile, and women figured prominently in various accounts of local opposition to collectivization.[86] The peasants themselves frequently told collectivizers that their womenfolk kept them from joining: "It would be heaven to go into a collective, but my wife won't hear of it." * In some cases the opposition of women to collectivization apparently led to the breakup of families.[87]

This is a familiar story, and there is no reason to doubt its accuracy. Yet it has another side. First of all, although many women were undoubtedly hostile to collectivization, their opposition provided a convenient screen for male peasants, who were more likely to be penalized for overt resistance. Furthermore, there is evidence that a growing number of women may have been won over to support the government's policies. After the Fifteenth Party Congress, Party propagandizers for collectivization paid an increasing amount of attention to women.[88] Meetings of women peasant delegates were held throughout the country in an attempt to involve rural women more closely with public life and to enlist their cooperation in local projects. In 1929 over 23,000 such meetings were held, attended by over 700,000 women delegates.[89] The success of this effort is indicated by the marked rise in the political participation of women in soviet elections. (See Table 23, p. 300.) Not only did peasant women vote in larger numbers than ever before (over half of all eligible peasant women voted in 1929), but many

* *Pravda*, June 7, 1929. Rumors circulating at the time included reports that all dresses would be taken away from women in collectives and that everyone would be forced to live in barracks. (Karavaev, p. 67.)

were elected members of rural soviets, and women became presidents in 7 percent of all rural soviets.[90] After the reelections in 1930 there were about 300,000 women in soviets at different levels throughout the country (about 20 percent of all delegates), and 5,000 women were serving as presidents of soviets.[91] Many soviets contained special women's sections.[92]

In some areas peasant women took an active part in establishing collectives. In mid-1929 the proportion of women in collectives was the same (52 percent) as their proportion in the rural population.[93] Because women were now more numerous than men, a significant number of rural households were headed by women.[94] Yet women generally found it difficult to work the fields unaided, and often resorted to hired labor. Collective farms offered special advantages to them, and some all-woman collectives were formed.[95] The first All-Russian Conference of Women Collective Farmers was held at the end of 1929, followed early in 1930 by their first all-Union congress.[96]

Much of the work of the collectivizers was concentrated on the women of the villages, and 8 percent of the "25,000-ers" sent out to the countryside were women.[97] Despite their initial resistance, the peasant women often responded positively to the propagandists after meetings and discussions. In some localities they themselves led the movement. Reports from a leading rural soviet in the Northern Caucasus indicated that women constituted over half of the 180 persons counted among the local activists. "In carrying out economic-political campaigns," announced the president of the soviet, "we rely on the women."[98] A number of accounts speak of the important part played by women peasants in the grain-collecting and sowing campaigns. In Tambov okrug, for example, an all-woman brigade organized by a female activist became the pacesetter in the "Red Star" collective in the spring sowing campaign in 1930.[99]

Such women's work brigades were often staffed by young peasants, whereas the strongest opposition to the collectives was said to come from women over 40.[100] The generational difference emphasized by the new group of rural sociologists in the late 1920's affected mothers and daughters as well as fathers and sons, and it may help to explain the contradictory reports about women's attitudes toward collectivization. Just a few days after *Pravda* published a complaint in June 1929 about the resistance of peasant women to collectivization, another article in the same newspaper presented Krupskaia's report on a Moscow conference of young peasants in which the girls were said to be the most insistent about the need for immediate collectivization.[101] Young people in general were more willing to embark on the great experiment of collectivization, and Young Communists of both sexes were in the fore-front of the movement.[102] Thus the shifting age profile of the decade was an extremely important element in the socioeconomic transforma-tion of the countryside.

The massive transfer of the peasants "by whole villages" into collec-tives meant the conversion of communes into collective farms and the disappearance of the commune from the countryside. The changeover was formalized by legislation adopted in 1930. The first explicit step was taken in the Ukraine, where all land societies were declared abol-ished by decree in January 1930.[103] This move was followed shortly by an all-Union statute of February 3, 1930, on the organization of rural soviets.[104] According to Article 14 of this law, the rural soviet was henceforth to supervise all land use in its territory and to "direct all the activity of land societies" in the interests of the socialist reconstruction of agriculture. The soviet now had "the right to repeal, modify, and confirm the rulings of land societies." There was no stipulation of a legal or even a social basis for rejecting the commune's decisions; the soviet was given complete and arbitrary control of that institution. This was relevant, however, only where there was a commune to control. The final statement read: "In regions of solid collectivization, land so-cieties are liquidated. All their rights and obligations are fully trans-ferred to the rural soviets."

The process of liquidation was delayed by the mass exodus from col-lectives in the spring. There were references in April to the role of the land societies in connection with the spring sowing campaign,[105] but by the summer elimination of the commune was back on the legislative agenda. An RSFSR decree of July 30, 1930, on land societies (amplify-ing Article 14 of the statute of February 3) specified that such societies were to be liquidated by the rural soviet wherever 75 percent of the households had joined collectives. The agricultural lands and inven-tory of the land societies were to be turned over to the collectives formed on their territory, and the remainder of their land and property was to go to the rural soviets. The division of property between the soviet and the collective was to be decided by the raion executive com-mittee. All agricultural contracts that had been signed by a land society remained binding on its former members, even after the society had been dissolved.[106] Two weeks later the right to collect and ex-pend funds by self-taxation was given to rural soviets throughout the country.[107]

The commanding role given to the rural soviet culminated a process of relocating local authority that had been a legislative goal for several years, and was therefore a logical development. Yet it was also a curious outcome, because the rural soviets played a quite insignificant part in collectivization. They were roundly criticized at the time for their lackluster performance in the matter, and suggestions were made that they be replaced.[108] Local authorities actually dissolved some rural soviets, assigning their functions to the collectives. This, however, was declared impermissible. Officials were instructed to put a firm halt to any transfer of the rights or functions of rural soviets to collectives and not to permit any fusion of the two institutions. An announcement issued at the end of January 1930 described rural soviets as the local representatives of state authority, with responsibility for distributing all land funds, supervising the use of land by collectives, and performing a number of other new functions connected with those institutions. At the same time it was acknowledged that the soviets had been standing passively on the sidelines, or trailing behind the collectivization movement. To ensure their more active application to the tasks facing them, the announcement called for reelections in which the poorer peasants were to be given a major role.[109]

The list of the responsibilities of the rural soviets made clear why they could not be fused with the collective farm administration. The soviets were official administrative units. Among their other duties, they were to see to it that the collective farms fulfilled "all their responsibilities to the proletarian state (grain procurements, contracting, taxes, and so forth)."[110] Collective farms, on the other hand, were "production units" concerned with quite different functions. This distinction is a good part of the reason why the rural soviet made so little headway against the commune throughout the postrevolutionary years, and why the commune disappeared at the time of collectivization. Although communes were perceived as rivals to the rural soviets, they were considered indispensable as organizers of agricultural production. The soviet could not replace the commune in this essential respect. The collective farm, however, could. Together, the collective and the soviet provided a bypass around the commune, but it took both to circumvent the older unit, because the commune was both a production unit and an administrative unit. Individual peasant households gained coherence as components of an economic system only through the organization of the commune. The socialization of agriculture required a new form of economic-technological organization, which the collective farm was capable of providing. This was clear to the opponents of the commune, who viewed the traditional institution as a barrier to the modernization of agriculture (as well as a baneful relic of the old regime, a stronghold of the kulak, and a harbor of neo-Populist illusions).

One curious aspect of collectivization was the rationalization that the creation of large-scale production units everywhere and at once was essential for the industrialization of agriculture. Much of the land work of the 1920's—the breakup of large communes, the formation of the new *vyselki* and *poselki*—had been based on the economies of scale demonstrated by contemporary investigations: under prevailing conditions, land that was organized in large production units could often be worked more efficiently when reorganized in smaller units. The collectivizers too argued for economies of scale, but for those at the other end of the scale: larger fields would permit optimal use of agricultural machinery. There would have been no contradiction in policy lines if the level of mechanization called for a change in the mode of production. Yet at the time of collectivization and for some years afterward, the limited stock of agricultural machinery available curtailed the advantages of large-scale organization. Thus it is not surprising that in late 1930, once the paroxysm of official gigantomania had subsided, the average collective farm returned to about the same number of households as the average commune it was replacing.[111]

Yet the collective farm faced new problems. The wholesale destruction of livestock that accompanied collectivization caused a serious loss of draft power, and the combined horsepower of machines and animals in agriculture by 1933 was only about two-thirds of what it had been in 1929.[112] When adverse climatic conditions in the early 1930's once again contributed to a famine, the loss of livestock directly affected the food supply. Famine victims joined the list of the casualties of collectivization. The cost of the move from the commune to the collective was high; however, state grain procurements did rise as the commune dissolved.[113] Opinions differ about the extent to which Soviet agriculture actually paid for the industrialization of the country,[114] but there is little question that the Soviet peasants paid for the collectivization of agriculture.[115]

The decline in the peasants' standard of living that accompanied the disappearance of the commune can hardly be viewed as the direct result of that disappearance; both developments were by-products of collectivization, or rather, of the manner in which collectivization was effected. Yet the fact that the commune was no longer upholding local community interests against the interests of the state, defending peasants against the world outside and the authorities above, meant that the peasants were in a weaker position in confrontations with those forces. This was well understood at the time. Stalin, hardly an ardent culture buff, was fond of the legend of Antaeus, the giant who lost his strength when he broke personal contact with the earth. As the Soviet leader was well aware, the historical point of contact between the Russian peasant and the land had been the commune.

Conclusion

Throughout its history the modern commune served the interests of the state. If it was not created by the state, the redistributional land commune was nonetheless developed and extended as a result of state policies and, in its later phases, with direct state support. As a responsible fiscal agent, as the primary unit of local self-administration, and as the basic form of economic production and social organization, the commune gave structural coherence to the human and territorial content of the state.

By the late nineteenth century, as a result of the shift toward indirect taxation, the appearance of the new organs of rural self-government (the zemstvos), the changes in production stemming from the commercialization of agriculture, and the transformation of social relationships caused by the emancipation, the commune might have been expected to fade away. But at the time of emancipation the peasants were locked into it in the interests of social and political stability. The allocation of peasant lands (along with financial responsibility for redemption payments) to the commune rather than to individual peasants blocked the dissolution of the institution.

Communal organization, however, impeded technological progress and contributed to the backwardness of Russian agriculture. The pressure of a growing population against relatively static resources and techniques in agriculture created mounting tensions in the economy. Taxation policies designed to underwrite industrialization placed additional stresses on the peasants, straining a fragile political equilibrium and contributing to the outbreak of revolution in 1905.

Once the revolution proved the commune no guarantor of political order, the government swung around to a policy intended to catabolize the institution by the establishment of independent, personally owned farms. The decision to back individual peasants with a "stake in society" was a victory for economic liberalism, and it came at a time when semiconstitutional innovations in the structure of government signaled the advance of political liberalism. Yet despite the opening of a legal exit from the commune and official encouragement of departures in the Stolypin era, the commune did not disappear.

Although it served the interests of the state, the commune also served the interests of the peasants. Because it provided a modicum of economic and social security, the hard-pressed peasants were, on the whole, hesitant to abandon it. After an initial wave of departures by those who had extra land and by poor peasants who left in order to sell small allotments, the rate of separations fell off. Individuals continued to leave to set up independent farms, but in the course of a decade the entire group of consolidators amounted to only a tenth of all peasant households.

The peasants' reluctance to leave the commune stemmed from two related factors: (1) unwillingness, in the face of generally adverse conditions, to give up the commune's "group insurance," and (2) lack of the capital necessary to establish independent farming operations. Because of incentive provisions written into the legislation to promote separations, many of those who left the commune did so at the expense of those who remained behind. As a result, a great resentment of individual farmers and a negative attitude toward the "antisocial" aspects of independent farming had built up by the time of the revolutions of 1917. Up to that point the commune had seemed headed for inexorable decline under the pressure of government policies, although the peasants' tenacity promised to make the process a prolonged one. The agrarian problem was still running in a closed circle: the communal system blocked agricultural progress, but until conditions improved the peasants would hesitate to leave the commune.

The fine study of rural Russia produced by Geroid Robinson half a century ago pursued its subject only to the eve of the First World War, leaving the reader with a number of questions about subsequent developments: "What would [the peasants] do when the rules were all off, and the bars all down? Were they by this time so comfortable and so full of the sense of private property that they would not fight [landlords] for the land? . . . Suppose the peasants did seize the land, what would they try to do with it—and with the land already in their possession? Would they push on still farther toward a system of petty holding and independent cultivation—or would they build upon what still remained of the old common interests and the old collective practices? The questions were to have their answer. The great scene, so often rehearsed in part, would be played out this time to the finish."[1] That answer, that great scene, has been witnessed in these pages.

What happened to the traditional socioeconomic structure of rural

Russia involved not only the political and physical conditions of life, not only questions of war and revolution, food and weather, demography and technology, but the impact of all these phenomena on and within a particular cultural and ideological framework. A revolutionary egalitarianism found roots in the folk myth of the *chernyi peredel*. Other revolutions nurtured in the soil of oppression and want have produced the same democratic impulse, but historical circumstances in Russia provided a unique institutional housing for it in the redistributional land commune. The release of antagonism toward individual tenure and the prospect of personal gain fed and found justification in an upwelling demand for egalitarian land redistribution. Under the circumstances, and given the need for a practical means of redistributing newly acquired lands, the commune was dramatically revived and extended in and after 1917.

The abandonment of the zemstvo system in 1917 enhanced the role of the commune in rural self-government, and the establishment of new agencies of local administration (notably, the rural soviets) failed to diminish its importance in the life of the village. The growth of communal landholding was tolerated as a political necessity by a government more apprehensive about elements of individualism in the commune than attracted by its elements of collectivism. Early attempts to introduce collectivized agriculture met with limited success and were played down after 1921 in the face of economic crisis.

Comparison of official rural policy after the revolutions of 1905 and 1917 shows an interesting pattern of change and continuity. Following the first revolution of the century the state, having decided that the collectivism of the commune was politically undesirable and economically detrimental, attempted to propel the peasants into individual forms of tenure. After 1917 the new government, having reached exactly the same conclusions about the individualism of the commune, attempted to propel the peasants into collective forms of tenure.

The NEP period was one of declared neutrality toward the commune. The institution, retaining its basic structure and previous functions, encompassed the great majority of the rural population and extended over most of the agricultural land. As in the Stolypin period, there was a significant tendency toward individual farming only in western and northwestern regions, where special conditions prevailed. Yet even there the commune was dominant. During this interval when they were left to their own devices, when the "rules were all off," the peasants overwhelmingly returned to the middle ground of the commune.

In the end the Stolypin anticommunal policy was consummated by

Soviet collectivization. The NEP period witnessed mounting uneasiness about socioeconomic differentiation and its political implications. Behind the assault on the kulak, however, lay anxieties about the political reliability of the entire peasantry (which was viewed as a petty bourgeois social stratum) and about the solidarity of the peasant-proletarian alliance on which the state was theoretically founded. This concern was heightened by grain-supply difficulties that threatened state economic control and planning. The Soviet state, like the tsarist state, was confronted with the constraints agriculture imposed on industrialization. Both governments saw the economic problem as inextricably bound up with political considerations, but they differed in their approach to the situation. Under tsarist rule taxation of the peasants was viewed simply as a means of obtaining funds for the state, and the commune was used as an instrument to secure tax receipts. Under the Soviet government taxation became an instrument of social as well as economic policy, an instrument that was effectively turned against the commune both externally and from within.

Many have puzzled over how it was possible to achieve a sweeping transformation of the countryside almost overnight. A decade of concerted effort in the prerevolutionary period, after all, had yielded limited results in dissolving the communal structure; yet within a matter of months in the first tsunamic wave of collectivization that edifice collapsed, and in the course of the next few years it was entirely washed away. In dealing with the question of how this was accomplished, most Western writers have pointed to the element of naked coercion that was brought to bear on the peasantry. The use of physical force is clear enough, but it is evident also that the moral force of the commune was a critical element in the process of its own destruction. The fact that communal assemblies were manipulated and pressured into taking decisions on collectivization did not lessen the traditional responsibility of all members to accept those decisions. The principle of unanimity in the face of a ruling by the commune (democratic centralism writ small) was deep-rooted in the institution. This last point is something of a commonplace in the literature, and the demand for unanimity, whether viewed positively (*sobornost'*) or negatively (authoritarianism) is often presented as a peculiarity of the Russian political mind. Yet considering the historical experience of the hard-pressed Russian peasantry, the protracted struggle for survival in a bare subsistence economy, it seems quite possible that the roots of that demand can be traced to the system of intermixed landholdings. Given that system and the limitations of the physical environment, life-sustaining production might have been impossible for all without the agreement of each. But this is merely to speculate.

The ultimate question, and the one that was finally to decide the fate of the commune, was the familiar *kto kogo?*—the question of control. The answer was found in collectivization. The precapitalist communal structure seen by some as a possible bridge to advanced noncapitalist society had, as the result of increasing concern about social differentiation and economic development, become widely identified with rural capitalist elements. The commune was said to be dominated by kulaks. Yet the problem was not that the kulaks had control, but that the government lacked it. Rural soviets had failed to secure control of the countryside, and in the village the commune remained a potent and more or less independent authority. Collectivization provided a bypass, and the commune became a casualty of an economic campaign in a politically inspired social war.

The government's unexpectedly complete victory in that campaign may have been due in some measure to a factor that played little part in its calculations and has received little attention: the nature of peasant field layout. Another factor that may have contributed more to rural developments at this time than has generally been recognized is the rapidly growing involvement of women in the political life of the villages. This took place for the most part outside of the commune, but growing participation in the rural soviets may have lessened the resistance of some peasant women, particularly younger women, to the introduction of collectivization and the abandonment of the commune.

These are just a few of the many topics only brushed against in this study that call for closer investigation. The whole system of peasant values, beliefs, and attitudes toward the commune still needs to be approached from ethnographic and sociological perspectives. But if parts of the picture remain to be filled in, the major outline appears clear. The final phase of the commune's history encompasses developments in the agrarian economy as well as features of the political scene because both affected rural policy and, ultimately, the commune. This was true both before and after 1917, but in the 1920's the government felt unable to take direct action against the institution. It was not official concern about the commune alone that led to its disappearance, but an aggregation of concerns about productivity, procurement, planning, and political power.

One of the many ironies in the commune's history is that uneasiness about social differentiation should have played a part in its elimination. Over the course of time the leveling effects of communal tenure had a significant effect on the political development of Russian society. The absence of a "territorial aristocracy" as a restraining factor in the evolution of the autocracy has been much discussed; the absence of a "territorial bourgeoisie" was hardly less important in the gradual shaping of political institutions and the formation of attitudes that became part of the political culture of Soviet society.

In some ways the commune seemed a model of democratic self-government. Within its narrow framework it provided a forum for public opinion and a means of participating in community life. Yet it has been argued that Western traditions of self-government and the practice of the commune were entirely at odds. According to a European observer, writing a century ago, "One is founded on respect for the rights of the individual, the other on the authority of the community."[2]

Every culture seeks its own resolution of the dichotomy between man and society, and the conflicting elements of individualism and collectivism have been reconciled in various ways. To the extent that the commune accustomed Russian society to a particular form of reconciliation, it helped to provide a historical base for the later socio-economic system and political culture, for socialism and Soviet "socialist democracy." The question of whether the communal order could survive under the Communist state was perhaps an even more difficult one than Marx had reckoned. Political perceptions (and preconceptions) proved no less important in determining the fate of the commune than "objective" realities.

Yet the extent to which the outcome of the decade was "determined" is an open question. The end of the commune could be viewed in retrospect as the inevitable climax of long-term historical trends. But there were contingencies—unintended consequences, bypassed options, and an illogic in certain acts—that give its disappearance the special post facto inevitability of the accident that happened.

The collectivization drive at the end of the 1920's might appear to have settled the old debate on the uses of the commune in the transition to socialism. Yet the debate goes on, although it has taken a new turn. For half a century before the revolution scholars looking ahead to the future disputed whether the commune could be used in the transition to a new order. A half century after the revolution scholars were looking back to the introduction of that order and debating whether the commune was so used. Some contend that the technological limitations of the system precluded the use of the commune in the transition to socialized agriculture; others suggest that the commune actually did serve as a valuable mechanism in the changeover through such measures as agricultural contracting.[3]

The debate remains vital in the context of developments in other countries of the modern world. Marx and Engels spoke of the need for a foreign as well as a domestic proletarian revolution to permit utilization of the commune as a stepping-stone to socialism. Russians lacked outside support in their own efforts to build a socialist society, yet the success of their own and of other modern socialist revolutions now holds out the prospect of outside support to those aspiring to socialism. Under contemporary conditions, claims a Soviet scholar, the economically undeveloped countries of Asia, Africa, and Latin America "can rapidly travel the path of noncapitalist development to socialism using the surviving elements of a communal structure."[4]

The uses of the "Soviet model," however, appear to be limited. The developments traced here suggest that the experience of a society in a revolutionary transition is shaped by a complex of factors so historically specific as to render the whole notion of a model suspect. Circumstances vary, and the variables in human affairs are many. Soviet historian Danilov points out quite reasonably that there is more than one possible approach to the contemporary commune in countries moving toward socialism. The basic content of the institution, he holds, is transformed "as a result of social change, and not through administrative influence."[5] The limits of the change achieved by the Stolypin reform and by Soviet legislation in the 1920's tend to confirm that judgment. Yet the historical record shows that the form, if not the content, of the institution can indeed be transformed when "administrative influence" is exerted with sufficient force. Whether this is socially desirable in particular circumstances, or at all, is quite another question. Yet to deny that it is possible would be to ignore the evidence of the past. A society can change its form of state through revolution, and the state can change the forms of its society.

According to the widely adopted sociological scheme first elaborated by Ferdinand Tönnies, all institutions fall into one of two basic structural configurations.[6] One type of institution, the gesellschaft (society, association, or company) serves the self-interest of the rational individual. It is formed on the basis of particular interests that its members have in common, and those interests are defined and limited. There is a contractual, or quasi-contractual, assumption of obligations by members with respect to the purposes for which the association is formed, and fulfillment of these responsibilities is enforced through a system of sanctions that may be moral or legal. Members of a gesellschaft have no obligations toward one another beyond what has been explicitly agreed upon.

The other form of institution is the gemeinschaft (community, commune, or collective). Institutions of this sort serve social objectives by equating the interests of the individual with those of society at large. Ties between members are based on widely shared interests that need not be formally defined since they are implicit in the relationship. Similarly, the obligations of members to one another extend beyond any formal responsibilities, and are enforced by the expression of deep-rooted social attitudes. Community sentiments, traditions, and morals govern the norms of social behavior.

Two things are immediately apparent from even this sketchy description: the commune can immediately be recognized as a gemeinschaft, and it is clear that this type of institution is inherently more resistant to social change. The broad scope of social relationships, the character of members' mutual obligations, and the nature of social sanctions combine to create a comprehensive, interlocking institutional structure. Since modifications in one sector produce repercussions in others, change, particularly rapid change, is difficult to control. The threat of destabilization, therefore, promotes social conservatism.

This theoretical conclusion merely confirms what the historical record has already indicated. The theory suggests further that the Russian land commune would have been difficult to abolish in short order other than by drastic means; it also helps to explain why abrupt displacement of the institution by the collective farm in the early 1930's so profoundly disrupted the lives of the peasants. Although the early collective farms cushioned somewhat the transition from gemeinschaft to gesellschaft, the costs of the institutional retooling of the countryside were many and high.

The topic of social change leads to a final observation. It was Max Weber's contention that modern societies move toward ever greater rationalization of human activity.[7] Modernization means, among other things, the rationalization of social systems. Insofar as gemeinschaft institutions are sustained by sentiments and attitudes, they are intrinsically less rational than gesellschaft institutions. In the last analysis, then, the commune might be thought of as an outmoded system succumbing to the forces of modernization in a Soviet rationalization of the countryside; the fact that greater economic rationality was the announced objective of the Soviet leadership in pursuing collectivization argues for such an interpretation. Whether that objective was achieved, and whether it was pursued by rational means, are questions for another discussion.

Reference Matter

Appendix

Communal Tenure and Population Growth in European Russia, 1861–1914

The table on the following pages correlates communal tenure with rates of birth and death, and corresponding population growth, for the fifty provinces of European Russia. Although the commune has been blamed for the population increase that put pressure on the land, the data show that higher birthrates in communal provinces were offset by even higher death rates, resulting in a lower overall rate of population increase than in noncommunal provinces. (For a summary of the data, see Table 2, p. 31.)

Sources for the Appendix are TsSK, *Statistika zemlevladeniia 1905*, pp. xxxii–xxxiii; and Rashin, *Naselenie*, pp. 44–45, 167–68, and 187–88.

Region/province	Percent of households in communes, 1905	Average birth rate per 1,000, 1861–1913	Average death rate per 1,000, 1861–1913	Percent of increase in population, 1863–1914
1 *Mid-Volga region*	100%			65%
Kostroma	100	46.7	34.9	69
Kazan	100	46.4	34.0	78
Nizhnii Novgorod	100	52.1	39.8	61
Iaroslavl	100	40.3	32.8	33
Simbirsk	99	50.9	37.0	75
2 *Lake region*	100			115
Pskov	100	46.7	33.1	98
Novgorod	100	42.0	31.4	66
St. Petersburg	98	35.2	32.7	167
3 *Trans-Volga region*	99			115
Perm	100	55.9	43.3	68
Orenburg	100	58.2	40.0	186
Ufa	98	49.6	32.1	
Viatka	99	53.1	39.3	77
Samara	99	57.2	40.2	125
4 *Volga-Don region*	98%			80%
Saratov	100	52.0	37.5	94
Tambov	97	49.4	33.9	79
Penza	97	52.2	38.0	62

Region/province	Percent of households in communes, 1905	Average birth rate per 1,000, 1861–1913	Average death rate per 1,000, 1861–1913	Percent of increase in population, 1863–1914
5 *Southern Steppe region*	98			241
Astrakhan	100	55.7	39.0	250
Don oblast	100	54.4	31.7	308
Ekaterinoslav	99	52.9	30.1	187
Taurida	92	47.7	27.6	239
6 *Northern region*	97			74
Olonets	98	46.6	37.4	57
Vologda	97	45.7	32.7	80
Arkhangel	97	40.5	27.6	70
7 *Central region*	97			82
Moscow	100	43.6	37.6	130
Kaluga	100	48.3	36.1	53
Smolensk	99	51.6	37.9	90
Tver	99	45.5	34.0	58
Vladimir	97	48.9	38.0	66
Riazan	97	48.5	33.0	96
Tula	85	51.6	38.5	64
8 *Dnepr-Don region*	68			94
Voronezh	99	52.3	36.6	87
Kharkov	93	49.2	32.7	115
Orel	90	52.0	37.7	81
Kursk	70	49.8	34.5	78
Chernigov	52	47.2	31.1	111
Poltava	18	44.8	28.4	98
9 *Northwestern region*	28			142
Mogilev	81	47.2	27.7	167
Vitebsk	53	41.8	25.6	152
Kovno	—	34.8	23.9	76
Grodno	—	42.1	27.5	129
Minsk	—	44.9	25.6	203
Vilno	—	40.3	24.6	130
10 *Trans-Dnepr region*	23			148
Kherson	93	46.6	29.8	182
Bessarabia	28	43.4	28.8	159
Kiev	9	47.2	31.0	138
Volynia	2	47.2	29.6	161
Podolia	—	45.7	30.1	117
11 *Baltic region*	—			68
Estland	—	30.2	21.9	62
Lifland	—	30.3	21.7	89
Kurland	—	28.6	19.1	38
50 provinces	77%	48.9	34.0	108.8%

Notes

Complete authors' names, titles, and publication data for works referred to below can be found in Works Cited, pp. 431–47. The following abbreviations have been used in the Notes and Works Cited:

Annales ESC — *Annales: économies, sociétés, civilisations.*
APSV — *Agrarnaia politika sovetskoi vlasti, 1917–1918 gg: dokumenty i materialy.* Moscow, 1954.
ARS — S. M. Sidel'nikov, ed. *Agrarnaia reforma Stolypina.* Moscow, 1973.
CREES — Centre for Russian and East European Studies, University of Birmingham, England.
EPR — *Ekonomicheskoe polozhenie Rossii nakanune Velikoi Oktiabr'skoi sotsialisticheskoi revoliutsii. Dokumenty i materialy.* Vol. 3. *Sel'skoe khoziaistvo i krest'ianstvo.* Leningrad, 1967.
NAF — *Na agrarnom fronte.*
NKRKI — Narodnyi komissariat raboche-krest'ianskoi inspektsii (People's Commissariat of Workers' and Peasants' Inspection [Workers' and Peasants' Inspectorate]).
NKVD — Narodnyi komissariat vnutrennikh del (People's Commissariat of Internal Affairs).
NKZ — Narodnyi komissariat zemledeliia (People's Commissariat of Agriculture).
PSS — V. I. Lenin. *Polnoe sobranie sochineniia.* 5th ed. 55 vols. Moscow, 1958–65.
SDD — Viktor Petrovich Danilov. *Sovetskaia dokolkhoznaia derevnia.* Vol. 1. *Naselenie, zemlepol'zovanie, khoziaistvo.* Moscow, 1977. Vol. 2. *Sotsial'naia struktura, sotsial'nye otnosheniia.* Moscow, 1979.
SDZZ — *Sbornik dokumentov po zemel'nomu zakonodatel'stvu SSSR i RSFSR, 1917–1954.* Moscow, 1954.
SNK — Sovet narodnykh komissarov (Council of Peoples' Commissars).
Sovety — *Sovety v epokhu voennogo kommunizma: sbornik dokumentov.* Moscow, 1928.
SS — V. I. Lenin. *Sobranie sochineniia.* 20 vols. Moscow, 1920–27.
TsGAOR — Tsentral'nyi gosudarstvennyi arkhiv Oktiabr'skoi revoliutsii (Central State Archive of the October Revolution).
TsGIA — Tsentral'nyi gosudarstvennyi istoricheskii arkhiv (Central State Historical Archive).
TsIK — Tsentral'nyi ispolnitel'nyi komitet (Central Executive Committee [of Soviets of the USSR]).
TsSK — Tsentral'nyi statisticheskii komitet (Central Statistical Committee).
TsSU — Tsentral'noe statisticheskoe upravlenie (Central Statistical Administration).

TsUNKhU   Tsentral'noe upravlenie narodno-khoziaistvennogo ucheta. Gosplan, SSSR (Central Administration of National Economic Accounting. State Planning Commission, USSR).

VTsIK   Vserossiskii tsentral'nyi ispolnitel'nyi komitet (All-Russian Central Executive Committee [of Soviets]).

VZP   *Vestnik zemleustroistva i pereseleniia.*

Preface

1. Trapeznikov, 1: 372.
2. *Sovetskaia istoricheskaia entsiklopediia,* 10: 423.
3. For example: S. M. Sidel'nikov, comp., *Agrarnaia reforma Stolypina;* S. M. Dubrovskii, *Stolypinskaia zemel'naia reforma;* and George Pavlovsky, *Agricultural Russia on the Eve of the Revolution.*
4. Kachorovskii, "Russian Land Commune," p. 573.
5. Vladimir P. Timoshenko, *Agricultural Russia and the Wheat Problem;* Naum Jasny, *The Socialized Agriculture of the USSR;* and Lazar Volin, *A Century of Russian Agriculture.*
6. Moshe Lewin, *Russian Peasants and Soviet Power;* E. H. Carr, *A History of Soviet Russia;* and R. W. Davies, *The Industrialization of Soviet Russia.*
7. Yuzuru Taniuchi, *The Village Gathering in the Mid-1920's.*
8. Donald J. Male, *Russian Peasant Organisation Before Collectivisation.*
9. Teodor Shanin, *The Awkward Class: Political Sociology of Peasantry in a Developing Society, Russia 1910–1925.*
10. Viktor Petrovich Danilov, "Zemel'nye otnosheniia v sovetskoi dokolkhoznoi derevne"; and *idem, Sovetskaia dokolkhoznaia derevnia.*
11. V. Ia. Osokina, *Sotsialisticheskoe stroitel'stvo v derevne i obshchina, 1920–1933.*

Chapter 1

1. See Karelin, *Obshchinnoe vladenie v Rossii.*
2. Kachorovskii, *Russkaia obshchina,* pp. 424–25.
3. Wallace, p. 266.
4. Grekov, *Kievskaia Rus',* p. 58, and his *Kratkii ocherk istorii russkogo krest'ianstva,* pp. 52–60.
5. *Entsiklopedicheskii slovar'* (Brokgauz-Efron), s.v. "Pozemel'naia obshchina," 24: 215.
6. In defining *mir,* Vladimir Dal's classic vernacular-based dictionary *Tolkovyi slovar'* (Moscow, 1955) offers *obshchina* as a synonym, but his skimpy definition of *obshchina* does not mention *mir.* Grant traces the usage of the terms in "*Obshchina* and *Mir.*"
7. When used in the last two meanings, the word was spelled differently in the nineteenth century. Its multiple meanings have intrigued many students of the commune, including Baron August Haxthausen, who discussed them in *Russian Empire,* 1: xiii; 2: 220.
8. Kovalevsky, p. 134.
9. The old German Mark had a similar tradition of unanimity, and the meanings of the name of its communal assembly—the *universitatis*—resem-

ble those of the term *mir* (Pavlov-Sil'vanskii, p. 37). It has long been suggested that communal organization marks a universal, or at least a common, stage in the evolution of societies; however, comparing ancient Russian communes with those of other societies is difficult because the history of early communes in Russia is still obscure. See Grekov, *Kievskaia Rus'*, pp. 52–65.

10. Aleksandrov, p. 182; Gorskaia, p. 231.

11. The word *volost* was originally synonymous with *vlast* ("power, authority") and designated a territory subject to a particular authority. On the "black volost" (the volost commune), see Alekseev, pp. 71–103; *Agrarnaia i sotsial'naia istoriia*, pp. 140–67; and *Agrarnaia istoriia severo-zapada*, pp. 53–57, 83–85, 201–2, 281–83, 285–90.

12. The history and significance of the traditional formula are analyzed by Smith, p. 17.

13. Kachorovskii, *Russkaia obshchina*, p. 219.

14. Liubavskii, pp. 466–68. The confiscatory policies of Ivan III, who caused 87 percent of the extensive lands of Novgorod to change hands in the latter part of the fifteenth century, are a dramatic illustration of the assumption of land rights by the Muscovite state. About half of this land, previously hereditary estates or Church property, was taken over directly by the ruler; most of the rest became *pomest'e* land. (*Agrarnaia istoriia severo-zapada*, p. 333.)

15. On the property rights of state peasants in land in medieval Russia, see Shapiro, pp. 70–71; Cherepnin, p. 182; Pipes, pp. 69–71; and N. N. Pokrovskii, pp. 103–14.

16. Vodarskii, p. 134.   17. Baklanova, p. 154.

18. Lappo-Danilevskii, p. 91.   19. *Ibid.*, pp. 282ff.

20. Baklanova, pp. 16–17, 99; Gorskaia, pp. 224–29.

21. Earlier instances of land redistribution were often prompted by estate owners in connection with a reassessment of peasant obligations. See Pavlov-Sil'vanskii, pp. 125–35; Semevskii, 1: 102, 2: 644; Aleksandrov, pp. 79, 182, 187–202; and Pushkarev, part 1, pp. 126–32.

22. Baklanova, pp. 144–54; Gorskaia, p. 231.

23. Aleksandrov, p. 219.   24. Rozhkov, pp. 86–88.

25. Aleksandrov, pp. 206–7.   26. Miller, p. 213.

27. Semevskii and Aleksandrov agree on this point, but Pushkarev (part 2, pp. 186, 196, 222) argues that redistributional practices did not predominate until the end of the eighteenth century.

28. Gorskaia, p. 232.

29. Semevskii, 2: 633–43; Vorontsov, "Nachalo peredelov."

30. Vorontsov, "Ucheniia," p. 226; Miller, p. 343.

31. Semevskii, 1: 106; 2: 761.

32. Kovalevsky, p. 81; Blum, pp. 520–21.

33. Gorskaia, p. 231; cf. Pushkarev, part 2.

34. Aleksandrov, p. 203; Baklanova, p. 154.

35. Aleksandrov, p. 302.

36. Luchitskii, pp. 502–3.

37. Kaufman, *Russkaia obshchina*, p. 59.

38. *Entsiklopedicheskii slovar'* (Brokgauz-Efron), s.v. "Pozemel'naia obshchina," 24: 222.

39. Kaufman, "K voprusu o proiskhozhdenii zemel'noi russkoi obshchiny," in his *Sbornik statei*, pp. 46–122.

40. Kachorovskii, *Russkaia obshchina*, p. 216.
41. See Vorontsov, "Nachalo peredelov"; Rozhkov, pp. 85–86.
42. Blum, pp. 505–7.
43. Kachorovskii, "Russian Land Commune," p. 569.
44. The only exceptions were the Baltic provinces, where serfs had already been emancipated, and the recently acquired southwestern province of Bessarabia.
45. Ignatovich, pp. 46–52. In the 20 central provinces that contained the bulk of the serf population in the eighteenth century, the number of serfs paying labor dues was about equal to the number paying nonlabor dues. A century later these provinces held less than half of all serfs due to the expansion of the empire and the growth of population beyond the center. In the entire area for which Ignatovich calculated mid-nineteenth-century data (40 provinces and the Don Region), labor dues were required from about two-thirds of the serf tiaglo units.
46. Interestingly, Alekseev observed that the juridical position of peasants paying nonlabor dues in the fifteenth and sixteenth centuries suggests an expansion of communal self-government (*Agrarnaia istoriia severo-zapada*, p. 217).
47. Kachorovskii, among others, notes that the first instances of communal land redistribution often occurred soon after the introduction of the three-field system (*Russkaia obshchina*, p. 226).

48. Aleksandrov, p. 176.	49. Confino, p. 344.
50. Semevskii, 1: 45–46.	51. Ignatovich, pp. 186–91.
52. Rubinshtein, p. 159; Baklanova, p. 111.	
53. Aleksandrov, p. 312.	
54. Semevskii, 1: 126.	

Chapter 2

1. On the Kiselev reforms, see Druzhinin, *Gosudarstvennye krest'iane*; Haxthausen, *Russian Empire*. Haxthausen's work provided ammunition for the Slavophiles and a target for the Westerners.
2. Blum, p. 24.
3. Aleksandrov, p. 3.
4. The historiographic controversy over the commune is discussed in the first chapter of Aleksandrov's study. See also: Dubrovskii, "Rossiiskaia obshchina," pp. 348–61; "Pozemel'naia obshchina"; Goehrke, *Theorien*; Laptin; Petrovich, pp. 206–18; Pushkarev, pp. 95–108; Vdovina, pp. 33, 50; and Vorontsov, "Ucheniia."
5. Emmons, p. 188.
6. Alexander II is known to have read Herzen's *Kolokol*, and Chernyshevsky addressed himself directly to Alexander's brother Konstantin, who was actively involved in the emancipation. Venturi, p. 152, credits Herzen with an effective role in changing the government's original intent of landless emancipation to an emancipation with land. However, Emmons, pp. 57–61, shows that a landed emancipation was intended from the start.
7. Herzen, pp. 122–26.
8. *Sovremennik*, 1858, nos. 1 and 9. Steklov, p. 72, states that "no one did as much to popularize the idea of communal tenure among the Russian public

as Chernyshevsky." Kachorovskii (*Russkaia obshchina*, p. 21) credited Voron-tsov with having done most in the investigation of the commune, but dedi-cated his own classic work to Chernyshevsky. For Chernyshevsky's role in the debate on the commune, see Dudzinskaia, "Chernyshevskii."

9. According to the report of the Valuev Commission in 1872, peasants paid 94 percent of all taxes collected from agriculture. (Liashchenko, *History of the National Economy*, p. 446.)

10. See Starr, *Decentralization and Self-government*.

11. Only those whose objections to the commune were based on principles of Manchester liberalism wanted immediate abolition. *Ekonomicheskii uka-zatel'*, their leading journal, stated in February 1857 that communal usage of land was an obstacle to increased productivity and cited as evidence the higher yield of the peasant's hereditary garden plot—a point still of interest in discus-sions of collectivized agriculture.

12. Skrebitskii, 2: 465–68.

13. Manuilov, "Reforma 19 fevralia," p. 66.

14. Skrebitskii, 2: 515.

15. Kachorovskii, *Russkaia obshchina*, p. 380, n. 2.

16. Skrebitskii 2: 529n.; *Vysochaishe utverzhdeniia 19 fevralia 1861 goda. Polozheniia* (hereafter *Polozheniia*); General Statute, Article 54, point 3, Local Statute for Great Russia, Article 114.

17. General Statute, Article 20, *Polozheniia*, p. 16.

18. General Statute, Articles 42–45, *Polozheniia*, pp. 16–17.

19. Czap, p. 393.

20. Robinson, pp. 68–69.

21. Statute on Redemption, Article 173, *Polozheniia*, p. 121.

22. Statute on Redemption, Article 165, *Polozheniia*, pp. 119–20.

23. Kachorovskii, *Russkaia obshchina*, p. 412. The provision requiring the consent of the commune to the separation of members who had fully redeemed their allotment was an extension of a restriction imposed previously only on former state peasants.

24. Emmons, p. 422. See also Zaionchkovskii, p. 148.

25. On the labor supply, see Gerschenkron, "Agrarian Policies." The exis-tence of a general shortage of labor is open to question, yet as Herzen had ob-served (p. 124), as long as a peasant was guaranteed a share of communal land, the factory was obliged to pay him more than he could earn in the field. Thus to the extent that the existence of the commune modified the "iron law" of wages proclaimed by the classical economists (i.e., a natural tendency of wages to fall to subsistence levels because of workers' competition for jobs), it may have exerted a negative influence on industrial development.

26. The overall reduction was only 4.1 percent. If the large, politically moti-vated western allotments are eliminated, however, along with the large allot-ments of infertile northern and desert lands, the reduction amounted to 13–16 percent of pre-emancipation peasant land according to official data. (Anisimov, p. 94.) Liashchenko, p. 384, calculated a reduction of 18 percent for the 36 provinces covered in the Great Russian Statute. More recent studies suggest that the loss may have been even greater; see Pershin, *Agrarnaia revoliutsiia v Rossii*, 1: 13–14.

27. The average holding of the contemporary French peasant, for example,

was considerably smaller than the average peasant allotment in Russia, but the productivity of the French land was far greater due to natural conditions, and to more advanced agrotechnology. (Robinson, p. 95.)

28. Zaionchkovskii, pp. 242–43.

29. Anisimov, pp. 90–91.

30. Robinson, p. 289, n. 9. For a discussion of the agricultural significance of the ratios, see Pavlovsky, pp. 84–85. Vinogradov, pp. 6–19, offers a different interpretation of the decline of peasant pasture land.

31. Pushkarev, part 3, p. 129.

32. Dubrovskii, *Stolypinskaia reforma*, p. 68.

33. Kachorovskii, *Russkaia obshchina*, pp. 291, 328; Liashchenko, p. 443.

34. Loginov, p. 10.

35. "Pozemel'naia obshchina," p. 216; Miller, pp. 324–25.

36. Kachorovskii, *Russkaia obshchina*, pp. 292, 298.

37. *Ibid.*, p. 415; "Pozemel'naia obshchina," p. 219. The original emancipation legislation had exempted members of small rural societies (having less than 21 souls) from mutual tax responsibility, but had neglected to make clear that members who bought their way out of the commune would be released from mutual responsibility. This was established by supplementary legislation in 1866. (Chernukha, pp. 196–200.)

38. Pavlovsky, p. 83. The same view has been expressed by a number of scholars, including Leroy-Beaulieu, 1: 573; and Dubrovskii, *Stolypinskaia reforma*, p. 50.

39. Treadgold, p. 44.

40. Chambers, pp. 35–36.

41. Tugan-Baranovskii, p. 71; Rashin, *Naselenie*, pp. 188–93.

42. Pershin, *Agrarnaia revoliutsiia*, 1: 81.

43. Liashchenko, pp. 468–69; cf. Egiazarova, pp. 70–76, 84–85.

44. Anfimov, *Zemel'naia arenda*, p. 15. If nonagricultural land is not included, the proportion of private land rented by peasants may have reached 60 percent.

45. Pavlovsky, p. 155.

46. "Pozemel'naia obshchina," p. 219; Kachorovskii, *Russkaia obshchina*, p. 412.

47. It has been pointed out, however, that official policies placed serious constraints on industrialization by limiting the development of a domestic market. See Arcadius Kahan, "Government Policies and the Industrialization of Russia," *Journal of Economic History*, 27 (1967): 460–77.

48. See Atkinson, "Zemstvo."

49. Egiazarova, p. 171.

50. Liashchenko, p. 447.

51. Chernyshev, *Agrarnyi vopros*, p. 93.

52. Chernyshev, "Zadacha," p. 41.

53. Rittikh, p. 2.

54. Witte, *Zapiska*, p. 85.

55. Iurdanskii, "Otmena krugovoi poruki."

56. Memorandum presented to the first Duma by the Minister of Internal Affairs, June 6, 1906; excerpts in *ARS*, pp. 32–34. See also Dubrovskii, *Stolypinskaia reforma*, p. 71.

57. *ARS*, p. 303, n. 15.

58. Dubrovskii, *Stolypinskaia reforma*, p. 81.
59. *ARS*, p. 300.
60. Chernyshev, "Zadacha," p. 48.

Chapter 3

1. Oganovskii, *Revoliutsiia*, p. 3; Tiumenev, chap. 1.
2. Official policies and practices in regard to colonization at this time are discussed by Treadgold in *The Great Siberian Migration*.
3. Glavnoe upravlenie zemleustroistva i zemledeliia, *Sbornik statistikoekonomicheskikh svedenii*, pp. 81–101.
4. *Vestnik sel'skogo khoziaistva*, 1910, no. 30, p. 5.
5. A——skii, *Skol'ko zemli*.
6. Those who argued this point relied on accumulating statistical evidence such as that presented by Karyshev, "Khoziaistvo," p. 66.
7. *Vestnik sel'skogo khoziaistvo*, 1910, no. 30, p. 6.
8. S. Witte, *Vospominaniia*, 2: 491.
9. The historiography of the dynamics of rural disturbances in 1905–7 is reviewed by Tropin, pp. 149–63. Cf. Dubrovskii, *Krest'ianskoe dvizhenie*, p. 42; and Piaskovskii, pp. 267–70.
10. *1905. Materialy i dokumenty. Agrarnoe dvizhenie v 1905–1907*, pp. 50, 63, 244.
11. Dubrovskii, *Krest'ianskoe dvizhenie*, p. 42.
12. *Zakonodatel'nye akty perekhodnogo vremeni (1904–1906 gg.)*, 1st ed., pp. 254–58 (hereafter *Zakonodatel'nye akty*); *ARS*, pp. 46–47. Although redemption payments were not collected after 1906, the government continued to collect arrears on them until 1917.
13. Gerschenkron, "Agrarian Policies," p. 781.
14. Dubrovskii, *Krest'ianskoe dvizhenie*, pp. 38, 42.
15. Piaskovskii, p. 267; Tropin, p. 150. The difficulty in calculating the extent of the revolutionary disturbances is illustrated by a recent study of Samara province. By one accounting the peasant movement extended to 62 percent of the province (190 out of 306 volosts); another approach suggests that only 23 percent of the province was affected (569 villages out of 2,477); and a third indicates that 39 percent is the correct figure (151,651 households in these villages out of 386,500 in the province). See Bukhovets, p. 100.
16. Fortunatov, p. 37; Pershin, *Agrarnaia revoliutsiia*, 1: 48–49.
17. Perrie, p. 107; Pershin, *Agrarnaia revoliutsiia*, 1: 239.
18. *Vestnik sel'skogo khoziaistva*, 1905, no. 24, p. 18.
19. Data of the Ministry of Internal Affairs for estate property damage in 1905, in *ARS*, p. 30; TsGAOR, *f*. DP oo, 1905, *ed. khr.* 390, *l*. 12.
20. TsGAOR, *f*. DP oo, 1905, *ed. khr.* 390, *l*. 24.
21. For a discussion of the myth and its uses, see Daniel Field, *Rebels in the Name of the Tsar* (Boston, 1976).
22. TsGIA, *f*. 91, *op*. 2, *d*. 800, *ll*. 137–38. Analyses of prigovory of the period are available in Bukhovets and in Vasilevskii, "Sotsial'no-ekonomicheskoe soderzhanie," pp. 121–46.
23. "Doklad predsedatelia Soveta ministrov S. Iu. Vitte po agrarnomu voprosu," January 10, 1906, in *ARS*, p. 52.
24. Dubrovskii, *Stolypinskaia reforma*, p. 89; *ARS*, p. 305.
25. *Zakonodatel'nye akty* (1st ed.), pp. 407–11; *ARS*, pp. 63–65. For an ac-

count stressing the basic (though ultimately ineffective) role of the March 4 decree in the early stages of the evolution of agrarian policy, see Hennessy, *Agrarian Question*.

26. "Proekt osnovnykh polozhenii zakona o svobodnom vykhode krest'ian iz obshchiny . . . ," *ARS*, pp. 58–61.

27. Witte, *Vospominaniia*, 2: 242.

28. For the projects of "the 42," "the 104," and "the 33," see *ARS*, pp. 70–80.

29. TsGAOR, *f*. DP oo, 1906 (II), *ed. khr.* 717 (1), *l*. 86.

30. *Ibid*., *ed. khr.* 715 (1), *l*. 59.

31. TsGAOR, *f*. 102, 1906, *op*. 6, *ed. khr.* 241, *ll*. 9, 14, 19.

32. *Pravitel'stvennyi vestnik*, no. 137 (June 20, 1906); *ARS*, p. 89.

33. TsGAOR, *f*. DP oo, 1906 (II), *ed. khr.* 715 (1), *l*. 1.

34. TsGIA, *f*. 91, *op*. 1, *d*. 837, *ll*. 12, 31–34.

35. *Krest'ianskii deputat* (St. Petersburg), July 2, 1906, p. 3. See also TsGAOR, *f*. DP oo, 1906 (II), *ed. khr.* 717 (1), *l*. 140.

36. TsGAOR, *f*. DP oo, 1906, *ed. khr.* N565, *l*. 1. Radical criticisms of the Duma that were aired by deputies during its sessions were made known to the peasants through extensive press coverage of Duma debates. For an example of the detailed coverage available in the provincial press, see *Smolenskii vestnik*, May 24, 1906.

37. TsGAOR, *f*. DP oo, 1906 (II), *ed. khr.* 715 (2), *ll*. 6, 20. A great many reports of the political agitation stirred up by Duma deputies throughout the countryside have been preserved in this police archive, in *ed. khr.* 715 (1 and 2) and 717 (1 and 2).

38. TsGAOR, *f*. DP oo, 1906, *ed. khr.* N565, *l*. 1.

39. TsGAOR, *f*. DP oo, 1906 (II), *ed. khr.* 717 (2), *l*. 183.

40. *Ibid*., *ed. khr.* 715 (1), *l*. 27.

41. *Ibid*., *l*. 20. In this communication to the governor of Mogilev, Stolypin also ordered that the police keep a close watch on and arrest agitators supporting the positions of the Peasant Union or the Labor Group; he noted, however, that members of the Duma were considered personally inviolable and not subject to "administrative measures."

42. Chernyshev, "Zadacha," p. 46.

43. *Trudy pervogo s"ezda upolnomochennykh dvorianskikh obshchestv 29 gubernii, 21–28 maia 1906 g*., pp. 3, 29–30. For the background, views, and influence of this group, see Geoffrey A. Hosking and Roberta Thompson Manning, "What Was the United Nobility," in Haimson, ed., *The Politics of Rural Russia, 1905–1914*, pp. 142–83.

44. *ARS*, p. 310.

45. *Ibid*., p. 311.

46. Dubrovskii, *Krest'ianskoe dvizhenie*, p. 42.

47. *Pravitel'stvennyi vestnik*, June 20, 1906; *ARS*, pp. 84–89.

48. TsGAOR, *f*. DP oo, 1906 (II), *ed. khr.* 715 (2), *ll*. 51–136.

49. Dubrovskii, *Stolypinskaia reforma*, p. 102.

Chapter 4

1. Gurko's account of the agrarian reform (*Features and Figures of the Past*) tends to downplay Stolypin's role, doubtless because of a keener appreciation of his own substantial part in formulating the reform legislation. In April 1906,

when P. I. Durnovo was dismissed as part of Witte's government, Gurko became the acting head of the Ministry of Internal Affairs. According to his memoirs, it was he who advised selecting Stolypin as the next minister. Gurko met Stolypin on his arrival in the capital and at once took the opportunity to urge the abolition of the commune. "But it seemed to me," he recorded, "that Stolypin knew little about the subject; he seemed to lack even a clear understanding of what the land commune was" (p. 461). Yet Stolypin advocated the reform policy in his official audience the next day, and had Gurko draw up the legislative project that he brought before the Council of Ministers in October 1906. This became the famous decree of November 9, but the Prime Minister declined to present it under his own signature since he was "not thoroughly acquainted with the matter" (p. 500). Gurko concedes, however, that Stolypin gave the reform his full support. For a more positive version of Stolypin's contribution, see Conroy, chap. 1. According to Conroy (p. 6), Stolypin stated that his views on the peasant question were shaped by his early administrative experiences in Kovno. Yet neither there nor in Grodno, where he served as governor in 1902–3, did the peasants hold land in communal tenure. It was the inefficiency of the widespread system of stripholding, prevalent outside of communes as well as within them, that first drew his attention to the problem of peasant landholding. Only after 1903, when he became governor of Saratov, did he have an opportunity to familiarize himself with the negative aspects of communal tenure.

2. See his gubernatorial report for 1904 (*Krasnyi arkhiv*, 1926, no. 17), which demonstrates a conviction that individual rather than communal land ownership was the key to peasant prosperity and political stability.

3. *Zakonodatel'nye akty* (2d ed.), pp. 673–81; *ARS*, pp. 99–105.

4. Gurko, p. 501.

5. "Postanovlenie I-i podkomissii agrarnoi komissii II Gosudarstvennoi Dumy . . . ," *ARS*, pp. 240–44. The lone supporter of the government's measure is described on p. 324, n. 154, as a "well-off peasant."

6. The changes in the Duma electoral systems are discussed by Leopold Haimson in "Russian Landed Nobility," pp. 1–29.

7. For the modifications introduced by the Duma Land Commission, see *ARS*, pp. 105–12. The law of June 14 follows on pp. 112–23.

8. In 1908 the Land Commission of the Third Duma had narrowly approved a provision recognizing hereditary tenure de facto wherever general redistribution had not occurred within the past 24 years. This was modified by the State Council (with Stolypin's approval) because of a concern that the peasants would feel forced out of communal tenure and would react negatively (*ARS*, p. 316, n. 99).

9. For provinces and regions covered in the Great Russian and Little Russian Statute, the limit was six times the maximum allotment; for provinces in the northwest and southwest, three times; for Bessarabia, two times (Article 56).

10. *Svod zakonov Rossiiskoi Imperii*.

11. "Ukaz . . . o vydache Krest'ianskim pozemel'nym bankom ssud pod zalog nadel'nykh zemel'," *ARS*, pp. 153–57.

12. Veselovskii, *Istoriia zemstva*, 4: 178.

13. *ARS*, p. 131.

14. Pavlovsky, p. 132.

15. Dubrovskii, *Stolypinskaia reforma*, pp. 268–69.

16. Pershin, *Ocherki*, p. 26; Dubrovskii, *Stolypinskaia reforma*, pp. 245, 247. Dubrovskii's posthumously published *Sel'skoe khoziaistvo*," p. 191, states that 18.5 percent of all peasant households completed land organization work under the Stolypin reform; although it is not apparent from his text, the higher rate is derived inappropriately from the number of peasant households existing in 1905.

17. *ARS*, p. 144, Table 64; Dubrovskii, *Stolypinskaia reforma*, pp. 266–67.

18. Oganovskii and Kondrat'ev, p. 60. Data are for 47 provinces. For a description of the founding and growth of the bank, see Pavlovsky, pp. 146–61.

19. Karyshev, "Nash zemel'nyi kredit," part 2, p. 11.

20. Pavlovsky, p. 155.

21. Oganovskii and Kondrat'ev, p. 65. Though not encouraged to buy through the bank, individual peasants had increased their private landholdings over the period also, and in 1905 they held 13.2 million desiatins—slightly over half of the private property in land owned by the peasantry.

22. Kosinskii, pp. 50–51.

23. Dubrovskii, *Stolypinskaia reforma*, p. 310. For the effect of the "Great Fear" on the politics of the nobility, see Manning, "Zemstvo," pp. 30–66.

24. Anfimov and Makarov, pp. 85–87. According to data tabulated on p. 87, the lands of the nobility had declined from 1863 to 1915 by 54 percent (58 percent in the black soil region and 51 percent in the non–black soil region).

25. *ARS*, p. 172.

26. *ARS*, pp. 152–57. Such mortgage loans could also be made to free the land from indebtedness to private lenders, which was necessary in some cases to make it eligible for land organization work.

27. Anfimov and Makarov, p. 85; cf. Robinson, p. 270 and p. 272, n. 5.

28. Pershin, *Ocherki*, p. 29.

29. Calculated from data in *ARS*, pp. 173–74, 178. The number of peasants who received loans from the bank as individual purchasers was 270,340 but 920,637 peasant households were beneficiaries of loans made to collectives. The figures include loans for land purchased with the help of the bank as well as for purchases of bank land.

30. Pershin, *Uchastkovoe zemlepol'zovanie*, p. 47.

Chapter 5

1. Land data for 1905 are from TsSK, *Statistika zemlevladeniia 1905 g.*, pp. xxx, 174–75. There were 12 million peasant households at the time, holding 124 million desiatins of allotment land, among them 9.2 million households in communes with 101 million desiatins of land. To these must be added some 280,000 Cossack households with almost 15 million desiatins in communal tenure.

2. Note that these figures are for households, whereas those given above were for (male) "souls." By 1905 the average amount of allotment land per soul was down to 2.24 desiatins. Cossack holdings in communes in the Don region, Orenburg, and Astrakhan averaged 53 desiatins per household.

3. The size of the average holding of allotment land varies in different sources and even within a single source using different bases of calculation. Data in *Statistika zemlevladeniia, 1905 g.* yield the following household aver-

ages for 50 provinces and 12.3 million households of European Russia: all allotment holdings and Cossack lands, 11.3 desiatins; all allotment holdings without Cossack lands, 10.3 desiatins; holdings in communes, including Cossack lands, 12.2 desiatins; holdings in communes, excluding Cossack lands, 10.9 desiatins; holdings under hereditary tenure (no Cossack lands), 8.1 desiatins. Pershin, *Agrarnaia revoliutsiia*, 1: 85, presents an overall figure of 11.1 desiatins; whereas Oganovskii and Kondrat'ev, p. 73, give an average of 10.7 desiatins for 42 provinces and 11.2 million households.

4. The smallest holdings of allotment land were in the provinces of Podolia, Volynia, Kiev, and Poltava, where over half of the peasant households had allotment holdings below five desiatins. (Oganovskii and Kondrat'ev, pp. 68–73.)

5. Kachorovskii, *Russkaia obshchina*, pp. 385–86. Cf. his "Russian Land Commune," p. 569.

6. Krestovnikov, p. 7; *ARS*, p. 317, n. 101. Although these figures may minimize the incidence of general redistributions, they indicate a dynamic that contradicts any picture of frequent and rapidly increasing redistributions soon after emancipation, such as that offered recently by Druzhinin, *Russkaia derevnia*, p. 122.

7. Chernyshev, *Obshchina*, p. xx.

8. Karpov, foldout table, p. 203; Dubrovskii, *Stolypinskaia reforma*, p. 581.

9. *Izvestiia zemskogo otdela Ministerstva vnutrennikh del*, 1911, no. 2, p. 87, in *ARS*, pp. 136–37.

10. Kachorovskii, "Russian Land Commune," p. 571.

11. Oganovskii and Chaianov, pp. 26–27.

12. Manuilov, "Noveishee zakonodatel'stvo," p. 248.

13. Pershin, *Uchastkovoe zemlepol'zovanie*, p. 7. An additional 300,000 consolidations were formed on lands of the Peasant Land Bank. Some of the 1.3 million consolidations generally described as "on allotment land" actually included non-allotment land, though apparently only a limited number. See Kofod, p. 109.

14. Sovet s''ezdov, *Statisticheskii ezhegodnik na 1913 god*, p. 17.

15. According to one estimate, half a million peasants in communes that had not redistributed land had already appropriated their holdings before June 1910. See Lositskii, p. 53.

16. For a discussion of statistical evaluations of the impact of the reform on the commune, see Atkinson, "Statistics," pp. 773–87.

17. Oganovskii, *Revoliutsiia naoborot*, p. 99; Dubrovskii, *Stolypinskaia reforma*, p. 108; Trapeznikov, 1: 203.

18. TsSK, *Statisticheskii ezhegodnik 1915*, section 6: 1.

19. In the article cited in n. 16 above, a question was raised concerning Dubrovskii's use (*Stolypinskaia reforma*, p. 205, Table 12) of the figure 10,176,100 as the number of peasant households in communes in 1915. A subsequent check of the archival source cited by Dubrovskii failed to uncover any basis for the figure, and it appears that it may well have been taken from Lositskii's estimate for 1912.

20. Kofod, p. 22. In one sample covering some 17,000 households on allotment land, 429 households had divided before consolidation and 352 house-

holds had split after consolidation. Some divisions led to the establishment of several new households, since a total of 752 households arose from the latter group alone.

21. *Predvaritel'nye itogi vserossiiskoi sel'sko-khoziaistvennoi perepisi 1916 goda*, part 1, *Evropeiskaia Rossiia* (Petrograd, 1916), pp. 462–624. The census gave a total of 15.5 million households, but did not include Grodno, Kovno, or Kurland. The number of households in these provinces can be estimated at .2 million on the basis of population-growth data for 1897–1914 in Rashin, p. 45. The 1916 census covered households "of peasant type" (see pp. xxxiii–xxxiv) and according to A. Vainshtein may be inflated by 3 percent due to the inclusion of rural nonpeasant households. This amount has therefore been deducted from the total. See *Statisticheskoe obozrenie*, 1929, no. 7, p. 17.

22. Oganovskii and Chaianov, pp. 26–27, gives a total of 16.3 million desiatins; *ARS*, p. 145, provides data totaling 16.9 million desiatins.

23. Anfimov and Makarov, pp. 88–89.

24. *ARS*, pp. 173–74.

25. Calculated from data in *ARS*, p. 178. Pavlovsky is one of many enthusiasts who stress the development of the "individualistic trend" in the bank's work after 1906 (p. 159), neglecting the other side of land transfers.

26. Pershin, *Uchastkovoe zemlepol'zovanie*, p. 29.

27. For data on the rising amounts of grain brought to market after the turn of the century, see Kitanina, p. 127; Liashchenko, *National Economy*, pp. 736–37.

28. Mozzhukhin, *Zemleustroistvo*, pp. 34–37; see also his *Agrarnyi vopros*, p. 38; and Lositskii, p. 31.

29. See Bilimovich, pp. 340–41; Treadgold, pp. 233–35.

30. Pershin, *Uchastkovoe zemlepol'zovanie*, p. 14.

31. Chernyshev, *Obshchina*, p. 178.

32. *Ibid.*, p. 52.   33. *Ibid.*, p. 164.

34. Nikonov-Smorodin, p. 62.   35. *Ibid.*, p. 67.

36. See the reports of peasants in Chernyshev, *Obshchina*, pp. 18, 46, 75, 127; Dubrovskii, *Stolypinskaia reforma*, pp. 209–13, 239. Lositskii, p. 9, admits "a degree of compulsion" but states it was exaggerated in the press.

37. *ARS*, pp. 269–72.

38. *Ibid.*, pp. 261–64.

39. Dubrovskii, *Stolypinskaia reforma*, pp. 578–81.

40. Pershin, *Uchastkovoe zemlepol'zovanie*, pp. 12–13.

41. Mozzhukhin, *Zemleustroistvo*, pp. 34–35.

42. Chernyshev, *Obshchina*, pp. 23–24, 50–52, 79–82, 108–9, 128, 168.

43. *Ibid.*, p. 167.

44. Mozzhukhin, *Zemleustroistvo*, p. 153.

45. Dubrovskii, *Stolypinskaia reforma*, pp. 219, 221.

46. Pavlovsky, pp. 134, 140.

47. See Brutskus, p. 92; Oganovskii, *Revoliutsiia*, p. 26. Oganovskii states that the belief that both extremes were leaving the commune was widespread among contemporaries. His own view was that mainly the poor peasants were separating; in support he shows that the average holding of separators in all regions was smaller than that of the communal average for the region.

48. *Stoimost' proizvodstva glavneishikh khlebov*, *vyp*. 1 (St. Petersburg, 1915), pp. 446–49, cited by Anfimov, "Krest'ianstvo."

49. Dubrovskii, *Sel'skoe khoziaistvo*, p. 191. This unsupported figure seems excessively high as a general description, but may be valid for local areas. See his *Stolypinskaia reforma*, p. 257.

50. Pershin, *Uchastkovoe zemlepol'zovanie*, pp. 46–47.

51. Lositskii, p. 21; Sovet s"ezdov, *Statisticheskii ezhegodnik na 1913*, p. 17.

52. Dubrovskii, *Stolypinskaia reforma*, p. 255.

53. Calculated from Pershin's data, *Uchastkovoe zemlepol'zovanie*, pp. 8, 47. Pavlovsky, p. 135, gives a general average of 9.2 desiatins; Dubrovskii, *Stolypinskaia reforma*, p. 250, states that the average consolidated holding was 9.7 desiatins.

54. Dubrovskii, *Stolypinskaia reforma*, pp. 258–60.

55. *Kratkie biudzhetnye svedeniia po khutorskim i obshchinnym krest'ian-skim khoziaistvam Simbirskoi gub.* (Simbirsk, 1916), pp. 153–54, cited by Dubrovskii, *Stolypinskaia reforma*, p. 262.

56. Pershin, *Agrarnaia revoliutsiia*, 1: 101–2; Mozzhukhin, *Zemleustroistvo*, pp. 200, 214. Consolidators also retained rights to undivided lands remaining in communal use. Pershin calculated this at 6.7 percent of their total land (*Uchastkovoe zemlepol'zovanie*, p. 46).

57. Mozzhukhin, *Zemleustroistvo*, pp. 184–93.

58. Pershin, *Uchastkovoe zemlepol'zovanie*, p. 33.

59. *Ibid.*, pp. 46–49; Dubrovskii, *Stolypinskaia reforma*, pp. 248, 252, 255. The government did not distinguish between khutors and otrubs in statistics published after 1911, and Dubrovskii believes this was an attempt to conceal the unsatisfactory rate of development of khutors. His data, derived from Pershin, indicate that 22 percent of all consolidated farms were khutors. Pershin avoided calculating the proportion since information is completely absent for 21, and only partial for 4, of the 47 provinces listed.

60. Glavnoe upravlenie zemleustroistva i zemledeliia, *Zemleustroennye khoziaistva*.

61. Chernyshev, *Obshchina*, p. xxiv.

62. According to Veselovskii, however, the higher investment of capital (in particular, the use of hired labor) accounted for the superior performance of the khutor (*Utopizm*, p. 6).

63. Chernyshev, *Obshchina*, pp. 23, 79; Brutskus, p. 183; Mozzhukhin, *Agrarnyi vopros*, p. 45; idem, *Zemleustroistvo*, p. 232.

64. Veselovskii, *Utopizm*, pp. 5–7. In Veselovskii's view, the establishment of the "gentry-khutors" suggested a return to Potemkin villages.

65. Mozzhukhin, *Zemleustroistvo*, p. 214.

66. Oganovskii and Chaianov, p. 20; Brutskus, p. 113; Rikhter, *Agrarnye voprosy v Rossii*, Part 2, p. 10. Sales from the Peasant Bank's own land fund were made at a lower average price (121 rubles per desiatin) than sales of private lands for which it arranged mortgages (141 rubles per desiatin). The bank paid higher prices for the land than it charged the peasants, the deficit being covered by a state subsidy—one-third of which was ultimately paid by the peasants in the form of taxes. See Anfimov, "O dolge krest'ianstva," p. 112; and *ARS*, pp. 80–81, 85.

67. Litvinov, p. 93.

68. See, for example, Kosinskii, pp. 270–71. The development of the school is described by Basile Kerblay in Daniel Thorner et al., eds., *A.V.*

Chayanov on the Theory of Peasant Economy (Homewood, Ill., 1966), pp. xxv–lxxv.

69. Oganovskii, *Individualizatsiia*, p. 62.

70. Glavnoe upravlenie zemleustroistva i zemledeliia, *Zemleustroennye khoziaistva*, Table 4; Pershin, *Agrarnaia revoliutsiia*, 1: 102–3.

71. Simonova, p. 401.

72. Pershin, *Agrarnaia revoliutsiia*, 1: 88.

73. Rikhter, p. 18; Anfimov, *Rossiiskaia derevnia*, pp. 72, 327. Pershin, *Agrarnaia revoliutsiia*, 1: 87.

74. Antsiferov, p. 75.

75. Mozzhukhin, *Zemleustroistvo*, p. 124.

76. Simonova, p. 401.

77. This is Simonova's conclusion, and her views on this point closely parallel those presented in Tiumenev's earlier work (see his *Ot revoliutsii*, p. 279). Simonova's valuable study is based on data of the Ministry of Justice and of the Land Department of the Ministry of the Interior, particularly the records of individual sales of allotment land. The later records provide new types of information, but a degree of methodological insouciance is notable: local officials were instructed to include under the category of "sales due to maintenance from outside employment" those sales concluded by peasants whose "outside employment" was "beggary."

78. Simonova, pp. 432–33.

79. *Ibid.*, p. 416; cf. Liashchenko, *Istoriia*, 2: 269–70.

80. Simonova, p. 451; cf. Tiumenev, p. 203.

81. Mozzhukhin, *Zemleustroistvo*, pp. 117–52.

82. Gurko, p. 136.

83. Simonova, p. 425. Voronezh was chosen for investigation because it was judged to be a typical European province and because complete data were available.

84. Kosinskii, p. 237; Mozzhukhin, *Zemleustroistvo*, p. 129.

85. Dubrovskii, *Stolypinskaia reforma*, pp. 337–41.

86. Mozzhukhin, *Agrarnyi vopros*, p. 36. Simonova, p. 402, contends that sales rose steadily through 1914, but the data cited do not support that conclusion. It may be, however, that the decline in sales starting in 1914 noted by Kosinskii, p. 235, was merely a result of wartime disruption. Tiumenev, pp. 201–4, argues that increased sales after 1910 disprove the "populist thesis" that the sellers were largely those who had already left the land. It is likely, however, that the "automatic conversion" clause of the 1910 legislation was responsible for the spurt. In 1910 the number of certifications was only slightly over 8,000; by 1911 it had climbed to 167,000. It fell steadily thereafter.

87. Mozzhukhin, *Zemleustroistvo*, p. 124.

Chapter 6

1. See the symposium *Osobennosti agrarnogo stroia Rossii v period imperializma. Materialy sessii nauchnogo soveta po probleme "Istoricheskie predposylki velikoi Oktiabr'skoi sotsialisticheskoi revoliutsii."*

2. Dubrovskii, *Sel'skoe khoziaistvo*, pp. 37–38, 43, 46.

3. *Ibid.*, p. 206.

4. *Ibid.*, p. 220.

5. Anfimov, *Rossiiskaia derevnia*, pp. 63–68.

6. Dubrovskii, *Sel'skoe khoziaistvo*, pp. 220–21.

7. *Ibid.*, p. 215.

8. *Ibid.*, pp. 223, 230. Anfimov, *Rossiiskaia derevnia*, p. 285. About one-fourth of the grain harvest was marketed outside of the local village.

9. Kitanina, pp. 41, 161; Oganovskii and Kondrat'ev, pp. 194–97, 300–303.

10. Kitanina, p. 126. For marketing by social sectors, see Anfimov, *Krupnoe pomeshchich'e khoziaistvo*, pp. 221–22.

11. Kitanina, pp. 38, 161.

12. Anfimov, *Zemel'naia arenda*, p. 175.

13. Dubrovskii, *Sel'skoe khoziaistvo*, p. 249.

14. Kayden and Antsiferov, p. 14; Dubrovskii, *Sel'skoe khoziaistvo*, pp. 359–60.

15. Dubrovskii, *Sel'skoe khoziaistvo*, p. 205; Anfimov, *Rossiiskaia derevnia*, p. 257.

16. Dubrovskii, *Sel'skoe khoziaistvo*, p. 215.

17. Glavnoe upravlenie zemleustroistva i zemledeliia, *Sbornik statistiko-ekonomicheskikh svedenii*, pp. 113–14; see also Obukhov, pp. 82–83.

18. Oganovskii and Chaianov, pp. 157–58, 194; Dubrovskii, *Sel'skoe khoziaistvo*, pp. 216–19.

19. See Iatsunskii, p. 217. The rate of natural increase in European Russia actually declined slightly in this period: from 1.72 in 1899–1906, it dropped to 1.65 in 1907–14. Both the birth rate and the death rate fell slightly. Recent and extremely interesting work that challenges longstanding assumptions about the influence of industrialization on demographic developments has opened up a host of new questions that invite investigation of the effect of communal organization on Russian marriage patterns and fertility rates. See Coale et al., *Fertility*.

20. Rashin, *Naselenie*, p. 45. Dubrovskii (*Sel'skoe khoziaistvo*, p. 35) cites an estimate for population increase of 41 percent in European Russia between 1897 and 1915; Anfimov places the increase in the rural population of the territory from 1901 to 1913 at 28 percent (*Krupnoe pomeshchich'e khoziaistvo*, pp. 370–71).

21. Kitanina, p. 42.

22. Kir'ianov, p. 198.

23. Nifontov, pp. 306–7.

24. Dubrovskii, *Sel'skoe khoziaistvo*, p. 204.

25. Kitanina, pp. 275–76; Litvinov, p. 95; Oganovskii and Kondrat'ev, p. 335.

26. Anfimov, *Zemel'naia arenda*, pp. 174–75.

27. *Ibid.*, p. 178. Anfimov's data on rental costs, rye yield, and prices from the turn of the century to 1914 (p. 201) indicate that rental could be profitable in this period when grain was marketed, especially on large farms (those of over 50 desiatins). (See *ibid.*, Appendices 5 and 6, pp. 199–202.) However, except for the south and southeast, most rented land was devoted to subsistence farming rather than market production. (See *ibid.*, Table 49, pp. 112–14.)

28. Liashchenko, *National Economy*, p. 734; Anfimov, *Rossiiskaia derevnia*, pp. 147–48, 198–99.

29. Dubrovskii, *Sel'skoe khoziaistvo*, p. 262.

30. Brutskus, p. 13; Anfimov, *Rossiiskaia derevnia*, p. 210.

31. Anfimov, *Krupnoe pomeshchich'e khoziaistvo*, pp. 370–71.

32. Dubrovskii, *Sel'skoe khoziaistvo*, pp. 266, 334.

33. Kitanina, p. 124; Pershin, *Agrarnaia revoliutsiia*, 1: 49, 52–53.

34. Oganovskii and Kondrat'ev, p. 303.

35. Anfimov, *Rossiiskaia derevnia*, p. 74.

36. *ARS*, p. 178; Anfimov, *Rossiiskaia derevnia*, pp. 72, 258.

37. Vasilevskii, *Ideinaia bor'ba*, p. 88. On the dynamics of peasant unrest see Mal'tsev, p. 126, and Ierusalimskii, p. 119.

38. Anfimov, "Krest'ianstvo," Table 9, p. 47a.

39. Haimson, "Problem of Social Stability," 23: 634–36; Tiumenev, pp. 223–40; Antonova. *Vliianie stolypinskoi agrarnoi reformy.*

40. Antonova, pp. 173–74. On the number of industrial enterprises see Antonova, Appendix 5, pp. 222–23; on the increase in the industrial labor force see Rashin, *Formirovanie*, p. 43.

41. Johnson, pp. 160–61. Many rural residents went off regularly for more or less temporary work in industry. According to Rashin, *Formirovanie*, p. 343, the number of such *otkhodniki* among the rural populace at the beginning of the century was eleven million.

42. Anfimov, *Rossiiskaia derevnia, passim*. A similar view is presented by Simonov in "Sel'skoe khoziaistvo Rossii," pp. 60–70. For a more recent overview that makes judicious use of Anfimov's account see Keep, chap. 3.

43. Antsiferov et al., *Russian Agriculture During the War.*

44. *Khar'kovskii oblastnoi gosudarstvennyi arkhiv, f.* 304, *op.* 1, *d.* 2065, *l.* 38, cited by Anfimov, *Rossiiskaia derevnia*, pp. 273–75.

45. Anfimov "Krest'ianstvo," p. 52.

46. See *Krest'ianskoe dvizhenie v Rossii v gody pervoi mirovoi voiny, Iiul' 1914 g.–fevral' 1917 g: sbornik dokumentov.*

47. TsSU, *Rossiia v mirovoi voine*, p. 21.

48. Anfimov, *Rossiiskaia derevnia*, p. 362.

49. Bilimovich, p. 358; Anfimov, *Rossiiskaia derevnia*, p. 335.

50. Alexander Gerschenkron, "Economic Backwardness in Historical Perspective," and "Russia: Patterns and Problems of Economic Development," in his *Economic Development*, pp. 5–30, 119–42.

51. Kachorovskii declared, rather uncharitably, that the "weaklings" drank up the profits from their speculative land sales ("The Russian Land Commune," p. 574).

52. Dubrovskii, *Sel'skoe khoziaistvo*, pp. 218–19.

53. Members of this group who have been cited here include Antsiferov, Kosinskii, Pavlovsky, Treadgold, and Yaney.

54. See, for example, Mozzhukhin, *Agrarnyi vopros*, p. 48; Oganovskii, *Individualizatsiia*, p. 49. The views of Anfimov, *Rossiiskaia derevnia*, pp. 70–84, Dubrovskii, *Stolypinskaia reforma*, pp. 567–68, and Litvinov, pp. 104–15, are typical of Soviet historiography, though Litvinov (writing in the 1920's) was more willing to acknowledge constructive elements in the reform. Pershin's recent work reflects the negative Soviet view (see his *Agrarnaia revoliutsiia*, 1: 273), but compare his 1922 *Uchastkovoe zemlepol'zovanie*. For a description of the debate among contemporary observers on the reform's impact on the commune, see Oreshkin, pp. 166–75.

Part III, Introduction

1. TsSU, *Trudy*, 7: 1: 250, 252. The average temperature in February 1917 was −14.5° C in Petrograd, −16.7° C in Moscow. The February average for the earlier war years (1914–16) was −4.2° C in Petrograd, −3.7° C in Moscow.

Chapter 7

1. On the wartime labor force, see *EPR*, pp. 33–73.
2. *Ibid.*, pp. 151, 153, 158; Anfimov, *Rossiiskaia derevnia*, p. 280.
3. *EPR*, pp. 167, 169, p. 471 n. 76, pt. 3.
4. *Ibid.*, pp. 159–89.
5. *Ibid.*, p. 206.
6. *Vestnik vremennogo pravitel'stva*, March 3, 1917, pp. 2–3. For objections to the requisition order by the Provisional Committee of the Duma, see *Ibid.*, p. 207.
7. Gill, pp. 50, n. 64, 51, 98. This work provides a more detailed discussion of the problems and central administrative structure of food supply.
8. *Ibid.*, p. 61; Keep, p. 176.
9. Gill, pp. 76–77; *Vestnik vremennogo pravitel'stva*, May 16, 1917, June 25, 1917.
10. *EPR*, p. 191. At the provincial level the commissars replaced the governors. For the peasants' negative reaction to the appointment of the presidents of zemstvo boards as special commissars of the Provisional Government, see Gaponenko, *Revoliutsionnoe dvizhenie posle sverzheniia*, p. 671.
11. *EPR*, pp. 204–5; Gill, p. 179.
12. *EPR*, p. 158.
13. *Ibid.*, pp. 454, 456.
14. *Ibid.*, pp. 196–97.
15. *Ibid.*, pp. 197–203.
16. *Ibid.*, pp. 207–10.
17. *Ibid.*, p. 209.
18. Gaponenko, *Revoliutsionnoe dvizhenie v aprele*, p. 316; *EPR*, p. 215.
19. Pershin, *Agrarnaia revoliutsiia*, 1: 295. Membership on the council of the Main Land Committee was enlarged by twelve additional representatives of the All-Russian Soviet of Peasant Deputies at the beginning of June. Additional changes designed to broaden committee membership were proposed by an organizational commission created early in July but were rejected by the government. See *EPR*, p. 231; Kostrikin, *Zemel'nye komitety*, pp. 152–53; Osipova, *Klassovaia bor'ba*, p. 142.
20. Kostrikin, *Zemel'nye komitety*, p. 140.
21. *Ibid.*, p. 143; Pershin, *Agrarnaia revoliutsiia*, 1: 350–51.
22. Kostrikin, *Zemel'nye komitety*, pp. 124–25, 137; Pershin, *Agrarnaia revoliutsiia*, 1: 353–54, and Osipova, *Klassovaia bor'ba*, pp. 140–41.
23. Gaponenko, *Revoliutsionnoe dvizhenie v aprele*, p. 613.
24. Kirillov, p. 20.
25. *EPR*, p. 231 and footnotes; pp. 279, 280, 292, 316, 343, 375.
26. Ginev, "Fevral'skaia burzhuazno-demokraticheskaia revoliutsiia," p. 331; *EPR*, p. 233.
27. Oreshkin, p. 177.
28. TsGIA, *f.* 91, *op.* 2, *d.* 1179 (1917), *l.* 1.
29. *Ibid.*, *l.* 3.
30. *Ibid.*, *ll.* 33–50; Oreshkin, pp. 182–86.
31. Gertsenshtein.

32. Gaponenko, *Revoliutsionnoe dvizhenie v aprele*, p. 596; Pershin, *Agrarnaia revoliutsiia*, 1: 302; *EPR*, pp. 349, 377.

33. *EPR*, p. 481, n. 11; Pershin, *Agrarnaia revoliutsiia*, 1: 302.

34. *EPR*, p. 235.

35. Pershin, *Agrarnaia revoliutsiia*, 1: 299.

36. Sidel'nikov, *Agrarnaia politika*, p. 275.

37. *EPR*, pp. 325–26.

38. *Ibid.*, p. 327.

39. Gaponenko, *Revoliutsionnoe dvizhenie v aprele*, p. 634.

40. *EPR*, p. 228.

41. *Ibid.*, p. 483, no. 130, n. 1.

42. *Ibid.*, p. 484, no. 132, n. 1.

43. Ginev, *Agrarnyi vopros*, pp. 153–60; *EPR*, pp. 258–59, 263–73.

44. On the participation of the local land committees in land seizures and other activity unacceptable to the central authorities, see Kostrikin, *Zemel'nye komitety*, esp. chap. 5.

45. *EPR*, p. 485, no. 132, n. 1.

Chapter 8

1. Rosenberg, p. 27.

2. *Ibid.*, pp. 85–89, 127–29.

3. Morokhovets, p. 144.

4. *Ibid.*, pp. 148–49.

5. *Rech'*, May 10, 1917, p. 2.

6. Sharapov, p. 77.

7. *Rech'*, April 15, 1917, pp. 1–2. Needless to say, the Kadets' enthusiasm for the committees waned as it became evident that some of them were involved with peasant land seizures and other unlawful activities. See Rosenberg, pp. 149–50, 192–93, and *EPR*, pp. 237, 241.

8. Rosenberg, p. 90.

9. P. P. Maslov, *Kritika*, p. 38.

10. Morokhovets, pp. 62–63. On this point, Lenin charged the Mensheviks with condemning the peasant to a perpetual "ghetto" of allotment land. The negative features of stripholding, distant plots, and so forth would be locked in and the free mobilization of land blocked. (Lenin, "Agrarnaia programma sotsial-demokratii v russkoi revoliutsii 1905–1907 godov," *PSS*, 16: 258).

11. P. P. Maslov, *Politicheskie partii*, p. 29.

12. Morokhovets, pp. 68–69.

13. P. P. Maslov, *Kritika*, pp. 10, 40.

14. Baron, pp. 94–101.

15. Anweiler, p. 123.

16. Ginev, *Agrarnyi vopros*, pp. 35–36.

17. Ginev (*Agrarnyi vopros*, pp. 182–84, and "Fevral'skaia burzhuazno-democraticheskaia revoliutsiia," pp. 330–31) suggests that there may have been some readiness to compromise on the issue of compensation, but the party program was unequivocal on this point.

18. Shishko, pp. 45–47.

19. Chernov, *Zemlia*, pp. 208–10.

20. *Ibid.*, p. 130.

21. Pershin, *Agrarnaia revoliutsiia*, 1: 295.

22. Kostrikin, pp. 322–27.

23. Radkey, *Agrarian Foes*, p. 213.

24. Chernov, *Great Russian Revolution*, p. 9.
25. Radkey, *Agrarian Foes*, p. 249.
26. *Ibid.*, p. 421.
27. Ginev, *Agrarnyi vopros*, pp. 126–38. Ginev's discussion of the proposal to transfer authority over land relations to the land committees is ambivalent. His account echoes Lenin's charge that the party supported the proposal solely as a means of preserving some gentry land and placating the wealthier peasants. The Left SRs, however, are said to have backed the measure as a radical, democratic move in the interests of the peasantry. Cf. *ibid.*, pp. 156–60 and 130–32.
28. Radkey, *Agrarian Foes*, p. 456.
29. Morokhovets, p. 73.
30. Kostrikin, *Zemel'nye komitety*, p. 327; Dubrovskii, *Krest'ianstvo*, p. 111.
31. Lenin, "Agrarnaia programma russkoi sotsial-demokratii," *PSS*, 6: 333.
32. S. P. Trapeznikov, who has analysed Lenin's agrarian views at length, does not credit him with originality on this point but presents him as the first Russian to apprehend the significance of the *Marxist* conception of an alliance between the proletariat and the peasantry "which became one of the cornerstones of Leninism." (*Leninizm*, 1: 69–70, 121.)
33. Lenin, "Agrarnaia chast' programmy RSDRP priniataia na II s"ezde," in *SS*, 9: 727.
34. Lenin, "Peresmotr agrarnoi programmy rabochei partii," *PSS*, 12: 244. Trapeznikov (1: 77), referring to Lenin's differences on this issue with the editors of *Iskra* in 1902, states that Lenin was ready then to include nationalization of all land in the Social Democratic program. However, the original manuscript and details of the controversy published in the *Leninskii sbornik* (3: 352–54, 383–87) show that Lenin was prepared to accept nationalization "at a certain revolutionary moment," but considered it inexpedient at the time.
35. Lenin, "Peresmotr," *PSS*, 12: 253.
36. For some of his own criticism of other programs, see "Poleznaia polemika," *PSS*, 13: 231.
37. Lenin, "Proekt agrarnoi programmy," *PSS*, 12: 269–70.
38. Lenin, "Doklad ob ob"edinitel'nom s"ezde RSDRP," *PSS*, 13: 28–29.
39. Lenin, "Rezoliutsiia ob"edinitel'nogo s"ezda ob otnoshenii k krest'ianskomy dvizheniiu," *SS*, 9: 716–17.
40. Lenin, "Agrarnaia programma . . . 1905–1907 gg.," *PSS*, 16: 291.
41. Lenin, "Doklad na VII (Aprel'skoi) Vserossiiskoi konferentsii RSDRP (b)," *APSV*, p. 73.
42. Lenin, "K kharakteristike ekonomicheskogo romantizma," *PSS*, 2: 213–14.
43. Pershin, *Agrarnaia revoliutsiia*, 1: 195. The demand was included in the projected program of the *Osvobozhdenie truda* group.
44. Lenin, "Agrarnaia programma RSD," *PSS*, 6: 344–45.
45. Lenin, "Chto delaetsia v derevne," *PSS*, 20: 77; "Ob otsenke tekushchego momenta," *PSS*, 18: 275; "Agrarnaia programma . . . 1905–1907," *PSS*, 26: 254.
46. In Lenin's view, socialism was "nothing but state-capitalist monopoly put to the benefit of all the people." ("Groziashchaia katastrofa i kak s nei borot'sia," *PSS*, 34: 192.)

47. Gaponenko, *Velikii oktiabr'*, pp. 59–62. The theses are dated April 4, the day after Lenin's return from abroad. They were published in Pravda on April 7.

48. *APSV*, pp. 107–9.

49. Lenin, "Vserossiiskii s"ezd krest'ianskikh deputatov," *PSS*, 32: 186–87.

50. *APSV*, p. 108.

51. *Pravda*, May 12, 1917.

52. Pershin, *Agrarnaia revoliutsiia*, 1: 297.

53. Lenin, "O 'samochinnom zakhvate' zemli," *PSS*, 32: 131–34.

54. Lenin, "Otkrytoe pis'mo k delegatam vserossiiskogo s"ezda krest'ian-skikh deputatov," *PSS*, 32: 43.

55. *APSV*, p. 107.

56. In his discussion of the Model Instruction (*Krest'ianskie s"ezdy*, p. 160), A. S. Smirnov mentions some of the demands listed by the peasants, including prohibition of commercial transactions in land and repeal of the laws permitting separation from communes. Then follows Lenin's statement that only the Bolsheviks could realize such a program. The juxtaposition is misleading since, as Lenin was well aware, by the time of his statement on August 29 both of these demands (formulated for the Peasant Congress in May) had been satisfied by the Provisional Government.

57. Lenin, "Krizis nazrel," in Gaponenko, *Velikii oktiabr'*, pp. 272–73; idem, "Iz dnevnik publitsista," *PSS*, 34: 115.

Chapter 9

1. For example, Kostrikin, *Zemel'nye komitety*; Keep, *Russian Revolution*; Volkhov; A. S. Smirnov, *Krest'ianskie s"ezdy*; N. F. Bugai, *Revkomy* (forthcoming). On the lack of earlier study and on source problems, see A. S. Smirnov, *Krest'ianskie s"ezdy*, p. 101; Anweiler, p. 273n.

2. *Birzhevye vedomosti*, July 9, 1917, cited by Keep, p. 219.

3. A. S. Smirnov, *Krest'ianskie s"ezdy*, p. 40.

4. Gaponenko, *Revoliutsionnoe dvizhenie posle sverzhaniia*, p. 440.

5. See the resolution on the agrarian question adopted by the congress and part 4 of the Model Instruction of the peasant delegates. (*EPR*, pp. 347, 411.) The wording of the latter, however, may reveal the hand of the SR leadership rather than the sentiments of the rank and file.

6. Kostrikin, "Krest'ianskoe dvizhenie," p. 13; Osipova, *Klassovaia bor'ba*, p. 60.

7. Kostrikin, "Krest'ianskoe dvizhenie," pp. 30–32. On the background of peasant attitudes toward the zemstvo, see the articles by Rosenberg and Atkinson in Emmons and Vucinich, eds.. *The Zemstvo in Russia*.

8. Kravchuk, pp. 69–70; A. S. Smirnov, *Bol'sheviki*, pp. 187–99.

9. On the dispatch of urban workers to the countryside in 1917, see Selunskaia, *Rabochii*.

10. A. S. Smirnov, *Bol'sheviki*, pp. 101–19; Kravchuk, pp. 70–74. According to Smirnov, p. 119, the Petrograd zemliachestvos sent out "several thousand" agitators to the countryside; Kravchuk, p. 74, reports that they dispatched over ten thousand agitators in September and October alone.

11. Tsypkina, pp. 6–7, 24–27, 55.

12. *Derevenskaia bednota*, October 25, 1917, cited by Tsypkina, p. 52.

13. For the text of the resolution, see A. S. Smirnov, *Krest'ianskie s"ezdy*, pp. 124–25.

14. Osipova, *Klassovaia bor'ba*, pp. 106–16; Gill, pp. 125–26. On the congress, see Shestakov, 1: 1: 121–61, and on the Peasant Union, pp. 161–220.

15. According to *EPR*, p. 498, there were 1,115 delegates from provincial congresses of peasants and from the army. Osipova, *Klassovaia bor'ba*, p. 106, and Smirnov, *Krest'ianskie s"ezdy*, p. 115, give a total of 1,353 delegates, including 672 peasants and 681 soldiers. For accounts showing a slightly higher proportion of peasants, see Keep, p. 233.

16. *EPR*, p. 499, no. 214.

17. Keep, p. 229.

18. Osipova, *Klassovaia bor'ba*, p. 116; A. S. Smirnov, *Bol'sheviki*, p. 132; Lepeshkin, *Sovety*, pp. 58–59; Anweiler, p. 121.

19. Moiseeva, p. 29.

20. Makarova, pp. 117–18; A. S. Smirnov, *Bol'sheviki*, p. 197.

21. Moiseeva, pp. 171–74. According to Abramov, p. 200, a questionnaire distributed in fourteen provinces of the central industrial region in April 1918 showed that volost soviets had been formed in less than two percent of the volosts before October. For a review of the sources see Makarov, pp. 114–15.

22. See, for example, Osipova, *Klassovaia bor'ba*, p. 116; Moiseeva, p. 39.

23. Anweiler, p. 121.

24. Gaponenko, *Revoliutsionnoe dvizhenie posle sverzheniia*, pp. 625–709.

25. *EPR*, p. 209.

26. Gaponenko, *Revoliutsionnoe dvizhenie posle sverzheniia*, pp. 693–97.

27. *EPR*, pp. 211–13; Gaponenko, *Revoliutsionnoe dvizhenie posle sverzheniia*, p. 308. According to Pershin, citing archival sources in *Agrarnaia revoliutsiia*, 1: 306, similar instances of rejection of locally adopted measures occurred in Pskov, Kazan, Poltava, Kursk, and elsewhere.

28. Pershin, *Agrarnaia revoliutsiia*, 1: 385–86, 392.

29. *EPR*, pp. 213–15; Pershin, *Agrarnaia revoliutsiia*, 1: 291.

30. Gaponenko, *Revoliutsionnoe dvizhenie posle sverzheniia*, pp. 326–29.

31. *EPR*, p. 249; Pershin, *Agrarnaia revoliutsiia*, 1: 381–82.

32. Kostrikin, "Krest'ianskoe dvizhenie," p. 27.

33. *EPR*, p. 489, no. 141, n. 2.

34. Kostrikin, *Zemel'nye komitety*, pp. 217–18; *idem*, "Krest'ianskoe dvizhenie," pp. 28, 35–36, 39–42; Pershin, *Agrarnaia revoliutsiia*, 1: 419; Gill, p. 189. For accounts of local events by the peasants themselves (collected in 1925 by rural correspondents of *Krest'ianskaia gazeta*), see Igritskii.

35. Kostrikin, "Krest'ianskoe dvizhenie," p. 36.

36. Fulin, p. 72.

37. Kostrikin, "Krest'ianskoe dvizhenie," pp. 30, 36.

38. Osipova, *Klassovaia bor'ba*, pp. 166–67.

39. *EPR*, pp. 325, 368–69, 381–82; Pershin, *Agrarnaia revoliutsiia*, 1: 415.

40. Osipova, *Klassovaia bor'ba*, pp. 162–65.

41. Kostrikin, "Krest'ianskoe dvizhenie," pp. 33–34; Igritskii, pp. 70–71; Rubach, pp. 203–4.

42. Osipova, *Klassovaia bor'ba*, p. 168. Some of Bykhovskii's data are provided by Shestakov, 1: 1: 254–56.

43. Dubrovskii, *Krest'ianstvo*, p. 56.

44. Osipova, *Klassovaia bor'ba*, p. 169.

45. Kostrikin, *Zemel'nye komitety*, p. 313. In his later essay, "Krest'ianskoe dvizhenie," Kostrikin cites Osipova's data and omits reference to his previous calculation.

46. Osipova, *Klassovaia bor'ba*, p. 169. The total indicated here is based on incidents recorded in materials of the Main Land Committee, the agrarian section of the Petrograd Soviet, the reports of commissars to the Ministry of Internal Affairs, and local sources. The figure does not indicate the number of individual households involved in each reported incident. Cf. Pershin, *Agrarnaia revoliutsiia*, 1: 417, which indicates lower rates of conflict among peasants.

47. Osipova, *Klassovaia bor'ba*, pp. 168, 170. Unlike holdings of allotment land, holdings of purchased nonallotment land had no limitation on their size. Therefore peasant owners of consolidated farms often had much in common with nonpeasant proprietors.

48. Shestakov, 1: 2: 161.

49. *Ibid.*, p. 165.

50. *EPR*, p. 273.

51. Igritskii, p. 14.

52. *EPR*, pp. 490–91, no. 151, n. 1.

53. On the effects of the season and the agricultural cycle, see Gill, pp. 113–14, 145–46; Keep, p. 193. For further discussion of statistical inadequacies, see Mel'gunov, pp. 198–204; Keep, pp. 187–89; Pershin, *Agrarnaia revoliutsiia*, 1: 407–8; Osipova, *Klassovaia bor'ba*, pp. 158ff.

54. For a summary of different viewpoints in these debates, see Kostrikin, "Krest'ianskoe dvizhenie," pp. 37–38.

55. *APSV*, p. 70. Emphasis in the original.

56. Lenin, "Krizis nazrel," in Gaponenko, *Veliki oktiabr'*, pp. 272–78.

Chapter 10

1. *Sovetskaia istoricheskaia entsiklopediia*, 3: 886, presents different figures from a number of sources. Yet another set may be found in *Krasnyi arkhiv*, 1937, no. 84, pp. 12, 16.

2. Aver'ev, "Sovety," p. 26. Although the peasant soviets amounted to less than 5 percent of soviets represented at the congress, 23 percent of the delegates there were peasants according to TsSU, *Itogi, 1917–1927*, p. 7.

3. John Reed, *Ten Days That Shook the World*, p. 137.

4. *SDZZ*, p. 11.

5. Lutskii, "Krest'ianskie nakazy," pp. 113–61. The archive of the newspaper that originally compiled the Model has not been preserved, but Lutskii was able to locate 151 of the 242 peasant instructions in contemporary newspapers and later documentary publications.

6. *Ibid.*, p. 158.

7. Even Ginev's thoughtful account, *Agrarnyi vopros*, is routinely punctuated with the familiar chorus on SR "deceit."

8. Lenin, *PSS*, 35: 27. Lutskii, "Leninskii dekret," p. 20.

9. Dubrovskii, *Krest'ianstvo*, p. 145.

10. Ginev, *Agrarnyi vopros*, pp. 198–201.

11. Lenin, *PSS*, 35: 27. An attempt by Lutskii to present egalitarian land distribution as a deliberate Bolshevik tactic in 1917 evoked a storm of protest in Soviet historical circles. See his "O sushchnosti uravnitel'nogo zemlepol'zovaniia," in *Voprosy istorii*, 1956, no. 9, pp. 59–71, and the reply of G. V. Sharapov in the same journal, 1957, no. 3, pp. 113–19. Although he

agrees with the critics that Lutskii erred about the Bolshevik attitude toward egalitarian land distribution, Ginev (*Agrarnyi vopros*, p. 205, n. 70), has pointed to strong points in Lutskii's work and has described the criticism as excessively severe at times.

12. Danilov et al., p. 40.

13. *Ibid.*, p. 37.

14. Grekov, *Krest'iane*, 1: 184, 517; 2: 92.

15. Plekhanov, *Chernyi peredel*, no. 1, January 15, 1880; *Sochineniia*, 1: 48.

16. Chernov, *Great Russian Revolution*, p. 147.

17. Lutskii, "Likvidatsiia," p. 22.

18. Lenin, "Otvet na zaprosy krest'ian," *PSS*, 35: 56–57.

19. *SDZZ*, no. 6, pp. 16–23.

20. Lutskii, "Likvidatsiia," p. 29.

21. Nelidov, pp. 496–98.

22. *SDZZ*, no. 8, pp. 23–31.

23. Tsypkina, pp. 101, 103.

24. The material summarized in *Materialy po zemel'noi reforme* covers 33 provinces and includes local statutes and regulations on redistribution collected by NKZ. See also Pershin, *Agrarnaia revoliutsiia*, 2: 289, 295–302; Fulin, p. 92.

25. Gerasimiuk, "Uravnitel'noe raspredelenie," pp. 95–96. Cf. Snegirev, "Velikaia Oktiabr'skaia sotsialisticheskaia revoliutsiia," pp. 12–13.

26. Several such incidents are described by Keep, pp. 214–15, 400.

27. Pershin, *Agrarnaia revoliutsiia*, 2: 231; Zybkovets, pp. 29–32.

28. *Vestnik statistiki*, 1923, nos. 1–3, pp. 131–53. (Data from 29 provinces.)

29. *Materialy po zemel'noi reforme*, part 1, p. 9.

30. Osipova, "Razvitie," p. 51; Pershin, *Agrarnaia revoliutsiia*, 2: 233–34. In some cases khutor and otrub inventory was exempted from confiscation on the grounds that its owners worked the land. (*Materialy po zemel'noi reforme 1918 goda*, part 6, *Otchuzhdenie i ispol'zovanie sel'skokhoziaistvennogo inventariia* [Moscow, 1918], p. 6.)

31. Pershin, *Uchastkovoe zemlepol'zovanie*, p. 36.

32. Fulin, p. 91.

33. *Materialy po zemel'noi reforme*, part 1, p. 9; Osipova, "Razvitie," pp. 51–52; Pershin, *Agrarnaia revoliutsiia*, 2: 233. Cf. Iakovtsevskii, p. 68. Iakovtsevskii states that allotment land was never considered part of the redistributable land fund, and that land purchased or rented by peasants was very rarely included. The source he cites was published in 1918 and may have covered only the initial stage of redistribution.

34. Nikonov-Smorodin, p. 81.

35. *Materialy po zemel'noi reforme*, part 1, pp. 3, 8.

36. Osipova, "Razvitie," p. 52.

37. Gerasimiuk, "Uravnitel'noe raspredelenie," p. 98. Pershin provides detailed information on local norms of distribution in *Agrarnaia revoliutsiia*, 2: 257–89.

38. Sobolev, p. 121; *Vestnik statistiki*, 1923, nos. 1–3, p. 141.

39. Pershin, *Agrarnaia revoliutsiia*, 2: 260–61.

40. Medvedev, p. 144; Fulin, p. 93.

41. Pershin, *Agrarnaia revoliutsiia*, 2: 285; Fulin, p. 94.

42. For an example of such an approach (Karachevskii district, Orel province), see Pershin, *Agrarnaia revoliutsiia,* 2: 286.

43. *Ibid.,* 2: 225; Fulin, p. 98.

44. *Krasnyi arkhiv,* 1938, no. 88–90, p. 34; Lutskii, "K istorii konfiskatsii," p. 515.

45. Fulin, p. 94.

46. *Vestnik statistiki,* 1923, nos. 1–3, pp. 142–44.

47. Fulin, p. 97.

48. Pershin, *Agrarnaia revoliutsiia,* 2: 225; *SDZZ,* pp. 140–44.

49. Danilov, "Pereraspredelenie," p. 263.

50. *APSV,* pp. 498–506, 536, n. 146.

51. Snegirev, "Velikaia Oktiabr'skaia sotsialisticheskaia revoliutsiia," p. 23.

52. For example, Danilov et al., p. 39; Selunskaia, *Izmeneniia, 1917–1920,* p. 209.

53. Danilov, "Ob itogakh pereraspredeleniia," p. 200; see also his "Pereraspredelenie."

54. As an example of the sort of problems encountered, compare the data on land redistribution in Astrakhan presented in different parts of the volume containing Danilov's critique (Mints, *Leninskii dekret*). According to data on p. 170, peasant allotment land in the province in 1917 amounted to 1.90 million desiatins, but peasant holdings had risen to 8.17 million desiatins in 1918. On p. 291 Danilov presents data (obtained by A. S. Nifontov from NKZ RSFSR in 1923, and supposedly "corrected" the previous year) showing about the same amount of prerevolutionary peasant land (1.87 million desiatins), but gains of only 3 percent as of 1922. Danilov warns that, although these statistics supply important information for some areas, "a significant part of the data is defective." Other data he provides, on pp. 286–87, place peasant landholding in Astrakhan at 11.8 million desiatins before the revolution, with an increase of 19 percent by 1919.

55. Danilov, "Pereraspredelenie," pp. 296–97.

56. *Ibid.,* p. 300.

57. *Ibid.,* p. 304. Danilov's text reads "77 million desiatins," but appears intended to refer to hectares. Data are presented in both units throughout the article, and "hectares" accords numerically with the other data, whereas "desiatins" does not. The figures are often (necessarily) imprecise. For example, the amount of land gained by peasants in the autonomous republics of the RSFSR is said to be "8 to 9.5 million hectares" (p. 303).

58. A gain of 72 desiatins (79 hectares) would mean an increase of less than 33 percent. In 1928 Molotov criticized the TsSU data showing an overall increase of 31 percent as much too low and a "most pernicious economic and political error." (*Piatnadtsatyi s"ezd vsesoiuznoi kommunisticheskoi partii (b), Stenograficheskii otchet,* 2: 1177.)

59. Dubrovskii, *Sel'skoe khoziaistvo,* p. 153.

60. Fulin, p. 99.

61. Danilov, "Pereraspredelenie," pp. 306–7.

62. For examples of local redistribution, see Pershin, *Agrarnaia revoliutsiia,* 2: 289–338.

63. Gerasimiuk, "Uravnitel'noe raspredelenie," p. 100; Kirillov, p. 114; see also the map in Knipovich, "Napravlenie," p. 31; Fulin, p. 100.

64. Lutskii, "Peredel zemli," p. 243; Snegirev, "Raspredelenie," p. 24.

65. Carr, *Socialism in One Country*, 1: 35.
66. Fedorov, p. 19.
67. Knipovich, *Ocherk*, p. 6.
68. Anfimov, "O dolge krest'ianstva," pp. 111–12; Danilov et al., p. 39.
69. M. Kubanin, "Anti-sovetskoe krest'ianskoe dvizhenie v gody grazhdan-skoi voiny (voennogo kommunizma)," *NAF*, 1926, no. 2, p. 39; Trapeznikov, 1: 362.
70. *Vestnik statistiki*, 1923, nos. 1–3, p. 146.
71. *Istoriia sovetskogo krest' ianstva*, p. 139.
72. Lenin, *PSS*, 44: 30.
73. Kachorovsky, "Russian Land Commune," p. 575.
74. TsSU, *Trudy*, vol. 8, part 1, pp. 284–332. Karnaukhova, p. 18, places 99 percent of all land outside of that in the state land fund in communal tenure in 1920.

Chapter 11

1. Gimpel'son, p. 35.
2. *Ibid.*, p. 29.
3. Danilov et al., p. 52.
4. Chernobaev, p. 9.
5. Sharapov, p. 176.
6. Drobizhev, pp. 74–75. The list included cloth, thread and yarn, clothing, leather, harness and saddle gear, shoes and overshoes, matches, soap, candles, kerosene, lubricating oil, agricultural machinery and equipment, wire, sheet iron, horseshoes, rope goods, glass, dishes, tobacco and tobacco products, salt, and sugar and tea along with their substitutes.
7. Danilov et al., p. 52.
8. *APSV*, p. 128.
9. *Ibid.*, p. 31; Anfimov, *Rossiiskaia derevnia*, pp. 205–12.
10. Zhmurovskii, pp. 75–76.
11. Sharapov, p. 60.
12. *APSV*, pp. 177–81.
13. Chernobaev, p. 79.
14. Selunskaia, *Rabochii klass*, p. 171.
15. *Ibid.*, pp. 198, 172–73.
16. Gerasimiuk, "Kombedy," pp. 122, 125, and his "Nekotorye dannye," p. 209. The number of committees equaled 57 percent of the number of populated localities within the 33 provinces, but large settlements sometimes had two or more committees.
17. Aver'ev, *Komitety bednoty*, 1: 21–22; Selunskaia, *Rabochii klass*, p. 205. Though the decree establishing the Committees of the Poor spoke only of village and volost committees, others were formed at higher (district and provincial) levels. See Selunskaia, *Rabochii klass*, p. 201, and Nelidov, pp. 313, 315.
18. Lenin, "Tezisy doklada o taktike RKP," *PSS*, 44: 7.
19. Sobolev, pp. 155–69, 205–18.
20. Lenin, "Rech' na ob''edinennom zasedanii VTsIK, moskovskogo soveta i vserossiiskogo s''ezda professional'nykh soiuzov 17 ianvaria 1919 g.," *PSS*, 37: 419. The harvest season naturally improved collection prospects, but the 67.5 million puds collected by the Commissariat of Food Supply was only half of the required amount. See Kovalenko, p. 378.
21. Kovalenko, p. 357; Chernobaev, p. 108.
22. Chernobaev, p. 93; Kon'kova, p. 142.
23. Nelidov, pp. 273, 313; Sobolev, p. 253.

24. Mikhailov, *Mestnoe sovetskoe upravlenie*, pp. 170–75.

25. There are various interpretations in Soviet literature of the policy shift from "neutralization" to alliance with the middle peasantry. Sobolev, pp. 292–93, holds that the new policy resulted from a change within the middle peasantry itself, a greater readiness to cooperate with the government once it became apparent that the Soviet regime was winning out in the struggle against its various opponents.

26. For examples of the resistance to dissolution of the committees that did occur despite the government's cautious policy, see Zhmurovskii, pp. 115–16.

27. Aver'ev, "Ot neitralizatsii," pp. 70–76; Selunskaia, *Rabochii klass*, pp. 225–40.

28. Zhmurovskii, p. 81.

29. Abramov, p. 200.

30. Cf. Lepeshkin, *Sovety*, p. 98; Abramov, p. 200; and Makarova, p. 116.

31. Danilov et al., p. 42.

32. *Sovety*, 1: 247–48; Mikhailov, pp. 170–71.

33. Poliakov, p. 170.

34. Mikhailov, p. 75. The same point is made in nearly identical language by Nelidov, p. 272.

35. *Voprosy istorii*, 1956, no. 10, p. 104.

36. Selunskaia, *Rabochii klass*, p. 251; Gimpel'son, p. 53.

37. Gimpel'son, pp. 55–69.   38. Aver'ev and Ronin, p. 56.

39. Gimpel'son, pp. 56–60, 63.   40. Zhmurovskii, pp. 321–22.

41. Gimpel'son, p. 65.   42. *Ibid.*, pp. 60, 484.

43. Lepeshkin, p. 187.

44. Gimpel'son, pp. 138–50; *Sovety*, 2: 9.

45. Mikhailov, p. 77. The statute is included in the documentary section, pp. 245–50, and in *Sovety*, 2: 9–14.

46. For a view of the nature of democratic centralism in the relationship between local and central soviets 50 years after the October Revolution, see Aimbetov et al., pp. 35–37.

47. Mikhailov, pp. 77–78. The statement on p. 77 referring to an attempt to substitute the *volispolkom* for the *sel'sovet* (rather than for the *ispolkom* of the *sel'sovet*) appears to be simply a slip. A note to Article 8 of the decree states that "In villages where there is a volost executive committee the latter is the executive organ of the rural soviet of the given village."

48. Mikhailov, p. 79.   49. *Ibid.*, pp. 250–52.

50. Gimpel'son, pp. 186–87.   51. *Ibid.*

52. *Ibid.*, pp. 200, 496–98.

53. Lepeshkin, p. 18; Gimpel'son, pp. 496, 498.

54. Gimpel'son, pp. 187, 191, 194, 494–98.

55. *Ibid.*, pp. 489–92.

56. "Postanovleniia VII Vserossiiskogo s"ezda Sovetov o sovetskom stroitel'stve (dekabr' 1919 g.)," in Mikhailov, pp. 241–45. This measure was considered a victory for local forces protesting "vertical centralization" at the Seventh Party Congress since it established the authority of the executive committee over its departments as well as confirming that of the superior department (the principle of "dual subordination"). See Mikhailov's discussion (pp. 46–50) of "the extraordinary centralization of the economic and administrative apparatus with the development of War Communism."

57. Nelidov, pp. 272, 274 n. 95.

58. *APSV*, pp. 197–99, 231–51.

59. Nelidov, p. 501.

60. Gimpel'son, p. 371; *Statisticheskii spravochnik po narodnomu khoziaistvu*, part 1, *Sel'skoe khoziaistvo (1920–1921 g.g.)* (Moscow, 1923), p. 8.

61. The organization and functions of the land departments are defined in the "Polozhenie o zemel'nykh otdelakh gubernskikh, uezdnykh i volostnykh ispolkomov," *APSV*, pp. 231–51.

62. Gimpel'son, p. 372.

63. Grishaev, *Stroitel'stvo*, p. 55.

64. Sobolev, p. 128; Grishaev, *Stroitel'stvo*, p. 61.

65. Lepeshkin, pp. 210–14.

66. Grishaev, *Stroitel'stvo*, pp. 62–63.

67. Poliakov, p. 173. Poliakov states that more complete data are not available. For discussion of the materials that are available, see Belogurov, pp. 197–231. According to Kukushkin, p. 23, there were approximately 100,000 rural soviets in the RSFSR by 1921.

68. Poliakov, pp. 169–73; Kukushkin, p. 24.

Chapter 12

1. Plotnikov, "Krest'ianskaia obshchina," pp. 34–36.

2. Gimpel'son, p. 385.   3. *SDZZ*, pp. 83–84.

4. *Ibid*., p. 88.   5. Gimpel'son, p. 387.

6. TsSU, *Trudy*, 8: 1: 284–322. Almost all of the territory in the 39 provinces or areas, and all but a small number of the households covered in the data, were in European Russia. For 1922 see *Trudy*, 8: 5: 181, and 18: 98.

7. Snegirev, "Zemleustroistvo," p. 27. According to Knipovich, *Ocherk*, p. 24, central land officials claimed that a staff of 35,000 was required for adequate land organization work.

8. NKZ, *Sovetskoe zemleustroistvo*, p. 22.

9. Snegirev, "Zemleustroistvo," p. 29.

10. Kachorovskii, "Budushchee obshchiny," p. 346.

11. Oganovskii, "Obshchina," p. 82.

12. *Ibid*., p. 87, italics in the original.

13. Kirillov, p. 65; Pershin, *Uchastkovoe zemlepol'zovanie*, p. 44.

14. *Materialy po zemel'noi reforme*, 1: 9.

15. Kirillov, pp. 60–61.

16. Pershin, *Uchastkovoe zemlepol'zovanie*, p. 39.

17. *Ibid*., p. 39.

18. Pershin, who was sympathetic to the khutor at this time, cites primarily reports that give evidence of a desire to form individual farms; Kirillov, on the other hand, favored the small settlement, and the evidence he cites suggests that this was popular also. Taken together they reinforce the conclusion that there was a significant movement in the northwest toward a more individualized form of tenure.

19. Pershin, *Uchastkovoe zemlepol'zovanie*, p. 42.

20. *Ibid*., p. 43.

21. TsSU, *Trudy*, 8: 5: 181; *Trudy*, 18: 98.

22. Kirillov suggests (pp. 61–62) that familiarity with the model of the prosperous khutor stimulated the peasants' interest in this form of tenure, whereas

fear of the unknown was responsible for their hostility to collective forms of land use.

23. Zelenin, pp. 35–37.

24. Grishaev, *Kommuny*, p. 59; Poliakov, p. 157.

25. Lenin, "Stranichki iz dnevnika," *PSS*, 45: 367.

26. *APSV*, p. 136, Article 11(d).

27. There has been much discussion about whether nationalization in the sense of state ownership was actually introduced by either the Decree on Land or the Law on Socialization. These measures had specifically included "state lands" among those alienated from their former owners. It has been argued, however, that nationalization was the clear intent of both pieces of legislation and that it was incontrovertibly established by Article 17 of the Law on Socialization, which gave the state the right to collect differential rent on land (i.e., "surplus income" deriving from favorable physical traits of the land or its location with respect to markets). The debate, active in the early years after the revolution, was revived in the late 1950's and early 1960's when the land rights of collective farms came under discussion. See Pershin, *Agrarnaia revoliutsiia*, 2: 49–56; Ginev, pp. 250–59.

28. *APSV*, pp. 417–31.

29. Zelenin, p. 37.

30. Cf. NKZ data in *APSV*, pp. 508 and 512 (for 1919–20), and *Sovetskoe zemleustroistvo*, p. 20; Zelenin, p. 189; Grishaev, *Kommuny*, p. 66; Poliakov, pp. 154–59.

31. NKZ, *Sovetskoe zemleustroistvo*, p. 43.

32. Knipovich, "Napravlenie," p. 43.

33. Zelenin, p. 191.

34. Knipovich, "Napravlenie," pp. 35–40; Zelenin, p. 197.

35. See Dyshler, *Novye formy* and *Organizatsiia*.

36. Kubanin, "Anti-sovetskoe dvizhenie," pp. 38–39.

37. Grishaev, *Kommuny*, p. 59.

38. *Ibid.*, p. 60.

39. *Ibid.*, pp. 14–22, 73; Knipovich, "Napravlenie," p. 44.

40. *APSV*, pp. 400–403, 433–41.

41. Kraev, p. 209.

42. Grishaev, *Kommuny*, p. 20.

43. See Wesson, *Soviet Communes*, for interesting case histories.

44. Zhmurovskii, p. 113.

45. Sutton, pp. 126–29; Grishaev, *Kommuny*, pp. 71–72.

46. NKZ data (*APSV*, p. 512) show an increase in 1921; however, Knipovich, in his *Ocherk* (p. 20) and "Napravlenie" (p. 42), states that the *kommuny* declined in number after July 1919. His data show only half as many *kommuny* existing in 1921 as do Snegirev's data in Table 16. According to *Sel'skoe i lesnoe khoziaistvo*, 1923, no. 9, p. 27, there were only 1,710 *kommuny* in 1921, averaging 134 desiatins apiece.

47. Grishaev, *Kommuny*, p. 66. The data cover 32 provinces in the European part of the RSFSR.

48. Kalinin, p. 91.

49. Selunskaia, *Rabochii klass*, p. 266.

50. *APSV*, pp. 462–70. Later versions were less liberal.

51. Knipovich, *Ocherk*, pp. 18, 44.

52. *Ibid.*, p. 44.

53. Grishaev, *Kommuny*, p. 64.

54. Knipovich, *Ocherk*, p. 18. According to this source, 613,000 individuals were in collectives in the RSFSR in November 1920.

55. NKZ, *Sovetskoe zemleustroistvo*, p. 52.

Chapter 13

1. Steven Wheatcroft has pursued a number of questions raised in a discussion of the grain statistics by Jerzy Karcz and R. W. Davies in *Soviet Studies* (April 1967, January and October 1970). Wheatcroft summarizes the data revisions, analyzes the bases of changes, and points out the implications of the data modifications in "The Reliability of Russian Prewar Grain Output Statistics," pp. 157–80. See also Jasny, *Socialized Agriculture*, pp. 725–27.

2. Moshkov, p. 20 n. 1. The explanation of the latest downward revision offered here appears to be standard in recent Soviet literature (e.g., *SDD*, 1: 284).

3. See Karcz, "Grain Front," p. 270.

4. Poliakov, pp. 56–60. The figures in Table 17 have been rounded to the nearest whole number and therefore show a drop of 15 or 30 percent.

5. Oganovskii and Kondrat'ev, p. 113.

6. Poliakov, pp. 63–64.

7. TsSU, *Sel'skoe khoziaistvo SSSR, statisticheskii sbornik* (1971), p. 33; Jasny, *Socialized Agriculture*, p. 201; see also Pestrzhetskii, p. 48.

8. TsSU, *Trudy*, 18: 100. The regions covered were: Far North, Lake, Moscow-Industrial, Central Agricultural, Cis-Ural, Lower Volga, and Western Siberia. Data incomplete.

9. TsSU, *Predvaritel'nye itogi*, pp. 3–4.

10. Poliakov, p. 54.

11. TsSU, *Trudy*, 8: 1: 344.

12. *Ibid.*, 18: 116, 136–37.

13. Oganovskii and Kondrat'ev, p. 132; Knipovich, *Ocherk*, p. 47.

14. Oganovskii and Kondrat'ev, pp. 308–9.

15. *APSV*, pp. 516–17.   16. Timoshenko, p. 159.

17. TsSU, *Trudy*, 18: 122–25.   18. Timoshenko, pp. 437–40.

19. Despite official interdiction, the private grain trade was said to have supplied more than half of all grain and flour consumed by the urban population in 1918–19 and up to 20 percent in 1920. (Larin, p. 37.)

20. Marx and Engels, p. 16.

21. TsSU, *Trudy*, 7: 1: 7: 5–55.

22. *Ibid.*, 18: 123.

23. TsSU, *Itogi, 1917–1927*, p. 357.

24. TsSU, *Trudy*, 18: 137.

25. *Ibid.*, 8: 6: 2: 202.

26. *Ibid.*, p. 220.

27. TsSU, *Itogi, 1917–1927*, p. 356.

28. Lenin, "Doklad o prodovol'stvennom naloge," *PSS*, 43: 303.

29. See Donkov, *Antonovshchina*, and Radkey, *Unknown Civil War*.

30. Radkey, *Unknown Civil War*, p. 229.

31. Lenin, "Doklad o zamene razverstki natural'nym nalogom," *PSS*, 43: 60.
32. Miliukov, 1: *Ocherk* 3.
33. Kirillov, p. 244.

Chapter 14

1. Lenin, "Doklad o zamene razverstki natural'nym nalogom," *PSS*, 43: 57.
2. M. N. Pokrovskii, p. 10.
3. Radkey, *Unknown Civil War*, 261.
4. NKZ, *Novoe zakonodatel'stvo*, p. 1.
5. Tsybul'skii, pp. 31–42. Barter proved unsuccessful, partly because of "tradition and the awesome force of habit of money" (p. 40).
6. *SDZZ*, no. 83, p. 127.
7. Danilov, "Nekotorye itogi," p. 25.
8. *SDZZ*, pp. 155–79, 182–83.
9. Although the term had not been used in prerevolutionary legislation, it had been considered and rejected in connection with the law of May 29, 1911. (Plotnikov, "Zemel'noe obshchestvo," p. 36.) According to Novitskii, it was first used officially in connection with the Statute on Land Organization issued on March 11, 1919. ("Zemel'noe obshchestvo," p. 72.)
10. Plotnikov, "Organizatsiia," p. 9.
11. Kozlov, p. 5.
12. Taniuchi, *Village Gathering*, p. 21.
13. Novitskii, "Zemel'noe obshchestvo," p. 77.
14. *Ibid.*, p. 72, n. 1.
15. Danilov, "Zemel'nye otnosheniia," pp. 97–98, 100 n. 46.
16. *Ibid.*, p. 89.
17. Kozlov, p. 21.
18. Anfimov and Zyrianov, p. 33.
19. *Sobranie ukazonenii RSFSR*, 1927, no. 51, art. 333.
20. Novitskii, "Zemel'noe obshchestvo," pp. 78, 81, 95 n. 2.
21. *SDD*, 1: 53.
22. *SDZZ*, p. 655.
23. *SDD*, 1: 98; Novitskii, p. 98 n. 1.
24. Karpinskii, "Nekotorye techenie," pp. 24–25.
25. *Sobranie ukazonenii RSFSR*, 1924, no. 60, art. 586.
26. *SDZZ*, p. 650–51.
27. Novitskii, "Zemel'noe obshchestvo," p. 86.
28. *SDZZ*, pp. 161, 190, 200.
29. *Zemel'nyi kodeks RSFSR*, pp. 180–83.
30. Rudin, p. 21.
31. Shul'gin, p. 23.
32. *SDZZ*, pp. 159–60. For a useful diagrammatic summary of the rural administrative structure dealing with land affairs, see Male, pp. 102, 104.
33. *SDD*, 1: 96.
34. Chugunov, *Rabota*, p. 126; Rezunov, p. 43.
35. *Bednota*, March 3, 1925.
36. For the 1922 data see Belogurov, pp. 204–9; for 1924/25, Kukushkin, p. 123; for 1927, *Pravda*, March 15, 1929, and May 29, 1929.
37. Carr, *Socialism*, 1: 249.
38. Relevant data from the 1926 census are conveniently summarized and

analyzed by Danilov, *SDD*, vol. 1, chap. 1. For the data cited here see pp. 24–25, 30, 39, 41–42. Changing fertility patterns can be traced in Coale et al., pp. 16, 20–23.

39. *SDD*, 1: 46–47.

40. Gazalova, *Droblenie, 1921–1928*, pp. 13–14.

41. *SDZZ*, p. 163.

42. *SDD*, 1: 213–16. Danilov believes the data on households may be exaggerated by 3 to 5 percent and suggests that 24 million is probably a more realistic figure. The official data must be utilized, however, for comparison with other statistical materials.

43. Gazalova, "Statisticheskie istochniki," pp. 273–74.

44. Gazalova, *Droblenie, 1921–1928*, p. 7.

45. Chaianov, "Peasant Farm Organization," in Thorner, pp. 58–60, 68, 77–80.

46. L. N. Kritsman, "O vnutrennikh protivorechiiakh krest'ianskogo dvora," in *Proletarskaia revoliutsiia i derevnia* (Moscow, 1929), pp. 506–10. The article was published as an introduction to M. I. Kubanin's *Klassovaia sushchnost' protsessa drobleniia krest'ianskikh khoziaistv*. It appeared also in *NAF*, 1929, no. 3, pp. 7–26.

47. *SDD*, 1: 46–47.

48. Quoted in *SDD*, 1: 236.

49. TsSU, *Statisticheskii spravochnik za 1928 g.*, p. 74. On the rural reaction, see Farnsworth, pp. 139–65.

50. *Krest'ianskaia entsiklopediia*, 2–3: 358.

51. Kindeev, *Voprosy zemleustroistva*, pp. 71–72.

52. Gazalova, "Zemel'nyi sud," p. 211.

53. *SDD*, 1: 155.

54. *Piatnadtsatyi s"ezd*, 2: 1362.

55. Pershin, "Vnutriselennaia cherespolosnost'," p. 32; *SDD*, 1: 126.

56. Spektor, "Raspad," pp. 22–26.

57. *SDD*, 1: 157.

58. See Article 134, Law of May 22, 1922. Most land organization was undertaken at the request of the land users, but work could be initiated by the land agencies in cases specified under Article 168 of the Land Code.

59. TsIK, 4 sessiia, 4 sozyv, *Biulleten*, no. 13, p. 7.

60. Pershin, "Vnutriselennaia cherespolosnost'," p. 42.

61. TsSU, *Sel'skoe khoziaistvo SSSR, 1925–1928*, p. 454; *SDD*, 1: 169.

62. TsIK, 4 sessiia, 4 sozyv, *Biulleten*, no. 13, p. 5; *SDD*, 1: 169.

63. On the extent of multi-field rotations, cf. Carr, *Foundations*, 1: 1: 231 and *SDD*, 1: 278. Carr's sources show 13.7 million hectares under multi-field rotation in the spring of 1928; Danilov gives a figure of 17.7 million hectares for 1927. For the effectiveness of land organization in improving rotation in the various sectors, see Kindeev, *Voprosy zemleustroistva*, p. 81. Data on the average size of peasant holdings and cultivated area are from *SDD*, 1: 224.

64. TsIK, 4 sessiia, 4 sozyv, *Biulleten*, no. 13, p. 5.

65. *SDD*, 1: 127.

66. *Ibid.*, pp. 131–36.

67. TsIK, 4 sessiia, 4 sozyv, *Biulleten*, no. 13, p. 5; *SDD*, 1: 163–64.

68. Spektor, "Raspad," p. 40.   69. Trapeznikov, 2: 75.

70. *SDD*, 1: 160–61.   71. *Pravda*, January 12, 1928.

72. *Ibid.*, February 22, 1928; May 18, 1928.

73. *Stenograficheskii otchet tret'ego vserossiiskogo soveshchaniia zemorganov, 28 fevralia–7 marta 1926 g.*, p. 425.

74. Mirtov, p. 9.

75. *Kollektivist*, 1925, no. 4, p. 61.

76. *Pravda*, January 12, 1928.

77. *SDD*, 1: 140.

78. *SDZZ*, pp. 219–20.

79. Danilov, "Zemel'nye otnosheniia," p. 112.

80. *SDZZ*, p. 250.

81. *Ibid.*, p. 257.

82. *Pravda*, November 26, 1927; *SDZZ*, pp. 341–44.

83. *Pravda*, November 19, 1929.   84. *Ibid.*, October 25, 1929.

85. I. Smirnov, p. 27.   86. Murav'ev, p. 334.

87. Nikonov-Smorodin, pp. 98–99; *Pravda*, December 9, 1928.

88. *Kollektivist*, 1925, no. 4, p. 61; M. I. Kubanin, "Raspredelenie," part 1, pp. 19–20; part 2, p. 59.

89. Novitskii, "Novye formy," p. 100.

90. *SDD*, 1: 187; *Pravda*, January 5, 1928.

91. NKZ, *Sovetskoe zemleustroistvo*, p. 205; *Krest'ianskaia entsiklopediia*, 2–3: 312; Spektor, "Zemel'naia registratsiia," pp. 16–19.

92. Among them, Trapeznikov (1: 374–75), Ivanov (p. 5), Kozlov (pp. 3–8), and Suchkov ("O formakh zemlepol'zovaniia," pp. 77–82).

93. *Statisticheskii spravochnik za 1928 g.* (Moscow, 1929), p. 290; *Pravda*, April 2, 1929.

94. For example, *Pravda*, November 24, 1928; January 4, 1929.

95. Rezunov, pp. 24–30; I. Kozhikov, p. 67.

96. *SDD*, 1: 97 n. 80.

97. Kukushkin, p. 23. For other estimates on rural soviets see Poliakov, p. 173.

98. Lepeshkin, *Mestnye organy*, p. 124.

99. NKVD, p. 13.

100. Kukushkin, p. 120.

101. Mikhailov, *Mestnoe sovetskoe upravlenie: konspekt i materialy*, p. 447; NKVD, pp. 13–14.

102. Lepeshkin, *Mestnye organy*, p. 132 n. 3. This was after the consolidation of rural soviets had begun, but before Pskov had become an okrug.

103. Osokina, p. 47.

104. The first figure comes from Miliutin's report in TsIK, 3 sessiia, 4 sozyv, p. 724; the second is from *Derevenskii kommunist*, 1928, no. 22, p. 14, as cited by Taniuchi, *Village Gathering*, p. 12. Neither figure appears to be exact. Miliutin warned that he was not sure his data were complete, and eight months later referred more loosely to "over 300,000" land societies. See his report in TsIK, 4 sessiia, 4 sozyv, p. 22. Unfortunately, there appear to be no data beyond these global figures on the total number of communes in the 1920's.

105. NKVD, 1928, p. 14.

106. *SDD*, 1: 213.

107. TsSU, *Trudy*, 8: 5: 182. Data have been converted from desiatins.

Chapter 15

1. Lenin, "Piat let rossiiskoi revoliutsii i perspektiv mirovoi revoliutsii (doklad na IV kongresse kominterna 13 noiabria [1922])," *PSS*, 45: 285.

2. See Wheatcroft, "Reliability," pp. 177–78.

3. TsSU, *Statisticheskii spravochnik za 1928*, pp. 2–5.

4. See Wheatcroft, "Climatic and Weather Change." Even before the change of regime Russia had been a leader in this field. Study of the relationship between meteorological factors and grain yields was advanced in the NEP period by the eminent TsSU statisticians V. M. Obukhov and N. S. Chetverikov. Articles by both appeared in a book edited by A. V. Chaianov in 1926 (*Problemy urozhaia*), and in the following year more of Obukhov's work was published in a collection edited by V. G. Groman (*Vliianie neurozhaev*). In 1928 Chetverikov produced a major volume of prewar crop data, intended to facilitate analysis of the influence of climatological factors on yields. As the decade drew to a close, however, changed political conditions limited the potential of scientific work in this area. In 1949, four years after his death, a collection of Obukhov's writing was published under S. G. Strumilin's editorship (*Urozhainost*). The work is cited by Danilov (*SDD*, 1: 282), whose frequent references to the effect of climatological factors on agrarian developments of the 1920's reflect a revival of interest in the topic. Chetverikov's investigations were recently reprinted as *Statisticheskie issledovaniia*.

5. Iakovlev, *K voprosu*, p. 382.

6. TsSU, *Statisticheskii spravochnik za 1928*, p. 722. Exceptions to the general decline were tractors (none in 1913) and electrical machinery (7,400 tons in 1913; 9,000 tons in 1927/28). For the ruble value and tonnage of imports of agricultural machinery and tractors for 1913 and 1920–32, see *Sotsialisticheskoe stroitel'stvo SSSR*, 1934, pp. 386–89.

7. Danilov, *Sozdanie*, pp. 387–90; *SDD*, 1: 275.

8. Danilov, *Sozdanie*, p. 415.

9. *Ibid.*, pp. 436–37.

10. On December 4, 1928, *Pravda* reported 28,000 tractors in agriculture, with 25,500 of these in cooperatives. On April 4, 1929, the number of tractors is given as 36,000; on April 16, 1929, as 37,000. According to TsSU, *Statisticheskii spravochnik za 1928*, p. 292, the number of domestically produced tractors in the country grew from 1,500 in 1925 to 3,700 in 1928; the number of imported tractors rose from 2,600 in 1924 to 32,000 in 1928.

11. Lenin's views on cooperativism evolved over time and have been subject to different interpretations. For a summary, see Carr, *Foundations*, 1: 2: 920–24; for amplification, see Kim, part 2, pp. 93–211.

12. The figures on and categorizations of cooperatives vary considerably in different sources. Prewar data are from TsSU, *Trudy*, 18: 334; later figures, from TsSU, *Itogi, 1917–1927*, p. 419, and *Statisticheskii spravochnik za 1928*, pp. 783–87, 791. The membership in 1929 was reported in Kalinin's speech to the Sixteenth Party Conference, *Pravda*, April 2, 1929.

13. TsSU, *Itogi, 1917–1927*, p. 357.

14. *Ibid.*, pp. 355–56.

15. *Ibid.*, p. 354.

16. *Ibid.*

17. TsSU, *Statisticheskii spravochnik za 1928*, pp. 2–5.

18. *Dvenadtsatyi s"ezd*, p. 393.

19. Carr, *Interregnum*, p. 98. The value of agricultural products marketed in 1923/24 was about a third less than in 1922/23 (in 1913 prices). See V. A. Arkhipov and L. F. Morozov, *Bor'ba protiv kapitalisticheskikh elementov v promyshlennosti i torgovle, 20ᵉ–nachalo 30ᵏʰ godov* (Moscow, 1978), p. 104.

20. *Dvenadtsatyi s"ezd*, p. 576.

21. *Trinadtsatyi s"ezd*, p. 396.

22. Carr, *Interregnum*, p. 99. Carr's monumental scholarship in laying out the developments of this entire period leaves all students of the 1920's in his debt, but one might question his acceptance of the official position on this point.

23. Millar, "Reformulation," p. 222.

24. *Ibid.*, p. 225.

25. Corinne A. Guntzel, "Soviet Agricultural Pricing Policy and the Scissors Crisis of 1922–23" (Ph.D. diss., University of Illinois, Urbana, 1972), cited by James Millar in *Problems of Communism* (July–August 1976), p. 51 n. 6.

26. TsSU, *Itogi, 1917–1927*, p. 354. For more detailed annual data see TsSU, *Trudy, 30, Sostoianie pitaniia.*

27. Carr, *Socialism*, 1: 207–9.

28. *Ibid.*, p. 209.

29. The slogan was first used by Zinov'ev, *Pravda*, July 30, 1924.

30. Carr, *Socialism*, 1: 305.

31. *Ibid.*, 1: 313–14.

32. *NAF*, 1926, no. 5–6, p. 121.

33. *Chetyrnadtsatyi s"ezd*, pp. 263–64, 416.

34. TsSu, *Itogi, 1917–1927*, p. 418.

35. *Ibid.*, p. 357.

36. *Ibid.*, pp. 360–61. Per capita grain consumption was down slightly in the towns, but the intake of meat, milk, and sugar was up.

37. TsUNKhU, p. 377.

38. *Pravda*, November 13, 14, and 15, 1925.

39. TsSU, *Itogi, 1917–1927*, p. 386.

40. TsUNKhU, pp. 377–79, 382–83.

41. Moshkov, p. 29.

42. TsSU, *Statisticheskii spravochnik za 1928*, pp. 703, 711; TsUNKhU, p. 383.

43. *Piatnadtsatyi s"ezd*, 2: 1359.

Chapter 16

1. Miliutin, "Vrednye mneniia ob industrializatsii," *NAF*, 1927, no. 6, p. 7.

2. Jasny, *Socialized Agriculture*, p. 773.

3. Belianova, pp. 28–37. One of the most prominent of those involved in discussing the declining curve was V. Bazarov; on the contributions of Bazarov and Groman see Jasny, *Soviet Economists*, pp. 126–27.

4. Preobrazhenskii's views are summarized in the excellent article by Alexander Erlich, "Preobrazhenskii and the Economics of Soviet Industrialization." The entire controversy is analyzed in Erlich's *The Soviet Industrialization Debate, 1924–1928.*

5. The question of plant obsolescence and of capital investment in industry

has been recently reviewed and reassessed, but the realities of the economic situation are of less concern here than the perceptions that motivated contemporaries in the debates of the 1920's.

6. Preobrazhenskii, *Novaia ekonomika*, pp. 57–59. The second edition of the work has been translated by Brian Pearce as *The New Economics*. Material from the lengthy foreword to the second edition is cited below from the English version. Preobrazhenskii credits the Soviet economist V. M. Smirnov with coining the term "primitive socialist accumulation."

7. Preobrazhenskii, *New Economics*, p. 38.

8. Preobrazhenskii, *Novaia ekonomika*, p. 58.

9. Preobrazhenskii, "Perspektivy," p. 201.

10. Preobrazhenskii, *New Economics*, pp. 39–40.

11. Bukharin, *Nekotorye voprosy*, pp. 63–70.

12. *Ibid.*, pp. 12–13.

13. For discussion of Bukharin's economic views, see Lewin, part 1, esp. pp. 41–48.

14. A discussion of the debate on agricultural policy as part of the political factionalism and the power struggle of the period is available in Bronger, *Kampf*.

15. Shanin, pp. 25–39. Shanin challenged Preobrazhenskii in a series of articles in *NAF*, 1926, nos. 9, 10, 11–12; 1927, no. 1.

16. S. Strumilin, *Na khoziaistvennom fronte* (Moscow, 1925), pp. 215–17. Cited by Carr, *Interregnum*, p. 22.

17. Varga, pp. 15–20.

18. Different uses and users of the term are discussed by Nikhulikhin, pp. 21–33.

19. TsUNKhU, p. 166; see also TsSU, *Statisticheskii spravochnik za 1928*, p. 292.

20. Preobrazhenskii, *Novaia ekonomika*, p. 208.

21. Lenin, "Doklad o rabote v derevne, 23 marta," *PSS*, 38: 204.

22. This was made clear in a 1922 publication in which Preobrazhenskii presented a "review" of NEP in the form of a lecture hypothetically delivered in 1970. (*Ot NEP^a k sotsializmu*, p. 27).

23. Preobrazhenskii, "Perspektivy," p. 203.

24. Lenin, "Doklad VTsIK^a i SNK^{ov} o vneshnei i vnutrennei politike," *PSS*, 42: 158. For an explanation of the comments on the flea market, see Smrukov and Matskevich, p. 11.

25. Dubrovskii, *Ocherk*, pp. 353–55.

26. See *NAF*, 1926, no. 5–6, pp. 219–32.

27. Jasny, *Socialized Agriculture*, p. 157n.

28. On the institutional organization of rural studies in the 1920's, see Solomon, pp. 22–27.

29. Chaianov, *Optimal'nye razmery*. In the mid-1920's Varga too supported the individual peasant farm.

30. Carr, *Foundations*, 1: 1: 20–21.

31. Even Carr's terminology shifts as his narrative moves along with the decade. Cf. *Interregnum*, p. 98, and *Socialism*, 1: 209. For a report on a debate on differentiation held in the Institute of Agricultural Economics in 1927, see Solomon, pp. 115–25.

32. *SDZZ*, pp. 112–13, 246. Provisions describing the personal property

that could be taken along by the evicted were supplied only in June. See *SDZZ*, p. 236.

33. Mikhailov, pp. 400–401.

34. On the article and its reception, see Carr, *Socialism*, 1: 306, 324–25.

35. The question was first raised as a historical and methodological problem by Lewin in "Who Was the Soviet Kulak?," pp. 189–212. It was pursued, along with the whole problem of stratification within the peasantry, in Lewin's *Russian Peasants*, pp. 41–81.

36. *Bednota*, July 3, 4, 5, 6, and 7, 1925.

37. *Ibid.*, April 5, 1925.

38. Gazalova, "Statisticheskie istochniki," pp. 267–68, 287.

39. Many of the reports of the Scientific Research Institute of Agricultural Economics were published in the NKZ publication *Puti sel'skogo khoziaistvo* in 1927; those of the Agrarian Section of the Communist Academy appeared in *NAF*.

40. *Piatnadtsatyi s"ezd*, 2: 1183.

41. A study by Larin, "Chastnyi kapital," pp. 43–49, although it stressed the fact of differentiation, placed only 2 percent of the peasantry in "the capitalist group." Dubrovskii, in "Rassloenie," pp. 31, 41, dismissed the kulak alarms of the Left as slander against the Party. He calculated that the kulak sector was under 5 percent, and growing slowly. A recent source, Selunskaia, *Izmeneniia 1921–* (p. 98), states that kulaks comprised 3.9 percent of the peasantry in 1926/27, but (in connection with another topic, p. 94) indicates that they were 2.2 percent of the rural population of the RSFSR in 1928/29.

42. NKRKI, *K voprosu o sotsialisticheskom pereustroistve sel'skogo khoziaistva: Materialy issledovaniia NKRKI SSSR* (Leningrad, 1928), p. xii.

43. Kriashcheva, pp. 82, 170–71.

44. Jasny, *Socialized Agriculture*, pp. 176–79; Litoshenko, p. 34.

45. Bokarev, p. 130.

46. *SDD*, 1: 224. Farming was not the only source of peasant income. A substantial part of rural income (from a third to a half) was derived from other sources, including work in trades, crafts, industry, forestry, construction, and mining.

47. Selunskaia, *Izmeneniia, 1921–*, pp. 89, 96–97.

48. Arguments for the position that households were impoverished by divisions are presented by Brysiakin, pp. 77–78. For alternative views, see Chernomorskii, "Vyborochnye obsledovaniia," pp. 38–39; and Gazalova, "Droblenie," p. 16.

49. Selunskaia, *Izmeneniia, 1921–*, p. 97; Dubrovskii, "Rassloenie," p. 31.

50. Selunskaia, *Izmeneniia, 1921–*, p. 91.

51. *Piatnadtsatyi s"ezd*, 2: 1183.

52. *SDD*, 2: 104.

53. *SDZZ*, p. 296. The term of leasing land now was reduced to a maximum of six years.

54. *SDD*, 2: 138.

55. Selunskaia, *Izmeneniia, 1921–*, p. 99.

56. There were approximately the same number of day workers (2.5 million) in agriculture in 1927. (Selunskaia, *Izmeneniia, 1921–*, p. 74; *SDD*, 2: 131.)

57. *SDD*, 2: 44.

58. *Ibid.*, p. 45.

59. L. Kamenev, *Stat'i i rechi*, 12 (Moscow, 1926): 357.

60. *Chetyrnadtsatyi s"ezd*, p. 264.

61. Nemchinov's absolute data are reproduced in Karcz, "Grain Problem," p. 402, with puds converted to tons.

62. For example, in *Pravda*, June 2, 1928, July 13, 1928, and April 3, 1929.

63. For a detailed discussion of the data, see Davies, "Grain Statistics"; Karcz, "Grain Problem"; and Wheatcroft, "Reliability." Soviet economist A. A. Barsov contends that the elimination of the more productive estates and of kulak holdings had little to do with the decline in marketing. In his view, the increased consumption of the previously underfed peasant masses was responsible for the marketing situation in the 1920's. See his *Balans*, pp. 22, 23.

64. There was talk of a "Right deviation" as early as the Fourteenth Party Congress, although it was not treated as seriously at that time as the Left heresy. See *Chetyrnadtsatyi s"ezd*, p. 416.

65. Bukharin and Preobrazhenskii, pp. 298–99.

66. Sukhanov, pp. 97–110; M. I. Kubanin, "Obshchina," pp. 111–26. The articles were reprinted in *Osnovnye nachala zemlepol'zovanii i zemleustroistva*, published by the Communist Academy (Moscow, 1927), pp. 86–124.

67. Sukhanov, pp. 103–4, 107.

68. This point was increasingly emphasized by defenders of the commune as the movement toward collectivization gained ground later. See Suchkov, "O formakh zemlepol'zovaniia," p. 79, and his "Dvor ili obshchina."

69. Sukhanov, p. 110.

70. *Arkhiv K. Marksa i F. Engel'sa*, 1: 265–86.

71. *Ibid.*, p. 285 (3d draft).

72. Kubanin, "Obshchina," p. 111.

73. See Zdanovich, p. 42.

74. Cf. Danilov, "Zemel'nye otnosheniia," pp. 110–11, for contrary evidence.

75. Kachorovskii had noted the similarities of Soviet and Stolypin legislation in an article published a short time earlier, "Budushchee obshchiny."

76. Marx's views on the Russian commune are discussed by Mitrany, pp. 56ff, and by Volin, *Russian Agriculture*, pp. 83–85.

77. E.g., Zenzinov, "Popravshaia gramota Marksa"; Suchkov, "O formakh zemlepol'zovaniia."

78. The drafts were found in Lafargue's collection of Marx's papers in 1911, but the letter itself turned up only in 1923 in Akselrod's papers in Berlin. Riazanov, who published all the material in 1924, states in his introduction (Marx and Engels, *Arkhiv*, p. 265) that Plekhanov, Zasulich, and possibly Akselrod had denied the existence of a letter in 1911. There was speculation at the time that it had been deliberately suppressed because of its affinities with Populist views. Another interesting thread is that Bukharin had collaborated with Riazanov in 1913 in establishing the sequence of the undated drafts. See Zenzinov, pp. 393–402.

79. As such, it could be cited in a variety of circumstances, and it proved most useful. Pershin, for example, used the drafts to bolster an attack on Preobrazhenskii.

80. *Pravda*, November 25, 1928.

81. *NAF*, 1926, no. 9, p. 117.

82. Zdanovich, p. 48.

83. *Ibid.*, p. 47.

Chapter 17

1. Nelidov, p. 513.
2. Mikhailov, pp. 264–70.
3. *SDZZ*, p. 144. The work of the commissions is described by Gazalova in "Zemel'nyi sud." They were abolished in October 1930.
4. *Sobranie uzakonenii i rasporiazhenii raboche-krest'ianskogo pravitel'stva RSFSR*, 1924, no. 82, art. 827.
5. Kolesnikov, pp. 18–20; Mikhailov, pp. 302–8; *SDZZ*, p. 221.
6. *Sobranie uzakonenii*, 1927, no. 51, art. 333. The title of the statute used the word *sobraniia* for "assemblies," but this was followed by *skhody* in parentheses.
7. E.g., Rezunov, pp. 24–26; Zdanovich, p. 41; I. Kozhikov, p. 68.
8. Chugunov, *Chto pokazali perevybory*, p. 6.
9. Kukushkin, p. 165.
10. *Ibid.*, p. 120; Rezunov, p. 36.
11. *Pravda*, March 2, 1929; May 18, 1929.
12. Kukushkin, p. 290.
13. NKVD, pp. 13–20. On p. 20 the average number of settlements per rural soviet in the European RSFSR is said to be six. However, data on the number of settlements and soviets on pp. 13–14 indicate an average of close to eight for both the RSFSR and the USSR. On p. 14 the total number of households in the USSR is given as 23.9 million, but according to Danilov, *SDD*, 1: 213, the number of peasant households in 1927 was 25 million.
14. *Bednota*, March 21, 1925.
15. Iakovlev, *Nasha derevnia*, p. 130.
16. *Vlast' sovetov*, August 15, 1926.
17. Kozhikov, p. 68.
18. Shirokov, p. 43; Rezunov, p. 33; Kozhikov, p. 67.
19. Rezunov, p. 47.
20. *Vlast' sovetov*, 1928, no. 23–24, p. 40.
21. Rezunov, pp. 27–29.
22. Kretov, pp. 77–78.
23. Iakovlev, *K voprosu*, p. 130.
24. Rezunov, pp. 33–34. Osokina's data (pp. 65–66) confirm the pattern for Siberia, although some change is evident from 1928.
25. Rezunov, pp. 42–44.
26. For the treatment of women in rural political life, see Carr, *Socialism*, 2: 344 n. 3.
27. Rezunov, p. 45.
28. The statement came originally from the NKRKI report. It is quoted by Kozhikov, p. 68, and Rezunov, p. 30, among others.
29. Rezunov, p. 31.
30. Chugunov, *Chto pokazali perevybory*, p. 11.
31. Rezunov, p. 36 (for the first set of figures); Angarov, p. 34.
32. Excerpts from the Ukrainian statute are included in Rezunov, pp. 74–76.
33. Chugunov, *Rabota*, pp. 26, 55.
34. *Piatnadtsatyi s"ezd*, 2: 1086, 1281.
35. *Pravda*, January 5, 1928.

36. *Bednota*, January 14, 1928.

37. *Pravda*, May 20, 1928. The report was made in March.

38. Pomotskii, p. 1.

39. Novitskii, "Novye formy," p. 105.

40. See Emmons and Vucinich, eds., *The Zemstvo in Russia*.

41. Podol'skii, pp. 8, 28.

42. Rezunov, p. 56; Kozhikov, pp. 75–76.

43. *Sobranie uzakonenii*, 1926, no. 92, art. 668; 1927, no. 79, art. 533.

44. The figure of 16 million rubles was reported by A. S. Enukidze at the Fifteenth Party Congress and was said to be for the USSR. The figure of 80 million rubles was attributed to the Commissariat of Finance, that of 100 million to NKRKI (*Piatnadtsatyi s"ezd*, p. 1112). *Pravda*, May 20, 1928, gives 16 million as the income of rural soviets in the RSFSR, and 70 million as the income of land societies there. Kukushkin also, p. 70, states that rural soviets had an income of 16 million rubles, but places the income of land societies in the RSFSR at approximately 40–50 million. Angarov, p. 55, reports that rural soviets had an income of 25,000 rubles in 1927/28. There was no official accounting of the budgets of land societies in the RSFSR. For some scattered data for other territories, see Kozhikov, p. 65.

45. Rezunov, p. 7.

46. Chugunov, *Rabota*, p. 72.

47. *Pravda*, May 18, 1929, and June 27, 1929; Osokina, p. 67; Zelenin, p. 324.

48. Zdanovich, p. 53.

49. *Pravda*, May 18, 1929.

50. Iakovlev, *Nasha derevnia*, pp. 129–30.

51. *Ibid.*, p. 130.

52. Rezunov, p. 35. According to Angarov, p. 17, only the kulaks looked on the rural soviet as an "organ for the extraction of taxes."

53. *Pravda*, May 20, 1928. Italics in the original.

54. Rezunov, pp. 14–15.

55. *Ibid.*, p. 11.

56. *Bednota*, March 6, 1925.

57. According to Kiselev, the main source of income of land societies was land rental. See *Pravda*, May 20, 1928. Osokina, citing archival materials, states (p. 71) that 50 percent of the income of the societies was from self-taxation. Rezunov's data is inconclusive, showing each source predominant in different cases.

58. *Sovetskoe stroitel'stvo*, 1927, no. 4, pp. 91–92; Rezunov, p. 13.

59. *Sobranie zakonov i rasporiazhenii raboche-krest'ianskogo pravitel'stva SSSR*, 1927, no. 51, art. 509. On self-taxation, see Carr, *Foundations*, 2: 464–68; Taniuchi, *Village Gathering*, pp. 53–67; Osokina, pp. 72–78.

60. *Sobranie zakonov*, 1928, no. 3, art. 29; *Pravda*, January 8, 1928.

61. *Sobranie uzakonenii*, 1928, no. 8, art. 73.

62. Carr, *Foundations*, 2: 257.

63. Kukushkin, p. 170; *Pravda*, May 20, 1928; Carr, *Foundations*, 2: 485. Some areas of the country had higher rates: in the Volga German ASSR all rural soviets had budgets after 1924; in the Northern Caucasus krai almost 40 percent had budgets in 1927; in Siberia 25 percent had budgets at the beginning of 1929. See Rezunov, p. 58; Osokina, p. 69.

64. Rezunov, pp. 34, 50.

65. Kozhikov, p. 75.

66. Zdanovich, p. 51.

67. *Pravda*, May 20, 1928.

68. *Piatnadtsatyi s"ezd*, 2: 1217, 1386–87.

69. See, for example, *Bednota*, June 15, 1928; Rezunov, pp. 33, 48–50; Zdanovich, p. 46.

Chapter 18

1. Davies and Wheatcroft, pp. 790–802.

2. *Sobranie zakonov*, 1927, no. 37, art. 373.

3. *Kollektivizatsiia*, p. 15.

4. *Ibid.*, p. 143.

5. *Piatnadtsatyi s"ezd*, 2: 1358–63. See also Davies and Wheatcroft, p. 797.

6. *Kollektivizatsiia*, p. 21 (emphasis in the original); Lewin, *Russian Peasants*, p. 209. For an informative discussion of the 1928 crisis, see chapter 9 of Lewin's work.

7. Article by M. Vol'f, chief of the agricultural division of the State Planning Commission, "Perezhivaem li my krizis zernogo khoziaistva?," *Pravda*, January 12, 1928. Vol'f himself questioned the existence of the "so-called crisis," but pointed to export problems.

8. *Pravda*, January 8, 1928.

9. *Ibid.*, January 12, 13, 18, 19, and 30, 1928.

10. *Ibid.*, April 14, 1928.

11. Carr, *Foundations*, 1: 2: 963–64, 967.

12. Davies, *Socialist Offensive*, p. 40; Malofeev, p. 115; *SDD*, 1: 295.

13. *Pravda*, May 25, 1929; *Kontrol'nye tsifry*, p. 413.

14. Rogachevskaia, p. 240.

15. TsSU, *Statisticheskii spravochnik*, 1928, p. 71.

16. Koniukhov, p. 201.

17. *Ibid.*, p. 119.

18. Stalin, "O khlebozagotovkakh i perspektivakh razvitiia sel'skogo khoziaistva," *Sochineniia*, 11: 4.

19. Stalin, "Pervye itogi zagotovitel'noi kampanii i dal'neishie zadachi partii," *Sochineniia*, 11: 12; *Pravda*, April 18, 1928.

20. *Pravda*, January 15, 1928.

21. The term was used occasionally at the time (e.g., by Stalin, "O pravom uklone v VKP[b]," *Sochineniia*, 12: 88, 90) and has been utilized by modern Western writers (Carr, *Foundations*, 1: 1: 101; 2: 468; Lewin, *Russian Peasants*, pp. 385–95; Davies, *Socialist Offensive*, pp. 59, 404–7). Soviet writers today generally refer to the method of "social influence." See Moshkov, pp. 52–53. The fullest treatment of the development of the Ural-Siberian method is to be found in Y. Taniuchi, "Ural-Siberian Method."

22. *Sobranie zakonov*, 1928, no. 3, art. 29.

23. Koniukhov, p. 20; Taniuchi, "Ural-Siberian Method," p. 23.

24. *Pravda*, April 19, 1928. It was Bukharin who revealed that people had been shot in connection with the campaign. See also Taniuchi, "Ural-Siberian Method," p. 15.

25. Koniukhov, p. 149.

26. *Kollektivizatsiia*, p. 47.

27. *Pravda*, April 18, 1928.

28. *Ibid.*, February 15, 1928; for the procurements data, *Kollektivizatsiia*, p. 46.

29. Stalin, *Sochineniia*, 11: 266.

30. *Pravda*, July 15, 1928.

31. *Ibid.*, September 5, 1928.

32. *Ibid.*, May 27, 1928.

33. *Kollektivizatsiia*, p. 78; *Pravda*, December 4, 1928.

34. *Kollectivizatsiia*, p. 80.

35. *Pravda*, December 2, 17, and 19, 1928.

36. *Ibid.*, June 2, 1928.

37. Danilov, "Ekonomicheskoe osnovy," p. 185; Davies, *Socialist Offensive*, p. 432.

38. *Pravda*, August 4, 1928.

39. Arkhipov and Morozov, p. 191.

40. Carr, *Foundations*, 1: 2: 960; *Pravda*, December 4, 1928.

41. For a lively description of the evolution of attitudes and the flow of political currents at this time, see Lewin, *Russian Peasants*, part 2. Bronger places the shift in Stalin's views in late 1927; Tucker (p. 399) sees evidence of a change somewhat earlier. For a Soviet review of the "Right deviation," see Vaganov, *Pravyi uklon*.

42. Zalesskii, pp. 38–50.

43. *Pravda*, April 20, 1928.

44. Zalesskii, pp. 55–66.

45. *Piatnadtsatyi s"ezd*, p. 1236. Lewin calls attention to Molotov's revealing phrase in *Russian Peasants*, pp. 208–9.

46. *Sobranie zakonov*, 1927, no. 61, art. 613.

47. Zalesskii, p. 74.

48. *Ibid.*, p. 74.

49. *Ibid.*, p. 80. Taxation of income from non-agricultural labor was introduced in 1927/28. The rate was fixed at up to 15 percent of such income.

50. *Kollektivizatsiia*, p. 26.

51. *Sobranie zakonov*, 1928, no. 24, art. 212.

52. Stalin, "Ob industrializatsii strany i o pravom uklone v VKP(b)," *Sochineniia*, 11: 264.

53. Zalesskii, pp. 80, 82. The local authorities indicated could raise the income level subject to the surtax and could set the rate of the surtax within the 5 to 25 percent range.

54. Gazalova, "Statisticheskie istochniki," pp. 288–89.

55. *Pravda*, December 9, 1928.

56. *Ibid.*, April 20, 1928; September 27, 1929. The latter issue gives 440 million as the amount actually collected. Carr, *Foundations*, 1: 2: 975, shows 449 million rubles income from the agricultural tax in 1928/29.

57. *Kollektivizatsiia*, pp. 153–54.

58. *Pravda*, February 8, 1929; *Kollektivizatsiia*, pp. 120–22.

59. Lewin, *Russian Peasants*, pp. 303–5, 322.

60. Zalesskii, p. 65. The total amount of payments of various sorts collected by the state from the countryside (including the peasants' overpayment for industrial goods due to "scissors" prices) amounted to 42 percent of the state budget in 1925/26, 36 percent in 1926/27, and 26 percent in 1927/28, according to the State Planning Commission. If the additional payments made by the peasants in the form of self-taxation, fees to cooperatives, state loans, and so

forth, are taken into account, the contribution of the peasants to the state budget in these years comes to 59, 51, and 42 percent respectively. (Danilov, "Ekonomicheskie osnovy," pp. 226–27.)

61. *Pravda*, April 14, 1928. According to the budget reconstructed by Davies, *Soviet Budgetary System*, pp. 82–83, the agricultural tax amounted to 7.7 percent of the total in 1927/28.

62. *Pravda*, September 23, 1928.

63. *Ibid.*, April 20, 1928.

64. *Ibid.*, November 22, 1928.

65. *Ibid.*, February 8, 1929; September 27, 1929.

66. *Ibid.*, September 27, 1929.

67. Danilov, "Ekonomicheskie osnovy," p. 201.

68. *Sobranie zakonov*, 1927, no. 35, art. 349; *Sobranie uzakonenii*, 1927, no. 115, art. 768.

69. Selunskaia, *Izmeneniia, 1921–*, p. 94.

70. Danilov, *Sozdanie*, p. 184; *Sobranie uzakonenii*, 1929, no. 29, art. 310.

71. *Sobranie uzakonenii*, 1928, no. 125, art. 805.

72. Danilov, *Sozdanie*, p. 185.

73. Danilov, "Material'no-technicheskaia baza," p. 14.

74. *SDD*, 2: 40–42.

75. Selunskaia, *Izmeneniia, 1921–*, p. 106.

76. Ivnitskii, p. 59.

77. Danilov, "Zemel'nye otnosheniia," pp. 126–27.

78. *Pravda*, July 13, 1928.

79. *Ibid.*, January 4, 1928; December 7, 1928.

80. *Ibid.*, November 3, 1928; February 2, 1929.

81. *Ibid.*, December 21, 1928.

82. Lewin, *Russian Peasants*, p. 394. Angarov, pp. 38–39, provides a table of instances of kulak activism in the electoral campaign of December–January 1928/29. See also Chamberlin, pp. 197–98; Kukushkin, p. 191; and Sharova, p. 156.

83. *Pravda*, December 14, 1928; March 30, 1929.

84. Strong, p. 16. Lewin, *Russian Peasants*, p. 394, suggests that the reason more complete data have not been published may be that the figures "might well cast some doubt on the official presentation of the kulak as a mortal enemy of the regime who was preparing to overthrow it by force of arms."

85. *Pravda*, April 26, 1929.

86. *SDD*, 1: 298.

87. See Bukharin's "Zametki ekonomista," *Pravda*, September 30, 1928. In December Rykov was careful to deny a regression in agriculture, yet the data he was presenting at the time indicated precisely such a development. See *Pravda*, December 4, 1928.

88. *Kollektivizatsiia*, pp. 89–96.

89. *Ibid.*, pp. 96–108.

90. *Pravda*, September 14, 1929.

91. *Ibid.*, May 18, 1929.

92. *Kollektivizatsiia*, pp. 116–20.

93. Angarov, p. 34.

94. *Pravda*, March 15, 1929; *Kollektivizatsiia*, pp. 177–79.

95. Carr, *Foundations*, 2: 485.

96. *Izvestiia*, March 1, 1929.

97. *Piatnadtsatyi s"ezd*, 2: 1199.

98. Morgenshtiern, p. 89.

99. *Pravda*, July 21, 1928.

100. *Ibid.*, September 7, 1928. The campaign was extended beyond the tar-

get date, and later reports were more encouraging. See *Pravda*, September 22, 1928.

101. *Pravda*, December 4, 1928; Carr, *Foundations*, 1: 2: 946.

102. *Pravda*, April 16, 1929.

103. Bulatov, p. 35. Cf. Trapeznikov, 2: 79–80.

104. *Kollektivizatsiia*, pp. 65–67.

105. *SDD*, 1: 190.

106. *Ibid.*, pp. 192–94.

107. *Kollektivizatsiia*, p. 196. According to Carr, *Foundations*, 1: 2: 946, the grain area under contract in 1928/29 reached 19 million hectares.

108. The Party's statement of August 26, 1929, on contracting was implemented by SNK legislation on October 7, 1929. (*Kollektivizatsiia*, pp. 196–98, 206–10.)

109. Lewin makes this point effectively in *Russian Peasants*, p. 408, noting that the contract was "unilateral in character, and purely an instrument of coercion."

110. *Pravda*, February 22, 1928.

111. *Ibid.*, January 12, 1928.

112. Despite the fact that collectives had been exempted from charges for land organization work in 1927, some land agencies had continued to press for payment. (*Pravda*, May 18, 1928.)

113. *Kollektivizatsiia*, pp. 99–100.

114 *Pravda*, January 4, 1929.

115. *Ibid.*, November 19, 1929.

116. *Ibid.*, October 2, 1928.

117. *Ibid.*, October 3, 1928. Kritsman's statement was soon followed in *Pravda* by Iakovlev's comments on the stifling effect of a lingering zemstvo tradition (October 28, 1928).

Chapter 19

1. According to a 1927 article in the journal of the Communist Academy (Volodkovich and Kulikov, p. 53), there was "almost no material on collectives" except for data establishing their "massive collapse" after the onset of NEP. Sharova (p. 62, n. 126) states that even basic information on the number of collectives is lacking or highly contradictory for the years before 1927.

2. Jasny, *Socialized Agriculture*, pp. 298–99, 303.

3. Zelenin, pp. 263, 265–66.

4. Ivnitskii, pp. 39, 59–60.

5. Jasny, *Socialized Agriculture*, p. 301.

6. *SDD*, 1: 303.

7. Danilov, *Ocherki*, p. 30; Kraev, p. 343; Sharova, p. 63.

8. *SDD*, 1: 306, 308.

9. *Ibid.*, pp. 305–7.

10. *Piatnadtsatyi s"ezd*, 1: 65, 2: 1185.

11. *SDD*, 1: 307.

12. Zelenin, pp. 339–40.

13. *Pravda*, June 2, 1928; Stalin, "Na khlebnom fronte," *Sochineniia*, 11: 85.

14. *Pravda*, July 18, 1928.

15. *Ibid.*, August 2, 1928; September 27, 1928.

16. *Ibid.*, December 4, 1928.
17. *Kollektivizatsiia*, p. 150.
18. Carr, *Foundations*, 1: 2: 942.
19. *Pravda*, November 21, 1929.
20. *Kollektivizatsiia*, pp. 61–62; emphasis added.
21. *Pravda*, November 10, 1928.
22. *Ibid.*, December 4, 1928.
23. *Ibid.*
24. Ivanov, p. 5.
25. *Kollektivizatsiia*, p. 149.
26. *Ibid.*, p. 155.

27. The harvest of 1927 was 72.3 million tons; that of 1928, 73.3 million. Procurements in 1927/28 were 11 million tons; in 1928/29, 10.8 million. But procurements of rye and wheat dropped in the latter year from 8.6 million tons to 6.9 million tons. See Davies, *Socialist Offensive*, pp. 424, 427–28.

28. *Pravda*, February 22, 1929; June 27, 1929.
29. *Ibid.*, April 27, 1929.
30. Zalesskii, pp. 65, 72–76.
31. *Ibid.*, p. 79.
32. *Piatnadtsatyi s"ezd*, p. 1086.
33. *Pravda*, April 12, 1929.

34. Stalin, "O pravom uklone v VKP(b)," *Sochineniia*, 12: 87–88. According to Vaganov, p. 127, the use of self-taxation techniques as an aid to grain collections had been proposed to the Central Committee by the Ural oblast committee and the Siberian krai committee.

35. Mikoian, p. 23.

36. *Sobranie uzakonenii*, 1929, no. 60, art. 591; art. 596.

37. *Ibid.*, no. 70, art. 681; *Pravda*, August 8, 1929.

38. When the inflated predictions proved erroneous, the realists among the statisticians were replaced. At the end of 1929 the TsSU was subordinated to the State Planning Commission. See Davies, *Socialist Offensive*, pp. 65–67, 71.

39. For harvest data see Table 20, p. 262. Davies, *Socialist Offensive*, pp. 65, 429.

40. Davies, *Socialist Offensive*, p. 96.

41. For a description of the work of the plenipotentiaries at this time, see Davies, *Socialist Offensive*, pp. 89–90.

42. Osokina, p. 140.

43. Davies, *Socialist Offensive*, pp. 96–97.

44. *Pravda*, January 11, 1929.

45. *Ibid.*, March 27, 1929.

46. Davies, *Socialist Offensive*, pp. 94, 98.

47. See Carr, *Foundations*, 1: 1: 259; Davies, *Socialist Offensive*, pp. 98, 100; Lewin, *Russian Peasants*, p. 488.

48. *Pravda*, August 2, 1929.

49. Vareikis, p. 65.

50. See *ibid.*, Kiselev's article in *Izvestiia*, April 19, 1930; and *Pravda*, January 6, 1930.

51. Cited by Jasny, *Socialized Agriculture*, p. 312.

52. *Pravda*, October 28, 1928.

53. For the archival evidence, see Fainsod, pp. 251–58.

54. *Pravda*, November 27, 1929.

55. Davies, *Socialist Offensive*, p. 158.

56. *Ibid.*, pp. 175–76. There had been earlier attempts to induce those economists to recant. The leaders of the school were arrested in 1930. See Solomon, pp. 158–60.

57. Stalin, "K voprosam agrarnoi politiki v SSSR," *Sochineniia*, 12: 170.

58. The resolution has been reconstructed in several accounts from various

sources. See Ivnitskii, pp. 178–79; Davies, *Socialist Offensive*, pp. 234–37.

59. *Pravda*, October 13, 1928; Davies, *Socialist Offensive*, p. 244.

60. Lewin, *Russian Peasants*, p. 413.

61. *Pravda*, June 27, 1929.

62. *Kollektivizatsiia*, p. 232.

63. Davies, *Socialist Offensive*, p. 112.

64. *SDD*, 1: 311.

65. Ivanov, p. 7, and similar articles in *Zemleustroitel'* throughout 1928. *Pravda*, October 2, 13, and 16, 1928; December 4, 1928; March 2, 1929.

66. *Pravda*, April 2, 1929 (Kalinin's theses). For the conference resolutions, see *Kollektivizatsiia*, p. 155.

67. Cited by Carr, *Foundations*, 1: 1: 215.

68. E.g., *Pravda*, September 12, 1929.

69. Stalin, "K voprosam agrarnoi politiki," *Sochineniia*, 12: 154.

70. *Pravda*, January 6, 1930.

71. Cited by Davies, *Socialist Offensive*, p. 114, n. 22.

72. Carr, *Foundations*, 1: 1: 173.

73. See above, p. 256, and Davies, *Collective Farm*, p. 184.

74. Vareikis, p. 65.

75. *Pravda*, November 7, 1929.

76. *Kollektivizatsiia*, pp. 227–34.

77. Ivnitskii, p. 85; Sharova, p. 173. Davies's data (*Collective Farm*, p. 185) show less movement in 1929.

78. Kukushkin, pp. 216–17.

79. V. Karpinskii, "O kolkhozakh," p. 30; Kukushkin, pp. 198–200; *SDD*, 1: 69.

80. *Kolkhozy*, p. xii.

81. *Izvestiia*, February 16, 1929. The decree was adopted by VTsIK and SNK, RSFSR, on December 31, 1928, but was not published until mid-February 1929.

82. *Sobranie uzakonenii*, 1930, no. 1, art. 1.

83. *Pravda*, March 2, 1930.

84. *Pravda*, January 1, 1928.

85. Karavaev, pp. 67–68; Chernomorskii, "Rol' rabochikh," p. 358; Fainsod, pp. 253–54.

86. Chernomorskii, "Rol' rabochikh" (see the letters from Tambov, pp. 331–89); *Pravda*, November 22, 1929; Davies, *Socialist Offensive*, pp. 100, 256.

87. Davies, *Socialist Offensive*, p. 125.

88. Sharova, p. 89; Mitiaeva, p. 62.

89. Shirokov, p. 46.

90. Kukushkin, p. 290; *Pravda*, May 18, 1929.

91. Shirokov, p. 46; *Pravda*, March 8, 1930.

92. Osokina, p. 82.

93. *SDD*, 1: 61.

94. *Derevenskii kommunist*, 1928, no. 10, p. 29. In 1913 the numbers of males and females in the population were almost equal.

95. Osokina, p. 55.

96. Mitiaeva, p. 65.

97. See Chernomorskii, "Rol' rabochikh," and Ezerskaia and Ivnitskii, pp. 390–519.

98. Kukushkin, p. 280.

99. Shirokov, p. 46; Sharova, p. 170.

100. Chernomorskii, "Rol' rabochikh," p. 347; Sharova, p. 170.

101. *Pravda*, June 7, 1929; June 11, 1929.

102. Danilov, *SDD*, 1: 25, points out that at the time of solid collectivization a full two-thirds of the rural population was under 25 years of age. According to Kukushkin, p. 196, 7 percent of all presidents of rural soviets in 1929
were Young Communists. See also Sharova, pp. 88–89, 170; Davies, *Socialist
Offensive*, p. 125.

103. Davies, *Socialist Offensive*, p. 227.

104. *Sobranie zakonov*, 1930, no. 16, art. 172; *Kollektivizatsiia*, pp. 269–
75.

105. Osokina, p. 147.

106. *Sobranie uzakonenii*, 1930, no. 5, art. 621.

107. Davies, *Socialist Offensive*, pp. 227–28.

108. Sharova, p. 150.

109. *Kollektivizatsiia*, pp. 245, 261–63.

110. *Ibid.*, p. 262.

111. Davies, *Collective Farm*, p. 184.

112. Jasny, *Socialized Agriculture*, p. 458; Davies, *Socialist Offensive*,
p. 448. Ia. A. Iakovlev minimized the impact of the loss of livestock in
Red Villages: The Five Year Plan in Soviet Agriculture (New York, 1931),
pp. 26–28.

113. Malofeev, pp. 175–77.

114. See Barsov, *Balans*; Millar, "Soviet Rapid Development" and "Mass
Collectivization"; and Ellman, "Agricultural Surplus."

115. One part of the cost paid by the peasants was a decline in food consumption. Over the period of the First Five-Year Plan (1928–32), per capita
consumption by the agricultural population fell in all food categories, and consumption of meat by over 50 percent. The urban populace too got less meat,
but was compensated with more grain. (Moshkov, p. 136.)

Conclusion

1. Robinson, p. 265.

2. Leroy-Beaulieu, 2: 55.

3. Trapeznikov, 2: 74–81.

4. Zak, pp. 40–41.

5. Danilov, "Obshchina," p. 54.

6. The general concepts are set forth in part one of his classic study, *Gemeinschaft und Gesellschaft*.

7. Weber developed this thesis most fully in his discussion of economic development. See vol. 1, part 1, chap. 2, of *Economy and Society*.

Works Cited

Abramov, P. N. "Oprosnyi list volostnogo soveta (1918 g.)." *Istoricheskii arkhiv*, 1960, no. 3.

Agrarnaia i sotsial'naia istoriia severo-vostochnoi Rusi XV–XVI vv. Moscow, 1966.

Agrarnaia istoriia severo-zapada Rossii vtoraia polovina XV–nachala XVI v. Leningrad, 1971.

Agrarnaia politika sovetskoi vlasti (1917–1918 gg.): dokumenty i materialy. Moscow, 1954.

Aimbetov, A., et al. *Problemy sovershenstvovaniia organizatsii i deiatel'nosti mestnykh sovetov*. Alma-Ata, 1967.

Aleksandrov, V. A. *Sel'skaia obshchina v Rossii (XVII–nachalo XIX v.)*. Moscow, 1976.

Alekseev, Iu. G. "Krest'ianskaia volost' v tsentre feodal'noi Rusi XV v." In *Problemy krest'ianskogo zemlevladeniia*.

Anfimov, A. M. "Krest'ianstvo Rossii v 1907–1914." Paper presented to the annual meeting of the American Historical Association, 1971.

———. *Krupnoe pomeshchich'e khoziaistvo Evropeiskoi Rossii*. Moscow, 1969.

———. "O dolge krest'ianstva Rossii Krest'ianskomu Pozemel'nomu Banku." *Voprosy istorii*, 1955, no. 1.

———. *Rossiiskaia derevnia v gody pervoi mirovoi voiny*. Moscow, 1962.

———. *Zemel'naia arenda v Rossii v nachale XX veke*. Moscow, 1961.

———, and Makarov, I. F. "Novye dannye o zemlevladenii Evropeiskoi Rossii." *Istoriia SSSR*, 1974, no. 1.

———, and Zyrianov, P. N. "Nekotorye cherty evoliutsii russkoi krest'ianskoi obshchiny v poreformennyi period (1861–1914 gg.)." *Istoriia SSSR*, 1980, no. 4.

Angarov, A. *Klassovaia bor'ba v derevne i sel'sovet*. Moscow, 1929.

Anisimov, V. I. "Nadely." In S. P. Dzhivelegov et al., eds., *Velikaia reforma: russkoe obshchestvo i krest'ianskii vopros v proshlom i nastoiashchem*. Vol. 6. Moscow, 1911.

Antonova, S. I. *Vliianie stolypinskoi agrarnoi reformy na izmeneniia v sostave rabochego klassa*. Moscow, 1951.

Antsiferov, A. N., et al. *Russian Agriculture During the War*. 1930. Reprint. New York, 1968.

Anweiler, Oskar. *The Soviets: The Russian Workers', Peasants,' and Soldiers' Councils, 1905–1921*. Translated by R. Hein. New York, 1974.

Arkhipa, V. A., and Morozov, L. F. *Bor'ba protiv kapitalisticheskikh elementov v promyshlennosti i torgovle, 20ᵉ–nachalo 30ᵏʰ godov*. Moscow, 1978.

Arkhiv K. Marksa i F. Engel'sa. Vol. 1. Moscow, 1924.

A——skii, V. P. *Skol'ko zemli v Rossii i gde est svobodnye zemli*. Odessa, 1906.

Atkinson, Dorothy. "The Statistics on the Russian Land Commune, 1905–1917." *Slavic Review*, December 1973.

——. "The Zemstvo and the Peasants." In Emmons and Vucinich, eds., *The Zemstvo in Russia*.

——, et al., eds. *Women in Russia*. Stanford, 1977.

Aver'ev, V. N. *Komitety bednoty: sbornik materialov*. Vol. 1. Moscow, 1933.

——. "Ot neitralizatsii seredniaka k soiuzu s nim," *Sovetskoe gosudarstvo i pravo*, 1934, no. 2.

——. "Sovety pered oktiabr'skoi sotsialisticheskoi revoliutsii (sentiabr'-oktiabr' 1917 g.)." *Sovetskoe gosudarstvo i pravo*, 1941, no. 1.

——, and Ronin, S. "Stroitel'stvo sovetov v derevne na pervom etape oktiabria (oktiabr' 1917 g.–iiun' 1918 g.)." *Sovetskoe gosudarstvo i pravo*, 1934, no. 4.

Baklanova, E. N. *Krest'ianskii dvor i obshchina na russkom severe*. Moscow, 1976.

Baron, Samuel H. *Plekhanov, the Father of Russian Marxism*. Stanford, 1963.

Barsov, A. A. *Balans stoimostnykh obmenov mezhdu gorodom i derevnei*. Moscow, 1969.

Belianova, A. M. *O tempakh ekonomicheskogo razvitiia SSSR*. Moscow, 1974.

Belugorov, M. G. "Statisticheskie istochniki o sostave sel'skikh sovetov v pervye gody vosstanovitel'nogo perioda (1921–1923)." In *Istochnikovedenie istorii sovetskogo obshchestva*, vol. 3. Moscow, 1978.

Bilimovich, A. D. "The Land Settlement." In A. N. Antsiferov et al., eds., *Russian Agriculture During the War*. New Haven, 1930.

Blum, Jerome. *Lord and Peasant in Russia from the Ninth to the Nineteenth Century*. Princeton, 1961.

Bokarev, Iu. P. "Metodika izucheniia krest'ianskikh biudzhetov 20ᵏʰ godov." In *Istochnikovedenie istorii sovetskogo obshchestva*, vol. 3. Moscow, 1978.

Bronger, Dirk. *Der Kampf um die sowjetische Agrarpolitik 1925–1929: Ein Beitrag zur Geschichte der kommunistischen Opposition in Sowjet-Russland*. Cologne, 1967.

Brutskus, B. D. *Agrarnyi vopros i agrarnaia politika*. Petrograd, 1922.

Brysiakin, S. K. "Sotsial'no-ekonomicheskaia kharakteristika krest'ianskogo khoziaistva nakanune kollektivizatsii." Kishenevskii gosuniversitet. *Uchenye zapiski*, 16 (istoricheskii), 1952.

Bukharin, N. I. *Nekotorye voprosy ekonomicheskoi politiki*. Moscow, 1925.

——. "Zametki ekonomista." *Pravda*, September 30, 1928.

——, and Preobrazhenskii, E. *The ABC of Communism*. Ann Arbor, 1967.

Bukhovets, O. G. "K metodike izucheniia 'prigovornogo' dvizheniia v 1905–1907 godakh." *Istoriia SSSR*, 1979, no. 3.

Bulatov, I. G. "Kontraktsiia i ee rol' v podgotovke sploshnoi kollektivizatsii." *Voprosy istorii*, 1953, no. 4.

Carr, E. H. *A History of Soviet Russia*.

    The Bolshevik Revolution, 1917–1923. 3 vols. New York, 1950–53.

    The Interregnum, 1923–1924. New York, 1954.

    Socialism in One Country, 1924–1926. 3 vols. New York, 1958–64.

Foundations of a Planned Economy, 1926–1929. Vol. 1 (in 2 parts), co-authored with R. W. Davies. New York, 1969. Vol. 2. New York, 1971.

Chaianov, A. V. *Optimal'nye razmery sel'skokhoziaistvennikh khoziaistv*. 3 eds. Moscow, 1922, 1924, 1928.

———, ed. *Problemy urozhaia*. Moscow, 1926.

Chamberlin, W. H. *Soviet Russia*. Boston, 1931.

Chambers, J. D. *Population, Economy, and Society in Pre-Industrial England*. New York, 1972.

Cherepnin, L. V. *Obrazovanie russkogo tsentralizovannogo gosudarstva v XIV–XV vekakh*. Moscow, 1960.

Chernobaev, A. *Kombed*. Moscow, 1978.

Chernomorskii, M. N. "Rol' rabochikh brigad v bor'be za sploshnuiu kollektivizatsiiu v Tambovskoi derevne." In *Materialy po istorii SSSR*, vol. 1. Moscow, 1955.

———. "Vyborochnye obsledovaniia i krest'ianskie biudzhety kak istochniki po istorii sotsial'no-ekonomicheskikh otnoshenii v derevne v gody nepa." *Trudy moskovskogo gosudarstvennogo istoriko-arkhivnogo instituta*, 4 (1954).

Chernov, V. *The Great Russian Revolution*. New Haven, 1936.

———. *Zemlia i pravo: sbornik statei*. Petrograd, 1919.

Chernukha, V. G. *Krest'ianskii vopros v pravitel'stvennoi politike Rossii*. Leningrad, 1972.

Chernyshev, I. V. *Agrarnyi vopros v Rossii*. Kursk, 1927.

———. *Obshchina posle 9 noiabria 1906 g.: po ankete Vol'nogo Ekonomicheskogo Obshchestva*. Vol. 1. Petrograd, 1917.

———. "Zadacha Gosudarstvennoi Dumy v oblasti reformy krest'ianskogo prava." *Trudy Vol'nogo Ekonomicheskogo Obshchestva*, 1907, no. 1–3.

Chetverikov, N. S. *Statisticheskie issledovaniia*. Moscow, 1975.

———, ed. *Svod urozhainikh svedenii za gody 1883–1915 gg*. Moscow, 1928.

Chetyrnadtsatyi s"ezd vsesoiuznoi kommunisticheskoi partii (b). Stenograficheskii otchet. Moscow, 1926.

Chugunov, S. I. *Rabota sel'skikh sovetov*. Moscow, 1926.

———. *Chto pokazali poslednie perevybory sovetov*. Moscow, 1926.

Coale, Ansley J., et al. *Human Fertility in Russia since the Nineteenth Century*. Princeton, 1979.

Confino, Michael. *Systèmes agraires et progrès agricole: l'assolement triennal en Russie aux XVIII–XIX siècles*. Paris, 1969.

Conroy, Mary S. *Peter Arkad'evich Stolypin: Practical Politics in Late Tsarist Russia*. Boulder, Colo., 1976.

Czap, Peter. "P. A. Valuev's Proposal for a Vyt' Administration, 1864." *Slavonic and East European Review*, July 1967.

Danilov, Viktor Petrovich. "Ekonomicheskoe osnovy soiuza rabochego klassa i krest'ianstva v pervye gody sotsialisticheskoi rekonstruktsii narodnogo khoziaistva SSSR." In *Rol' rabochego klassa*.

———. "Material'no-tekhnicheskaia baza sel'skogo khoziaistva SSSR nakanune sploshnoi kollektivizatsii." *Voprosy istorii*, 1956, no. 7.

———. "Nekotorye itogi nauchnoi sessii po istorii sovetskoi derevni." *Voprosy istorii*, 1962, no. 2.

———. "Ob itogakh pereraspredeleniia zemel'nogo fonda Rossii i rezultate pervykh agrarnykh preobrazovanii sovetskoi vlasti." In *Tezisy dokladov i soobshchenii 8-i sessii simpoziuma po agrarnoi istorii Vostochnoi Evropy.* Moscow, 1965.

———. "Obshchina u narodov SSSR v posleoktiabr'skii period." *Narody azii i afriki,* 1973, no. 3.

———. "Pereraspredelenie zemel'nogo fonda Rossii v rezultate Velikoi Oktiabr'skoi revoliutsii." In Mints, *Leninskii dekret v deistvii.*

———. *Sovetskaia dokolkhoznaia derevnia.* Vol. 1. *Naselenie, zemlepol'zovanie, khoziaistvo.* Moscow, 1977. Vol. 2. *Sotsial'naia struktura, sotsialnye otnosheniia.* Moscow, 1979.

———. *Sozdanie material'no-tekhnicheskikh predposylok kollektivizatsii sel'skogo khoziaistva SSSR.* Moscow, 1957.

———. "Zemel'nye otnosheniia v sovetskoi dokolkhoznoi derevne," *Istoriia SSSR,* 1958, no. 3.

———, ed. *Ocherki istorii kollektivizatsii sel'skogo khoziaistva v soiuznykh respublikakh.* Moscow, 1963.

———, et al., eds. *Sovetskoe krest'ianstvo.* Moscow, 1970.

Davies, R. W. *The Development of the Soviet Budgetary System.* London, 1958.

———. *The Industrialisation of Soviet Russia.* Vol. 1. *The Socialist Offensive: The Collectivisation of Soviet Agriculture, 1929–1930.* Vol. 2. *The Soviet Collective Farm, 1929–1930.* Cambridge, Mass., 1980.

———. "A Note on Grain Statistics." *Soviet Studies,* 1970, no. 3.

———, and Wheatcroft, S. G. "Further Thoughts on the First Soviet Five-Year Plan." *Slavic Review,* December 1975.

Donkov, I. D. *Antonovshchina: zamysly i deistvitel'nost'.* Moscow, 1977.

Drobizhev, V. Z., ed. *Sbornik dokumentov po istorii SSSR: epokha sotsializma, 1917–1920.* Moscow, 1978.

Druzhinin, N. M. *Gosudarstvennye krest'iane i reforma P.D. Kiseleva.* 2 vols. Moscow, 1946–58.

———. *Russkaia derevnia na perelome, 1860–1880 gg.* Moscow, 1978.

Dubrovskii, S. M. *Krest'ianskoe dvizhenie v revoliutsii 1905–1907 gg.* Moscow, 1956.

———. *Krest'ianstvo v 1917 g.* Moscow, 1927.

———. "Marks i Engel's ob obshchine i o vozmozhnosti nekapitalisticheskogo razvitiia Rossii." *Agrarnye problemy,* 1933, no. 4–6.

———. *Ocherki russkoi revoliutsii.* Part 1. *Sel'skoe khoziaistvo.* Moscow, 1923.

———. "Rassloenie krest'ianstva i zadachi partii v derevne." *NAF,* 1927, no. 11–12.

———. "Rossiiskaia obshchina v literature XIX i nachale XX v." In *Voprosy istorii sel'skogo khoziaistva, krest'ianstva i revoliutsionnogo dvizheniia v Rossii: sbornik statei k 75 letniu akademika Nikolai Mikhailovicha Druzhinina.* Moscow, 1961.

———. *Sel'skoe khoziaistvo i krest'ianstvo Rossii v period imperializma.* Moscow, 1975.

———. *Stolypinskaia zemel'naia reforma.* Moscow, 1963.

Dudzinskaia, E. A. "Chernyshevski i spor o russkoi obshchine." *Istoriia SSSR,* 1978, no. 5.

Dvenadtsatyi s"ezd rossiiskoi kommunisticheskoi partii (b). Stenograficheskii otchet. Moscow, 1923.

Dyshler, P. Ia. *Novye formy sel'skogo khoziaistva*. Part 2. Petrograd, 1918.
————. *Organizatsiia kollektivnykh trudovykh khoziaistv*. Petrograd, 1920.
Efimenko, Aleksandra. *Issledovaniia narodnoi zhizni*. Moscow, 1884.
Egiazarova, N. A. *Agrarnyi krizis kontsa XIX veka v Rossii*. Moscow, 1959.
Ekonomicheskoe polozhenie Rossii nakanune velikoi oktiabr'skoi sotsialisticheskoi revoliutsii: dokumenty i materialy. Vol. 3. *Sel'skoe khoziaistvo i krest'ianstvo*. Leningrad, 1967.
Ellman, Michael. "Did the Agricultural Surplus Provide the Resources for the Increase in Investment During the First Five Year Plan?" *Economic Journal*, December 1975.
Emmons, Terence. *The Russian Landed Gentry and the Peasant Emancipation of 1861*. Cambridge, Eng., 1968.
————, and Vucinich, Wayne S., eds. *The Zemstvo in Russia: An Experiment in Self-Government*. New York, 1982.
Erlich, Alexander. "Preobrazhenskii and the Economics of Soviet Industrialization." *Quarterly Journal of Economics*, 64 (1950), no. 1.
————. *The Soviet Industrialization Debate, 1924–1928*. Cambridge, Mass., 1960.
Ezerskaia, D. M., and Ivnitskii, N. A. "Dvadtsatipiatitysiachniki i ikh rol' v kollektivizatsii sel'skogo khoziaistva v 1930 g." In *Materialy po istorii SSSR*, vol. 1.
Fainsod, Merle. *Smolensk under Soviet Rule*. New York, 1958.
Farnsworth, Beatrice Brodsky. "Bolshevik Alternatives and the Soviet Family: The 1926 Marriage Law Debate." In Atkinson et al., *Women in Russia*.
Fedorov, Evgenii. "Faktory vliiaiushchie na razvitie semeino-imushchestvennykh razdelov." *Zemleustroitel'*, 1925, no. 10.
Fortunatov, A. *Ekonomika i statistika sel'skogo khoziaistva*. Moscow, 1925.
Fulin, Iu. V. "Osushchestvlenie dekreta o zemle v Tsentral'no-zemledel'cheskom raione." In Mints, *Leninskii dekret o zemle v deistvii*.
Gaponenko, L. S., ed. *Revoliutsionnoe dvizhenie v Rossii posle sverzheniia samoderzhaviia: dokumenty y materialy*. Moscow, 1957.
————. *Revoliutsionnoe dvizhenie v Rossii v aprele 1917 g.: dokumenty i materialy*. Moscow, 1958.
————. *Velikii oktiabr': sbornik dokumentov*. Moscow, 1961.
Gazalova, K. M. *Droblenie krest'ianskikh khoziaistv v Evropeiskoi Rossii v 1921–1928 gg*. Avtoreferat. Moscow, 1967.
————. "Statisticheskie istochniki o droblenii krest'ianskikh khoziaistv v 1921–1929 gg." *Istochnikovedenie istorii sovetskogo obshchestva*. Vol. 2. Moscow, 1968.
————. "Zemel'nyi sud RSFSR i poriadok rassmotreniia spornykh del o semeino-imushchestvennykh razdelakh krest'ianskikh khoziaistv (1921–1928)." *Trudy moskovskogo gosudarstvennogo istoriko-arkhivnogo instituta*. Vol. 19. *Po istorii gosudarstvennykh uchrezhdenii SSSR*. Moscow, 1965.
Gerasimiuk, V. R. "Kombedy rossiiskoi federatsii v tsifrakh." *Istoriia SSSR*, 1960, no. 4.
————. "Nekotorye novye statisticheskie dannye o Kombedakh RSFSR." *Voprosy istorii*, 1963, no. 6.
————. "Uravitel'noe raspredelenie zemel' v evropeiskoi chasti rossiiskoi federatsii v 1918." *Istoriia SSSR*, 1965, no. 1.
Gerschenkron, Alexander. "Agrarian Policies and Industrialization, Russia

1861–1917." In *Cambridge Economic History*, vol. 6, part 2. Cambridge, Eng., 1965.

―――. *Economic Development in Historical Perspective*. Cambridge, Mass., 1962.

Gertsenshtein, M. Ia. *Konfiskatsiia ili vykup*. Moscow, 1917.

Gill, Graeme J. *Peasants and Government in the Russian Revolution*. New York, 1979.

Gimpel'son, E. G. *Sovety v gody interventsii i grazhdanskoi voiny*. Moscow, 1968.

Ginev, V. N. *Agrarnyi vopros i melkoburzhuaznye partii v Rossii v 1917 g.* Leningrad, 1977.

―――. "Fevral'skaia burzhuazno-demokraticheskaia revoliutsiia i agrarnyi vopros u eserov." In *Problemy krest'ianskogo zemlevladeniia*.

Glavnoe upravlenie zemleustroistva i zemledeliia. *Sbornik statistiko-ekonomicheskikh svedenii po sel'skomu khoziaistvu Rossii i nekotorykh inostrannykh gosudarstv*. Vol. 8. Petrograd, 1915.

―――. *Zemleustroennye khoziaistva*. Petrograd, 1915.

Goehrke, C. *Die Theorien uber Entstehung und Entwicklung des "Mir."* Wiesbaden, 1964.

Gorskaia, N. A. *Monastyrskie krest'iane tsentral'noi Rossii v XVII veke*. Moscow, 1977.

Grant, Steven. *"Obshchina* and *Mir."* *Slavic Review*, December 1976.

Grekov, B. D. *Kievskaia Rus'*. Moscow, 1944.

―――. *Kratkii ocherk istorii russkogo krest'ianstva*. Moscow, 1958.

―――. *Krest'iane na Rusi*. 2d ed. 2 vols. Moscow, 1952–54.

Grishaev, V. V. *Sel'skokhoziaistvennye kommuny Sovetskoi Rossii, 1917–1929.* Moscow, 1976.

―――. *Stroitel'stvo sovetov v derevne v pervyi god sotsialisticheskoi revoliutsii*. Moscow, 1967.

Groman, V. G., ed. *Vliianie neurozhaev na narodnoe khoziaistvo Rossii*. Moscow, 1927.

Gurko, V. I. *Features and Figures of the Past: Government and Opinion in the Reign of Nicholas II*. Edited by J. E. W. Sterling et al. Translated by L. Matveev. Stanford, 1939.

Haimson, Leopold. "The Problem of Social Stability in Urban Russia, 1905–1917." *Slavic Review*, 23 (1964), no. 4, and 24 (1965), no. 1.

―――. "The Russian Landed Nobility and the System of the Third of June." In his *The Politics of Rural Russia*.

―――, ed. *The Politics of Rural Russia*. Bloomington, Ind., 1979.

Haxthausen, August. *The Russian Empire: Its People, Institutions, and Resources*. Translated and abridged by R. Farie. 2 vols. London, 1856.

Hennessy, Richard. *The Agrarian Question in Russia, 1905–1907*. Giessen, Germany, 1977.

Herzen, Aleksandr. "O sel'skoi obshchine v Rossii." In *O razvitii revoliutsionnykh idei v Rossii*. Moscow, 1958.

Iakovlev, Ia. A. *K voprosu o sotsialisticheskom pereustroistve sel'skogo khoziaistva (materialy issledovaniia NKRKI SSSR)*. Leningrad, 1928.

―――. "Kolkhoznoe dvizhenie na perelom." *NAF*, 1927, no. 4.

―――. *Nasha derevnia*. 4th ed. Moscow, 1925.

―――. *Partiia v bor'be s biurokratizmom*. Moscow, 1928.

Iakovtsevskii, V. N. *Agrarnye otnosheniia v SSSR v period stroitel'stva sotsializma.* Moscow, 1964.

Iatsunskii, V. K. "Izmeneniia v razmeshchenii naseleniia Evropeiskoi Rossii v 1724–1916 gg." *Istoriia SSSR*, 1957, no. 1.

Ierusalimskii, A. F. "Krest'ianskoe dvizhenie v Rossii nakanune i v nachale pervoi mirovoi voiny." *Istoriia SSSR*, 1967, no. 3.

Ignatovich, I. I. *Pomeshchich'e krest'iane nakanune osvobozhdeniia.* Moscow, 1910.

Igritskii, I. V., comp. *1917 god v derevne.* Moscow, 1967.

Istoriia sovetskogo krest'ianstva i kolkhoznogo stroitel'stva v SSSR. Moscow, 1963.

Iurdanskii, N. "Otmena krugovoi poruki." *Mir Bozhii*, May 1903.

Ivanov, V. "Zemel'nye obshchestva i rol' ikh v sotsialisticheskom sektore." *Zemleustroitel'*, 1928, no. 6.

Ivnitskii, N. A. *Klassovaia bor'ba v derevne i likvidatsiia kulachestva kak klassa.* Moscow, 1972.

Jasny, Naum. *The Socialized Agriculture of the USSR.* Stanford, 1949.

———. *Soviet Economists of the Twenties.* New York, 1972.

Johnson, Robert E. *Peasant and Proletarian.* New Brunswick, N.J., 1979.

Kachorovskii (Kachorovsky), K. R. "Budushchee obshchiny." *Sovremennye zapiski*, 26 (1925).

———. *Russkaia obshchina.* St. Petersburg, 1900.

———. "The Russian Land Commune in History and Today." *Slavonic and East European Review*, 7 (1929).

Kalinin, M. I. *O derevne.* Moscow, 1925.

Karavaev, A. "Kolkhoznoe dvizhenie i kulachestvo." *NAF*, 1928, no. 11.

Karcz, Jerzy. "Back on the Grain Front." *Soviet Studies*, October 1970.

———. "Thoughts on the Grain Problem." *Soviet Studies*, April 1967.

Karelin, A. A. *Obshchinnoe vladenie v Rossii.* St. Petersburg, 1893.

Karnaukhova, E. C. *Zemel'nye otnosheniia v sotsialisticheskom obshchestve.* Moscow, 1967.

Karpinskii, V. "Nekotorye techenie v nashei politike (k voprosu o rasshirenii kruga izbirateli." *Bol'shevik*, 1926, no. 1.

———. "O kolkhozakh i kulake." *Bol'shevik*, 1929, no. 11.

Karpov, N. I. *Agrarnaia politik Stolypina.* Leningrad, 1925.

Karyshev, N. A. "Nash zemel'nyi kredit dlia chastnykh i dlia krest'ian." *Russkoe bogatstvo*, 1894, no. 3.

———. "Podvornoe i obshchinoe khoziaistvo: statisticheskie paralleli." *Russkoe bogatstvo*, 1894, no. 6.

Kaufman, A. A. *Russkaia obshchina v protsesse ee zarozhdenie i rosta.* Moscow, 1908.

———. *Sbornik statei: Obshchina, Pereselenie, Statistika.* Moscow, 1915.

Kayden, Eugene M., and Antsiferov, Alexis N. *The Cooperative Movement in Russia During the War.* New Haven, 1929.

Keep, John L. *The Russian Revolution.* New York, 1976.

Kerblay, Basile. "L'Evolution de l'alimentation rurale en Russie (1896–1960)." *Annales ESC* 17 (1962).

Kim, M. P., ed. *Problemy agrarnoi istorii sovetskogo obshchestva.* Moscow, 1971.

Kindeev, K. Ia. "O formakh zemlepol'zovaniia." *Zemleustroitel'*, 1925, no. 10.

————. *Voprosy zemleustroistva*. Moscow, 1925.

Kir'ianov, Iu. I. *Zhiznennyi uroven rabochikh Rossii*. Moscow, 1979.

Kirillov, I. A. *Ocherki zemleustroistva za tri goda revoliutsii 1917–1920 gg.* Petrograd, 1922.

Kitanina, T. M. *Khlebnaia torgovlia Rossii v 1875–1914 gg.* Leningrad, 1978.

Knipovich, B. N. "Napravlenie i itogi agrarnoi politiki 1917–1920 gg." in *O zemle*.

————. *Ocherk deiatel'nosti Narodnogo Komissariata Zemledeliia za tri goda (1917–1920)*. Moscow, 1920.

Kofod, A. A. *Russkoe zemleustroistvo*. 2d ed. St. Petersburg, 1914.

Kolesnikov, A. "Novoe polozhenie o VIK akh i sel'sovetakh i rabota zemleustroitelia." *Zemleustroitel'*, 1925, no. 4.

Kolkhozy v 1929. Moscow, 1931.

Kollektivizatsiia sel'skogo khoziaistva: vazhneishie postanovleniia kommunisticheskoi partii i sovetskogo pravitel'stva 1927–1935. Moscow, 1957.

Koniukhov, G. A. *KPSS v bor'be s khlebnymi zatrudneniiami v strane, 1928–1929*. Moscow, 1960.

Kon'kova, A. S. *Bor'ba kommunisticheskoi partii z soiuz rabochego klassa s bedneishim krest'ianstvom v 1917–1918 gg.* Moscow, 1974.

Kontrol'nye tsifry narodnogo khoziaistva SSSR na 1928–1929 g. Moscow, 1929.

Kosinskii, V. A. *Osnovnye tendentsii v mobilizatsii zemel'noi sobstvennosti i ikh sotsial'no-ekonomicheskie faktory*. Prague, 1925.

Kostrikin, V. I. "Krest'ianskoe dvizhenie nakanune oktiabria." In *Oktiabr' i sovetskoe krest'ianstvo*.

————. *Zemel'nye komitety v 1917 gody*. Moscow, 1975.

Kovalenko, D. A., ed. *Sovety v pervyi god proletarskoi diktatury*. Moscow, 1967.

Kovalevsky, M. M. *Modern Customs and Ancient Laws of Russia*. London, 1891.

Kozhikov, I. "Sel'skie sovety i zemel'nye obshchestva." *NAF*, 1928, no. 5.

Kozlov, N. I. *O zemel'nom obshchestve*. Moscow, 1926.

Kraev, M. A. *Pobeda kolkhoznogo stroia v SSSR*. Moscow, 1954.

Kravchuk, N. A. *Massovoe krest'ianskoe dvizhenie v Rossii nakanune Oktiabria*. Moscow, 1971.

Krest'ianskaia reforma v Rossii 1861 goda: sbornik zakonodatel'nykh aktov. Moscow, 1954.

Krest'ianskaia sel'sko-khoziaistvennaia entsiklopediia. Vol. 2–3. *Ekonomika i blagoustroistva derevni*. Moscow, 1925.

Krestianskoe dvizhenie v Rossii v gody pervoi mirovoi voiny, iiul' 1914 g.–fevral' 1917 g.: sbornik dokumentov. Moscow, 1965.

Krestovnikov, G. A. *Mogut-li byt' peredely nadel'noi zemli krest'ian posle okonchaniia vykupnoi operatsii?* Moscow, 1908.

Kretov, F. *Derevnia posle revoliutsii*. Moscow, 1925.

Kriashcheva, A. I. *Gruppy i klassy v krest'ianstve*. 2d ed. Moscow, 1926.

Kritsman, L. N. *Klassovoe rassloenie sovetskoi derevni*. Moscow, 1926.

————. *Proletarskaia revoliutsiia i derevnia*. Moscow, 1929.

Kubanin, M. I. "Anti-sovetskoe krest'ianskoe dvizhenie v gody grazhdanskoi voiny (voennogo kommunizma)." *NAF*, 1926, no. 2.

————. *Klassovaia sushchnost' protsessa drobleniia krest'ianskikh khoziaistv*. Moscow, 1929.

———. "Obshchina pri diktature proletariata." *NAF*, 1926, no. 11–12.

———. "Raspredelenie zemli v usloviiakh raznykh form zemlepol'zovaniia." *VZP*, 1928, no. 9–10; 1929, no. 1.

Kukushkin, Iu. S. *Sel'skie sovety i klassovaia bor'ba v derevne (1921–1932 gg.)*. Moscow, 1968.

Lappo-Danilevskii, A. *Organizatsiia priamogo oblozheniia v moskovskom gosudarstve*. St. Petersburg, 1890.

Laptin, P. F. *Obshchina v russkoi istoriografii poslednei treti XIX–nachala XX v.* Kiev, 1971.

Larin, Iu. "Chastnyi kapital v sel'skom khoziaistve." *NAF*, 1927, no. 4.

Lefebvre, Henri. *The Sociology of Marx*. Translated by Norman Guterman. New York, 1969.

Lenin, V. I. *Leninskii sbornik*. 39 vols. Moscow, 1924–80.

———. *Polnoe sobranie sochineniia*. 5th ed. 55 vols. Moscow, 1958–65.

———. *Sobranie sochineniia*. 20 vols. Moscow, 1920–27.

Leninskii dekret "O zemle" i sovremennost'. Moscow, 1970.

Lepeshkin, A. I. *Mestnye organy vlasti sovetskogo gosudarstva*. Moscow, 1959.

———. *Sovety—vlast' trudiashchikhsia, 1917–1936*. Moscow, 1966.

Leroy-Beaulieu, Anatole. *The Empire of the Tsars and the Russians*. 3 vols. New York, 1893.

Lewin, Moshe. *Political Undercurrents in Soviet Economic Debates*. Princeton, 1974.

———. *Russian Peasants and Soviet Power: A Study of Collectivization*. Evanston, Ill., 1968.

———. "Who Was the Soviet Kulak?" *Soviet Studies*, 18 (1966).

Liashchenko, Peter I. *History of the National Economy of Russia to the 1917 Revolution*. Translated by L. M. Herman. New York, 1949.

Litoshenko, L. "L'économie rurale." In *La situation économique de l'Union Sovietique*. Paris, 1926.

Litvinov, I. I. *Ekonomicheskie posledstviia stolypinskogo agrarnogo zakonodatel'stva*. Moscow, 1929.

Liubavskii, M. K. *Oblastnoe delenie i mestnoe upravlenie litovsko-russkogo gosudarstva ko vremeni izdaniia pervogo litovskogo statuta*. Moscow, 1892–93.

Loginov, A. "Mirskie peredely." *Vestnik sel'skogo-khoziaistva*, 1906, no. 14.

Lositskii, A. E. *K voprosu ob izuchenii stepeni i form raspadeniia obshchiny*. Moscow, 1916.

Luchitskii, I. V. "Etudes sur la propriété communale dans la Petite-Russie." *Revue internationale de sociologie*, 3 (1895).

Lutskii, E. A. "K istorii konfiskatsii pomeshchich'ikh imenii v 1917–1918 godakh." *Izvestiia akademii nauk SSSR. Seriia istorii i filosofii*, 5 (1948), no. 6.

———. "Krest'ianskie nakazy 1917 g. o zemle." In *Istochnikovedenie istorii sovetskogo obshchestva*, part 2. Moscow, 1968.

———. "Leninskii dekret o zemle." In Mints, *Leninskii dekret v deistvii*.

———. "Likvidatsiia Glavnogo Zemel'nogo Komiteta (1917–1918 gody)." *Trudy moskovskogo gosudarstvennogo istoriko-arkhivnogo instituta*, 9 (1957).

———. "O sushchnosti uravnitel'nogo zemlepol'zovaniia v Sovetskoi Rossii." *Voprosy istorii*, 1956, no. 9.

———. "Peredel zemli vesnoi 1918 goda." *Izvestiia akademii nauk SSSR. Seriia istorii i filosofii*, 6 (1949), no. 3.

Makarova, S. L. "K voprosu o vremeni likvidatsii pomeshchich'ego zemlevla-deniia." In Volkhov, *Oktiabr' i sovetskoe krest'ianstvo.*

Male, Donald J. *Russian Peasant Organisation Before Collectivisation.* Cambridge, Eng., 1971.

Malofeev, A. N. *Istoriia tsenoobrazovaniia v SSSR, 1917–1963.* Moscow, 1964.

Mal'tsev, N. A. "O kolichestve krest'ianskikh vystuplenii v period stolypinskoi agrarnoi reform (3 iiuna 1907 g.–1 avguste 1914 g.)." *Istoriia SSSR,* 1965, no. 1.

Manning, Roberta Thompson. "What Was the United Nobility?" In Haimson, *The Politics of Rural Russia.*

———. "The Zemstvo and the Nobility." In Haimson, *The Politics of Rural Russia.*

Manuilov, A. A. "Noveishee zakonodatel'stvo o zemel'noi obshchine." *Vestnik Evropy,* November 1912.

———. "Reforma 19 fevralia i obshchinnoe zemlevladenie." In S. P. Dzhivelo-gov et al., eds., *Velikaia reforma: Russkoe obshchestvo i krest'ianskii vopros v proshlom i v nastoiashchem,* vol. 6. Moscow, 1911.

Marx, Karl, and Engels, Friedrich. *The German Ideology.* Edited by R. Pascal. New York, 1947.

Maslov, P. P. *Kritika agrarnykh programm.* Moscow, 1905.

———. *Politicheskie partii i zemel'nyi vopros.* Moscow, 1917.

Maslov, Semon. *K voprosu ob usloviiakh sushchestvovaniia obshchin.* Moscow, 1914.

Materialy po istorii SSSR: dokumenty istorii sovetskovo obshchestva. Moscow, 1955.

Materialy po zemel'noi reforme 1918 goda. Part 1. *Raspredelenie zemli v 1918 godu.* Moscow, 1919. Part 6. *Otchuzhdenie i ispol'zovanie sel'skokhoziaist-vennogo inventariia.* Moscow, 1918.

Medvedev, E. I. "Agrarnye preobrazovaniia oktiabr'skoi revoliutsii v srednem povolzh'e." In Volkhov, *Oktiabr' i sovtskoe krest'ianstvo.*

Mel'gunov, S. P. *The Bolshevik Seizure of Power.* Santa Barbara, Calif., 1972.

Mikhailov, G. S. *Mestnoe sovetskoe upravlenie.* Moscow, 1927.

———. *Mestnoe sovetskoe upravlenie: konspekt i materialy.* Moscow, 1927.

Mikoian, A. "Novaia khlebozagotovitel'naia kampaniia i zadachi partii." *Bol'she-vik,* 1929, no. 23–24.

Miliukov, P. N. *Ocherk istorii russkoi kul'tury.* 7th ed. Vol. 1. Moscow, 1918.

Miliutin, V. "Vrednye mneniia ob industrializatsii." *NAF,* 1927, no. 6.

Millar, James R. "Mass Collectivization and the Contribution of Soviet Agriculture to the First Five-Year Plan." *Slavic Review,* December 1974.

———. "A Reformulation of A. V. Chayanov's Theory of Peasant Economy." *Economic Development and Cultural Change,* January 1970.

———. "Soviet Rapid Development and the Agricultural Surplus Hypothesis." *Soviet Studies,* July 1970.

Miller, Alexandre. *Essai sur l'histoire des institutions agraires de la Russie centrale du XVIᵉ au XVIIIᵉ siècles.* Paris, 1926.

Minin, A. A. *Sel'sko-khoziaistvennaia kooperatsiia SSSR.* Moscow, 1925.

Mints, I. I., ed. *Leninskii dekret o zemle v deistvii.* Moscow, 1979.

Mirtov, I. "O formakh zemlepol'zovaniia." *Zemleustroitel',* 1924, no. 4–5.

Mitiaeva, O. I. *Kommunisticheskaia partiia: rukovoditel' kul'turnogo rosta krest'ianstva v gody kollektivizatsii.* Moscow, 1978.

Mitrany, David. *Marx Against the Peasant*. New York, 1961.

Moiseeva, O. N. *Sovety krest'ianskikh deputatov v 1917 gody*. Moscow, 1967.

Morgenshtiern, V. "Kontraktsiia zernovykh kul'tur." *NAF*, 1929, no. 1.

Morokhovets, E. A. *Agrarnye programmy rossiiskikh politicheskikh partii v 1917 gody*. Leningrad, 1929.

Moshkov, Iu. A. *Zernovaia problema v gody sploshnoi kollektivizatsii sel'skogo khoziaistvo SSSR*. Moscow, 1966.

Mozzhukhin, I. V. *Agrarnyi vopros v tsifrakh i faktakh deistvitel'nosti*. Moscow, 1917.

———. *Zemleustroistvo v Bogoroditskom uezde Tul'skoi gubernii*. Moscow, 1917.

Murav'ev, V. E. "Zemel'nye otnosheniia v ural'skoi derevne nakanune kollektivizatsii." *Uchenye zapiski permskogo universiteta*, 158 (1966).

Nelidov, A. A. *Istoriia gosudarstvennykh uchrezhdenii SSSR, 1917–1936 gg*. Moscow, 1962.

Nemchinov, V. S. *Sel'skokhoziaistvennaia statistika s osnovami obshchei teorii*. Moscow, 1945.

Nifontov, A. S. *Zernovoe proizvodstvo Rossii vo vtoroi polovine XIX veka*. Moscow, 1974.

Nikonov-Smorodin, M. Z. *Pozemel'no-khoziaistvennoe ustroistvo krest'ianskoi Rossii*. Sofia, 1939.

Nikulikhin, Ia. "O probleme industrializatsii sel'skogo khoziaistva." *NAF*, 1928, no. 6–7.

NKVD. Statisticheskii otdel. *Administrativno-territorial'noe delenie Soiuza SSR*. Moscow, 1928, 1931.

NKZ. *Novoe zakonodatel'stvo v oblasti sel'skogo khoziaistva: sbornik dekretov, instruktsii, i postanovlenii s 15 marta po 1 ianvaria 1923 goda*. Moscow, 1923.

———. *Sovetskoe zemleustroistvo i melioratsiia*. Moscow, 1925.

Novitskii, I. B. "Novye pravovye formy zemel'no-khoziaistvennykh otnoshenii." *VZP*, 1927, no. 3.

———. "Zemel'noe obshchestvo v sovetskom zakonodatel'stve," *VZP*, 1927, no. 1.

O zemle: sbornik statei o proshlom i budushchem zemel'no-khoziaistvennogo stroitel'stva. Moscow, 1921.

Obukhov, V. "Evoliutsiia urozhainosti rzhi za period 1883–1915 v Evropeiskoi Rossii." *Vestnik statistiki*, 1923, no. 7–12.

Oganovskii, N. P. *Individualizatsiia zemlevladeniia v Rossii i ee posledstviia*. Moscow, 1917.

———. "Obshchina i zemel'noe tovarishchestvo." In *O zemle*.

———. *Revoliutsiia naoborot: razrushenie obshchiny*. Petrograd, 1917.

———, and Chaianov, A. V., eds. *Statisticheskii spravochnik po agrarnomu voprosu*. Part 1. *Zemlevladenie i zemlepol'zovanie*. Moscow, 1917.

———, and Kondrat'ev, N. D., eds. *Sel'skoe khoziaistvo Rossii v XX veke: sbornik statistichesko-ekonomicheskikh svedenii za 1901–1922*. Moscow, 1923.

Oreshkin, V. V. *Volnoe Ekonomicheskoe Obshchestvo v Rossii, 1765–1917*. Moscow, 1963.

Osipova, T. V. *Klassovaia bor'ba v derevne v period podgotovki i provedeniia oktiabr'skoi revoliutsii*. Moscow, 1974.

―――. "Razvitie sotsialisticheskoi revoliutsii v derevne v pervyi god diktatury proletariata." In Volkhov, *Oktiabr' i sovetskoe krest'ianstvo.*

Osobennosti agrarnogo stroia Rossii v period imperializma. Materialy sessii nauchnogo soveta po probleme "Istoricheskie predposylki velikoi Oktiabr'skoi sotsialisticheskoi revoliutsii." Moscow, 1962.

Osokina, V. Ia. *Sotsialisticheskoe stroitel'stvo v derevne i obshchina, 1920–1933.* Moscow, 1978.

Pavlov-Sil'vanskii, N. P. *Feodalizm v udel'noi Rusi.* St. Petersburg, 1910.

Pavlovsky, George. *Agricultural Russia on the Eve of the Revolution.* New York, 1968.

Perrie, Maureen. *The Agrarian Policy of the Russian Social Revolutionary Party.* Cambridge, Eng., 1976.

Pershin, P. N. *Agrarnaia revoliutsiia v Rossii.* 2 vols. Moscow, 1966.

―――. *Ocherki zemel'noi politiki russkoi revoliutsii.* Moscow, 1918.

―――. *Uchastkovoe zemlepol'zovanie v Rossii. Khutora i otruba, ikh rasprostranenie za desiatiletie 1907–1916 gg. i sud'by vo vremia revoliutsii (1917–1920 gg.).* Moscow, 1922.

―――. "Vnutriselennaia cherespolosnost' i ee regulirovanie." *VZP,* 1927, no. 2.

Pestrzhetskii, D. I. *Okolo zemli.* Berlin, 1922.

Petrovich, Michael B. "The Peasant in Nineteenth Century Historiography." In Wayne S. Vucinich, ed., *The Peasant in Nineteenth Century Russia.* Stanford, 1968.

Piaskovskii, A. V. *Revoliutsiia 1906–1907 v Rossii.* Moscow, 1966.

Piatiletnii plan narodno-khoziaistvennogo stroitel'stva SSSR. Vol. 2. Moscow, 1929.

Piatnadtsatyi s"ezd vsesoiuznoi kommunisticheskoi partii (b). Stenografcheskii otchet. Moscow, 1928.

Pipes, Richard. *Russia under the Old Regime.* New York, 1974.

Plekhanov, G. V. *Chernyi peredel,* no. 1, January 15, 1880. In his *Socheneniia,* vol. 1. Moscow, 1923.

―――. *Sochineniia.* 2d ed. 24 vols. Moscow, 1920–27.

Plotnikov, V. E. "Krest'ianskaia obshchina piati uezdov moskovskoi gubernii." *Zemleustroitel',* 1925, no. 7.

―――. "Organizatsiia zemel'nykh obshchestv." *Sel'skoe i lesnoe khoziaistvo,* 1926, no. 4.

―――. "Zemel'noe obshchestvo i obosoblennyi zemlepol'zovatel'." *Zemleustroitel',* 1926, no. 10.

Podol'skii, A. *Volostnoi biudzhet.* Moscow, 1925.

Pokrovskii, M. N. *Kontr-revoliutsiia za 4 goda.* Moscow, 1922.

Pokrovskii, N. N. *Aktovye istochniki po istorii chernososhnogo zemlevladeniia v Rossii XIV–nachala XVI v.* Novosibirsk, 1973.

Poliakov, Iu. A. *Perekhod k nepu i sovetskoe krest'ianstvo.* Moscow, 1967.

Pomotskii, V. "Obshchee sobranie (skhod) grazhdan sela i sel'skii sovet." *Ezhemesiachnik sovetskoi iustitsii ASSR,* 1928, no. 2(3).

"Pozemel'naia obshchina." *Entsiklopedicheskii slovar'* (Brokgauz-Efron). Vol. 24. St. Petersburg, 1898.

Predvaritel'nye itogi vserossiiskoi sel'skokhoziaistvennoi perepisi 1916. Part 1. *Evropeiskaia Rossiia.* Petrograd, 1916.

Preobrazhenskii, Evgenii. *The New Economics.* 2d ed. Translated by Brian Pearce. London, 1965.

———. *Novaia ekonomika.* 1st ed. Moscow, 1926.

———. *Ot NEP^a k sotsializmu.* Moscow, 1922.

———. "Perspektivy novoi ekonomicheskoi politiki." *Krasnaia nov'*, 1921, no. 3.

Problemy krest'ianskogo zemlevladeniia i vnutrennoi politiki Rossii. Leningrad, 1972.

Pushkarev, S. G. *Krest'ianskaia pozemel'no-peredel'naia obshchina v Rossii.* Newtonville, Mass., 1976.

Radkey, Oliver H. *The Agrarian Foes of Bolshevism.* New York, 1958.

———. *The Unknown Civil War in Soviet Russia: A Study of the Green Movement in the Tambov Region, 1920–1921.* Stanford, 1976.

Rashin, Adol'f G. *Formirovanie rabochego klassa Rossii.* Moscow, 1958.

———. *Naselenie Rossii za 100 let (1811–1913 gg.): statisticheskie ocherki.* Moscow, 1956.

Reed, John. *Ten Days That Shook the World.* New York, 1935.

Rezunov, M. *Sel'skie sovety i zemel'nye obshchestva.* Moscow, 1928.

Rikhter, D. I. *Agrarnye voprosy v Rossii. Part 1. Gosudarstvennye banki v Rossii i ikh dal'neishaia sud'ba. Part 2. Gosudarstvennye zemel'nye banki v Rossii i ikh dal'neishaia sud'ba.* Petrograd, 1917.

Rittikh, A. A., comp. *Vysochaishche uchrezhdenoi Osobie Soveshchanie o nuzhdakh sel'skokhoziaistvennoi promyshlennosti. Krest'ianskoe delo.* St. Petersburg, 1903.

Robinson, Gerold T. *Rural Russia under the Old Regime.* Reprint. Berkeley, 1967.

Rogachevskaia, L. S. "K voprosu preobrazovanii sel'skogo khoziaistva i likvidatsii bezrabotitsy v SSSR." In *Rol' rabochego klassa.*

Rol' rabochego klassa v sotsialisticheskom preobrazovanii derevni v SSSR. Moscow, 1968.

Rosenberg, William G. *Liberals in the Russian Revolution.* Princeton, 1974.

Rozhkov, N. A. *Gorod i derevnia v russkoi istorii.* Petrograd, 1918.

Rubach, M. A. "Leninskii dekret o zemle i razvertyvanie vtoroi sotsial'noi voiny v ukrainskoi derevne." In Mints, *Leninskii dekret v deistvii.*

Rubinshtein, N. L. *Sel'skoe khoziaistvo Rossii vo vtoroi polovine XVIII v.* Moscow, 1957.

Rudin, N. "O formakh zemlepol'zovaniia." *Zemleustroitel'*, 1925, no. 3.

Rybinskii, M. I. "O pomoshchi trudiashchikhsia zarubezhnykh stran sovetskomu sel'skomu khoziaistvu 1921–1925 gg." *Istoricheskii arkhiv*, 1961, no. 4.

Sbornik dokumentov po zemel'nomu zakonodatel'stvu SSSR i RSFSR, 1917–1954. Moscow, 1954.

Seleznev, V. A., and Gumarov, N. N. *Nachalo massovogo kolkhoznogo dvizheniia na severo-zapade RSFSR, 1930–1932.* Leningrad, 1972.

Selunskaia, V. M. *Rabochii klass i Oktiabr' v derevne.* Moscow, 1968.

———, ed. *Izmeneniia sotsial'noi struktury sovetskogo obshchestva, oktiabr' 1917–1920.* Moscow, 1976.

———, ed. *Izmeneniia sotsial'noi struktury sovetskogo obshchestva 1921–seredina 30^{kh} godakh.* Moscow, 1979.

Semevskii, V. I. *Krest'iane v tsarstvovanie Ekateriny II.* 2 vols. St. Petersburg, 1903.

Shanin, L. "Ekonomicheskaia priroda nashego bestovar'ia." *Ekonomicheskoe obozrenie*, November 1925.

Shanin, Teodor. *The Awkward Class: Political Sociology of Peasantry in a Developing Society, Russia 1910–1925.* Oxford, 1972.

Shapiro, A. L. "O prirode feodal'noi sobstvennosti na zemliu." *Voprosy istorii,* 1969, no. 12.

Sharapov, G. V. *Razreshenie agrarnogo voprosa v Rossii posle pobedy oktiabr'skoi revoliutsii (1917–1920 gg.).* Moscow, 1961.

Sharova, P. N. *Kollektivizatsiia sel'skogo khoziaistva v tsentral'no-chernozemnoi oblasti, 1928–1932.* Moscow, 1932.

Shestakov, A. V., ed. *Sovety krest'ianskikh deputatov i drugie krest'ianskie organizatsii.* 2 vols. Moscow, 1929.

Shirokov, M. M. "Rabota kommunisticheskoi partii po ovladeniiu zemel'nymi obshchestvami i perevodu ikh na sotsialisticheskii put' razvitiia (1927–1929 gg.)." *Vestnik moskovskogo universiteta.* Seriia 9. *Istoriia,* 1966, no. 4.

Shishko, L. *Po programmnym voprosam.* Moscow, 1906.

Shul'gin, M. "O iuridicheskom ravnopravii form zemlepol'zovaniia." *Zemleustroitel',* 1924, no. 6–7.

Shuvaev, K. M. *Staraia i novaia derevnia: s prilozhenium knigi A. I. Shingareva, Vymiraiushchaia derevnia.* Moscow, 1937.

Sidel'nikov, S. M. *Agrarnaia politika samoderzhaviia v period imperializma.* Moscow, 1980.

———, comp. *Agrarnaia reforma Stolypina.* Moscow, 1973.

Simonov, N. V. "Sel'skoe khoziaistvo Rossii v gody pervoi mirovoi voiny." *Voprosy istorii,* 1955, no. 3.

Simonova, M. S. "Mobilizatsiia krest'ianskoi nadel'noi zemli v period Stolypinskoi agrarnoi reformy." *Materialy po istorii sel'skogo khoziaistva i krest'ianstva SSSR.* Vol. 5. Moscow, 1962.

Skrebitskii, Aleksandr. *Krest'ianskoe delo v tsarstvovanie imperatora Aleksandra II.* 4 vols. Bonn, 1862–68.

Smirnov, A. S. *Bol'sheviki i krest'ianstvo v oktiabr'skoi revoliutsii.* Moscow, 1976.

———. *Krest'ianskie s"ezdy v 1917 gody.* Moscow, 1979.

Smirnov, I. "Po sledam Stolypina." *Zemleustroitel',* 1929, no. 11–12.

Smith, R. E. F. *Peasant Farming in Muscovy.* Cambridge, Eng., 1977.

Smrukov, M., and Matskevich, A. "Sem'ia ne bez uroda." *Zemleustroitel',* 1928, no. 12.

Snegirev, M. A. "Velikaia Oktiabr'skaia sotsialisticheskaia revoliutsiia i raspredelenie zemel' v 1917–1918 godakh." *Voprosy istorii,* 1947, no. 11.

———. "Zemleustroistvo v RSFSR po 'Polozheniiu o sotsialisticheskom zemleustroistve i o merakh perekhoda k sotsialisticheskomu zemledeliiu' (1919–1921 gg.)." *Trudy moskovskogo instituta inzhenerov zemleustroistva,* 9 (1960).

Sobolev, P. N. *Uprochnenie soiuza rabochikh i krest'ian v pervyi god proletarskoi diktatury.* Moscow, 1977.

Sobranie uzakonenii i rasporiazhenii raboche-krest'ianskogo pravitel'stva RSFSR.

Sobranie zakonov i rasporiazhenii raboche-krest'ianskogo pravitel'stva SSSR.

Solomon, Susan Gross. *The Soviet Agrarian Debate: A Controversy in Social Science, 1923–1929.* Boulder, Colo., 1977.

Sovet s"ezdov predstavitelei promyshlennosti i torgovli. Statisticheskii ezhegodnik na 1913 god. St. Petersburg, 1913.

Sovety v epokhe voennogo kommunizma: sbornik dokumentov. Moscow, 1928.

Spektor, G. V. "Raspad mnogodvornykh obshchin v samarskoi gubernii." *VZP*, 1929, no. 1.

―――. "Zemel'naia registratsiia." *Zemleustroitel'*, 1926, no. 1.

Stalin, I. V. *Sochineniia*. 13 vols. Moscow, 1946–1955.

Starr, Frederick S. *Decentralization and Self-Government in Russia, 1830–1870*. Princeton, 1972.

Steklov, Iu. "N. G. Chernyshevskii i krest'ianskii vopros." *NAF*, 1928, nos. 5, 6–7.

Stenograficheskii otchet tret'ego vserossiiskogo soveshchaniia zemorganov, 28 fevralia–7 marta 1926 g. Moscow, 1926.

Strong, Anna L. *The Soviets Conquer Wheat*. New York, 1931.

Suchkov, A. "Dvor ili obshchina." *Sel'sko-khoziaistvennaia zhizn'*, 1927, no. 10.

―――. "Kak ne nado rassmatrivat' vopros o formakh zemlepol'zovaniia." *Bol'shevik*, 1928, no. 2.

Sukhanov, N. "Obshchina v sovetskom agrarnom zakonodatel'stve." *NAF*, 1926, no. 11–12.

Sutton, Anthony C. *Western Technology and Soviet Economic Development, 1917–1930*. Stanford, 1968.

Svod zakonov Rossiisskoi Imperii. Vol. 10, part 3. *Polozhenie o zemleustroistve*. St. Petersburg, 1912.

Taniuchi, Yuzuru. *A Note on the Ural-Siberian Method*. Soviet Industrialization Project Series. CREES, University of Birmingham, no. 17. Birmingham, Eng., 1979.

―――. *The Village Gathering in Russia in the Mid-1920s*. Birmingham, Eng., 1968.

Thorner, Daniel, et al., eds. *A. V. Chayanov on the Theory of Peasant Economy*. Homewood, Ill., 1966.

Timoshenko, Vladimir P. *Agricultural Russia and the Wheat Problem*. Stanford, 1932.

Tiumenev, A. *Ot revoliutsii k revoliutsii: iz obshchestvenno-ekonomicheskikh itogov revoliutsii 1905 goda*. Leningrad, 1925.

Tönnies, Ferdinand. *Gemeinschaft und Gesellschaft*. Leipzig, 1887. Translated and edited by Charles Loomis as *Community and Society*. East Lansing, Mich., 1957.

Trapeznikov, S. P. *Leninizm i agrarno-krest'ianskii vopros*. Vol. 1. *Agrarnyi vopros i Leninskie agrarnye programmy v trekh russkikh revoliutsiiakh*. Vol. 2. *Istoricheskii opyt KPSS v osushchestvlenii Leninskogo kooperativnogo plana*. Moscow, 1967.

Treadgold, Donald. *The Great Siberian Migration*. Princeton, 1957.

Trinadtsatyi s"ezd RKP(b). Stenograficheskii otchet. Moscow, 1924.

Tropin, V. I. *Bor'ba bol'shevikov za rukovodstvo krest'ianskim dvizheniem v 1905 g*. Moscow, 1970.

Trudy pervogo s"ezda upolnomochennykh dvorianskikh obshchestv 29 gubernii, 21–28 maia 1916 g. St. Petersburg, 1906.

TsIK SSSR. 3 sessiia, 4 sozyv, zasedanie 7. *Stenograficheskii otchet*. Moscow, 1928.

―――. 4 sessiia, 4 sozyv, zasedanie 4. *Biulleten'*, no. 13. Moscow, 1928.

TsSK. *Statistika zemlevladeniia 1905 g.: svod dannykh po 50 guberniiam Evropeiskoi Rossii*. St. Petersburg, 1907.

TsSU. *Itogi desiatiletiia sovetskoi vlasti v tsifrakh, 1917–1927*. Moscow, 1927.

————. *Predvaritel'nye itogi perepisi naseleniia 28 avgusta 1920 g.* Moscow, 1921.

————. *Rossiia v mirovoi voine 1914–1918 goda (v tsifrakh).* Moscow, 1925.

————. *Sel'skoe khoziaistvo SSSR, 1925–1928: sbornik statisticheskikh svedenii.* Moscow, 1929.

————. *Sel'skoe khoziaistvo SSSR: statisticheskii sbornik.* Moscow, 1960.

————. *Sel'skoe khoziaistvo SSSR: statisticheskii sbornik.* Moscow, 1971.

————. *Statisticheskii spravochnik za 1928 g.* Moscow, 1929.

————. *Trudy.*

Vol. 6, part 3. *Ekonomicheskoe rassloenie krest'ianstva v 1917 i 1919 g.* Moscow, 1922.

Vol. 7, part 1. *Statisticheskii sbornik za 1913–1917 gg.* Moscow, 1921.

Vol. 8, part 1. *Statisticheskii ezhegodnik 1918–1920 gg.* Moscow, 1921–22.

Vol. 8, part 5. *Statisticheskii ezhegodnik 1922 i 1923.* Moscow, 1924.

Vol. 18. *Sbornik statisticheskii svedenii po Soiuza SSSR, 1918–1923.* Moscow, 1924.

Vol. 30. *Sostoianie pitaniia.* Moscow, 1919–.

TsUNKhU. *Sotsialisticheskoe stroitel'stvo SSSR: statisticheskii ezhegodnik.* Moscow, 1934.

Tsybul'skii, V. A. "Tovaroobmen mezhdu gorodom i derevnei v pervye mesiatsy NEP[a]." *Istoriia SSSR,* 1968, no. 4.

Tsyl'ko, F. "Osnovnye vekhi kolkhoznogo dvizheniia." *NAF,* 1930, no. 5.

Tsypkina, R. G. *Sel'skaia krasnaia gvardiia v oktiabr'skoi revoliutsii.* Moscow, 1970.

Tucker, Robert C. *Stalin as Revolutionary, 1879–1929: A Study in History and Personality.* New York, 1973.

Tugan-Baranovskii, M. I. *Zemel'nyi vopros na zapade i v Rossii.* Moscow, n.d. *1905: materialy i dokumenty. Agrarnoe dvizhenie v 1905–1907.* Moscow, 1925.

Vaganov, F. M. *Pravyi uklon v VKP(b) i ego razgrom.* Moscow, 1970.

Vainshtein, A. "Chislennost i dinamika nalichnykh krest'ianskikh dvorov v predvoennoi Rossii." *Statisticheskoe obozrenie,* 1929, no. 7.

Vareikis, M. "O partiinom rukovodstve kolkhozami." *NAF,* 1929, no. 8.

Varga, Evgenii. "Agrarizatsiia i industrializatsiia." *NAF,* 1928, no. 6–7.

Vasilevskii, E. G. *Ideinaia bor'ba vokrug stolypinskoi agrarnoi reformy.* Moscow, 1960.

————. "Sotsial'no-ekonomicheskoe soderzhanie krest'ianskikh prigovorov i nakazov vo II gosudarstvennuiu Dumu (1907 g.)." *Uchenye zapiski MGU,* 179. *Trudy kafedry istorii narodnogo khoziaistva i ekonomicheskikh uchenii ekonomicheskogo fakulteta,* 1959.

Vdovina, L. N. "Vopros o proiskhozhdenii krest'ianskoi obshchiny v russkoi dorev. istoriografii." *Vestnik moskovskogo universiteta (istoriia),* 1973, no. 4.

Venturi, Franco. *Roots of Revolution.* New York, 1966.

Veselovskii, B. B. *Istoriia zemstva za sorok let.* 4 vols. St. Petersburg, 1909–11.

————. *Utopizm i "real'naia politika" v zemleustroistvo.* St. Petersburg, 1910.

Vinogradov, Eugene D. "The 'Invisible Hand' and the Russian Peasant." *Peasant Studies Newsletter,* July 1975.

Vodarskii, Ia. E. *Naselenie Rossii v kontse XVII–nachale XVIII veka.* Moscow, 1977.

Volin, Lazar. *A Century of Russian Agriculture: From Alexander II to Khrushchev*. Cambridge, Mass., 1970.

Volkhov, I., ed. *Oktiabr' i sovetskoe krest'ianstvo, 1917–1927 gg.* Moscow, 1977.

Volodkovich, I., and Kulikov, P. "K voprosu o razvitii kollektivizatsii v derevne." *NAF*, 1927, no. 1.

Vorontsov, V. P. "Nachalo peredelov na severe Rossii." *Russkaia mysl'*, 1897, nos. 11 and 12.

———. "Ucheniia o proiskhozhdenii zemel'noi obshchiny v Rossii." *Vestnik Evropy*, 1910, no. 4.

Vysochaishe utverzhdeniia 19 fevralia 1861 goda. *Polozheniia o krest'ianakh vyshedshikh iz krepostnoi zavisimosti, s dopolneniiami ko nim po 31 marta 1863 goda*. N.p., n.d.

Wallace, D. M. *Russia on the Eve of War and Revolution*. New York, 1961. (First published in 1877.)

Weber, Max. *Economy and Society: An Outline of Interpretive Sociology*. Ed. Guenther Roth and Claus Wittich. 2 vols. Berkeley, 1978.

Wesson, Robert G. *Soviet Communes*. New Brunswick, N.J., 1963.

Wheatcroft, Steven G. "The Reliability of Russian Prewar Grain Output Statistics." *Soviet Studies*, April 1974.

———. "The Significance of Climatic and Weather Change on Soviet Agriculture (with Particular Reference to the 1920s and 1930s)." Discussion paper. CREES. University of Birmingham, Birmingham, Eng., 1977.

Witte, Sergei Iu. *Vospominaniia*. 2 vols. Moscow, 1960.

———. *Zapiska po krest'ianskomu delu*. St. Petersburg, 1904.

Zaionchkovskii, P. A. *Otmena krepostnogo prava v Rossii*. 2d ed. Moscow, 1960.

Zak, S. D. "Marksizm o prirode i sud'bakh obshchinnoi sobstvennosti i razvaiushchiesia strany." *Itogi i perspektivy sotsial'no-ekonomicheskogo razvitiia molodykh suverennykh gosudarstv. Materialy nauchnoi konferentsii kafedry ekonomiki sovremennogo kapitalizma*. Leningrad, 1965.

Zakonodatel'nye akty perekhodnogo vremeni (1904–1906 gg.). 1st ed. St. Petersburg, 1906. 2d ed. St Petersburg, 1907. (The first edition extends through March 1906; the second covers all of 1906 but omits some of the material included in the earlier edition.)

Zalesskii, M. Ia. *Nalogovaia politika sovetskogo gosudarstva v derevne*. Moscow, 1940.

Zdanovich, S. "Sel'skie sovety i zemel'nye obshchestva." *Bol'shevik*, 1928, no. 6.

Zelenin, I. E. *Sovkhozy v pervoe desiatiletie sovetskoi vlasti, 1917–1927*. Moscow, 1972.

Zemel'nyi kodeks RSFSR. 2d ed. Moscow, 1928.

Zenzinov, V. M. "Popravshaia gramota Marksa o russkoi obshchine." *Sovremennye zapiski*, 24 (1925).

Zhmurovskii, D. P. *Organizatorskaia rabota kommunisticheskoi partii v derevne (1918–1920 gg.)*. Minsk, 1970.

Zybkovets, V. F. "Likvidatsiia monastyrskogo zemlevladeniia v sovetskoi Rossii (1917–1921 gg.)." In Kim, *Problemy agrarnoi istorii*.

Index